FOURTH EDITION

ORGANIZATION AND PEOPLE

Readings, Exercises, and Cases in Organizational Behavior

FOURTH EDITION

ORGANIZATION AND PEOPLE

Readings, Exercises, and Cases in Organizational Behavior

J. B. RITCHIE and PAUL THOMPSON
Brigham Young University

WEST PUBLISHING COMPANY
St. Paul • New York • Los Angeles • San Francisco

Photos:
George Gardner **151**
Jeffrey Grosscup **152, 153, 154**

Cartoons:
Malcolm Hancock

Text Design:
Lucy Lesiak

COPYRIGHT © 1976   By WEST PUBLISHING COMPANY
COPYRIGHT © 1980   By WEST PUBLISHING COMPANY
COPYRIGHT © 1984   By WEST PUBLISHING COMPANY
COPYRIGHT © 1988   By WEST PUBLISHING COMPANY
                   50 W. Kellogg Boulevard
                   P.O. Box 64526
                   St. Paul, MN 55164–1003

Printed in the United States of America
95 94 93 92 91 90   8 7 6 5 4 3 2 1

Library of Congress Cataloging-in-Publication Data

Organization and people.

    Includes index.
    1. Organizational behavior.   2. Management.
I. Ritchie, J. B.   II. Thompson, Paul, 1938–
HD58.7.067   1988   658.4   87–31586
ISBN 0–314–65672–3

PREFACE

Organizational behavior is both a very old and a very new field. It is old in the sense that people have been behaving in organizations for a very long time. In fact, we suspect that some of the earliest debates in primitive society had to do with the advantages and disadvantages of different types of organizations. But organizational behavior is a *new* field of study. In spite of the traditional and pervasive nature of organizations, the formal development of an area of study entitled *organizational behavior* is still in its infancy. Sociology, psychology, industrial relations, and various programs in administration (business, education, public, hospital) have probed facets of the behavior of people in organizations, but only recently have we attempted to bring it all together in a single field of study.

The synthesis is important. In most societies, but especially in those in an advanced state of industrialization, people are members of many different organizations—family, social, political, religious, athletic, military, educational, service, economic. And they must relate to even more, all of them competing for time, money, loyalty—perhaps even people's fundamental values. But, although some memberships are mutually advantageous, others produce severe role conflicts, and coping with these multiple, and often conflicting, roles occupies increasing amounts of each person's energy. More and more, individual well-being is affected by the quality of organizational relationships, and that quality depends largely on the degree of understanding of increasingly complex organizations.

Students are taught these relationships in several ways. Some books in the field present a large number of readings, primarily from academic journals. Others contain many case studies and a few theoretical articles. Still others include numerous exercises designed to increase student involvement. As the title indicates, this book contains all three: readings, cases, and exercises. We recognize that for a given group of students (and instructors) one approach may be more useful than another in understanding a given concept. Furthermore, for most students a combination of approaches is better than one exclusive technique. We have followed the maxim that "a change of medium reduces the tedium." We feel that a textbook in organizational behavior need not be boring or extremely complex for students to learn a great deal from it. A course should not only promote optimum learning, but it should also be interesting and fun. Our personal experience with the material has convinced us that it really does help students enjoy the course as well as understand the subject.

The readings are intended to provide the students with a wide variety of perspectives regarding the day-to-day operations of organizations. They were selected from such diverse sources as *Time, Black Enterprise, Psychol-*

ogy Today, Harvard Business Review, and *Organizational Dynamics.* This affords flexibility. The instructor can explore and develop a variety of concepts from articles written on different levels of complexity. The theoretical models can be used in analysis of organizational phenomena, and the empirical evidence can be analyzed, debated, and extended. Interviews offer provoking shotgun comments on issues; other readings contain prescriptions for specific problems. Finally, some contributions are fun, or frightening, depending on your viewpoint. Breadth, rather than depth, is clearly our intent.

The cases also represent a spectrum of situations from which students or instructors can choose a setting appropriate for analysis or application of various organizational concepts. Our experience with cases in introductory courses suggests that students learn more if they can move back and forth between a theory in an article and a problem in a case. They need both teaching tools if they are going to develop skill in identification and analysis of problems, as well as in development of plans for dealing with those problems.

The exercises add still another dimension. For example, students will experience some of the frustrations and competitive feelings that commonly arise in group decision making. Since people often find it easier to discuss concepts and theories rather than apply them, involvement in exercises and role plays can help them to achieve certain introspective and applied skill objectives as well as various theoretical insights. There seems to be a trend toward designing courses that use such activities almost exclusively. But, while such exercises can be very useful tools, we advocate a more balanced approach, using a variety of vehicles rather than the singular approach.

The book is organized into five sections with introductory comments for each section. We have intended that these comments be used in the transition between sections of a course. The first section, an introduction to the book, raises issues that are explored more thoroughly in what follows. The second section focuses on individuals and on issues such as motivation, career development, and decision making. Section 3 presents material on people in groups of two or more: interpersonal, group, and intergroup behavior. Leadership is the focus in Section 4. Section 5 turns to the future and some of the environmental forces pressing for change in organizations.

Our focus is not on a single type of organization, but, because business organizations are dominant in society, they are the subject in a majority of the discussions. Also, while our primary goal is a broad understanding of organizations in general, a corollary effect is the preparation of individuals for management and leadership roles.

A major issue in this collection is the confrontation between organizational pressures and human values. Current journals are replete with evidence of immoral and unethical use of organizations by members at the top and the bottom of the hierarchy. We feel that at all levels in all types of organizations there is an urgent need for increased honesty and integrity and, most important, increased development of the individual.

Our assumption is that this material will be used in an introductory course at either a graduate or an undergraduate level. We feel that the variety of perspectives raised and issues discussed will enrich any introductory course dealing with the phenomena of organizations and people.

Although it is difficult to mention each person who has contributed to this collection, we want to acknowledge the efforts of the following graduate students: Ross Davidson, Maureen Fisher, Hal Gregersen, Deborah Hutson, Mike Linford, Gordon Meyer, Kerry Patterson, Lois Ritchie, Mary Delamar-Shaefer, Tim Shurtleff, Mike Silva, and Randy Stott. In a more general sense, however, the most significant contribution has come from the thousands of students in our introductory courses in organizational behavior at Harvard, Berkeley, Michigan, Stanford, and Brigham Young.

J. B. Ritchie
Paul H. Thompson

CONTENTS

CROSS-REFERENCE GUIDE

The primary purpose of this Cross-Reference Guide is to provide a link between a variety of topical areas in organizational behavior and the material in this book. An additional purpose is to suggest the breadth of the field by referencing additional material. The items mentioned, of course, are only illustrative (an extensive list would defy reproduction), but they indicate the diverse avenues which might be used in better understanding organizational behavior. Fiction, non-fiction, and films all provide a useful vehicle for exploring topics which are illuminated by the artist's sensitivity in addition to the researcher's measurements.

Topic	Articles (Page)	Cases/Exercises (Page)	Related Materials Outside Book
Assumptions	We Need a Nation of Scholar-Leaders (5) On the Folly of Rewarding A, . . . (76) The Managers Job: Folklore and Fact (255) Participative Management: Quality vs. Quantity (299) It's Time to Punt Macho Metaphors (324)	An Ancient Tale (53) Washington Elementary (64) Intergroup Exercise (233) Supervisory Style Exercise (327) L.J. Summers Company (344) DMG Corporation (435)	(M)* Productivity and Self-Fulfilling Prophecy: The Pygmalion Effect; (A) "Floundering in Fallacy: Seven Quick Ways to Kid Yourself," C. Offir, Psychology Today, April 1975; (MH) Absence of Malice; (MH) Tootsie; (MH) Godfather; (MH) The Great Santini.
Authority	See Leadership		
Behavior Modification	See Reinforcement		

*(M) Instructional Movie   (MH) Hollywood Movie   (B) Book   (N) Novel   (A) Article
(P) Play   (SS) Short Story

Topic	Articles (Page)	Cases/Exercises (Page)	Related Materials Outside Book
Career Development	The Cultural Awareness Hierarchy (16) Who Gets the Parachutes? (21) A Conversation with Peter F. Drucker (23) Managing Your Manager (40) Urge to Achieve (86) Tear Down the Pyramids (123) On Wasting Time (128) Formal Mentoring Programs are no Panacea (320)	Margaret Jardine (165) Career Exercise (156) Ranch Supplies Company (239) Universal Bank (431)	(A) Building Personal and Professional Networks, R. Keele and C. Jacobs, Networks and Organizations; (M) The Blue Color Trap; (M) Factory (M) Cage (B) What Color Is Your Parachute?, R. Bolles; (B) Career Satisfaction Success, B. Haldane; (P) Death of a Salesman, A. Miller; (TV) What If They Succeed?; (A) "Adult Life Stages: Growth Toward Self-Tolerance," R. Gould, Psychology Today, Feb. 75.
Change	Who Gets the Parachutes? (21) Choosing Strategies for Change (353) Today's Success—Tomorrow's Challenge (415)	Washington Elementary (64) The Reluctant Account Executive (158) Organizational Profile Exercise (425) What, Me Change? (427) Hovey and Beard Company (441) Metropolitan Police Department (444)	(M) Human Nature and Organizational Reality; (M) A Time for Burning; (M) How to Overcome Resistance to Change; (A) "The Management of Change," P. Hersey and K. Blanchard, Training and Development, Journal, Jan., Feb., and March 72; (B) The Planning of Change, W. Bennis, K. Benne, and R. Chin; (MH) The Last Emperor; (B) The Changemasters, Kanter; (B) The Executive Challenge, Managing Change and Ambiguity, McCaskey; (B) Strategies for Change, Quinn; (MH) Brubaker.

*(M) Instructional Movie   (MH) Hollywood Movie   (B) Book   (N) Novel   (A) Article
(P) Play   (SS) Short Story

CROSS-REFERENCE GUIDE

Topic	Articles (Page)	Cases/Exercises (Page)	Related Materials Outside Book
Communication	That's Easy for You to Say (10) Managing Your Manager (40) On the Folly of Rewarding A, While Hoping for B (76) Tear Down the Pyramids (123)	Washington Elementary (64) The Reluctant Account Executive (158) Ranch Supplies Company (239) The Great Majestic Company (242) Fables for Management (343) L. J. Summers Company (344)	(M) Is It Always Right To Be Right?; (M) A Charie Tale; (M) In the Company of Men; (M) Avoiding Communications Breakdown; (M) Effective Listening; (M) Communication: The Nonverbal Agenda; (A) "The One Way/Two Way Communication Exercise: Some Ghosts Laid to Rest," F. Tesch, L. Lansky, and D. Lundgren, JABS, Nov./Dec. 72.
Cross-Culture	That's Easy for You to Say (10) The Cultural Awareness Hierarchy (16) A Big Winner in Two Leagues (115) Performance Lies are Hazardous to Organizational Health (191) Today's Success—Tomorrow's Challenge (415)	Gemini Electronics (66) Giant Food Company (234) Universal Bank (431)	(B) The Japanese Employee, R.J. Ballon; (A) "Made In America Under Japanese Management," R. Johnson and W. Ouchi, HBR, Sept.–Oct. 74; (A) "What We Can Learn From Japanese Management," P. Drucker, HBR, March–April 71; (B) Theory Z, Ouchi; (B) In Search of Excellence, Peters and Waterman; (B) Novations, Dalton/Thompson; (B) Megatrends, Naisbitt.
Decision-making	We Need a Nation of Scholar-Leaders (5) Phantoms Fill Boy Scout Rolls (35) How to Make an Intelligent Decision (130)	The Tinkertoy Exercise (52) An Ancient Tale (53) Mountain View Hospital (108)	(A) Beyond the Analytic Manager, H. Leavitt, Calif. Mgt. Review SP 1975; (A) The Nature of Problems, E. Schumacher, A Guide for the Perplexed; (MH) Twelve Angry Men;

*(M) Instructional Movie   (MH) Hollywood Movie   (B) Book   (N) Novel   (A) Article
(P) Play   (SS) Short Story

CROSS-REFERENCE GUIDE

Topic	Articles (Page)	Cases/Exercises (Page)	Related Materials Outside Book
Decision-making (*continued*)	Managerial Problem Solving (**134**) Assets and Liabilities in Group Problem Solving (**171**)	NASA/Winter Exercise (**229**) Giant Food Company (**234**) Who's in Charge Around Here? (**333**)	(M) Effective Decisions; (M) Focus on Tomorrow; (MH-B) Fail-Safe, E. Burdick; (N) Decision Making in the White House, T. Sorenson; (N) The Double Helix, J. Watson; (TV) "The Missiles of October"; (A) "Decision Making: Organization Choice," W. Gueck, Personnel Psychology, Spring 74; (A) "Decisions, Decisions, Decisions," J. Hall, Psychology Today, Nov. 71; (B) Groupthink, Janis.
Discrimination	Breaking Through—Women on the Move (**378**) The Touchy Issue of Sexual Harassment (**384**) Black Managers: The Dream Deferred (**387**) Whistleblowing (**409**)	An Ancient Tale (**53**) Supervision, Jazz and Beards (**54**) Giant Food Company (**234**) Who's in Charge Around Here? (**333**) L.J. Summers Company (**344**) DMG Corporation (**435**)	(A) Women in Management; Obstacles and Opportunities they Face, C. Hay, Personnel Administrator, April 1980; (M) Women in Management: Threat or Opportunity?; (B) Breakthrough: Women in Management, R. Loring and T. Wells; (M) Bill of Rights in Action: Equal Opportunity; (M) I'm a Man; (B) Black Americans in White Business, E. Epstein and Hampton; (MH) The Grapes of Wrath; (MH) Nine to Five; (MH) Tootsie; (MH) The China Syndrome.

*(M) Instructional Movie   (MH) Hollywood Movie   (B) Book   (N) Novel   (A) Article
(P) Play   (SS) Short Story

CROSS-REFERENCE GUIDE

Topic	Articles (Page)	Cases/Exercises (Page)	Related Materials Outside Book
Ethics	A Conversation with Peter F. Drucker (23) Phantoms Fill Boy Scout Rolls (35) Scouting Motto Forgotten... (37) Rise and Fall of an Insider (118) Performance Lies (191) "Why Should My Conscience Bother Me?" (207) A Billion Levi's Later (372)	An Ancient Tale (53) A Question of Ethics (60) Winter Survival Exercise (231) Intergroup Exercise (233) Ranch Supplies (239)	(A) Blowing the Whistle on Corporate Misconduct, D. Clutterbuck, International Management, Jan. 1980; (A) Corporate Responsibility, B. Moskal, Industry Week, July 26, 1982; (M) The Lottery; (M) Obedience; (M) Moral Development; (M) Whether to Tell the Truth; (N) All the President's Men, C. Bernstein and B. Woodward; (A) "Stimulus/Response: Social Scientists Ought to Stop Lying," D. Warwick, Psychology Today, Feb. 75; (MH) Silkwood; (MH) Serpico; (MH) The China Syndrome; (B) In the Name of Profit; (MH) Breaker Morant; (MH) Brubaker; (MH) One Flew Over the Cuckoo's Nest; (MH) The Verdict.
Groups	Assets and Liabilities In Group Problem Solving (171) The Abilene Paradox (181) "Why Should My Conscience Bother Me?" (207) Issues in Observing Groups (220)	The Tinkertoy Exercise (52) NASA Exercise (229) Winter Survival (231) Intergroup (233) Giant Food Company (234) Hovey and Beard Company (441)	(M) Social Animal; (M) Group Dynamics: "Groupthink"; (M) Group Pressure; (MH) Cool Hand Luke; (MH-N) Lord of the Flies, W. Golding; (A) "Productivity and Group Success: Team Spirit vs. the Individual," A. Zander, Psychology Today, Nov. 74;

*(M) Instructional Movie (MH) Hollywood Movie (B) Book (N) Novel (A) Article
(P) Play (SS) Short Story

CROSS-REFERENCE GUIDE

Topic	Articles (Page)	Cases/Exercises (Page)	Related Materials Outside Book
Groups (continued)			(MH) Twelve Angry Men; (M) ZUBIN MEHTA! Commitment and Fulfillment as a Way of Life; (MH-B) All the President's Men.
Intergroup	Intergroup Problems in Organizations (200) "Why Should My Conscience Bother Me?" (207) Working Man and Management (253)	The Tinkertoy Exercise (52) Intergroup Exercise (233) Northwest Industries (245) Hovey and Beard Company (441)	(B) Groups in Harmony and Tension, M. and C. Sherif; (A) "Organization and Conflict," K. Boulding, Journal of Conflict Resolution, 1957, 1; (B) Managing Intergroup Problems in Organizations, R. Blake, H. Shepard, J. Mouton; (MH) Bridge on the River Kwai.
Leadership	We Need a Nation of Scholars-Leaders (5) Who Gets the Parachutes? (21) Managing Your Manager (40) Motivation—A Diagnostic Approach (94) Thinking and Learning About Leadership (271) Power Failure in Management Circuits (285) Participative Management: Quality vs. Quantity (299) Getting the Best from Foreign Employees (309)	The Tinkertoy Exercise (52) Supervision, Jazz and Beards (54) The Reluctant Account Executive (158) Leadership Exercise (328) Who's in Charge Around Here? (333) How Iacocca Won the Big One (337) L.J. Summers Company (344)	(A) MacGregor, A. Carlisle, Organizational Dynamics, SU 1976; (A) He's Hired to be Fired, R. Fimrite, Sports Illustrated, April 1981; (MH) Patton; (MH) Twelve O'clock High; (MH-N) The Flight of the Phoenix, E. Trevor; (MH-N) The Bridge on the River Kwai, P. Boulle; (MH-N) The Caine Mutiny, H. Wouk; (B) Theories of Management, R.E. Miles; (B) Leadership and Effective Management, F. Fiedler and M. Chemers; (B) Leaders, Bennis; (B) Iaccoca;

*(M) Instructional Movie   (MH) Hollywood Movie   (B) Book   (N) Novel   (A) Article
(P) Play   (SS) Short Story

Topic	Articles (Page)	Cases/Exercises (Page)	Related Materials Outside Book
Leadership (*continued*)	Formal Mentoring (**320**) It's Time to Punt (**324**) A Billion Levi's Later (**372**) Business Ethics, A Manager's Primer (**399**)		(MH) Brubaker; (MH) Gandhi; (MH) Platoon; (MH) Being There; (M) ZUBIN MEHTA! Commitment and Fulfillment as a Way of Life; (B) Men and Women of Corporation, Kanter; (A) The Four Competencies of Leadership, T & D Journal, Aug. 84, Warren—Bennis.
Life Planning	See Career Development		
Management Style	See Leadership, Reinforcement or Participation		
Motivation	On the Folly of Rewarding A, While Hoping for B (**76**) That Urge to Achieve (**86**) Motivation—A Diagnostic Approach (**94**) A New Strategy for Job Enrichment (**102**) Participative Management: Quality vs. Quantity (**299**) Getting the Best from Foreign Employees (**309**) Today's Success—Tomorrow's Challenge . . . (**415**)	Supervision, Jazz and Beards (**54**) Motivational Style Exercise (**145**) Perception Exercise (**150**) The Reluctant Account Executive (**158**) State Bank (**161**) Margaret Jardine (**165**)	(M) Maslow and Self-Actualization; (M) Motivation in Perspective; (M) Understanding Motivation; (M) Herzberg Series—Job Enrichment in Action, Motivation Through Job Enrichment, etc.; (M) Motives Moving Business; (M) Need to Achieve; (M) Self-motivated Achievers; (B) Motivation to Work, F. Herzberg, B. Mausner, and B. Snyderman; (B) Motivation Through the Work Itself, R. Ford;

*(M) Instructional Movie   (MH) Hollywood Movie   (B) Book   (N) Novel   (A) Article

(P) Play   (SS) Short Story

Topic	Articles (Page)	Cases/Exercises (Page)	Related Materials Outside Book
Motivation (*continued*)			(A) "Beyond Stick and Carrot: Hysteria Over the Work Ethic," P. Drucker, Psychology Today, Nov. 73; (A) "Power Driven Managers—Good Buys Make Bum Bosses," D. McClelland and D. Burnham, Psychology Today, Dec. 75; (MH) Chariots of Fire; (MH) Bridge on the River Kwai; (MH) An Officer and A Gentleman.
Participation	Assets and Liabilities in Group Problem Solving . . . (**171**) Participative Management: Quality vs. Quantity (**299**) Choosing Strategies for Change (**353**) Hardhats in the Boardroom (**362**)	Washington Elementary (**64**) Giant Food Company (**234**) L.J. Summers Company (**344**) Hovey and Beard Company (**441**)	(B) The Changemasters, R. Kanter; (B) The Human Organization: Its Management and Value, R. Likert; (B) Organizational Behavior (chapt. 3), G. Strauss; (B) Incentive Management: A New Approach to Human Relationships in Industry, J.F. Lincoln; (A) "Human Relations or Human Resources?," R. Miles, HBR, July–Aug. 65; (MH) Nine to Five.
Perception	On the Folly of Rewarding A, While Hoping for B (**76**) It's Time to Punt Those Macho Old Metaphors (**324**)	The Reluctant Account Executive (**158**) Giant Food Company (**234**) Ranch Supplies Company (**239**) Who's in Charge Around Here? (**333**)	(M) Powers of Ten; (M) The Eye of the Beholder; (M) Is It Always Right to be Right?; (M) In the Name of the Law; (M) Meanings Are in People; (M) The Way I See It;

*(M) Instructional Movie   (MH) Hollywood Movie   (B) Book   (N) Novel   (A) Article
(P) Play   (SS) Short Story

CROSS-REFERENCE GUIDE

Topic	Articles (Page)	Cases/Exercises (Page)	Related Materials Outside Book
Perception (*continued*)		Universal Bank (**431**) DMG Corporation (**435**)	(A) "Perception: Implications for Administration," S. Zalkind and T. Costello, ASQ Sept. 62; (MH) Being There; (MH) The China Syndrome; (MH) The Chosen.
Power	Who Gets the Parachutes? (**21**) Phantoms Fill Boy Scout Rolls (**35**) That Urge to Achieve (**86**) "Why Should My Conscience Bother Me?" (**207**) Workingman and Management (**253**) Power Failure in Management Circuits (**285**)	Supervision, Jazz and Beards (**54**) Intergroup Exercise (**233**) Who's in Charge Around Here? (**333**) How Iacocca Won the Big One (**337**) L.J. Summers Company (**344**) Hovey and Beard Company (**441**)	(MH-N) A Man For All Seasons, R. Bolt; (MH) Brubaker; (MH) Gandhi; (MH) Apocalypse Now; (MH) Citizen Kane; (B) Iacocca; (B) Power and Influence; (B) Innovations; (B) The Sovereign State of I.T.T., A. Sampson; (B) Management and Machiavelli, A. Jay; (B) In the Name of Profit, B. Heilbroner et al.; (A) "Two Faces of Power," D. McClelland, Journal of International Affairs, Vol. 24, #1.
Reinforcement	On the Folly of Rewarding A, While Hoping for B (**76**) Performance Lies are Hazardous to Organizational Health (**191**)	The Reluctant Account Executive (**158**) Mountain View Hospital (**188**)	(M) Business, Behaviorism and the Bottom Line; (M) Kita, or What Have You Done For Me Lately? (B) Walden Two, B.F. Skinner; (B) Contingency Management in Education and Other Equally Exciting Places, R. Mallott; (A) "Performance Audit, Feedback and Positive Reinforcement," E. Feeney, Training and Development Journal, Nov. 72.

*(M) Instructional Movie   (MH) Hollywood Movie   (B) Book   (N) Novel   (A) Article
(P) Play   (SS) Short Story

Topic	Articles (Page)	Cases/Exercises (Page)	Related Materials Outside Book
Systems	"Why Should My Conscience Bother Me?" (207) The Manager's Job, Folklore and Fact (255)	The Tinkertoy Exercise (52) Framework for Organizational Analysis (57) Ranch Supplies Company (239) DMG Corporation (435) Hovey and Beard Company (441)	(M) The Factory; (B) Systems Analysis and Organizational Behavior, J. Seller; (B) The Systems Approach, C. Churchman; (A) "A Structural Approach to Organizational Change," V. Averch, JABS, Sept.–Oct. 73; (A) "Understanding Your Organization's Characteristics," R. Harrison, HBR, May–June 72; (MH) One Flew Over the Cuckoo's Nest.

*(M) Instructional Movie   (MH) Hollywood Movie   (B) Book   (N) Novel   (A) Article
(P) Play   (SS) Short Story

FOURTH EDITION

ORGANIZATION AND PEOPLE

Readings, Exercises, and Cases in Organizational Behavior

Organizations Can Be Found Just About Everywhere

"Some days it would be nice to have a little stronger organization."

1

In Search of Organizational Behavior

If visitors from another planet were to travel to Earth, it would not take them long to recognize one of the more poignant debates of our time, that is, the significance, dominance, and controversial nature of contemporary organizations. They would hear of monumental achievements and colossal failures, humanitarian causes and deceptive exploitation, optimistic forecasts and doomsday predictions, the promise and the threat of multinational organizations, the fear of big organizations and the impotence of small ones, the advent of exciting new concepts of administration and the bankruptcy of modern theories.

Through all these judgments, however, runs a theme by no means unique to the contemporary setting, namely, how to better utilize organizational resources for achieving worthwhile goals. *Worthwhile*, of course, can be defined in terms of a global objective (eliminating smallpox or gaining military supremacy), a more limited activity (winning a ball game or increasing production by 10 percent), or an individual goal (achieving a position or finding meaningful work). In each case, an organization is a means to pursue an end *someone* thinks is important. And there lies the essential problem of organizations—individuals define organizational goals, values, and success from their own perspective. We need to understand the impact of these individual perspectives. To understand their impact means to remember that organizations do not behave; rather, *people* behave in organizations. Similarly, organizations do not have goals; *people* have goals in organizations. Of course, people articulate the goals they want the organization to achieve, but such statements may or may not determine the direction of behavior. The sum of the behavior of all the individual members adds up to the dynamic phenomenon we call *organization*.

Each person occupies a unique combination of roles in different organizations, and each, therefore, has unique needs and objectives in any one of those organizations. An individual may be a manager of a large work force attempting to achieve a complex task. If so, she may find that problems of motivation, control, and coordination are the most important. However, an individual may also find himself as the president of a union negotiating for ten cents in a collective bargaining session with a firm. Another individual may be a student in a university who is struggling with a variety of communication and power techniques to convince a committee that she really does deserve a staff parking sticker or that he should not be dismissed from school. Such issues are included in the study of organizational behavior.

Another set of important considerations for students of contemporary organizations comes from the changing nature of the society in which we live. Our affluent society has created the imperative for justice, equality, and the "good life" in addition to the conventional measures of success. Demands from women, minorities, and special interest groups for an equitable share of opportunities and rewards have added a new dimension to the challenge of dealing with organizations.

In a very general sense we define organizational behavior as the *analysis of factors that influence and are influenced by the behavior of people in organizations.* This means that an organizational behavior course can turn into an applied management class, a course in individual development, a theoretical review of research findings, or one of many other variations. Regardless of the orientation, however, we always return to the issue of how an individual identifies his or her organizational role.

We are all part of many organizations with a variety of forces continually pushing or pulling at us. This leaves us with three alternatives: to be victimized by the system without ever knowing what happened, to understand the process and try to protect ourselves, or to attempt to change the organization. If we fail, we should at least have a better understanding of the reasons why (although it may afford small consolation).

This section is intended to suggest different perceptions of an individual's role in an organization. Our intent is to confront people with many different dimensions of involvement in contemporary organizations.

READINGS

We Need a Nation of Scholar–Leaders

J.B. RITCHIE

Personal Responsibility and Organizations: We Need
a Nation of Scholar-Leaders

In the book, *The Once and Future King*, T.H. White retells the legend of King Arthur. In so doing, he captures an interesting dimension of growing up, learning, and accepting responsibility. When the young Arthur, affectionately referred to as "Wart" in the account, is despondent, a little confused, and sad, he goes to Ector and asks what he should do. Ector says he should go see the magician, Merlin, for some advice as to how to handle his frustrations. When he approaches the magician, Merlin responds as follows:

"The best thing for being sad," replied Merlin, beginning to puff and blow, "is to learn something. That is the only thing that never fails. You may grow old and trembling in your anatomies, you may lie awake at night listening to the disorder of your veins, you may miss your only love, you may see the world about you devastated by evil lunatics, or know your honor trampled in the sewers of baser minds. There is only one thing for it then—to learn. Learn why the world wags and what wags it. That is the only thing which

Reprinted courtesy of *Exchange*, a publication of the Brigham Young University School of Management, Fall 1980.

the mind can never exhaust, never alienate, never be tortured by, never fear or distrust, and never dream of regretting. Learning is the thing for you. Look at what a lot of things there are to learn—pure science, the only purity there is. You can learn astronomy in a lifetime, natural history in three, literature in six. And then after you have exhausted a milliard of lifetimes in biology and medicine and theocriticism and geography and history and economics why, you can then start to make a cartwheel out of the appropriate wood, or spend fifty years learning to begin to learn to beat your adversary at fencing. After that you can start again on mathematics, until it is time to learn to plough."

LEARNING: A SOLUTION TO LIFE'S FRUSTRATIONS

I subscribe to that advice. The solution to life's aggravations is to learn. And the solution to a frustrating life is to develop an attitude of learning. Each of us needs to develop an attitude toward life, toward organizations, toward the university, toward the Church, toward the state, toward the corporation, and toward each other of learning and of growing. We reduce the anxieties and confusions of life by developing a criterion for thinking that is based on analysis, interpretation, extrapolation, and extension of ideas rather than on judgment, classification, and rigid acceptance or rejection.

STUDENT VERSUS SCHOLAR PERSPECTIVE

The term *student* is a revered term to me. Although I will suggest a metaphor that may not reflect my reverence toward students, I do so only to make a point. Students are like computers. The system sits there waiting for an input to be determined by something like a professor, a textbook, or an expert source that tells the student what is appropriate or what is desirable or what is true. The information is put into the computer and, by some previously designed operational system, is classified, perhaps processed a bit, and then stored in some way for easy retrieval. That retrieval is triggered by something like a question in a classroom, an assignment to write a paper, or a question on an examination.

I wonder if our student model has corrupted us in the ability to learn and to grow. I wonder if we have simply mastered the art of taking a class. That can be pretty empty. There is life after college!

We should develop an eternal perspective rather than a semester perspective. We have different people reviewing and evaluating rather than a single teacher, and sometimes the student model gets in the way. Sometimes the student model undercuts our capacity to cope in a complex world. What is needed today is a scholar model.

A student asks what to do, a scholar searches and proposes what to do. A student blames the system for failure, a scholar has no need to blame anyone. He or she accepts responsibility for cor-

recting a failed system. A student listens to judge, a scholar listens to learn. A student transfers to the university, to the professor, to the boss, or to God both credit and blame that the individual should accept. In the process of so doing, we default in the most important function we have to perform: to decide what the meaning of life is.

THE SCHOLAR AND PERSONAL RESPONSIBILITY

From the scholar perspective, we do not search for the meaning of life, we define it, we develop it, we create it. We don't seek out who we are. Our identity is not found by searching across the land. Our identity is something we decide. Students expect someone else to define them; scholars accept the responsibility of defining themselves. Students expect the textbook to have the answer, and they want to know whether it is A or B.

I was intrigued recently in reading Norman Cousins's book, *Anatomy of an Illness*, where he describes how he accepted the joint responsibility with his doctor for his own health. He was told that his odds for getting better were 500–1 against, and he said when that announcement was made he decided he had to become a participant in this process in a way he had not considered previously. Norman Cousins, as the editor of the *Saturday Review*, had available to him a research staff. He sent his research staff out to do a survey of various medical findings, and he found that what his doctors were prescribing was not accurate. Norman Cousins did not blindly accept the diagnosis and prescriptions his doctor had arrived at working with incomplete data. Norman Cousins took the scholar-leader role and asked why. He found that the prescribed medication and the hospital environment were inappropriate. He determined that what he really needed was some Vitamin C, some laughter, and a pleasant environment. He moved himself out of a hospital into a nice hotel room. He started taking Vitamin C and watching Laurel and Hardy movies *and he got better.*

Cousins became part of the healing process. He applied the power of the participant, rather than to sit back and defer to the expert doctor.

Another example touches upon an uncomfortable and a difficult issue, but one that I find terribly compelling. Victor Frankl in *Man's Search for Meaning*, describes the fate of people in the concentration camps in Nazi captivity. He argues that what was needed was a fundamental change in attitude. Attitudes towards life, he said, had become too self-indulgent, too narcissistic, too self-serving, to really understand what was going on and to survive the brutality of the camp. In talking about the men in his camp, he said, "what was really needed was a fundamental change in our attitude towards life. We had to learn ourselves and furthermore we had to teach others that the issue was not what we expected from life but what life expected from us. We needed to stop asking what the meaning of life was and instead think of ourselves as those who were being questioned by life daily and hourly."

BEYOND "LOOKING OUT FOR NUMBER ONE"

Our answers must consist not simply in talk and meditation, but in right action and conduct. Life ultimately means accepting responsibility to define appropriate answers to each problem as it comes up. The more you look for the meaning of life, I would argue, the less you would find it. We can only be trapped by the contemporary pop psychology of "looking out for No. 1," "winning through intimidation," "pulling your own strings," "being your own best friend," and the whole raft of pop psychology books that tell you how to beat the system, take care of your-

self, indulge yourself at the expense of other people, be calloused and insensitive to the needs of the world around you in order to come out on top and win that game of competition with each other. The more we become victimized by such philosophies, the less capable we are of turning each of life's events into a learning experience rather than just an historical occurrence. We have got to become an involved part of the dynamic, rather than a simple part of a static system.

This issue of self-service is not new. It is not a product of our most recent five years. I refer to John Steinbeck's comments in *Grapes of Wrath*, where he described some of the landowners of the 1930s: "Some were kind because they hated what they had to do. Some of them were angry because they hated to be cruel. Some of them were cold because they long ago found that one could not be an owner unless one were cold. And all of them were caught up in something larger than themselves. Some of them hated the mathematics that drove them and were afraid. Some worshipped the mathematics that drove them because it provided a refuge from thought and from feeling."

THE STUDENT AND OVERRELIANCE ON ORGANIZATIONS

I think we have overdemanded our organizations to the point that we can only, ultimately, feel betrayed. Our economic, political, academic, social, and religious systems cannot answer all of the demands that we place on them. They cannot be aware enough. They cannot have an efficient enough information processing system to cope with the exponential explosion of information. They cannot acquire, digest, analyze, and resolve all of the complex and contradictory data received.

There is growing evidence of the failure of organizations just as there is growing evidence of shortcomings in the student perspective of life. Consider the following examples.

Fifty Percent of Organizational Decisions Ignored. For the past 15 years, I have been collecting observations of managers, executives, people who seemingly are in positions where others expect them to run an organization. One of the things I found interesting was that about 50 percent of the decisions these people make are never carried out in organizations. Not 50 percent of the random comments in a hall "why don't you look into this, Sue," but 50 percent of the formal decisions you can trace to board minutes, to memoranda that are distributed in an organization. Half of those decisions are not carried out! Why are they not carried out? Because no one person knows enough to account for all the variables in making those decisions. No one person nor one group—not the Soviet Politburo, not the Board of Directors of Exxon—can make all the decisions that will dictate the behavior of every member of that organization. "Democracy by default" may not sound elegant, but I think it comes from the inability to account for or control all the variables. The result of these decisions based on incomplete information: 50 percent of the decisions are not carried out.

When I was collecting my observations on this particular issue, I attempted to ask many people for their evaluations. When I would fly in an airplane, I would try to sit next to a person I felt was a business executive. (Sometimes I was badly mistaken, and that was an interesting experiment in itself.) I would sit next to someone that looked like an executive and I would say, "I am doing a research project, and I have been working in an organization where I find that half of the decisions made are not carried out. What do you think? It seems high to me. Can you believe that that is really true?" The responses I got were almost all confirming. In fact, one individual said, "Gee, I think that is right

and maybe it is even a little low. If 50 percent of my decisions got carried out, I would be delighted."

The Wrong Decisions Are Carried Out. This same respondent went on to make another point about failings in organizations. After confirming that many decisions are, in fact, ignored, he went on to say, "But I would argue that the survival and success of business depends on that 50 percent that are not carried out."

That is a telling argument, the fact that many decisions *shouldn't* be carried out. Now again, that is not comfortable to the administrator or the executive who sits back frustrated because orders are not followed. And, unfortunately, I have observed that ofttimes it is the wrong 50 percent that are not carried out. The good decisions are resented by the rebellious deviants, and the bad decisions are implemented by enthusiastic zealots. Somehow we need a nation of scholars, a nation of leaders, to discriminate as to which decisions *ought* to be carried out. But the more important point is not to sit back in judgment of which 50 percent, but to become part, in a responsible way, of that process.

There Is a Crisis in Organizational Leadership. I have been collecting other data about organizations which reveal an interesting trend. There is a crisis of leadership. There is, indeed, a crisis of confidence in our institutions: government, corporate, union, and military. I have been measuring the attitudes that people have toward those above and below them in organizations. I found it interesting that 15 years ago when I started studying this, I asked people to rate some of their character traits on seven-point scales. Consistently, these self-ratings came out about 5.7. Now there is nothing very significant about that particular point until we use it as a reference for comparison.

In the course of this research I also

asked people to rate, using the same seven-point scales, their bosses and their subordinates. Fifteen years ago, they saw their bosses at about a 6.0 (three-tenths of a point above themselves) and they saw their subordinates at a 4.2 (about a point and a half below them). That was a consistent pattern regardless of organizational level. Vice presidents saw the president at about a 6, themselves at 5.7, and the department heads at about a 4.2. First-line supervisors saw themselves at about a 5.7, their foreman at about 6.0 and their subordinates at about the same point of 4.2. These people saw themselves as a lot better than their subordinates, and almost as good as their boss. Therefore, when they communicate with the boss, they expected the boss to have full confidence in them and to think they were almost as good as the boss. Conversely, however, they expect subordinates to be inferior clods, and they talk down to them, disregard them, and belittle them. They have little confidence in subordinates' ability to function, and, therefore, they overcontrol them and harass them.

Those indicators held for several years. But as the 1970s began, I started getting different data. People still rated themselves at 5.7 on an average, still put their subordinates at about a 4.2, but now the bosses were coming in at a 5.7 also. So now my conclusions about their relationships changed. They now saw themselves as a lot better than subordinates, and as good as their boss. Many people now felt that they could do the boss's job as well as the boss. They were losing confidence in their superiors. By the middle of the seventies the data changed again. Starting in 1975 or 1976 the data started to look this way: Individuals still rated themselves at 5.7, subordinates about 4.2 and bosses were averaging 5.3. Now my interpretation changed one more time: they now see themselves as a lot better than their subordinates and quite a bit better than the boss. They concluded that there is nobody

in the world as good as themselves!

Organizational Lying. One further bit of evidence of the failing organization was reflected in a recent study of organizational lying—outright misstatements of the truth. The study discussed the external pressures on organizations to misrepresent their performance. The emphasis is on the facade rather than substance. Organizational rewards come from positive external reports, valid or not, instead of the internal criterion of genuine service.

There are pressures to lie and to misrepresent in all organizations. These need to be identified.

THE ORGANIZATION AS A HAVEN FROM SELF-RESPONSIBILITY

The organization has become a mechanism that many of us use to absolve ourselves of the burden of making decisions that only we can make and of accepting responsibility for thinking. Organizations will not and cannot replace the individual's need to become a scholar-leader who participates in the dynamic process of deciding. We cannot be spectators. We cannot shift the burden for self-development to others. Besides, organizations simply don't work that well.

As a "student" society, we have come to expect of organizations functions that only we as individuals can be responsible for. And when they fail to meet these expectations, our confidence in organizational leadership drops. We all need to be scholar-leaders. Our contemporary society is so complex, that it behooves each of us to become not only minimally informed, not passive members, but incredibly well-informed, active members. The burden is severe on all of us to be scholars and leaders, to develop the analytical tools to understand what organizations in our societies are doing, and to make fewer demands upon them. Not fewer demands in terms of morality or ethics, but fewer demands in terms of the universality of organizations serving needs we must ultimately be responsible for as individuals. We must demand of leaders of essential organizations, dignity and morality. We must expect less in terms of total output.

Our civilization depends on that informed citizenry in a way we have never depended on it before. The information available is too complex, the demands and opportunities for misrepresentation are too great, and the opportunity for organizational encroachment in private lives is too great.

But the positive opportunities are also great for accepting responsibility for our own involvement in life as scholars, defin-

ing our own learning and performance objectives, evaluating ourselves, making proposals instead of simply asking questions, and listening to learn rather than to judge. I hope we can do that. I hope we can become enthused, committed, informed participants rather than ones who sit back condemning the system because it does not define things our way. And in the process, I hope that we clearly can gain an increased confidence in ourselves. I hope that we don't wait for the university or for the nation, or the state, or the corporation to change our world—but instead, accept responsibilities for being part of it. When organizations fail, don't just blame the system, but accept the opportunity to become part of a changing process of the world in which we live.

That's Easy for You to Say

LUCIEN RHODES

An Obsession With "Corporate Culture" Can Be Worse Than No Culture at All. Just Ask the Man Who Wrote *the* Book on the Subject

It all began on Labor Day Weekend in 1982. Allan A. Kennedy was sitting in a low beach chair on the shore in front of his cottage on Cape Cod. Next to him was his friend and fellow consultant Tony

Merlo. As they relaxed there, watching the sailboats drift across Cape Cod Bay, drinking beer, and listening to a Red Sox game on the radio, Kennedy turned to Merlo and, with the majestic eloquence suited to great undertakings, said: "Gee, Tony, you know, we ought to start some kind of business together."

This identical thought has, of course, passed between countless friends ever since the discovery of profit margins. Coming from most people, it would have fallen into the general category of loose talk. But Kennedy was not most people. For one thing, he was a 13–year veteran of McKinsey & Co., the management consulting firm, and partner in charge of its Boston office. More to the point, he was the co-author of a recently published book that offered a startling new perspective on corporate life—one that challenged the whole way people thought about business.

The book was entitled *Corporate Cultures*, a term that was itself new to the language, and it dealt with an aspect of business that, up to then, had been largely ignored. Broadly speaking, that aspect involved the role played by a company's values, symbols, rites, and rituals in determining its overall performance. Citing examples from some of the country's most dynamic companies, Kennedy and co-author Terrence E. Deal showed that these "cultural" factors had a major effect on the attitudes and behavior of a company's employees, and were thus of critical importance to its long-term success.

By any measure, the book was a ground-breaking work, challenging, as it did, the rational, quantitative models of corporate success that were so popular in the 1960s and '70s. But its impact had as much to do with its timing as its content. Published in June 1982, during a period of economic stagnation—with unemployment at 9.5%, the prime over 16%, and trade deficits soaring to record levels—*Corporate Cultures* offered a welcome antidote to the doom and gloom that was abroad in the land. Like *In Search of Excellence*, which appeared a few months later, it suggested that Japan was not the only nation capable of producing strong, highly motivated companies that could compete effectively in the international arena. America could produce—in fact,

was already producing—its own.

What the book did not detail, however, was how corporate cultures were actually constructed. The authors could describe a particular culture and demonstrate its effects, but they offered few clues as to how a company might develop a culture in the first place. So the news that Allan Kennedy was going into business was greeted with more than passing interest among the followers of corporate culture. Here was an opportunity to find out how a living, breathing culture could be created, and the creator would be none other than the man who wrote the book.

After an extensive survey of business opportunities, Kennedy and Merlo decided to develop microcomputer software for sales and marketing management. They felt this was their most promising option, given the anticipated growth of the microcomputer market and their own experience as consultants. Acting on that assessment, they resigned from McKinsey and, in February 1983, formally launched Selkirk Associates Inc. with four of their friends.

Kennedy had lofty ambitions for Selkirk. More than a business, he saw it as a kind of laboratory for his theories. He wanted it to function as a society of professional colleagues committed to building a culture and a company that would stress collaboration, openness, decentralization, democratic decisions, respect, and trust. In this society, each individual would be encouraged to devise his or her own entrepreneurial response to the challenges of the business.

For Kennedy, this was not a long-term goal, something that would evolve naturally in the fullness of time. On the contrary, it was a pressing, immediate concern. Accordingly, he focused all his attention on creating such a culture from the start. "I spent lots of time," he says, "trying to think about what kind of values the company ought to stand for and therefore what kind of behavior I expected from people." These thoughts eventually went into a detailed statement of "core beliefs," which he reviewed and amplified with each new employee. In the same vein, Kennedy and his colleagues chose a "guiding principle," namely, a commitment to "making people more productive." They would pursue this ambition, everyone agreed, "through the products and services we offer" and "in the way we conduct our own affairs."

And, in the beginning at least, Selkirk seemed to be everything Kennedy had hoped for. The company set up shop in Boston, in an office that consisted of a large, rectangular room, with three smaller attachments. Each morning, staff members would pile into the main room and sort themselves out by function—programmers and systems engineers by the windows, administrators in the middle, sales and marketing folk at the other end. In keeping with Kennedy's cultural precepts, there were no private offices or, indeed, any physical demarcations between functions.

It was a familial enterprise, informed with the very qualities Kennedy had laid out in his statement of core beliefs. The work was absorbing, the comradeship inspiring. Most mornings, the staff feasted on doughnuts, which they took to calling "corporate carbos," as a wordplay on "corporate cultures." They began a scrapbook as an impromptu cultural archive. Included among the memorabilia was "The Ravin'," an Edgar Allan Poe takeoff that commemorated Selkirk's first stirrings in earlier temporary headquarters:

Once upon an April morning, disregarding every warning,
In a Back Bay storefront, Selkirk software was begun:
True, it was without a toilet, but that didn't seem to spoil it.

To strengthen their bonds even further, the staff began to experiment with so-called rites, rituals, and ceremonies—all

important elements of a corporate culture, according to Kennedy's book. Selkirk's office manager, Linda Sharkey, recalls a day, for example, when the whole company went out to Kennedy's place on Cape Cod to celebrate their common purpose with barbecues on the beach. "The sun was shining, and we were all there together," she says. "It was a beautiful day. That's the way it was. We didn't use the terms among ourselves that Allan uses in the book. With us, corporate culture was more by seeing and doing." Sharkey remembers, too, Friday afternoon luncheons of pizza or Chinese food, at which everyone in the company had a chance to talk about his or her accomplishments or problems, or simply hang out.

Kennedy was pleased with all this, as well he might be. "We were," he says, "beginning to develop a real culture."

Then the walls went up.

The problem stemmed from the situation in the big room, where the technical people were laboring feverishly to develop Selkirk's first product, while the salespeople were busy preselling it. The former desperately needed peace and quiet to concentrate on their work; the latter were a boisterous lot, fond of crowing whenever a prospect looked encouraging. In fact, the salespeople crowed so often and so loudly that the technicians complained that they were being driven to distraction. Finally, they confronted Kennedy with the problem. Their solution, which Kennedy agreed to, was to erect five-foot-high movable partitions, separating each functional grouping from the others.

In the memory of Selkirk veterans, "the day the walls went up" lives on as a day of infamy. "It was terrible," says Sharkey. "I was embarrassed."

"It was clearly a symbol of divisiveness," says Kennedy.

"I don't know what would have been the right solution," says Reilly Hayes, Selkirk's 23–year-old technical wizard, "but the wall certainly wasn't. It blocked out the windows for the other end of the room. Someone [in marketing] drew a picture of a window and taped it to the wall. The whole thing created a lot of dissension."

Indeed, the erection of the walls touched off a feud between engineering and marketing that eventually grew into "open organizational warfare," according to Kennedy. "I let the wall stand, and a competitive attitude developed where engineering started sniping at marketing. We had two armed camps that didn't trust each other."

As if that weren't bad enough, other problems were beginning to surface. For one thing, the company was obviously overstaffed, having grown from 12 people in June 1983 to 25 in January 1984, without any product—or sales—to show for it. "That was a big mistake," says Kennedy. "We clearly ramped up the organization too fast, particularly given the fact that we were financing ourselves. I mean, for a while, we had a burn rate of around $100,000 per month."

Even more serious, however, was the problem that emerged following the release of the company's initial product, Correspondent, in February 1984. Not that there was anything wrong with the product. It was, in fact, a fine piece of software, and it premiered to glowing reviews. Designed as a selling tool, it combined database management, calendar management, word processing, and mail merge—functions that could help customers organize their accounts, track and schedule sales calls and follow-ups, and generate correspondence. And it did all that splendidly.

The problem had to do with the price tag, a whopping $12,000 per unit. The Selkirk team members had come up with this rarefied figure, not out of greed, but out of a commitment to customer service—a goal to which they had pledged themselves as part of their cultural mission. In order to provide such service, they fig-

ured, a Selkirk representative might have to spend two or three weeks with each customer, helping to install and customize the product. Trouble was, customers weren't willing to *pay* for that service, not at $12,000 per unit anyway. After a brief flurry of interest, sales dropped off.

"We just blew it," says Kennedy. "We were arrogant about the market. We were trying to tell the market something it wasn't interested in hearing. We took an arbitrary cultural goal and tried to make it into a strategy, rather than saying we're a market-driven company and we've got to find out what the market wants and supply it." Unfortunately, six months went by before Kennedy and his colleagues figured all this out and began to reduce Correspondent's price accordingly.

By then, however, Selkirk's entire sales effort was in shambles, a victim of its commitment to employee autonomy. Sales targets were seldom realized. Indeed, they were scarcely even set. At weekly meetings, salespeople would do little more than review account activity. "If a salesman said each week for three weeks in a row that he expected to close a certain account, and it never happened," says Merlo, "well, we didn't do anything about it. In any other company, he would probably have been put on probation." As it was, each of the participants entered the results of the meeting in a red-and-black ledger book and struck out once again to wander haphazardly through uncharted territory. "The mistake we made," reflects Merlo, "was using real money in a real company to test hypotheses about what sales goals should be."

Finally, in June 1984, Kennedy took action, laying off 6 people. In July, Correspondent's price was dropped to $4,000 per unit, but sales remained sluggish. In September, Kennedy laid off 5 more people, bringing the size of the staff back to 12.

One of those laid off was the chief engineer, a close friend of Kennedy's, but a man whose departure brought an immediate ceasefire between the warring factions. That night, the remaining staff members took down the walls and stacked them neatly in the kitchenette, where they repose to this day. "We felt," says Sharkey, "like we had our little family back together again."

With morale finally rebounding, Selkirk again cut Correspondent's price in the early fall, to $1,500. This time, sales responded, and, in November, the company enjoyed its first month in the black.

But Selkirk was not yet out of the woods. What remained was for Kennedy to figure out the significance of what had happened, and to draw the appropriate conclusions. Clearly, his experiment had not turned out as he had planned. His insistence on a company without walls had led to organizational warfare. His goal of providing extraordinary service had led to a crucial pricing error. His ideal of employee autonomy had led to confusion in the sales force. In the end, he was forced to fire more than half of his staff, slash prices by 87%, and start over again. What did it all mean?

Merlo had one answer. "We're talking about an experiment in corporate culture failing because the business environment did not support it," he says. "The notion of corporate culture got in the way of tough-minded business decisions." He also faults the emphasis on autonomy. "I don't think we had the right to be organized the way we were. I think we should have had more discipline."

Kennedy himself soon came around to a similar view. "Look in [the statement of core beliefs] and tell me what you find about the importance of performance, about measuring performance or about the idea that people must be held accountable for their performance," he says. "That stuff should have been there. I'm not discounting the importance of corporate culture, but you have to worry about

the business at the same time, or you simply won't have one. Then you obviously won't *need* a culture. Where the two come together, I think, is in the cultural norms for performance, what kind of performance is expected of people. And that's a linkage that wasn't explicit in my mind three years ago. But it is now." He adds that, if the manuscript of *Corporate Cultures* were before him today, he would include a section on performance standards, measurement systems, and accountability sanctions.

On that point, he might get an argument from his co-author, Terrence Deal, a professor at Vanderbilt University and a member of Selkirk's board of directors since its inception. Deal does not disagree about the importance of discipline and performance standards, but he questions the wisdom of trying to impose them from above. The most effective performance standards, he notes, are the ones that employees recognize and accept as the product of their own commitment, and these can emerge only from the employees' experience. "One of the things that we know pretty handsomely," says Deal, "is that it's the informal performance standards that really drive a company."

In fact, Kennedy may have gotten into trouble not by doing too little, but by doing too much. Rather than letting Selkirk's culture evolve organically, he tried to impose a set of predetermined cultural values on the company, thereby retarding the growth of its own informal value system. He pursued culture as an end in itself, ignoring his own caveat, set down in his book, that "the business environment is the single greatest influence in shaping a corporate culture." Instead, he tried to shape the culture in a vacuum, without synchronizing it with the company's business goals.

In so doing, Kennedy reduced corporate culture to a formula, a collection of generic "principles." It was a cardinal error, if not an uncommon one. "There are a lot of people," says Deal, "who take our book literally and try to design a culture much as if they're trying to design an organization chart. My experience across the board has been that, as soon as people make it into a formula, they start making mistakes." By following the "formula," Kennedy wound up imposing his own set of rules on Selkirk—although not enough of them, and not the right kind, he now says. The irony is that a real corporate culture allows a company to manage itself *without* formal rules, and to manage itself better than a company that has them.

Deal makes another point. Kennedy, he observes, might be less concerned with performance today if he had not hired so many friends at the beginning. Friends are nice to have around, but it's often hard to discipline them, or subject them to a company's normal sanctions. Over the long run, Deal says, their presence at Selkirk probably undermined the development of informal performance standards.

Kennedy himself may have played a role in that, too. He estimates that, over the past year, he has spent only one day a week at Selkirk. The rest of the time he has been on the road as a consultant, using his fees to help finance the company. In all, he has sunk some $1 million of his own money into Selkirk, without which the company might not have survived. But it has come at a price. "Nobody had to pay attention to things like expenses, because there was a perception of an infinite sink of money," Kennedy says.

The danger of that perception finally came home to him last summer, when three of Selkirk's four salespeople elected to take vacations during the same month. The result was that sales for the month all but vanished. Kennedy had had enough. "I told the people here that either you sustain the company as a self-financing entity, or I will let it go under. I'm unwilling to put more money on the table."

And yet, in the end, it was hard to avoid the conclusion that a large part of Selkirk's continuing problem was Allan Kennedy himself—a thought that did not escape him. "I've got a lot to learn about running a business successfully," he says, "about doing it myself, I mean. I think I know everything about management except how to manage. I can give world-class advice on managing, but—when it comes right down to it—I take too long and fall into all the traps that I see with the managers I advise."

Whatever his shortcomings as a manager, there is one thing Kennedy can't be faulted for, and that is lack of courage. Having drawn the inevitable conclusion, he went out looking for someone who could help him do a better job of managing the company. For several months, he negotiated with the former president of a Boston-based high-tech firm, but the two of them were unable to come to terms. Instead, Kennedy has made changes at Selkirk that he hopes will achieve the same effect. In the new structure, Merlo is taking charge of the microcomputer end of the business, while Betsy Meade—a former West Coast sales representative—has responsibility for a new minicomputer version of Correspondent, to be marketed in conjunction with Prime Computer Corp. As for Kennedy, he will concern himself with external company relations, product-development strategies, and, of course, corporate culture.

Kennedy is full of optimism these days. He points out that, despite its checkered history, Selkirk has emerged with a durable product and an installed base of about 1,000 units. In addition, the company will soon be bolstered with the proceeds from a $250,000 private placement. Meanwhile, he says, some of the company's previous problems have been dealt with, thanks to the introduction of a reliable order-fulfillment process, the decision to put sales reps on a straight commission payment schedule, and the establishment of specific sales targets for at least the next two quarters. "I think we have much more focused responsibility," he says, "and much more tangible measures of success for people in their jobs."

Overall, Kennedy looks on the past three years as a learning experience. "There are times when I think I should charge up most of the zigs and the zags to sheer rank incompetence," he admits. "But then there are other times when I look back and say, 'Nobody's that smart, and you can't do everything right.' In life, you have to be willing to try things. And if something doesn't work, you have to be willing to say, 'Well, that was a dumb idea,' and then try something else." Now, he believes, he has a chance to do just that.

In the meantime, he is in the process of writing another book. He already has a proposal circulating among publishers. In his idle moments, he occasionally amuses himself by inventing titles. One of those titles speaks volumes about where he has been: *Kicking Ass and Taking Names*.

The Cultural Awareness Hierarchy: A Model for Promoting Understanding

PETER MUNIZ and ROBERT CHASNOFF

Frequently, trainers are called upon to conduct training sessions that help participants increase their understanding of another culture. We trainers are tempted to rush in with what has been asked for—instant information and understanding. We bring films, speakers, reading materials (often fancy brochures), foods, entertainment and case studies about the culture under discussion.

This kind of information is valuable in learning about another culture. However, several preliminary sets of understanding are required before understanding of another culture can be achieved.

This article presents the Cultural Awareness Hierarchy, a conceptual model

that outlines six levels necessary for a full understanding of another culture. A training approach used to introduce the hierarchy is presented, as well.

THE AGREE–DISAGREE QUESTIONNAIRE

To help participants become involved in the topic and the training session, a questionnaire similar to that shown in Figure 1 is distributed. Before continuing to read this article, take a moment now to complete the questionnaire. Read each statement quickly, and decide whether you strongly agree (SA), agree (A), disagree (D) or strongly disagree (SD).

In training sessions, the questionnaire is used in the following manner:

• Each participant completes the questionnaire individually.

- The participants form subgroups to determine a group answer for each item. The subgroups are instructed to address each statement, to make their decisions unanimous (or, at the very least, to arrive at them by consensus) and to avoid voting or merely giving in.
- The subgroups post their answers on large easel sheets, identifying which were "trouble" items.
- The entire group looks at the data. Participants are instructed to examine those items where responses of the subgroups are distributed over both "agree" and "disagree"; and those items with which the subgroups had the most difficulty reaching a decision.

Following discussion of the questionnaire data, the Cultural Awareness Hierarchy is introduced.

THE CULTURAL AWARENESS HIERARCHY

The Cultural Awareness Hierarchy con-sists of six levels (Figure 2). To achieve knowledge and understanding at level VI, one must first gain knowledge and understanding at levels I through V. Cultural awareness training programs that concentrate *only* on level VI risk failure.

The model is universal. It is applicable in a highly heterogeneous country or one with an apparently homogeneous cultural base. The hierarchy also may be used to deal with subcultures within one nation. The model may refer to specialized groups within a culture, such as a group of professionals as one population and their clients as another.

Level I—The Self

The concept of self-understanding is the foundation of the hierarchy. It is based on personal factors, such as the individual's health, culture and subculture, education, work and other experiences, values and interpersonal ability. Understanding at this step is fulfilled when an individual can describe how he or she relates to others and how others relate to him or her.

Why is understanding at this level so

FIGURE 1. Agree/Disagree Items

1. Hostile relations between countries often cancel any benefits that may be gained through cultural awareness training programs.	SA	A	D	SD
2. Many people cannot understand *other* cultures because they don't know or understand their *own* culture.	SA	A	D	SD
3. Highly skilled technicians who have very little self-awareness (or self-under-standing) and who cannot communicate with people in their *own* country, will *not* be able to understand or accept another country's culture.	SA	A	D	SD
4. The words we use to describe our own behavior, in contrast with words we use to describe the behavior of people from other countries, often serve as greater intercultural barriers than our lack of cultural understanding. (Example: "*We* are patriotic. *They* are nationalistic.")	SA	A	D	SD
5. "Cultural differences" are merely different ways of coping with universal human feelings and situations.	SA	A	D	SD
6. An excellent technician who has no intercultural knowledge will succeed in another country more easily than the technician who has a lot of intercultural knowledge but very little technical skill.	SA	A	D	SD
7. When selecting people to go to another country, the best candidates are those individuals who have a subcultural (minority group) background that is the same as the culture of the country to which the individual will be assigned.	SA	A	D	SD

crucial before engaging in training about another culture? Take, for example, the case of a hostile individual with very little self-understanding, who alienates many people in his or her own culture. Very likely, such a person also will alienate people when working in another culture. Large doses of knowledge of the other culture will be rendered useless because of the general negative behavior and lack of self-awareness.

Level II—Technical or Professional Skills

Level II goes beyond personal traits and focuses on a person's technical or professional skills. An incompetent technician or professional working in another country will fail regardless of his or her knowledge about that country's culture.

Trainers and managers may be tempted to infuse large amounts of "cultural understanding" as a substitute for either confronting an individual's lack of technical/professional skills or implementing

the necessary technical competency criteria in selecting individuals for assignment to other cultures.

People in host countries may have little patience with incompetent individuals who are supposed to be helping or working with them. They may view the incompetent individual as officially representing the sending country. They may believe they are held in low regard and thus receive the discards of the sending organization or country.

Level III—Factors Beyond "Culture" Which May Influence Behavior

In the August 1980 *Training and Development Journal*, Luke L. Batdorf wrote, "... what is called a cultural problem is frequently not a cultural problem, but a problem of a different sort." (Batdorf 1980, 28–41) When relationships between cultural groups are strained, there is a tendency to place the blame on lack of cultural understanding or, more politely,

---

FIGURE 2. The Cultural Awareness Hierarchy

VI The Other Culture	Knowledge, understanding about the other culture or subculture.
V Factors Specific to One's Own Country	Understanding, knowledge about, recognition of the differences among monoculture, multiculture and "melting pot."
IV One's Own Culture	Recognition, understanding, acceptance of *own* culture/subculture.
III Factors Beyond "Culture" Which May Influence Behavior	The dynamics of poverty, sexism, racism; knowledge, understanding, empathy.
II Technical or Professional Skills	The individual's technical or professional skills; how the individual relates to others.
I The Self	Self-awareness, interpersonal ability, culture/subculture, background, experience, education, values.

Source: ©1979, By Peter Muniz & Company, Somerset, N.J.

---

to refer to "the differences between the cultures." Frequently, this type of explanation deftly avoids the real issue—the "problem of a different sort." Level III focuses on factors *other* than obvious cultural differences as a way to confront the real issues that influence relationships and productivity.

At this level the emphasis is on identifying and understanding organizational and individual behavior in specific events, and distinguishing that behavior from what is often referred to as "cultural." Suppose, for example, people from one group are rich and people from another group are poor. The behaviors between the two groups may greatly depend upon such factors as their degree of hunger, self-interests, satisfaction of aspirations, skills and capability to function successfully. When the two groups represent different cultures or subcultures, there is a tendency to blame negative behaviors on cultural differences rather than on the real motivating forces.

Level IV—One's Own Culture

Most of us take our own culture for granted. We have seen it, heard it, felt it and tasted it all our lives. It is reality, and it feels right. If we were never to deal with another culture, perhaps we would never have to stop to understand our own.

However, once we need to relate to another culture, we must come to grips with our culture. After we have examined some of our basic cultural experiences, we are better able to see how people of other cultures deal with the same experiences. This examination is particularly important in the United States, where people who prepare to work in other countries generally know only one language and have had few contacts with people from other countries.

Participants' reactions to this approach are predictable. At first, they resist openly or question politely: "I came here to learn about other cultures, not my own." But after the initial difficulties, participants describe the activities as revealing, important and satisfying.

In the U.S., a frequent cultural issue relates to the fact that one generation (or more) buried cultural aspects of their original, "native" country or culture as a price for assimilation into the dominant culture. Participants describe experiences and family stories they thought they had forgotten—about children being told not to speak their "native" tongue outside the home or to dress or behave in certain ways. These remembered events frequently are touched by rage, a sense of inferiority or shame related to one's own cultural ties.

Level V—Factors Specific to One's Country

After dealing with one's culture, the next question is: What should one know about one's country? There are many topics and issues that must be understood. One issue that always emerges is diversity.

Again, using the U.S. as an example, diversity is the rule. But what kind of diversity? For generations, the U.S. was described as a "melting pot." The cultural ingredients were believed to lose their original identities and blend into a common product. More recently, however, the multicultural quality of the nation has been described as a "salad bowl." The latter image indicates a uniting of the ingredients, with each maintaining its own identity. The civil rights movement of Blacks, Hispanics, Native Americans, women and other groups have underscored the multicultural "salad bowl" quality of the U.S.

Level VI—The Other Culture

Once levels I through V have been covered, level VI finally can be addressed.

Trainers and consultants should apply levels I to V to themselves before attempting to train others in another country's culture. Self-awareness is extremely important for intercultural trainers.

We live by our perspectives. In her seminal study *Patterns of Culture*, Ruth Benedict warns about our temptation to view other cultures with our own as the standard. (Benedict 1959) To do so leads to biased analyses and presentations of other cultures. We are in. They are out. We use such judgmental terms as *those* people, uncultured, barbaric, backwards, uncivilized, nationalistic, politically inexperienced, primitive, living in the dark ages. We accept terminology without thinking. For example, the whole world accepted a certain perspective for centuries, in using the terms Far East and Mid East without realizing that they referred to distance from London.

Oversimplification that denies the modern, overlooks diversity or distorts the past may lead to misrepresentation. There are universals, alternatives and specialties in every culture of every country. Oversimplification can give trainees a neat set of notes and a few catch phrases. Oversimplification can also lead to distortions that insult, reduce intercultural understanding, create conflict and diminish productivity.

FLEXIBILITY IN THE HIERARCHY

The questionnaire that introduces the hierarchy should be adapted and developed according to a diagnosis of organizational and training needs. A good questionnaire contains about 18 items and touches on material at all levels of the hierarchy. Of course, the questionnaire is merely a vehicle. It rapidly moves into the background, and the major focus is on the hierarchy.

Some trainers familiar with the hierarchy have suggested that levels III, IV and V be interchanged; that levels III and V be interchanged; or that levels III and IV be interchanged. Another variation is to deal with these three intertwining levels starting with IV, then V, then III. Regardless of the position the three levels take in relation to one another, they must appear above levels I and II, and below level VI.

Traditional approaches to learning about another culture ensure a familiarity with superficial aspects of the culture. The kind of approach offered by the Cultural Awareness Hierarchy—involving, introspective, building progressively on the known—delivers a far deeper, lasting understanding of the culture and the individual's unique response to it. In addition, the hierarchy offers a practical, methodical training system that can be adapted easily for a variety of circumstances.

Who Gets the Parachutes?

JERRY FLINT

When did you last pick up a newspaper without reading about another big layoff? That, unfortunately, is the dark side of the current improvement in efficiency.

In this issue we cite instance after instance of U.S. companies slimming down to fighting weight. Call it rationalization, call it restructuring, call it just common sense, but the plain fact is that a good deal of this efficiency is being achieved at the expense of a lot of laid-off workers and executives. That these layoffs are necessary for keeping businesses in business is obvious. We ought not forget, however, that some people are paying a heavier price than others for improving U.S. efficiency.

Lee Iacocca was becomingly blunt about it in his story of saving Chrysler: "When we finally held the victory parade, a lot of our soldiers were missing. A lot of people—blue-collar, white-collar and dealers—who had been with us in 1979 were no longer around to enjoy the fruits of victory."

Hardly a day goes by without a headline on some major bloodletting: AT & T to cut its payroll by 27,000, IBM letting go 10,000, GM chopping 29,000, United Technologies 11,000, the merged Burroughs/Sperry (Unisys) 10,000, Eastern Air Lines another 1,500, Illinois Central Gulf Railroad also 1,500. Wang, Tenneco, RCA, Exxon, Alcoa. Why go on? The list seemingly never stops. (When did you last read

about a big company hiring on a large scale?)

Despite the move from recession in 1980 to good times in 1985, 40% of The Forbes 500 companies had fewer employees than five years earlier. Were it not for the continued vigor of small business and service business, unemployment might be staggering.

Is there a missing ingredient here? Yes. What might be called the human face of capitalism—at least some symbols, if not the reality, of equality of sacrifice.

After all, those workers from the production line now laid off and those middle managers now adrift didn't hire themselves. They didn't create bureaucratic bloat. They didn't make the foolish acquisitions or product choices. Yet too often the executives who made mistakes escape the sacrifice. Fire enough, cut costs enough, and profits climb, stock options are worth more, and so are the bonuses. At worst, the unsuccessful managers bail out with golden parachutes, and the new managers bayonet the wounded.

In all this, business is building up a good deal of resentment that will one day come to haunt it, perhaps in the form of ill-considered legislation. Iacocca cut his pay to $1 a year. Sure, Lee Iacocca was rich, but it was a symbol. Leadership means setting the example. The good officer feeds his men before he feeds himself. The army that doesn't bring out its wounded with it will find its fighters ready to break and run when the battle gets hot. There are some unwritten rules in business, too: Loyalty up requires loyalty down.

But how? At the Toyota-GM car plant in Fremont, Calif., the management pledged to cut its own pay before it lays off production workers. At Hewlett-Packard, during bad times employees have gone on short time, taking a day off without pay every two weeks, and executives have taken 10% pay cuts to avoid firings. At Delta Air Lines back when times were bad in 1983, the executives and the board took up to 10% pay cuts, and the employees took voluntary pay cuts or donated money to buy the company a new $30 million jetliner. "Some Japanese called us to find out where in Japan we had trained. They figured we must have trained in Japan to have anything like that," laughed a Delta man. But Delta didn't learn this from the Japanese. It's just a good-old-boy, old-fashioned airline with a southern-gentleman attitude.

Maybe more bosses should be fired when things go wrong, if for no other reason than to set an example. That's a tough sell. But the bosses and the boards could be tougher on themselves and others at the top. They should be willing to cut their own pay and perks and to eliminate bonuses before layoffs are necessary. Once the head-chopping starts, it's necessary. Laurence Tisch has ordered layoffs at CBS, for example, but he also closed executive dining rooms and cut back on limousines.

Business people like to point out that they aren't heartless in their layoffs. They pay early retirement bonuses and boost pensions when they push people out. They carry hospital insurance for them and hire job counselors. That helps, but it doesn't change the fact that the privates and junior officers are too often the ones who are laid off, while the generals get medals for cleaning up the mess they themselves made.

The final issue is what happens after the pressure for cost-cutting eases; it will, it always has. Is it back to the good old days, meaning back to corporate bloat? If that's what happens, the sacrifices of today's victims will be for nought.

A Conversation With Peter F. Drucker: Or the Psychology of Managing Management

MARY HARRINGTON HALL

Peter Drucker is perhaps the most respected management consultant in this country, and his clients include some of the nations most respected companies. Born in Vienna, educated in Austria, England, and Germany, he received his law degree from Frankfurt University. After working as a newspaperman in Europe, he became an economist with a London international banking house. Drucker came to this country in 1937, continuing as an economist until 1942, when he began a seven-year association with Bennington College as professor of politics. In 1957, he was awarded the American Marketing Association's Parlin Award, and now is on the New York University faculty. His books include *The Practice of Management,* shown by a *Harvard Business Review* survey to be read by more top executives than any other book in the field, as well as *Managing for Results,* and *The Effective Executive,* both rapidly becoming bibles for students of the business world.

Mary Harrington Hall: How can young people today know just where they might fit in this wide-open kind of world? How can they choose?

Peter Drucker: Here I am 58, and I still don't know what I am going to do when I grow up. My children and their respective spouses think I am kidding when I say that, but I am not. You know what I mean; they don't. Nobody tells them that life is not that categorized. And nobody tells them that the only way to find what you want is to create a job. Nobody worth his salt has ever moved into an existing job. That's for post office clerks.

Hall: Whether they actually are in the post office or not.

Drucker: Primarily, out of the post office. But if you told this to the 22–year-old, I don't think it would register. He doesn't understand it, and no one can make him understand. There are a few elementary things you can say.

Hall: And what are they?

Drucker: First, you know what you don't want to do, but what you *do* want to do you don't know. There is no way of finding out but by trying. Second, one doesn't marry a job. A job is your opportunity to find out—that's all it is. You owe no loyalty to your employer other than not betraying secrets. Be ruthless about finding out whether you belong; I am. Finally, looking around doesn't get you anywhere. One can always quit. Don't try to reason out those things one can learn only from experience. Do you know enough about yourself? There are things you can know, even at age 20.

Hall: When I was 20 I knew so many things. I knew that life was exciting and romantic and a great adventure. What should my career thoughts have been?

Drucker: To start out, I think one of the most important things would be to know if you like pressure or if you cannot take it at all. There may be people who can take pressure or leave it alone, but I have never met any of them. I am one who needs pressure. You are one, too, Mary. If there is no deadline staring us in the face, we have to invent one. I am sluggish, lethargic, a lizard, until the adrenaline starts pouring. A low metabolism—psychologically. People differ so. One of the men I am closest to goes to pieces under pressure. He is one of the best urologists. But he spends nights at the bedside of a critically ill patient, and it is obvious he is going to pieces before the patient dies. Mind you, he pulls a lot of them through, but he cannot take the pressure. He's a wreck—which probably makes him a good doctor.

Hall: What else should you know besides your ability to stand pressure?

Drucker: You have to know whether you belong in a big organization. In a big organization, you don't see results, you are too damn far away from them. The enjoyment is being a part of the big structure. If you tell people you work for General Electric, everyone knows what G.E. is. And I think you need to know whether you want to be in daily combat as a dragon-slayer or if you want to think things through, to an-

alyze, prepare. Do you enjoy surmounting the daily crisis, or do you really get your satisfaction out of anticipating and preventing the crisis? These things I believe one *does* know about oneself at age 20.

Hall: What is the hardest thing to know?

Drucker: There is one great question I don't think most young people can answer: "Are you a perceptive or an analytical person?" This is terribly important. Either you start out with an insight and then think the problem through, or you start out with a train of thought and arrive at a conclusion. One really needs to be able to do both, but most people can't. I am totally unanalytical and completely perceptive. I have never in my life understood anything that I have not seen.

Hall: What about being a listener or a reader?

Drucker: That's another thing most young people don't know—are they readers or listeners? And this is something they can check easily.

Hall: It's like being right or left-handed, isn't it?

Drucker: That's right. The only ambidextrous people are trial lawyers—they both read and listen. Nobody else can. I am a listener; I can read after I listen but not before. Probably I can't even write first, but that's pathological.

Hall: But what is the most important thing about the choice of the job, apart from the personality of the person?

Drucker: Job content. The question is not, am I interested in biology. That interest may or may not change. You can't tell. This issue is: when you work, do you want to sit down to a stack of information reports and to plot figures for two weeks, or do you want to go around and pick people's brains? Do you enjoy being alone, or do you have to be a member of a team? How do you really function? There is a fabulous amount of misinformation about jobs, because there is not one job pattern that is clear. You just can't tell by the field.

Hall: I've always thought maybe a university graduate school faculty was a more conformist bunch than a group of bankers.

Drucker: There are businesses that are quite conformist, but there is nothing as conformist as a graduate faculty. The Ph.D. program is even worse.

There are businesses that are wide open, like positions in the international divisions of some big banks—the Bank of America, Chase Manhattan, or First National City Bank of New York are examples. Their young men are really entrepreneurs. They invent new services and new branches, and no one says them nay. And there are government jobs meant for the kind of fellow who draws to an inside royal flush.

John Lindsay in New York has that kind of government job, or Richard Lee in New Haven. There are terrific opportunities in Washington in the Office of Health, Education, and Welfare. Not in the education section, though. That's dead. Another place for the creative guy is in the environmental sciences section of the Department of Commerce. You've got to be good there. They are ruthless, as they should be, if you don't come up with solid, original ideas.

Hall: Are job stereotypes changing?

Drucker: Jobs cannot be typified, cannot be classified. Ten or twenty years ago bankers were good Anglo-Saxons who parted their hair in the middle. That is no longer necessarily so. In New York a fellow with a red beard who goes barefoot to work is vice-president of a commercial bank today.

Hall: Is that *really true*, Peter Drucker?

Drucker: Yes, he can do it so long as he stays in the data-processing department. I met him at lunch today. He's a vice-president of one of the very big banks and is very young. I don't think it's necessary for him to pretend he's 19 any longer, but that's his business.

Hall: How old is he, really?

Drucker: About 36, I would say.

Hall: What on earth has happened to banking in the past ten years?

Drucker: Nothing has happened to banking. Banks have discovered that if they have a computer that costs a million dollars a month, they had better have somebody who can make it produce. And if he goes barefoot and has a red beard and wears a blue undershirt, you just make damn sure you don't expose him to the clientele. Nobody has to see him except the computer, and the computer has no great fashion preferences. On the other hand, no university faculty would dare to hire him. And for good reasons.

Hall: Would that be the unpopularity of the image because of current student style?

Drucker: It wouldn't be his red beard, his going barefoot, or his peculiar sweat-shirt that the university would mind. It would be the fact that they have to expose him. Chances are that he cannot get along with human beings. He talks so much about love that everybody hates him. The university needs somebody much more conformist than this. But the bank will set him up. I imagine the older credit officers of the bank are duly shocked, but then you know that puritans need to be shocked twice a day anyhow.

Hall: Yes, good for their livers.

Drucker: Right. Exactly.

Hall: So it's not a matter of the field, biology or education or medicine or psychology or engineering, but the specific kind of job within the field.

Drucker: Right. And there's another highly important matter. No matter what job it is, it ain't final. The first few years are trials. The probability that the first choice you make is right for you is roughly one in a million. If you decide your first choice is the right one, chances are you are just plain lazy. People believe that if they take their job for General Electric or New York University or *Psychology Today* that they have taken their vows, that the world will come to an end if it doesn't work out.

Hall: How many of us know from the very beginning what we want to be?

Drucker: There are a very few who know at, say, age 11, "This is where I want to be." They are either musicians or mathematicians or physicians. And, incidentally, the physicians all go through a horrible identity crisis when they reach the age of 28.

Hall: Why is that?

Drucker: Because medical school is unspeakably boring. They all go into medicine because they are dedicated. Then it is so Goddam scientific for seven or eight years. They are taught to be callous and to learn the bones of the body, only to forget them tomorrow. Then, when they have finished their internship or their residency, they have a terrible crisis. Only yesterday I wrote a long letter to a very sweet boy who just finished his medical training. Now he wants to go back to school and learn philosophy, because he is so terribly distraught. He doesn't realize that almost any sensitive young doctor goes through this. The medical faculties don't tell the kids. They think it's a good idea not to warn them that they will undergo a crisis. Most of them come back to medicine when they discover that once you are out of medical school, you *do* deal with people and you don't really know very much. Then they rediscover medicine. But medical school is a great place to be weaned away from being a physician.

Hall: You say that it's important to know yourself before you can know what kind of job best suits you. How early do you think this assessment can be made?

Drucker: Contrary to everything that modern psychologists tell you, I am convinced that one can acquire knowledge, one can acquire skills, but one cannot change his personality. Only the Good Lord changes personality—that's His business. I have had four great children, and I can assure you that by the time they were six months old, they were set in concrete. After six months, parents get educated, but not children.

One can take a child and try to bring him out of excessive timidity, but you won't ever make a bold one out of him. Or, you can take a bold one, a rash one, and try to teach him how to count to ten before shooting with the hope that he will count at least to three. But that is all one can do. One can take a charmer and try to get him— charmers are mostly boys—to work to catch up with what he has improvised. And one can get one of those awful, horrible, overplanners to jump once in a while. But you are not going to change the basic structure. It is much more important that in this age of psychology people tell the kids that what you *are* matters, and your values matter.

Hall: Now, what about going to graduate school? Suppose one has learned all he can about himself. Should he go on to graduate school before he tries his first job?

Drucker: As long as you go to graduate school to avoid the draft, it's rational. I don't criticize that at all. If Uncle Sam set up the draft in such a way that you are rewarded for getting out of it, don't complain if this is done. People always behave as they are rewarded. If the present draft system is immoral, and God help me, it is, then it is the draft that is to blame and not the kids who react to a clear incentive.

I'm not sure that it wouldn't be a smart thing for all of them to go into the Army at the age of 18. Military service is juvenile. At the age of 18, one enjoys it; at 21 or 22, one has outgrown it.

But apart from staying out of the draft, in graduate school they are going to postpone *themselves,* and they will do so with the peculiar idea that *academia* is a free environment. They soon discover that graduate school is our least vented environment. The arrogance, the petty restrictions of the learned are horrible. Nothing is more demeaning than to be forced to be conventionally unconventional.

Hall: Politics in the groves of academe fascinate and appall me. The infighting is worse than in the old Kansas City or Boston wards. And the academicians are far more shrewd and vicious.

Drucker: There's only one kind of politics that's worse. We have only 2,000 colleges, and *academia* is not so narrow here as in Europe. But look at musicians. This country has never been able to support more than 25 pianists. If you are a first-rate pianist, you take the bread out of somebody's mouth. That's not quite true of *academia,* but there is a horrible frustration if you are not Number One. In *academia* there are numerous jobs for the merely competent man, but not room for him. The kids don't understand this.

Hall: Would you say, go into the Peace Corps first, before going to graduate school?

Drucker: No! The Peace Corps is a great disappointment.

Hall: How can you say that? Why?

Drucker: I always thought the kids would get a tremendous amount out of the Peace Corps, but I have seen too many when they came back. In their personal development, they are exactly where they were when they left. The Peace Corps is just a postponement, a delay. My conclusion is that one belongs in the Peace Corps in his thirties, not in his twenties. In the twenties he belongs in the city administration of San Pedro, or out selling Gallo wine.

Hall: Out selling wine? Gallo?

Drucker: Let me tell you about one of the nicest boys I know. He took a job as a salesman for one of the large wineries. His parents were beside themselves. I asked him why he went to work as a salesman. "To find out what I can do," he answered. "But why did you go to work for a winery?" I asked. You see, he had offers from Ford and IBM and Minneapolis-Honeywell. "At the winery," he answered, "I'm the only one who can read and write."

Now he's a bright boy. I don't think he'll stay long with the winery unless he's made president within five years. That might happen. Or he might go back to law school. This boy knows exactly what he's doing. He is trying himself out. If he does a good job, he will be right at the top. If he doesn't work out, nothing has happened. Too many kids with too many opportunities are just playing around. They know only what they don't want.

Hall: I see what you mean. You think that any good young person should go out and jump in somewhere, anywhere.

Drucker: Yes, and not with the typical question the kids ask the recruiters: Is this the right place to stay for the next 25 years? Hell, the answer in all likelihood is no. There is a right question to ask the recruiter: Is this a place where I can learn something for two years and have fun for two years, and where I will have a change if I produce?

Hall: All right. I believe you. You'd put off graduate school?

Drucker: I'd put off elementary school if I had my way. I am not a great believer in school. School is primarily an institution for perpetuation of adolescence.

Hall: If you don't believe in school how would you educate?

Drucker: That is an entirely different question. The thought that school educates is not one I have accepted yet. No, I am not joking.

Hall: I know you are not joking.

Drucker: No, Mary, I would be much happier if kids at age 17 were young adults among adults. Those who wanted to go back to school could come back later. They would be better students and much happi-

er people. But I don't control the universe. In the university we expect everybody to sit on his butt through the full natural life span of man—which is about 25. All I can say is, thank God I am not young. I could not survive this horror. The only thing my secondary school faculty and I were in total agreement on was that I sat too long and did not belong in school. In this we were in total agreement. Otherwise, we had few points of contact. Adolescence is a man-made problem. It is not a stage of nature.

Hall: Do you think this has some bearing on the unrest and rioting on college campuses?

Drucker: I am not a bit surprised that the kids riot. I am surprised that they are so placid, because they are all so unspeakably bored. Seriously, though, I am not at all opposed to graduate school *per se.* I am opposed to graduate school as a delaying action. I am opposed to a graduate school as hibernation. And I am opposed to graduate school as education, which it is not.

Hall: Just how would you define graduate school?

Drucker: Graduate school is not focused on forming a human being but on imparting a finer set of skills. The purpose is not education, but specialization. My guess is that 20 years from now, the existing academic departments will all be gone. There is not a single one left that makes any sense.

Today knowledge exists in action, not in hard-covered books. But I am very biased. I am a doer, not a contemplator, a perceiver, not a thinker. I am one of those who has to listen to himself to know what he is thinking or saying all the time. These are all very undesirable characteristics, so I am not at all the type that graduate schools look for. There are plenty of kids to fill them up.

Hall: Did you go from the university into management consultant work, or was it the other way around?

Drucker: I have always taught on the side, because I like to teach. I started teaching at 20 when I was in law school out of sheer boredom. It was the only way to stay alive. I was working and studying and teaching too. After I finished secondary school, I went to work in England as an apprentice clerk in a woolen-export house. I was the first person to start apprenticeship as late as 18. All my bosses' sons started at 14. And I was the first who did not live over the premises—solely because a fire had destroyed the premises.

And I was the first not to start off with a goose-quill pen. That was the year they discovered they couldn't buy goose-quill pens anymore. I told all this to a friend of mine who said that only showed I didn't start off in a high-class establishment. When he began as an apprentice at a merchant bank, the banker bought a goose farm when he found out he couldn't buy goose-quill pens.

Hall: That sounds like something out of Charles Dickens. How did you get there?

Drucker: Well, I grew up in Vienna, but my family had very close ties with England.

By the way, the only connection I can claim with psychology is that my family knew Freud. My father knew him from boyhood and put him on a pedestal as a genius who could do no wrong. My mother's reaction was quite different. When she was a young medical student, she was one of Freud's favorites. (She was one of the first women to go to medical school. She had to go to Zurich to do it.) She understood why he was important but at the same time she refused to have anything to do with him. Freud loved her but she couldn't stand him.

Hall: Why couldn't she stand Freud?

Drucker: She felt that he was an evil man. She was a perceptive person. My father saw this man as a genius, and felt that geniuses should be allowed anything.

Hall: Why did your mother feel that Freud was an evil man?

Drucker: Because he was, period. He was a man who had to domineer.

Hall: Let's get back to your own life. Where did you go from your apprenticeship in the export business?

Drucker: I went to Germany. I went into investment banking there. In 1929, as you may have heard, there was a slight unpleasantness. Investment banking came to an end, and I became a newspaperman. But all the time, I was enrolled as a law student.

Hall: I didn't know that you had been a journalist.

Drucker: In a way I have never ceased being one. But for two periods in my life this was my main occupation. For a few years in the late twenties and early thirties when I worked on the Continent primarily as one of the editors of a German daily paper and then in the late thirties when I first came to the United States as American correspondent for a group of British papers. But I have really been writing all my life, and it is the only thing I claim any skill in. And in between my newspaper jobs, for four years right after the Nazis came to power, I was in London as an investment banker and economist.

Hall: You did quite a few things as a young man.

Drucker: Yes, until I was 30 I was really a drifter. I knew perfectly well all the things I didn't want to do with myself. In retrospect, I realize that I must have been a very sorry specimen and I do marvel at my parents' patience with me. It was not until I came to this country that I realized what I wanted.

Hall: But you were very successful in that interim period.

Drucker: I looked successful, but I wasn't. This is why I have such sympathy with today's young people. What saved me, they don't have. I had to have a job to pay the rent. And they, instead, have Uncle Sam with a graduate grant, which makes finding yourself a good deal harder than hard times did for my generation.

Hall: Your background and your family's is about as broad as one could ask. I know your father was an important figure in the Austrian government, an international lawyer, and a founder of the Salzburg Festival.

Drucker: Narrowness is no fun. As a writer, I think your interviews with B.F. Skinner, the father of operant conditioning, and with the humanist Rollo May, were totally marvelous.

You made so clear what Skinner has really been talking about.

Hall: Skinner was incredibly patient in making it clear to me.

Drucker: I wish I were one-tenth as brilliant as Fred Skinner. But he is so totally a prisoner of his work that he doesn't realize what he has done.

Hall: How can you say that?

Drucker: I overstate because I worry that he may be "advertising" his work under wrong labels. He has contributed a fantastic amount, and I worry that it may get lost. God, I

wish there were more of him.

You were wonderful to Rollo May. You made him mean things he didn't know he knew.

Hall: He is an impressive thinker and a great man.

Drucker: Well, you brought out what some of us had suspected. May is a wise man. A very wise man.

I have a close friend in New York who is the diagnostician's diagnostician, and six months ago I wrote to him about a friend and he wrote back that the man didn't need a psychiatrist, he needed a friend. This is what Rollo May has been to our generation. And he doesn't know it, and you brought it out.

Hall: You came to the United States before the Second World War?

Drucker: Yes. In April, 1937. Here I also taught on the side. I taught philosophy at Bennington, then I came here to New York University. I am not a proper model for anything.

Hall: Oh, I think you are a swinging model.

Drucker: No, no, no. I am not a scholar; I am a writer. You know the difference?

Hall: Yes, there can be a vast sea between the two.

Drucker: Few people are aware of it. I am proud of not being a scholar. I am a writer, but I am not good enough to write novels. I always like to teach, because I like young people and I like the excitement of people discovering things.

Hall: When did you switch entirely to management consulting?

Drucker: I haven't. The book I am working on has nothing to do with management. It's about discontinuities—in politics, in economy. I don't have a title for it yet.

Hall: Tell me about it.

Drucker: For years and years I have

been writing slowly on a book about basic American experiences, such as the separation of church and state. The only chapter I have finished is called "The Education of a Pretender." It's about Henry Adams. The title of the book probably will be *The American Political Genius* or *The American Patriot*. I am tired of management books.

Hall: You may be tired of management books, but our readers want to know about careers. Young people want to know how to find their particular round hole, or square—depending on their shape. You said the young person looking for a career should figure: "Do I fit into the large corporation?" or "Should I be on my own?" But what is the opportunity for being on one's own? Isn't the large corporation most likely?

Drucker: Even in General Electric there are places where you can be on your own, plenty of them. But let's go back to examples once again. I know two young men, each of whom decided he would like to be completely on his own. One is building a very nice business as a computer consultant on the West Coast. The other one is in the East, building his own design engineering firm. These young men are loners, they are extremes. I am one myself. But take a more typical case. Yesterday, I had a young scientist here. He had been with a medium-sized company for eight years, was their number two man in research. He wanted a change, but refused to go into a big company. He knew he'd get better pay there, but he said that unless he was in on a whole project, from the formulation of the proposal to NASA all the way to the prototype delivery, he wasn't interested. This morning, I think I found him the job he wants.

Hall: What kind of job?

Drucker: A job as head of the field in instrumentation design at one of the country's largest hospitals. He knows nothing about biochemistry, but he can learn. He will work with the surgeons there and will head a small group of a half a dozen engineers and biochemists. Now the hospital is a hell of a big organization—1,800 patient beds—but he won't even see the big organization.

Hall: He must be darned bright.

Drucker: On the contrary. I wouldn't send a bright boy to a hospital. It would be a great waste; they wouldn't know what to do with him.

Hall: You keep running into complaints about technology. Clark Kerr has said that we can't really make our peace with technology. How can the individual survive and function in this technology?

Drucker: There is no war; there is fear. The attitude of this generation is, what can we do for the computer? The next generation will solve the problem; their attitude will be: What will the computer do for me? It doesn't ever pay to be permissive and pleasant about mechanical gadgets. Be nasty. Throw it out if it doesn't perform.

Hall: I wonder if people were afraid of the light switch once.

Drucker: That's right. I don't know whether you know that the first advanced management training course was one that the German Post Office used in 1888. Its topic was the use of the telephone. Believe me, the next generation is going to look upon the computer the way today's teenager looks upon the telephone. At the moment you realize that you can always pull the plug, the fear is ended. Once you know what you want to do, either it can do it for you or it can't. The computer is a tool. If the tool can't do something for you, leave it in the tool box.

Hall: And careers are a tool, too.

Drucker: Precisely. The smart way to look at a career is, What does it do for me? What do I want to accomplish?

Hall: Are there any special things to look for in a company?

Drucker: Yes. You want old age at top management. You know, one question the young career seeker never asks the company recruiter is, "How old are the department heads?"

Hall: You want old ones so you can come up, right?

Drucker: Oh, my yes. You don't want the First National City Bank in the city, for instance.

Hall: They're all young?

Drucker: Oh, yes; the executive vice president is 36. Too many companies are actually lopsided. You want a company with some old and some young at the head.

Hall: Then I don't want Edgar Bronfman's Seagram's and assorted enterprises?

Drucker: Anyone would want a company run by him. He's creative. But you would prefer to have him be 90 years old if you plan to inherit his job.

Hall: People are younger longer now. How has this changed the job picture?

Drucker: The real career crisis is the extension of the working-life span. In the time of our grandparents, man's working life was over at 45. By then, few people were physically or mentally capable of working. It was a rural civilization and the preindustrial farmer was either worn out or had been killed by an accident by age 45. The Chinese or Irish who built our railroads had a five-year working life. Within five years they were gone—by liquor, or syphilis, or accident, or hard work.

Now suddenly, you have people reaching the age of 65 in the prime of physical and mental health. This is due partly to the movement of people from the farm to the city—accidents occur on the farm with about ten times the frequency of that in the most dangerous industrial employment—and partly to scientific management taking the toil out of labor. We have pushed up education to compensate for this.

Hall: What possible solution is there other than a continual increasing of life-long education programs?

Drucker: I am absolutely convinced that one of the greatest needs is the systematic creation of second careers. At 45, after having been a market research man, or a professor of English or psychology, or an officer in the armed services for 20 years, man is spent. At least he thinks so. But he is mentally, biologically, and physically sound. His kids are grown up and the mortgage is paid off and he has plenty to contribute to society.

You know, one of the most thrilling things that has happened in the last 20 years is the new careers for the crop of military officers who are being axed by the military services at age 47. They've reached lieutenant colonel or lieutenant commander, gone as far as they can go, and they're out.

Hall: What does one do after 20 years as an officer?

Drucker: That's exactly what they want to know. They are absolutely sure there is nothing they can do. They are terribly conscious that they have been in an insulated, artificial environment.

Hall: I should think they'd be scared to death.

Drucker: They *are,* scared out of their wits. Most of them think they need a graduate degree or some kind of guidance. All they need is for someone to say: "Look, Jack, there's nothing wrong with you." They can apply to one of the big downtown law firms for a job as office manager. These have 99 people who know nothing but law, and they need someone to organize them. There are jobs as business managers of law firms or accounting firms or small colleges. All kinds of good jobs.

Hall: It would be like starting life all over again.

Drucker: Six months after these former service men have taken on their new jobs, they are 20 years younger. They have recovered enthusiasm, they are growing, they have ideas. Their wives are enchanted. They are exciting again.

Hall: Not everybody would be a success as an office manager. Are there any other jobs that are especially suited to second careers?

Drucker: Indeed there are. The older professions are best suited to become second careers. Middle age is really the best time to switch to being the lawyer, the teacher, the priest, the doctor—I shocked you—and the social worker. Twenty years from now, we'll have few young men in these fields.

Hall: However would you train a man to be a doctor as a second career?

Drucker: It is not very difficult to be a good doctor, a good physician. I am not saying these men could do good heart transplants or diagnose some obscure tropical disease, but they would know full well that this diagnosis is not right and maybe the patient ought to go see a specialist. But they could do the work the average general practitioner faces.

Hall: What has been the reaction of the medical schools to this idea?

Drucker: I've talked to them. I said: "Take men of 45, engineers, weather forecasters, career officers, how would you make doctors of them in one year?" The medical schools said it couldn't be done. I said, "What do you mean it couldn't be done? With the amount of ignorance you have, I could teach you in three weeks." They answered, "It can't be done. They have to learn the bones of the body." But they can look that up, you know. Very rarely does a bone of the throat move into the knee.

And I talked to the archdioceses about putting these men in the parishes as priests in six months. "Can't be done," I was told. But it is going to be done. Most training for these old professions consists of trying to simulate experience. Hell, these people *have* experience.

Hall: Is it being done anywhere?

Drucker: We are putting men into the classroom to teach at the University in six months.

Hall: How?

Drucker: How? By putting them into the classroom, period. Eight out of ten will swim. And, once they swim I work on polishing their style. If they sink, I jump in with a life preserver. What I can't do is to teach them how to swim.

Hall: And if they sink, you pull them out so they can do something else?

Drucker: No, I dry them off and throw them in again.

Hall: In my mind, you are the ideal management consultant. But what you have been describing to me partly is a personal employment agency. How did you ever get into this wonderful thing? I wanted to be a missionary when I was a little girl. You *are* one.

Drucker: Well, I have students, and friends who have kids. And it has gotten around that if you get thrown out of the U.S. Navy on the Eastern seaboard, there is a peculiar character around named Drucker of whom most people strongly disapprove. I'm too frivolous for them.

Hall: What's it like, being a management consultant?

Drucker: Any man who has been a consultant has dealt in the unlicensed practice of psychiatry. The great weakness of an organization is that you can't have a confidant. You are always either boss or subordinate. And people are terribly lonely, terribly lonely. Here comes an outsider, the licensed lunatic, and you just start spilling. What clients tell me is incredible. I know too much about them. Every management consultant has the same experience.

Hall: Doesn't this knowledge help you as a consultant?

Drucker: No.

Hall: It doesn't help at all?

Drucker: Oh, sometimes, But more often, one has to suppress it. I have never liked to be cruel, and as I get older, I hate cruelty more and more. But one has to force oneself to do what is right. Sometimes that means cutting off heads. Then the question is, How do we do it in a compassionate way? If the compassion enters into the initial decision, you get sentimental. In the end, you do much more harm. The real cruelty is always that of sentimental people. And so, one has to force oneself to eliminate all one knows about that poor devil and only bring it in afterwards. You say, Now that we have cut off his head, what do we do with him so that he doesn't feel it? But first, his head must be cut off.

Hall: What happens with the thousands and thousands of people who are stuck, working out their years of retirement?

Drucker: I think company managers will have to learn to sit down and say: "Look, Jack, do you want to stay here or do you really want to do something? If you stay here, you are about as far as you will ever get. Oh, maybe two more raises." Most so-called promotions are not promotions, but raises, you know. It just changes the title. And the boss should say: "You are going to remain a quality control manager. Do you want to do that for 20 more years? We are perfectly happy to have you stay around here. On the other hand, you have all the mortgages paid off. What have you always wanted to do? If you want to become a priest, well, we'll help you." Does this make any sense to you, Mary?

Hall: It makes all the sense in the world.

Phantoms Fill Boy Scout Rolls

DAVID YOUNG

The Boy Scouts have been a tradition in America for most of this century. To the public, scouting conjures up images of camping in the woods, hikes, and troop meetings. But there is another side of scouting that is not seen, a *Tribune* reporter discovered during a four-month investigation. It includes massive cheating on the part of paid professional staff members to make their quotas. This is the first of a two-part report on the problem.

The Boy Scouts of America—that venerable institution devoted to keeping boys physically strong, mentally aware, and morally straight—is in trouble.

A $65 million national campaign to expand scouting by more than 2 million boys in 1976 is nearly two years behind schedule.

And professionals within the Scout organization claim the problem has been aggravated by extensive cheating which has inflated membership figures. Scouting officials claim to have 4.8 million boys enrolled nationwide.

Like most charitable organizations, scouting also has been plagued with the problem of finding enough adult volunteers to run programs and raising enough money to keep up with inflation, Scout officials concede.

Many officials blame scouting's problems on the inability to recruit and keep volunteers, especially in the inner cities.

But the root of the problem is scouting's Boypower 76 program—a national effort to increase the membership rolls to include one-third of all eligible boys in

Reprinted, courtesy of the *Chicago Tribune*, Sunday, June 9, 1974.

America—an estimated 6 million youngsters.

Dissidents within scouting's 4,600-member professional staff, which raises funds and recruits boys and volunteers, also claim that efforts to streamline the organization and use improved business techniques have encouraged cheating.

What has happened, past and present Scout professionals claim, is that many professionals under pressure continually to make increasing membership quotas have been meeting those quotas with nonexistent boys belonging to nonexistent units. The boys exist only on rosters filed away in Scout offices throughout the country.

Actually, the cheating is confined largely to the professional organization and has had little or no effect on existing Scout programs operated by adult volunteers. Once started, the troops, packs, and posts operate almost independently of the professional organization.

Thus, the 15 Cub Scouts who meet each week in a Detroit ghetto church aren't aware that their unit has 65 members on official Scout reports. And the PTA of a West Side Chicago school is not aware it is sponsoring a nonexistent, 44–member

Boy Scout troop.

Scout professionals interviewed during the *Tribune's* four-month investigation revealed that sometimes they cheat with federal money. The nonexistent boys and units were paid for with poverty funds from Washington.

"This thing is national in scope," claimed one Scout executive from the national organization. He asked that his name be withheld.

"They don't know themselves how many boys they have," he said.

"As far as they are concerned, the name on a roster is a Scout until someone proves it different."

An independent report on scouting in the New York area in 1971 by the Institute of Public Affairs said that many Scout professionals believe that the pressure to meet membership goals there resulted in a "numbers game and a possible cause of paper troops." The report never was publicly released.

But nowhere is the problem more critical than in Chicago—the place where scouting started in America in 1910 and the city that gave America the Boypower 76 program.

Some Scout professionals here estimated that anywhere from 25 to 50 percent of the 87,000 Cub Scouts, Boy Scouts, and Explorers registered in the Chicago Area Council are inactive or exist only on paper.

A suppressed 1968 audit of Scout operations in Chicago shows that of the council's 2,555 units, 1,694 were substandard and 623 were phony. Though Scout officials in Chicago claimed at the time to have 75,000 boys enrolled, the actual number of Scouts was less than 40,000, the audit showed. The Scout official who ordered the audit was quietly reassigned elsewhere.

Joseph Klein, the head of scouting in Chicago, claims to have 87,000 members—making Chicago the largest council in the nation.

However, confidential membership reports obtained by the *Tribune* show that on April 12 the actual membership was about 52,000 boys—nearly 40 percent less than quoted.

Though cheating also exists in the suburbs, it is worse in the inner city, Scout professionals said. They claim that it is extremely difficult to determine the exact extent of the cheating, but said that Scout districts with widely fluctuating membership totals and few promotions indicate large numbers of phony boys and units. Nonexistent boys can't be promoted.

Though 2,321 Boy Scouts were registered in the Midwest District on the West Side last December, only 117 boys received promotions to the six ranks of scouting. Only 32 boys were promoted to Tenderfoot—an almost automatic jump.

The adjacent Fort Dearborn District listed no promotions for its 1,511 Boy Scouts, although the predominantly white Timber Trails District on the Southwest Side had 245 promotions for its 850 registered boys for the same period.

Membership in the Midwest District has fluctuated widely since 1966, confidential Scout records show. On December 31, 1972, the district reported having 4,577 Scouts, but 2,797 of them—more than half—had evaporated in just two months. The district claimed to have recruited 3,270 new boys during its membership drive last fall, making it the largest district in the city, with 5,050 boys. But by the beginning of April 2,981 boys—nearly 60 percent of the district—had somehow disappeared.

The seven Scout districts on the West Side claim to have recruited 8,630 new Scouts during last fall's membership drive, but lost 9,000 in the following three months. The six South Side districts in the Chicago Council lost more than 8,000 scouts during the same period—nearly half of the total membership.

The worst cheating actually occurs in the federally funded programs administered through the Chicago Model Cities program, the professionals claim. The programs, collectively known as Project 13, pay the Scout dues and fees for inner city blacks and Latins, many of whom live in housing projects.

The Chicago Council has received $341,000 in federal funds for the program during the last four years, reportedly to provide a Scouting program for more than 40,000 poor youngsters, federal records show.

"It's not hard to paper your project (13) boys," bragged one Scout professional who asked to remain anonymous. "You register all the boys in December. You can put an extra 1,000 boys in a unit because they drop out in two months and there's no record of them," he said.

An official of the Lawndale Urban Progress Center, which sponsors one federally funded program on the West Side, said that not more than 500 of the 2,000 boys on the books are actually Scouts.

Scout professionals, past and present, admitted to a *Tribune* interviewer that they registered thousands of nonexistent boys to meet their quotas.

One of the most common ploys the professionals claim they used was to re-register units year after year without bothering to check to see whether the units actually exist.

"You simply change a few names so the charter looks different, then re-register it," said one former professional. "Who's going to walk through those housing projects to check you out?"

"We've got to clean the cheating up," he said. "The minute we find it (cheating) we terminate the professional."

Klein said he constantly lectures his staff on maintaining a quality scouting program, "but maybe they're not hearing me."

"I firmly believe there's a hell of a lot more good in this program than there is bad," he said.

Scouting Motto Forgotten in Signup Drive

With great fanfare the Boy Scouts of America announced in 1968 it was beginning a program to make scouting more relevant.

Boypower 76, it was called.

And its goal was to raise $65 million and to bring into scouting one-third (about 6 million) of all eligible boys 8 to 20 years old in the country by 1976.

Scouting wanted the poor black youths from the ghetto, and the Puerto Ricans

Reprinted, courtesy of the *Chicago Tribune*, Monday, June 10, 1974.

from Spanish Harlem. It wanted the whites from the suburbs and the sons of steelworkers from Gary.

To make the traditional scouting program more relevant to the recruits, the Boy Scouts revised handbooks to include subjects of interest to urban dwellers, translated manuals into Spanish, and asked for federal funds to pay for programs for the poor.

But somewhere in the more than five years that Boypower 76 has been with us, something went wrong.

Professional Scout staff members have detailed to the *Tribune* widespread cheating to meet the Boypower quotas imposed on them—including cheating in the federally funded programs.

"This thing is national in scope," claimed one Scout executive assigned to the national organization.

The officials claim they were forced to cheat to make their goals. If they didn't make the goals, they were out. Scout executive Alden G. Barber conceded he is aware cheating has occurred.

"Some of our people cheat—quite frankly," Barber said.

He conceded that Boypower 76 is now two years behind schedule. The problem is economic, he said. There just isn't enough money to get the job done.

Though the national organization has raised $33 million and placed nearly 500 additional professionals on local staffs, donors who gave to the national effort apparently cut back on their contributions to local Scout councils. Many local councils were forced to cut back their staffs as a result.

"The actual net gain is close to 80 professionals," Barber said.

In Chicago, the local Scout council was faced with a $340,000 deficit and was forced to chop 10 professionals from its staff although the council was expected to increase its membership from 75,000 to 100,000. The result was cheating.

Past and present Scout professionals in Chicago estimate that from 25 to 50 percent of the 87,000 Scouts registered here exist only on paper.

The professionals also detailed how the cheating has gradually moved into the suburbs—the traditional bastions of the Boy Scout movement.

One South Suburban professional estimated that when he was transferred into his district he found about 20 percent of his Scouts existed only on paper.

A North Suburban staff member discovered one day that several hundred boys had somehow mysteriously appeared on his rolls. He was later told by a supervisor that the boys were put there to make a quota.

A Southwest Suburban volunteer told of how he held an anguished meeting with his professional late one night because the district was 200 boys short of its quota. The volunteer resigned himself to missing the quota, but early the next morning he got a call from a friend congratulating him for making it.

"I don't know where the boys came from," the volunteer said. "Our meeting ended at 11 P.M. and by 8 A.M. the next day we were on target."

But cheating in the suburbs is minor compared to the inflating of membership rolls going on in the inner city, professionals claim.

"When I left the Fort Dearborn District (West Side) in 1972, I had 3,000 Scouts on the books, but only 300 of them were real," said Andre Miller, a former professional.

"We had 850 boys registered in the Altgeld Gardens project on the South Side," said Bart Kencade, another former professional. "Realistically, there were 30 Scouts active."

A Detroit supervisor told his staff members to meet their quotas even if they had to register bodies in a cemetery to do it.

Nearly 20 charters for Cub Scout packs on the West Side in 1973 list as den mother a Mrs. Ollie Carter, 130 E. Franklin St. Mrs. Carter is in fact an employee of the Boy Scouts in their equipment store at that address. She said she wasn't sure why her name appeared on so many unit rosters.

"I haven't done anything with any units for four or five years," she said.

Edward Meier, a suburban Oak Lawn businessman, is listed on those same rosters as an official of the units.

"I haven't been in the area for years," he said. "Years ago," he claimed he allowed a professional to use his name for promotional purposes in Oak Lawn.

One professional sat in his suburban apartment one night and detailed to a *Tribune* interviewer just how the cheating is accomplished.

His favorite tactic is known in the business as "diming them in." In November and December near the end of the scouts' annual membership drive, the practice becomes common "because in those months you only have to pay a dime (dues are 10 cents a month) to register a boy for the Dec. 31 deadline. So you can sign up 100 boys for $10."

"You can go to a business for a contribution to pay the tab, you can hold back some money you raised earlier, or you can go to your field director (supervisor) for contingency funds," he said.

Some professionals admitted they paid the phony boys' dues out of their own pocket.

They claimed they got the phony names from telephone books or by visiting elementary schools to have boys fill out applications and pay their dues in advance. Once the registration cards and dues were collected, the professionals never returned to organize units, they said.

Still others claimed they reregistered entire units without checking to see whether the units still existed. In this way, units which have dissolved are carried on the books for years.

The school ploy angered the mothers at Brown Elementary School, 54 N. Hermitage Ave.

"Last September ... a Scout representative came through the school and recruited 30 to 40 boys," one mother said. "I called them downtown (Scout headquarters) and told them we had collected the boys' money.

"They came out and picked it up but that's the last we ever saw of them."

The Scout professionals—the men who admitted cheating—blamed the problem on the Scout organization and Boypower 76.

"If you didn't make a majority of your goals, you were fired," said one 11–year veteran who was forced out after he refused to cheat.

"Membership is at one of its lowest points in the history of the district," said John P. Costello, Chicago's assistant Scout executive, in a letter to one professional last year. "Camp is 30 per cent off target," he continued.

"Failure to show dramatic progress ... will place you in a terminal employment position with the Chicago Area Council," the letter continued.

"I couldn't send anyone to camp because paper Boy Scouts can't go to camp," said the professional. He claimed he was transferred into the district only a few months before receiving Costello's letter and discovered that 33 of his 47 registered units were nonexistent.

Another Scout professional was fired last year after he attempted to organize a union among the other professionals. The firing occurred a few days after the National Labor Relations Board refused to hear a complaint he filed against the Chicago Council charging it was threatening to fire employees trying to organize the union.

"I didn't want the union," the former professional said. "I wanted to find some way we could put an end to all these abuses."

Raymond N. Carlen, a steel company executive and president of the Chicago Area Council, has adopted a hard-nosed attitude toward the dissident professionals:

"If you don't enjoy what your are doing, look for something else to do," he said.

However, Barber believes that many of the problems of cheating could be curbed by better training of professionals and their supervisors.

"I assumed the middle management people knew the techniques necessary to achieve the goals," he said.

Barber, who was the Scout executive in Chicago before being named national chief executive, is credited with streamlining the Scout organization, imposing the quota system, and making the professionals accountable for making the quotas. He engineered the "Years of Decision" Scout program in Chicago during the early 1960s. "Boypower 76 was an outgrowth of that program."

He also is credited with engineering the attempt by the Scout organization to reach the inner city.

"I felt that if scouting was to reach its potential, it had to be as meaningful to the boy in the inner city as to the boy in suburbia."

Managing Your Manager: The Effective Subordinate

NORMAN C. HILL and PAUL H. THOMPSON

After weeks of futile maneuvering to save his job, Lee Iacocca, 53, the hard-driving, cigar-chomping president of the world's fourth largest manufacturing company, found himself quite bluntly sacked by his equally toughminded boss, Chairman Henry Ford II. It was the culmination of months of behind-the-scenes quarreling between two of the auto industry's most respected—and often feared—executives.

As president of the Ford Motor Company, Lee Iacocca was widely respected as one of the most skillful managers in the auto industry's history; but his problems with his boss apparently cost him his job.

People at all levels in organizations have difficulties with their bosses. And the name doesn't have to be Lee Iacocca, Andrew Young, Billy Martin, or Midge Constanza for the word to get around. A career may be terminated, jeopardized, or, at the very least, slowed by failing to establish a workable superior-subordinate relationship.

Nearly everyone is a subordinate to

Reprinted from Fall/Winter 1978 *Exchange*, a publication of the Brigham Young University School of Management, 730 TNRB, Provo, Utah 84602.

someone, no matter how high he or she rises in the organizational hierarchy. The value of a widespread concern for a better understanding of the relationship between superiors and subordinates would appear obvious—especially when so many managers are frustrated by their subordinates' lack of motivation and general low level of performance. Likewise, individuals often complain about their bosses' apparent lack of interest, supervision, or concern. Yet from university classrooms to slick paperbacks, the focus has been largely limited to "management style"—i.e., building your career by successfully directing those *beneath* you. Little attention has been paid to the other side of the issue—establishing your career based on your ability to manage those who formally manage you.

In the traditional role definition, the boss gives the orders and the subordinate carries them out. Many individuals expect a manager to define the job, make assignments, and then check to see that the work is completed. When the boss doesn't behave in this manner, frustration for many is evident. However, for professionals and other highly trained employees, the relationship is seldom that simple. Very often the two parties have different expectations about roles. These differing expectations can lead to tension, conflicts, missed deadlines, and even transfers or terminations.

A way to avoid these problems for some individuals is to have the two parties clarify expectations right at the beginning. One highly regarded manager described doing this:

> Whenever I get a new boss, I sit down with him and ask him to make his expectations explicit. We try to list not my job activities but the main purposes of my job. To do that, we continue each statement of activity with "In order to . . .," and try to complete the sentence. By recording my job purposes, we get a clear picture of what I should be accomplishing; and that's what counts—results.

This approach works very well for this individual, but most bosses are not able (or willing) to be nearly that clear about their expectations. In most cases, communication between superiors and subordinates is an ongoing, shifting dynamic. Most issues are not resolved in a one-shot conversation. In writing about superior-subordinate communications, Rensis Likert concluded:

> A number of recent studies are providing disturbing evidence that communications between managers and supervisors is seriously deficient on such important matters as what a subordinate understands his job to be. The data shows that superiors fail to

make clear to subordinates precisely what the job is and what is expected of them. Moreover, the subordinates do not tell the superior about the obstacles and problems they encounter in doing the job. (New Pattens of Management, McGraw-Hill, New York, 1961, pp. 52–53.)

What is so difficult about communications in this relationship? Why do so many people have trouble spelling out their expectations? First, frequent changes in work assignments and relationships lead to frequent changes in expectations. Many professionals work on projects for periods of two weeks to six months. In addition, they may be working on two or three projects at the same time. This might even involve two or more bosses simultaneously. In such environments there is seldom adequate time to develop mutually agreed upon expectations.

Second, an effective working relationship is complex and involves a number of different facets. Specific issues need to be resolved in building an effective relationship. It obviously takes time and skill for two people to reach a mutual understanding in so many areas. It is probably not possible to resolve these issues in one two-hour session, but sooner or later they need to be addressed either explicitly or implicitly.

JOB CONTENT

Reaching agreement on the subordinate's responsibilities is an important issue in defining the relationship. However, this is often difficult for professional jobs. It is seldom easy to define measurable standards of performance. For example, how do you define individual performance measures for a team of engineers designing a computer component? It is possible to set objectives in terms of time (meeting deadlines), cost, and quality. But engineers often do not have control over all of these factors. Furthermore, if the objectives are not achieved, how do you decide which engineer(s) is to blame? In addition, as mentioned earlier, job assignments change frequently, so there is often inadequate time to spell out responsibilities in detail. Many professionals are given "state of the art" assignments, so the work has never been done before. If professionals are exploring a new field, it is difficult to write a detailed job description of just how to proceed on the project. For these reasons, detailed job descriptions may be of little value for most professional workers. However, job descriptions may be more useful where assignments are more stable and the work more routine. (For example, it may be quite realistic to define responsibilities for a team conducting a routine audit of a division that the firm has audited many times before.)

TAKING INITIATIVE

A good subordinate is one who thinks of the things I would do before I do them. What this means is that he tries to adopt my perspective and look at things from my position in the organization, not just his own.

Another executive said:

I have people coming back to me all of the time saying they couldn't do what I ask because of such and such or so and so. They may call a guy and he's sick or on vacation or something else. But they don't ask themselves, "Is there some other way to get this information?" They just report back to me, thinking that I'll accept their efforts and good intentions as a substitute for what I need.

The message becomes evident: individuals are expected to take initiative on the job. However, the degree of initiative varies with each manager. One boss means that a person should be willing to complete an assignment even when there are obstacles to overcome. Another wants a subordinate to anticipate what the boss wants done. These different perspectives suggest an important point: a person needs to find out how much initiative is expected. Some bosses may be threatened by subordinates who anticipate their desires, others would welcome it.

A means of resolving this dilemma is to look at the different levels of initiative that might be exercised. One article suggests that there are five degrees of initiative that an individual can exercise in relation to the boss. (W. Oncken, Jr., and D.L. Wass, *Harvard Business Review*, Nov.-Dec. 1974, p. 79.) These are:

1. Wait until told (i.e., "But I haven't been told yet to put out the fire.")
2. Ask what to do.
3. Recommend, then take resulting action.
4. Act, but advise at once.
5. Act on own, then routinely report (i.e., "September 5—Fire in factory. Damage: approximately $25,000. Cause: Under Investigation.")

A famous case is brought to mind. A technician at a large company invented a transparent adhesive. But he found no one that was particularly interested in his discovery. Everyone ignored what he felt would be a useful product. During a break in the company's board of directors meeting, the technician taped all the directors' papers to the table. It was the beginning of Scotch tape and a windfall for the 3M Company. Of course, the technician jumped ten levels in the organization to find a responsive audience, and this degree of initiative, itself, is not without risk.

Rather than asking the boss, "What are your expectations?", it might be more useful to talk about levels of initiative. A discussion of those alternatives is likely to lead to a better understanding of the expectations. However, using such an approach could result in oversimplifying the relationship. On some matters the boss may want the subordinate to operate on level five, but on other matters he or she may prefer that the subordinate operate on level two. This suggests that they may also need to talk about activities inside the department versus outside the department—decisions that are within existing policies versus those that might require a change of policy, etc. Individuals should not merely ask how they are expected to operate, but also *observe* carefully over a period of months the boss's reaction when they take different levels of initiative on various kinds of problems. This can do much to clarify expectations.

KEEPING THE BOSS INFORMED

The information-to-the-boss issue is closely tied to initiative, but there are some aspects that deserve separate consideration. Subordinates need to learn how to keep the boss advised on *appropriate* matters.

One rule of thumb to follow is letting the boss know about the progress that is being made on particular projects and avoid reporting all of the *activities* engaged in to achieve those results.

Some subordinates think they must report everything they do. Those who do may find their boss becoming increasingly inaccessible to them. Managers have neither the time nor the desire to know all that the subordinate knows about a particular situation. If the boss has to spend that much time on a project, of what use is the subordinate?

One of the most difficult issues in this area concerns negative information. Often individuals fail to call attention to problems, mistakes, or misjudgments because they believe that "someone up there must know what's going on around here." Individuals may feel that they do not have all of the facts in a situation and thus say nothing. By assuming that superiors have complete information or answers, subordinates ease themselves out of taking responsibility for what goes on in the division or organization. Taking the "it's-not-my-job" position shifts more burden from a subordinate back to the boss—a burden that few bosses need or want to carry.

John and Mark Arnold have documented a number of cases where subordinates in an organization knew that something was wrong, but failed to do anything about it. Two examples:

> The president of a manufacturing company ordered work to begin on a new type of photocopying machine. Although those with direct responsibility believed the machine would take two years to build, they cooperated in forecasting that it could be developed in a matter of months. Working furiously, they managed to complete a prototype to meet their deadline. The president inspected and left the test room with assurances that it was ready for production. Shortly after, however, the machine burst into flames and was destroyed.
>
> In one electronics firm, shipments were being predated and papers falsified to meet sales targets. Sales representatives had accepted the targets rather than complain for fear that they would be labeled as uncommitted. It took months before upper-level managers realized what was happening. (The *Wall Street Journal*, June 5, 1978, p. 9.)

Even though these may be extreme cases, they are real examples, and they are repeated on a smaller scale hundreds of times every day.

Reasons given for withholding negative information from the boss are varied. While the subordinate's well-meant *intent* might be to protect others (the manager or the organization), the *outcome*, generally, will negatively impact any or all of them. Frequent comments in this area include:

> "Don't worry the boss about this, she's got enough trouble as it is."
> "Don't tell Frank, he has a terrible temper and he'll really chew you out."
> "We need to insulate Mr. Layton from all of these details or he'll get overloaded and won't be able to get anything done."

These are nice rationalizations, but managers need negative as well as positive information.

ASKING FOR HELP

A sensitive matter for both the manager and the subordinate is the issue of requesting help. Some bosses want to be deeply involved in a project, and they use requests for help as an opportunity to teach their subordinates. Others only want to see the final product and do not want to be bothered with frequent questions. A bank manager presented his views on this issue:

> Some subordinates will take an assignment, work as hard on it as possible, then come back to you when they get stuck or when it's completed. Other people start coming back to you to do their work for them. People in the second group don't do very well in our bank.

Asking for help too often undermines the manager's confidence in the subordinate. However, there are times when the individual is new or has a difficult assignment and a great deal of help is needed. One way to solve this dilemma is to seek help from peers in the department. The more experienced people are usually able to help, and such requests are less likely to affect the boss's opinion of the employee's ability.

Another factor to consider is the amount of risk involved in a situation. A promising young accountant described his strategy on seeking advice from the boss:

> My boss had high expectations for me when he hired me, and I believe I have lived up to them. To ensure that I would perform successfully, I adopted a strategy of taking risks—not gambles—but calculated risks. If a decision involved a high level of risk, I would consult with my boss and didn't assume full responsibility on my own. However, if a job was not overly risky or of cru-

cial importance, I would do as much of it on my own as I could and not waste my boss's time with the details. I assumed it was important to look out for my boss's welfare, not just my own. If I could make him look good or make his job easier and less time consuming, then it would benefit me as well. However, when I made a decision that turned out to be a mistake, I told my boss about it and didn't try to cover my errors.

This suggests some important guidelines in deciding when to go to the boss for help and when an individual should handle the situation alone:

Take risks, not gambles (and recognize the differences between the two).

Handle the details, but keep the manager informed.

Check with the boss on decisions that will impact work units outside the department.

Take the boss a recommendation each time he asks for an analysis of a project.

Initiate an appointment only when prepared to suggest some action that should be taken.

The last recommendation may meet with mixed reactions. For some managers it works very well, but others want to be kept informed and have the opportunity to talk through the issues as work progresses. This is another area where the boss's style must be considered.

FREQUENCY AND LENGTH OF CONTACT

Many individuals are upset because they don't get more time with their managers. They feel that the boss doesn't appreciate them because he doesn't spend more time with them. Often subordinates feel they are delayed on projects waiting for a decision. On the other hand, many managers are frustrated because they lack information from their subordinates. They don't want to be continually checking up on their people, but neither do they want to be surprised because projects aren't done on time.

The amount of time spent working together involves the previous issues of keeping informed and asking for help, but is also concerns the nature of the relationship. Differing expectations about frequency of contact and the amount of time spent together can be a major sore spot. In practice, people take quite different approaches in deciding how often to get together, including:

Getting together whenever something comes up. (These contacts might be initiated by the superior or the subordinate).

Setting up another appointment at the end of each session together.

Establishing regular meetings (e.g., Wednesday at 9:00 *a.m.*) with one individual or an entire staff.

Any of these approaches can be effective depending on the nature of the relationship. However, it is important that both individuals work out an agreement regarding their approach to this issue.

A RECIPROCAL RELATIONSHIP

The young accountant in the last example made an important point that should not be overlooked. He said:

"I assumed it was important to look out for my boss's welfare, not just my own. If I could make him look good or make his job easier and less time consuming, then it would benefit me as well."

The most effective superior-subordinate relationships are reciprocal. Both individuals gain substantial benefits from the relationship. The boss gains because the accountant saves him time and produces high-quality work. The boss rewards the subordinate by spending extra time with him, giving him challenging work assignments, and increasing his responsibilities. In addition, the young accountant is given opportunities to make presentations to higher levels of management, thus providing him visibility in the firm. This kind of reciprocity contributes to a productive relationship and increases the motivation level of both individuals. When a manager and employee see that the efforts of each individual contribute to the reputation of both, they begin to see the reciprocal process. A boss who thoroughly outlines pitfalls in a specific project or a client's past association with the organization may invest several hours, but he will be rewarded with extra time to devote to other assignments. Undoubtedly he must recognize that his reputation will, to a great extent, rest with his subordinates and the quality of work they produce. Likewise, subordinates' reputations will, to a large degree, stem from the extent to which they are able to handle increasingly complex, significant, or otherwise valued assignments. Investing time in doing a highly competent job for a manager will put both the boss and subordinate in a good light. Future assignments and other rewards will generally reflect the manager's opinion of extra-mile work. The wise subordinate should take the stance of what-I-do-for-my-boss-I-do-for-myself.

Such an alliance contributes to a mentor-protégé relationship, a reciprocal coalition in which the boss, serving as a mentor, agrees to let the subordinate gain the experience and acquire the skills valued in the organization. In exchange, the subordinate must be prepared to perform the necessary detail work that goes with every project and assure its accuracy. He must do the routine but essential groundwork—and do it well—if he expects to gain a reputation that both will value.

The advantages of having a mentor are many. As the primary link in the development of coalitions, a mentor can do such things as guide a subordinate through the unwritten rules and policies that govern routine affairs or show the protégé how to design and carry a project to successful completion. Moreover, as his or her advocate, a mentor can show how to have upward influence with other managers and even be a force in getting the subordinate's ideas accepted.

At this point it must be acknowledged that all organizations are, by definition, political entities, and individuals must manage their careers with this in mind. To say that organizations are by their very nature political is to neither commend nor condemn them. This political aspect is simply an expression of the network of power relationships that may or may not be represented on formal organizational charts. Unfortunately, many professionals view the power relationships from one of two extremes: either they cynically ignore them and claim to be above politics, or they pursue their goals with Machiavellian tactics and coercive techniques. Neither approach optimizes either personal objectives or organizational goals. Nevertheless, mentors can be extremely valuable to those trying to learn the political ropes of the organization.

DEVELOPING A CONDITION OF TRUST WITH THE BOSS

E.E. Jennings suggests that an effective subordinate achieves a condition of trust with his superior (See *The Mobile Manager*, New York, McGraw-Hill, 1967, pp. 47–50). He views four conditions as being necessary for trust to develop.

Accessibility. This is defined as a person who takes in ideas easily and gives them out freely. Both individuals need to demonstrate that they value each other's ideas. If two people are going to develop a productive relationship they must respect each other's ideas and give them careful thought and consideration. A subordinate

who does not respect the boss's ideas will never be trusted and will not obtain the help needed in developing his own ideas. This does not mean that two people always have to agree with one another. "The minimum requirement of trust in this sense is that the subordinate respects new and different ideas enough to think them through carefully and energetically" (Jennings, p. 48).

Availability. This subordinate should be attentive and available physically, mentally, and emotionally when the manager is under pressure and needs support. Recently, one of the authors was under pressure to complete several projects with very tight deadlines. One of his subordinates became upset because he was not receiving the help he needed on a project that the author felt was of less importance. Another subordinate took a different approach. In one of their meetings, he said:

> I know you're under a lot of pressure right now trying to complete high-priority projects. This article we're working on is less important, so I'm quite willing to let it wait for a while. In addition, if I can be of help on any of your projects, just let me know. I've got a little extra time, and I'm willing to pitch in and help any way I can.

The second subordinate was invited to work on two of the projects and not only helped his boss but helped himself as well. It is not difficult to guess which individual received the most favorable letters of recommendation.

Predictability. By predictability, Jennings means that the subordinate will handle delicate administrative circumstances with good judgment and thoroughness. This bears on the kinds of assignments a manager will feel free to give a subordinate. If an individual demonstrates early that he can be trusted to handle relationships with customers on a sensitive project, this will free the manager to work on other projects. However, if the subordinate lacks sensitivity or interpersonal skills and jeopardizes relationships with the customer, it means that in the future the subordinate will not be as trusted, and thus, will be of much less value to the boss.

Predictability has another important facet that relates to dependability. An accounting manager described the importance of this factor:

> Recently, I was supervising some tax work with one of our major clients. I assigned one member of the team to a specific part of the project. He kept saying, "I can do it." Each time I checked he'd say, "I will get it done," but it was not ready when I went out to the job on Friday night. We had to make a major adjustment that night in order to meet a filing deadline. The client had gone to Las Vegas and was very upset when we called him. You can be sure that I don't take that young accountant's word anymore on important matters.

Needless to say, managers don't like surprises that embarrass them or make them look bad.

Loyalty. In this context Jennings is not referring to organizational loyalty but personal loyalty. A manager is not likely to trust a subordinate with important information if he or she fears that the information might be used to further the subordinate's own interests at the manager's expense.

But loyalty must also be considered in a broader context. There are times when loyalty to an immediate superior will come in conflict with loyalty to the organization or to society. What is good for the boss is not always good for the organization; and what is good for the organization is not always good for society. But recognizing and acting upon such situations is not without costs to the individual. A case in a Big 8 accounting firm relates such a conflict: A housing project

was being audited, and a supervisor in the firm wanted to give a qualified opinion. A partner in charge of the audit said that the project should be given a clear opinion. The supervisor refused to have his name associated with the working paper unless he could include a memo stating his objections. While some others involved in the case also sided with the supervisor and admired him for stating his view, he remained the only one who held out. Today he has yet to make promotion to manager.

Other professionals work to maintain a certain distance, a degree of objectivity, about projects—even those that appear to be critical to the organization's future success. One highly regarded middle manager described his strategy:

> I'm not a yes man. I know the importance of speaking up and saying what's on my mind. I also know that other people in the organization may have a better perspective than I do. So I follow this rule of thumb: I argue forcefully one time for my position. If my boss then does not accept my recommendation, I try to make his decision an effective one through my support and commitment. That is, of course, unless I feel a conflict with my personal values.

Watergate brings to mind a wide range of activities associated with the problems of conflicting loyalties. Focusing on the role of subordinates does not imply that a person should always be a loyal subordinate at the expense of individual conscience, the organization, or society. Rather, individuals need to understand their own values and adhere to them even if it means running into conflict with the boss or losing a job. In fact, an individual should take the initiative and seek out another boss when there is a major conflict of values. Some things are far more important than being an "effective subordinate" to a manager of doubtful or even differing values.

The relationship between two individuals in a superior-subordinate relationship is critical, and mutual expectations must be achieved if the individual is to become a valued subordinate.

Those subordinates interested in accomplishing this objective are advised to remember the following points:

> Very few bosses will do all that is necessary to clarify expectations in a superior-subordinate relationship.
>
> Most managers will respond favorably to a discussion of the manager-subordinate relationship. However, managers have varying styles, so an individual is well advised to find out how the boss is *likely* to respond before initiating such a discussion.
>
> Subordinates will usually learn more in such a discussion if they present their perceptions of the expectations and ask for a response. Just asking "What are my responsibilities?" will not generate as much dialogue as, "My understanding of my assignment is that I am to . . . and . . . Is this in agreement with your viewpoint?"

"And God created the organization and gave it dominion over man."
Peter Townsend, *Up the Organization*

"Why are the nations with the most developed systems of professional management education, the United States and Great Britain, performing so poorly, when two nations that provide almost no professional management training, Germany and Japan, have been the outstanding successes of the postwar period?"
David Vogel, School of Business Administration University of California, Berkeley

"The secret of managing is to keep the five guys who hate you away from the five who are undecided."
Casey Stengel

In contemporary America the needs of organization overwhelm all other considerations, whether those of family, religion, art, science, law or the individual. This has had a shattering impact on us, for it has caused us to become a different people than we thought we would be.
D.K. Hart and W.G. Scott, *The Organizational Imperative*

I was to learn later in life that we tend to meet any new situation by reorganizing; and a wonderful method it can be for creating the illusion of progress while producing confusion, inefficiency, and demoralization.
Petronius Arbiter (Circa A.D. 60)

EXERCISES

Group Observer Instructions

Often when a group has a task to perform, the group becomes so involved in the *task* of organizing for the activity that it is not able to remember accurately the process by which the task was accomplished. It can be useful for a neutral person who is not involved in the activity to observe and give feedback about the behavior of individuals during the excitement of an exercise. The observation process can also serve to sensitize group members, as well as the observer, to be more aware of the subtleties of group behavior in their day-to-day involvement.

Your task as group observer is to provide feedback to group members about their behavior in the exercise or experience you are observing. You are to take no active part, but you should position yourself at a point where you can hear what is being said, see nonverbal behavior of as many participants as possible, and observe people on the periphery of the group.

Listed below are a number of issues that often emerge in group interaction. Use them as a guide for increasing your observation skills. Familiarize yourself with them so that you will notice them when they occur. As the exercise proceeds, take notes of specifically what happens, who is involved, and so forth, so that you can refer to them when you verbally elaborate on them to the group members after they have completed the exercise. Avoid evaluations such as *good* and *bad*, simply describe the behavior of the people involved.

In your examination of the group process, focus on the emergence of leaders, communication (both talking and listening), conflict, evaluation of ideas, and facilitating or disruptive behavior. The following items are intended to trigger discussion of group processes. Consider each of them and concentrate on the issues that seem most relevant.

1. Who are high participators, and who are low participators? Are there any shifts in participation as the exercise proceeds?
2. Which members seem to listen the most, and which seem to listen the least to other members' points of view? Discuss the evidence that supports your choice. How are silent people treated? Ignored? Asked for input? Do any members continually interrupt?
3. Which members receive the most attention while they make their points? Does a leader emerge whom the others are willing to follow? How do members indicate agreement? Disagreement?
4. How are decisions made? Does the majority rule? Do powerful individuals dominate decisions? Do some suggestions go unnoticed? How does that person respond?

5. How does the group decide to proceed with the task? Does the group as a whole decide on a procedure, or does a procedure just emerge? Does one person or a faction control the process, or do all share equally in the decision? What is the response of people whose suggestions are rejected or voted down?

6. What is the general group climate? What specific examples of behavior can you give to illustrate this?

7. How do group members express their feelings? How are these received?

8. Recall and discuss comments that tended to turn the group away from or back to the problem at hand. Did any members continually make side-tracking comments?

9. What kind of roles emerge during this exercise? Is there a "taskmaster" who tries to get the job done? Is there a person who tries to draw out silent members? Is anyone openly concerned about maintaining a good atmosphere among people during the discussion? Cite specific behavior.

10. If there is an emergent leader or leaders, what do they or the group members do that put them in that position?

The Tinkertoy Exercise

To approach the field of organizational behavior it is useful to have a shared experience that students can use to define issues. This exercise provides a brief experience in which problems of organizing, planning, decision making, leadership, implementation, communication, and many others can be identified. It seems easier to appreciate organizational problems when they are experienced and discussed with actual tasks rather than abstract definitions. It also serves the purpose of bringing students together early in the term in a group activity.

Exercise objective. To build the tallest self-support structure with the contents of one box of Tinkertoys.

"Tinkertoy" is a registered trademark of the Questor Corporation.

Exercise rules. The class should be divided into groups of from three to eight members. Each group is given a regular size box of Tinkertoys (120–130 pieces). The group has 20 minutes to plan their work. It is most important, however, that during the planning period there is *no* assembly of parts. The pieces can be looked at, but not even a trial assembly of any two pieces is allowed. At the end of the 20 minutes, all pieces go back in the box. Then the construction phase starts. The construction phase lasts *40* seconds! It is important that the instructor only start and stop the planning and construction periods. He or she should not give advice or amount of time remaining.

There are obviously many variations which can be employed with this exercise. Criteria can be stated in terms of aesthetic dimensions, number of pieces used, functional performance (how far a car will roll), etc. Monetary incentives can be used (if available), groups can be of different size, and learning can be tested with future repetitions.

An Ancient Tale

In attempts to understand, analyze, and improve organizations, it is imperative that we be able to think carefully through the issue of who is responsible for what activities in different organizational settings. Often we hold someone responsible who has no control over the outcome, or we fail to teach or train someone who could make the vital difference.

To explore this issue, the following exercise could be conducted with either an individual or a group. It provides an opportunity to see how different individuals assign responsibility for an event. It is also a good opportunity to discuss the concept of organizational boundaries (what is the organization, who is in or out, and so forth).

You should read the short story and respond quickly to the first three questions. Then take a little more time on questions 4 and 5. The results, criteria, and implications could then be discussed in class, in groups, or in a more formal manner, such as in a mock trial in which different individuals present an argument for or against different characters and a jury decision assigns responsibility (or, alternately, a policy decision could be made on how to improve the environment in the kingdom).

Long ago in an ancient kingdom there lived a princess who was very young and very beautiful. The princess, recently married, lived in a large and luxurious castle with her husband, a powerful and wealthy lord. The young princess was not content, however, to sit and eat strawberries by herself while her husband took frequent and long journeys to neighboring kingdoms. She felt neglected and soon became quite unhappy. One day, while she was alone in the castle gardens, a handsome vagabond rode out of the forest bordering the castle. He spied the beautiful princess, quickly won her heart, and carried her away with him.

Following a day of dalliance, the young princess found herself ruthlessly abandoned by the vagabond. She then discovered that the only way back to the castle led through the bewitched forest of the wicked sorcerer. Fearing to venture into the forest unaccompanied, she sought out her kind and wise godfather. She explained her plight, begged forgiveness of the godfather, and asked his assistance in returning home before her husband returned. The godfather, however, surprised and shocked at her behavior, refused forgiveness and denied her any assistance.

Discouraged but still determined, the princess disguised her identity and sought the help of the most noble of all the kingdom's knights. After hearing the sad story, the knight pledged his unfailing aid—for a modest fee. But, alas, the princess had no money and the knight rode away to save other damsels.

The beautiful princess had no one else from whom she might seek help and decided to brave the great peril alone. She followed the safest path she knew, but when she was almost through the forest, the wicked sorcerer spied her and caused her to be devoured by the fire-breathing dragon.

1. Who is most responsible for the death of the beautiful princess?

2. Who is next most responsible?
3. Who is least responsible?
4. What is your criterion for the above decisions?
5. What are the implications for *organizational behavior*?

	Most responsible	Next most responsible	Least responsible
Princess			
Husband			
Vagabond			
Godfather			
Knight			
Sorcerer			

Check one character in each column.

Supervision, Jazz and Beards

ROLE FOR MICHELLE JONES, LINE SUPERVISOR

You are the supervisor for a work group of nineteen people on a line where microchips are manufactured. You have been working at the facility since it first started producing chips several years ago, know your job well, and get along well with your group. You have just been notified that Quality Control has rejected another batch of particle-contaminated chips. Had the chips made it into finished computers the results would have had a very negative impact on the company. Microchip production is very automated and the machines require limited supervision by relatively unskilled workers. At the same time, microchips must be produced in a completely particle-free environment. While quality is a top priority in the highly competitive microchip industry, Quality Control has been rejecting an increasingly high percentage of chips since two new operators joined your work group a few months ago. The two always seem to be caught without their protective, sterilized face masks, even though theirs is one of the most critical stations on the line. One is Bob, black, 22 years old, and generally cooperative. The other is Ted, white, 20 years old and a little grumpy. They appear to be friends and each seems to be able to talk his way out of any problem. Bob even suggested you buy a different mask for him because he didn't like the standard one issued. You gave them one warning after a bad batch of chips was traced directly to them. The next incident means they are laid off without pay for three days, and the third means termination. You want to give them a fair hearing and have called them in to tell them about the new batch of bad chips. They are coming now.

ROLE FOR BOB

You are a 22–year–old black who has worked on a microchip production line for three months. When you first came to work the job looked pretty good. But now you and your best friend, Ted, are getting a lot of flack from your line supervisor, Michelle. She has been on your back about not wearing a dumb face mask for weeks and just won't let up. Just because *one* lousy chip had a speck of dust in it you have to look silly in an uncomfortable mask. And you have to wear one of the masks provided by the company, even though the largest one is too small to cover your beard. You have complained about the size of the mask several times, but Michelle doesn't pay attention. You have even offered to bring your own, but the "rules" require a certain kind. Besides, several women at other stations pull the masks down below their chins all the time, and Michelle never says anything to them. Of course, the supervisor is a woman and so she lets them get away with it. Someone suggested that you shave your beard so that the mask wouldn't be so uncomfortable, but you and Ted play in a jazz quartet at night, and shaving your beard would ruin your whole image.

Michelle has asked you to come in to see her. You and Ted are on your way to her office now.

ROLE FOR TED

You are a 20–year–old white who has worked on a microchip production line for three months. You and your best friend, Bob, are getting a lot of flack from your line supervisor, Michelle, for not wearing a stupid face mask while at your station. She even threatened to suspend you just because Quality Control found dust in a chip they claim came from your station. There are lots of other places on the line where you believe the dust could have gotten in. Anyway, several female operators at other stations pull the masks down below their chins all the time. Of course, Michelle doesn't say anything to them because they are women. One worker even suggested that you shave your beard so that the mask would fit better, but you and Bob play in a jazz quartet at night. Shaving your beard would ruin your whole image. You only took the job in the first place because it seemed like a good way to provide extra money while you and Bob got your jazz quartet off the ground. The job wouldn't be too bad if Michelle would just do away with that dumb mask requirement. There really aren't any better jobs; so maybe you could put up with a little discomfort. On the other hand, Michelle said that she wants to talk to you and Bob, and you don't know what to expect.

You and Bob are on your way to Michelle's office now.

The Whole Concept of Organization Depends on Some Degree of Collective Action

"I did it! I just fired all 324 of them! I'm going to run the plant by myself."

CASES

Framework for Organizational Analysis

Before an examination of nearly any situation, it is generally helpful to know what key areas might be analyzed. Whether you are discussing your own work setting, a news account of a government agency, or a case in this book, a "road map" can allow you to zero in quickly on central organizational issues. The tendency for many is to move rapidly to solutions, to the action stage. Failure to analyze available information restricts an individual's understanding and insights and thus limits the number of alternatives that are considered. Another pitfall is that students go to one of two extremes: Either there is only one correct answer, or there aren't any answers ("It depends on how you see it"). Avoiding these two extremes and opening up options depends upon your ability to carefully consider the task, people, social, organizational, and environmental factors that are provided in the setting. The following questions are presented as an aid in organizational analysis:

I. What is the problem?
   A. What hurts in the organization?
   B. What factors are contributing to the pain?
   C. What output of the system is not living up to the manager's expectations?

II. Analysis
   A. Task—nature of the business as defined by top management.
      1. What does the organization need to do well in order to succeed? (What are the key variables?)
      2. Important aspects of the task
         a. The amount of uncertainty in the environment
         b. The amount of interdependence required between subunits
         c. The time span of the performance cycle
   B. People
      1. What skills and abilities are required of them?
         a. What are their skills and abilities?
         b. How long does it take to develop those skills?
         c. How necessary is on-the-job training?
      2. What types of rewards are they seeking from their jobs?
      3. What types of rewards are they getting from their jobs?
      4. How do the people in the various subunits differ from one another in—
         a. Goal orientation (e.g., a scientist vs. a production manager)
         b. Time orientation
         c. Interpersonal orientation
   C. Social factors
      1. What is the nature of the ex-

isting social system?
  a. What are the norms of
     the group?
  b. How strong is the group's
     influence on individual
     performance?
  2. How much trust exists be-
     tween management and em-
     ployees?
  3. What are the management-
     union relationships?
D. Organization
  1. Organizational structures
     a. Division of work
     b. Span of control
     c. Management hierarchy
  2. Measurement and evaluation
     practices
     a. Control system
     b. Performance appraisal
  3. Compensation
  4. Recruiting and selection
  5. Training
E. Environment
  1. What boundary separates the
     inside and outside of the or-
     ganization?
  2. How does the organization
     relate to other organizations
     within this particular indus-
     try?
  3. What is the nature of the in-
     dustry?
     a. Degree of competition
     b. Degree of interdepen-
        dence
     c. Types of suppliers
  4. In what ways is the govern-
     ment involved with the orga-
     nization's activities?
  5. What outside special-interest

groups are important for the
organization to work with?
F. Fit
  1. Is there a fit between task,
     people, social, organizational,
     and environmental variables?
  2. Are these variables compati-
     ble with one another? (e.g.,
     does the control system fit
     the structure?)

III. Action
  A. Which parts of the organization
     should be changed?
  B. Who is in a position to change
     them?
  C. How much change is necessary?
     1. Change only in the manager's
        behavior
     2. Change in design and imple-
        mentation of a new system
     3. Change covering a large num-
        ber of persons or groups
  D. What are the appropriate steps
     for implementing the change?

IV. Framework for organizational anal-
    ysis
  A. What are the relationships
     among these factors?
  B. Are the task, people, social, or-
     ganizational, and environmental
     variables compatible?
  C. Is there an adequate fit among
     them?

V. Environment
  A. Industry atmosphere
  B. Special-interest groups
  C. Government influence
  D. Local culture

GROUP OBSERVER INSTRUCTIONS

Framework for organizational analysis

What are the relationships among these factors?
Are the task, people, social, organizational,
   and environmental variables compatible?
Is there an adequate fit among them?

Actual work performed
Physical conditions and demands
Spatial arrangements
Interdependence of work groups
Degree of structure vs. uncertainty
Performance cycle time span
   etc.

Division of work
Span of control
Management hierarchy
Rules and procedures
Performance evaluation
   and control
Rewards and compensation
Recruiting and selection
   etc.

Educational backgrounds
Age
Sex
Skill level
Ethnicity
Supply of labor
Individuals' motivation(s)
Attitudes toward work
   etc.

Social structure
Group norms
Leadership patterns, roles
Morale, climate
Influence, status
   etc.

Industry atmosphere
Special-interest groups
Government influence
Local culture

A Question of Ethics

J.B. RITCHIE and THOMAS W. DUNFEE

How Would Your Moral Code Hold Up in the Face of a Make-
or-Break Career Decision?

Every decade has its scandals, but the 1980s seem to have had an extra portion. Top officials at two of the nation's power centers—Wall Street and the White House—currently face continuing investigation, perhaps prosecution. Their names read like a who's who of recent headlines: Ivan Boesky, Oliver North, David Levine, Robert McFarlane, Martin Siegel, Michael Deaver.

Telling as they are, the headlines are mere symptoms of a larger problem. Politicians and investment bankers certainly have no monopoly on misdealings. The vast majority of questionable business practices, like most crimes, no doubt go unreported. Hence the standard one-liner about "business ethics" being an oxymoron. . . .

Many of the young people entering today's business world fail to see the humor in the wisecrack. In talking to college seniors from around the nation last semester, we found a real quandary on the topic of workplace ethics. Most realized that they would face ethical dilemmas, probably early in their careers. Some had pondered the issue already, trying to pick companies compatible with their values

Taken from *The Wall Street Journal:* The College Edition of the National Business Employment Weekly, Spring, 1987. Reprinted by permission of authors.

and beliefs.

But few students felt confident in their ability to think through murky questions of morality. One of them, a history major from Los Angeles, summarized the sentiment when he said, "We could really use a framework for analyzing ethical issues."

Easier said than done, of course. Philosophers have been debating ethics for centuries. Dilemmas, by definition, defy clearcut solutions. But this article is our attempt to offer some of the clearest reasoning available on the subject.

First, we outline the situation of a young business school graduate caught in a moral dilemma on his first job. We then present responses from two professors who have dedicated their careers to thinking and teaching about ethics in organizations. Their insights provide surprisingly practical guidelines for dealing with an age-old problem.

A CASE STUDY

After earning an undergraduate degree in history and an M.B.A. in finance, Robert was offered a position with a medium-sized real estate development firm in his hometown. Much to his liking, the job involved working in the firm's "community projects" area, where he would oversee the books for the company's

construction of low-cost housing projects.

The opportunity to work in finance while also aiding the public good appealed to Robert. When interviewing for other jobs in finance and real estate, he didn't like the competitive atmosphere at larger firms where the size of salaries and bonuses seemed to be the overriding concern of most new hires.

After a few weeks in his position, Robert discovered a discrepancy in the books of one of his firm's housing projects. Six separate checks for $10,000 each had been written by Robert's boss over the past year, and each was made payable to "Cash" with no further explanation. When Robert approached his boss, he was told that they were just another cost of doing business and to inflate the cost of other items to cover for the payments.

Through further investigation, Robert learned that the checks were being paid to building inspectors to overlook the use of certain substandard materials. Robert again protested to his boss, who responded with obvious irritation. He said such payments were common and the use of substandard materials wouldn't affect safety.

The boss implied that significant cost savings on materials were necessary for the firm to build low-income housing on a profitable basis. He noted that the cost of each unit would increase by only $2,000 to cover the payments, and that the eventual owners probably expect that they'll have to upgrade their units from time to time anyway.

Robert knew that, at the least, replacements or repairs would be needed after only two or three years because of the substandard materials. Concerned that a wrong was being committed and fearful that he might personally become entangled in the mess, Robert protested to his boss's supervisor. The supervisor told Robert that "he would look into it." Robert hasn't heard anything in the three weeks since and has just discovered that a seventh $10,000 check payable to cash has come through. What should Robert do now?

PRACTICE VS. PRINCIPLE

J. Bonner Ritchie

Robert is caught in a dilemma that we all face repeatedly in our careers. While our situations may not involve bribes or low-income housing, the basic question is the same: Where do we draw the line between *practice* and *principle*? The answer is rarely cut and dried, and usually involves some compromise of individual or organizational well-being—or both.

In this case, Robert must decide where practice may be compromised and where principle must be honored. His choice is complicated by a number of conflicting values and goals, including:

- the community's need for adequate low-cost housing.
- the profitability and reputation of the construction firm.
- the importance of a good working relationship with the firm's upper management.
- the opportunity to remain with the firm long enough to make a *real* difference.
- the need to hold on to his job in a tight market.

Each of these criteria bears *consideration* and could be used to justify a particular course of action. But they miss what is perhaps the most important factor: the value Robert brings to the company.

Robert's worth to any organization (current or future) is a function of the resources he brings to the job. I assume that honesty and integrity are driving forces in Robert's life. Given that position, he cannot continue with business as usual; to do so would destroy the most important resource he offers the organization.

How drastic an action need he take in order to preserve his integrity? Here again, his decision will hinge on where he strikes the compromise between personal and organizational well-being. His options are:

- Report the matter to higher level management. Since he has done this already, some would argue that he has cleared himself from any responsibility in the matter.
- If the company doesn't take acceptable actions, mobilize resources within the company to fight the questionable practice.
- Mobilize forces outside the company (county attorney or the media) to put pressure on company management.
- Quit and walk away quietly from the situation, without burning too many bridges.
- Quit *and* report the matter to legal or media representatives.

Robert also must consider the timing of the recent check. This is the first such transaction since he joined the firm; it could well be the "test." His superior knows Robert is aware and disapproves of past practice. Failure to act now will signal a "buy in" to the supervisor's policy. Robert would become an accomplice.

Considering all of these factors, I suggest that Robert:

1. Document the whole matter. Make a log of conversations and a copy of all relevant records.
2. Start a low-key job search, testing the waters without tipping his hand.
3. Prepare his resignation addressed to the CEO and, for now, keep it in his briefcase.
4. Make another appointment to see his boss's supervisor. The previous discussion with this individual didn't produce any immediate harmful effects. Robert should operate on the assump-

tion that his manager is "looking into it" with honest intent. Maybe he wasn't aware of the problem and is taking the necessary investigative and corrective steps.

5. In the discussion, Robert should restate his concern, with information regarding the additional $10,000 check.
6. If he isn't satisfied that adequate organizational and legal steps are being taken, he should "make his speech," indicating that he will tender his resignation (with a report of his reasons) to the CEO immediately.
7. After resigning, since there is a criminal issue with the payoffs to the inspectors, he should then contact the city or county attorney's office with a formal complaint and all the supporting documents.
8. Finally, he should shift the low-key job search into high gear and lose sleep over the problem of finding a new job rather than wondering how to regain his integrity.

BLOWING THE WHISTLE

Thomas W. Dunfee

I'm sure that few students believe they'll ever face a choice similar to Robert's. The odds are to the contrary, however. Most managers will confront situations involving illegal or unethical behavior at some point in their careers.

Robert is in a position where he must make a decision. The alluring alternative is to do nothing and hope that nothing bad happens. But a head-in-the-sand approach fails to confront the critical ethical issues.

Before reaching a decision, Robert should attempt to get the facts straight. At this point, his only source of information is his boss's statement that the payments are essential and that tenant safety isn't being compromised. Robert should seek independent evidence.

Next, Robert should make sure that senior management knows about the payments. The company's president and chief financial officer likely would care about payments that could seriously harm the firm if disclosed. Robert already has mentioned the payments to his boss and his boss's supervisor. If the company has a formal procedure for internal whistle-blowing, now is the time for Robert to use it. If such a procedure doesn't exist, he should at least relay his information to a company attorney.

If Robert informs top management and nothing happens, then as a third step, he must decide whether to stay with the company and whether to blow the whistle to outsiders. If Robert decides to stay with the company despite their inaction with the problem, he likely will continue to encounter a never-ending series of incidents in which his values clash with those of his peers and superiors.

Whether Robert should blow the whistle to outsiders depends on the answers to four questions:

1. Is his evidence believable?
2. Will the disclosures produce results?
3. Will disclosing have an unacceptable impact on his life and career?
4. Do the code violations threaten the safety of the owners?

Whistle-blowing becomes more ethically mandatory as the dangers to human safety increase.

The utilitarian argument that the bribes being paid directly benefit low-income housing recipients—or the situationalist argument that they are common practice in the industry, even if true—doesn't justify continuation of the payments. For the utilitarian argument to be valid, the benefits to society must be greater than the costs. The likely major beneficiary of the bribes is Robert's firm, not the public.

In addition, there are significant costs associated with the bribes. Low-income people will be defrauded by the substandard components. Even worse, they may be subjected to safety hazards despite what Robert's boss says.

If the system for setting low-income housing specifications doesn't work well, it's not up to the company to take it upon itself to correct the problem. Further, the fact that many people pay bribes doesn't make bribing ethical. Bribes to building inspectors violate the law and represent a fundamental violation of the public trust. Therefore, the situationalist argument that the company is following industry customs can't be justified.

It's understandable that some people in Robert's position may be reluctant to blow the whistle. They fear being branded a pariah, which will make it difficult for them to find other jobs. They may try notifying outsiders anonymously by calling or writing a reporter. Such muted whistle-blowing may be less effective because there isn't an insider publicly supporting the charge of wrongdoing. Nor would it be possible to remain anonymous if Robert were one of just a handful of people who know about the practice.

The payments to public inspectors violate criminal law and produce "cooked books" that may be part of Robert's direct responsibility. At the minimum, he should inform senior management and make sure he doesn't participate in the bribe in any way. If the company fails to take action, Robert should look for another job and strongly consider blowing the whistle.

Washington Elementary School

Washington Elementary School is located in an upper socio-economic area of Lincoln, Nebraska. Most parents of Washington Elementary's students are professionals and university professors. Population growth in the area has increased the number of students attending the school, but recent funding requests for an additional school in the Lincoln School District have been rejected by the voters. The result has been larger classes in most grades and a considerable drop in teacher morale.

Jack Adams, a Lincoln native and a former junior high school teacher, has been the principal at Washington for four years. In his early thirties, he is about in the middle of the faculty in age and experience. Jack is a highly regarded administrator whom the teachers perceive to be supportive, reasonable, and fair. His sense of humor is frequently exploited as the faculty plays good-natured jokes on him or on others. He is viewed as one of the team, rather than a different "animal," and he reinforces this image with activities in the teachers' organization.

Jack's classroom visits are infrequent, usually only what the district requires for twice-a-year evaluations of the staff. Teachers are assumed to be responsible and capable, and therefore not in need of his services unless something unusual happens.

The twenty-one-member faculty at Washington usually includes two or three new teachers and a majority of returning

This case was prepared by Hal B. Gregersen and Judyth Peterson under the direction of Paul H. Thompson, Brigham Young University.

teachers, five or six of whom have been there over ten years. The older teachers are very influential in determining the activities at the school, and it is difficult to initiate any changes without their support.

Earlier administrations of Lincoln School District had conducted business in a colleaguial fashion. There was little differentiation between teachers and administrators and the loyalty was generally mutual. Several years ago, however, some teachers suggested striking over a particular issue. In response to this threat, the superintendent indicated that a strike would be just fine, as he could replace them all within twenty-four hours. Because the local supply of elementary teachers had been high, Washington's teachers were unwilling to buck the powers that be. Instead, they chose to suffer in silence.

Recently, a new superintendent was hired for the Lincoln School District. She had an intense desire to update the instructional methods and practices in the district as economically as possible. Previously, teachers had "done their own thing" and liked it that way. In spite of the district's proximity to a local university, Lincoln's teaching techniques were seen by many as very outdated. During this district curriculum transition, Sue Erickson joined the faculty of Washington Elementary. She perceived that the emphasis in the district was on teaching practices which had been used in California ten years earlier and were subsequently discarded because of their ineffectiveness.

As a result of the superintendent's desire to improve the district's educational offering, a science program was developed through the cooperation of the local teachers. The design of this program required that teachers not only cover textbook material but also develop more creative learning opportunities. The district supported the curriculum improvement effort by making an investment in materials and equipment for the teachers to use. There was some grumbling and griping about the extra effort required to implement this innovative program; however, most teachers used the ideas at least enough to make some difference in their curriculum.

On the heels of the major science changes, preparations were made for a significant overhaul of the reading program. Sue Erickson, a second-grade teacher, was assigned to the language arts curriculum committee because she had had experience using the kind of techniques which the district was going to require, as well as specific professional training in reading instruction. Most of the other teachers on the committee, she discovered, were unaware of recent developments in this area but seemed open to suggestions. One of the priorities in implementing the program was the persuasion of middle and upper-grade teachers to make significant changes in their methods, going from total group instruction to small ability groups and individualization.

From time to time, Jack Adams would ask for a report in faculty meetings from Sue on the progress of the language arts committee. Although she tried very hard to articulate the committee's action in non-threatening terms, there were two or three teachers who indicated regularly that they were content with their own teaching methods and felt no need to make any changes. Jack usually made no comment after her report.

The controversy came to a head one afternoon at a special faculty meeting to which Kathy Hadley, the district curriculum development specialist, had been invited. Washington's teachers had been informed that Kathy would be presenting the new district reading instruction guidelines for them to consider and that the district would be open to the teachers' suggestions or comments. Kathy began her presentation, and at first there were no problems; however, when she distributed a small packet of materials outlining the program, three teachers started muttering to each other, flipping through the pages, and shaking their heads. When she came to the section expressing the district's commitment to meeting individual needs of students and outlining suggestions for personalization of instruction, the tension became obvious as the faculty began voicing their opinions.

Neil Decker, a fourth-grade teacher who was considering leaving the profession because of the inadequate salary, was the first to speak. "I've got 34 children in my class. How can I handle this individual stuff? What do the other 25 kids do while I'm working with a group?"

"That's just what I'd like to know!" Jeri Wade, another fourth-grade teacher, joined in. "And another thing—what's wrong with the way we're doing it now? Our students do well on the achievement tests."

"We're not implying that your children aren't learning," Kathy said. "We just think their needs could be met more effectively. Teaching thirty children all together at the same time in the same reading skills results in a lot of wasted time for some children and pushes other children beyond what they're prepared to learn."

Neil said, "It's impossible to do. You guys come down from your ivory tower and tell us how to teach. I don't have time to do any more than I'm already doing." Several of the other teachers nodded their heads in agreement.

Kathy replied, "Of course, this isn't

something we would expect you to implement all at once. We realize that you are used to your own way of teaching, and we just hope to encourage you to be moving in this direction, so that perhaps over a reasonable period of time—"

Dixie Dearden, a third-grade teacher, broke in. "We're doing the best we can with these big classes. Why don't you spend some of that district money on relieving our class loads instead of thinking up more work for us?"

"We can't do this," Neil repeated. "It's just not possible."

"First and second-grade teachers teach this way all the time," Sue said. But no one was listening. The other first and second-grade teachers failed to comment on Sue's position, leaving her alone in her efforts. The faculty immediately broke into small, heated discussion groups. Caught off guard by the hostility to her proposal, Kathy was embarrassed about the teachers' reactions. Jack had to make some quick decisions; What should he do to restore order in the meeting, and how could he not only persuade his teachers to accept the new program in principle but also motivate them to implement it in the classroom?

Gemini Electronics

MANUFACTURING PERSPECTIVE

Part A

"This is a flaming disaster," fumed Bob Reynolds, COO of Gemini Electronics Company. "We'd better have a deliverable system on time," he told Calvin Webber, head production engineer, "because my job is riding on this project."

Reynolds's outburst was not without cause. He had just attended a design review with the Houtin-Smith (a client) display development team. Already well on their way to using up their budget—and halfway into the manufacturing process—the team had encountered a number of unforeseeable problems in getting the system built. Prospects of meeting the con-

This case was prepared by Kurt Sandholtz and Robert A Page, Jr., under the direction of Alan Wilkins, Brigham Young University, August, 1985.

tract deadline looked dim. "I think our relationship with the design engineers hit an all-time low at that point," explained Webber.

Antipathy between the two factions was certainly nothing new. Prior to the Houtin-Smith crisis, Manufacturing's relationship with Engineering had been rocky at best. Webber, who had recently come to Starr from Ajax Motors, recalled his first few days on the job. "My starting assignment was production engineer on the Houtin-Smith development effort. I was personally responsible for all the manufacturing processes and procedures needed to build the display. It was exciting—we were dealing with a lot of brand new, untouched areas. But one of the first things my fellow workers told me was: 'Watch out for the engineers. They're a bunch of slobs.'"

Initially surprised by such an open expression of bad blood, Webber soon understood the motivation behind the sentiment. "In manufacturing, we really felt like underdogs. I mean, we designed parts, incorporated the latest technology into our processes—everything that the design engineers did, we did. But we got paid less for it." The perceived inequity was aggravated by the company's decision to build a modern new facility specifically for the engineers. "Engineering really had a holier-than-thou attitude towards us," remarked Webber.

Despite this history of antagonism, both Manufacturing and Engineering demonstrated apparent willingness to co-operate on the Houtin-Smith development effort. In early cross-functional meetings, the design engineers agreed to work as much as possible within the standard manufacturing procedures, and Manufacturing agreed to remain more flexible than usual. "It looked like we might actually work together for once," Webber recalled.

Such hopes proved premature, however. "I remember an early attempt to help the design engineers," explained Webber. "One of our first technical challenges was to figure out a way to encapsulate the CRT unit in a liquid-cooled casing. I came up with a way to do it, and took it to Stan Bower, the head design engineer. I'll never forget his response. He looked real disgusted and asked me, 'Who do you think you are? Why did you do that?' That was my first exposure to the 'You jerk!' attitude of the engineers. The situation deteriorated from there."

The main sore spot for the manufacturing people was Engineering's reluctance to document design changes. Webber related an example that he called "typical": "Gemini Electronics buys printed circuit boards from a Florida company called ELR. For the Houtin-Smith project, the engineers completely rebuilt ELR's stock PC boards. Trying to document those changes was a nightmare. We needed to-

tal ability to duplicate the changes that they'd made, but the engineers wanted to bypass the documentation. They'd rebuild a board, then hand it to us and say, 'Make the rest of the boards look like this one.' We'd say 'We can't do that. You have to give us a list of components and specific assembly instructions.' Without those things, we would have no idea what new parts they used, the steps they used to make the board, or how it was supposed to work. In the end, one of our production engineers had to sit down and figure out what they'd done—a reverse engineering process right here in our own company."

According to Webber, the engineers' avoidance of documentation was partially a result of the laborious drafting procedures associated with Engineering Change Orders (ECOs). "The people in Engineering Services had to produce a whole set of working drawings for each ECO," explained Webber. "That took time, but we needed those drawings to build the final system. The engineers were complaining that it took too long. I think they had a blow-up over that one."

John Meyors, head of Engineering Services, acknowledged that there had been some heated discussions with the engineers over the issue of documentation. "We had a lot of gripes about how long it took to get mechanical sketches into finished drawings. The engineers would bring us the drawing for an entire assembly, hand sketched on a single piece of graph paper. We'd have to extract three views of each separate component, then extract the detail for piece part drawings. It was a time-consuming process. If the engineer that designed the part would do a little more detail work, it would make our job a lot easier."

"The quality question is another can of worms," continued Meyors. "How good do the drawings have to be? It's a decision that the project engineers have to make. Unless they specify otherwise, we go with inked drawings. It takes 30 percent more time to ink drawings, but that level of quality is what a lot of customers—especially high-quality operations like Houtin-Smith—demand. The design engineers literally exploded when they found out we were inking the drawings. But what do they expect us to do, read their minds?"

Shortly after the blow-up with Engineering Services, the development team held the fateful design review in which Bob Reynolds, the COO, labeled the project a "flaming disaster." "That's when we really started to feel the heat," observed Webber. Paul Taylor, the program manager for the entire Houtin-Smith contract, began imposing deadlines on both the design engineers and the manufacturing people. "He thought that would solve the problem," said Webber.

Taylor's deadlines, however, actually intensified the problem. "It put the engineers under the gun to get their design finalized," explained Webber, "and their reaction was to stop doing ECOs altogether. From that point, they did everything at a PECO (Preliminary Engineering Change Order) level. ECOs go through Engineering Services, Quality Control, and Test Engineering before they are approved. PECOs remain in engineering and require only three signatures. They're designed to facilitate development, but Manufacturing won't build at a PECO level. It's a prototype level—we have no control over it.

"Anyway, the design engineers started using PECOs to avoid the hassles and expense of formal ECOs. That made development real messy. We were never sure what changes were going on at what level. Changes would go through engineering without us hearing about them. The result was that we'd end up producing equipment from specs that were obsolete before we even started—like the high-voltage power supply assembly that we built, put in the stores, and then had to completely rebuild four times. We were about ready to throw up our hands and say to the engineers, 'OK, build the damn thing yourselves.' "

Part B

Pete Jones, the VP of Manufacturing, was faced with a dilemma: he could either stop the abuse of the PECOs, and thereby almost guarantee that the system would be delivered late; or he could allow the system to be designed and built at a PECO level, thus forfeiting any vestige of quality control over the finished product. Fearing the consequences of a late delivery, Jones chose a middle course. He had Stan Bower, the head design engineer, sign a statement accepting full contractual responsibility for the quality and performance of the product.

"That was a good move on the part of Jones," commented Webber. "If he hadn't made that compromise, the system would never have been shipped, plain and simple. I just hope it doesn't establish a precedent. We can't let the engineers have free reign to change things then send them out the door."

ENGINEERING PERSPECTIVE

Part A

"This is a flaming disaster," fumed Bob Reynolds, COO of Gemini Electronic Company. "We'd better have a deliverable system on time, he told Stan Bower, head design engineer, "because my job is riding on this project."

Reynolds's outburst was not without cause. He had just attended a design review with the Houtin-Smith display development team. Already well on their way to using up their budget—and halfway into the manufacturing process—the team had encountered a number of unforeseeable problems in getting the system built. Prospects of meeting the contract deadline looked dim. "It was at about this time that I started praying," recalled Bower.

The situation had not always been so dismal for the Houtin-Smith display team. When Gemini Electronics reached a formal agreement with the Houtin-Smith Engineering Facility to provide the display unit for a first-of-its-kind computer system, Bower had been ecstatic. "I wanted to build the best display unit ever built," he explained, "and Houtin-Smith looked like the vehicle for doing it. They were interested in cutting-edge technology. They had been exploring some of the things that we had been talking about. It was a near-perfect fit."

In early cross-functional meetings, this sense of excitement translated into an ostensible bond of cooperation. "Before we ever tried to build the system," Bower remembered, "we had a meeting with the people from Manufacturing. Everyone acted like one big happy family, like they were going to give their support. I walked out thinking, 'Great. We're all working together on this.' "

The euphoria was short lived, however. Bower found that the expertise required to design and build a complex display system was not available within the company. "I had to hire a whole new staff—13 or 14 people—in less than a year. Some of them turned out to be real duds." On top of the difficulties of working with a group of unknowns, Bower found the technology itself unfamiliar. "This kind of thing had never been done before by *anyone, anywhere.* We were plowing full speed through uncharted territory."

The burden of this technological uncertainty began to weigh more heavily under the pressure of contract deadlines. "Under normal development conditions," remarked Bower, "it wouldn't have mattered if we'd missed a few targets along the way. But when you're working towards a specified delivery date, the whole picture changes. You have no slack. It's do or die."

"Part of the problem," he continued, "is that under that kind of pressure, you have to be a little bit more dictatorial. My engineers would come to me with a new way of solving a problem, and I'd have to say, 'That looks interesting, but we're going to do it this other way.' That was hard on a lot of them."

Indeed, the development effort began to take its toll on the entire team. Severe personnel problems developed. Engineers started quitting. "We had been working 14–hour days for a period of many months," observed Bower. "No one took any vacation. A lot of days, we'd come in before sunrise and leave long after dark."

Amidst these intense pressures, the development team ran into its most formidable obstacle: the Manufacturing Department.

"There's a series of manufacturing procedures around here that must have evolved the same way as the streets of London," Bower exclaimed. "No planning, no logical reasoning behind it, just a bunch of cow paths that eventually got cemented over and that people have had to follow ever since."

The procedures that incurred Bower's wrath centered around the issue of documentation. But Bower was not the only one complaining about Manufacturing's requirements. Steve Kendericks, one of the Vice Presidents of Engineering, commented on the incongruity of the manufacturing procedures. "As it now stands," he explained, "the manufacturing people are supposed to build the first prototype as if they were going to build 1000 of the things. That requires extensive documentation—instructions so detailed that anyone off the street could walk in and put the thing together. The process is excruciatingly slow and cumbersome in the development phase, when designs are being changed constantly and documentation takes more time than the actual development work. By the time you actually get the thing built, you're ready to build a bunch of them but there's a very narrow market window."

For Bower and his team of engineers, however, the problem was not one of market windows but of delivery deadlines. "We kept track once," he related, "and found that it took between 80 and 120 man hours of documentation per design change—and we're talking thousands of changes. That's an awful lot of time and money." They tried to negotiate around the requirements, arguing that it made no sense to spend all those resources documenting changes—especially on a one-time contract with a tight deadline.

At first, it appeared that the engineers' negotiations might pay off. "We'd get together in meetings," explained Hank Ross, one of the engineering supervisors over the entire Houtin-Smith project, "and agree on some compromises. But then we'd leave the meeting, and everything would go back to normal. The manufacturing people would go back to their rules, and the engineering people would go back to changing their drawings every three hours. It was a cesspool of non-communication—an absolute morass."

The engineers were successful in changing some procedures, but not without significant effort. "Any time we altered the design at all," recalled Bower, "the people in Engineering Services had to produce a whole new set of drawings. Manufacturing would not work from red lined corrections on the existing prints. It was taking forever, so one day I went over there to see what was going on. I couldn't believe what I saw: those idiots were inking the drawings—*inking* them! It's incredible that in a company that prides itself on doing state-of-the-art CAD development these draftsmen were still inking drawings by hand. I asked them why on earth they were doing it, and they said something about specifications requiring that final drawings maintain their line quality for 40 years—40 years! At this point, I lost my cool. 'Holy crap' I yelled, 'the part will be obsolete in five years!' They insisted that the rule was 40 years

and that the drawings therefore had to be inked.

"That was the last straw. I stormed into their boss's office and asked, 'Why are they inking drawings out there?' He said, 'They're not inking drawings.' I said, 'Like hell they're not.' He said, 'No one inks drawings anymore. I told them not to.' So I went out and grabbed a drawing, brought it in, and laid it on his desk. He just about went through the ceiling. After that, they stopped inking drawings."

Shortly after this incident, the development team held the fateful design review in which Bob Reynolds, the COO, labeled the project a "flaming disaster." "That really hurt," recalled Bower, "but I tried to shield the team from it. It wasn't easy. We all felt that if the project was a failure, Bob would be out with the rest of us. On top of that, every two weeks or so we had the Houtin-Smith people calling us, telling us that we had to have the system delivered on time because the mayor of Seattle was going to attend the grand opening and they didn't want to be embarrassed.

"We really had our backs to the wall—and on top of everything else, the manufacturing people were insisting that we jump through all these ridiculous hoops. I'd initially thought that they were working together with us on the project, but I was hopelessly naive. They were actually self-appointed company watchdogs, in charge of making sure that the engineers didn't sneak any inferior products out under their noses. Some of the guys in my group were literally ready to kill the people over in manufacturing."

Part B

Not long after the "flaming disaster" episode, Bower realized that following the formal product development procedures would practically guarantee the late delivery of the system. As a last resort, he approached John Meyors, an old friend and manager of Engineering Services. "I asked him why it was so difficult to get things through," recalled Bower. "He explained that they *had* to be strict. They were aware of Houtin-Smith's quality standards; they couldn't afford any mistakes. One malfunction or missing spec, and they knew they'd be dead meat. So I asked him if he'd feel good about having a group of our engineers sign a statement saying something like, 'To the best of our knowledge, this equipment is free from flaws and will perform properly.' He said, 'OK.' It took him off the hook. From then on, things went a lot smoother. If it weren't for my friendship with John, we might never have delivered that system. He really stuck his neck out for me.

"In the early days of the company, Engineering controlled everything. Now we've become a manufacturing company. Engineering, by definition, means 'make it better'; Manufacturing means 'leave it alone.' When you bring the two together, you've got a real rip tide, a fissure between two continental plates. I hope I'm never caught in the middle like that again. Engineers should be left to solve the major technical problems, and should be given the latitude to do whatever they need to do to solve them."

People Work for Different Reasons

"Basically people like to work. However, from time to time they need some incentive ...

"... so today we're firing Murphy, Gross, and Finstrap!"

2

Some Perspectives on Individual Behavior in Organizations

People spend a good part of their lives trying to understand individual behavior. Sometimes we think we're experts. ("Haven't I been dealing with people ever since I was born?") At other times, when people seem so hard to understand, we think that we know nothing about the subject. ("You have to be a psychologist to manage people.") But whether we consider ourselves expert or incompetent, most of us agree that possession of such a skill is important.

This section focuses on individual behavior within organizations. Because work organizations occupy a major part of most people's lives, the quality of the relationship between the individual and the organization is critical. When the relationship is positive, both the individual and the organization seem to benefit. When it is negative, both parties would like to terminate it. Of course, it is expected that individuals are likely to have both positive and negative experiences in their relationship with an organization.

People beginning their work life soon find that their goals do not perfectly match the goals of others in the organization, notably its supervisors or top management. And when beginners discover this discrepancy, they can adopt any of a number of approaches.

1. They can respond by trying to identify and adopt their superiors' goals. These subordinates work hard to live up to the expectations of their superiors. They are eager to get ahead and believe that this approach will help them most.
2. They can try to change the goals of their superiors. For example, they might set out to make the organization more human, to make

it more conscious of pollution, or to make it less exploitative of customers. Such an approach seems to be occurring more frequently in recent years.

3. They can try to avoid "selling out" to the organization. These individuals, thinking it impossible to reconcile their goals with those of management, invest as little of themselves as possible in the organization and seek fulfillment outside the job. They say, "The only thing I want from the organization is a paycheck," and in return they ask only that people in the organization not try to influence or change them. But in practice, it is virtually impossible to avoid being influenced by the organization. That relationship is too much a part of their lives.

We have mentioned just a few possible responses to organizations; but, whatever the response, individuals are influenced by organizations and need to understand more about the influence.

Motivation is a theme pervading all attempts to influence people in organizations. Managers are always searching for new and more effective means of motivation. Thousands of articles and numerous conferences and workshops claim to answer the question, "How do I motivate people?" and those aspiring to become managers will no doubt have an interest in motivation. It is taken for granted that knowledge of some current theories of motivation and how to apply them is valuable to administrators. But it may also be worthwhile for subordinates to learn something about the topic. If they have some knowledge of motivation theory, they may be able to identify what the organization is doing to try to motivate them.

This section of the book presents several different theories of motivation. Some people are confused by all these theories. They want to know which one is the "truth" so that they can use it. Unfortunately for these people a theory is not an all-encompassing explanation of developments in a complex world. Rather, it is just one way of looking at and trying to understand a phenomenon. We suggest that the test of a theory is its usefulness, which depends upon the situation. This section presents several theories so that the student might be exposed to a variety of approaches to motivation and be in a position to choose the best one at the right time.

Another theme in the relationship between individuals and organizations is career development. Rewards that might motivate a 22–year–old employee may be of little interest to a 52–year–old. One way to think about career development is to think about starting in an entry-level job in an organization and working hard to rise to the top. However, the dream of working up from messenger boy to president, fairly common in the first half of the twentieth century, is no longer a very realistic one for most people in our society, because organizations have grown so large and complex. As a result, we need some better ways to think about career development, ways to think about ourselves, our interests, and how those interests might change over time. We also need ways to understand the people with whom we work, including superiors, peers, and subordinates.

We have selected a number of ideas and theories designed to improve the understanding of individual behavior in organizations. It is safe to say that individual behavior is difficult to understand. However, with the help of some concepts and theories and some practice in applying these ideas, we are optimistic that students will have a better understanding of individual behavior within organizations.

READINGS

On the Folly of Rewarding A, While Hoping for B

STEVEN KERR

Whether dealing with monkeys, rats, or human beings, it is hardly controversial to state that most organisms seek information concerning what activities are rewarded, and then seek to do (or at least pretend to do) those things, often to the virtual exclusion of activities not rewarded. The extent to which this occurs of course will depend on the perceived attractiveness of the rewards offered, but neither operant nor expectancy theorists would quarrel with the essence of this notion.

Nevertheless, numerous examples exist of reward systems that are fouled up in that behaviors which are rewarded are those which the rewarder is trying to *discourage*, while the behavior he desires is not being rewarded at all.

In an effort to understand and explain this phenomenon, this paper presents examples from society, from organizations in general, and from profit making firms in particular. Data from a manufacturing company and information from an insurance firm are examined to demonstrate the consequences of such reward systems for the organizations involved, and possible reasons why such reward systems continue to exist are considered.

Reprinted with the permission of the publisher and author from the *Academy of Management Journal*, Volume 18, No. 4 (1975), pp. 769–783.

SOCIETAL EXAMPLES

Politics

Official goals are "purposely vague and general and do not indicate ... the host of decisions that must be made among alternative ways of achieving official goals and the priority of multiple goals ..." (Perrow 1969, 66). They usually may be relied on to offend absolutely no one, and in this sense can be considered high-acceptance, low-quality goals. An example might be "build better schools." Operative goals are higher in quality but lower in acceptance, since they specify where the money will come from, what alternative goals will be ignored, etc.

The American citizenry supposedly wants its candidates for public office to set forth operative goals, making their proposed programs "perfectly clear," specifying sources and uses of funds, etc. However, since operative goals are lower in acceptance, and since aspirants to public office need acceptance (from at least 50.1 percent of the people), most politicians prefer to speak only of official goals, at least until after the election. They of course would agree to speak at the operative level if "punished" for not doing so. The electorate could do this by refusing to support candidates who do not speak at the operative level.

Instead, however, the American voter typically punishes (withholds support from) candidates who frankly discuss where the money will come from, rewards politicians who speak only of official goals, but hopes that candidates (despite the reward system) will discuss the issues operatively. It is academic whether it was moral for Nixon, for example, to refuse to discuss his 1968 "secret plan" to end the Vietnam war, his 1972 operative goals concerning the lifting of price controls, the reshuffling of his cabinet, etc. The point is that the reward system made such refusal rational.

It seems worth mentioning that no manuscript can adequately define what is "moral" and what is not. However, examination of costs and benefits, combined with knowledge of what motivates a particular individual often will suffice to determine what for him is "rational" (Simon 1957, 76–77).* If the reward system is so designed that it is irrational to be moral, this does not necessarily mean that immorality will result. But is this not asking for trouble?

War

If some oversimplification may be permitted, let it be assumed that the primary goal of the organization (Pentagon, Luftwaffe, or whatever) is to win. Let it be assumed further that the primary goal of most individuals on the front lines is to get home alive. Then there appears to be an important conflict in goals—personally rational behavior by those at the bottom will endanger goal attainment by those at the top.

But not necessarily! It depends on how the reward system is set up. The Vietnam war was indeed a study of disobedience and rebellion, with terms such as "frag-

* In Simon's terms, a decision is "subjectively rational" if it maximizes an individual's valued outcomes so far as his knowledge permits. A decision is "personally rational" if it is oriented toward the individual's goals.

ging" (killing one's own commanding officer) and "search and evade" becoming part of the military vocabulary. The difference in subordinates' acceptance of authority between World War II and Vietnam is reported to be considerable, and veterans of the Second World War often have been quoted as being outraged at the mutinous actions of many American soldiers in Vietnam.

Consider, however, some critical differences in the reward system in use during the two conflicts. What did the GI in World War II want? To go home. And when did he get to go home? When the war was won! If he disobeyed the orders to clean out the trenches and take the hills, the war would not be won and he would not go home. Furthermore, what were his chances of attaining his goal (getting home alive) if he obeyed the orders compared to his chances if he did not? What is being suggested is that the rational soldier in World War II, *whether patriotic or not*, probably found it expedient to obey.

Consider the reward system in use in Vietnam. What did the man at the bottom want? To go home. And when did he get to go home? When his tour of duty was over! This was the case *whether or not* the war was won. Furthermore, concerning the relative chance of getting home alive by obeying orders compared to the chance if they were disobeyed, it is worth noting that a mutineer in Vietnam was far more likely to be assigned rest and rehabilitation (on the assumption that fatigue was the cause) than he was to suffer any negative consequence.

In his description of the "zone of indifference," Barnard stated that "a person can and will accept a communication as authoritative only when ... at the time of his decision, he believes it to be compatible with his personal interests as a whole" (Barnard 1964, 165). In light of the reward system used in Vietnam, would it not have been personally irrational for some orders to have been obeyed? Was not the military implementing a system which *rewarded* disobedience, while *hoping* that soldiers (despite the reward system) would obey orders?

Medicine

Theoretically, a physician can make either of two types of error, and intuitively one seems as bad as the other. A doctor can pronounce a patient sick when he is actually well, thus causing him needless anxiety and expense, curtailment of enjoyable foods and activities, and even physical danger by subjecting him to needless medication and surgery. Alternately, a doctor can label a sick person well, and thus avoid treating what may be a serious, even fatal ailment. It might be natural to conclude that physicians seek to minimize both types of error.

Such a conclusion would be wrong (Garland 1959).† It is estimated that numerous Americans are presently afflicted with iatrogenic (physician-caused) illnesses (Scheff 1965). This occurs when the doctor is approached by someone complaining of a few stray symptoms. The doctor classifies and organizes these symptoms, gives them a name, and obligingly tells the patient what further symptoms may be expected. This information often acts as a self-fulfilling prophecy, with the result that from that day on the patient for all practical purposes is sick.

Why does this happen? Why are physicians so reluctant to sustain a type 2 error (pronouncing a sick person well) that they will tolerate many type 1 errors? Again, a look at the reward system is needed. The punishments for a type 2 error are real: guilt, embarrassment, and the threat of lawsuit and scandal. On the other hand, a type 1 error (labeling a well

person sick) "is sometimes seen as sound clinical practice, indicating a healthy conservative approach to medicine" (Scheff 1965, 69). Type 1 errors also are likely to generate increased income and a stream of steady customers who, being well in a limited physiological sense, will not embarrass the doctor by dying abruptly.

Fellow physicians and the general public therefore are really *rewarding* type 1 errors and at the same time *hoping* fervently that doctors will try not to make them.

GENERAL ORGANIZATIONAL EXAMPLES

Rehabilitation Centers and Orphanages

In terms of the prime beneficiary classification (Blau and Scott, 1962, 42) organizations such as these are supposed to exist for the "public-in-contact," that is, clients. The orphanage therefore theoretically is interested in placing as many children as possible in good homes. However, often orphanages surround themselves with so many rules concerning adoption that it is nearly impossible to pry a child out of the place. Orphanages may deny adoption unless the applicants are a married couple, both of the same religion as the child, without history of emotional or vocational instability, with a specified minimum income and a private room for the child, etc.

If the primary goal is to place children in good homes, then the rules ought to constitute means toward that goal. Goal displacement results when these "means become ends in themselves that displace the original goals" (Blau and Scott 1962, 229).

To some extent these rules are required by law. But the influence of the reward system on the orphanage's management should not be ignored. Consider, for example, that the:

† In one study (Garland 1959, 25–38) of 14,867 films for signs of tuberculosis, 1,216 positive readings turned out to be clinically negative; only 24 negative readings proved clinically active, a ratio of 50 to 1.

1. Number of children enrolled often is the most important determinant of the size of the allocated budget.
2. Number of children under the director's care also will affect the size of his staff.
3. Total organizational size will determine largely the director's prestige at the annual conventions, in the community, etc.

Therefore, to the extent that staff size, total budget, and personal prestige are valued by the orphanage's executive personnel, it becomes rational for them to make it difficult for children to be adopted. After all, who wants to be the director of the smallest orphanage in the state?

If the reward system errs in the opposite direction, paying off only for placements, extensive goal displacement again is likely to result. A common example of vocational rehabilitation in many states, for example, consists of placing someone in a job for which he has little interest and few qualifications, for two months or so, and then "rehabilitating" him again in another position. Such behavior is quite consistent with the prevailing reward system, which pays off for the number of individuals placed in any position for 60 days or more. Rehabilitation counselors also confess to competing with one another to place relatively skilled clients, sometimes ignoring persons with few skills who would be harder to place. Extensively disabled clients find that counselors often prefer to work with those whose disabilities are less severe.*

Universities

Society *hopes* that teachers will not neglect their teaching responsibilities but *rewards* them almost entirely for research and publications. This is most true at the large and prestigious universities. Clichés

* Personal interviews conducted during 1972–1973.

such as "good research and good teaching go together" notwithstanding, professors often find that they must choose between teaching and research-oriented activities when allocating their time. Rewards for good teaching usually are limited to outstanding teacher awards, which are given to only a small percentage of good teachers and which usually bestow little money and fleeting prestige. Punishments for poor teaching also are rare.

Rewards for research and publications, on the other hand, and punishments for failure to accomplish these, are commonly administered by universities at which teachers are employed. Furthermore, publication-oriented resumés usually will be well received at other universities, whereas teaching credentials, harder to document and quantify, are much less transferable. Consequently it is rational for university teachers to concentrate on research, even if to the detriment of teaching and at the expense of their students.

By the same token, it is rational for students to act based upon the goal displacement which has occurred within universities concerning what they are rewarded for. If it is assumed that a primary goal of a university is to transfer knowledge from teacher to student, then grades become identifiable as a means toward that goal, serving as motivational, control, and feedback devices to expedite the knowledge transfer. Instead, however, the grades themselves have become much more important for entrance to graduate school, successful employment, tuition refunds, parental respect, etc., than the knowledge or lack of knowledge they are supposed to signify.

It therefore should come as no surprise that information has surfaced in recent years concerning fraternity files for examinations, term paper writing services, organized cheating at the service academies, and the like. Such activities constitute a personally rational response to a reward system which pays off for grades rather than knowledge.

BUSINESS RELATED EXAMPLES

Ecology

Assume that the president of XYZ Corporation is confronted with the following alternatives:

1. Spend $11 million for antipollution equipment to keep from poisoning fish in the river adjacent to the plant; or
2. Do nothing, in violation of the law, and assume a one in ten chance of being caught, with a resultant $1 million fine plus the necessity of buying the equipment.

Under this not unrealistic set of choices it requires no linear program to determine that XYZ Corporation can maximize its probabilities by flouting the law. Add the fact that XYZ's president is probably being rewarded (by creditors, stockholders, and other salient parts of his task environment) according to criteria totally unrelated to the number of fish poisoned, and his probable course of action becomes clear.

Evaluation of Training

It is axiomatic that those who care about a firm's well-being should insist that the organization get fair value for its expenditures. Yet it is commonly known that firms seldom bother to evaluate a new GRID, MBO, job enrichment program, or whatever, to see if the company is getting its money's worth. Why? Certainly it is not because people have not pointed out that this situation exists; numerous practitioner-oriented articles are written each year to just this point.

The individuals (whether in personnel, manpower planning, or wherever) who normally would be responsible for con-

ducting such evaluations are the same ones often charged with introducing the change effort in the first place. Having convinced top management to spend the money, they usually are quite animated afterwards in collecting rigorous vignettes and anecdotes about how successful the program was. The last thing many desire is a formal, systematic, and revealing evaluation. Although members of top management may actually *hope* for such systematic evaluation, their reward systems continue to *reward* ignorance in this area. And if the personnel department abdicates its responsibility, who is to step into the breach? The change agent himself? Hardly! He is likely to be too busy collecting anecdotal "evidence" of his own, for use with his next client.

Miscellaneous

Many additional examples could be cited of systems which in fact are rewarding behaviors other than those supposedly desired by the rewarder. A few of these are described briefly below.

Most coaches disdain to discuss individual accomplishments, preferring to speak of teamwork, proper attitude, and a one-for-all spirit. Usually, however, rewards are distributed according to individual performance. The college basketball player who feeds his teammates instead of shooting will not compile impressive scoring statistics and is less likely to be drafted by the pros. The ballplayer who hits to right field to advance the runners will win neither the batting nor home run titles, and will be offered smaller raises. It therefore is rational for players to think of themselves first, and the team second.

In business organizations where rewards are dispensed for unit performance or for individual goals achieved, without regard for overall effectiveness, similar attitudes often are observed. Under most Management by Objectives (MBO) systems, goals in areas where quantification is difficult often go unspecified. The organization therefore often is in a position where it *hopes* for employee effort in the areas of team building, interpersonal relations, creativitiy, etc., but it formally *rewards* none of these. In cases where promotions and raises are formally tied to MBO, the system itself contains a paradox in that it "asks employees to set challenging, risky goals, only to face smaller paychecks and possibly damaged careers if these goals are not accomplished" (Kerr 1973a, 40).

It is *hoped* that administrators will pay attention to long run costs and opportunities and will institute programs which will bear fruit later on. However, many organizational reward systems pay off for short run sales and earnings only. Under such circumstances it is personally rational for officials to sacrifice long-term growth and profit (by selling off equipment and property, or by stifling research and development) for short-term advantages. This probably is most pertinent in the public sector, with the result that many public officials are unwilling to implement programs which will not show benefits by election time.

As a final, clear-cut example of a fouled-up reward system, consider the cost-plus contract or its next of kin, the allocation of next year's budget as a direct function of this year's expenditures. It probably is conceivable that those who award such budgets and contracts really hope for economy and prudence in spending. It is obvious, however, that adopting the proverb "to him who spends shall more be given," rewards not economy, but spending itself.

TWO COMPANIES' EXPERIENCES

A Manufacturing Organization

A midwest manufacturer of industrial goods had been troubled for some time by aspects of its organizational climate it believed dysfunctional. For research purposes, interviews were conducted with many employees and a questionnaire was administered on a company-wide basis, including plants and offices in several American and Canadian locations. The company strongly encouraged employee participation in the survey, and made available time and space during the workday for completion of the instrument. All employees in attendance during the day of the survey completed the questionnaire. All instruments were collected directly by the researcher, who personally administered each session. Since no one employed by the firm handled the questionnaires, and since respondent names were not asked for, it seems likely that the pledge of anonymity given was believed.

A modified version of the Expect Approval scale (Litwin and Stringer 1968) was included as part of the questionnaire. The instrument asked respondents to indicate the degree of approval or disapproval they could expect if they performed each of the described actions. A seven-point Likert scale was used, with one indicating that the action would probably bring strong disapproval and seven signifying likely strong approval.

Although normative data for this scale from studies of other organizations are unavailable, it is possible to examine fruitfully the data obtained from this survey in several ways. First, it may be worth noting that the questionnaire data corresponded closely to information gathered through interviews. Furthermore, as can be seen from the results summarized in Table 1, sizable differences between various work units, and between employees at different job levels within the same work unit, were obtained. This suggests that response bias effects (social desirability in particular loomed as a potential concern) are not likely to be severe.

Most importantly, comparisons be-

SOME PERSPECTIVES ON INDIVIDUAL BEHAVIOR

TABLE 1 Summary of Two Divisions Data Relevant to Conforming and Risk-Avoidance Behaviors (Extent to Which Subjects Expect Approval)

Dimension	Item	Division and sample	Total responses	Percentage of workers responding		
				1, 2, or 3 Disapproval	4	5, 6, or 7 Approval
Risk avoidance	Making a risky decision based on the best information available at the time, but which turns out wrong.	A, levels 1–4 (lowest)	127	61	25	14
		A, levels 5–8	172	46	31	23
		A, levels 9 and above	17	41	30	30
		B, levels 1–4 (lowest)	31	58	26	16
		B, levels 5–8	19	42	42	16
		B, levels 9 and above	10	50	20	30
	Setting extremely high and challenging standards and goals, and then narrowly failing to make them.	A, levels 1–4	122	47	28	25
		A, levels 5–8	168	33	26	41
		A, levels 9+	17	24	6	70
		B, levels 1–4	31	48	23	29
		B, levels 5–8	18	17	33	50
		B, levels 9+	10	30	0	70
	Setting goals which are extremely easy to make and then making them.	A, levels 1–4	124	35	30	35
		A, levels 5–8	171	47	27	26
		A, levels 9+	17	70	24	6
		B, levels 1–4	31	58	26	16
		B, levels 5–8	19	63	16	21
		B, levels 9+	10	80	0	20
Conformity	Being a "yes man" and always agreeing with the boss.	A, levels 1–4	126	46	17	37
		A, levels 5–8	180	54	14	31
		A, levels 9+	17	88	12	0
		B, levels 1–4	32	53	28	19
		B, levels 5–8	19	68	21	11
		B, levels 9+	10	80	10	10
	Always going along with the majority.	A, levels 1–4	125	40	25	35
		A, levels 5–8	173	47	21	32
		A, levels 9+	17	70	12	18
		B, levels 1–4	31	61	23	16
		B, levels 5–8	19	68	11	21
		B, levels 9+	10	80	10	10
	Being careful to stay on the good side of everyone, so that everyone agrees that you are a great guy.	A, levels 1–4	124	45	18	37
		A, levels 5–8	173	45	22	33
		A, levels 9+	17	64	6	30
		B, levels 1–4	31	54	23	23
		B, levels 5–8	19	73	11	16
		B, levels 9+	10	80	10	10

tween scores obtained on the Expect Approval scale and a statement of problems which were the reason for the survey revealed that the same behaviors which managers in each division thought dysfunctional were those which lower-level employees claimed were rewarded. As compared to job levels 1 to 8 in Division B (see Table 1), those in Division A claimed a much higher acceptance by management of "conforming" activities. Between 31 and 37 percent of Division A employees at levels 1–8 stated that going along with the majority, agreeing with the boss, and staying on everyone's good side brought approval; only once (level 5–8 responses to one of the three items) did a majority suggest that such actions would generate disapproval.

Furthermore, responses from Division A workers at levels 1–4 indicate that behaviors geared toward risk avoidance were as likely to be rewarded as to be punished. Only at job levels 9 and above was it apparent that the reward system was positively reinforcing behaviors desired by top management. Overall, the same "tendencies toward conservatism and apple-polishing at the lower levels" which divisional management had complained about during the interviews were those claimed by subordinates to be the most rational course of action in light of the existing reward system. Management apparently was not getting the behaviors it was *hoping* for, but it certainly was getting the behaviors it was perceived by subordinates to be *rewarding*.

An Insurance Firm

The Group Health Claims Division of a large eastern insurance company provides another rich illustration of a reward system which reinforces behaviors not desired by top management.

Attempting to measure and reward accuracy in paying surgical claims, the firm systematically keeps track of the number of returned checks and letters of complaint received from policyholders. However, underpayments are likely to provoke cries of outrage from the insured, while overpayments often are accepted in courteous silence. Since it often is impossible to tell from the physician's statement which of two surgical procedures, with different allowable benefits, was performed, and since writing for clarifications will interfere with other standards used by the firm concerning "percentage of claims paid within two days of receipt," the new hire in more than one claims section is soon acquainted with the informal norm: "When in doubt, pay it out!"

The situation would be even worse were it not for the fact that other features of the firm's-reward system tend to neutralize those described. For example, annual "merit" increases are given to all employees, in one of the following three amounts:

1. If the worker is "outstanding" (a select category, into which no more than two employees per section may be placed): 5 percent.
2. If the worker is "above average" (normally all workers not "outstanding" are so rated): 4 percent.
3. If the worker commits gross acts of negligence and irresponsibility for which he might be discharged in many other companies: 3 percent.

Now, since (a) the difference between the 5 percent theoretically attainable through hard work and the 4 percent attainable merely by living until the review date is small and (b) since insurance firms seldom dispense much of a salary increase in cash (rather, the worker's insurance benefits increase, causing him to be further overinsured), many employees are rather indifferent to the possibility of obtaining the extra one percent reward and therefore tend to ignore the norm concerning indiscriminant payments.

However, most employees are not indifferent to the rule which states that, should absences or lateness total three or more in any six-month period, the entire 4 or 5 percent due at the next "merit" review must be forfeited. In this sense the firm may be described as *hoping* for performance, while *rewarding* attendance. What it gets, of course, is attendance. (If the absence-lateness rule appears to the reader to be stringent, it really is not. The company counts "times" rather than "days" absent, and a ten-day absence therefore counts the same as one lasting two days. A worker in danger of accumulating a third absence within six months merely has to remain ill (away from work) during his second absence until his first absence is more than six months old. The limiting factor is that at some point his salary ceases, and his sickness benefits take over. This usually is sufficient to get the younger workers to return, but for those with 20 or more years' service, the company provides sickness benefits of 90 percent of normal salary, tax-free! Therefore . . .)

CAUSES

Extremely diverse instances of systems which reward behavior A although the rewarder apparently hopes for behavior B have been given. These are useful to illustrate the breadth and magnitude of the phenomenon, but the diversity increases the difficulty of determining commonalities and establishing causes. However, four general factors may be pertinent to an explanation of why fouled-up reward systems seem to be so prevalent.

Fascination With An "Objective" Criterion

It has been mentioned elsewhere that:

> Most "objective" measures of productivity are objective only in that their subjective elements are a) determined in advance, rather than coming into play at the time of the formal evaluation, and b) well concealed on the rating instrument itself. Thus industrial firms seeking to devise objective rating systems first decide, in an arbitrary manner,

what dimensions are to be rated, . . . usually including some items having little to do with organizational effectiveness while excluding others that do. Only then does Personnel Division churn out official-looking documents on which all dimensions chosen to be rated are assigned point values, categories, or whatever (Kerr 1973b, 92).

Nonetheless, many individuals seek to establish simple, quantifiable standards against which to measure and reward performance. Such efforts may be successful in highly predictable areas within an organization, but are likely to cause goal displacement when applied anywhere else. Overconcern with attendance and lateness in the insurance firm and with number of people placed in the vocational rehabilitation division may have been largely responsible for the problems described in those organizations.

Overemphasis on Highly Visible Behaviors

Difficulties often stem from the fact that some parts of the task are highly visible while other parts are not. For example, publications are easier to demonstrate than teaching, and scoring baskets and hitting home runs are more readily observable than feeding teammates and advancing base runners. Similarly, the adverse consequences of pronouncing a sick person well are more visible than those sustained by labeling a well person sick. Team building and creativity are other examples of behaviors which may not be rewarded simply because they are hard to observe.

Hypocrisy

In some of the instances described the rewarder may have been getting the desired behavior, notwithstanding claims that the behavior was not desired. This may be true, for example, of management's attitude toward apple-polishing in the manufacturing firm (a behavior which subordinates felt was rewarded, despite management's avowed dislike of the practice). This also may explain politicians' unwillingness to revise the penalties for disobedience of ecology laws, and the failure of top management to devise reward systems which would cause systematic evaluation of training and development programs.

Emphasis on Morality or Equity Rather Than Efficiency

Sometimes consideration of other factors prevents the establishment of a system which rewards behaviors desired by the rewarder. The felt obligation of many Americans to vote for one candidate or another, for example, may impair their ability to withhold support from politicians who refuse to discuss the issues. Similarly, the concern for spreading the risks and costs of wartime military service may outweigh the advantage to be obtained by committing personnel to combat until the war is over.

It should be noted that only with respect to the first two causes are reward systems really paying off for other than desired behaviors. In the case of the third and fourth causes the system *is* rewarding behaviors desired by the rewarder, and the systems are fouled up only from the standpoints of those who believe the rewarder's public statements (cause 3), or those who seek to maximize efficiency rather than other outcomes (cause 4).

CONCLUSIONS

Modern organization theory requires a recognition that the members of organizations and society possess divergent goals and motives. It therefore is unlikely that managers and their subordinates will seek the same outcomes. Three possible remedies for this potential problem are suggested.

Selection

It is theoretically possible for organizations to employ only those individuals whose goals and motives are wholly consonant with those of management. In such cases the same behaviors judged by subordinates to be rational would be perceived by management as desirable. State-of-the-art reviews of selection techniques, however, provide scant grounds for hope that such an approach would be successful (for example, see Webster 1964).

Training

Another theoretical alternative is for the organization to admit those employees whose goals are not consonant with those of management and then, through training, socialization, or whatever, alter employee goals to make them consonant. However, research on the effectiveness of such training programs, though limited, provides further grounds for pessimism (for example, see Fieldler 1972).

Altering the Reward System

What would have been the result if:

1. Nixon had been assured by his advisors that he could not win reelection except by discussing the issues in detail?
2. Physicians' conduct was subjected to regular examination by review boards for type 1 errors (calling healthy people ill) and to penalties (fines, censure, etc.) for errors of either type?
3. The President of XYZ Corporation had to choose between (a) spending $11 million dollars for antipollution equipment, and (b) incurring a fifty-fifty chance of going to jail for five years?

Managers who complain that their workers are not motivated might do well to consider the possibility that they have installed reward systems which are paying off for behaviors other than those they are seeking. This, in part, is what happened in Vietnam, and this is what regularly frustrates societal efforts to bring about honest politicians, civic-minded managers, etc. This certainly is what happened in both the manufacturing and the insurance companies.

A first step for such managers might be to find out what behaviors currently are being rewarded. Perhaps an instrument similar to that used in the manufacturing firm could be useful for this purpose. Chances are excellent that these managers will be surprised by what they find—that their firms are not rewarding what they assume they are. In fact, such undesirable behavior by organizational members as they have observed may be explained largely by the reward systems in use.

This is not to say that all organizational behavior is determined by formal rewards and punishments. Certainly it is true that in the absence of formal reinforcement some soldiers will be patriotic, some president will be ecology minded, and some orphanage directors will care about children. The point, however, is that in such cases the rewarder is not *causing* the behaviors desired but is only a fortunate bystander. For an organization to *act* upon its members, the formal reward system should positively reinforce desired behaviors, not constitute an obstacle to be overcome.

It might be wise to underscore the obvious fact that there is nothing really new in what has been said. In both theory and practice these matters have been mentioned before. Thus in many states Good Samaritan laws have been installed to protect doctors who stop to assist a stricken motorist. In states without such laws it is commonplace for doctors to refuse to stop, for fear of involvement in a subsequent lawsuit. In college basketball additional penalties have been instituted against players who foul their opponents deliberately. It has long been argued by Milton Friedman and others that penalties should be altered so as to make it irrational to disobey the ecology laws, and so on.

By altering the reward system the organization escapes the necessity of selecting only desirable people or of trying to alter undesirable ones. In Skinnerian terms (as described in Swanson 1972, 704), "As for responsibility and goodness—as commonly defined—no one ... would want or need them. They refer to a man's behaving well despite the absence of positive reinforcement that is obviously sufficient to explain it. Where such reinforcement exists, 'no one needs goodness.' "

That Urge to Achieve

DAVID C. McCLELLAND

Most people in this world, psychologically, can be divided into two broad groups. There is that minority which is challenged by opportunity and willing to work hard

Reprinted by permission from *Think* magazine, published by IBM copyright 1966 by International Business Machines Corporation.

to achieve something, and the majority which really does not care all that much.

For nearly twenty years now, psychologists have tried to penetrate the mystery of this curious dichotomy. Is the need to achieve (or the absence of it) an accident, is it hereditary, or is it the result of environment? Is it a single, isolatable human motive, or a combination of motives—the desire to accumulate wealth, power, fame? Most important of all, is there some technique that could give this will to achieve to people, even whole societies, who do not now have it?

While we do not yet have complete answers for any of these questions, years of work have given us partial answers to most of them and insights into all of them. There is a distinct human motive, distinguishable from others. It can be found, in fact tested for, in any group.

Let me give you one example. Several years ago, a careful study was made of 450 workers who had been thrown out of work by a plant shutdown in Erie, Pennsylvania. Most of the unemployed workers stayed home for a while and then checked back with the United States Employment Service to see if their old jobs or similar ones were available. But a small minority among them behaved differently: the day they were laid off, they started job-hunting.

They checked both the United States and the Pennsylvania Employment Office; they studied the "Help Wanted" sections of the papers; they checked through their union, their church, and various fraternal organizations; they looked into training courses to learn a new skill; they even left town to look for work, while the majority when questioned said they would not under any circumstances move away from Erie to obtain a job. Obviously the members of that active minority were differently motivated. All the men were more or less in the same situation objectively: they needed work, money, food, shelter, job security. Yet only a minority showed initiative and enterprise in finding what they needed. Why? Psychologists, after years of research, now believe they can answer that question. They have demonstrated that these men possessed in greater degree a specific type of human motivation. For the moment let us refer to this personality characteristic as "Motive

A" and review some of the other characteristics of the men who have more of the motive than other men.

Suppose they are confronted by a work situation in which they can set their own goals as to how difficult a task they will undertake. In the psychological laboratory, such a situation is very simply created by asking them to throw rings over a peg from any distance they may choose. Most men throw more or less randomly, standing now close, now far away, but those with Motive A seem to calculate carefully where they are most likely to get a sense of mastery. They stand nearly always at moderate distances, not so close as to make the task ridiculously easy, nor so far away as to make it impossible. They set moderately difficult, but potentially achievable goals for themselves, where they objectively have only about a one-in-three chance of succeeding. In other words, they are always setting challenges for themselves, tasks to make them stretch themselves a little.

But they behave like this only if *they* can influence the outcome by performing the work themselves. They prefer not to gamble at all. Say they are given a choice between rolling dice with one in three chances of winning and working on a problem with a one-in-three chance of solving in the time allotted, they choose to work on the problem even though rolling the dice is obviously less work and the odds of winning are the same. They prefer to work at a problem rather than leave the outcome to chance or to others.

Obviously they are concerned with personal achievement rather than with the rewards of success *per se*, since they stand just as much chance of getting those rewards by throwing the dice. This leads to another characteristic the Motive A men show—namely, a strong preference for work situations in which they get concrete feedback on how well they are doing, as one does, say in playing golf, or in being a salesman, but as one does not in teaching, or in personnel counseling. A golfer always knows his score and can compare how well he is doing with par or with his own performance yesterday or last week. A teacher has no such concrete feedback on how well he is doing in "getting across" to his students.

THE *n* ACH MEN

But why do certain men behave like this? At one level the reply is simple: because they habitually spend their time thinking about doing things better. In fact, psychologists typically measure the strength of Motive A by taking samples of a man's spontaneous thoughts (such as making up a story about a picture they have been shown) and counting the frequency with which he mentions doing things better. The count is objective and can even be made these days with the help of a computer program for content analysis. It yields what is referred to technically as an individual's *n* Ach score (for "need for Achievement"). It is not difficult to understand why people who think constantly about "doing better" are more apt to do better at job-hunting, to set moderate, achievable goals for themselves, to dislike gambling (because they get no achievement satisfaction from success), and to prefer work situations where they can tell easily whether they are improving or not. But why some people and not others come to think this way is another question. The evidence suggests it is not because they are born that way, but because of special training they get in the home from parents who set moderately high achievement goals but who are warm, encouraging, and nonauthoritarian in helping their children reach these goals.

Such detailed knowledge about one motive helps correct a lot of common sense ideas about human motivation. For example, much public policy (and much business policy) is based on the simple minded notion that people will work harder "if they have to." As a first approxi-

mation, the idea isn't totally wrong, but it is only a half-truth. The majority of unemployed workers in Erie "had to" find work as much as those with higher *n* Ach but they certainly didn't work as hard at it. Or again, it is frequently assumed that *any* strong motive will lead to doing things better. Wouldn't it be fair to say that most of the Erie workers were just "unmotivated"? But our detailed knowledge of various human motives shows that each one leads a person to behave in *different* ways. The contrast is not between being "motivated" or "unmotivated" but between being motivated toward A or toward B or C, etc.

A simple experiment makes the point nicely: subjects were told that they could choose as a working partner either a close friend or a stranger who was known to be an expert on the problem to be solved. Those with higher *n* Ach (more "need to achieve") chose the experts over their friends, whereas those with more *n* Aff (the "need to affiliate with others") chose friends over experts. The latter were not "unmotivated"; their desire to be with someone they liked was simply a stronger motive than their desire to excel at the task. Other such needs have been studied by psychologists. For instance, the need for Achievement because both may lead to "outstanding" activities. There is a distinct difference. People with a strong need for Power want to command attention, get recognition, and control others. They are more active in political life and tend to busy themselves primarily with controlling the channels of communication both up to the top and down to the people so that they are more "in charge." Those with high *n* Pow are not as concerned with improving their work performance daily as those with high *n* Ach.

It follows, from what we have been able to learn, that not all "great achievers" score high in *n* Ach. Many generals, outstanding politicians, great research scientists do not, for instance, because their work requires other personality characteristics, other motives. A general or a politician must be more concerned with power relationships, a research scientist must be able to go for long periods without the immediate feedback the person with high *n* Ach requires, etc. On the other hand, business executives, particularly if they are in positions of real responsibility or if they are salesmen, tend to score high in *n* Ach. This is true even in a Communist country like Poland; Apparently there, as well as in a private enterprise economy, a manager succeeds if he is concerned about improving all the time, setting moderate goals, keeping track of his or the company's performance, etc.

MOTIVATION AND HALF–TRUTHS

Since careful study has shown that common sense notions about motivation are at best half-truths, it also follows that you cannot trust what people tell you about their motives. After all, they often get their ideas about their own motives from common sense. Thus a general may say he is interested in achievement (because he has obviously achieved), or a businessman that he is interested only in making money (because he has made money), or one of the majority of unemployed in Erie that he desperately wants a job (because he knows he needs one); but a careful check of what each one thinks about and how he spends his time may show that each is concerned about quite different things. It requires special measurement techniques to identify the presence of *n* Ach and other such motives. Thus what people say and believe is not very closely related to these "hidden" motives which seem to affect a person's "style of life" more than his political, religious or social attitudes. Thus *n* Ach produces enterprising men among labor leaders or managers, Republicans or Democrats, Catholics or Protestants, capitalists or Communists.

Wherever people begin to think often in *n* Ach terms, things begin to move. Men with high *n* Ach get more raises and are promoted more rapidly, because they keep actively seeking ways to do a better job. Companies with many such men grow faster. In one comparison of two firms in Mexico, it was discovered that all but one of the top executives of a fast-growing firm had higher *n* Ach scores than the highest-scoring executive in an equally large but slow-growing firm. Countries with many such rapidly growing firms tend to show above average rates of national economic growth. This appears to be the reason why correlations have regularly been found between the *n* Ach content in popular literature (such as popular songs or stories in children's textbooks) and subsequent rates of national economic growth. A nation which is thinking about doing better all the time (as shown in its popular literature) actually does do better economically speaking. Careful quantitative studies have shown this to be true in Ancient Greece, in Spain in the Middle Ages, in England from 1400–1800, as well as among contemporary nations, whether capitalist or Communist, developed or underdeveloped.

Contrast these two stories for example. Which one contains more *n* Ach? Which one reflects a state of mind which ought to lead to harder striving to improve the way things are?

Excerpt From Story A. (fourth-grade reader): "Don't Ever Owe a Man—The world is an illusion. Wife, children, horses, and cows are all just ties of fate. They are ephemeral. Each after fulfilling his part in life disappears. So we should not clamour after riches which are not permanent. As long as we live it is wise not to have any attachments and just think of God. We have to spend our lives without trouble, for is it not time that there is an end to grievances? So it is better to live knowing the real state of affairs. Don't get entangled in the meshes of family life."

Excerpt From Story B. (fourth-grade reader): "How I Do Like to Learn—I was sent to an accelerated technical high school. I was so happy I cried. Learning is not very easy. In the beginning I couldn't understand what the teacher taught us. I always got a red cross mark on my papers. The boy sitting next to me was very enthusiastic and also an outstanding student. When he found I couldn't do the problems he offered to show me how he had done them. I could not copy his work. I must learn through my own reasoning. I gave his paper back and explained I had to do it myself. Sometimes I worked on a problem until midnight. If I couldn't finish, I started early in the morning. The red cross marks on my work were getting less common. I conquered my difficulties. My marks rose. I graduated and went on to college."

Most readers would agree, without any special knowledge of the n Ach coding system, that the second story shows more concern with improvement than the first, which comes from a contemporary reader used in Indian public schools. In fact the latter has a certain Horatio Alger quality that is reminiscent of our own McGuffey readers of several generations ago. It appears today in the textbooks of Communist China. It should not, therefore, come as a surprise if a nation like Communist China, obsessed as it is with improvement, tended in the long run to outproduce a nation like India, which appears to be more fatalistic.

The n Ach level is obviously important for statesmen to watch and in many instances to try to do something about, particularly if a nation's economy is lagging. Take Britain, for example. A generation ago (around 1925) it ranked fifth among 25 countries where children's readers were scored for n Ach—and its economy was doing well. By 1950 the n Ach level had dropped to 27th out of 39 countries—well below the world average—and today, its leaders are feeling the severe economic effects of this loss in the spirit of enterprise.

ECONOMICS AND n ACH

If psychologists can detect n Ach levels in individuals or nations, particularly before their effects are widespread, can't the knowledge somehow be put to use to foster economic development? Obviously detection or diagnosis is not enough. What good is it to tell Britain (or India for that matter) that it needs more n Ach, a greater spirit of enterprise? In most such cases, informed observers of the local scene know very well that such a need exists, though they may be slower to discover it than the psychologist hovering over n Ach scores. What is needed is some method of developing n Ach in individuals or nations.

Since about 1960, psychologists in my research group at Harvard have been experimenting with techniques designed to accomplish this goal, chiefly among business executives whose work requires the action characteristics of people with high n Ach. Initially, we had real doubts as to whether we could succeed, partly because like most American psychologists we had been strongly influenced by the psychoanalytic view that basic motives are laid down in childhood and cannot really be changed later, and partly because many studies of intensive psychotherapy and counseling have shown minor if any long-term personality effects. On the other hand we were encouraged by the non-professionals: those enthusiasts like Dale Carnegie, the Communist ideologue or the Church missionary, who felt they could change adults and in fact seemed to be doing so. At any rate we ran some brief (7-to-10-day) "total push" training courses for businessmen, designed to increase their n Ach.

FOUR MAIN GOALS

In broad outline the courses had four main goals: (1) They were designed to teach the participants how to think, talk and act like a person with high *n* Ach, based on our knowledge of such people gained through 17 years of research. For instance, men learned how to make up stories that would code high in *n* Ach (i.e., how to think in *n* Ach terms), how to set moderate goals for themselves in the ring toss game (and in life). (2) The courses stimulated the participants to set higher but carefully planned and realistic work goals for themselves over the next two years. Then we checked back with them every six months to see how well they were doing in terms of their own objectives. (3) The courses also utilized techniques for giving the participants knowledge about themselves. For instance, in playing the ring toss game, they could observe that they behaved differently from others—perhaps in refusing to adjust a goal downward after failure. This would then become a matter for group discussion and the man would have to explain what he had in mind in setting such unrealistic goals. Discussion could then lead on to what a man's ultimate goals in life were, how much he cared about actually improving performance vs. making a good impression or having many friends. In this way the participants would be freer to realize their achievement goals without being blocked by old habits and attitudes. (4) The courses also usually created a group *esprit de corps* from learning about each other's hopes and fears, successes and failures, and from going through an emotional experience together, away from everyday life, in a retreat setting. This membership in a new group helps a man achieve his goals, partly because he knows he has their sympathy and support and partly because he knows they will be watching to see how well he does. The same effect has been noted in other therapy groups like Alcoholics Anonymous. We are not sure which of these course "inputs" is really absolutely essential—that remains a research question—but we were taking no chances at the outset in view of the general pessimism about such efforts, and we wanted to include any and all techniques that were thought to change people.

The courses have been given: to executives in a large American firm, and in several Mexican firms; to underachieving high school boys; and to businessmen in India from Bombay and from a small city—Kakinada in the state of Andhra Pradesh. In every instance save one (the Mexican case), it was possible to demonstrate statistically, some two years later, that the men who took the course had done better (made more money, got promoted faster, expanded their businesses faster) than comparable men who did not take the course or who took some other management course.

Consider the Kakinada results, for example. In the two years preceding the course 9 men, 18 percent of the 52 participants, had shown "unusual" enterprise in their businesses. In the 18 months following the course 25 of the men, in other words nearly 50 percent, were unusually active. And this was not due to a general upturn of business in India. Data from a control city, some forty-five miles away, show the same base rate of "unusually active" men as in Kakinada before the course—namely, about 20 percent. Something clearly happened in Kakinada: the owner of a small radio shop started a chemical plant; a banker was so successful in making commercial loans in an enterprising way that he was promoted to a much larger branch of his bank in Calcutta; the local political leader accomplished his goal (it was set in the course) to get the federal government to deepen the harbor and make it into an all-weather port; plans are far along for establishing a steel rolling mill, etc. All this took place without any substantial capital from the outside. In fact, the only costs were for our 10–day courses plus some brief follow-up visits every six months. The men are raising their own capital and using their own resources for getting business and industry moving in a city that had been considered stagnant and unenterprising.

The promise of such a method of developing achievement motivation seems very great. It has obvious applications in helping underdeveloped countries, or "pockets of poverty" in the United States, to move faster economically. It has great potential for businesses that need to "turn around" and take a more enterprising approach toward their growth and development. It may even be helpful in developing more n Ach among low-income groups. For instance, data shows that lower-class Negro Americans have a very low level of n Ach. This is not surprising. Society has systematically discouraged and blocked their achievement striving. But as the barriers to upward mobility are broken down, it will be necessary to help stimulate the motivation that will lead them to take advantage of new opportunities opening up.

EXTREME REACTIONS

But a word of caution: Whenever I speak of this research and its great potential, audience reaction tends to go to opposite extremes. Either people remain skeptical and argue that motives can't really be changed, that all we are doing is dressing Dale Carnegie up in fancy "psychologese," or they become converts and want instant course descriptions by return mail to solve their local motivation problems. Either response is unjustified. What I have described here in a few pages has taken 20 years of patient research effort, and hun-

dreds of thousands of dollars in basic research costs. What remains to be done will involve even larger sums and more time for development to turn a promising idea into something of wide practical utility.

ENCOURAGEMENT NEEDED

To take only one example, we have not yet learned how to develop n Ach really well among low-income groups (see chart). In our first effort—a summer course for bright underachieving 14–year–olds—we found that boys from the middle class improved steadily in grades in school over a two-year period, but boys from the lower class showed an improvement after the first year followed by a drop back to their beginning low grade average. Why? We speculated that it was because they moved back into an environment in which neither parents nor friends encouraged achievement or upward mobility. In other words, it isn't enough to change a man's motivation if the environment in which he lives doesn't support at least to some degree his new efforts. Negroes striving to rise out of the ghetto frequently confront this problem: they are often faced by skepticism at home and suspicion on the job, so that even if their n Ach is raised, it can be lowered again by the heavy odds against their success. We must learn not only to raise n Ach but also to find methods of instructing people in how to manage it, to create a favorable environment in which it can flourish.

Many of these training techniques are now only in the pilot testing stage. It will take time and money to perfect them, but society should be willing to invest heavily in them in view of their tremendous potential for contributing to human betterment.

THAT URGE TO ACHIEVE

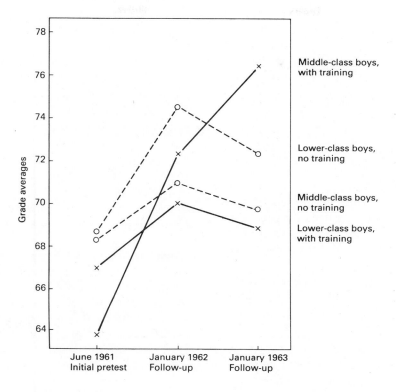

In a Harvard study, a group of underachieving 14-year-olds was given a six-week's course designed to help them do better in school. Some of the boys were also given training in achievement motivation, or n Ach (solid lines). As the graph reveals, the only boys who continued to improve after a two-year period were the middle-class boys with the special n Ach training. Psychologists suspect the lower-class boys dropped back, even with n Ach training, because they returned to an environment in which neither parents nor friends encouraged achievement.

Motivation—A Diagnostic Approach

DAVID A. NADLER and EDWARD E. LAWLER III

- What makes some people work hard while others do as little as possible?
- How can I, as a manager, influence the performance of people who work for me?
- Why do people turn over, show up late to work, and miss work entirely?

These important questions about employees' behavior can only be answered by managers who have a grasp of what motivates people. Specifically, a good understanding of motivation can serve as a valuable tool for *understanding* the causes of behavior in organizations, for *predicting* the effects of any managerial action, and for *directing* behavior so that organizational and individual goals can be achieved.

EXISTING APPROACHES

During the past twenty years, managers have been bombarded with a number of different approaches to motivation. The terms associated with these approaches are well known—"human relations," "scientific management," "job enrichment," "need hierarchy," "self-actualization," etc. Each of these approaches has something to offer. On the other hand, each of these different approaches also has its problems in both theory and practice. Running through almost all of the approaches

Reprinted by permissions of the authors from "Perspectives on Behavior in Organizations", Second Edition, 1983.

with which managers are familiar are a series of implicit but clearly erroneous assumptions.

Assumption 1: All Employees Are Alike. Different theories present different ways of looking at people, but each of them assumes that all employees are basically similar in their makeup: Employees all want economic gains, or all want a pleasant climate, or all aspire to be self-actualizing, etc.

Assumption 2: All Situations Are Alike. Most theories assume that all managerial situations are alike, and that the managerial course of action for motivation (for example, participation, job enlargement, etc.) is applicable in all situations.

Assumption 3: One best way. Out of the other two assumptions there emerges a basic principle that there is "one best way" to motivate employees.

When these "one best way" approaches are tried in the "correct" situation they will work. However, all of them are bound to fail in some situations. They are therefore not adequate managerial tools.

A NEW APPROACH

During the past ten years, a great deal of research has been done on a new approach to looking at motivation. This approach, frequently called "expectancy theory," still needs further testing, refining, and extending. However, enough is known that many behavioral scientists have concluded that it represents the most comprehensive, valid, and useful approach to understanding motivation. Further, it is apparent that it is a very useful tool for understanding motivation in organizations.

The theory is based on a number of specific assumptions about the causes of behavior in organizations.

Assumption 1: Behavior Is Determined By a Combination of Forces in the Individual and Forces in the Environment. Neither the individual nor the environment alone determines behavior. Individuals come into organizations with certain "psychological baggage." They have past experiences and a developmental history which has given them unique sets of needs, ways of looking at the world, and expectations about how organizations will treat them. These all influence how individuals respond to their work environment. The work environment provides structures (such as a pay system or a supervisor) which influence the behavior of people. Different environments tend to produce different behavior in similar people just as dissimilar people tend to behave differently in similar environments.

Assumption 2: People Make Decisions About Their Own Behavior in Organizations. While there are many constraints on the behavior of individuals in organizations, most of the behavior that is observed is the result of individuals' conscious decisions. These decisions usually fall into two categories. First, individuals make decisions about *membership behavior*—coming to work, staying at work, and in other ways being a member of the organization. Second, individuals make decisions about the amount of *effort* they will direct *towards performing their jobs.* This includes decisions about how hard to work, how much to produce, at what

quality, etc.

Assumption 3: Different People Have Different Types of Needs, Desires, and Goals. Individuals differ on what kinds of outcomes (or rewards) they desire. These differences are not random; they can be examined systematically by an understanding of the differences in the strength of individuals' needs.

Assumption 4: People Make Decisions Among Alternative Plans of Behavior Based on Their Perceptions (Expectancies) of the Degree to Which a Given Behavior Will Lead to Desired Outcomes. In simple terms, people tend to do those things which they see as leading to outcomes (which can also be called "rewards") they desire and avoid doing those things they see as leading to outcomes that are not desired.

In general, the approach used here views people as having their own needs and mental maps of what the world is like. They use these maps to make decisions about how they will behave, behaving in those ways which their mental maps indicate will lead to outcomes that will satisfy their needs. Therefore, they are inherently neither motivated nor unmotivated; motivation depends on the situation they are in, and how it fits their needs.

THE THEORY

Based on these general assumptions, expectancy theory states a number of propositions about the process by which people make decisions about their own behavior in organizational settings. While the theory is complex at first view, it is in fact made of a series of fairly straightforward observations about behavior. Three concepts serve as the key building blocks of the theory:

Performance-Outcome   Expectancy.

Every behavior has associated with it, in an individual's mind, certain outcomes (rewards or punishments). In other words, the individual believes or expects that if he or she behaves in a certain way, he or she will get certain things.

Examples of expectancies can easily be described. An individual may have an expectancy that if he produces ten units he will receive his normal hourly rate while if he produces fifteen units he will receive his hourly pay rate plus a bonus. Similarly an individual may believe that certain levels of performance will lead to approval or disapproval from members of her work group or from her supervisor. Each performance can be seen as leading to a number of different kinds of outcomes and outcomes can differ in their types.

Valence. Each outcome has a "valence" (value, worth, attractiveness) to a specific individual. Outcomes have different valences for different individuals. This comes about because valences result from individual needs and perceptions, which differ because they in turn reflect other factors in the individual's life.

For example, some individuals may value an opportunity for promotion or advancement because of their needs for achievement or power, while others may not want to be promoted and leave their current work group because of needs for affiliation with others. Similarly, a fringe benefit such as a pension plan may have great valence for an older worker but little valence for a young employee on his first job.

Effort-Performance Expectancy. Each behavior also has associated with it in the individual's mind a certain expectancy or probability of success. This expectancy represents the individual's perception of how hard it will be to achieve such behavior and the probability of his or her successful achievement of that behavior.

For example, you may have a strong expectancy that if you put forth the effort, you can produce ten units an hour, but that you have only a 50–50 chance of producing fifteen units an hour if you try.

Putting these concepts together, it is possible to make a basic statement about motivation. In general, the motivation to attempt to behave in a certain way is greatest when:

a. The individual believes that the behavior will lead to outcomes (performance-outcome expectancy)
b. The individual believes that these outcomes have positive value for him or her (valence)
c. The individual believes that he or she is able to perform at the desired level (effort-performance expectancy)

Given a number of alternative levels of behavior (ten, fifteen, and twenty units of production per hour, for example) the individual will choose that level of performance which has the greatest motivational force associated with it, as indicated by the expectancies, outcomes, and valences.

In other words, when faced with choices about behavior, the individual goes through a process of considering questions such as, "Can I perform at that level if I try?" "If I perform at that level, what will happen?" "How do I feel about those things that will happen?" The individual then decides to behave in that way which seems to have the best chance of producing positive, desired outcomes.

A GENERAL MODEL

On the basis of these concepts, it is possible to construct a general model of behavior in organizational settings (see Figure 1). Working from left to right in the model, motivation is seen as the force on the individual to expend effort. Motivation leads to an observed level of effort by the individual. Effort, alone, however, is not enough. Performance results from a combination of the effort that an individ-

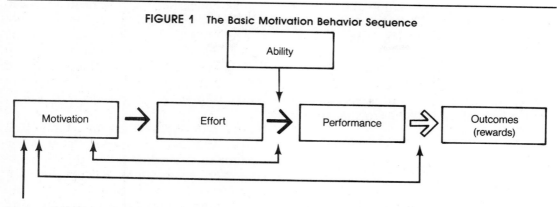

FIGURE 1   The Basic Motivation Behavior Sequence

A person's motivation is a function of: a. Effort-to-performance expectancies
b. Performance to outcome expectancies
c. Perceived valence of outcomes

ual puts forth *and* the level of ability which he or she has (reflecting skills, training, information, etc.). Effort thus combines with ability to produce a given level of performance. As a result of performance, the individual attains certain outcomes. The model indicates this relationship in a hollow arrow, reflecting the fact that sometimes people perform but do not get desired outcomes. As this process of performance-reward occurs, time after time, the actual events serve to provide information which influences the individual's perceptions (particularly expectancies) and thus influences motivation in the future.

Outcomes, or rewards, fall into two major categories. First, the individual obtains outcomes from the environment. When an individual performs at a given level he or she can receive positive or negative outcomes from supervisors, coworkers, the organization's rewards systems, or other sources. These environmental rewards are thus one source of outcomes for the individual. A second source of outcomes is the individual. These include outcomes which occur purely from the

performance of the task itself (feelings of accomplishment, personal worth, achievement, etc.). In a sense, the individual gives these rewards to himself or herself. The environment cannot give them or take them away directly; it can only make them possible.

SUPPORTING EVIDENCE

Over fifty studies have been done to test the validity of the expectancy-theory approach to predicting employee behavior. Almost without exception, the studies have confirmed the predictions of the theory. As the theory predicts, the best performers in organizations tend to see a strong relationship between performing their jobs well and receiving rewards they value. In addition they have clear performance goals and they feel they can perform well. Similarly, studies using the expectancy theory to predict how people choose jobs also show that individuals tend to interview for and actually take those jobs which they feel will provide the rewards they value. One study, for example, was able to correctly predict for 80 percent of the people studied which of several jobs they would take. Finally, the theory correctly predicts that beliefs about the outcomes associated with performance (expectancies) will be better predictors of performance than will feelings of job satisfaction since expectancies are the critical causes of performance and satisfaction is not.

QUESTIONS ABOUT THE MODEL

Although the results so far have been encouraging, they also indicate some problems with the model. These problems do not critically affect the managerial implications of the model, but they should be noted. The model is based on the assumption that individuals make very rational decisions after a thorough exploration of all the available alternatives and on weighing the possible outcomes of all these alternatives. When we talk to or observe individuals, however, we find that their decision processes are frequently less thorough. People often stop considering alternative behavior plans when they find one that is at least moderately satisfying, even though more rewarding plans remain to be examined.

People are also limited in the amount of information they can handle at one time, and therefore the model may indicate a process that is much more complex than the one that actually takes place. On the other hand, the model does provide enough information and is consistent enough with reality to present some clear implications for managers who are concerned with the question of how to motivate the people who work for them.

IMPLICATIONS FOR MANAGERS

The first set of implications is directed toward the individual manager who has a group of people working for him or her

and is concerned with how to motivate good performance. Since behavior is a result of forces both in the person and in the environment, you as manager need to look at and diagnose both the person and the environment. Specifically, you need to do the following:

Figure Out What Outcomes Each Employee Values. As a first step, it is important to determine what kinds of outcomes or rewards have valence for your employees. For each employee you need to determine "what turns him or her on." There are various ways of finding this out, including (a) finding out employees' desires through some structured method of data collection, such as a questionnaire, (b) observing the employees' reactions to different situations or rewards, or (c) the fairly simple act of asking them what kinds of rewards they want, what kind of career goals they have, or "what's in it for them." It is important to stress here that it is very difficult to change what people want, but fairly easy to find out what they want. Thus, the skillful manager emphasizes diagnosis of needs, not changing the individuals themselves.

Determine What Kinds of Behavior You Desire. Managers frequently talk about "good performance" without really defining what good performance is. An important step in motivating is for you yourself to figure out what kinds of performances are required and what are adequate measures of indicators of performance (quantity, quality, etc.). There is also a need to be able to define those performances in fairly specific terms so that observable and measurable behavior can be defined and subordinates can understand what is desired of them (e.g., produce ten products of a certain quality standard—rather than only produce at a high rate).

Make Sure Desired Levels of Performance Are Reachable. The model states that motivation is determined not only by the performance-to-outcome expectancy, but also by the effort-to-performance expectancy. The implication of this is that the levels of performance which are set as the points at which individuals receive desired outcomes must be reachable or attainable by these individuals. If the employees feel that the level of performance required to get a reward is higher than they can reasonably achieve, then their motivation to perform well will be relatively low.

Link Desired Outcomes to Desired Performances. The next step is to directly, clearly, and explicitly link those outcomes desired by employees to the specific performances desired by you. If your employee values external rewards, then the emphasis should be on the rewards systems concerned with promotion, pay, and approval. While the linking of these rewards can be initiated through your making statements to your employees, it is extremely important that employees see a clear example of the reward process working in a fairly short period of time if the motivating "expectancies" are to be created in the employees's minds. The linking must be done by some concrete public acts, in addition to statements of intent.

If your employee values internal rewards (e.g., achievement), then you should concentrate on changing the nature of the person's job, for he or she is likely to respond well to such things as increased autonomy, feedback, and challenge, because these things will lead to a situation where good job performance is inherently rewarding. The best way to check on the adequacy of the internal and external reward system is to ask people what their perceptions of the situation are. Remember it is the perceptions of people that determine their motivation, not reality. It doesn't matter for example whether you feel a subordinate's pay is

related to his or her motivation. Motivation will be present only if the subordinate sees the relationship. Many managers are misled about the behavior of their subordinates because they rely on their own perceptions of the situation and forget to find out what their subordinates feel. There is only one way to do this: ask. Questionnaires can be used here, as can personal interviews.

Analyze the Total Situation for Conflicting Expectancies. Having set up positive expectancies for employees, you then need to look at the entire situation to see if other factors (informal work groups, other managers, the organization's reward systems) have set up conflicting expectancies in the minds of the employees. Motivation will only be high when people see a number of rewards associated with good performance and few negative outcomes. Again, you can often gather this kind of information by asking your subordinates. If there are major conflicts, you need to make adjustments, either in your own performance and reward structure, or in the other sources of rewards or punishments in the environment.

Make Sure Changes in Outcomes Are Large Enough. In examining the motivational system, it is important to make sure that changes in outcomes or rewards are large enough to motivate significant behavior. Trivial rewards will result in trivial amounts of effort and thus trivial improvements in performance. Rewards must be large enough to motivate individuals to put forth the effort required to bring about significant changes in performance.

Check the System for Its Equity. The model is based on the idea that individuals are different and therefore different rewards will need to be used to motivate different individuals. On the other hand, for a motivational system to work it must be a fair one—one that has equity (not equality). Good performers should see that they get more desired rewards than do poor performers, and others in the system should see that also. Equity should not be confused with a system of equality where all are rewarded equally, with no regard to their performance. A system of equality is guaranteed to produce low motivation.

IMPLICATIONS FOR ORGANIZATIONS

Expectancy theory has some clear messages for those who run large organizations. It suggests how organizational structures can be designed so that they increase rather than decrease levels of motivation of organization members. While there are many different implications, a few of the major ones are as follows:

Implication 1: The Design of Pay and Reward Systems. Organizations usually get what they reward, not what they want. This can be seen in many situations, and pay systems are a good example. Frequently, organizations reward people for membership (through pay tied to seniority, for example) rather than for performance. Little wonder that what the organization gets is behavior oriented towards "safe," secure employment rather than effort directed at performing well. In addition, even where organizations do pay for performance as a motivational device, they frequently negate the motivational value of the system by keeping pay secret, therefore preventing people from observing the pay-to-performance relationship that would serve to create positive, clear, and strong performance-to-reward expectancies. The implication is that organizations should put more effort into rewarding people (through pay, promotion, better job opportunities, etc.) for the performances which are desired, and that to

keep these rewards secret is clearly self-defeating. In addition, it underscores the importance of the frequently ignored performance evaluation or appraisal process and the need to evaluate people based on how they perform clearly defined specific behaviors, rather than on how they score on ratings of general traits such as "honesty," "cleanliness," and other, similar terms which frequently appear as part of the performance appraisal form.

Implication 2: The Design of Tasks, Jobs, and Roles. One source of desired outcomes is the work itself. The expectancy-theory model supports much of the job enrichment literature, in saying that by designing jobs which enable people to get their needs fulfilled, organizations can bring about higher levels of motivation. The major difference between the traditional approaches to job enlargement or enrichment and the expectancy-theory approach is the recognition by expectancy theory that different people have different needs and, therefore, some people may not want enlarged or enriched jobs. Thus, while the design of tasks that have more autonomy, variety, feedback, meaningfulness, etc., will lead to higher motivation in some, the organization needs to build in the opportunity for individuals to make choices about the kind of work they will do so that not everyone is forced to experience job enrichment.

Implication 3: The Importance of Group Structures. Groups, both formal and informal, are powerful and potent sources of desired outcomes for individuals. Groups can provide or withhold acceptance, approval, affection, skill training, needed information, assistance, etc. They are a powerful force in the total motivational environment of individuals. Several implications emerge from the importance of groups. First, organizations should consider the structuring of at least a portion of rewards around group members who have to cooperate with each other to produce a group product or service, and where the individual's contribution is often hard to determine. Second, the organization needs to train managers to be aware of how groups can influence individual behavior and to be sensitive to the kinds of expectancies which informal groups set up and their conflict or consistency with the expectancies that the organization attempts to create.

Implication 4: The Supervisor's Role. The immediate supervisor has an important role in creating, monitoring, and maintaining the expectancies and reward structures which will lead to good performance. The supervisor's role in the motivation process becomes one of defining clear goals, setting clear reward expectancies, and providing the right rewards for different people (which could include both organizational rewards and personal rewards such as recognition, approval, or support from the supervisor). Thus, organizations need to provide supervisors with an awareness of the nature of motivation as well as the tools (control over organizational rewards, skill in administering those rewards) to create positive motivation.

Implication 5: Measuring Motivation. If things like expectancies, the nature of the job, supervisor-controlled outcomes, satisfaction, etc., are important in understanding how well people are being motivated, then organizations need to monitor employee perceptions along these lines. One relatively cheap and reliable method of doing this is through standardized employee questionnaires. A number of organizations already use such techniques, surveying employees' perceptions and attitudes at regular intervals (ranging from once a month to once every year-and-a-half) using either standardized surveys or surveys developed specifically for the organization. Such information is useful

both to the individual manager and to top management in assessing the state of human resources and the effectiveness of the organization's motivational systems.

Implication 6: Individualizing Organizations. Expectancy theory leads to a final general implication about a possible future direction for the design of organizations. Because different people have different needs and therefore have different valences, effective motivation must come through the recognition that not all employees are alike and that organizations need to be flexible in order to accommodate individual differences. This implies the "building in" of choice for employees in many areas, such as reward systems, fringe benefits, job assignments, etc., where employees previously have had little say. A successful example of the building in of such choice can be seen in the experiments at TRW and the Educational Testing Service with "cafeteria fringe benefits plans" which allow employees to choose the fringe benefits they want, rather than taking the expensive and often unwanted benefits which the company frequently provides to everyone.

SUMMARY

Expectancy theory provides a more complex model of man for managers to work with. At the same time, it is a model which holds promise for the more effective motivation of individuals and the more effective design of organizational systems. It implies, however, the need for more exacting and thorough diagnosis by the manager to determine (a) the relevant forces in the individual, and (b) the relevant forces in the environment, both of which combine to motivate different kinds of behavior. Following diagnosis, the model implies a need to act—to develop a system of pay, promotion, job assignments, group structures, supervision, etc.—to bring about effective motivation by providing different outcomes for different individuals.

Performance of individuals is a critical issue in making organizations work effectively. If a manager is to influence work behavior and performance, he or she must have an understanding of motivation and the factors which influence an individual's motivation to come to work, to work hard, and to work well. While simple models offer easy answers, it is the more complex models which seem to offer more promise. Managers can use models (like expectancy theory) to understand the nature of behavior and build more effective organizations.

A New Strategy for Job Enrichment

J. RICHARD HACKMAN,[1] GREG OLDHAM,[2] ROBERT JANSON,[3] and KENNETH PURDY [4]

Practitioners of job enrichment have been living through a time of excitement, even euphoria. Their craft has moved from the psychology and management journals to the front page and the Sunday supplement. Job enrichment, which began with

[1] J. Richard Hackman is Associate Professor of Administrative Sciences and of Psychology at Yale University. He is the author of numerous articles on organizational behavior and co-author of the recent book *Behavior in Organizations*.

[2] Greg Oldham is Assistant Professor of Business Administration at the University of Illinois. His work has been published in several leading journals, and his current research interests include leadership, job design, and motivation.

[3] Robert Janson is Vice-President of Roy W. Walters & Associates, a consulting firm specializing in applications of the behavioral sciences to the solution of organizational problems. He has contributed numerous articles to personnel and training journals, as well as to books on motivation and work design.

[4] Kenneth Purdy is a senior associate with Roy W. Walters & Associates. He has written numerous articles on job design and the quality of work.

the pioneering work of Herzberg and his associates, originally was intended as a means to increase the motivation and satisfaction of people at work—and to improve productivity in the bargain. (Herzberg 1966, 1968; Herzberg, Mausner, and Snyderman 1959; Paul, Robertson, and Herzberg 1969; Ford 1969). Now it is being acclaimed in the popular press as a cure for problems ranging from inflation to drug abuse.

Much current writing about job enrichment is enthusiastic, sometimes even messianic, about what it can accomplish. But the hard questions of exactly what should be done to improve jobs, and how, tend to be glossed over. Lately, because the harder questions have not been dealt with adequately, critical winds have begun to blow. Job enrichment has been described as yet another "management fad," as "nothing new," even as a fraud. And reports of job enrichment failures are beginning to appear in management and psychology journals.

This article attempts to redress the excesses that have characterized some of the recent writings about job enrichment. As the technique increases in popularity as a management tool, top managers inevitably will find themselves making decisions about its use. The intent of this paper is to help both managers and behavioral scientists become better able to make those decisions on a solid basis of fact and data.

Succinctly stated, we present here a new strategy for going about the redesign of work. The strategy is based on three years of collaborative work and cross-fertilization among the authors—two of whom are active practitioners in job enrichment. Our approach is new, but it has been tested in many organizations. It draws on the contributions of both management practice and psychological theory, but it is firmly in the middle ground between them. It builds on and complements previous work by Herzberg and others, but provides for the first time a set of tools for *diagnosing* existing jobs—and a map for translating the diagnostic results into specific action steps for change.

What we have, then, is the following:

1. A theory that specifies when people will get personally "turned on" to their work. The theory shows what kinds of jobs are most likely to generate excitement and commitment about work, and what kinds of employees it works best for.
2. A set of action steps for job enrichment based on the theory, which prescribe in concrete terms what to do to make jobs more motivating for the people who do them.
3. Evidence that the theory holds water and that it can be used to bring about measurable—and sometimes dramatic—improvements in employee work behavior, in job satisfaction, and in the financial performance of the organizational unit involved.

THE THEORY BEHIND THE STRATEGY

What makes people get turned on to their work? For workers who are really prospering in their jobs, work is likely to be a lot like play. Consider, for example, a golfer at a driving range, practicing to get rid of a hook. His activity is *meaningful* to him; he has chosen to do it because he gets a "kick" from testing his skills by playing the game. He knows that he alone is *responsible* for what happens when he hits the ball. And he has *knowledge of the results* within a few seconds.

Behavioral scientists have found that the three "psychological states" experienced by the golfer in the above example also are critical in determining a person's motivation and satisfaction on the job.

* *Experienced meaningfulness:* The individual must perceive his work as worthwhile or important by some system of values he accepts.
* *Experienced responsibility:* He must believe that he personally is accountable for the outcomes of his efforts.
* *Knowledge of results:* He must be able to determine, on some fairly regular basis, whether or not the outcomes of his work are satisfactory.

When these three conditions are present, a person tends to feel very good about himself when he performs well. And those good feelings will prompt him to try to continue to do well—so he can continue to earn the positive feelings in the future. That is what is meant by "internal motivation"—being turned on to one's work because of the positive internal feelings that are generated by doing well, rather than being dependent on external factors (such as incentive pay or compliments from the boss) for the motivation to work effectively.

What if one of the three psychological states is missing? Motivation drops markedly. Suppose, for example, that our golf-

FIGURE 1 · Relationships Among Core Job Dimensions, Critical Psychological States, and On-the-Job Outcomes

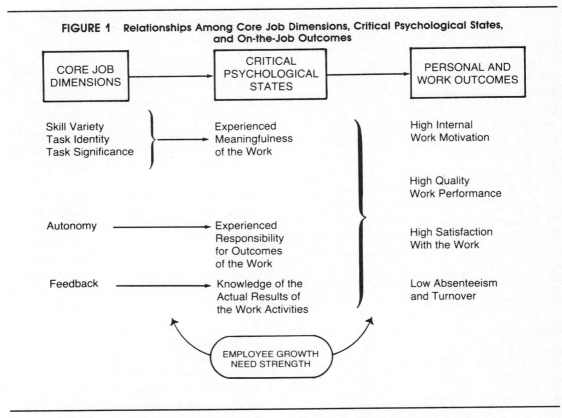

er has settled in at the driving range to practice for a couple of hours. Suddenly a fog drifts in over the range. He can no longer see if the ball starts to tail off to the left a hundred yards out. The satisfaction he got from hitting straight down the middle—and the motivation to try to correct something whenever he didn't—are both gone. If the fog stays, it's likely that he soon will be packing up his clubs.

The relationship between the three psychological states and on-the-job outcomes is illustrated in Figure 1. When all three are high, then internal work motivation, job satisfaction, and work quality are high, and absenteeism and turnover are low.

What Job Characteristics Make it Happen? Recent research has identified five

"core" characteristics of jobs that elicit the psychological states described above. (Turner and Lawrence 1965; Hackman and Lawler 1971; Hackman and Oldham 1974). These five core job dimensions provide the key to objectively measuring jobs and to changing them so that they have high potential for motivating people who do them.

• Toward meaningful work. Three of the five core dimensions contribute to a job's meaningfulness for the worker;

1. Skill variety—the degree to which a job requires the worker to perform activities that challenge his skills and abilities. When even a single skill is involved, there is at least a seed of potential meaningfulness. When several are involved, the job has the potential

of appealing to more of the whole person, and also of avoiding the monotony of performing the same task repeatedly, no matter how much skill it may require.

2. Task identity—the degree to which the job requires completion of a "whole" and identifiable piece of work—doing a job from beginning to end with a visible outcome. For example, it is clearly more meaningful to an employee to build complete toasters than to attach electrical cord after electrical cord, especially if he never sees a completed toaster. (Note that the whole job, in this example, probably would involve greater skill variety as well as task identity.)

3. Task significance—the degree to which the job has a substantial and perceivable impact on the lives of other people, whether in the immediate organization or the world at large. The worker who tightens nuts on aircraft brake assemblies is more likely to perceive his work as significant than the worker who fills small boxes with paper clips—even though the skill levels involved may be comparable.

Each of these three job dimensions represents an important route to experienced meaningfulness. If the job is high in all three, the worker is quite likely to experience his job as very meaningful. It is not necessary, however, for a job to be very high in all three dimensions. If the job is low in any one of them, there will be a drop in overall experienced meaningfulness. But even when two dimensions are low the worker may find the job meaningful if the third is high enough.

• Toward personal responsibility. A fourth core dimension leads a worker to experience increased responsibility in his job. This is *autonomy,* the degree to which the job gives the worker freedom, independence, and discretion in scheduling work and determining how he will carry it out. People in highly autonomous jobs know that they are personally responsible for successes and failures. To the extent that their autonomy is high, then, how the work goes will be felt to depend more on the individual's own efforts and initiatives rather than on detailed instructions from the boss or from a manual of job procedures.

• Toward knowledge of results. The fifth and last core dimension is *feedback.* This is the degree to which a worker, in carrying out the work activities required by the job, gets information about the effectiveness of his efforts. Feedback is most powerful when it comes directly from the work itself—for example, when a worker has the responsibility for gauging and otherwise checking a component he has just finished and learns in the process that he has lowered his reject rate by meeting specifications more consistently.

• The overall "motivating potential" of a job. Figure 1 shows how the five core dimensions combine to affect the psychological states that are critical in determining whether or not an employee will be internally motivated to work effectively. Indeed, when using an instrument to be described later, it is possible to compute a "motivating potential score" (MPS) for any job. The MPS provides a single summary index of the degree to which the objective characteristics of the job will prompt high internal work motivation. Following the theory outlined above, a job high in motivating potential must be high in at least one (and hopefully more) of the three dimensions that lead to experienced meaningfulness and high in both autonomy and feedback as well. The MPS provides a quantitative index of the degree to which this is in fact the case. As will be seen later, the MPS can be very useful in diagnosing jobs and in assessing the effectiveness of job enrichment activities.

Does the Theory Work for Everybody?

Unfortunately not. Not everyone is able to become internally motivated in his work, even when the motivating potential of a job is very high indeed.

Research has shown that the *psychological needs* of people are very important in determining who can (and who cannot) become internally motivated at work. Some people have strong needs for personal accomplishment, for learning and developing themselves beyond where they are now, for being stimulated and challenged, and so on. These people are high in "growth-need strength."

Figure 2 shows diagrammatically the proposition that individual growth needs have the power to moderate the relationship between the characteristics of jobs and work outcomes. Many workers with high growth needs will turn on eagerly when they have jobs that are high in the core dimensions. Workers whose growth needs are not so strong may respond less eagerly—or, at first, even balk at being "pushed" or "stretched" too far.

Psychologists who emphasize human potential argue that everyone has within him at least a spark of the need to grow and develop personally. Steadily accumulating evidence shows, however, that unless that spark is pretty strong, chances are it will get snuffed out by one's exper-

iences in typical organizations. So, a person who has worked for twenty years in stultifying jobs may find it difficult or impossible to become internally motivated overnight when given the opportunity.

We should be cautious, however, about creating rigid categories of people based on their measured growth-need strength at any particular time. It is true that we can predict from these measures who is likely to become internally motivated on a job and who will be less willing or able to do so. But what we do not know yet is whether or not the growth-need "spark" can be rekindled for those individuals who have had their growth needs dampened by years of growth-depressing experience in their organizations.

Since it is often the organization that is responsible for currently low levels of growth desires, we believe that the organization also should provide the individual with the chance to reverse that trend whenever possible, even if that means putting a person in a job where he may be "stretched" more than he wants to be. He can always move back to the old job—and in the meantime the embers of his growth needs just might burst back into flame, to his surprise and pleasure, and for the good of the organization.

FIGURE 2 The Moderating Effect of Employee Growth-Need Strength

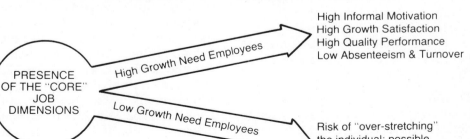

FROM THEORY TO PRACTICE: A TECHNOLOGY FOR JOB ENRICHMENT

When job enrichment fails, it often fails because of inadequate *diagnosis* of the target job and employees' reactions to it. Often, for example, job enrichment is assumed by management to be a solution to "people problems" on the job and is implemented even though there has been no diagnostic activity to indicate that the root of the problem is in fact how the work is designed. At other times, some diagnosis is made—but it provides no concrete guidance about what specific aspects of the job require change. In either case, the success of job enrichment may wind up depending more on the quality of the intuition of the change agent—or his luck—than on a solid base of data about the people and the work.

In the paragraphs to follow, we outline a new technology for use in job enrichment which explicitly addresses the diagnostic as well as the action components of the change process. The technology has two parts: (1) a set of diagnostic tools that are useful in evaluating jobs and people's reactions to them prior to change—and in pinpointing exactly what aspects of specific jobs are most critical to a successful change attempt; and (2) a set of "implementing concepts" that provide concrete guidance for action steps in job enrichment. The implementing concepts are tied directly to the diagnostic tools; the output of the diagnostic activity specifies which action steps are likely to have the most impact in a particular situation.

The Diagnostic Tools.   Central to the diagnostic procedure we propose is a package of instruments to be used by employees, supervisors, and outside observers in assessing the target job and employees' reactions to it. (Hackman and Oldham 1975). These instruments gauge the following:

1. The objective characteristics of the jobs themselves, including both an overall indication of the "motivating potential" of the job as it exists (that is, the MPS score) and the score of the job on each of the five core dimensions described previously. Because knowing the strengths and weaknesses of the job is critical to any work redesign effort, assessments of the job are made by supervisors and outside observers as well as the employees themselves—and the final assessment of a job uses data from all three sources.

2. The current levels of motivation, satisfaction, and work performance of employees on the job. In addition to satisfaction with the work itself, measures are taken of how people feel about other aspects of the work setting, such as pay, supervision, and relationships with co-workers.

3. The level of growth-need strength of the employees. As indicated earlier, employees who have strong growth needs are more likely to be more responsive to job enrichment than employees with weak growth needs. Therefore, it is important to know at the outset just what kinds of satisfactions the people who do the job are (and are not) motivated to obtain from their work. This will make it possible to identify which persons are best to start changes with, and which may need help in adapting to the newly enriched job.

What, then, might be the actual steps one would take in carrying out a job diagnosis using these tools? Although the approach to any particular diagnosis depends upon the specifics of the particular work situation involved, the sequence of questions listed below is fairly typical.

• *Step 1.   Are motivation and satisfaction central to the problem?* Sometimes organizations undertake job enrichment to improve the work motivation and satis-faction of employees when in fact the real problem with work performance lies else-where—for example, in a poorly designed production system, in an error-prone computer, and so on. The first step is to examine the scores of employees on the motivation and satisfaction portions of the diagnostic instrument. (The question-naire taken by employees is called the Job Diagnostic Survey and will be referred to hereafter as the JDS.) If motivation and satisfaction are problematic, the change agent would continue to Step 2; if not, he would look to other aspects of the work situation to identify the real problem.

• *Step 2. Is the job low in motivating potential?* To answer this question, one would examine the motivating potential score of the target job and compare it to the MPS's of other jobs to determine whether or not *the job itself* is a probable cause of the motivational problems docu-mented in Step 1. If the job turns out to be low on the MPS, one would continue to Step 3: if it scores high, attention should be given to other possible reasons for the motivational difficulties (such as the pay system, the nature of supervision, and so on).

• *Step 3. What specific aspects of the job are causing the difficulty?* This step in-volves examining the job on each of the five core dimensions to pinpoint the spe-cific strengths and weaknesses of the job as it is currently structured. It is useful at this stage to construct a "profile" of the target job, to make visually apparent where improvements need to be made. An illustrative profile for two jobs (one "good" job and one job needing improve-ment) is shown in Figure 3.

Job A is an engineering maintenance job and is high on all of the core dimen-sions; the MPS of this job is a very high 260. (MPS scores can range from 1 to about 350; an "average" score would be about 125.) Job enrichment would not be recommended for this job; if employees working on the job were unproductive and unhappy, the reasons are likely to have little to do with the nature or design of the work itself.

Job B, on the other hand, has many problems. This job involves the routine and repetitive processing of checks in the "back room" of a bank. The MPS is 30, which is quite low—and indeed, would be even lower if it were not for the moderate-ly high task significance of the job. (Task significance is moderately high because the people are handling large amounts of other people's money, and therefore the quality of their efforts has potentially im-portant consequences for their unseen cli-ents.) The job provides the individuals with very little direct feedback about how effectively they are doing it; the employ-ees have little autonomy in how they go about doing the job; and the job is moder-ately low in both skill variety and task identity.

For Job B, then, there is plenty of room for improvement—and many avenues to examine in planning job changes. For still other jobs, the avenues for change often turn out to be considerably more specific: for example, feedback and autonomy may be reasonably high, but one or more of the core dimensions that contribute to the experienced meaningfulness of the job (skill variety, task identity, and task sig-nificance) may be low. In such a case, at-tention would turn to ways to increase the standing of the job on these latter three dimensions.

• *Step 4. How "ready" are the employ-ees for change?* Once it has been docu-mented that there is need for improve-ment in the job—and the particularly troublesome aspects of the job have been identified—then it is time to begin to think about the specific action steps which will be taken to enrich the job. An important factor in such planning is the level of growth needs of the employees, since employees high on growth needs

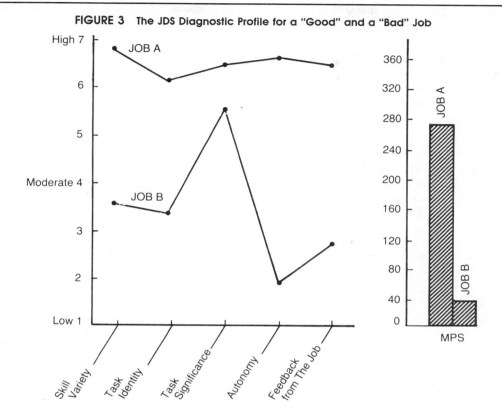

FIGURE 3 The JDS Diagnostic Profile for a "Good" and a "Bad" Job

usually respond more readily to job enrichment than do employees with little need for growth. The JDS provides a direct measure of the growth-need strength of the employees. This measure can be very helpful in planning how to introduce the changes to the people (for instance, cautiously versus dramatically), and in deciding who should be among the first group of employees to have their jobs changed.

In actual use of the diagnostic package, additional information is generated which supplements and expands the basic diagnostic questions outlined above. The point of the above discussion is merely to indicate the kinds of questions which we believe to be most important in diagnosing a job prior to changing it. We now turn to how the diagnostic conclusions are translated into specific job changes.

The Implementing Concepts. Five "implementing concepts" for job enrichment are identified and discussed below. (Walters and Associates 1975). Each one is a specific action step aimed at improving both the quality of the working experience for the individual and his work productivity. They are: (1) forming natural work units, (2) combining tasks, (3) establishing client relationships, (4) vertical loading, (5) opening feedback channels.

The links between the implementing concepts and the core dimensions are shown in Figure 4—which illustrates our theory of job enrichment, ranging from the concrete action steps through the core dimensions and the psychological states to the actual personal and work outcomes.

After completing the diagnosis of a job, a change agent would know which of the core dimensions were most in need of remedial attention. He could then turn to Figure 4 and select those implementing concepts that specifically deal with the most troublesome parts of the existing job. How this would take place in practice will be seen below.

• Forming natural work units. The notion of distributing work in some logical way may seem to be an obvious part of the design of any job. In many cases, however, the logic is one imposed by just about any consideration except jobholder satisfaction and motivation. Such considerations include technological dictates, level of worker training or experience,

"efficiency" as defined by industrial engineering, and current workload. In many cases the cluster of tasks a worker faces during a typical day or week is natural to anyone *but* the worker.

For example, suppose that a typing pool (consisting of one supervisor and ten typists) handles all work for one division of a company. Jobs are delivered in rough draft or dictated form to the supervisor, who distributes them as evenly as possible among the typists. In such circumstances the individual letters, reports, and other tasks performed by a given typist in one day or week are randomly assigned. There is no basis for identifying with the work or the person or department for whom it is performed, or for placing any personal value upon it.

The principle underlying natural units of work, by contrast, is "ownership"—a worker's sense of continuing responsibility for an identifiable body of work. Two steps are involved in creating natural

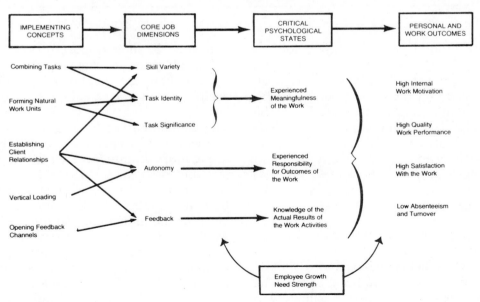

FIGURE 4   The Full Model: How Use of the Implementing Concepts Can Lead to Positive Outcomes

work units. The first is to identify the basic work items. In the typing pool, for example, the items might be "pages to be typed." The second step is to group the items in natural categories. For example, each typist might be assigned continuing responsibility for all jobs requested by one or several specific departments. The assignments should be made, of course, in such a way that workloads are about equal in the long run. (For example, one typist might end up with all the work from one busy department, while another handles jobs from several smaller units.)

At this point we can begin to see specifically how the job-design principles relate to the core dimensions (cf. Figure 4). The ownership fostered by natural units of work can make the difference between a feeling that work is meaningful and rewarding and the feeling that it is irrelevant and boring. As the diagram shows, natural units of work are directly related to two of the core dimensions: task identity and task significance.

A typist whose work is assigned naturally rather than randomly—say, by departments—has a much greater chance of performing a whole job to completion. Instead of typing one section of a large report, the individual is likely to type the whole thing, with knowledge of exactly what the product of the work is (task identity). Furthermore, over time the typist will develop a growing sense of how the work affects co-workers in the department serviced (task significance).

• Combining tasks. The very existence of a pool made up entirely of persons whose sole function is typing reflects a fractionalization of jobs that has been a basic precept of "scientific management." Most obvious in assembly-line work, fractionalization has been applied to non-manufacturing jobs as well. It is typically justified by efficiency, which is usually defined in terms of either low costs or some time-and-motion type of criteria.

It is hard to find fault with measuring efficiency ultimately in terms of cost-effectiveness. In doing so, however, a manager should be sure to consider all the costs involved. It is possible, for example, for highly fractionalized jobs to meet all the time-and-motion criteria of efficiency, but if the resulting job is so unrewarding that performing it day after day leads to high turnover, absenteeism, drugs and alcohol, and strikes, then productivity is really lower (and costs higher) than data on efficiency might indicate.

The principle of combining tasks, then, suggests that whenever possible existing and fractionalized tasks should be put together to form new and larger modules of work. At the Medfield, Massachusetts plant of Corning Glass Works the assembly of a laboratory hot plate has been redesigned along the lines suggested here. Each hot plate now is assembled from start to finish by one operator, instead of going through several separate operations that are performed by different people.

Some tasks, if combined into a meaningfully large module of work, would be more than an individual could do by himself. In such cases, it is often useful to consider assigning the new, larger task to a small *team* of workers—who are given great autonomy for its completion. At the Racine, Wisconsin plant of Emerson Electric, the assembly process for trash disposal appliances was restructured this way. Instead of a sequence of moving the appliance from station to station, the assembly now is done from start to finish by one team. Such teams include both men and women to permit switching off the heavier and more delicate aspects of the work. The team responsible is identified on the appliance. In case of customer complaints, the team often drafts the reply.

As a job-design principle, task combination, like natural units of work, expands the task identity of the job. For example, the hot plate assembler can see and identify with a finished product ready for shipment, rather than a nearly invisible junction of solder. Moreover, the more tasks that are combined into a single worker's job, the greater the variety of skills he must call on in performing the job. So task combination also leads to greater skill variety—the third core dimension that contributes to the overall experienced meaningfulness of the work.

• Establishing client relationships. One consequence of fractionalization is that the typical worker has little or no contact with (or even awareness of) the ultimate use of his product or service. By encouraging and enabling employees to establish direct relationships with the clients of their work, improvements often can be realized simultaneously on three of the core dimensions. Feedback increases, because of additional opportunities for the individual to receive praise or criticism of his work output directly. Skill variety often increases, because of the necessity to develop and exercise one's interpersonal skills in maintaining the client relationship. And autonomy can increase because the individual often is given personal responsibility for deciding how to manage his relationships with the clients of his work.

Creating client relationships is a three-step process. First, the client must be identified. Second, the most direct contact possible between the worker and the client must be established. Third, criteria must be set up by which the client can judge the quality of the product or service he receives. And whenever possible, the client should have a means of relaying his judgments directly back to the worker.

The contact between worker and client should be as great as possible and as frequent as necessary. Face-to-face contact is highly desirable, at least occasionally. Where that is impossible or impractical, telephone and mail can suffice. In any case, it is important that the performance criteria by which the worker will be rated by the client must be mutually understood and agreed upon.

• Vertical loading. Typically the split between the "doing" of a job and the "planning" and "controlling" of the work has evolved along with horizontal fractionalization. Its rationale, once again, has been "efficiency through specialization." And once again, the excess of specialization that has emerged has resulted in unexpected but significant costs in motivation, morale, and work quality. In vertical loading, the intent is to partially close the gap between the doing and the controlling parts of the job—and thereby reap some important motivational advantages.

Of all the job-design principles, vertical loading may be the single most crucial one. In some cases, where it has been impossible to implement any other changes, vertical loading alone has had significant motivational effects.

When a job is vertically loaded, responsibilities and controls that formerly were reserved for higher levels of management are added to the job. There are many ways to accomplish this:

• Return to the jobholder greater discretion in setting schedules, deciding on work methods, checking on quality, and advising or helping to train less experienced workers.

• Grant additional authority. The objective should be to advance workers from a position of no authority or highly restricted authority to positions of reviewed, and eventually, near-total authority for their own work.

• Time management. The jobholder should have the greatest possible freedom to decide when to start and stop work, when to break, and how to assign priorities.

• Troubleshooting and crisis decisions. Workers should be encouraged to seek problem solutions on their own, rather than calling immediately for the supervisor.

• Financial controls. Some degree of knowledge and control over budgets and other financial aspects of a job can often be highly motivating. However, access to this information frequently tends to be restricted. Workers can benefit from knowing something about the costs of their jobs, the potential effect upon profit, and various financial and budgetary alternatives.

When a job is vertically loaded it will inevitably increase in *autonomy*. And as shown in Figure 4, this increase in objective personal control over the work will also lead to an increased feeling of personal responsibility for the work, and ultimately to higher internal work motivation.

• Opening feedback channels. In virtually all jobs there are ways to open channels of feedback to individuals or teams to help them learn whether their performance is improving, deteriorating, or remaining at a constant level. While there are numerous channels through which information about performance can be provided, it generally is better for a worker to learn about his performances *directly as he does his job*—rather than from management on an occasional basis.

Job-provided feedback usually is more immediate and private than supervisor-supplied feedback, and it increases the worker's feelings of personal control over his work in the bargain. Moreover, it avoids many of the potentially disruptive interpersonal problems that can develop when the only way a worker has to find out how he is doing is through direct messages or subtle cues from his boss.

Exactly what should be done to open channels for job-provided feedback will vary from job to job and organization to organization. Yet in many cases the changes involve simply removing existing blocks that isolate the worker from naturally occuring data about performance—rather than generating entirely new feedback mechanisms. For example:

• Establishing direct client relationships often removes blocks between the worker and natural external sources of data about his work.

• Quality control efforts in many organizations often eliminate a natural source of feedback. The quality check on a product or service is done by a person other than those responsible for the work. Feedback to the workers—if there is any—is belated and diluted. It often fosters a tendency to think of quality as "someone else's concern." By placing control close to the worker (perhaps even in his own hands), the quantity and quality of data about performance available to him can dramatically increase.

• Tradition and established procedure in many organizations dictate that records about performance be kept by a supervisor and transmitted up (not down) in the organizational hierarchy. Sometimes supervisors even check the work and correct any errors themselves. The worker who made the error never knows it occurred—and is denied the very information that could enhance both his internal work motivation and the technical adequacy of his performance. In many cases it is possible to provide standard summaries of performance records directly to the worker (as well as to his superior), thereby giving him personally and regularly the data he needs to improve his performance.

• Computers and other automated operations sometimes can be used to provide the individual with data now blocked from him. Many clerical operations, for example, are now performed on computer consoles. These consoles often can be programmed to provide the clerk with immediate feedback in the form of a CRT display or a printout indicating that an error has been made. Some systems even have been programmed to provide the operator with a positive feedback message when a period of error-free performance has been sustained.

Many organizations simply have not recognized the importance of feedback as a motivator. Data on quality and other aspects of performance are viewed as being of interest only to management. Worse still, the *standards* for acceptable performance often are kept from workers as well. As a result, workers who would be interested in following the daily or weekly ups and downs of their performance, and in trying accordingly to improve, are deprived of the very guidelines they need to do so. They are like the golfer we mentioned earlier, whose efforts to correct his hook are stopped dead by fog over the driving range.

CONCLUSIONS

In this article we have presented a new strategy for the redesign of work in general and for job enrichment in particular. The approach has four main characteristics:

1. It is grounded in a basic psychological theory of what motivates people in their work.
2. It emphasizes that planning for job changes should be done on the basis of *data* about the jobs and the people who do them—and a set of diagnostic instruments is provided to collect such data.
3. It provides a set of specific implementing concepts to guide actual job changes, as well as a set of theory-based rules for selecting *which* action steps are likely to be most beneficial in a given situation.
4. The strategy is buttressed by a set of findings showing that the theory holds water, that the diagnostic procedures are practical and informative,

and that the implementing concepts can lead to changes that are beneficial both to organizations and to the people who work in them.

We believe that job enrichment is moving beyond the stage where it can be considered "yet another management fad." Instead, it represents a potentially powerful strategy for change that can help organizations achieve their goals for higher quality work—and at the same time further the equally legitimate needs of contempory employees for a more meaningful work experience. Yet there are pressing questions about job enrichment and its use that remain to be answered.

Prominent among these is the question of employee participation in planning and implementing work redesign. The diagnostic tools and implementing concepts we have presented are neither designed nor intended for use only by management. Rather, our belief is that the effectiveness of job enrichment is likely to be enhanced when the tasks of diagnosing and changing jobs are undertaken *collaboratively* by management and by the employees whose work will be affected.

Moreover, the effects of work redesign on the broader organization remain generally uncharted. Evidence now is accumulating that when jobs are changed, turbulence can appear in the surrounding organization—for example, in supervisory-subordinate relationships, in pay and benefit plans, and so on. Such turbulence can be viewed by management either as a problem with job enrichment, or as an opportunity for further and broader organizational development by teams of managers and employees. To the degree that management takes the latter view, we believe, the oft-espoused goal of achieving basic organizational change through the redesign of work may come increasingly within reach.

The diagnostic tools and implementing concepts we have presented are useful in deciding on and designing basic changes in the jobs themselves. They do not address the broader issues of who plans the changes, how they are carried out, and how they are followed up. The way these broader questions are dealt with, we believe, may determine whether job enrichment will grow up—or whether it will die an early and unfortunate death, like so many other fledgling behavioral science approaches to organizational change.

A Big Winner, in Two Leagues

NANCY J. PERRY

When the Amazin' Mets won the 1986 World Series, sweeping New York into a frenzy, one Very Important Person remained curiously out of sight. Nelson Doubleday, chairman of Doubleday & Co., which bought the Mets six years ago when they were down and almost out, did not appear in the locker room after the game, wasn't on hand to accept the World Series trophy from Baseball Commissioner Peter Ueberroth. He did not even attend the ticker tape parade thronged by two million ecstatic New Yorkers, held to honor the town's newest heroes. There was *no way*, he said later, that he wanted all that public attention. If, as New York Yankees owner George Steinbrenner insists, "every single owner of a major league franchise has an ego," well, somebody forgot to inform Doubleday.

He bought the team, he says, to provide entertainment for New York; he has no desire to see his name in lights. Sure, he intends to make money with the Mets, but more than the typical entrepreneur Doubleday wants to have fun, to "give somebody some fun they otherwise couldn't have had."

It is Wednesday, the day following the fete on Wall Street, and the publicity-shy Doubleday is sitting hunched forward on a sofa in his sunny Park Avenue office, struggling to describe how he felt when the Mets clinched the championship. It is tough for him; self-revelations do not come easy to this intensely private, emotional man. "The thing I never realized during the last two weeks," he finally says, "was the involvement of the city of New York. I think I was involved with the Mets and with winning, but . . ." His voice quavers and he breaks off, unable to continue. Tears glisten in his eyes, trickle down his cheeks. "I had no *concept*," he whispers after a moment. "I really had no concept of just how much this meant to a lot of people." He brushes the tears from his face, embarrassed, but they keep coming. "I guess I surprise myself when I do something right," he says.

It has been an amazing year for Nelson Doubleday. In a play as dramatic as Ray Knight's winning World Series home run, he agreed in September to sell Doubleday & Co., the family-owned publishing business founded in 1897 by his grandfather, to Bertelsmann AG, a West German communications conglomerate. The price: a lofty $500 million. Friends say that Doubleday agonized over the decision for months—long after directors began urging him to sell. "I think he felt a tremendous loyalty to his family name," says Peter Shea, a Doubleday director and Nelson's close friend since childhood. "There was a lot of soul-searching."

In August, prompted in part by pending tax law changes, Doubleday asked for bids on the business, of which he and his family control over 51%. Bertelsmann, eager to expand its presence in the U.S., made an offer. The deal surprised analysts. For almost a decade Doubleday's publishing operations have been in trouble and the company's overall performance has been poor. In the fiscal year that ended April 30, Doubleday & Co. earned only $7 million on sales of $472 million, and $5 million of that came from the Mets.

The Mets, however, were not included in the sale. In a separate transaction, Doubleday and Fred Wilpon, a real estate investor who already owned 2.5% of the team, arranged to pay $85 million to buy the Mets from Doubleday & Co. before it was sold to Bertelsmann. The two men, who will be equal partners, assumed some $15 million in player contracts and other liabilities, bringing the total value of the franchise to $100 million. That is the highest price ever paid for a sports franchise, and five times what it cost in 1980 when Doubleday & Co. bought it.

At the moment it is hard to tell whether the publishing-cum-sports magnate is more elated about his multimillion-dollar deal, the Mets' World Series victory, or an upcoming hunting trip with his buddies. Tall and robust, Doubleday, 53, is a fine Scotch blend: two parts Locust Valley, Long Island, WASP—pampered, patrician, and exceedingly preppie—and one part earthy Scot, with deep voice, hearty chuckle, bawdy humor. A man's man. He likes people, parties, practical jokes, and, it appears, ducks. Paintings of wild ducks decorate his office walls, rows of bright yellow ducks swim across his navy-blue necktie; he and his wife, Sandra, own a rambling house on Duck Pond Road. He also shoots ducks—but those don't count, he quips, because they are "dead ducks."

Preparing to embark on an annual pheasant-shooting vacation in Somerset, England, with a bunch of pals, Doubleday is in his usual ebullient spirits, playfully deflecting sound away from the reporter's tape recorder with an ashtray—"It's a satellite dish"—and making wisecracks: "I shoot anything that moves. Reporters, anything." Characteristically flippant, he is only half kidding. Nelson Doubleday does not encroach on other people's territory (he *never* visits the Mets dugout), and he expects the same in return. Tread too close, push too far, ask for instance if you might chat with his wife or daughters, and his mood changes. He becomes brusque, dismissive; you-be-damned.

He is understandably delighted to talk about the Mets. Six years ago, he says, everybody thought he was crazy to pay $21 million for a team that had finished last in the National League's Eastern Division for three seasons in a row and was losing money. Friends laughed. Some Doubleday directors questioned his judgment. Worst of all, the Cuckoo Convoy thought he was nuts. Back then Doubleday was in a group of citizens' band radio freaks who met over the airwaves on their daily commute into Manhattan. A diverse group ranging from a maintenance man to a phone booth manufacturer to a big-time book publisher, they nicknamed themselves the Cuckoo's Nest Convoy. Doubleday's on-air name was the Bookworm. For five years, before CBs gave way to cellular car phones, he and his good buddies met to kibitz, talk sports, and tell jokes. He invited them to lunch at "21," greeted them at Shea Stadium by flashing "Welcome Cuckoos" on the scoreboard, and chattered with them nonstop on the CB. "It seemed a hideaway for him," says Miles Godin, an advertising executive known to CBers as Magic Pencil. "At Doubleday everyone did things because he was Doubleday. But with us he was just the Bookworm."

The day after he bought the Mets, Doubleday stopped as he did every morning for coffee with the Cuckoos at the McDonald's on Astoria Boulevard in Queens. "What are you buying a crummy team like the Mets for?" they razzed him over Egg McMuffins. His reply was prophetic. "Just you wait," he retorted. "Give me five or six years, and they will be a first-place team." He might have added that they would also begin to coin cash. Attendance at Shea Stadium surged to three million in 1986, up from a low of 700,000 in 1980. Between May and October the Mets earned over $6 million.

Doubleday's interest in sports dates back to his early days in Oyster Bay, an exclusive Long Island suburb where he and his younger sister, Neltje, grew up. "We were two rich kids sitting in a big house with lots of nannies and maids," recalls Neltje, now a painter on a ranch in Banner, Wyoming. "We lived a very isolated life." So the youngsters looked to each other for amusement. Says Neltje: "I learned to play baseball pretty young." (Their great-great-granduncle Abner popularized baseball but did not invent it, as widely believed.) Friends claim to still have ribbons from the "Nelson and Neltje Field Day" that Nelson organized every year on his birthday.

The dollar scion went on to attend Deerfield Academy in Massachusetts and Princeton University, where he majored in economics. He excelled in club sports, particularly football, baseball, and hockey. But he was always mindful of his destiny. His father, Nelson Sr., had died of lung cancer when Nelson was only 15, and so, he says, "I was always aimed at

publishing. And I'd always said to my mother, 'Look, I reserve the right not to go into it. But I'll go into it until I say, Hey—enough. I don't like it.'"

After graduating from college in 1955, he worked briefly as a copywriter at Doubleday, then left to serve three years in the U.S. Air Force, where he found his penchant for pranks squelched by "something called a commanding officer." Despite urgings from his superiors to make the Air Force a career. Doubleday returned to publishing in 1959, this time for good. He started as an editorial assistant in the advertising and promotion department. Two years later, at 28, he became manager of Doubleday's trade publishing division and joined the board of directors. In the Sixties and Seventies he also invested in a couple of pro hockey teams, the Oakland Seals and the New York Islanders. In 1978 he took over as president. Doubleday admits that his own rapid rise "had something to do with my last name." In 1985 he was elected chairman of the board.

He insists that he was never bored with his job. But he certainly was not fascinated by it, which partly explains the publishing operations' poor performance. Some people think that had there been two brothers Doubleday would have been content to take his inheritance and run—preferably to the nearest ballpark. "There is an axiom in this field: You go into it because you love books," says Scott Meredith, a top literary agent who worked with Doubleday's father. "Nelson is a smart man. But he never had the passion."

It is not that Doubleday dislikes books, just that his passion for living does not necessarily extend to selling them. Below the surface is a part of Doubleday that is still a kid, that just wants to have fun, to be one of the boys. Hence the pranks, the sports teams, the Cuckoos. He gets a bang out of sending farm animals to his friends at Brown Brothers Harriman, the staid brokerage—chickens, for instance, or a crate full of squealing piglets. Says Tom Guinzburg, former president of Viking Press and an old friend: "Trapped inside that large body there are another couple of people."

The Rise and Fall of an Insider

STEVEN BRILL

This is the exclusive account of the seduction, corruption and destruction of a brilliant young lawyer who got trapped in Wall Street's biggest scandal. Here is how, and why, a rising star in a pre-eminent law firm let a crooked operator talk him into leaking trading tips on multimillion-dollar takeover deals. What happened to Ilan Reich—who went from law school to full partnership in his firm to the federal dock in seven years—may serve, he hopes, as a lesson to other young professionals in the world of law and finance who suddenly find unimaginable riches at their fingertips.

Ilan Reich insisted that Dennis Levine meet him in Central Park that Saturday morning. He didn't want to risk being overheard. So they met in front of the Plaza Hotel, walked into the park, and then stopped and sat on a bench. And on March 22, 1980, in this very public place chosen for a very private conversation, Ilan Reich, just 10 months out of law school and six months into what was to be a meteoric career at Wachtell, Lipton, Rosen & Katz, said he still had mixed feelings but that, yes, yes, he would do it. Yes, he would tip Levine to deals being done at Wachtell.

Levine, smiling his winning smile, assured his young friend once again that the scheme was foolproof. He told Reich that he'd start him out with $20,000 in a trading account that Levine would use on Reich's behalf to trade on Reich's tips in

concert with Levine's larger trades. As the scheme prospered, the young associate could draw cash from his "account."

Four years and six months later, on the morning of July 14, 1986, Ilan Reich, a 31–year–old, $500,000–a–year partner at Wachtell, Lipton, was sitting with his feet propped on his desk. He was savoring his latest master stroke in a poison-pill defense of a takeover fight when he got the call that signaled the end. He had never taken a cent from Dennis Levine, who had gone on to become a managing director at Drexel Burnham Lambert, and he had long since dropped out of Levine's trading scheme. There had never been a scrap of paper with his name on it. He had never told anyone about what he'd done, not even his wife. It was, he says, a "skeleton in my closet that I thought had long since gone away, as if it had never happened."

Reich had first met Levine in October

of 1979. Reich was 25 years old, and the deal, a friendly merger of two large cement companies, was the second he'd worked on at the firm. He remembers coming into a conference room and seeing a pin-striped man about his age standing off in a corner chatting easily with several other, older people. It was an amiability that came easily to Dennis Levine, then a 27–year–old banker with Smith Barney, Harris Upham.

SOMETHING OF A LONER

Reich was impressed that Levine, though apparently so young, was dressed so investment-banker rich and seemed to fit in so well. It was something Reich—who had thought of himself as something of a loner at Columbia Law School and who still didn't know more than a few lawyers at his own firm—instantly envied. In what now seems to have been a pattern Levine followed in the relationships he would build with the three other young professionals whom he recruited as tipsters in his elaborate and now infamous insider-trading scheme, Levine and Reich became fast friends, with Levine doing the courting.

Their first 2–hour lunch led to another, then another and another. Until, at the fourth or fifth lunch in early March of 1980, Levine popped the question. As Reich recalls, Levine began by saying that as much as he loved his work, he was sick and tired of being an adviser and not a principal in these deals. Within a few years, he said, he wanted to have $10 million or $20 million so he, too, could be a player. He'd be independent. He'd hire lawyers and bankers, not be one. He'd be bigger than the arbs.

Reich laughed and asked how Levine intended to do that. On cue, Levine spelled out his scheme. Using information he got on deals that were about to pop and working through an elaborate network of untraceable foreign accounts, he'd make

millions trading stock in companies soon to be acquired. That's illegal, Reich said. And, besides, it leaves a paper trail. You're bound to get caught.

Everybody does it, Levine countered, especially the arbs. They're in *the business* of doing it, he added, and no one bothers them. So why couldn't he join them? Why should we—that's the pronoun he used—have to sit by while so many other guys not nearly as smart get so much richer? The key to not getting caught would be to get information early enough so that he could trade weeks, rather than days, before a deal. Then the SEC wouldn't suspect anything. Besides, he'd figured out how to do the trading overseas so that it would be completely untraceable. In five years, Levine concluded, he'd have his $10 million to $20 million. (The SEC charges against Levine would later spell out $12.6 million in profits that he had made by early 1986.)

Then came the question. Levine was going to need help, and he'd already recruited a banker or two at key firms. He needed a lawyer at a firm like Wachtell, which was in on so many of the deals he'd want to know about. Did Reich want to come in on it? Reich did not then bolt from the table, and shrinks and cops and Reich himself can forever debate why. Reich says now that he was in a fog that day, stemming from deep-seated emotional problems that he is beginning to appreciate only now that he's in psychotherapy. He says that these problems, the attraction of a friendship with Levine and, yes, the money—although he wasn't then or later ever any kind of high liver—all played a role.

His first response was that he was so low on the totem pole at Wachtell that he doubted he could give Levine anything of value. Levine shrugged that off. The whole point of his plan, he said, was to gather several pretty good sources—not necessarily one sure-fire source whom the SEC could catch—and pool their information, just the way the arbs did. Levine stressed that Reich's involvement would be secret and that there'd never be any paper work because the trading accounts, shielded anyway in foreign accounts, would all be in Levine's name. So that Saturday morning, Reich, as he puts it, "crossed the line, never to be able to take that moment back." He said he'd do it.

For the next two years, Reich would call Levine for lunch when he thought he had some information. If not, Levine would check in with him regularly. The foreplay in the restaurant would be small talk about families, deals and the mechanics and people behind deals. Then they'd go out into the street and walk. And Reich would pass the information. Reich says he felt "sick about myself" after each meeting.

By this time, as is now known from the SEC charges and the corresponding guilty pleas, Levine had recruited young bankers who would end up at Shearson Lehman Brothers, Goldman, Sachs & Company and Lazard Frères. Once, in early 1981, Levine invited Reich and his wife to brunch. Reich accepted until Levine responded enthusiastically by promising that Reich would have a chance there to meet some of the other people involved in the trading scheme. Reich said Levine had to be crazy, that Reich didn't want to know who they were (Levine had already told him about a source at Lazard), and he sure didn't want them to know who he was.

Early on, the results, at least according to what Reich says Levine told him, were mixed. The first few deals brought Reich's "account" from $20,000 up over $100,000. Reich never took any of the money, despite Levine's repeated offers. Reich says he still felt ambivalent or worse about what he was doing and that he didn't consider that he was really doing it all the way until he actually took some money. Besides, he wasn't sure what he'd do with the money anyway. But as the months

passed, Levine reported that some deals had turned sour and that the account had dropped back to about $40,000. Then the account went up again to about $100,000 in November, 1982. It was then, says Reich, that he pulled out of the scheme because he was "sick of the whole thing; I just didn't like myself." He told Levine he didn't want any of the money he'd already earned, either. In all, he had tipped on eight deals.

But he continued to see Levine for lunch, and in May, 1984, he got back in. Reich says he needed the money for personal and emotional problems. What he hesitates to say is that he thought his marriage was in trouble and that the extra money would be used for what he thought would be alimony and support for his baby son.

From May through August, 1984, Reich tipped Levine on four more deals, including the acquisitions of G.D. Searle & Company and SFN Companies—two deals on which Levine allegedly made more than $900,000. After the Searle tip, in late August, 1984, Reich got out again because, he says, the problem for which he needed the money had solved itself—his marriage was back on track—and because, again, he hated himself for what he was doing. By now, Reich's account with Levine was up over $300,000. But again, he told Levine to keep the money.

In November, 1984, Reich was told that he'd made partner, effective January 1. Tall, well dressed, good-looking despite prematurely grayed hair, and thoroughly charming to secretaries and CEO's alike, Reich was now a star of the legal world. The years from the summer of 1984 to the summer of 1986 were, says Reich, "about the two most pleasant years of my life.... Once I said no to Dennis the final time," he adds, "I assumed that the skeleton in my closet had gone away."

Reich continued to see Levine occasionally for lunch, but the two never talked about how the plot was faring. In

April, 1986, Reich and his wife went to Levine's Park Avenue apartment for brunch, the first time their families had socialized. Reich remembers Levine's remarking coyly that he was now doing so well as a managing director of Drexel Burnham that "it's enough to make an honest man out of me."

NAMING NAMES

Reich was talking to another investment banker on the phone at about 5 p.m. on May 12, 1986, when the banker asked if he'd heard the news about Dennis Levine that had come across the Dow Jones ticker that afternoon. What news? Reich asked. The SEC had sued Levine for $12.6 million for insider trading. Over the next four weeks, when he had time to himself to ponder the skeleton in the closet, Reich was nervous and depressed. There were now rumors on Wall Street and reports in the press that Levine was turning, naming names.

On a red-eye flight home from Los Angeles, Reich found what he calls an inner peace. Taking out a yellow legal pad, he wrote down all the facts arrayed against him and discovered that there were no "external facts," as he described them to himself. No documents. No money passing hands and, therefore, no bank deposits or expenditures beyond the ordinary. And no one in the information loop. It was just Levine's word against his. And that he could handle if it came to that. He knew he would prevail, or so he told himself.

The subpoena served on Wachtell, Lipton by the SEC in early July shattered all that. Broad gauged as it was (documents covering dozens of the firm's deals over the past six years were demanded), the partners assumed it was part of an SEC fishing expedition incited vaguely by the Levine case. Reich suspected otherwise. Still, he kept up the front, helping his partners gather material for the subpoena.

On Friday, July 11, SEC enforcement director Gary Lynch called one of Wachtell, Lipton's senior litigation partners and told him that the firm ought to get an outside lawyer to represent Reich separately. The Wachtell, Lipton lawyers demanded more specifics before they would agree to abandon a partner. Finally, Lynch (or perhaps another SEC staffer; memories are hazy on this point) blurted out that, as one participant puts it, "Reich is guilty as hell," whereupon he offered a specific list of 12 deals Levine had claimed to have traded on based on Reich's tips.

Reich recalls that he couldn't bear it when he heard that his partners wouldn't represent him because they no longer trusted him. He insisted that they talk about it, that he wanted to listen to anything they'd heard from the SEC or the prosecutors and that he'd respond to it.

For the better part of 2 hours, he denied everything, doodling furiously throughout. Perhaps Reich had just been indiscreet with the wily Levine, one of the partners suggested, hopefully, and he hadn't intentionally leaked to an insider trader. Reich, hunkering down, said he was sure he hadn't been indiscreet. Then someone said that the SEC claimed that one of Levine's other coconspirators had told the investigators that Levine had told him he had a tipster at Wachtell, Lipton. This was contemporaneous hearsay, one of the ex-prosecutors explained, and would, therefore, be admissible. Reich now was shaken. Suddenly, there was an external fact he hadn't counted on.

Reich started sobbing. Still, he denied everything. Levine had told the SEC that Reich had stopped in the fall of 1984, one of the partners noted. Wasn't that when Reich had become aware that he was going to get a partnership? And, conversely, hadn't he been afraid in the years before that that he wouldn't make it, which would make a plot with Levine a timely hedge against failure?

This line of questioning soon began to break Reich emotionally, for it led to a long discussion about which partners he'd not gotten along with. These same partners had stood by him in the last week, always assuming his innocence, he was told. Was he now betraying them? And was he betraying his friends at the firm? He'd never been good at making friends, Reich replied, sobbing. Even with his wife, although that relationship had improved dramatically in the last two years. But these people, his partners, had been his real friends, his first real friends. So, too, had Levine. Now his friends at the firm no longer trusted him, and Levine had squealed on him. It was, says one partner, "the most cathartic thing I had ever seen. The man just unraveled."

At about 9 p.m., carrying not even a briefcase, Reich left Wachtell, Lipton. Reich sat out on Long Island for the rest of the summer, explaining to his inquiring 4–year–old that he wasn't going to work any more because he was changing jobs.

SUFFER THE CONSEQUENCES

On October 9, Reich, his pregnant wife alternately clutching and patting his bicep as she sat next to him, waited in Federal District Judge Robert Sweet's courtroom. Reich's father sat on the other side. When the case was called, Reich approached the bench, buttoning his suit jacket, standing up straight, swaying a bit on his heels and pleaded guilty to two counts of fraud— each punishable by five years in prison. Afterward, Reich's lawyer distributed a statement in which Reich apologized and said he is ready "to suffer the consequences of my actions."

At the same time, the SEC released documents announcing that the commission had that morning sued Reich for fraud and that Reich had simultaneously settled the case by agreeing to pay $485,000 in cash and property to the government and to cooperate in the ongoing investigation.

Reich, of course, has little to offer the investigators. Unlike Levine, who subsequently traded up and turned in Ivan Boesky, Reich has no one to turn in. He knows nothing about the mechanics of Levine's scheme. And he never had any idea that Levine had teamed up with Boesky—a linkup that, according to SEC's charges, began at least six months after Reich dropped out of the scheme.

Reich's $485,000 disgorgement called for him to turn over all of his assets. The only exceptions are his modest West Side apartment, items in that home or the Long Island place worth less than $2,000, his Oldsmobile and $10,000 in cash. He agreed to sell the house on Long Island, to clean out his and his wife's savings and checking accounts, to cash in some tax shelters in which he had invested and to turn over $195,000 worth of capital accounts and retirement funds held at Wachtell, Lipton. All of that would go to the government. He also can never practice law again. The felony conviction means automatic disbarment in New York.

Reich faces up to 10 years, and at sentencing next January 23, Judge Sweet will have no easy time measuring how much, if any, of that time to give him. Sweet will have standing in front of him a man who, at 32, already talks about most of his life in the past tense. A man who'll be standing there in clothes he'll probably never be able to afford to replace. A man who has already shamed his proud family beyond anything imaginable and who, if it comes to that, will have no easy time explaining to his 4–year–old and his 2–year–old that he's going away. A man who has already gone from riches to near bankruptcy, from honor to humiliation, from the top of his career to no career at all— all for no money and for a criminal conspiracy that he walked away from on his own well before it reached its prime.

But he will also have standing in front of him a man who broke the only rule of his game that really counts—a man who betrayed his partners, his clients and his profession in the most fundamental way.

Whether he goes for four months or 18 months or not at all is almost beside the point of the larger tragedy here, which is that Reich may be emblematic of a dark side of the get-rich '80s, in which the best and brightest kids are thrown, thoroughly unready, into a world of everybody's-getting-rich megadeals.

Like children suddenly being told that their Monopoly money is real, they find that they have affluence, influence and opportunity so far beyond what they're used to that some overdose on it. And in a frenzy to get even richer faster, some, especially those with some weak underpinning in their emotional lives, fall—and not because they burn out physically from the supposedly brutal hours and high tension, but because their ethical compasses burn out. They lose their souls out there.*

* Author's note: It was Reich's strong preference that this article not be published until after he is sentenced on January 23. He said he did not want to use this story in any attempt to affect the judge's decision. I want to make it clear that I, not he, controlled the timing of publication. Reich agreed to these interviews, only after much persuasion, in hopes they might dramatize for other lawyers the onerous consequences of transgressions such as his.

Tear Down the Pyramids

PAUL H. THOMPSON

It's not unusual to hear managers comment on the difficulties they have managing their professional employees. The most visible evidence of this problem has been union activity. An increasing number of doctors, teachers, and engineers are walking picket lines and pressing for improvements in pay, hours, and working conditions. Membership in professional unions or associations involved in collective bargaining has increased dramatically in the last decade.

Much of that increase has been in the public sector. For example, last year the American Federation of Teachers claimed

Reprinted from *Exchange,* a publication of the Brigham Young University School of Management, 730 TNRB, Provo, Utah 84602.

450,000 members, four and one-half times their 1963 membership. Nearly 20 percent of the college and university professors on 420 campuses have been organized.

However, the private sector cannot afford to ignore these developments because there has been a high level of interest in unionization among scientists, engineers, and other professional employees. And this is not the only evidence of unrest among what Peter Drucker calls "knowledge workers." Research interviews with over 400 accountants, scientists, engineers, bank loan officers, and professors have indicated frequent disenchantment with professional employment.

"Engineering doesn't have the prestige

it once had. The glamour has worn off."

"I'd never let my son go into this field."

"My brother makes more money as a plumber than I do with a Ph.D."

MANAGING "KNOWLEDGE WORKERS"

We are not doing a very good job of managing our professional work force. Peter Drucker has written on our inadequate knowledge in managing this type of worker.

> We also do not know how to satisfy the knowledge worker and to enable him to gain the achievement he needs. Nor do we as yet fully understand the social and psychological needs of the knowledge worker.... We also do not know how to manage the knowledge worker so that he wants to contribute and perform. But we do know that he must be managed quite differently from the way we manage the manual worker. (*The Age of Discontinuity*, Harper and Row, 1968, pp. 287–288).

Organizations are having difficulty with their professional employees because firms tend to think of career growth only in terms of climbing the corporate ladder. With that concept, career development consists of moving as high and as fast as possible. Whether the ladder is called the hierarchy, organization chart, or pyramid, upward movement has become the symbol of corporate success.

However, this concept of career growth can be completely inappropriate for professional organizations. We need a new way to think about careers if professionals are going to be motivated and productive members of organizations. Yet the pyramid problem must be studied before we can develop workable alternatives.

WINNERS AND LOSERS

In the last 15 to 20 years almost all medium-to-large organizations have employed increasing numbers of professionals—accountants, engineers, lawyers, scientists, and the like. As the numbers in each of these specialties increased, it seemed only natural to create a hierarchy and appoint supervisors, managers, vice-presidents, and so forth. Since many of these specialists were bright and well educated, some of the most competent were promoted into the top management to help the organization cope with increasingly complex situations. No one would argue that these professionals should not be promoted into top management. But management went beyond just promoting some capable people; they designed a whole reward system that inadvertently gave the signal that professional contributions were valued—but only secondarily. The reward system encouraged all the brightest people to move out of their specialties and into the management ranks as fast as possible. Those who had been promoted into management were labeled *winners*, and those still performing the prime tasks of the organization were pegged *losers*. In these organizations it became extremely difficult for anyone to take pride in himself as a professional. Most power and status were given to the managers.

A recent article in *Business Week* advocates "career pathing" for those who want to "make something" of themselves. In describing "career pathing," the article gives some advice that illustrates the point very well:

> Get out of your specialty fast, unless you decide that's all you ever want to do. This means rapid rejection of the notion that you are a professional engineer, lawyer, scientist, or anything but a manager.

This advice makes it very difficult for a person to feel successful if he chooses to make a contribution in his specialty. But organizations do more than just imply that promotion means success and not being promoted means failure. They tie most of the important rewards to the hierarchy.

"MAHOGANY ROW"

Most pay systems are designed on the basis of a hierarchical system which emphasizes factors such as the number of people supervised. Before long, a chemist, who has the ability to develop a new product that may mean millions of dollars in profits, decides that he wants to become a manager because that's where the money is. The status symbols are also tied to the hierarchy. Most organizations make major distinctions between managers and nonmanagers—the accountants have desks in a large bull pen and their supervisor gets a large office on "Mahogany Row." Furthermore, for each promotion, the manager gets a larger office, more expensive furniture, and a parking space closer to the front door. These symbols don't go to those making significant contributions in nonmanagement areas. Such distinctions are often a real disincentive to individual contributors.

Managers are not deliberately trying to push all the best people out of professional work. They are aware that a chemical company needs top-notch chemists in the labs and an engineering company needs first-rate engineers at the drafting tables. If all the best professionals go into management, what will there be left to manage? The problem remains that managers and professionals alike have been locked into the concept of pyramid scaling. An alternative system is necessary.

INDIVIDUAL SPECIALISTS, MENTORS ...

Looking at careers of professionals, one becomes aware that many individuals remain high performers while others slip into mediocrity after age 35 or 40. Examination of these patterns makes it clear that the careers of professionals develop by stages. Each stage differs from the others in activities, relationships, and psychological adjustments. Moreover, successful performance at each stage is a prerequisite for moving on to the next. Individuals who continue to move through these stages retain their high performance ratings; those who do not move tend to be less valued by the organization. Four stages are identified in the accompanying box, with Stage I noted as the apprenticeship period. Here an individual works under relatively close supervision and direction. In addition, most highly successful professionals have an informal "mentor" at this time. Surprisingly, some people stay in this stage most of their careers and are never able to assume independent responsibility for their own work. However, that group represents a small minority. The majority of professionals make a successful transition into Stage II—the independent specialist.

A majority of professionals look forward to having their own project or area of responsibility. Earning this opportunity and taking advantage of it moves a person into Stage II. Most of the solid professional work in the organization is done by individuals in this category. About 40 percent of professionals are in Stage II. However, from an individual point of view, it is risky to remain in this stage because managers have rising expectations as a person's age and salary level increase. As a result those who remain in this stage after age 40 tend to receive lower performance ratings. Professionals who move into Stages III and IV are quite successful in avoiding that fate.

The last two stages are characterized by greater breadth of interest and activities and by involvement in the careers and development of others in the organization. The activities in Stages III and IV are highly valued in professional organizations, and people in these stages receive

Stage I

Works under the supervision and direction of a more senior professional in the field

Is never entrusted with work entirely his own but is given assignments which are a portion of larger project or activity being overseen by senior professional

Lacks experience and status in organization

Is expected to accept supervision and direction willingly

Is expected to do most of the detailed and routine work on a project

Is expected to exercise "directed" creativity and initiative

Learns to perform well under pressure and accomplish a task within the time budgeted

Stage II

Goes into depth in one problem or technical area

Assumes responsibility for a definable portion of the project, process, or clients

Works independently and produces significant results

Develops credibility and a reputation

Relies less on supervisor or mentor for answers, develops more of his own resources to solve problems

Increases in confidence and ability

Stage III

Involved enough in his own work to make significant technical contributions but begins working in more than one area

Greater breadth of technical skills and application of those skills

Stimulates others through ideas and information

Involved in developing people in one or more of the following ways:
a. acts as an idea man for a small group
b. serves as a mentor to younger professionals
c. assumes a formal supervisory position

Deals with the outside to benefit others in organizations, i.e., works and relationships with client organizations, developing new

business, etc.

Stage IV

Influences future direction of organization through:
a. original ideas, leading the organization into new areas of work
b. organizational leadership and policy formation
c. integrating the work of others to a significant end

Influence gained on the basis of:
a. past ability to assess environmental trends
b. ability to deal effectively with outside
c. ability to affect others inside the organization

Has the ability to engage in wide and varied interactions:
a. at all levels of the organization
b. with individuals and groups outside the organization

Involved in the development of future key people; a sponsor for promising people in other stages

---

high performance rankings. The following table presents the average performance rating for the four stages in one research organization that was studied.

Stage	Average performance ranking
I	17th percentile
II	34th percentile
III	65th percentile
IV	89th percentile

Some have commented that these stages are just descriptions of different levels of management and that all that has been done is to give the pyramid another name. Yet research does not support this observation. In an effort to better understand this concept, third-level managers in five organizations were asked to list each person in their departments in one of the four stages. We then compared the descriptions with current performance rankings. On the average, people in the later stages were rated higher than those in early stages, as the table indicates. But an analysis of proportion of managers and nonmanagers in each stage reveals some interesting results:

Stage	Proportion of nonmanagers
I	100 percent
II	100 percent
III	65 percent
IV	26 percent

It is true there are many managers in Stages III and IV, but those stages are by no means reserved exclusively for managers. In fact, a majority of the people in Stage III were individual contributors. This indicates that a *person can remain an individual contributor doing work primarily in his specialty and still be highly valued by the organization.* Unfortunately, the pyramid and associated reward system in many organizations make it difficult, if not impossible, for managers to show the individual contributors in Stages III and IV that they are highly valued. It becomes evident that major changes must be made if organizations are going to succeed in keeping competent professionals working hard at their professional work.

TOPPLING THE CORPORATE LADDER

In order to manage professionals effectively, executives need to tear down the pyramids. Instead of highlighting the corporate ladder and tying all rewards to promotion, that aspect of rewards needs to be substantially deemphasized. Some concrete recommendations may be helpful in meeting that objective.

Focus on Stages, Not Ladders

Promotion as an indicator of career growth has serious consequences for a professional organization, but very few managers and professionals have had satisfactory ways to evaluate careers. The concept of career stages is one alternative. This idea has been received positively when presented to both professionals and their managers. They seem almost relieved that there is an alternative way to examine careers. The four-stage system is a useful tool in seminars focusing on careers as well as on a one-to-one basis in performance appraisal and long-range planning sessions between professionals and their supervisors.

Reward Professional Contributions

If an organization is going to keep talented employees doing professional work, it must provide meaningful rewards to high-performing individual contributors. An individual should be paid for his performance and not for his position or the number of people he supervises. If an individual contributor is doing Stage IV work, he should be paid more than the manager doing Stage III work.

A critical incentive for an experienced professional is the confidence that he is influential in making important decisions. The manager who makes all decisions on the basis of the authority of his position has a stifling effect on the whole organization. Managers who make use of the expertise of individual contributors have found the practice pays off.

One reason promotion into management is an important sign of success is that it provides increased visibility, often in the form of status symbols such as a private office, reserved parking, and the like. The distinction between managers and nonmanagers in these areas is often counterproductive. If distinctions must be made, it would be better to use stages as a basis rather than managerial status.

The pyramid, or corporate hierarchy, may be a major cause of unrest and disenchantment in the ranks of professional employees in organizations. Many competent professionals want to make their contribution to the corporation in their area of speciality. If they can believe that such a contribution is valued and rewarded, they will remain highly productive. It will not be an easy task for managers to communicate this view to their professionals, but tearing down the pyramid is a step in the right direction.

On Wasting Time

JAMES A. MICHENER

We all worry about wasting time, about the years sliding past, about what we intend to do with our lives. We shouldn't. For there is a divine irrelevance in the universe that defies calculation. Many men and women win through to a sense of greatness in their lives only by first stumbling and fumbling their way into patterns that gratify them and allow them to utilize their endowments to the maximum.

If Swarthmore College in 1925 had employed even a halfway decent guidance counselor, I would have spent my life as an assistant professor of education in some Midwestern university. Because when I reported to college it must have been apparent to everyone that I was destined for some kind of academic career. Nevertheless, I was allowed to take Spanish, which leads to nothing, instead of French or German, which everyone knows are important languages studied by serious students who wish to gain a Ph.D.

I cannot tell you how often I was penalized for having taken a frivolous language like Spanish instead of a decent, self-respecting tongue like French. In fact, it led to the sacrifice of my academic career.

Still, I continued to putter around with Spanish, eventually finding a deep affinity for it. In the end, I was able to write a book about Spain which will probably live longer than anything else I've done. In other words, I blindly backed into a minor masterpiece. There are thousands of people competent to write about France, and if I had taken that language in college I would have been prepared to add no new ideas to general knowledge. It was Spanish that opened up for me a whole new universe of concepts and ideas.

Actually, I wrote nothing at all until I was 40. This tardy beginning, one might say delinquency, stemmed from the fact that I had spent a good deal of my early time knocking around the country and Europe, trying to find out what I believe in, what values were large enough to enlist my sympathies during what I sensed would be a long and confused life. Had I committed myself at age 18, as I was encouraged to do, I would not even have known the parameters of the problem, and any choice I might have made then would have had to be wrong.

It took me 40 years to find out the facts.

As a consequence, I have never been able to feel anxiety about young people who are fumbling their way toward the enlightenment that will keep them going. I doubt that a young man—unless he wants to be a doctor or a research chemist in which case a substantial body of specific knowledge must be mastered within a prescribed time—is really capable of wasting time, *regardless* of what he does. I believe you have until 35 to decide finally on what you are going to do, and that any exploration you pursue in the process will in the end turn out to have been creative.

Indeed, it may well be that the years observers describe as "wasted" will prove to have been the most productive of those insights which will keep you going. The trip to Egypt. The two years spent working as a runner for a bank. The spell you spent on the newspaper in Idaho. Your apprenticeship at a trade. These are the ways in which a young man ought to spend his life ... the ways of "waste" that lead to true knowledge.

Two more comments. First, I have recently decided that the constructive work of the world is done by an appallingly small percentage of the general population. The rest simply don't give a damn ... or they grow tired ... or they have failed to acquire when young the ideas that would vitalize them for the long decades.

I am not saying that such people don't matter. They are among the most precious items on earth. But they cannot be depended upon either to generate necessary new ideas or to put them into operation if someone else generates them. Therefore, those men and women who do have the energy to form new constructs and new ways to implement them just do the work of many. I believe it to be an honorable aspiration to want to be among those creators.

Second, I was about 40 when I retired from the rat race, having satisfied myself that I could handle it if I had to. I saw then that a man could count his life a success if he survived—merely survived—to age 70 without having ended up in jail (because he couldn't adjust to the minimum laws that society requires) or having landed in the booby hatch (because he could not bring his personality into harmony with the personalities of others).

I believe this now without question: income, position, the opinion of one's friends, the judgment of one's peers and all the other traditional criteria by which human beings are generally judged are for the birds. The only question is, "Can you hang on through the crap they throw at you and not lose your freedom or your good sense?"

I am now 67¾, and it looks as if I've made it. Whatever happens now is on the house ... and of no concern to me.

How to Make an Intelligent Decision

ROBERT L. HEILBRONER

There is nothing in the world so common and ordinary and yet so agonizingly difficult as a tough decision. Most of us have marched up to some crossroad in our lives—whether or not to get married, to change jobs, to choose this or that career—and experienced the awful feeling of not knowing which route to choose. Worse yet, many of us have known what it is like, after a paralyzing wait, to start down one road with the sinking sensation that we've picked the wrong one.

Ever since Adam and Eve made the wrong one, decisions have been bedeviling people. Damn-fool decisions and half-cocked decisions lie behind much of the unhappiness of life. More pathetic yet is the misery caused by no-decision. "Everything comes to him who waits," writes Bill Gibson, in *The Seesaw Log,* "—too late."

What makes us decide things badly, when we "know better?" What is it that sometimes stalls our decision-making machinery entirely? There is no single or simple reason why decisions are the pitfall of our lives. A high school senior who sits with his pencil wavering between the True and False answers on an examination may be baffled by the difficulty of the questions, or may simply be reduced to a blue funk by the pressure of taking an exam. A young woman in the throes of indecision over a marriage proposal may be trying to weigh the pros and cons of a

tangled life situation, or may be panicked by the thought of marriage itself. Foolish decisions and indecision are the consequence not only of the complexity of the world about us, but of the complicated crosscurrents of the world within us.

Whatever their causes, the agonies of decision making are often magnified because we go about making up our minds so ineffectively. Faced with a hard choice, we allow our thoughts to fly around, our emotional generators to get overheated, rather than trying to bring our energies to bear as systematically as we can.

There is no ABC for decision making. But, there are a few guidelines that have helped others, and we can use them to help ourselves.

MARSHAL THE FACTS

A lot of the mental anguish of decision making comes because we often worry in a factual vacuum. An endless amount of stewing can be avoided if we do what all good executives do with a problem that can't be settled: send it back for more data. Dale Carnegie once quoted a distinguished university dean as saying, "If I have a problem that has to be faced at three o'clock next Tuesday, I refuse to try to make a decision about it until Tuesday arrives. In the meantime I concentrate on getting all the facts that bear on the problem. And by Tuesday, if I've got all the facts, the problem usually solves itself."

But just gathering facts won't solve

hard problems. "The problem in coming to a firm and clear-sighted decision," says Lt. General Thomas L. Harrold, veteran infantry commander and now Commandant of the National War College, "is not only to corral the facts, but to marshal them in good order. In the Army," General Harrold explains, "we train our leaders to draw up what we call an Estimate of the Situation. First, they must know their objective. Unless you know what you want, you can't possibly decide how to get it. Second, we teach them to consider *alternative* means of attaining that objective. It's very rarely that a goal, military or any other, can be realized in only one way. Next we line up the pros and cons of each alternative, as far as we can see them. Then we choose the course that appears most likely to achieve the results we want. That doesn't guarantee success. But at least it allows us to decide as intelligently as the situation permits. It prevents us from going off on a half-baked hunch that may turn out to be disastrous."

Some people, however, *misuse* the idea of fact collecting. They go on and on getting advice, gathering data, and never seem to be able to clinch the case. When we find ourselves assembling more and more facts without coming to any clear conclusions, without acting, it's time to be suspicious. Frequently we are merely waiting for the "right" fact which will rationalize a decision we have already made.

An executive of a New York placement agency tells of a young man who couldn't make up his mind whether or not to take a job that involved a move out of town. He kept coming back for more and more information until one day he learned that the company had had tough sledding during the 30's and nearly closed down. That clinched it. With obvious relief the young man "reluctantly" turned the job down.

"Actually," the placement official comments, "it was clear that he didn't want to move. But he had to find a 'fact' to make this decision respectable in his own eyes."

When we reach this point, it is time to stop fact collecting.

CONSULT YOUR FEELINGS

The psychiatrist Theodore Reik, when still a young man, once asked Sigmund Freud about an important decision he had to make. "I can only tell you of my personal experience," Freud replied. "When making a decision of minor importance I have always found it advantageous to consider all the pros and cons. In vital matters, however, such as the choice of a mate or a profession, the decision should come from the unconscious, from somewhere within ourselves. In the important decisions of our personal life, we should be governed, I think, by the deep inner needs of our nature."

We can usually tell when a decision accords with our nature by the enormous sense of relief that it brings. Good decisions are the best tranquilizers ever invented; bad ones often increase our mental tension. When we have decided something against the grain, there is a nagging sense of incompletion, a feeling that the last knot has been pulled out of the string.

TIMING

We must learn to distinguish between our deep-running characteristics and our transient moods. There is an old rule that we should sleep on big decisions, and contemporary psychological research has established that the rule is sound.

Data from questionnaires answered by some 500 persons at Columbia University's Bureau of Applied Social Research show that our behavior is affected by our passing moods. When we are blue, low, our actions tend to be aggressive and destructive; when we are in good spirits, all fired up, our behavior swings toward tolerance and balance. Everyone knows that the boss is more apt to make lenient decisions when he's in a good mood, and that it's no time to ask him for a raise when he comes into the office glowering. We do well to take account of our emotional temperatures before we put important decisions on our *own* desks. On paydays, for example, we are all apt to be a little happy-go-lucky, especially about money decisions; on days when we've had a run-in with our wife or the day's work has gone all wrong, we are apt to decide things harshly, pessimistically, sourly.

A sense of timing also requires that we know when *not* to make a decision. "In surgery," says Dr. Abram Abeloff, Surgeon at New York's Lenox Hill Hospital, "a doctor often studies a situation for days or even weeks until he feels reasonably confident to go ahead. Time itself is an essential component of many decisions. It brings uncertain situations to a head. Premature decisions are the most dangerous a person can make."

In ordinary life, as well as in business and medicine, many of the most involved and difficult decisions are best not "made," but allowed to ripen. Facts accumulate, feelings gradually jell and, as Barnard says, other people take a hand in the situation. By holding ourselves back—refusing to plunge in the moment our adolescents ask us, "Should I go to college?" "Should I enlist in the Army now, or should I wait?"—we give complicated situations a chance to work themselves out, and sometimes save ourselves a great deal of exhausting and useless brain-cudgeling.

Consciously postponing a decision—deciding not to decide—is not the same as indecision. As Chester I. Barnard, first president of the New Jersey Bell Telephone Company, has put it in a famous book on business leadership, *The Functions of the Executive:* "The fine art of executive decision consists in not deciding questions that are not now pertinent, in not deciding prematurely, in not making decisions that others should make."

FOLLOW–THROUGH

We all know that decisions do not mean much unless we back them with the will to carry them out. The alcoholic decides a thousand times to give up drink; the smoker vows again and again that this is his last cigarette. Many times an inability to make up our minds reflects just such an unwillingness to *go through* with a decision. "Thinking," wrote the great Swiss psychiatrist, Otto Fenichel, "is preparation for action. People who are afraid of actions increase the preparation."

Thus indecision can sometimes help us *clarify* our minds. It can be the signal flag that forces us to look beyond the immediate point at issue into the follow-through that a decision demands of us. Frequently, when we make fools of ourselves at a retail counter, trying to decide which gift to buy, we are really wrestling with a quite different problem—such as our unconscious feelings about the person for whom we're selecting the gift. At a more serious level, an unhappily married woman, endlessly debating with herself whether or not to ask for a divorce, may in fact be avoiding the more difficult question of what she would do with her life if she were divorced.

FLEXIBILITY

Part of the worrisomeness of decision making comes from a natural tendency to overstress the *finality*, the once-and-for-allness of our choices. There is much more "give" in most decisions than we are aware. Franklin D. Roosevelt, for example, was a great believer in making flexible decisions. "He rarely got himself sewed tight to a program from which there was no turning back," his Secretary of Labor, Frances Perkins, once observed.

"We have to do the best we know how at the moment," he told one of his aides.

"If it doesn't turn out all right, we can modify it as we go along."

Too many of us find decisions painful because we regard them as final and irrevocable. "Half the difficulties of man," Somerset Maugham has written, "lie in his desire to answer every question with yes or no. Yes or no may neither of them be the answer; each side may have in it some yes and some no."

Sometimes, naturally, we have to answer a question with a firm yes or no. But even then it is often possible to modify our answer later. That's why some advisers counsel: "When in doubt, say no. It's a lot easier to change a no to a yes, than vice versa."

THE FINAL INGREDIENT

Finally, there is one last consideration to bear in mind. In making genuinely big decisions we have to be prepared to stand a sense of loss, as well as gain. A student who hesitates between a lifetime as a teacher or businessman, a talented young girl trying to make up her mind between marriage and a career, face choices in which sacrifice is involved, *no matter what they do*. That's one reason why big decisions in contrast to little ones, do not leave us exhilarated and charged with confidence, but humble and prayerful.

It helps to talk big decisions over with others—not only because another's opinion may illumine aspects of the dilemma that we may have missed, but because in the process of talking we sort out and clarify our own thoughts and feelings. Talk, as a clergyman and the psychiatrist both know, has a cathartic effect; it gives vent to feelings which may otherwise be expressed, not always wisely, in actions.

After this, meditation, reflections—letting the problem stew in its own juice—can also help. But in the end, after talk and thought, one ingredient is still essential. It is courage.

"One man with courage makes a majority," said Andrew Jackson; and this was never more true than in the election in our minds where the one vote we cast is the deciding one.

Managerial Problem-Solving Styles

Some people are naturals in certain organizational roles. A model is presented for differentiating problem-solving styles and matching them with roles in which they are most effective.

DON HELLRIEGEL and JOHN W. SLOCUM, JR.*

What does your ideal organization look like? How do you go about solving problems? Is there really only one way to solve problems? Can your problem-solving style interact with different situational factors to increase or decrease the probability of effective decisions? If so, can you learn to modify your problem-solving style to fit certain basic situational requirements?

This article will explore different managerial problem-solving styles. Either consciously or subconsciously, managers are able to exercise somewhat different styles to cope with different situational requirements and personal needs, although they often have a natural tendency to use one problem-solving style more than the others. Personality may have a strong influence on the use of particular problem-solving styles, but differences in individual styles should not be synonymous with differences in personality. We do not attempt to discuss the numerous perspectives or conflicting positions existing within the field of personality theory. For our purposes, personality is defined as how a person affects others, how he understands and views himself, and his pattern of inner and outer measurable traits.

Our major objectives are the following: to present and explain a model for differentiating problem-solving styles of managers; to develop an understanding of some contingencies under which certain problem-solving styles are likely to be more effective for managerial and organizational performance; to develop the ability to diagnose and recognize one's own and other's problem-solving styles; and to increase empathy and understanding of individual differences.

PERSONALITY THEORY

The theoretical and empirical basis for our discussion of managerial problem-solving styles was developed by Carl Jung (Jung 1953). We draw primarily upon this work for the orientation of personality, including extroversion or introversion, and the four basic psychological functions—thinking, feeling, sensing and intuiting. Before discussing some specific characteristics of Jung's personality theory, it should be useful to mention a few of his major themes.

First, Jung maintained that the individual's behavior is influenced by his past as well as by his goals and aspirations for the future. The individual is not simply a

* Don Hellriegel is a faculty member in management at Texas A & M University. John W. Slocum, Jr., is a faculty member in administrative studies at Ohio State University in Columbus.
Business Horizons © 1975 by the School of Business at Indiana University. Reprinted by permission.

slave to the past, but can also be proactive in selecting goals and influencing his own destiny. Second, Jung's personality theory assumes an optimistic view of the individual's potential for growth and change, stating that constant creative development is possible. Third, Jung suggests an open systems view of personality. Personality consists of a number of differentiated but interacting subsystems. These subsystems can be receptive to inputs and exchanges between each other. Also, the personality as a whole, or one of its subsystems, can change as a result of inputs and interactions with the external environment, particularly through influences from other individuals. The subsystems within Jung's personality theory that we will consider include the ego, personal unconscious, basic attitudes (extroversion-introversion) and the psychological functions (thinking, feeling, sensing and intuiting).

The ego refers to the conscious mind. It consists of feelings, thoughts, perceptions and memories we are aware of and can articulate to others. The personal unconscious includes experiences and wishes which have been repressed (suppressed below the level of consciousness); feelings and thoughts that lie below conscious awareness but have never gone through the process of repression; and feelings and thoughts that have not yet reached consciousness, but which are the basis for certain forms of future consciousness such as creativity. The personal unconscious is often first expressed in the form of dreams and fantasies, and can change its content in coordination with the conscious mind.

The personal unconscious and conscious are often in a compensatory relationship to one another. Compensation is a key element in Jung's personality principles, and consists of the theory that for the normal personality, one subsystem may compensate for another subsystem. A period of intense, extroverted behavior may be followed by a period of introverted behavior. A manager who is characterized by the psychological functions of thinking and feeling in the conscious mind may emphasize the intuitive and sensation functions in the unconscious mind. Thus, contrasting types equalize, preventing the personality from becoming neurotically unbalanced (Hall 1970, 90–91).

BASIC ATTITUDE–TYPES

According to Jungian theory, the two orientations of the personality are extroversion and introversion. Although these are opposing orientations, they are both present in our personality. One of them is usually dominant and exists in the conscious mind, and the other is subordinate and exists in the unconscious. The introvert attitude is "normally characterized by a hesitant, reflective, retiring nature that keeps to itself, shrinks from objects, is always slightly on the defensive and prefers to hide behind mistrustful scrutiny." The extrovert is "normally characterized by an outgoing, candid, and accommodating nature that adapts itself easily to a given situation, quickly forms attachments, and, setting aside any possible misgivings, will often venture forth with careless confidence into unknown situations" (Wehr 1971, 64–65).

The introverted manager needs quiet for concentration, must work without interruptions, has problems communicating with co-workers and usually works best alone. Extroverts "like variety and action, are impatient with long, slow jobs, usually communicate well, like to have people around, and are good at greeting people" (Myers and Briggs 1962). Most of us can probably think of individuals that characterize the extremes of introversion and extroversion. However, most individuals vary by the degree to which they are extroverted, introverted or relatively balanced between the extremes.

The managerial occupation seems to be disproportionately represented by extroverts. Some research even suggests that extroversion is important to managerial success. Since the manager's role often involves identifying and solving problems with and through other individuals, a certain degree of extroversion is likely to be functional. However, an extreme extrovert can literally sacrifice himself to external conditions and demands. The manager who becomes totally immersed in his job at the cost of all other concerns is one example of this. His limitation is one of getting "sucked" into external objects or demands and completely losing himself in them.

At the other extreme is the introvert, who tends to be more concerned with personal factors than with external factors. As a consequence, the introvert may choose courses of action that do not readily fit the external situation. Jung emphasized that when external understanding is overvalued, the subjective or personal factor is repressed, thus causing a denial of self. Perception and cognition (in other words, knowledge and understanding) are not simply externally determined, but are also subjectively determined and conditioned. The world exists not merely in itself, but also as it appears to us.

PSYCHOLOGICAL FUNCTIONS

Although extroversion and introversion can be directly related to differences in managerial problem-solving styles, they can operate indirectly as well through the four psychological functions. We will first consider the basic relationships between these four functions. The thinking and feeling functions represent the two opposite types which managers may prefer for making decisions. As with introversion-extroversion, the feeling-thinking functions are paired opposites which should be thought of as ranging in intensity along a continuum, with feeling at one extreme and thinking at the other. These extremes of individual decision-making orientations influence evaluations and judgments of external facts and the fact world.

The psychological functions of sensation and intuition are also paired opposites, and may be thought of as ranging in intensity along a continuum. Sensation and intuition represent the extreme orientations to perceptions which may be preferred by managers. As used here, perception refers to the ways by which we become aware of people, things and situations.

Only one of the four functions is likely to dominate in each individual. But the dominant function is normally supported by one of the functions from the other set of paired opposites. For example, thinking may be backed by sensation, or sensation may be supported by thinking. These two combinations are regarded as most characteristic of modern man in Western industrialized societies. As a consequence, feeling and intuition are functions which are apparently disregarded, undeveloped or repressed. We will first consider each of the four psychological functions as a dominant type and then consider the two perceptual orientations (sensation and intuition) in combination with the two decision-making orientations (thinking and feeling).

Feeling–Thinking Orientations

Feeling types are "... aware of other people and their feelings, like harmony, need occasional praise, dislike telling people unpleasant things, tend to be sympathetic, and relate well to most people" (Myers and Briggs 1962). They are inclined to be conformists who accommodate themselves to others. This type of manager tends to make decisions that will win the approval of his peers, subordinates and superiors, and tends to avoid problems that will result in disagreements. When avoidance or smoothing of differences is not possible, the feeling type is prone to change his position to one more acceptable to others. The establishment and maintenance of friendly relations may even supersede, and possibly interfere with, a concern for achievement, effectiveness and sound decision (Boyatzis 1974, 183–7). A feeling type manager may find it extremely difficult to suspend or discharge a subordinate for inadequate performance that is widely recognized by others, including the poor performer's own peers. In sum, the feeling type emphasizes affective and personal processes in decision making.

At the other extreme, thinking types are "... unemotional and uninterested in people's feelings, like analysis and putting things into logical order, are able to reprimand people or fire them when necessary, may seem hardhearted, and tend to relate well only to other thinking types" (Myers and Briggs 1962). This manager is constantly trying to make his activities and decisions dependent on intellectual processes, and has a tendency to fit problems and their solutions into standardized formulas. He applies external data and impersonal formulas to decisions, often forgetting to consider his own welfare. For the sake of some goal, this manager may neglect his health, finances, family or other interests. In terms of a problem-solving style, thinking managers are likely to

    make a plan and look for a method to
        solve the problem
    be extremely concerned with the approach they take to a problem
    define carefully the specific constraints in the problem
    proceed by increasingly refining their analysis
    search for additional information in a very orderly manner (McKenney and Keen 1974, 79–90).

There are many similarities between the thinking type, elements in the scientific method, and what our society often characterizes as rational problem solving. Our educational institutions have also been most concerned with developing the thinking type of function. The elements of this type are obviously crucial to any advanced industrialized society, but Jung's concern and ours is with the too frequent one-dimensional emphasis on thinking over feeling.

Sensation–Intuition Orientations

In terms of individual perceptual orientations, the sensation types of individuals "... dislike new problems unless there are standard ways to solve them, like an established routine, must usually work all the way through to reach a conclusion, show patience with routine details, and tend to be good at precise work" (Myers and Briggs 1962). The sensation type usually dislikes unstructured problems which contain considerable uncertainty that requires some degree of judgment. Sensation types are satisfied and are good performers as detail persons or bureaucrats. As used here, bureaucrat refers to a manager whose organizational life revolves primarily around the implementation and use of rules, regulations and standard operating procedures. Lower level managerial roles are often designed like this. Sensation types may adequately fill such roles because they have a minimal need to exercise discretion.

A sensation type manager may experience considerable anxiety over the uncertainties inherent in making decisions in gray areas because of his orientation to realism, external facts and concrete experiences. Along with his preference for concrete reality, this manager is not inclined toward personal reflection and introspection.

The routine and structured role enjoyed by a sensation type is likely to be performed poorly by an intuitive type. An intuitive type is one who "... likes solving new problems, dislikes doing the same things over and over again, jumps to conclusions, is impatient with routine details, and dislikes taking time for precision" (Myers and Briggs 1962). Whereas the sensation type tends to perceive the external environment in terms of details and parts, the intuitive type manager tends to perceive the whole or totality of the external environment. In terms of a problem-solving style, intuitives tend to:

> keep the total problem continuously in mind as the problem-solving process develops
> continuously redefine the problem as the process unfolds
> rely on hunches and unverbalized cues
> almost simultaneously consider a variety of alternatives and options
> jump around or back and forth in the elements or steps in the problem-solving process. After presumably defining a problem, identifying alternatives to the problem, and evaluating consequences of each alternative, the intuitive manager may suddenly jump back to a reassessment of whether the true problem has even been identified.
> very quickly consider and discard alternatives (McKenney and Keen 1974).

Unlike the sensation type, the intuitive manager is suffocated by stable conditions and constantly seeks out and creates new possibilities. Intuitives are often found among business tycoons, politicians, speculators, entrepreneurs, stockbrokers and the like. The intuitive type can be extremely valuable to the economy and society as an initiator and promoter of new enterprises, services, concepts and innovations within organizations. If the intuitive is more people oriented than thing oriented, he may be exceptionally good at diagnosing the abilities and potentials of other individuals.

The discussion of problem-solving style to this point has focused on the four pure and dominant psychological functions for differentiating managers. As suggested earlier, each dominant type is likely to be supported by one of the other paired opposite types. Thus, the analysis for differentiating managerial problem-solving styles must be carried one step further. This will be accomplished by considering the four pure composite styles that might be derived when combining the two decision-making orientations with the two perceptual orientations.

COMPOSITE MODEL

The accompanying figure presents a composite model of managerial problem-solving styles. This model is derived from the decision-making orientations of thinking and feeling and the perceptual orientations of sensation and intuition. Since we have already presented the nature of the four psychological functions when each is dominant in an extroverted individual, the following will briefly review the four pure combined types. Then, a profile of a specific manager who seems to approximate the attributes of the combined type is presented. Since the classification of these managers is based on secondary data, the reader should be more concerned with the behaviors described than whether the specific individuals are truly of a particular composite type.

SENSATION–FEELING TYPE

Managers in cell A of the accompanying figure rely primarily on sensation for purposes of perception and feeling for purposes of decision making. These managers are interested in facts that can be collected and verified directly by the senses. They approach these facts with personal and human concern because they are more interested in facts about people than about things. When asked to write a paragraph or two on their perception of the ideal organization, these individuals often describe an organization with a well-defined hierarchy and set of rules that exist for the benefit of members and society. The ideal organization would also satisfy member needs and enable them to communicate openly with one another (Kilman and Taylor 1974) (Mitroff and Kilman 1974).

Stewart Rowlings Mott, multimillionaire liberal and philanthropist, seems to manifest a number of attributes of the sensation-feeling type (Ross 1974, 134–5). Stewart Mott inherited his fortune from his father, who was one of the biggest stockholders of General Motors. Through 1974, Mott's annual income ranged from $950,000 to $1.5 million. He greets individuals with a friendly and open smile and is quite willing to discuss any aspect of his life in an open and candid manner. His Park Avenue penthouse in New York serves as his office and home. Mott's main office is filled with piles of papers scattered around the room in an organized manner. He says, "I don't know how to throw things out—people, old newspapers or cigarette boxes." Details fascinate him. He works long hours, constantly reviewing reports and memoranda to keep informed on all the major and minor activities of the organizations he helps to support.

Mott contends that the two major problems facing the world are population control and arms control, and much of the $6 million he has donated between 1964 and

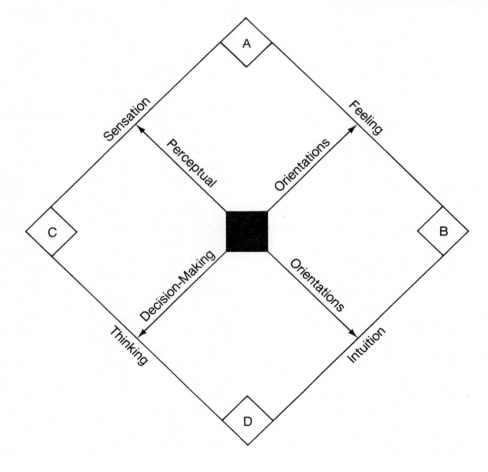

1974 has gone to charitable and political groups concerned with these two causes. Although Mott is an activist for people causes, he is not interested in taking the time for abstract reflection or considering global philosophies. Mott says, "I'm no idealogue. I feel uncomfortable when asked to explain in some cogent, complete, lucid way a blueprint of my political perceptions. I believe in chipping away at the defects in the present system without attempting to change the way it fundamentally works."

INTUITION–FEELING TYPE

Managers in cell B of the figure rely primarily on intuition for purposes of perception and feeling for purposes of decision making. These managers focus on new projects, new approaches, new truths, possible events and the like. They approach these possibilities in terms of meeting or serving the personal and social needs of people in general. Intuitive-feeling types avoid specifics, and focus instead on broad themes that revolve around the human purposes of organizations, such as serving mankind or the organization's clientele. The ideal organization for these individuals would be decentralized, with flexible and loosely defined lines of authority, and few required rules and standard operating procedures. Intuitive-feeling types emphasize long-term goals and desire organizations that are flexible and adaptive.

Our example of the intuitive-feeling type is Steve Carmichael, a project manager with nine subordinates who worked for a federally funded neighborhood youth corps. The following excerpt is from Studs Terkel's book, *Working* (Terkel 1974, 341–3). At the time of the interview, Steve was twenty-five years old, married and had one child.

Steve said, "They say I'm unrealistic. One of the fellas that works with me said, 'It's a dream to believe this program will take sixteen-, seventeen-year-old dropouts and make something of their lives.' This may well be true, but if I'm going to think that I can't believe my job has any worth.... We've got five or six young people who are burning to get into an automotive training program. Everybody says, 'It takes signatures, it takes time.' I follow up on these things because everybody else seems to forget there are people waiting. So I'll get that phone call, do some digging, find out nothing's happened, report that to my boss, and call back and make my apologies.... The most frustrating thing for me is to know that what I'm doing does not have a positive impact on others. I don't see this work as meaning anything. I now treat my job disdainfully...."

SENSATION–THINKING TYPE

The sensation plus thinking type, in cell C of the accompanying figure, emphasizes external factual details and specifics of a problem. The facts of a problem are often analyzed through a logical step-by-step process of reasoning from cause to effect. This manager's problem-solving style tends to be practical and matter-of-fact. When asked to describe his ideal organization, this individual often describes an extreme form of bureaucracy, characterized by its extensive use of rules and regulations, a well-defined hierarchy, emphasis on high control, specificity and certainty, and its concern with realistic, limited and short-term goals. Although he is not an extreme sensation-thinking type, John deButts, chairman of the board of the American Telephone and Telegraph Company, revealed some attributes of this type in a published interview (Harvard Business Review 1974, 34–42). From this interview, he appears to focus on short-term problems, using standard operating procedures to solve problems, and keep the system under control.

DeButts stated that the quality of decisions depends on the quality of input, on how unvarnished information is after it has passed up the chain of command. "And I do get information of that quality," said deButts, "The constant contacts I have with the key people at AT & T and the top people of our subsidiaries give me that quality. The organizational structure we have here helps provide quality information, too.... Every other week I meet with all the officers of AT & T; and practically every month I meet with all the presidents of our subsidiaries. In between I have many conversations with individuals in these groups. These contacts give me a lot of my input."

When asked if he ever finds himself unprepared for something, deButts responded, "Seldom is there a significant surprise. Naturally, details come up with which I am not familiar. That's why we have discussions.... The key, for me, has been to set up my broad objectives and then deal with the tasks within that framework...."

Asked how he spends his time, deButts replied, "Usually, before I arrive at the office, I try to get into my mind the things I want to accomplish that day. I also jot down notes to myself. Today, for example, I've got several things I need to talk to people about. Then I'll try to take care of the mail. Incidentally, I read every letter that's addressed to me, either by name or by title. Nobody signs my name but me."

INTUITION–THINKING TYPE

The fourth pure composite type is shown in cell D. Intuitive-thinking managers tend to focus on possibilities, but approach them through impersonal analysis. Rather than dealing with the human element, they consider possibilities which are more often theoretical or technical. These managers are likely to enjoy positions which are loosely defined and require abstract skills, such as long-range planning, marketing research and search-

ing for new goals. The ideal organization for these individuals would be impersonal and conceptual. Goals of the organization should be consistent with environmental needs (such as pure air, clear water and equal opportunity) and the needs of organizational members. However, these issues are considered in an abstract and impersonal frame of reference.

Our example of the intuitive-thinking type is Irving Shapiro, who at the age of fifty-seven, became chairman of the board and chief executive officer of E.I. duPont de Nemours and Company in 1974 (Vanderwicken 1974, 70–81). Others at duPont regard Shapiro as well qualified to deal with the wide ranging changes affecting duPont and all other multinational corporations. It is said that no one else in duPont's top management has his ability to analyze risks, comprehend complex issues of law and politics, and negotiate and devise solutions that the company— and those watching it—can accept. Shapiro holds strong opinions but listens carefully to others. He is cautious but willing, if the odds are right, to take big risks.

At the start of World War II, Shapiro went to work at the Office of Price Administration (OPA), where he helped set up rationing systems for sugar, automobiles and bicycles. After a while, bored with the OPA, Shapiro soon had a job in the criminal division of the Justice Department. Shapiro soon had a reputation as an outstanding writer of briefs, with the ability to grasp the critical issues in a case, clarify them, and argue in support of the government's position. The Justice Department at that time was divided into two factions, both of which considered Shapiro a member—he was smart enough to debate the intellectuals and practical enough to satisfy the activists. Soon after joining duPont in 1951, Shapiro became known as the "can do" lawyer. Instead of putting up legal roadblocks, he suggested ways by which duPont's management could accomplish their objectives legally.

Shapiro's associates say that one of his greatest gifts is his ability to put complex and often emotional issues into simple, practical terms. One executive tells about a personnel problem he was unable to resolve. He phoned Shapiro at home one afternoon and was immediately invited over for a drink. The executive said he laid out three alternatives, and after talking for only fifteen minutes, the best alternative became obvious.

The validity and long-term utility of this model for considering differences in managerial problem-solving styles is still being developed. Previous research and our own applied research suggest it is worthy of recognition, discussion and consideration. The model presented is also consistent with a number of key assumptions and findings from other models of individual decision making. Among these assumptions and findings are:

Individual differences in judgment reflect the characteristic styles in which individuals perceive, construe and organize their environment.

These individual differences are reflected in differences in the weighting and combining of stimuli in the situation.

Judgmental differences are themselves intervened by and functionally related to a wide variety of characteristics of individuals (which were not investigated in our model of problem-solving styles) such as intelligence and values.

The dimensions of the stimuli in the environment as well as the individual need to be assessed (Wiggins 1973) (Taylor and Dunnette 1974, 420–23).

We have discussed four pure composite problem-solving styles, but do not mean to suggest that every manager can be characterized as one of the four pure types. A manager could exist any place along the grid shown in the figure. According to Jung, the developing individual tends to move toward a balance and integration of the four psychological functions. This balance would exist in the center of the figure. Since all individuals are so rich in variety and complex in nature, we need to be especially cautious of categorizing managers by inferring that they cannot adapt to situations that do not fit their preferred style. We hope this article has served to develop an empathy and understanding of differences between managers; help managers understand their characteristic style and how it might influence their actions and reactions to certain problems and provide a framework for possible forms of desired personal growth and development. No single composite style is inherently better than another. We have suggested that the requirements of certain organizational roles may be more natural to one style than another.

"Most people need less management than you think."
Jim Treybig, Tandem Computers, *Fortune* (June 28, 1982)

Biff Loman: To suffer fifty weeks of the year for the sake of a two-week vacation, when all you really desire is to be outside with your shirt off. And always to have to get ahead of the next fella. And still that's how you build a future.
Arthur Miller, *Death of a Salesman*

"The team that makes the most mistakes will probably win." There is much truth in that statement if you analyze it properly. The doer makes mistakes, and I want doers on my team—players who make things happen.
John Wooden, *They Call Me Coach*

Taking a look back at his 37 years in the automobile business, Iaccoca reflected not long ago: "I don't know what the hell I rushed for, It's a long race. I was trying to sprint all the time. Maybe if I had to do it again I would slow down a little." The thought is so outlandish that not even Lee Iacocca can sell it.
Time (March 21, 1983)

Many of our young managers are looking six steps ahead and pushing for every promotion while trying to break so and so's record to vice-president. In the meantime, they seem to have forgotten what they were hired to do. They have lost interest in learning skills.
Fifty-year-old bank manager

The inquiring reporter asked the young man why he wanted to be a mortician. "Because," he said, "I enjoy working with people."
The San Francisco Chronicle

EXERCISES

Motivational Style Exercise

We all have assumptions with respect to the motivating forces in behavior. Sometimes we find people have conflicting assumptions. Also, it often turns out that when we are required to state our assumptions we may not like some of them. An exercise such as this one allows you to approximate some of your own assumptions and then develop a profile where you can look at yourself compared to other students. Also, you can compare your adjusted score to that of the average middle manager.

Motivational Style Questionnaire

Instructions

Think about what you would do in a supervisory role in relation to handling your subordinates. There are 36 pairs of statements which may describe what you would do in that setting. Read each pair of statements and decide which one best applies to you. Then mark an "X" in the

box next to that statement. For instance, if you think that the first statement in item 1 best describes what you would do in your job, then place an "X" in the box which appears under column B.

You must answer all questions. Some questions you will find hard to distinguish because both seem to apply or neither seem to apply. Nevertheless a choice must be made as to which of the two is more characteristic of you.

Please be sure that you place your "X" in the box next to the statement you have chosen.

1. I believe that once the goals have been set, then each man should have enough motivation to achieve them.
   or
   I will give responsibility, but take it away if performance is not forthcoming.

2. I tell subordinates not to worry about others' performance but rather to concentrate on self-improvement.
   or

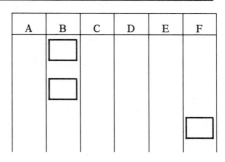

SOME PERSPECTIVES ON INDIVIDUAL BEHAVIOR

	A	B	C	D	E	F

I feel that reports are not very necessary in a situation where trust has been established. ☐(E)

3. I have high standards of performance and have less sympathy for those whose performance falls short. ☐(B)
   or
   When a subordinate's plan is inappropriate, I stimulate him to re-think and come up with another plan. ☐(F)

4. I believe that human rights and values are more important than the immediate job on hand. ☐(D)
   or
   I reward good work and feel that punishment for non-performance has limited use. ☐(E)

5. I suggest alternative ways of doing things rather than indicate the way I prefer it myself. ☐(F)
   or
   I think that subordinates should be able to overcome difficulties in the way to achievement by themselves. ☐(B)

6. When alternatives are described to me I am not long in indicating the course of action I prefer. ☐(C)
   or
   When a subordinate disagrees with me, I am careful to give my reasons why I want it done a certain way. ☐(C)

7. I think that disciplining employees does more harm than good. ☐(D)
   or
   I develop a close personal relationship with subordinates because I believe this marks out a good manager. ☐(D)

8. I reward good work and feel that punishment for non-performance has limited use. ☐(D)
   or
   When a subordinate fails to perform I let him know of the failure in a firm and reasoned manner. ☐(C)

9. I expect my subordinates to carry out plans I have prepared. ☐(A)
   or
   I think that subordinates should be able to overcome difficulties in the way to achievement by themselves. ☐(B)

10. When I make a decision, I take the additional step of persuading my subordinates to accept it. ☐(C)
    or
    I feel that accepted plans should generally represent the ideas of my subordinates. ☐(D)

11. I feel that people develop best in a trusting environment. ☐(D)
    or
    I believe that once goals have been set, then each man should have enough motivation to achieve them. ☐(B)

12. When I discipline a subordinate I am definite in letting him know what he has done wrong. ☐(A)
    or
    I feel that reports are not very necessary in a situation where trust has been established. ☐(E)

MOTIVATIONAL STYLE EXERCISE

	A	B	C	D	E	F

13. I believe that firm discipline is important to keep the work moving.

    or

    I insist subordinates submit detailed reports on their activities.

    [A ☐] [A ☐]

14. I believe that a popular leader is better than an unpopular one.

    or

    I believe that subordinates should not be too discouraged by setbacks in the job, but rather should be able to clear blockages themselves.

    [D ☐] [B ☐]

15. I believe that it is a manager's job to arouse the will to achieve in subordinates.

    or

    I am constantly concerned with high standards of performance and encourage subordinates to reach these standards.

    [F ☐] [F ☐]

16. I am available to subordinates as a consultant and adviser when it is agreed they need help.

    or

    I feel that people develop best in a trusting environment.

    [E ☐] [E ☐]

17. When a subordinate's plan is inappropriate, I stimulate him to re-think and come up with another plan.

    or

    I often give orders in the form of a suggestion, but make clear what I want.

    [F ☐] [C ☐]

18. I believe that job security and benefits such as super-annuation plans are important for employee happiness.

    or

    When a subordinate's plan is inappropriate I stimulate him to re-think and come up with another plan.

    [D ☐] [F ☐]

19. In the long run, I will fire a man I consider to be unmanageable.

    or

    I discourage arguments which upset the harmony amongst subordinates.

    [A ☐] [D ☐]

20. I feel that reports are not very necessary in a situation where trust has been established.

    or

    I expect my subordinates to carry out plans I have prepared.

    [E ☐] [A ☐]

21. I am not so concerned with establishing close personal relationships as in getting subordinates to follow my example.

    or

    I believe that human rights and values are more important than the immediate job on hand.

    [B ☐] [D ☐]

22. I watch for improvement in individual performance rather than insist on high level performance from subordinates.

    or

    I discourage arguments which upset the harmony amongst subordinates.

    [F ☐] [D ☐]

23. I believe that subordinates should not be too discouraged by setbacks in the job, but rather should be able to clear blockages themselves.

    [B ☐]

SOME PERSPECTIVES ON INDIVIDUAL BEHAVIOR

Statement	A	B	C	D	E	F
or When I make a decision, I take the additional step of persuading my subordinates to accept it.			☐			
24. When a subordinate disagrees with me, I am careful to give my reasons why I want it done a certain way.			☐			
or I think that disciplining employees does more harm than good.				☐		
25. I am constantly concerned with high standards of performance and encourage subordinates to reach these standards.						☐
or I believe that firm discipline is important to keep the work moving.	☐					
26. I discourage arguments which upset the harmony amongst subordinates.				☐		
or I expect my subordinates to follow my instructions closely.	☐					
27. I develop a close personal relationship with subordinates because I believe this marks out a good manager.				☐		
or When alternatives are described to me I am not long in indicating the course of action I prefer.			☐			
28. When a subordinate fails to perform I let him know of the failure in a firm and reasoned manner.			☐			
or I am not so concerned with establishing close personal relationships as in getting subordinates to follow my example.		☐				
29. I expect my subordinates to follow my instructions closely.	☐					
or I often give orders in the form of a suggestion, but make it clear what I want.				☐		
30. I will give responsibility, but take it away if performance is not forthcoming.		☐				
or I am available to subordinates as a consultant and adviser when it is agreed that they need help.					☐	
31. I think that subordinates should be able to overcome difficulties in the way to achievement by themselves.		☐				
or When I discipline a subordinate I am definite in letting him know what he has done wrong.	☐					
32. I tend to rely on self-direction and self-control rather than doing much controlling myself.					☐	
or I suggest alternative ways of doing things rather than indicate the way I prefer it myself.						☐
33. I seek to reduce resistance to my decision by indicating what subordinates have to gain from my decision.			☐			
or I watch for improvement in individual performance rather than insist on high level performance from subordinates.						☐

MOTIVATIONAL STYLE EXERCISE

	A	B	C	D	E	F

34. I often give orders in the form of a suggestion, but make clear what I want.

    or

    In the long run, I will fire a man I consider to be unmanageable.

35. I insist subordinates submit detailed reports on their activities.

    or

    I am constantly concerned with high standards of performance and encourage subordinates to reach these standards.

36. I feel that accepted plans should generally represent the ideas of my subordinates.

    or

    I believe that a popular leader is better than an unpopular one.

Scoring Key and Profile

To compute your motivational style, count the number of Xs you made in column A; then do the same for those you made in column B and so forth through column F.

Put the number of Xs for each column here:

A	B	C	D	E	F	
$+1$	0	$+2$	0	$+1$	-2	$=36$
A=	B=	C=	D=	E=	F=	

To shade in your Motivation Style Profile, simply shade the space using your adjusted score above. For instance, if your "A" for Coercer score is 6, then you shade your profile thus:

	1	2	3	4	5	6	7	8	9	10	11+
A ☐ Coercer	/////////////////////////										

	1	2	3	4	5	6	7	8	9	10	11+
A ☐ Coercer											
B ☐ Pace-setter											
C ☐ Authoritarian											
D ☐ Affiliator											
E ☐ Democrat											
F ☐ Coach											

To further analyze your profile, you could compare yourself to the average middle manager adjusted score of 6 on each of the six scales. Also, you should turn back to the McClelland article, "That Urge to Achieve," and review his classification of needs. The categories in this profile fit McClelland's framework as follows:

n Ach	Pace Setter	(I)
	Coach	(II)
n Power	Coercer	(I)
	Authoritarian	(II)
n Aff	Affiliator	(I)
	Democrat	(II)

You also might note that the "I" variable in each need category is the strongest or more extreme indicator of the need. The "II" variable is a less extreme emphasis. This means that you lean in that direction, but it is a more facilitating rather than obsessive force.

Perception Exercise

Imagination and creative ability can be very useful to you in analyzing and interpreting organizational phenomena. The following exercise gives you the opportunity to use your imagination to describe and interpret common situations that occur in organizations. Four pictures are provided to give you a starting point from which you should describe, using your imagination, the people involved, their relationships, what has and what will happen, what they are saying or thinking, etc. Do not merely describe the picture, but make up a story based upon it. The pictures are intentionally very general and can be interpreted in many different ways. Look at the pictures briefly, then begin to write your stories.

Take no more than five minutes to write each story. They need not be long but should be as complete and yet as spontaneous as you can make them in the time allowed. When you have completed one, go directly to the next one. It is not necessary to go back and refine and revise your stories; just write what comes to mind as you interpret the pictures.

In order for this to be a meaningful learning experience, avoid looking ahead at the scoring key until you have completed your stories.

After you have completed your stories, form into groups of three. Each person in turn should read one story to the other two. Using the scoring summary, discuss the themes and motives that appear to be dominant in the story. Try to determine whether the story is primarily concerned with n Aff, n Ach, or n Pow. Try to understand why the story suggests the different needs that become evident as you relate the content of the story to the three basic needs that McClelland identified. How does the operation of these needs in yourself affect the manner in which you behave in organizations?

After you have each read and analyzed one of your stories, go on to another one and continue the process until you have completed all of your stories or until you run out of time.

The purpose of this exercise is not so much to analyze each individual's inner drives as to understand, through personal experience with these concepts, how these motives affect your behavior in relation to other people in organizations.

Just look at the picture briefly (10–15 seconds), and write the story it suggests.

Just look at the picture briefly (10–15 seconds), and write the story it suggests.

PERCEPTION EXERCISE

Just look at the picture briefly (10–15 seconds), and write the story it suggests.

Just look at the picture briefly (10–15 seconds), and write the story it suggests.

Scoring Summary

Over the last twenty years, David McClelland has done a great deal of research into the inner motivations of people. In his research, he developed the Thematic Apperception Test, which consists of showing a series of pictures to his subjects asking them to respond to them in an imaginative story about what the people in the pictures were doing or thinking. He analyzed the content of these stories for a great number of people and determined that there were three basic motives or needs which occur in different mixtures in different people. He called these three motives: need for achievement (n Ach), need for affiliation (n Aff), and need for power (n Pow). Other researchers used the same projective techniques as McClelland and included hunger, sex, fear, aggression, and a number of other drives in their research. For our purposes, we are primarily concerned with n Aff, n Ach, and n Pow as they relate to behavior of people in organizations.

The differing mixtures of these three factors in people may result in different behavior patterns in interpersonal relationships. The relationships between people, which are determined by the interplay of their behaviors, are strongly affected by the motives of the individuals involved. These factors influence many, if not all, of the interpersonal and organizational dynamics that are commonly observed where people must organize to accomplish some goal.

The following is a summary of the basic themes that McClelland and his associates used to identify their motives in scoring the T.A.T. Since we do not need the complexity and sophistication that McClelland developed, we have simplified and summarized the scoring key. Use the following key as a guideline to understand the motives evident in your stories.

Need for Achievement

Achievement motive, n Ach, is reflected in behavior which strives for performing excellence. Three main indications of n Ach are the following:

1. Competition with a standard of excellence
   a. Some competitive activity where winning or doing as well as or better than others is explicitly stated; winning a competition, the desire to show that one can indeed accomplish some stated task.
   b. The statement that someone feels "good" over success or "bitter" over a failure, anticipation of good feelings when a task is successfully completed, etc.
   c. Evidence of concern for a standard of excellence must be present; a statement that someone is "working hard" or accomplishing something, without mention of a goal or standard, should not be considered n Ach.
2. Unique accomplishment
   a. Someone is concerned with accomplishing something out of the ordinary, such as an invention, an artistic creation, or some other extraordinary accomplishment. An explicit statement of a goal or standard of excellence is not necessary when the task is unique and will be accepted as a personal accomplishment when completed.
3. Long-term involvement
   a. A character is concerned with or involved in the attainment of a long-term achievement goal. Career involvement or preparations for a profession make possible the inference of a standard of excellence unless some other primary reason is clearly stated.
   b. The relationship of a limited task to a long-term goal must be clearly stated if it is to be considered n Ach.

Need for Affiliation

Affiliation Motive, n Aff, is concerned with the need to be with, liked by, and accepted by other people.

1. n Aff is scored when concern for establishing, maintaining, or restoring a positive affective relationship with another person is stated. Friendship is a key word. There must be a statement of liking or desire for acceptance or forgiveness concerning a relationship. Mere mention of a relationship, e.g., father-son, husband-wife, does not indicate affiliation motive—only social states.
2. Negative reaction toward a separation or disruption in social or interpersonal ties may be scored as n Aff.
3. Positive statement about generally accepted affiliation activities, such as parties, reunions, visits, bull sessions, can be considered evidence for n Aff.
4. Nurturant actions, such as consoling, helping, being concerned about the happiness or well-being of others, are evidence for n Aff.

Need for Power

Power motive, n Pow, is evident where one person in the story is concerned with control of the means of influence of other people in the story. *n* Pow is characterized by the following:

1. Statements of feelings about attainment or maintenance of the control of the means of influencing a person. Feeling about winning an argument; feeling about the avoidance of weakness; desires to teach, inspire other people out of the context of teacher; etc.

2. A definite statement about someone actually doing something to gain control of the means of influence of another person, e.g., a character must be arguing a point, demanding or forcing something, giving a command, punishing someone, telling someone off, etc.

3. A statement of an interpersonal relationship which is culturally defined as a superior/subordinate one and in which there is some control of the means of influencing a person. There must be some mention of both the superior and the subordinate and some mention of the effect of the superior on the subordinate.

Career Exercise

1. Write twelve different answers to the question "Who am I?" You may choose to answer in terms of the roles and responsibilities you have in life, in terms of groups you belong to and beliefs you hold, in terms of certain qualities or traits you have as a person, in terms of behavior patterns, needs or feelings that are characteristic of you, etc. Try to list those things which are really important to your sense of yourself: things that, if you lost them, would make a radical difference to your identity and the meaning of life for you.

2. *Identity Review:* Consider each item on your list of "Who am I's" separately. Try to imagine, try to feel how it would be if that item were no longer true of you. (For example, if "husband" or "wife" is one of the items, what would the loss of your spouse mean to you? How would you feel? What would you do? What would your life be like?) After reviewing each item in this way, rank-order the items on the list by putting a number in the box to the right of each item. Put "1" beside the item which is most essential to your sense of yourself, which loss would require the greatest struggle to adjust to. Put "12" beside the item which is least essential to your sense of yourself. Try to rank-order all items in this way, without any items tying for first place, second place, third place, etc. If some items on your list are aspects of you that you dislike and would like to be rid of, they don't necessarily fall in the lower end of the rank-order. The questions for rank-ordering is how big would the adjustment struggle be if you lost that item. Some aspects of yourself that you dislike might be very hard to give up!

3. *Eulogy:* The purpose of this exercise is to explore your future. The task is to

write the eulogy that you wish it would be possible and realistic to have delivered about you at your funeral. Don't write the eulogy that could realistically be delivered if you died tomorrow; unless that represents all you want to be in the future. So give yourself time, hope and even allow yourself some fantasy and wishful thinking in composing a eulogy to your life. As in the "Who am I" exercise, this exercise requires reflection, silence, being alone with yourself.

4. *Fantasy Day:* Construct a fantasy day sometime in the future. The day can be a "special day" that you would really love to experience, or it can be the kind of "typical day" that you really wish would characterize your life. Or you can create a week instead of a day, etc. The important thing is to create an experience you really want some time in the future.

5. *Life Inventory:* In this exercise you generate as many answers as you can to a list of seven questions about your values and the resources you have for realizing those values.

A useful procedure for construction of your life inventory is to take a few minutes alone to write down as many answers to the seven questions as come to mind quickly and without thinking too deeply. In fact, the more spontaneous you can let yourself be, the better. After you have answered all of the questions, go back over each answer and see if you still agree with your response. Also compare the answers to see if some things would be better listed under another item.

A. When do I feel fully alive? What things, events, activities, etc., make me feel that life is really worth living, that it's great to be me and to be alive?

B. What do I do well? What do I have to contribute to the lives of others; what skills have I mastered?

C. Given my current situation and given my aspirations, what do I need to learn how to do?

D. What wishes should I be turning into plans? Are there any dreams I've discarded as "unrealistic" that I should start dreaming again?

E. What underdeveloped or misused resources do I have? (Resources might be material things, talents, or friends)

F. What should I start doing now?

G. What should I stop doing now?

6. What do the answers to all the above questions mean for my career plans for the future? What do they imply about the general direction of my life? What specific changes or plans should I now make to make my life and career congruent?

Additional considerations in the conduct of this exercise:

Often people benefit from sharing their life and career values with other individuals. This may be done with a spouse or close friends who know you well and could give you useful feedback or suggestions regarding some of your insights. This may help you to better understand who your are and where you want to go.

If this exercise is used as a class group project, it is important to realize that no one should be forced to share their personal values or perceptions. While group sharing can have beneficial outcomes, it should not be done in situations which may compromise private feelings.

The Reluctant Account Executive

ROLE FOR CHARLIE SHORE, SUPERVISOR

You are the supervisor for an advertising account group of sixteen individuals in a large advertising agency. You have the typical problems any supervisor must deal with—extended lunch hours, some absenteeism and tardiness—but basically a very good team. The group has consistently been recognized for the high quality of its work. The client has now asked your agency to take on a brand extension of your current product. Because of the increased administrative demands—budgets, meetings, and so on—you and your management supervisor have decided that you need an assistant supervisor.

You are certain that your management supervisor is going to be promoted and that you are most likely to be his replacement. This means that the assistant you choose will probably make supervisor himself. In reviewing your team, you have observed that the majority of the members are young and too inexperienced to be considered good prospects for the assistant account supervisor position.

There is one individual, however, who stands out as an excellent prospect for the job—if he would just change his attitude. Marc Stanton is a young man, about 26, who joined your account group as an assistant account executive right out of college. He is now the senior account executive on your staff and has had exposure in all areas—media, creative and administrative—of your brand's marketing plan. He knows the brand's needs and has an excellent working relationship with the client.

The problem is that, whenever you have asked him to work on the brand's long-term strategic issues, he doesn't seem interested. Although he has the best overall picture of the brand's needs, Marc is now content to limit his work to the day-to-day administrative duties on the brand. Many times you have told him that he has a good future with the agency and you would like to help him develop his leadership ability. Again and again, he shows little interest. You still think he is your best prospect, however, and so you have decided to talk to him once more about his attitude. He is on his way to your office now.

ROLE FOR MARC STANTON, SENIOR ACCOUNT EXECUTIVE

You are the senior account executive on a sixteen-member advertising account group at a large advertising agency. Charlie Shore is your account supervisor. Most of the members of your group are much younger than you and are simply "paying their dues" in jobs that are simple and mundane. The advertising world is not at all what you had expected. Your job is mostly administrative in nature, the pay is not very good and agency work is not at all glamourous. You feel that talent, especially yours, goes unrewarded and that anyone would be crazy to stay with an advertising agency. But then, you really don't care. You are not going to be here much longer because you have already been accepted to graduate school. You want to get an MBA so that you can get a job in brand management. After all, the client side is where the real strategic brand decisions are made. You only took the agency job in the first place because it would make you a more attractive candidate for a top graduate business school.

There are some difficulties with your present position, however. You can't let Charlie know you are planning to return to school because you believe he will let you go. You need to work through the summer to save enough money for school. And lately he has been asking you to work on the long-term strategic plan for the brand, even though you know you won't be around to implement it. You just want to do what you're paid to do—the day-to-day administrative duties on the brand—and go home. Now Charlie wants to see you again. He has asked you to come to his office. You wonder if its about a problem yesterday when one of your assistants erased a computer spreadsheet your group had been working on. You weren't able to retrieve it and it looked a little like you were at fault, but it really wasn't a very big deal. Oh, well, you can stall for time—it has always worked before. You only have a month before you give notice anyway. You will just complain about the poor pay, long hours, inexperienced staff and low career potential. You are just about to knock on Jim's door.

Some Individuals Never See the Relationship Between Their Personal Needs and Organizational Realities.

"Frankly, I believe your resumé would be much stronger if you were to condense it a bit ... for instance ... you might consider leaving out this entire section dealing with your pet hamster."

CASES

State Bank

After graduating from college, I accepted a job with what I considered to be the best local bank, State Bank. My first year of employment consisted of a management development program that mixed a bit of formal book education with a generous amount of practical application. At the close of one year, I received a permanent assignment at the bank's computer processing and operations center as an operations officer. I received very little concrete explanation of my job from the officer I replaced. This was frustrating, considering that I now faced the task of overseeing seven departments that I knew very little about.

The first week on my own, Jack Freestone, the manager of the operations center, called me into his office to talk about a special assignment he had for me. Jack wanted me to give up one of my departments and take on the challenge of the Phone Inquiry Department. Trina Farr, the officer over the department, couldn't handle the job. Jack felt there was too much "goofing off," and discipline was terrible. My assignment was to "straighten things out" and "get some work out of those people." Jack told me to report to Fred Garcia, the assistant manager, about my progress in solving the problem (see Exhibit 1).

When I left Jack's office, I went right to Fred's desk to ask for some insight into the situation. Fred's response was, "You can ask Trina about the department, but she didn't get along well with the people there and probably won't have anything good to say. Jack does this once a year. He assigns that department to another officer and hopes they'll do something . . . Let me know if you come up with an idea."

THE PHONE INQUIRY DEPARTMENT

The Phone Inquiry Department was not essential to the work flow of the operations center. But it did play an important role in the check-cashing process for the branches. Tellers would call the phone operators to inquire as to whether the check they were about to cash would clear. The inquiry operator sat at a computer terminal, punched in the account number of the customer, checked for sufficient funds, and then reserved those funds on the computer until the check could be processed. If the operator gave permission to cash the check, the teller would go ahead with the transaction.

Phone Inquiry also handled customer questions, either directly or via branch personnel. Branch clerks would call to get information to solve the problems while customers waited. Customers could call to get their current balance and find out if a certain check had cleared the account. Sometimes operators would spend twenty minutes or more going through the processed checks of a particular account to help the customer balance his or her books. Both the computer terminals and cancelled checks waiting to be mailed in the next monthly statement were at the operators' disposal.

Fifteen young employees were employed in the department; twelve were full-time operators, two were alternates, and one was a supervisor. Each of the twelve full-time workers was assigned a small desk with a terminal on it. The desks were arranged in clusters of three, with partitions separating each work station (see Exhibit 2). Each desk had a phone board with twelve phone lines on it. No one was assigned to a particular line. When a phone rang, any free operator was expected to answer as quickly and courteously as possible. (The phones didn't actually ring, they beeped. The beep came over a central speaker in the middle of the department. If one phone needed answering the beep was slow. The speed of the beep increased in proportion to the number of phones needing answering. Calls came constantly from 8:30 A.M. to 6:00 P.M. each work day.)

The two alternates in the department filled in for ill employees. Sometimes two were not enough and the department ran short. Very rarely was there a day when no one was ill. If the alternates were not needed on the phones, they did other miscellaneous duties: stuffing statement envelopes or filing copies of charge notices. When calls slowed down, the other operators were also supposed to help with these tasks.

Twenty-three-year-old Mary Anderson supervised the department. Mary had come from another department about a year earlier. She hadn't worked in Phone Inquiry before but was selected for her

EXHIBIT 1   Operations Center Organization Chart

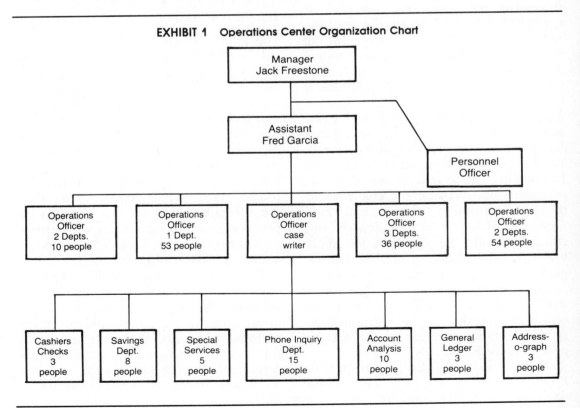

STATE BANK

EXHIBIT 2 Phone Inquiry Department Physical Layout

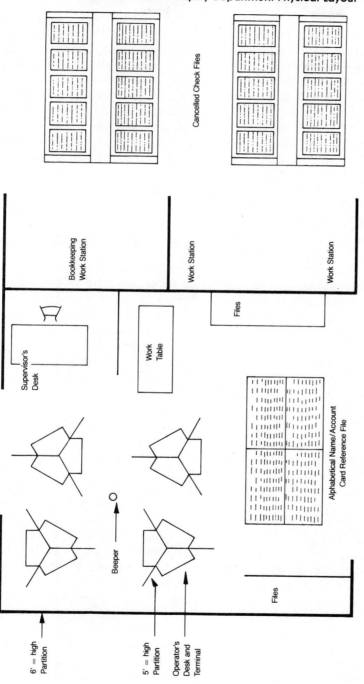

patience and her ability to relate to the young workers. When asked, all the operators said they liked Mary and thought she was easy to get along with. In her last annual appraisal Mary had been rated as "competent" in her position. Officer comments on the appraisal were "needs to be more strict." Her attendance had become a problem in the past few months due to problems with her pregnancy. Mary came at 8:00 A.M. each day, took a half-hour lunch, and left at 4:30 P.M. She gave daily work station assignments to the operators and determined where the alternates were needed. Operators "signed on" to their assigned terminal with a security code. This allowed the supervisor to monitor the number and length of time between transactions on each terminal daily and identify the operator who used the terminal. A hand tally of calls was also kept because (contrary to rules) operators sometimes used another operator's station. The total calls calculated by the computer and the total hand tallies for any given day usually did not match. Yet each operator insisted the tally they kept was accurate.

Operators were divided into three groups of four. Each group worked a shift for one week and then switched systematically to the next shift, which only varied by one-half hour. That is, Group 1 worked 8:30 to 5:00, Group 2 worked 9:00 to 5:30, and Group 3 worked 9:30 to 6:00. The next week Group 1 worked the middle shift, Group 2 the late shift, and Group 3 the early shift. The members of the group were changed only when someone was transferred to another department or quit—which occurred quite often.

Usually an operator was hired at a minimum wage because no previous experience or skill was required for the job. New employees trained with a more experienced worker for about two days and then were given their own station. After 90 days on the job an operator was evaluated on performance and given a ten to twelve percent raise. Shortly after the 90–day raise, most operators began to ask about opportunities in other departments. They wanted more challenge, were bored, or didn't like the other employees. Other departments had turnover problems too and were talking to the operators on the side. If a transfer was not granted, the operator would often quit. Only three workers had been in the department more than nine months. No other department wanted them.

TIME FOR CHANGE

The challenge of overseeing seven departments kept me quite busy for the first few days. But I did manage to spend a few minutes observing the Phone Inquiry Department each afternoon. It was obvious that the operators liked to gossip among themselves and were not eager to answer the beeping phones. It was a game to wait long enough that another operator would break down and answer first. The winner was the worker who eventually answered the phone last.

The gossip and talking sometimes led to loud laughter and an occasional outburst of shouts and chasing around the department. The noise didn't seem too serious when I was there, but early one morning I received a call from one of the bank vice-presidents. He had received numerous complaints from customers about the background noise they heard when they called the Phone Inquiry Department. He had decided to check it out and had called the department about 5:30 the previous evening, after I had gone for the day. He said the giggling, shouting, and general commotion, were not professional and did not portray the proper bank image.

Now I knew something had to be done right away. The vice-president would probably anonymously check on the department again very soon.

Margaret Jardine

(A)

Margaret Jardine was sure when she completed her bachelor's degree in business at Oregon State over thirteen years ago that she would go places at Pacific Security Bank. She had graduated with honors from OSU with an emphasis in finance and had joined PSB because she had felt it was a very progressive bank and sufficiently large to allow for movement into a variety of areas. She had done very well in the bank's credit training program and had gone, after one year with the bank, directly to the position of loan officer at the Albany branch of PSB. Albany was located in central Oregon about 100 miles south of Portland, where PSB had its headquarters.

She had been successful in her first assignment, she felt, because she had been able to work closely with Ben Compton, the branch manager, who had given her a good deal of direction and guidance on handling accounts during her first year or two. She had also put in a great deal of extra time in that assignment keeping up with pending loan requests and making sure of each analysis. The only disconcerting thing to Margaret was that she had spent a full seven years in the assignment. This, she felt, had been too long.

When Ben Compton left the bank, Margaret felt there were a lot of reasons why she should be his replacement.

When she did get the position as Albany branch manager, this confirmed her faith that she was on her way up in the bank. She was only the second woman in PSB to attain the position of branch manager. Recently, though, she had begun again to wonder about her future with the bank.

She had now been branch manager for over five years, and from her current perspective she could see what kind of opportunities were open to her in the bank. The fact was that there was very little movement among officers in the bank. There was only one other branch manager in the division who had been in his position less time than she had, and there were several who had been branch manager for ten years or more. The division manager, Dan Martin, was new but had himself been a branch manager for twelve years at Corvallis before becoming division manager. Recently at a bank dinner, Dan had introduced her to someone from another division and had referred to her as "one of our new branch managers."

In her four years at Albany, the branch had done well, with substantial increases in loans outstanding and earnings. Recently, though, she felt that she had lost some of her motivation. Now if she put in extra time, it was only out of necessity of getting something done that had to be done. It certainly was not voluntary.

SOME PERSPECTIVES ON INDIVIDUAL BEHAVIOR

Margaret felt trapped, pigeonholed in some way. She felt like she had no idea where she was going in the bank. Others who had joined the bank and gone through the training program with her had stayed near PSB headquarters in Portland and had gotten a somewhat broader experience than she had. They were probably more promotable now than she was. She was at the stage with the bank where, although her market value was still high, her salary increases were getting smaller and smaller and her options were becoming more limited. Recently, Margaret had turned down a very attractive offer from Northwestern Security and Exchange, a small finance company in Salem near Albany, because there, too, she thought there would be little opportunity for advancement. Now she wondered if it would have been better to take the opportunity.

Still, there was an ambiguity in Margaret's feelings about the bank. She felt that a move to corporate headquarters would be advantageous for her at this point in her career. At least that seemed like the next logical move; and if she could do that, there was a great likelihood she would be made an AVP. Yet she had really come to enjoy living in Albany. She was not sure that she wanted to leave Albany for the big city atmosphere of Portland even if a better opportunity presented itself there. Her dilemma was that as long as she stayed in Albany, there was no place for her to go in the bank, and realistically speaking, an offer to go to Portland was not exactly imminent.

After dialing Northwestern's number, only to hang up before it rang, Margaret decided she would put off any decision for at least a month so she could have plenty of time to think over her situation. Besides, Dan Martin had called from division headquarters and asked to see her on Monday morning. This would be a good time, she felt, to raise her concerns with Dan and to get his ideas.

(B)

Dan Martin had felt like he had it coming. After twelve years as manager of the Corvallis, Oregon, branch office of Pacific Security Bank, Dan had been made division manager of PSB's southern division. PSB was a large northwestern bank centered at Portland and the southern division covered most of the southern half of Oregon. Since division headquarters were in Corvallis, Dan had not had to move with the promotion.

Along with the benefits, the new position had brought its share of headaches. Dan's biggest challenge, he felt, was keeping the branch managers in his division motivated. Margaret Jardine, the branch manager at Albany, was of particular concern to Dan. Margaret was a very promising young employee who, at 36, still had a bright future with the bank Margaret's problem was not exactly motivation, since she was one of the most outstanding performers in the division and her branch had significantly bettered its financial position during her term as branch manager. Nor was her problem one of complacency or stagnation. While several of the other branch managers had been in their positions for ten years or more, Margaret had only been a branch manager for five years or so.

From Dan's point of view, Margaret's problem was simply that she had become dissatisfied with the bank. She apparently felt, from comments she had made to Dan and Ed Finnerty, the former division manager, that she had not had sufficient opportunity to move around within the bank and to gain a broad exposure to PSB's operation. She also felt according to Ed, that her advancement opportunities had not come quickly enough. Ed had said that he expected her to leave PSB sometime in the near future if she could not get the kind of opportunity she wanted within the bank.

Of late, Dan had noticed a subtle

change in her attitude. Margaret seemed to be less enthusiastic than Dan had come to expect of her and had been, on occasion, very critical of PSB's operations. One or two of the other branch managers in the division had described her as being "cynical" and even "apathetic." Dan decided he had better bring her in to talk over her situation.

Dan turned to her file to learn more about her background and her history with PSB. Margaret had been at the Albany branch for twelve of her thirteen years with the bank. She had spent only seven years as a loan officer before becoming the branch manager. That she had been very highly rated in her appraisals throughout her career also corroborated Dan's impression of her. Her salary increases had been generally quite high. Considering the age at which she had become a branch manager and the kind of increases she had received, it was difficult to understand her dissatisfaction.

Dan read through the appraisals Ed Finnerty had written on her in the last few years. The following comment from her most recent appraisal was typical:

"Margaret is a highly competent professional with sound quantitative skills and credit judgment as well as the skills necessary for bank leadership. She gets along well with the people who work with and for her and

the Albany branch has shown consistent improvement under her direction."

Dan found some of Ed's concluding remarks interesting:

"Margaret is anxious to continue her career at Pacific Security and looks forward in the future to taking on new and diverse assignments within the bank. She would like, however, to remain in the southern division and her preference would be to remain in or around Albany, where she has lived for some time."

It occurred to Dan that Margaret wanted to have her cake and eat it, too. She could never really advance in the bank without moving close to Portland. To remain in Albany was impossible if she really wanted to develop her career at the bank. Dan might be able to offer her a divisional assignment in Corvallis sometime down the line, but this would not really be a step up for her, and Dan was not sure she would want to move to Corvallis. Dan did not want to see her leave the bank, and he also felt that her present frame of mind needed to be changed if she ever wanted to advance beyond her present position at the bank. Not knowing exactly what he planned to say to Margaret or what he could do for her, Dan phoned her and arranged an appointment for the following Monday morning.

Mountain View Hospital

Motivation Dilemma

THE SETTING

Mountain View is a not-for-profit hospital in an urban setting. Built in 1964, many of the staff have been with the hospital since that time. "We have a family feeling" is a frequent response of the staff to questions about their employment. Many of the managers in all departments have moved up through the ranks.

The system, of which Mountain View is a member, has a Hay system for determining salaries. The current Personnel Director started as a secretary in the human resources division, but has little formal training in human resources. She is not highly regarded by the administrator because she tends to be very quiet and responds to orders rather than being proactive. She holds firm against any requests to deviate from or reframe policy, and always interprets policy in the most conservative way possible. She makes no attempt to help managers with a problem that derives from the Hay system: The employees who have been there the longest have reached the highest point in their range and so cannot be given more than a 1 percent increase unless they are judged to be distinguished in their annual performance appraisals.

One hospital in the system has heard of tentative movements toward unionization. Hearing that, the corporation ordered that no manager do anything that would fuel the fire of union organizing. Census at Mountain View has been declining, reaching 55 percent in 1985. The trend continues downward. Most managers have not replaced staff lost through attrition because they do not want to lay anyone off during the traditional decline of census in July and August. The pool of temporary employees is inadequate whenever the census goes above 51 percent, and weekends and holidays are a nightmare to staff. At the moment employees are receiving their shifts and keeping their benefits; hanging over everyone is the realization that if the census declines that may no longer be true.

THE PROBLEM

For years the emergency room had been extremely busy and an important feeder into the hospital. Since the development of free-standing "clinics" like Medfirst and Insta-Care, usage of the emergency room has declined precipitously.

A history of managers in emergency looked like a history of a military unit. The first manager was there for 15 years and "ran a tight ship." Then different M.D.'s were on call and available. Now there are emergency room physicians and specialized staff.

The second manager was equally authoritarian, and the staff had developed a distrust of any other units in the hospital. They did not report to nursing, but to an operations vp, and they came to believe that nobody cared about what happened to them. Half of the staff had been there more than 10 years. Several had left other units because they did not like the style of the manager. When the second manager's lack of support for nursing policies in the rest of the hospital and refusal to consider a new strategic place for the emergency room, he was fired as manager.

When Polly was hired from another department in the hospital, there was considerable distrust from the staff. Polly's style was participative but she was willing to make hard decisions. The staff was angry about the firing of their old manager; they didn't think Polly understood how misused they had been. Polly was charged with bringing all of the emergency room staff, including physicians, into a place where they could contribute to the new strategic directions instead of blocking them.

THE CHALLENGE

You are Polly's supervisor. How would you help her to assess the situation, determine the motivators for the group, and develop a plan of action? Be specific and realistic and relate your suggestions to motivation theory. (It is not helpful to say, "Show them we care.")

In the Future People May Demand More Than a Formal Role; They Want Genuine Meaning in Relationships

"Of course I love you. I'm your husband. That's my job!"

3

Differing Viewpoints on the Impact of Groups

Groups in organizations have become the subject of widely differing viewpoints in recent years. Many individuals underestimate the impact of groups; they believe that, to get along well in an organization, all they have to do is to meet their boss's expectations. For some it is surprising to discover that informal groups within an organization have real power to make their lives easy or difficult, depending on the acceptance of the individual into the group. Similarly, some managers tend to ignore informal groups and have little faith in committees. In their attempts to develop an effective organization, they focus exclusively on the relationship between manager and subordinates. These managers' attempts to introduce changes are often frustrated by resistance from informal groups.

On the other hand, some individuals overestimate the impact of groups. Such people focus only on the interests of the group and ignore the wishes of the boss. Usually that is a risky strategy. Likewise, some managers rely heavily on groups for making and implementing decisions. But involving every individual in every decision can lead to inefficiency and a very slow decision-making process.

These extreme positions are not helpful in dealing with work groups. However, the examples illustrate that groups do have a major impact on their members, on other groups, and on the parent organization. This section presents a variety of viewpoints on important issues concerning groups in organizations.

One area where groups can make a contribution is in decision making. A group can be an asset in some aspects, but a liability in others. A better understanding of when and how to use a group in decision making should reduce much of the frustration that people experience in the process. One problem in decision making concerns

DIFFERING VIEWPOINTS ON THE IMPACT OF GROUPS

the management of agreement. Most people want to be agreeable and get along with others. One negative result of this desire is that many times a group will agree to do something that none of the individuals want to do. The inability to cope with agreement rather than the inability to cope with conflict is the most pressing issue of modern organizations.

If we move up the organization ladder one more step, we see that organizations contain many groups that often compete for resources, prestige, power, and so forth. Being caught between conflicting groups can prove to be a very confusing and frustrating experience.

Finally, we look at some of the implications of power and obedience. We present a case study of managers who order their subordinates to carry out activities that are dishonest and unethical. The pressures in organizations that lead to these kinds of actions need to be carefully analyzed.

Group behavior involves a complex set of relationships. This section provides concepts and ideas to help bring order to that chaotic world. In addition, applying those ideas to the cases and exercises should help develop relevant skills as well as increase awareness of the importance of this topic.

READINGS

Assets and Liabilities in Group Problem Solving: The Need for an Integrative Function *

NORMAN R.F. MAIER

Research on group problem solving reveals that the group has both advantages and disadvantages over individual problem solving. If the potentials for group problem solving can be exploited and if its deficiencies can be avoided, it follows that group problem solving can attain a level of proficiency not ordinarily achieved. The requirement for achieving this level of group performance seems to hinge on developing a style of discussion leadership which maximizes the group's assets and minimizes its liabilities. Since members possess the essential ingredients for the solutions, the deficiencies that appear in group solutions reside in the processes by which group solutions develop. These processes can determine whether the group functions effectively or ineffectively. The critical factor in a group's potential is organization and integration. With training, a leader can supply these functions and serve as the group's central nervous system, thus permitting the group to emerge as a highly efficient entity.

* The research reported in the following reading was supported by Grant No. MH–02704 from the United States Public Health Service. Grateful acknowledgment is made for the constructive criticism of Melba Colgrove, Junie Janzen, Mara Julius, and James Thurber.

A number of investigators have raised the question of whether group problem solving is superior, inferior, or equal to individual problem solving. Evidence can be cited in support of each position so that the answer to this question remains ambiguous. Rather than pursue this generalized approach to the question, it seems more fruitful to explore the forces that

influence problem solving under the two conditions (see reviews by Hoffman 1965; Kelley and Thibaut 1954). It is hoped that a better recognition of these forces will permit clarification of the varied dimensions of the problem-solving process, especially in groups.

The forces operating in such groups include some that are assets, some that are liabilities, and some that can be either assets or liabilities, depending upon the skills of the members, especially those of the discussion leader. Let us examine these three sets of forces.

GROUP ASSETS

Greater Sum Total of Knowledge and Information

There is more information in a group than in any of its members. Thus problems that require the utilization of knowledge should give groups an advantage over individuals. Even if one member of the group (e.g., the leader) knows much more than anyone else, the limited unique knowledge of lesser-informed individuals could serve to fill in some gaps in knowledge. For example, a skilled machinist might contribute to an engineer's problem solving and an ordinary workman might supply information on how a new machine might be received by workers.

Greater Number of Approaches to a Problem

It has been shown that individuals get into ruts in their thinking (Duneker 1945; Maier 1930; Wertheimer 1959). Many obstacles stand in the way of achieving a goal, and a solution must circumvent these. The individual is handicapped in that he tends to persist in his approach and thus fails to find another approach that might solve the problem in a simpler manner. Individuals in a group have the same failing, but the approaches in which they are persisting may be different. For example, one researcher may try to prevent the spread of a disease by making man immune to the germ, another by finding and destroying the carrier of the germ, and still another by altering the environment so as to kill the germ before it reaches man. There is no way of determining which approach will best achieve the desired goal, but undue persistence in any one will stifle new discoveries. Since group members do not have identical approaches, each can contribute by knocking others out of ruts of thinking.

Participation in Problem Solving Increases Acceptance

Many problems require solutions that depend upon the support of others to be effective. Insofar as group problem solving permits participation and influence, it follows that more individuals accept solutions when a group solves the problem than when one person solves it. When one individual solves a problem he still has the task of persuading others. It follows, therefore, that when groups solve such problems, a greater number of persons accept and feel responsible for making the solution work. A low-quality solution that has good acceptance can be more effective than a higher-quality decision that lacks acceptance.

Better Comprehension of the Decision

Decisions made by an individual, which are to be carried out by others, must be communicated from the decision maker to the decision executors. Thus individual problem solving often requires an additional stage—that of relaying the decision reached. Failures in this communication process detract from the merits of the decision and can even cause its failure or create a problem of greater magnitude than the initial problem that was solved. Many organizational problems can be traced to inadequate communication of decisions made by superiors and transmitted to subordinates who have the task of implementing the decision.

The chances for communication failures are greatly reduced when the individuals who must work together in executing the decision have participated in making it. They not only understand the solution because they saw it develop, but they are also aware of the several other alternatives that were considered and the reasons why they were discarded. The common assumption that decisions supplied by superiors are arbitrarily reached therefore disappears. A full knowledge of goals, obstacles, alternatives, and factual information is essential to communication, and this communication is maximized when the total problem-solving process is shared.

GROUP LIABILITIES

Social Pressure

Social pressure is a major force making for conformity. The desire to be a good group member and to be accepted tends to silence disagreement and favors consensus. Majority opinions tend to be accepted regardless of whether or not their objective quality is logically and scientifically sound. Problems requiring solutions based upon facts, regardless of feelings and wishes, can suffer in group problem-solving situations.

It has been shown (Maier and Solem 1952) that minority opinions in leaderless groups have little influence on the solution reached, even when these opinions are the correct ones. Reaching agreement in a group often is confused with finding the right answer, and it is for this reason that the dimensions of a decision's acceptance and its objective quality must be distinguished (Maier 1963).

Valence or Solutions

When leaderless groups (made up of three or four persons) engage in problem solving, they propose a variety of solutions. Each solution may receive both critical and supportive comments, as well as descriptive and explorative comments from other participants. If the number of negative and positive comments for each solution are algebraically summed, each may be given a valence index (Hoffman and Maier 1964). The first solution that receives a positive valence value of .15 tends to be adopted to the satisfaction of all par-

ticipants about 85 percent of the time, regardless of its quality. Higher-quality solutions introduced after the critical value for one of the solutions has been reached have little chance of achieving real consideration. Once some degree of consensus is reached, the jelling process seems to proceed rather rapidly.

The critical valence value of .15 appears not to be greatly altered by the nature of the problem or the exact size of the group. Rather, it seems to designate a turning point between the idea-getting process and the decision-making process (idea evaluation). A solution's valence index is not a measure of the number of persons supporting the solution, since a vocal minority can build up a solution's valence by actively pushing it. In this sense, valence becomes an influence in addition to social pressure in determining an outcome.

Since a solution's valence is independent of its objective quality, this group factor becomes an important liability in group problem solving, even when the value of a decision depends upon objective criteria (facts and logic). It becomes a means whereby skilled manipulators can have more influence over the group process than their proportion of membership deserves.

Individual Domination

In most leaderless groups a dominant individual emerges and captures more than his share of influence on the outcome. He can achieve this end through a greater degree of participation (valence), persuasive ability, or stubborn persistence (fatiguing the opposition). None of these factors is related to problem-solving ability, so that the best problem solver in the group may not have the influence to upgrade the quality of the group's solution (which he would have had if left to solve the problem by himself).

Hoffman and Maier (1967) found that

the mere fact of appointing a leader causes this person to dominate a discussion. Thus, regardless of his problem-solving ability a leader tends to exert a major influence on the outcome of a discussion.

Conflicting Secondary Goal: Winning the Argument

When groups are confronted with a problem, the initial goal is to obtain a solution. However, the appearance of several alternatives causes individuals to have preferences and once these emerge the desire to support a position is created. Converting those with neutral viewpoints and refuting those with opposed viewpoints now enter into the problem-solving process. More and more the goal becomes that of winning the decision rather than finding the best solution. This new goal is unrelated to the quality of the problem's solution and therefore can result in lowering the quality of the decision (Hoffman and Maier 1967).

FACTORS THAT SERVE AS ASSETS OR LIABILITIES, DEPENDING LARGELY UPON THE SKILL OF THE DISCUSSION LEADER

Disagreement

The fact that discussion may lead to disagreement can serve either to create hard feelings among members or lead to a resolution of conflict and hence to an innovative solution (Hoffman 1961; Hoffman, Harburg, and Maier 1962; Hoffman and Maier 1961; Maier 1958, 1963; Maier and Hoffman 1965). The first of these outcomes of disagreement is a liability, especially with regard to the acceptance of solutions; while the second is an asset, particularly where innovation is desired. A leader can treat disagreement as undesirable and thereby reduce the probability of both hard feelings and innovation, or he can maximize disagreement and risk

hard feelings in his attempts to achieve innovation. The skill of a leader requires this ability to create a climate for disagreement which will permit innovation without risking hard feelings. The leader's perception of disagreement is one of the critical factors in this skill area (Maier and Hoffman 1965). Others involve permissiveness (Maier 1953), delaying the reaching of a solution (Maier and Hoffman 1960b; Maier and Solem 1962), techniques for processing information and opinions (Maier 1963; Maier and Hoffman 1960a; Maier and Maier 1957), and techniques for separating idea getting from idea evaluation (Maier 1960, 1963; Osborn 1953).

Conflicting Interests Versus Mutual Interests

Disagreement in discussion may take many forms. Often participants agree with one another with regard to solutions, but when issues are explored one finds that these conflicting solutions are designed to solve different problems. Before one can rightly expect agreement on a solution, there should be agreement on the goal, as well as on the various obstacles that prevent the goal from being reached. Once distinctions are made between goals, obstacles, and solutions (which represent ways of overcoming obstacles), one finds increased opportunities for cooperative problem solving and less conflict (Hoffman and Maier 1959; Maier 1960, 1963; Maier and Solem 1962; Solem 1965).

Often there is also disagreement regarding whether the objective of a solution is to achieve quality or acceptance (Maier and Hoffman 1964b), and frequently a stated problem reveals a complex of separate problems, each having separate solutions so that a search for a single solution is impossible (Maier 1963). Communications often are inadequate because the discussion is not synchronized and each person is engaged in discussing a different aspect. Organizing discussion to synchronize the exploration of different aspects of the problem and to follow a systematic procedure increases solution quality (Maier and Hoffman 1960a; Maier and Maier 1957). The leadership function of influencing discussion procedure is quite distinct from the function of evaluating or contributing ideas (Maier 1950, 1953).

When the discussion leader aids in the separation of the several aspects of the problem-solving process and delays the solution-mindedness of the group (Maier 1958, 1963; Maier and Solem 1962), both solution quality and acceptance improve; when he hinders or fails to facilitate the isolation of these varied processes, he risks a deterioration in the group processes (Solem 1965). His skill thus determines whether a discussion drifts toward conflicting interests or whether mutual interests are located. Cooperative problem solving can only occur after the mutual interests have been established and it is surprising how often they can be found when the discussion leader makes this his task (Maier 1952, 1963; Maier and Hayes 1962).

Risk Taking

Groups are more willing than individuals to reach decisions involving risks (Wallach and Kogan 1965; Wallach, Kogan, and Bem 1962). Taking risks is a factor in acceptance of change, but change may represent either a gain or a loss. The best guard against the latter outcome seems to be primarily a matter of a decision's quality. In a group situation this depends upon the leader's skill in utilizing the factors that represent group assets and avoiding those that make for liabilities.

Time Requirements

In general, more time is required for a group to reach a decision than for a single individual to reach one. Insofar as some problems require quick decisions, individual decisions are favored. In other situations acceptance and quality are requirements, but excessive time without sufficient returns also represents a loss. On the other hand, discussion can resolve conflicts, whereas reaching consensus has limited value (Wallach and Kogan 1965). The practice of hastening a meeting can prevent full discussion, but failure to move a discussion forward can lead to boredom and fatigue-type solutions, in which members agree merely to get out of the meeting. The effective utilization of discussion time (a delicate balance between permissiveness and control on the part of the leader), therefore, is needed to make the time factor an asset rather than a liability. Unskilled leaders tend to be too concerned with reaching a solution and therefore terminate a discussion before the group potential is achieved (Maier and Hoffman 1960b).

Who Changes

In reaching consensus or agreement, some members of a group must change. Persuasive forces do not operate in individual problem solving in the same way they operate in a group situation; hence, the changing of someone's mind is not an issue. In group situations, however, who changes can be an asset or a liability. If persons with the most constructive views are induced to change the end product suffers; whereas if persons with the least constructive point of view change, the end product is upgraded. The leader can upgrade the quality of a decision because his position permits him to protect the person with a minority view and increase his opportunity to influence the majority position. This protection is a constructive factor because a minority viewpoint influences only when facts favor it (Maier 1950, 1952; Maier and Solem 1952).

The leader also plays a constructive

role insofar as he can facilitate communications and thereby reduce misunderstandings (Maier 1952; Solem 1965). The leader has an adverse effect on the end product when he suppresses minority views by holding a contrary position and when he uses his office to promote his own views (Maier and Hoffman 1960b, 1962; Maier and Solem 1952). In many problem-solving discussions the untrained leader plays a dominant role in influencing the outcome, and when he is more resistant to changing his views than are the other participants, the quality of the outcome tends to be lowered. This negative leader influence was demonstrated by experiments in which untrained leaders were asked to obtain a second solution to a problem after they had obtained their first one (Maier and Hoffman 1960a). It was found that the second solution tended to be superior to the first. Since the dominant individual had influenced the first solution, he had won his point and therefore ceased to dominate the subsequent discussion which led to the second solution. Acceptance of a solution also increases as the leader sees disagreement as idea producing rather than as a source of difficulty or trouble (Maier and Hoffman 1965). Leaders who see some of their participants as troublemakers obtain fewer innovative solutions and gain less acceptance of decisions made than leaders who see disagreeing members as persons with ideas.

THE LEADER'S ROLE FOR INTEGRATED GROUPS

Two Differing Types of Group Process

In observing group problem solving under various conditions, it is rather easy to distinguish between cooperative problem-solving activity and persuasion or selling approaches. Problem-solving activity includes searching, trying out ideas on one another, listening to understand rather than to refute, making relatively short speeches, and reacting to differences in opinion as stimulating. The general pattern is one of rather complete participation, involvement. Persuasion activity includes the selling of opinions already formed, defending a position held, either not listening at all or listening in order to be able to refute, talking dominated by a few members, unfavorable reactions to disagreement, and a lack of involvement of some members. During problem solving the behavior observed seems to be that of members interacting as segments of a group. The interaction pattern is not between certain individual members, but with the group as a whole. Sometimes it is difficult to determine who should be credited with an idea. "It just developed," is a response often used to describe the solution reached. In contrast, discussions involving selling or persuasive behavior seem to consist of a series of interpersonal interactions with each individual retaining his identity. Such groups do not function as integrated units but as separate individuals, each with an agenda. In one situation the solution is unknown and is sought; in the other, several solutions exist and conflict occurs because commitments have been made.

The Starfish Analogy

The analysis of these two group processes suggests an analogy with the behavior of the rays of a starfish under two conditions; one with the nerve ring intact, the other with the nerve ring sectioned (Hamilton 1922; Moore 1924; Moore and Doudoroff 1939; Schneirla and Maier 1940). In the intact condition, locomotion and righting behavior reveal that the behavior of each ray is not merely a function of local stimulation. Locomotion and righting behavior reveal a degree of coordination and interdependence that is centrally controlled. However, when the nerve ring is sectioned, the behavior of one ray still can influence others, but internal coordination is lacking. For example, if one ray is stimulated, it may step forward, thereby exerting pressure on the sides of the other four rays. In response to these external pressures (tactile stimulation), these rays show stepping responses on the stimulated side so that locomotion successfully can occur on the basis of external control. If, however, stimulation is applied to opposite rays, the specimen may be "locked" for a time, and in some species the conflicting locomotions may divide the animal, thus destroying it (Crozier 1920; Moore and Doudoroff 1939).

Each of the rays of the starfish can show stepping responses even when sectioned and removed from the animal. Thus each may be regarded as an individual. In a starfish with a sectioned nerve ring the five rays become members of a group. They can successfully work together for locomotion purposes by being controlled by the dominant ray. Thus if uniformity of action is desired, the group of five rays can sometimes be more effective than the individual ray in moving the group toward a source of stimulation. However, if "locking" or the division of the organism occurs, the group action becomes less effective than individual action. External control, through the influence of a dominant ray, therefore can lead to adaptive behavior for the starfish as a whole, but it can also result in a conflict that destroys the organism. Something more than external influence is needed.

In the animal with an intact nerve ring, the function of the rays is coordinated by the nerve ring. With this type of internal organization the group is always superior to that of the individual actions. When the rays function as a part of an organized unit, rather than as a group that is physically together, they become a higher type of organization—a single intact organism. This is accomplished by the nerve ring, which in itself does not do the behaving. Rather, it receives and processes the data which the rays relay to it. Through this central organization, the responses of rays become part of a larger pattern so that together they constitute a single coordinated total response rather than a group of individual responses.

The Leader as the Group's Central Nervous System

If we now examine what goes on in a discussion group we find that members can problem-solve as individuals, they can influence others by external pushes and pulls, or they can function as a group with varying degrees of unity. In order for the latter function to be maximized, however, something must be introduced to serve the function of a nerve ring. In our conceptualization of group problem solving and group decision (Maier 1963), we see this as the function of the leader. Thus the leader does not serve as the dominant ray and produce the solution. Rather, his function is to receive information, facilitate communications between individuals, relay messages, and integrate the incoming responses so that a single unified response occurs.

Solutions that are the product of good group discussions often come as surprises to discussion leaders. One of these is unexpected generosity. If there is a weak member, this member is given less to do, in much the same way as an organism adapts to an injured limb and alters the function of other limbs to keep the locomotion on course. Experimental evidence supports the point that group decisions award special consideration to needy members of groups (Hoffman and Maier 1959). Group decisions in industrial groups often give smaller assignments to the less gifted (Maier 1952). A leader could not effectually impose such differential treatment on group members without being charged with discriminatory practices.

Another unique aspect of group discussion is the way fairness is resolved. In a simulated problem situation involving the problem of how to introduce a new truck into a group of drivers, the typical group solution involves a trading of trucks so that several or all members stand to profit. If the leader makes the decision the number of persons who profit is often confined to one (Maier and Hoffman 1962; Maier and Zerfoss 1952). In industrial practice, supervisors assign a new truck to an individual member of a crew after careful evaluation of needs. This practice results in dissatisfaction, with the charge of *unfair* being leveled at him. Despite those repeated attempts to do justice, supervisors in the telephone industry never hit upon the notion of a general reallocation of trucks, a solution that crews invariably reach when the decision is theirs to make.

In experiments involving the introduction of change, the use of group discussion tends to lead to decisions that resolve differences (Maier 1952, 1953; Maier and Hoffman 1961, 1964a, 1964b). Such decisions tend to be different from decisions reached by individuals because of the very fact that disagreement is common in group problem solving and rare in individual problem solving. The process of resolving differences in a constructive setting causes the exploration of additional areas and leads to solutions that are integrative rather than compromises.

Finally, group solutions tend to be tailored to fit the interests and personalities of the participants; thus group solutions to problems involving fairness, fears, facesaving, etc., tend to vary from one group to another. An outsider cannot process these variables because they are not subject to logical treatment.

If we think of the leader as serving a function in the group different from that of its membership, we might be able to create a group that can function as an intact organism. For a leader, such functions as rejecting or promoting ideas according to his personal needs are out of bounds. He must be receptive to information contributed, accept contributions without evaluating them (post contributions on a chalk board to keep them alive), summarize information to facilitate integration, stimulate exploratory behavior, create awareness of problems of one member by others, and detect when the group is ready to resolve differences and agree to a unified solution.

Since higher organisms have more than a nerve ring and can store information, a leader might appropriately supply information, but according to our model of a leader's role, he must clearly distinguish between supplying information and promoting a solution. If his knowledge indicates the desirability of a particular solution, sharing this knowledge might lead the group to find this solution, but the solution should be the group's discovery. A leader's contributions do not receive the same treatment as those of a member of the group. Whether he likes it or not, his position is different. According to our conception of the leader's contribution to discussion, his role not only differs in influence, but gives him an entirely different function. He is to serve much as the nerve ring in the starfish and to further refine this function so as to make it a higher type of nerve ring.

This model of a leader's role in group processes has served as a guide for many of our studies in group problem solving. It is not our claim that this will lead to the best possible group function under all conditions. In sharing it we hope to indicate the nature of our guidelines in exploring group leadership as a function quite different and apart from group membership. Thus the model serves as a stimulant for research problems and as a guide for our analyses of leadership skills and principles.

CONCLUSIONS

On the basis of our analysis, it follows that the comparison of the merits of group versus individual problem solving depends on the nature of the problem, the goal to be achieved (high quality solution, highly accepted solution, effective communication and understanding of the solution, innovation, a quickly reached solution, or satisfaction), and the skill of the discussion leader. If liabilities inherent in groups are avoided, assets capitalized upon, and conditions that can serve either favorable or unfavorable outcomes are effectively used, it follows that groups have a potential which in many instances can exceed that of a superior individual functioning alone, even with respect to creativity.

This goal was nicely stated by Thibaut and Kelley (1961) when they

> wonder whether it may not be possible for a rather small, intimate group to establish a problem-solving process that capitalizes upon the total pool of information and provides for great interstimulation of ideas

without any loss of innovative creativity due to social restraints (p. 268).

In order to accomplish his high level of achievement, however, a leader is needed who plays a role quite different from that of the members. His role is analogous to that of the nerve ring in the starfish which permits the rays to execute a unified response. If the leader can contribute the integrative requirement, group problem solving may emerge as a unique type of group function. This type of approach to group processes places the leader in a particular role in which he must cease to contribute, avoid evaluation, and refrain from thinking about solutions or group *products*. Instead he must concentrate on the group *process*, listen in order to understand rather than to appraise or refute, assume responsibility for accurate communication between members, be sensitive to unexpressed feelings, protect minority points of view, keep the discussion moving, and develop skills in summarizing.

The Abilene Paradox: The Management of Agreement

JERRY B. HARVEY

The July afternoon in Coleman, Texas (population 5,607) was particularly hot—

Excerpted, by permission of the publisher, from "The Abilene Paradox: The management of agreement" by Harvey, pp. 63–80, *Organizational Dynamics*, Summer 1974 © 1974 by AMACOM, a division of American Management Associations, New York. All rights reserved.

104 degrees as measured by the Walgreen's Rexall Ex-Lax temperature gauge. In addition, the wind was blowing fine-grained West Texas topsoil through the house. But the afternoon was still tolerable—even potentially enjoyable. There was a fan going on the back porch; there

was cold lemonade; and finally, there was entertainment. Dominoes. Perfect for the conditions. The game required little more physical exertion than an occasional mumbled comment, "Shuffle 'em," and an unhurried movement of the arm to place the spots in the appropriate perspective on the table. All in all, it had the makings of an agreeable Sunday afternoon in Coleman—that is, it was until my father-in-law suddenly said, "Let's get in the car and go to Abilene and have dinner at the cafeteria."

I thought, "What, go to Abilene? Fifty-three miles? In this dust storm and heat? And in an unairconditioned 1958 Buick?"

But my wife chimed in with, "Sounds like a great idea. I'd like to go. How about you, Jerry?" Since my own preferences were obviously out of step with the rest I replied, "Sounds good to me," and added, "I just hope your mother wants to go."

"Of course I want to go," said my mother-in-law. "I haven't been to Abilene in a long time."

So into the car and off to Abilene we went. My predictions were fulfilled. The heat was brutal. We were coated with a fine layer of dust that was cemented with perspiration by the time we arrived. The food at the cafeteria provided first-rate testimonial material for antacid commercials.

Some four hours and 106 miles later we returned to Coleman, hot and exhausted. We sat in front of the fan for a long time in silence. Then, both to be sociable and to break the silence, I said, "It was a great trip, wasn't it?"

No one spoke.

Finally my mother-in-law said, with some irritation, "Well, to tell the truth, I really didn't enjoy it much and would rather have stayed here. I just went along because the three of you were so enthusiastic about going. I wouldn't have gone if you all hadn't pressured me into it."

I couldn't believe it. "What do you mean 'you all'?" I said. "Don't put me in the 'you all' group. I was delighted to be doing what we were doing. I didn't want to go. I only went to satisfy the rest of you. You're the culprits."

My wife looked shocked. "Don't call me a culprit. You and Daddy and Mama were the ones who wanted to go. I just went along to be sociable and to keep you happy. I would have had to be crazy to want to go out in heat like that."

Her father entered the conversation abruptly. "Hell!" he said.

He proceeded to expand on what was already absolutely clear. "Listen, I never wanted to go to Abilene. I just thought you might be bored. You visit so seldom I wanted to be sure you enjoyed it. I would have preferred to play another game of dominoes and eat the leftovers in the icebox."

After the outburst of recrimination we all sat back in silence. Here we were, four reasonably sensible people who, of our own volition, had just taken a 106–mile trip across a godforsaken desert in a furnace-like temperature through a cloud-like dust storm to eat unpalatable food at a hole-in-the-wall cafeteria in Abilene, when none of us had really wanted to go. In fact, to be more accurate, we'd done just the opposite of what we wanted to do. The whole situation simply didn't make sense.

At least it didn't make sense at the time. But since that day in Coleman, I have observed, consulted with, and been a part of more than one organization that has been caught in the same situation. As a result, they have either taken a side trip, or, occasionally, a terminal journey to Abilene, when Dallas or Houston or Tokyo was where they really wanted to go. And for most of those organizations, the negative consequences of such trips, measured in terms of both human misery and economic loss, have been much greater than for our little Abilene group.

This article is concerned with that paradox—the Abilene Paradox. Stated simply, it is as follows: Organizations frequently take actions in contradiction to what they really want to do and therefore defeat the very purposes they are trying to achieve. It also deals with a major corollary of the paradox, which is that *the inability to manage agreement is a major source of organization dysfunction.* Last, the article is designed to help members of organizations cope more effectively with the paradox's pernicious influence.

As a means of accomplishing the above, I shall: (1) describe the symptoms exhibited by organizations caught in the paradox; (2) describe, in summarized case study examples, how they occur in a variety of organizations; (3) discuss the underlying causal dynamics; (4) indicate some of the implications of accepting this model for describing organizational behavior; (5) make recommendations for coping with the paradox; and, in conclusion (6) relate the paradox to a broader existential issue.

SYMPTOMS OF THE PARADOX

The inability to manage agreement, not the inability to manage conflict, is the essential symptom that defines organizations caught in the web of the Abilene Paradox. That inability effectively to manage agreement is expressed by six specific subsymptoms, all of which were present in our family Abilene group.

1. Organization members agree privately, as individuals, as to the nature of the situation or problem facing the organization. For example, members of the Abilene group agreed that they were enjoying themselves sitting in front of the fan, sipping lemonade, and playing dominoes.

2. Organization members agree privately, as individuals, as to the steps that would be required to cope with the situation or problem they face. For members of the Abilene group "more

of the same" was a solution that would have adequately satisfied their individual and collective desires.

3. Organization members fail to accurately communicate their desires and/or beliefs to one another. In fact, they do just the opposite and thereby lead one another into misperceiving the collective reality. Each member of the Abilene group, for example, communicated inaccurate data to other members of the organization. The data, in effect, said, "Yeah, it's a great idea. Let's go to Abilene," when in reality members of the organization individually and collectively preferred to stay in Coleman.

4. With such invalid and inaccurate information, organization members make collective decisions that lead them to take actions contrary to what they want to do, and thereby arrive at results that are counterproductive to the organization's intent and purposes. Thus, the Abilene group went to Abilene when it preferred to do something else.

5. As a result of taking actions that are counterproductive, organization members experience frustration, anger, irritation, and dissatisfaction with their organization. Consequently, they form subgroups with trusted acquaintances and blame other subgroups for the organization's dilemma. Frequently, they also blame authority figures and one another. Such phenomena were illustrated in the Abilene group by the "culprit" argument that occurred when we had returned to the comfort of the fan.

6. Finally, if organization members do not deal with the generic issue—the inability to manage agreement—the cycle repeats itself with greater intensity. The Abilene group, for a variety of reasons, the most important of which was that it became conscious

of the process, did not reach that point.

To repeat, the Abilene Paradox reflects a failure to manage agreement. In fact, it is my contention that the inability to cope with (manage) agreement, rather than the inability to cope with (manage) conflict is the single most pressing issue of modern organizations.

OTHER TRIPS TO ABILENE

The Abilene Paradox is no respecter of individuals, organizations, or institutions. Following are descriptions of two other trips to Abilene that illustrate both the pervasiveness of the paradox and its underlying dynamics.

Case no. 1: The boardroom

The Ozyx Corporation is a relatively small industrial company that has embarked on a trip to Abilene. The president of Ozyx has hired a consultant to help discover the reasons for the poor profit picture of the company in general and the low morale and productivity of the R & D division in particular. During the process of investigation, the consultant becomes interested in a research project in which the company has invested a sizable proportion of its R & D budget.

When asked about the project by the consultant in the privacy of their offices, the president, the vice-president for research, and the research manager each describes it as an idea that looked great on paper but will ultimately fail because of the unavailability of the technology required to make it work. Each of them also acknowledges that continued support of the project will create cash flow problems that will jeopardize the very existence of the total organization.

Furthermore, each individual indicates he has not told the others about his reservations. When asked why, the president says he can't reveal his "true" feelings because abandoning the project, which has been widely publicized, would make the company look bad in the press and, in addition, would probably cause his vice-president's ulcer to kick up or perhaps even cause him to quit, "because he has staked his professional reputation on the project's success."

Similarly, the vice-president for research says he can't let the president or the research manager know of his reservations because the president is so committed to it that "I would probably get fired for insubordination if I questioned the project."

Finally, the research manager says he can't let the president or vice-president know of his doubts about the project because of their extreme commitment to the project's success.

All indicate that, in meetings with one another, they try to maintain an optimistic facade so the others won't worry unduly about the project. The research director, in particular, admits to writing ambiguous progress reports so the president and the vice-president can "interpret them to suit themselves." In fact, he says he tends to slant them to the "positive" side, "given how committed the brass are."

The scent of the Abilene trail wafts from a paneled conference room where the project research budget is being considered for the following fiscal year. In the meeting itself, praises are heaped on the questionable project and a unanimous decision is made to continue it for yet another year. Symbolically, the organization has boarded a bus to Abilene.

In fact, although the real issue of agreement was confronted approximately eight months after the bus departed, it was nearly too late. The organization failed to meet a payroll and underwent a two-year period of personnel cutbacks, retrenchments, and austerity. Morale suffered, the most competent technical personnel resigned, and the organization's prestige in the industry declined.

Case no. 2: The Watergate

Apart from the grave question of who did what, Watergate presents America with the profound puzzle of why. What is it that led such a wide assortment of men, many of them high public officials, possibly including the President himself, either to instigate or to go along with and later try to hide a pattern of behavior that by now appears not only reprehensible, but stupid? (*The Washington Star and Daily News*, editorial, May 27, 1973.)

One possible answer to the editorial writer's question can be found by probing into the dynamics of the Abilene paradox. I shall let the reader reach his own conclusions, though, on the basis of the following excerpts from testimony before the Senate investigating committee on "The Watergate Affair".

In one exchange, Senator Howard Baker asked Herbert Porter, then a member of the White House staff, why he (Porter) found himself "in charge of or deeply involved in a dirty tricks operation of the campaign." In response, Porter indicated that he had had qualms about what he was doing, but that he "... was not one to stand up in a meeting and say that this should be stopped.... I kind of drifted along."

And when asked by Baker why he had "drifted along," Porter replied, "In all honesty, because of the fear of the group pressure that would ensue, of not being a team player," and "... I felt a deep sense of loyalty to him (the President) or was appealed to on that basis." (*The Washington Post*, June 8, 1973, p. 20.)

Jeb Magruder gave a similar response to a question posed by committee counsel Dash. Specifically, when asked about his, Mr. Dean's, and Mr. Mitchell's reactions to Mr. Liddy's proposal, which included bugging the Watergate, Mr. Magruder replied, "I think all three of us were appalled. The scope and size of the project were something that at least in my mind were not envisioned. I do not think it was

in Mr. Mitchell's mind or Mr. Dean's, although I can't comment on their states of mind at that time."

Mr. Mitchell, in an understated way, which was his way of dealing with difficult problems like this, indicated that this was not an "acceptable project." (*The Washington Post*, June 15, 1973, p. A14.)

Later in his testimony Mr. Magruder said, "... I think I can honestly say that no one was particularly overwhelmed with the project. But I think we felt that this information could be useful, and Mr. Mitchell agreed to approve the project, and I then notified the parties of Mr. Mitchell's approval." (*The Washington Post*, June 15, 1973, p. A14.)

Although I obviously was not privy to the private conversations of the principal characters, the data seem to reflect the essential elements of the Abilene Paradox. First, they indicate agreement. Evidently, Mitchell, Porter, Dean, and Magruder agreed that the plan was inappropriate. ("I think I can honestly say that no one was particularly overwhelmed with the project.") Second, the data indicate that the principal figures then proceeded to implement the plan in contradiction to their shared agreement. Third, the data surrounding the case clearly indicate that the plan multiplied the organization's problems rather than solved them. And finally, the organization broke into subgroups with the various principals, such as the President, Mitchell, Porter, Dean, and Magruder, blaming one another for the dilemma in which they found themselves, and internecine warfare ensued.

In summary, it is possible that because of the inability of White House staff members to cope with the fact that they agreed, the organization took a trip to Abilene.

ANALYZING THE PARADOX

The Abilene Paradox can be stated succinctly as follows: Organizations frequently take actions in contradiction to the data they have for dealing with problems and, as a result, compound their problems rather than solve them. Like all paradoxes, the Abilene Paradox deals with absurdity. On the surface, it makes little sense for organizations, whether they are couples or companies, bureaucracies or governments, to take actions that are diametrically opposed to the data they possess for solving crucial organizational problems. Such actions are particularly absurd since they tend to compound the very problems they are designed to solve and thereby defeat the purposes the organization is trying to achieve. However, as Robert Rapaport and others have so cogently expressed it, paradoxes are generally paradoxes only because they are based on a logic or rationale different from what we understand or expect.

Discovering that different logic not only destroys the paradoxical quality but also offers alternative ways for coping with similar situations. Therefore, part of the dilemma facing an Abilene-bound organization may be the lack of a map—a theory or model—that provides rationality to the paradox. The purpose of the following discussion is to provide such a map.

The map will be developed by examining the underlying psychological themes of the profit-making organization and the bureaucracy and it will include the following landmarks: (1) Action Anxiety; (2) Real Risk; (3) Separation Anxiety; and (4) the Psychological Reversal of Risk and Certainty. I hope that the discussion of such landmarks will provide harried organization travelers with a new map that will assist them in arriving at where they really want to go and, in addition, will help them in assessing the risks that are an inevitable part of the journey.

ACTION ANXIETY

Action anxiety provides the first landmark for locating roadways that by-

pass Abilene. The concept of action anxiety says that the reason organization members take actions in contradiction to their understanding of the organization's problems lies in the intense anxiety that is created as they think about acting in accordance with what they believe needs to be done. As a result, they opt to endure the professional and economic degradation of pursuing an unworkable research project or the consequences of participating in an illegal activity rather than act in a manner congruent with their beliefs. It is not that organization members do not know what needs to be done—they do know. For example, the various principals in the research organization cited *knew* they were working on a research project that had no real possibility of succeeding. And the central figures of the Watergate episode apparently *knew* that, for a variety of reasons, the plan to bug the Watergate did not make sense.

Such action anxiety experienced by the various protagonists may not make sense, but the dilemma is not a new one. In fact, it is very similar to the anxiety experienced by Hamlet, who expressed it most eloquently in the opening lines of his famous soliloquy:

> To be or not to be; that is the question:
> Whether 'tis nobler in the mind to suffer
> The slings and arrows of outrageous fortune
> Or to take arms against a sea of troubles
> And by opposing, end them? ... (*Hamlet*, Act III, Scene II)

REAL RISK

Risk is a reality of life, a condition of existence. John Kennedy articulated it in another way when he said at a news conference, "Life is unfair." By that I believe he meant we do not know, nor can we predict or control with certainty, either the events that impinge upon us or the outcomes of actions we undertake in response to those events.

Consequently, in the business environment, the research manager might find that confronting the president and the vice-president with the fact that the project was a "turkey" might result in his being fired. And Mr. Porter's saying that an illegal plan of surveillance should not be carried out could have caused his ostracism as a non-team player. There are too many cases when confrontation of this sort has resulted in such consequences. The real question, though, is not, Are such fantasized consequences possible? but, Are such fantasized consequences likely?

Thus, real risk is an existential condition, and all actions do have consequences that, to paraphrase Hamlet, may be worse than the evils of the present. As a result of their unwillingness to accept existential risk as one of life's givens, however, people may opt to take their organizations to Abilene rather than run the risk, no matter how small, of ending up somewhere worse.

Again, though, one must ask, What is the real risk that underlies the decision to opt for Abilene? What is at the core of the paradox?

FEAR OF SEPARATION

One is tempted to say that the core of the paradox lies in the individual's fear of the unknown. Actually, we do not fear what is unknown, but we are afraid of things we do know about. What do we know about that frightens us into such apparently inexplicable organizational behavior?

Separation, alienation, and loneliness are things we do know about—and fear. Both research and experience indicate that ostracism is one of the most powerful punishments that can be devised. Solitary confinement does not draw its coercive strength from physical deprivation. The evidence is overwhelming that we have a fundamental need to be connected, engaged, and related and a reciprocal need not to be separated or alone. Everyone of us, though, has experienced aloneness. From the time the umbilical cord was cut, we have experienced the real anguish of separation—broken friendships, divorces, deaths, and exclusions. C.P. Snow vividly described the tragic interplay between loneliness and connection:

"Each of us is alone; sometimes we escape from our solitariness, through love and affection or perhaps creative moments, but these triumphs of life are pools of light we make for ourselves while the edge of the road is black. Each of us dies alone."

That fear of taking risks that may result in our separation from others is at the core of the paradox. It finds expression in ways of which we may be unaware, and it is ultimately the cause of the self-defeating, collective deception that leads to self-destructive decisions within organizations.

Concretely, such fear of separation leads research committees to fund projects that none of its members want and, perhaps, White House staff members to engage in illegal activities that they don't really support.

THE PSYCHOLOGICAL REVERSAL OF RISK AND CERTAINTY

One piece of the map is still missing. It relates to the peculiar reversal that occurs in our thought processes as we try to cope with the Abilene Paradox. For example, we frequently fail to take action in an organizational setting because we fear that the actions we take may result in our separation from others, or, in the language of Mr. Porter, we are afraid of being tabbed as "disloyal" or are afraid of being ostracized as "non-team players." But therein lies a paradox within a paradox, because our very unwillingness to take such risks virtually ensures the separation and aloneness we so fear. In effect, we reverse "real existential risk" and "fantasized risk" and by doing so transform what is a probability statement into what, for all practical purposes, becomes a certainty.

Take the R & D organization described earlier. When the project fails, some people will get fired, demoted, or sentenced to the purgatory of a make-work job in an out-of-the-way office. For those who remain, the atmosphere of blame, distrust, suspicion, and backbiting that accompanies such failure will serve only to further alienate and separate those who remain.

The Watergate situation is similar. The principals evidently feared being ostracized as disloyal non-team players. When the illegality of the act surfaced, however, it was nearly inevitable that blaming, self-protective actions, and scapegoating would result in the very emotional separation from both the President and one another that the principals feared. Thus, by reversing real and fantasied risk, they had taken effective action to ensure the outcome they least desired.

One final question remains: Why do we make this peculiar reversal? I support the general thesis of Alvin Toffler and Philip Slater, who contend that our cultural emphasis on technology, competition, individualism, temporariness, and mobility has resulted in a population that has frequently experienced the terror of loneliness and seldom the satisfaction of engagement. Consequently, though we have learned of the reality of separation, we have not had the opportunity to learn the reciprocal skills of connection, with the result that, like the ancient dinosaurs, we are breeding organizations with self-destructive decision-making proclivities.

A POSSIBLE ABILENE BYPASS

Existential risk is inherent in living, so it is impossible to provide a map that meets the no-risk criterion, but it may be possible to describe the route in terms that make the landmarks understandable and that will clarify the risks involved. In order to do that, however, some commonly used terms such as victim, victimizer, collusion, responsibility, conflict, conformity, courage, confrontation, reality, and knowledge have to be redefined. In addition, we need to explore the relevance of the redefined concepts for bypassing or getting out of Abilene.

Victim and Victimizer. Blaming and fault-finding behavior is one of the basic symptoms of organizations that have found their way to Abilene, and the target of blame generally doesn't include the one who criticizes. Stated in different terms, executives begin to assign one another to roles of victims and victimizers. Ironic as it may seem, however, this assignment of roles is both irrelevant and dysfunctional, because once a business or a government fails to manage its agreement and arrives in Abilene, all its members are victims. Thus, arguments and accusations that identify victims and victimizers at best become symptoms of the paradox, and, at worst, drain energy from the problem-solving efforts required to redirect the organization along the route it really wants to take.

Collusion. A basic implication of the Abilene Paradox is that human problems of organization are reciprocal in nature. As Robert Tannenbaum has pointed out, you can't have an autocratic boss unless subordinates are willing to collude with his autocracy, and you can't have obsequious subordinates unless the boss is willing to collude with their obsequiousness.

Thus, in plain terms, each person in a self-defeating, Abilene-bound organization *colludes* with others, including peers, superiors, and subordinates, sometimes consciously and sometimes subconsciously, to create the dilemma in which the organization finds itself. To adopt a cliche of modern organization, "It takes a real team effort to go to Abilene." In that sense each person, in his own collusive manner, shares responsibility for the trip, so searching for a locus of blame outside oneself serves no useful purpose for either the organization or the individual. It neither helps the organization handle its dilemma of unrecognized agreement nor does it provide psychological relief for the individual, because focusing on conflict when agreement is the issue is devoid of reality. In fact, it does just the opposite, for it causes the organization to focus on managing conflict when it should be focusing on managing agreement.

Responsibility for Problem-Solving Action. A second question is, Who is responsible for getting us out of this place? To that question is frequently appended a third one, generally rhetorical in nature, with "should" overtones, such as, Isn't it the boss (or the ranking government official) who is responsible for doing something about the situation?

The answer to that question is no.

The key to understanding the functionality of the no answer is the knowledge that, when the dynamics of the paradox are in operation, the authority figure—and others—are in unknowing agreement with one another concerning the organization's problems and the steps necessary to solve them. Consequently, the power to destroy the paradox's pernicious influence comes from confronting and speaking to the underlying reality of the situation, and not from one's hierarchical position within the organization. Therefore, any organization member who chooses to risk confronting that reality possesses the necessary leverage to release the organization from the paradox's grip.

In one situation, it may be a research director's saying, "I don't think this project can succeed." In another, it may be Jeb Magruder's response to this question of Senator Baker:

If you were concerned because the action was known to you to be illegal, because you thought it improper or unethical, you thought the prospects for success were very meager, and you doubted the reliability of Mr. Liddy, what on earth would it have taken to decide against the plan?

Magruder's reply was brief and to the point:

Not very much, sir. I am sure that if I had fought vigorously against it, I think any of us could have had the plan cancelled. (*Time*, June 25, 1973, p. 12.)

Reality, Knowledge, Confrontation. Accepting the paradox as a model describing certain kinds of organizational dilemmas also requires rethinking the nature of reality and knowledge, as they are generally described in organizations. In brief, the underlying dynamics of the paradox clearly indicate that organization members generally know more about issues confronting the organization than they don't know. The various principals attending the research budget meeting, for example, knew the research project was doomed to failure. And Jeb Magruder spoke as a true Abilener when he said, "We knew it was illegal, probably, inappropriate." (*The Washington Post*, June 15, 1973, p. A16.)

Given this concept of reality and its relationship to knowledge, confrontation becomes the process of facing issues squarely, openly, and directly in an effort to discover whether the nature of the underlying collective reality is agreement or conflict. Accepting such a definition of confrontation has an important implication for change agents interested in making organizations more effective. That is, organization change and effectiveness may be facilitated as much by confronting the organization with what it knows and agrees upon as by confronting it with what it doesn't know or disagrees about.

THE ABILENE PARADOX AND THE MYTH OF SISYPHUS

In essence, this paper proposes that there is an underlying organizational reality that includes both agreement and disagreement, cooperation and conflict. However, the decision to confront the possibility of organization agreement is all too difficult and rare, and its opposite, the decision to accept the evils of the present, is all too common. Yet those two decisions may reflect the essence of both our human potential and our human imperfectability. Consequently, the choice to confront reality in the family, the church, the business, or the bureaucracy, though made only occasionally, may reflect those "peak experiences" that provide meaning to the valleys.

In many ways, they may reflect the experience of Sisyphus. As you may remember, Sisyphus was condemned by Pluto to a perpetuity of pushing a large stone to the top of a mountain, only to see it return to its original position when he released it. As Camus suggested in his revision of the myth, Sisyphus' task was absurd and totally devoid of meaning. For most of us, though, the lives we lead pushing papers or hubcaps are no less absurd, and in many ways we probably spend about as much time pushing rocks in our organizations as Sisyphus did in his.

Camus also points out, though, that on occasion as Sisyphus released his rock and watched it return to its resting place at the bottom of the hill, he was able to recognize the absurdity of his lot, and for brief periods of time, transcend it.

So it may be with confronting the Abilene Paradox. Confronting the absurd paradox of agreement may provide, through activity, what Sisyphus gained from his passive but conscious acceptance of his fate. Thus, through the process of active confrontation with reality, we may take respite from pushing our rocks on their endless journeys and, for brief moments, experience what C.P. Snow termed "the triumphs of life we make for ourselves" within those absurdities we call organizations.

Performance Lies Are Hazardous to Organizational Health

LEE T. PERRY and JAY B. BARNEY

When performance standards set by top management become increasingly difficult to attain, many employees resort to performance lies to protect their jobs. This avoidance of difficult issues and problems, the authors warn, only steers the organization toward obsolescence.

A new first-line supervisor at a large electronics firm was evaluating the performance of her production group. She found that her group had managed to meet the production goals set by the plant manager even though the centrifuge, a crucial piece of equipment in the production process, had been broken several times the previous month. Wondering how much more her group could produce with a centrifuge running properly full time, she decided to estimate its maximum capacity.

Her findings astonished her. Even running at full capacity and never breaking down, the centrifuge simply could not process enough units to meet the production goals. Yet a review of her records indicated that month after month, these "impossible" goals had been met.

When she told all this to her manager, his reply shocked her: "Don't tell anyone about what you've found—it means we've been shipping defective parts!"

The example depicts a kind of lie that we have found to be especially common in organizational life—the lie about individual or group performance. An organizational performance lie can be defined as any deliberate effort, either within or across organizational boundaries, by a person or group of persons to deceive an-

other person or group about performance levels. Such lies can occur in a wide range of situations—from lying to the payroll department about the number of hours worked to lying to the federal government about illegal payments made to foreign governments in exchange for lucrative contracts.

We'll begin by exploring the conditions that encourage performance lies in organizations. Then we present a case study of how one attempt to break out of or "forsake" a performance lie in a particular organization was thwarted. Finally, we analyze the activities that both encourage and preserve performance lies.

CAUSES OF PERFORMANCE LIES

Franz Kafka observed that "A man lies as little as he can only when he lies as little as he can, not when he is given the smallest opportunity to lie." The implication, of course, is that the opportunity to lie does not necessarily affect the telling of a lie; those who have a predisposition to lie will do so regardless of the situation facing them. This is a very individualistic view of lying behavior—either persons are liars or they are not.

An alternative view of lying can be taken from the legal concept of entrapment. Illegal entrapment involves inciting crimes that otherwise would not have been committed. Implicit in this is the assumption that circumstances can be created that make it very difficult for an individual or a group to refrain from committing a crime. When authorities create such conditions, those who commit crimes should not be held responsible. Applying the same logic to dishonesty in organizations suggests that situational circumstances may exist that make it very difficult to avoid telling performance lies or maintaining the lies that have been told by others. From this perspective, some of the causes of performance lies may be situational in nature, thus making individual responsibility more diffuse.

In any given case it is often difficult to distinguish between individual and situational causes of performance lies. Usually, both types of encouragement to lie are so interconnected that attempts to disentangle them are futile. Although we accept this interconnectedness, we have chosen here to avoid the moral conundrums that would confound any discussion of individual causes. Instead, we will explore the social forces that lead to organizational performance lies.

The Situational Causes of Performance Lies

First, we must emphasize one important point. The existence of situational causes of performance lies does not presuppose the existence of the lies themselves. The decision to lie is an individual one. However, situational causes of performance lies provide structural incentives to effect and structural buffers to preserve the lie. Therefore, they do increase the likelihood that persons will tell and be successful at telling performance lies.

A recent article from *Business Week* makes the observation that in the diversified corporation run by financial executives who have no feel for the fiber and texture of a business, the bottom line is all that matters. They manage the bottom line to produce a desired profit and then order division executives to produce their share—or else. This opens the door for widespread dishonesty that top management does not expect and cannot curtail because it does not understand the business.

Figure 1 presents a simple conceptual framework for understanding this observation. Initially, *performance expectations* are developed at Level IV by top management. These performance expectations are communicated downward, contributing to the performance expectations of both Level III and Level II managers. Whether *expected performance* levels are attained (represented by a plus sign) or not attained (represented by a minus sign) by Levels III, II, and I managers depends very much upon the standard set by the performance expectations at Level IV. The original standard can be either too high (resulting in expected performance that is seldom achieved) or too low (resulting in expected performance that is easily achieved). In periodic *evaluation* of managers at all levels, actual performance is compared with expected performance. Lower-level evaluations contribute to higher-level evaluations. Thus, when managers can give their subordinates high evaluations, they increase the likelihood that they themselves will be evaluated highly. Periodic evaluations both provide feedback for the setting of future performance expectations and are related to which *expected outcomes* are received.

The Coalition

A performance lie can occur at any level in the organization: In Figure 1, for example, it occurs at Level I. In making it appear that an unreached expected level of performance has been reached, the performance lie transforms a potentially negative performance evaluation into a positive or, at least, a neutral one. Because lower-level evaluations contribute to higher-level evaluations, a performance lie benefits both the teller and the receiver—and, in turn, the receiver's receiver. Expected outcomes are more positively valent for managers at all organizational levels as a result of the performance lie, even if the probability of receiving expected outcomes does not change. For this reason, managers at all levels have a clear self-interest in maintaining a performance lie.

In hierarchial organizations there is of course a clear power differential between top-management and lower-management levels. As Figure 1 illustrates, the performance expectations set by top management define successful performance at all organizational levels. Managers below the highest level have the power to administer performance policy, but not to *make* it. This power differential often has the effect of forming two distinct groups—those *with* and those *without* the discretion to set organizational performance goals. A principal function of the performance lie is to set up a barrier between these two groups—a barrier that affects the content of communications between them. Using

the lie, those managers lacking the power to set performance expectations insulate themselves from the control of top management and are able to exercise expanded self-control. Soon afterward, these individuals form a network of informal alliances that are held together by the benefits accruing from the lie and the potential negative consequences that would occur if the lie were discovered. We have chosen to call this network of informal alliances the *coalition to effect and preserve the organizational performance lie.*

The coalition is maintained primarily by the loyalty of each member—loyalty expressed through the continued support and use of the lie. If only one member of the coalition were to forsake it, the difference between his or her picture of performance and the picture distorted by the lie would predictably raise top management's suspicions. If this scenario were carried to its logical conclusion, the entire coalition could be undermined. Obviously, it is very important to the continued viability of the coalition that *all* its members choose to continue using the lie.

FIGURE 1

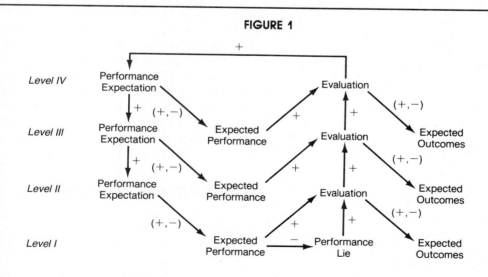

This is contrary to A.O. Hirschman's notion of loyalty. In exploring the relationship between "voice" and loyalty, he proposes that loyalty enhances voice. In other words, loyalty to the organization would encourage employees to deal openly with difficult problems and issues—to voice publicly their observations that performance expectations were unrealistic. Loyalty would also encourage them to take personal and interpersonal risks in dealing with any difficulties they perceive as undermining the efficacy of the organization.

The use of the performance lie is antithetical to the use of voice. Loyalty to the coalition in effecting and preserving the organizational performance lie is very different from loyalty to the organization. The former requires that its members conceal difficult issues and problems to avoid both personal and interpersonal risks. It invalidates upward communications by repressing accurate information flow and thus undermines the organizations ability to adapt to a changing environment. It becomes a policy of long-term irrationality.

The coalition employs subtle mechanisms for ensuring the loyalty of its members. For example, William H. Read's observation that there is a selective screening of information from the bottom up in industrial hierarchies can be reinterpreted in terms of top-down incentives to screen information. Within the coalition, supervisors influence the validity of the information they receive from subordinates by (1) the questions they ask, (2) the manner in which they ask these questions, and (3) the kinds of answers they want to hear. Subordinates reluctant to reveal unpleasant matters, errors, and difficulties are reinforced by supervisors who consciously choose not to probe. Thus the performance lie becomes easier to tell and maintain by subordinates.

More overt mechanisms are also used to protect a performance lie when the honesty of one of its members challenges loyalty to the coalition. The coalition can be perceived as a system of buffers that prevents a true picture of performance at one level from reaching higher levels. The situation in the large electronics firm mentioned above provides an illustration of this system of buffers. The first-line supervisor (Level I) discovered that a performance lie was being told by members of her production group and reported this discovery to her supervisor (Level II). However, because the supervisor knew that knowledge of the lie would affect his performance evaluation, he ordered her not to repeat it and he continued to ship defective parts. In effect, the supervisor acted in both his and the coalition's best interests by choosing to serve as a buffer against disclosure of the true picture of performance to top management.

In this examination of the situational causes of the performance lie, we've focused on elements that would increase an understanding of the coalition's need to effect and preserve the organizational performance lie. Under normal circumstances the activities of the coalition are not very clear-cut. They are disconnected and inconspicuous; coalition members may not even be aware of their interests. Only when revelation of a performance lie is threatened do the coalition's activities manifest themselves outwardly.

The case that follows involves an attempt to forsake a performance lie within a family service organization. The resistance forces that were mobilized illustrate how in this particular instance the coalition operated successfully to preserve the lie.

A CASE OF GOING PUBLIC

The Family Service Organization (FSO) was established over 100 years ago to assist member families in the development of Judeo-Christian brotherhood. Its current membership numbers in the millions. Structurally, the FSO closely resembles an eight-tiered business organization (see Figure 2). The president and board of directors formulate policy for the entire organization, and five lower levels of administrators execute various policies. The FSO relies upon a highly centralized, conservative management orientation, although a movement toward increased decentralization and liberalization of management practices within FSO is currently underway.

The home visiting program of the FSO has been in existence since the early 1960s. Its purpose is to offer assistance to FSO member families, thus linking the full resources of the FSO and its member families. If a family is experiencing financial difficulties, for example, a home visitor will inform his or her department manager, who in turn will inform the branch manager. The branch manager then will draw upon branch resources and, if necessary, district resources to financially assist the member family.

According to FSO policy the home visiting program is expected to meet three performance goals: (1) Every member family is to be visited at home at least once a month, (2) all home visits are to be made by two-person home visiting teams, and (3) no more than five families are to be assigned to each home visiting team.

The Eastern Branch Home Visiting Program

The eastern branch of the Atlantic Coast district had struggled with administration of the home visiting program for several years. Because of long travel distances involved and the limited number of qualified home visitors, it was impossible for the eastern branch to attain the expected performance level. Increasing pressures to improve performance were placed upon the eastern branch and, as a result, it used several lies to bolster performance reports: First, it increased the number of home visitors by splitting up the two-person teams; second, more than five families were assigned to each home visitor; and third, letters sent to marginally involved member families were reported to the district manager as home visits. None of these actions was formally approved by the district manager. Other branches in the Atlantic Coast district, however, employed similar performance lies. In fact, the eastern branch manager had decided to use the above performance lies after several informal conversations with the managers of these branches.

The way in which home-visiting reporting procedures were administered also encouraged the use of the performance lie. For example, reports involved only one statistic—the monthly percentage of families in a branch that were home-visited. If the reported percentage was high, the branch manager was commended by the district manager. No questions were asked about either the validity of the percentages or how they were obtained. If, however, the reported percentage was low, the district manager severely reprimanded the branch manager at the monthly meeting. In spite of these pres-

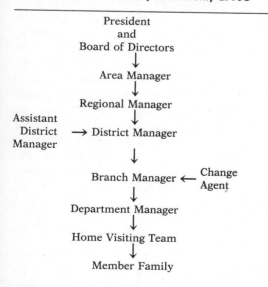

FIGURE 2   Hierarchy of Authority at FSO

President
and
Board of Directors
↓
Area Manager
↓
Regional Manager
↓
Assistant District Manager → District Manager
↓
Branch Manager ← Change Agent
↓
Department Manager
↓
Home Visiting Team
↓
Member Family

sures to do otherwise, the eastern branch manager still wanted to develop a method for effectively operating the program without having to resort to performance lies.

On September 16 the change agent, a staff assistant to the eastern branch manager with responsibility for the home visiting program, applied for and received permission from FSO's board of directors to design a pilot home visiting program for the eastern branch. The program was to be developed using input from the eastern branch home visitors over a period of several months and implementation was tentatively scheduled for the beginning of the following year. The district manager was notified about the pilot program by the regional manager, his direct superior. It was the change agent's understanding that the message communicated by the regional manager to the district manager was: "The eastern branch has permission from the board to conduct a pilot home visiting program. Do not meddle in it."

On October 7 the change agent was asked by the district manager to attend a meeting on the pilot program. During this meeting the change agent explained to the district manager the exploratory nature of the program, stating that he was committed to keeping the district manager informed of future program developments. The district manager requested a written statement of the intentions of the program from the change agent and got it on October 21.

A Pilot Program

Between September 24 and December 31 the change agent held several discussion sessions with eastern branch home visitors, and developed an initial design for the pilot program. The design of the pilot program and the current program were only marginally different, the major difference being that performance lies were not used in the design of the pilot program. The latter had three important features: First, not every family in the eastern branch would be visited monthly. Home visiting priority would be based on a family's level of involvement in FSO. The more the family used FSO's resources, the more likely it would be home visited monthly. Second, preassignment interviews would be conducted by department managers with each home visitor to determine (1) his or her present attitudes about home visiting, (2) criteria for pairing him or her with a home visiting partner, (3) criteria for making family assignments, and (4) the number of families he or she would like the team to visit. Third, one or two home-visiting teams would be assigned to visit annually all those families that did not regularly receive home visits.

The philosophy behind the pilot program was to develop long-term solutions to the eastern branch's inability to meet FSO performance goals, not to conceal these difficulties with a series of performance lies. The level of success of the program would ultimately be based upon the recruitment and development of additional home visitors, putting the original FSO goals within reach.

From October 21 to February 18, contact between the change agent and the district manager was limited to two communications, the first being a letter from the district manager to the change agent in which he outlined his performance expectations for the pilot program. The second communication was an announcement by the change agent to the district manager that the design of the pilot program would be presented to all eastern branch home visitors at a meeting to be held on February 18. The district manager later requested time to speak at that meeting.

A Challenge to the Program

During the meeting the change agent outlined the new eastern branch home visiting program to the branch's home visitors. Afterward the district manager pumped the change agent's hand, congratulating him on having done a fine job. The district manager then delivered his own speech about home visiting. The two main points of the district manager's speech were that everyone in the eastern branch should receive a home visit monthly, and that decisions about home visiting assignments should be made by department managers and approved by the branch manager, *not* tailored to the personal preferences of individual home visitors. In short, the district manager argued for a home-visiting program that basically adhered to the status quo and rejected the program just proposed by the change agent.

A meeting was scheduled by the change agent for that same day in which he had intended to discuss with the district manager future branch-district linkages and evaluation criteria for the program. The district manager did not attend this meeting. Instead, he sent the assistant district manager, who made it absolutely clear that his superior would under no circumstances attend the meeting and then turned the discussion to that morning's events. The assistant district manager argued that there was very little difference between the district manager's and the change agent's presentations. He explained that his superior had presented an ideal home visiting program, and the change agent merely proposed a means for reaching that ideal. After a period of intense debate over what the district manager did and did not say, the direction of the meeting shifted again, and the two men discussed what actions should now be taken to clear up the confusion that resulted from the district manager's speech. The results of these negotiations satisfied the change agent, but he still sensed that it was necessary to speak directly with the district manager.

Later that same day the change agent approached the district manager and said,

"I really think we have some fundamental differences about the administration of the home visiting program and I would be available to discuss them with you any time." The district manager responded, "That will not be necessary. I'm not the one you need to convince. Convince your branch manager; that's all you need to do."

Aftermath of the February 18 Meeting

On February 28 the change agent received a telephone call from the assistant district manager who wanted to discuss further the eastern branch home visiting program. A meeting was scheduled for the afternoon of March 1. At that meeting the assistant district manager gave the change agent some interesting information: (1) During the previous fall the district manager had, on several occasions, come close to eliminating the eastern branch's home visiting program because he did not feel right about it; (2) the district manager wanted to hear more from his superiors about the pilot program; (3) the message that had been communicated by the regional manager was not "do not meddle" but rather "The eastern branch will be conducting a pilot home visiting program. I don't like it. Don't let it spread." (It is unclear whether this was the actual message communicated by the regional manager or if the district manager somehow reinterpreted it according to his own feelings about the program.)

The assistant district manager and the change agent agreed that a statement of guidelines for the eastern branch home visiting program should be prepared before March 17 and 18—the days on which a district conference attended by the area manager would be held. This statement was to outline the roles and responsibilities of all those involved in the program, the parameters established by the board of directors of FSO concerning program development, and future evaluation criteria. In this statement, there was to be a clause specifying that it was within the district manager's authority to terminate the pilot program whenever he considered such an action necessary. This statement was to be approved by the area manager during his visit or the pilot program would be stopped immediately. At the conclusion of the meeting, both the assistant district manager and the change agent felt that their ability to work together had been strengthened. Commitments were made to communicate at more regular intervals over the coming months.

On the evening of March 17, two meetings were scheduled for the Atlantic Coast district conference and were attended by the change agent. Between these two meetings, the assistant district manager asked the change agent to fill a vacant position at the district level. Though surprised, the change agent accepted. Later, he discovered that he could not continue to oversee the eastern branch home visiting program in his new position.

The next day the change agent discussed his new position with the assistant district manager, who happened to comment that it was under the area manager's direction that the change agent had been asked to fill the position. Later, while speaking with the area manager, the change agent asked him very candidly why he had suggested this change, and the area manager responded that all he had done was tell the district manager that he had the authority to promote the change agent to a district-level position. He then briefly questioned the change agent about his role in the eastern branch home visiting program. He noted that the ideas behind the pilot program had a great deal of merit, and requested that the change agent meet with him sometime to develop them further. Finally, the area manager said: "I think we need to take *your* home visiting program away from this setting. I hope you'll help me with that."

Activities of the Coalition to Effect the Performance Lie

In this case, encouragement to lie about the home visitors' performance took several forms. Initially, it had been the unattainable performance goals (that is, all families should be home visited once a month, all visits should be made by two-person teams, and no team should have more than five families assigned to it) set by FSO that encouraged the telling of the performance lie. There were not enough qualified home visitors in the eastern branch to meet these goals. Without the performance lie, it was impossible for the branch to show top management that it could perform at the expected level.

The reporting system also encouraged the use of the performance lie. Information concerning the performance of the home visiting program was conveyed by the eastern branch manager to the district manager through a single statistic—the percentage of families in the branch that were home-visited monthly. No questions were ever asked about the statistic's source or its validity. If the statistic communicated to the district manager was high, compared with that of other branches, the eastern branch manager was duly commended. However, if the statistic was comparably low, the eastern branch manager was criticized by the district manager in front of his peers at a monthly meeting. Moreover, each time the eastern branch manager reported an acceptable percentage of families home-visited, the district manager raised his performance expectations. (Of course, the district manager was only responding to the performance expectation imposed on him by the regional manager and originally created by FSO's president and board of directors.) Thus acceptable performance became increasingly more difficult to attain until it finally became impossible.

In an attempt to please the district manager and avoid the negative sanctions resulting from unacceptable home visiting performance, branch managers throughout the Atlantic Coast district adopted strategies of lying about home visiting performance. Either uninvolved families were not assigned home visiting teams, two-person home visiting teams were divided; or teams were assigned more than five families to raise perceived performance levels. The performance lie took a more obvious form when letters sent to FSO families were counted as personal visits in the statistics reported to the district manager.

Peer-group encouragements to effect the performance lie were also observed. Among themselves, the branch managers were very open about their truth-bending practices. The eastern branch manager, for example, knew that his *actual* performance was probably comparable to that of any other branch manager. It was not actual performance, however, that seemed to concern the district manager— it was *reported* performance. The eastern branch manager soon discovered that reporting actual performance always made him appear in a comparatively unfavorable light to the district manager. Under these circumstances, using the performance lie became a pragmatic rationalization for the eastern branch manager.

Activities of the Coalition to Preserve the Performance Lie

The actions taken by the eastern branch to forsake the performance lie were disloyal to the coalition. The regional manager's reaction—"I don't like it; don't let it spread"—revealed the dominant attitude taken by members of the coalition toward the eastern branch home visiting program. In the end, the pilot program was terminated by the district manager (also a coalition member) through the cooperation of the change agent. By so doing, the coalition effectively preserved lies about home visiting performance in the Atlantic

Coast district.

The progress of the coalition's conspiracy to preserve the performance lie can be traced throughout the case. The district manager, of course, was most centrally involved in these activities. Being the immediate superior to those forsaking the performance lie, he was the principal buffer protecting it. His February 18 speech was the initial outward show of resistance to forsaking the lie. The speech, to all intents and purposes, undermined the eastern branch home visiting program while presenting a mien of innocence. It also tested the district manager's power against the support that the change agent had been granted by the board of directors. It was an attack and then pull-back-to-see-what-happens strategy that provided the district manager with an initial reading of what he could and could not do.

The March 1 meeting between the assistant district manager and the change agent was a follow-up to the February 18 speech by the district manager. During that meeting, the assistant district manager informed the change agent that the regional manager was not on his side but on the side of the district manager. The assistant district manager also revealed to the change agent that the district manager was uncomfortable with the pilot program—something he had refused to admit previously. Finally, the assistant district manager asked the change agent to prepare a statement of guidelines that explicitly recognized the district manager's authority to terminate the program. This was the important litmus test. It assured the district manager that he had ultimate control over the pilot program.

Nevertheless, the district manager knew that it would be politically unwise to terminate the pilot program unless he had a compelling reason for doing so. The program did, after all, have the support of FSO's board of directors. However, in promoting the change agent to a district-level position, the district manager found a convenient way to terminate the program without having to take a more obvious, direct approach. When he asked the area manager if it was within his authority to place the change agent in a district-level position, the district manager was actually asking the area manager if he would support the removal of the change agent from the agent's staff position in the eastern branch—the only position in which he had authority to supervise the pilot program. The area manager, of course, confirmed the district manager's authority to promote the change agent, reaffirming traditional lines of authority based upon standard FSO policy. Using this strategy, both managers were able to defuse the eastern branch home visiting program and preserve lies about home visiting performance.

SUMMARY

Performance lies arise both from individual and from situational causes, but in this article, the attention is on situational causes. These are generally triggered by loyalty to the coalition, which is expressed through the continued use of performance lies. Because performance lies help create a boundary around the coalition that insulates its activities from top management, performance lies enable members of the coalition to exercise a greater degree of internal control. Naturally, such lies are dysfunctional, resulting in the avoidance of difficult issues and problems and compromising the organization's ability to adapt to a changing environment based on accurate information.

Intergroup Problems in Organizations

EDGAR H. SCHEIN

The first major problem of groups in organizations is how to make them effective in fulfilling both organizational goals and the needs of their members. The second major problem is how to establish conditions *between groups* which will enhance the productivity of each without destroying intergroup relations and coordination. This problem exists because as groups become more committed to their own goals and norms, they are likely to become competitive with one another and seek to undermine their rivals' activities, thereby becoming a liability to the organization as a whole. The overall problem, then, is how to establish high-productive, *collaborative* intergroup relations.

SOME CONSEQUENCES OF INTERGROUP COMPETITION

The consequences of intergroup competition were first studied systematically by Sherif in an ingeniously designed setting. He organized a boys' camp in such a way

Intergroup problems in organizations (Edgar H. Schein) Schein, *Organizational Psychology*, 2d ed., © 1970, Englewood Cliffs, New Jersey.

that two groups would form and would become competitive. Sherif then studied the effects of the competition and tried various devices for reestablishing collaborative relationships between the groups (Sherif et al. 1961). Since his original experiments, there have been many replications with adult groups; the phenomena are so constant that it has been possible to make a demonstration exercise out of the experiment. (Blake and Mouton 1961). The effects can be described in terms of the following categories:

A. What happens *within* each competing group?
 1. Each group becomes more closely knit and elicits greater loyalty from its members; members close ranks and bury some of their internal differences.
 2. Group climate changes from informal, casual, playful to work and task oriented; concern for members' psychological needs declines while concern for task accomplishment increases.
 3. Leadership patterns tend to change from more democratic toward more autocratic; the group becomes more willing to tolerate autocratic leadership.
 4. Each group becomes more highly structured and organized.
 5. Each group demands more loyalty and conformity from its members in order to be able to present a "solid front."

B. What happens *between* the competing groups?
 1. Each group begins to see the other groups as the enemy, rather than merely a neutral object.
 2. Each group begins to experience distortions of perception—it tends to perceive only the best parts of itself, denying its weaknesses, and tends to perceive only the worst parts of the other group, denying

its strengths; each group is likely to develop a negative stereotype of the other ("they don't play fair like we do").
 3. Hostility toward the other group increases while interaction and communication with the other group decrease; thus it becomes easier to maintain negative stereotypes and more difficult to correct perceptual distortions.
 4. If the groups are forced into interaction—for example, if they are forced to listen to representatives plead their own and the others' cause in reference to some task—each group is likely to listen more closely to their own representative and not to listen to the representative of the other group, except to find fault with his presentation; in other words, group members tend to listen only for that which supports their own position and stereotype.

Thus far, I have listed some consequences of the competition itself, without reference to the consequences if one group actually wins out over the other. Before listing those effects, I would like to draw attention to the generality of the above reactions. Whether one is talking about sports teams, or interfraternity competition, or labor-management disputes, or interdepartmental competition as between sales and production in an industrial organization, or about international relations and the competition between the Soviet Union and the United States, the same phenomena tend to occur. If you will give just a little thought to competing groups of which you have been a member, you will begin to recognize most of the psychological responses described. I want to stress that these responses can be very useful to the group in making it more effective and highly motivated in task accomplishment. However, the same factors which improve *intra-group* effectiveness may have negative consequences for *intergroup* effectiveness. For example, as we have seen in labor-management or international disputes, if the groups perceive themselves as competitors, they find it more difficult to resolve their differences.

Let us look at the consequences of winning and losing, as in a situation where several groups are bidding to have their proposal accepted for a contract or as a solution to some problem. Many intraorganizational situations become win-or-lose affairs, hence it is of particular importance to examine their consequences.

C. What happens to the *winner?*
1. Winner retains cohesion and may become even more cohesive.
2. Winner tends to release tension, lose its fighting spirit, become complacent, casual, and playful (the "fat and happy" state).
3. Winner tends toward high intra-group cooperation and concern for members' needs, and low concern for work and task accomplishment.
4. Winner tends to be complacent and to feel that winning has confirmed the positive stereotype of itself and the negative stereotype of the "enemy" group; there is little basis for reevaluating perceptions, or reexamining group operations in order to learn how to improve them.

D. What happens to the *loser?*
1. If the situation permits because of some ambiguity in the decision (say, if judges have rendered it or if the game was close), there is a strong tendency for the loser to deny or distort the reality of losing; instead, the loser will find psychological escapes like "the judges were biased," "the judges didn't really understand our solu-

tion," "the rules of the game were not clearly explained to us," "if luck had not been against us at the one key point, we would have won," and so on.
2. If loss is accepted, the losing group tends to splinter, unresolved conflicts come to the surface, fights break out, all in the effort to find the cause for the loss.
3. Loser is more tense, ready to work harder, and desperate to find someone or something to blame—the leader, itself, the judges who decided against them, the rules of the game (the "lean and hungry" state).
4. Loser tends toward low intra-group cooperation, low concern for members' needs, and high concern for recouping by working harder.
5. Loser tends to learn a lot about itself as a group because positive stereotype of itself and negative stereotype of the other group are upset by the loss, forcing a reevaluation of perceptions; as a consequence, loser is likely to reorganize and become more cohesive and effective, once the loss has been accepted realistically.

The net effect of the win-lose situation is often that the loser is not convinced that he lost, and that intergroup tension is higher than before the competition began.

REDUCING THE NEGATIVE CONSEQUENCES OF INTERGROUP COMPETITIONS

The gains of intergroup competition may under some conditions outweigh the negative consequences. It may be desirable to have work groups pitted against one another or to have departments become cohesive loyal units, even if interdepartmental coordination suffers. Other times, however, the negative consequences outweigh the gains, and management seeks ways of reducing intergroup tension. Many of the ideas to be mentioned about how this might be accomplished also come from the basic researches of Sherif and Blake; they have been tested and found to be successful. As we will see, the problems derive not so much from being unable to think of ways for reducing intergroup conflicts as from being *unable to implement some of the most effective ways.*

The fundamental problem of intergroup competition is the conflict of goals and the breakdown of interaction and communication between the groups; this breakdown in turn permits and stimulates perceptual distortion and mutual negative stereotyping. The basic strategy of reducing conflict, therefore, is to find goals upon which groups can agree and to reestablish valid communication between the groups. The tactics to employ in implementing this strategy can be any combination of the following:

Locating a Common Enemy. For example, the competing teams of each league can compose an all-star team to play the other league, or conflicts between sales and production can be reduced if both can harness their efforts to helping their company successfully compete against another company. The conflict here is merely shifted to a higher level.

Inventing a Negotiation Strategy Which Brings Subgroups of the Competing Groups Into Interaction With Each Other. The isolated group representative cannot abandon his group position but a subgroup which is given some power can not only permit itself to be influenced by its counterpart negotiation team, but will have the strength to influence the remainder of the group.

Locating a Superordinate Goal. Such a goal can be a brand-new task which requires the cooperative effort of the previously competing groups or can be a task like analyzing and reducing the intergroup conflict itself. For example, the previously competing sales and production departments can be given the task of developing a new product line that will be both cheap to produce and in great customer demand; or, with the help of an outside consultant, the competing groups can be invited to examine their own behavior and reevaluate the gains and losses from competition.

Reducing Intergroup Competition Through Laboratory Training Methods

The last procedure mentioned above has been tried by a number of psychologists, notably Blake, with considerable success. (Blake and Mouton 1962). Assuming the organization recognizes that it has a problem, and assuming it is ready to expose this problem to an outside consultant, the laboratory approach to reducing conflict might proceed as follows: (1) The competing groups are both brought into a training setting and the goals are stated to be an exploration of mutual perceptions and mutual relations. (2) Each group is then invited to discuss its perceptions of and attitudes toward itself and the other group. (3) In the presence of both groups, representatives publicly share the perceptions of self and other which the groups have generated, while the groups are obligated to remain silent (the objective is simply to report to the other group as accurately as possible the images that each group has developed in private). (4) Before any exchange has taken place, the groups return to private sessions to digest and analyze what they have heard; there is a great likelihood that the representative reports have revealed great discrepancies to each group between its self-image and the image that the other group holds of it; the private session is partly devoted to an analysis of the reasons for the discrepancies, which forces each group to review its actual behavior toward the other group and the possible consequences of that behavior, regardless of its intentions. (5) In public session, again working through representatives, each group shares with the other what discrepancies they have uncovered and their analysis of the possible reasons for them, with the focus on the actual behavior exhibited. (6) Following this mutual exposure, a more open exploration is then permitted between the two groups on the *now-shared goal* of identifying further reasons for perceptual distortions.

Interspersed with these steps are short lectures and reading assignments on the psychology of intergroup conflict, the bases for perceptual distortion, psychological defense mechanisms, and so on. The goal is to bring the psychological dynamics of the situation into conscious awareness and to refocus the groups on the common goal of exploring jointly the problem they share. In order to do this, they must have valid data about each other, which is provided through the artifice of the representative reports.

The Blake model described above deals with the entire group. Various other approaches have been tried which start with numbers. For example, groups A and B can be divided into pairs composed of an A and B member. Each pair can be given the assignment of developing a joint product which uses the best ideas from the A product and the B product. Or, in each pair, members may be asked to argue for the product of the opposing group. It has been shown in a number of experiments that one way of changing attitudes is to ask a person to play the role of an advocate of the new attitude to be learned. (Janis and King 1954). The very act of arguing for another product, even if it is purely an exercise, exposes the person to some of its virtues which he had previously denied. A practical application of these points might be to have some members of the sales department spend time in the production department and be asked to represent the production point of view to some third party, or to have some production people join sales teams to learn the sales point of view.

Most of the approaches cited depend on a recognition of some problem by the organization and a willingness on the part of the competing groups to participate in some training effort to reduce negative consequences. The reality, however, is that most organizations neither recognize the problem nor are willing to invest time and energy in resolving it. Some of the unwillingness also arises from each competing group's recognition that in becoming more cooperative it may lose some of its own identity and integrity as a group. Rather than risk this, the group may prefer to continue the competition. This may well be the reason why, in international relations, nations refuse to engage in what seem like perfectly simple ways of resolving their differences. They resist partly in order to protect their integrity. Consequently, the *implementation* of strategies and tactics for reducing the negative consequences of intergroup competition is often a greater problem than the development of such strategies and tactics.

PREVENTING INTERGROUP CONFLICT

Because of the great difficulties of reducing intergroup conflict once it has developed, it may be desirable to prevent its occurrence in the first place. How can this be done? Paradoxically, a strategy of prevention must bring into question the fundamental premise upon which organization, through division of labor, rests. Once it has been decided by a superordinate authority to divide up functions among different departments or groups, a bias has already been introduced toward intergroup competition; for in doing its own job well, each group must to some degree compete for scarce resources and rewards from the superordinate authority. The very concept of division of labor implies a reduction of communication and interaction between groups, thus making it possible for perceptual distortions to occur.

The organization planner who wishes to avoid intergroup competition need not abandon the concept of division of labor, but he should follow some of the steps listed in creating and handling his different functional groups.

1. Relatively greater emphasis given to *total organizational effectiveness* and the role of departments in contributing to it; departments measured and rewarded on the basis of their *contribution* to the total effort rather than their individual effectiveness.
2. *High interaction* and *frequent communication* stimulated between groups to work on problems of intergroup coordination and help; organizational *rewards given partly on the basis of help* which groups give to each other.
3. Frequent *rotation of members* among groups of departments to stimulate high degree of mutual understanding and empathy for one another's problems.
4. *Avoidance of any win-lose situation;* groups never put into the position of competing for some organizational reward; emphasis always placed on pooling resources to maximize organizational effectiveness; rewards shared equally with all the groups or departments.

Most managers find the last of the above points particularly difficult to accept because of the strong belief that performance can be improved by pitting people or groups against one another in a competitive situation. This may indeed

be true in the short run, and in some cases may work in the long run, but the negative consequences we have described are undeniably a product of a competitive win-lose situation. Consequently, if a manager wishes to prevent such consequences, he must face the possibility that he may have to abandon competitive relationships altogether and seek to substitute intergroup collaboration toward organizational goals. Implementing such a preventive strategy is often more difficult, partly because most people are inexperienced in stimulating and managing collaborative relationships. Yet it is clear from observing organizations, such as those using the Scanlon Plan, not only that it is possible to establish collaborative relationships, even between labor and management, but also that where this has been done, organizational and group effectiveness have been as high as or higher than under competitive conditions.

THE PROBLEM OF INTEGRATION IN PERSPECTIVE

I have discussed two basic issues in this chapter, both dealing with psychological groups: (1) the development of groups within organizations which can fulfill both the needs of the organization and the psychological needs of its members; and (2) the problems of intergroup competition and conflict. To achieve maximum integration, the organization should be able to create conditions that will facilitate a balance between organizational goals and member needs and minimize disintegrative competition between the subunits of the total organization.

Groups are highly complex sets of relationships. There are no easy generalizations about the conditions under which they will be effective, but with suitable training, many kinds of groups can become more effective than they have been.

Consequently, group dynamics training by laboratory methods may be a more promising approach to effectiveness than attempting *a priority* to determine the right membership, type of leadership, and organization. All the factors must be taken into account, with training perhaps weighted more heavily than it has been, though the training itself must be carefully undertaken.

The creation of psychologically meaningful and effective groups does not solve all of the organization's problems if such groups compete and conflict with each other. We examined some of the consequences of competition under win-lose conditions and outlined two basic approaches for dealing with the problem: (1) reducing conflict by increasing communication and locating superordinate goals, and (2) preventing conflict by establishing from the outset organizational conditions which stimulate collaboration rather than competition.

The prevention of intergroup conflict is especially crucial if the groups involved are highly interdependent. The greater the interdependence, the greater the potential loss to the total organization of negative stereotyping, withholding of information, efforts to make the other group look bad in the eyes of the superior, and so on.

It is important to recognize that the preventative strategy does not imply absence of disagreement and artificial "sweetness and light" within or between groups. Conflict and disagreement at the level of the group or organizational *task* is not only desirable but essential for the achievement of the best solutions to problems. What is harmful is *interpersonal* or *intergroup* conflict in which the task is not as important as gaining advantage over the other person or group. The negative consequences we described, such as mutual negative stereotyping, fall into this latter category and undermine rather than aid overall task performance. And it is these kinds of conflicts which can be reduced by establishing collaborative relationships. Interestingly enough, observations of cases would suggest that task-relevant conflict which improves overall effectiveness is greater under collaborative conditions because groups and members trust each other enough to be frank and open in sharing information and opinions. In the competitive situation, each group is committed to hiding its special resources from the other groups, thus preventing effective integration of all resources in the organization.

"Why Should My Conscience Bother Me?"

KERMIT VANDIVIER

The B.F. Goodrich Co. is what business magazines like to speak of as "a major American corporation." It has operations in a dozen states and as many foreign countries, and of these far-flung facilities, the Goodrich plant at Troy, Ohio, is not the most imposing. It is a small, one-story building, once used to manufacture airplanes. Set in the grassy flatlands of west-central Ohio, it employs only about six hundred people. Nevertheless, it is one of the three largest manufacturers of aircraft wheels and brakes, a leader in a most profitable industry. Goodrich wheels and brakes support such well-known planes as the F111, the C5A, the Boeing 727, the XB70 and many others. Its customers include almost every aircraft manufacturer in the world.

Contracts for aircraft wheels and brakes often run into millions of dollars, and ordinarily a contract with a total value of less than $70,000, though welcome, would not create any special stir of joy in the hearts of Goodrich sales personnel. But purchase order P–23718, issued on June 18, 1967, by the LTV Aerospace Corporation, and ordering 202 brake assemblies for a new Air Force plane at a total price of $69,417, was received by Goodrich with considerable glee. And there was good reason. Some ten years previously, Goodrich had built a brake for

LTV that was, to say the least, considerably less than a rousing success. The brake had not lived up to Goodrich's promises, and after experiencing considerable difficulty, LTV had written off Goodrich as a source of brakes. Since that time, Goodrich salesmen had been unable to sell so much as a shot of brake fluid to LTV. So in 1967, when LTV requested bids on wheels and brakes for the new A7D light attack aircraft it proposed to build for the Air Force, Goodrich submitted a bid that was absurdly low, so low that LTV could not, in all prudence, turn it down.

Goodrich had, in industry parlance, "bought into the business." Not only did the company not expect to make a profit on the deal; it was prepared, if necessary, to lose money. For aircraft brakes are not something that can be ordered off the shelf. They are designed for a particular aircraft, and once an aircraft manufacturer buys a brake, he is forced to purchase all replacement parts from the brake manufacturer. The $70,000 that Goodrich would get for making the brake would be a drop in the bucket when compared with the cost of the linings and other parts the Air Force would have to buy from Goodrich during the lifetime of the aircraft. Furthermore, the company which manufacturers brakes for one particular model of an aircraft quite naturally has the inside track to supply other brakes when the planes are updated and improved.

Thus, that first contract, regardless of the money involved, is very important, and Goodrich, when it learned that it had been awarded the A7D contract, was determined that while it may have slammed the door on its own foot ten years before, this time, the second time around, things would be different. The word was soon circulated throughout the plant: "We can't bungle it this time. We've got to give them a good brake, regardless of the cost."

There was another factor which had undoubtedly influenced LTV. All aircraft brakes made today are of the disk type, and the bid submitted by Goodrich called for a relatively small brake, one containing four disks and weighing only 106 pounds. The weight of any aircraft part is extremely important. The lighter a part is, the heavier the plane's payload can be. The four-rotor, 106–pound brake promised by Goodrich was about as light as could be expected, and this undoubtedly had helped move LTV to award the contract to Goodrich.

The brake was designed by one of Goodrich's most capable engineers, John Warren. A tall, lanky blond and a graduate of Purdue, Warren had come from the Chrysler Corporation seven years before and had become adept at aircraft brake design. The happy-go-lucky manner he usually maintained belied a temper which exploded whenever anyone ventured to offer any criticism of his work, no matter how small. On these occasions, Warren would turn red in the face, often throwing or slamming something and then stalking from the scene. As his coworkers learned the consequences of criticizing him, they did so less and less readily, and when he submitted his preliminary design for the A7D brake, it was accepted without question.

Warren was named project engineer for the A7D, and he, in turn, assigned the task of producing the final production design to a newcomer to the Goodrich engineering stable, Searle Lawson. Just turned twenty-six, Lawson had been out of the Northrup Institute of Technology

only one year when he came to Goodrich in January 1967. Like Warren, he had worked for a while in the automotive industry, but his engineering degree was in aeronautical and astronautical sciences, and when the opportunity came to enter his special field, via Goodrich, he took it. At the Troy plant, Lawson had been assigned to various "paper projects" to break him in, and after several months spent reviewing statistics and old brake designs, he was beginning to fret at the lack of challenge. When told he was being assigned to his first "real" project, he was elated and immediately plunged into his work.

The major portion of the design had already been completed by Warren, and major assemblies for the brake had already been ordered from Goodrich suppliers. Naturally, however, before Goodrich could start making the brakes on a production basis, much testing would have to be done. Lawson would have to determine the best materials to use for the linings and discover what minor adjustments in the design would have to be made.

Then, after the preliminary testing and after the brake was judged ready for production, one brake assembly would undergo a series of grueling, simulated braking stops and other severe trials called qualification tests. These tests are required by the military, which gives very detailed specifications on how they are to be conducted, the criteria for failure, and so on. They are performed in the Goodrich plant's test laboratory, where huge machines called dynamometers can simulate the weight and speed of almost any aircraft. After the brakes pass the laboratory tests, they are approved for production, but before the brakes are accepted for use in military service, they must undergo further extensive flight tests.

Searle Lawson was well aware that much more had to be done before the A7D brake could go into production, and he knew that LTV had set the last two weeks in June 1968, as the starting dates for flight tests. So he decided to begin testing immediately. Goodrich's suppliers had not yet delivered the brake housing and other parts, but the brake disks had arrived, and using the housing from a brake similar in size and weight to the A7D brake, Lawson built a prototype. The prototype was installed in a test wheel and placed on one of the big dynamometers in the plant's test laboratory. The dynamometer was adjusted to simulate the weight of the A7D and Lawson began a series of tests, "landing" the wheel and brake at the A7D's landing speed, and braking it to a stop. The main purpose of these preliminary tests was to learn what temperatures would develop within the brake during the simulated stops and to evaluate the lining materials tentatively selected for use.

During a normal aircraft landing the temperatures inside the brake may reach 1000 degrees, and occasionally a bit higher. During Lawson's first simulated landings, the temperature of his prototype brake reached 1500 degrees. The brake glowed a bright cherry-red and threw off incandescent particles of metal and lining material as the temperature reached its peak. After a few such stops, the brake was dismantled and the linings were found to be almost completely disintegrated. Lawson chalked this first failure up to chance and, ordering new lining materials, tried again.

The second attempt was a repeat of the first. The brake became extremely hot, causing the lining materials to crumble into dust.

After the third such failure, Lawson, inexperienced though he was, knew that the fault lay not in defective parts or unsuitable lining material but in the basic design of the brake itself. Ignoring Warren's original computations, Lawson made his own, and it didn't take him long to discover where the trouble lay—the brake was too

small. There simply was not enough surface area on the disks to stop the aircraft without generating the excessive heat that caused the linings to fail.

The answer to the problem was obvious but far from simple—the four-disk brake would have to be scrapped, and a new design, using five disks, would have to be developed. The implications were not lost on Lawson. Such a step would require the junking of all the four-disk brake subassemblies, many of which had now begun to arrive from the various suppliers. It would also mean several weeks of preliminary design and testing and many more weeks of waiting while the suppliers made and delivered the new subassemblies.

Yet, several weeks had already gone by since LTV's order had arrived, and the date for delivery of the first production brakes for flight testing was only a few months away.

Although project engineer John Warren had more or less turned the A7D over to Lawson, he knew of the difficulties Lawson had been experiencing. He had assured the young engineer that the problem revolved around getting the right kind of lining material. Once that was found, he said, the difficulties would end.

Despite the evidence of the abortive tests and Lawson's careful computations, Warren rejected the suggestion that the four-disk brake was too light for the job. Warren knew that his superior had already told LTV, in rather glowing terms, that the preliminary tests on the A7D brake were very successful. Indeed, Warren's superiors weren't aware at this time of the troubles on the brake. It would have been difficult for Warren to admit not only that he had made a serious error in his calculations and original design but that his mistakes had been caught by a green kid, barely out of college.

Warren's reaction to a five-disk brake was not unexpected by Lawson, and seeing that the four-disk brake was not to be abandoned so easily, he took his calculations and dismal test results one step up the corporate ladder.

At Goodrich, the man who supervises the engineers working on projects slated for production is called, predictably, the projects manager. The job was held by a short, chubby and bald man named Robert Sink. A man truly devoted to his work, Sink was as likely to be found at his desk at ten o'clock on Sunday night as ten o'clock on Monday morning. His outside interests consisted mainly of tinkering on a Model–A Ford and an occasional game of golf. Some fifteen years before, Sink had begun working at Goodrich as a lowly draftsman. Slowly, he worked his way up. Despite his geniality, Sink was neither respected nor liked by the majority of the engineers, and his appointment as their supervisor did not improve their feelings about him. They thought he had only gone to high school. It quite naturally rankled those who had gone through years of college and acquired impressive specialites such as thermodynamics and astronautics to be commanded by a man whom they considered their intellectual inferior. But, though Sink had no college training, he had something even more useful: a fine working knowledge of company politics.

Puffing upon a Meerschaum pipe, Sink listened gravely as young Lawson confided his fears about the four-disk brake. Then he examined Lawson's calculations and the results of the abortive tests. Despite the fact that he was not a qualified engineer, in the strictest sense of the word, it must certainly have been obvious to Sink that Lawson's calculations were correct and that a four-disk brake would never have worked on the A7D.

But other things of equal importance were also obvious. First, to concede that Lawson's calculations were correct would also mean conceding that Warren's calculations were incorrect. As projects manager, he not only was responsible for Warren's activities, but, in admitting that

Warren had erred, he would have to admit that he had erred in trusting Warren's judgment. It also meant that, as projects manager, it would be he who would have to explain the whole messy situation to the Goodrich hierarchy, not only at Troy but possibly on the corporate level at Goodrich's Akron offices. And, having taken Warren's judgment of the four-disk brake at face value (he was forced to do this since, not being an engineer, he was unable to exercise any engineering judgment of his own), he had assured LTV, not once but several times, that about all there was left to do on the brake was pack it in a crate and ship it out the back door.

There's really no problem at all, he told Lawson. After all, Warren was an experienced engineer, and if he said the brake would work, it would work. Just keep on testing and probably, maybe even on the very next try, it'll work out just fine.

Lawson was far from convinced, but without the support of his superiors there was little he could do except keep on testing. By now, housings for the four-disk brake had begun to arrive at the plant, and Lawson was able to build up a production model of the brake and begin the formal qualification tests demanded by the military.

The first qualification attempts went exactly as the tests on the prototype had. Terrific heat developed within the brakes and, after a few, short, simulated stops, the linings crumbled. A new type of lining material was ordered and once again an attempt to qualify the brake was made. Again, failure.

Experts were called in from lining manufacturers, and new lining "mixes" were tried, always with the same result. Failure.

It was now the last week in March 1968, and flight tests were scheduled to begin in seventy days. Twelve separate attempts had been made to formally qualify the brake, and all had failed. It was no longer possible for anyone to ignore the glaring truth that the brake was a dismal failure and that nothing short of a major design change could ever make it work.

In the engineering department, panic set in. A glum-faced Lawson prowled the test laboratory dejectedly. Occasionally, Warren would witness some simulated stop on the brake and, after it was completed, troop silently back to his desk. Sink, too, showed an unusual interest in the trials, and he and Warren would converse in low tones while poring over the results of the latest tests. Even the most inexperienced of the lab technicians and the men who operated the testing equipment knew they had a "bad" brake on their hands, and there was some grumbling about "wasting time on a brake that won't work."

New menaces appeared. An engineering team from LTV arrived at the plant to get a good look at the brake in action. Luckily, they stayed only a few days, and Goodrich engineers managed to cover the true situation without too much difficulty.

On April 4, the thirteenth attempt at qualification was begun. This time no attempt was made to conduct the tests by the methods and techniques spelled out in the military specifications. Regardless of how it had to be done, the brake was to be "nursed" through the required fifty simulated stops.

Fans were set up to provide special cooling. Instead of maintaining pressure on the brake until the test wheel had come to a complete stop, the pressure was reduced when the wheel had decelerated to around 15 mph, allowing it to "coast" to a stop. After each stop, the brake was disassembled and carefully cleaned, and after some of the stops, internal brake parts were machined in order to remove warp and other disfigurations caused by the high heat.

By these and other methods, all clearly contrary to the techniques established by the military specifications, the brake was coaxed through the fifty stops. But even

using these methods, the brake could not meet all the requirements. On one stop the wheel rolled for a distance of 16,000 feet, nearly three miles, before the brake could bring it to a stop. The normal distance required for such a stop was around 3500 feet.

On April 11, the day the thirteenth test was completed, I became personally involved in the A7D situation.

I had worked in the Goodrich test laboratory for five years, starting first as an instrumentation engineer, then later becoming a data analyst and technical writer. As part of my duties, I analyzed the reams and reams of instrumentation data that came from the many testing machines in the laboratory, then transcribed it to a more usable form for the engineering department. And when a new-type brake had successfully completed the required qualification tests, I would issue a formal qualification report.

Qualification reports were an accumulation of all the data and test logs compiled by the tests, and were documentary proof that a brake had met all the requirements established by the military specifications and was therefore presumed safe for flight testing. Before actual flight tests were conducted on a brake, qualification reports had to be delivered to the customer and to various government officials.

On April 11, I was looking over the data from the latest A7D test, and I noticed that many irregularities in testing methods had been noted on the test logs.

Technically, of course, there was nothing wrong with conducting tests in any manner desired, so long as the test was for research purposes only. But qualification test methods are clearly delineated by the military, and I knew that this test had been a formal qualification attempt. One particular notation on the test logs caught my eye. For some of the stops, the instrument which recorded the brake pressure had been deliberately miscalibrated so that, while the brake pressure used during the stops was recorded as 1000 psi (the maximum pressure that would be available on the A7D aircraft), the pressure had actually been 1100 psi!

I showed the test logs to the test lab supervisor, Ralph Gretzinger, who said he had learned from the technician who had miscalibrated the instrument that he had been asked to do so by Lawson. Lawson, said Gretzinger, readily admitted asking for the miscalibration, saying he had been told to do so by Sink.

I asked Gretzinger why anyone would want to miscalibrate the data-recording instruments.

"Why? I'll tell you why," he snorted. "That brake is a failure. It's way too small for the job, and they're not ever going to get it to work. They're getting desperate, and instead of scrapping the damned thing and starting over, they figure they can horse around down here in the lab and qualify it that way."

An expert engineer, Gretzinger had been responsible for several innovations in brake design. It was he who had invented the unique brake system used on the famous XB70. A graduate of Georgia Tech, he was a stickler for detail and he had some very firm ideas about honesty and ethics. "If you want to find out what's going on," said Gretzinger, "ask Lawson, he'll tell you."

Curious, I did ask Lawson the next time he came into the lab. He seemed eager to discuss the A7D and give me the history of his months of frustrating efforts to get Warren and Sink to change the brake design. "I just can't believe this is really happening," said Lawson, shaking his head slowly. "This isn't engineering, at least not what I thought it would be. Back in school, I thought that when you were an engineer, you tried to do your best, no matter what it cost. But this is something else."

He sat across the desk from me, his chin proped in his hand. "Just wait," he warned. "You'll get a chance to see what

I'm talking about. You're going to get in the act, too, because I've already had the word that we're going to make one more attempt to qualify the brake, and that's it. Win or lose, we're going to issue a qualification report!"

I reminded him that a qualification report could only be issued after a brake had successfully met all military requirements, and therefore, unless the next qualification attempt was a success, no report would be issued.

"You'll find out," retorted Lawson. "I was already told that regardless of what the brake does on test, It's going to be qualified." He said he had been told in those exact words at a conference with Sink and Russell Van Horn.

This was the first indication that Sink had brought his boss, Van Horn, into the mess. Although Van Horn, as manager of the design engineering section, was responsible for the entire department, he was not necessarily familiar with all phases of every project, and it was not uncommon for those under him to exercise the what-he-doesn't-know-won't-hurt-him philosophy. If he was aware of the full extent of the A7D situation, it meant that matters had truly reached a desperate stage—that Sink had decided not only to call for help but was looking toward that moment when blame must be borne and, if possible, shared.

Also, if Van Horn had said, "regardless what the brake does on test, it's going to be qualified," then it could only mean that, if necessary, a false qualification report would be issued! I discussed this possibility with Gretzinger, and he assured me that under no circumstances would such a report ever be issued.

"If they want a qualification report, we'll write them one, but we'll tell it just like it is," he declared emphatically. "No false data or false reports are going to come out of this lab."

On May 2, 1968, the fourteenth and final attempt to qualify the brake was begun. Although the same improper methods used to nurse the brake through the previous tests were employed, it soon became obvious that this too would end in failure.

When the tests were about half completed, Lawson asked if I would start preparing the various engineering curves and graphic displays which were normally incorporated in a qualification report. "It looks as though you'll be writing a qualification report shortly," he said.

I flatly refused to have anything to do with the matter and immediately told Gretzinger what I had been asked to do. He was furious and repeated his previous declaration that under no circumstances would any false data or other matter be issued from the lab.

"I'm going to get this settled right now, once and for all," he declared. "I'm going to see Line [Russell Line, manager of the Goodrich Technical Services Section, of which the test lab was a part] and find out just how far this thing is going to go!" He stormed out of the room.

In about an hour, he returned and called me to his desk. He sat silently for a few moments, then muttered, half to himself, "I wonder what the hell they'd do if I just quit?" I didn't answer and I didn't ask him what he meant. I knew. He had been beaten down. He had reached the point when the decision had to be made. Defy them now while there was still time—for knuckle under, sell out.

"You know," he went on uncertainly, looking down at his desk, "I've been an engineer for a long time, and I've always believed that ethics and integrity were every bit as important as theorems and formulas, and never once has anything happened to change my beliefs. Now this . . . Hell, I've got two sons I've got to put through school and I just . . ." His voice trailed off.

He sat for a few more minutes, then, looking over the top of his glasses, said hoarsely, "Well, it looks like we're licked.

The way it stands now, we're to go ahead and prepare the data and other things for the graphic presentation in the report, and when we're finished, someone upstairs will actually write the report.

"After all," he continued, "we're just drawing some curves, and what happens to them after they leave here, well, we're not responsible for that."

He was trying to persuade himself that as long as we were concerned with only one part of the puzzle and didn't see the completed picture, we really weren't doing anything wrong. He didn't believe what he was saying, and he knew I didn't believe it either. It was an embarrassing and shameful moment for both of us.

I wasn't at all satisfied with the situation and decided that I too would discuss the matter with Russell Line, the senior executive in our section.

Tall, powerfully built, his teeth flashing white, his face tanned to a coffee-brown by a daily stint with a sun lamp, Line looked and acted every inch the executive. He was a crossword puzzle enthusiast and an ardent golfer, and though he had lived in Troy only a short time, he had been accepted into the Troy Country Club and made an official of the golf committee. He had been transferred from the Akron offices some two years previously, and an air of mystery surrounded him. Some office gossips figured he had been sent to Troy as the result of some sort of demotion. Others speculated that since the present general manager of the Troy plant was due shortly for retirement, Line had been transferred to Troy to assume that job and was merely occupying his present position to "get the feel of things." Whatever the case, he commanded great respect and had come to be well liked by those of us who worked under him.

He listened sympathetically while I explained how I felt about the A7D situation, and when I had finished, he asked me what I wanted him to do about it. I said that as employees of the Goodrich

Company we had a responsibility to protect the company and its reputation if at all possible. I said I was certain that officers on the corporate level would never knowingly allow such tactics as had been employed on the A7D.

"I agree with you," he remarked, "but I still want to know what you want me to do about it."

I suggested that in all probability the chief engineer at the Troy plant, H.C. "Bud" Sunderman, was unaware of the A7D problem and that he, Line, should tell him what was going on.

Line laughed, good-humoredly. "Sure, I could, but I'm not going to. Bud probably already knows about this thing anyway, and if he doesn't, I'm sure not going to be the one to tell him."

"But why?"

"Because it's none of my business, and it's none of yours. I learned a long time ago not to worry about things over which I had no control. I have no control over this."

I wasn't satisfied with this answer, and I asked him if his conscience wouldn't bother him if, say, during flight tests on the brake, something should happen resulting in death or injury to the test pilot.

"Look," he said, becoming somewhat exasperated, "I just told you I have no control over this thing. Why should my conscience bother me?"

His voice took on a quiet, soothing tone as he continued. "You're just getting all upset over this thing for nothing. I just do as I'm told, and I'd advise you to do the same."

He had made his decision, and now I had to make mine.

I made no attempt to rationalize what I had been asked to do. It made no difference who would falsify which part of the report or whether the actual falsification would be by misleading numbers or misleading words. Whether by acts of commission or omission, all of us who contributed to the fraud would be guilty. The

only question left for me to decide was whether or not I would become a party to the fraud.

Before coming to Goodrich in 1963, I had held a variety of jobs, each a little more pleasant, a little more rewarding than the last. At 42, with seven children, I had decided that the Goodrich Company would probably be my "home" for the rest of my working life. The job paid well, it was pleasant and challenging, and the future looked reasonably bright. My wife and I had bought a home and we were ready to settle down into a comfortable, middle-age, middle-class rut. If I refused to take part in the A7D fraud, I would have to either resign or be fired. The report would be written by someone anyway, but I would have the satisfaction of knowing I had had no part in the matter. But bills aren't paid with personal satisfaction, nor house payments with ethical principles. I made my decision. The next morning, I telephoned Lawson and told him I was ready to begin on the qualification report.

In a few minutes, he was at my desk, ready to begin. Before we started, I asked him, "Do you realize what we are going to do?"

"Yeah," he replied bitterly, "we're going to screw LTV. And speaking of screwing," he continued, "I know now how a whore feels, because that's exactly what I've become, an engineering whore. I've sold myself. It's all I can do to look at myself in the mirror when I shave. I make me sick."

I was surprised at his vehemence. It was obvious that he too had done his share of soul-searching and didn't like what he had found. Somehow, though, the air seemed clearer after his outburst, and we began working on the report.

I had written dozens of qualification reports, and I knew what a "good" one looked like. Resorting to the actual test data only on occasion, Lawson and I proceeded to prepare page after page of elaborate, detailed engineering curves, charts, and test logs, which purported to show what had happened during the formal qualification tests. Where temperatures were too high, we deliberately chopped them down a few hundred degrees, and where they were too low, we raised them to a value that would appear reasonable to the LTV and military engineers. Brake pressure, torque values, distances, times—everything of consequence was tailored to fit the occasion.

Occasionally, we would find that some test either hadn't been performed at all or had been conducted improperly. On those occasions, we "conducted" the test—successfully, of course—on paper.

For nearly a month we worked on the graphic presentation that would be a part of the report. Meanwhile, the fourteenth and final qualification attempt had been completed, and the brake, not unexpectedly, had failed again.

During that month, Lawson and I talked of little else except the enormity of what we were doing. The more involved we became in our work, the more apparent became our own culpability. We discussed such things as the Nuremberg trials and how they related to our guilt and complicity in the A7D situation. Lawson often expressed his opinion that the brake was downright dangerous and that, once on flight test, "anything is liable to happen."

I saw his boss, John Warren, at least twice during that month and needled him about what we were doing. He didn't take the jibes too kindly but managed to laugh the situation off as "one of those things." One day I remarked that what we were doing amounted to fraud, and he pulled out an engineering handbook and turned to a section on laws as they related to the engineering profession.

He read the definition of fraud aloud, then said, "Well, technically I don't think what we're doing can be called fraud. I'll admit it's not right, but it's just one of those things. We're just kinda caught in the middle. About all I can tell you is, do like I'm doing. Make copies of everything and put them in your SYA file."

"What's an 'SYA' file?" I asked.

"That's a 'save your ass' file." He laughed.

Although I hadn't known it was called that, I had been keeping an SYA file since the beginning of the A7D fiasco. I had made a copy of every scrap of paper connected even remotely with the A7D and had even had copies of 16mm movies that had been made during some of the simulated stops. Lawson, too, had an SYA file, and we both maintained them for one reason: Should the true state of events on the A7D ever be questioned, we wanted to have access to a complete set of factual data. We were afraid that should the question ever come up, the test data might accidentally be "lost."

We finished our work on the graphic portion of the report around the first of June. Altogether, we had prepared nearly two hundred pages of data, containing dozens of deliberate falsifications and misrepresentations. I delivered the data to Gretzinger, who said he had been instructed to deliver it personally to the chief engineer, Bud Sunderman, who in turn would assign someone in the engineering department to complete the written portion of the report. He gathered the bundle of data and left the office. Within minutes, he was back with the data, his face white with anger.

"That damned Sink's beat me to it," he said furiously. "He's already talked to Bud about this, and now Sunderman says no one in the engineering department has time to write the report. He wants us to do it, and I told him we couldn't." The words had barely left his mouth when Russell Line burst in the door. "What the hell's all the fuss about this damned report?" he demanded loudly.

Patiently, Gretzinger explained. "There's no fuss. Sunderman just told me that we'd have to write the report down here, and I said we couldn't. Russ," he went on, "I've told you before that we weren't going to write the report. I made my position clear on that a long time ago."

Line shut him up with a wave of his hand and, turning to me, bellowed, "I'm getting sick and tired of hearing about this damned report. Now, write the goddam thing and shut up about it!" He slammed out of the office.

Gretzinger and I just sat for a few seconds looking at each other. Then he spoke.

"Well, I guess he's made it pretty clear, hasn't he? We can either write the thing or quit. You know, what we should have done was quit a long time ago. Now, it's too late."

Somehow, I wasn't at all surprised at this turn of events, and it didn't really make that much difference. As far as I was concerned, we were all up to our necks in the thing anyway, and writing the narrative portion of the report couldn't make me any more guilty than I already felt myself to be.

Still, Line's order came as something of a shock. All the time Lawson and I were working on the report, I felt, deep down, that somewhere, somehow, something would come along and the whole thing would blow over. But Russell Line had crushed that hope. The report was actually going to be issued. Intelligent, law-abiding officials of B.F. Goodrich, one of the oldest and most respected of American corporations, were actually going to deliver to a customer a product that was known to be defective and dangerous and which could very possibly cause death or serious injury.

Within two days, I had completed the narrative, or written portion of the report. As a final sop to my own self-respect, in the conclusion of the report I wrote, "The B.F. Goodrich P/N 2–1162–3 brake assembly does not meet the intent or the requirements of the applicable specification documents and therefore is not quali-

fied."

This was a meaningless gesture, since I knew that this would certainly be changed when the report went through the final typing process. Sure enough, when the report was published, the negative conclusion had been made positive.

One final and significant incident occurred just before publication.

Qualification reports always bear the signature of the person who has prepared them. I refused to sign the report, as did Lawson. Warren was later asked to sign the report. He replied that he would "when I received a signed statement from Bob Sink ordering me to sign it."

The engineering secretary who was delegated the responsibility of "dogging" the report through publication, told me later that after I, Lawson, and Warren had all refused to sign the report, she had asked Sink if he would sign. He replied, "On something of this nature, I don't think a signature is really needed."

On June 5, 1968, the report was officially published and copies were delivered in person to the Air Force and LTV. Within a week, flight tests were begun at Edwards Air Force Base in California. Searle Lawson was sent to California as Goodrich's representative. Within approximately two weeks, he returned because some rather unusual incidents during the test had caused them to be canceled.

His face was grim as he related stories of several near crashes during landings—caused by brake troubles. He told me about one incident in which, upon landing, one brake was literally welded together by the intense heat developed during the test stop. The wheel locked, and the plane skidded for nearly 1500 feet before coming to a halt. The plane was jacked up and the wheel removed. The fused parts within the brake had to be pried apart.

Lawson had returned to Troy from California that same day, and that evening, he and others of the Goodrich engineering department left for Dallas for a high-level conference with LTV.

That evening I left work early and went to see my attorney. After I told him the story, he advised that, while I was probably not actually guilty of fraud, I was certainly part of a conspiracy to defraud. He advised me to go to the Federal Bureau of Investigation and offered to arrange an appointment. The following week he took me to the Dayton office of the FBI, and after I had been warned that I would not be immune from prosecution, I disclosed the A7D matter to one of the agents. The agent told me to say nothing about the episode to anyone and to report any further incident to him. He said he would forward the story to his superiors in Washington.

A few days later, Lawson returned from the conference in Dallas and said that the Air Force, which had previously approved the qualification report, had suddenly rescinded that approval and was demanding to see some of the raw test data taken during the tests. I gathered that the FBI had passed the word.

Omitting any reference to the FBI, I told Lawson I had been to an attorney and that we were probably guilty of conspiracy.

"Can you get me an appointment with your attorney?" he asked. Within a week he had been to the FBI and told them of his part in the mess. He too was advised to say nothing but to keep on the job reporting any new development.

Naturally, with the rescinding of Air Force approval and the demand to see raw test data, Goodrich officials were in a panic. A conference was called for July 27, a Saturday morning affair at which Lawson, Sink, Warren and myself were present. We met in a tiny conference room in the deserted engineering department. Lawson and I, by now openly hostile to Warren and Sink, arranged ourselves on one side of the conference table while Warren sat on the other side. Sink, chairing the meeting, paced slowly in

front of a blackboard puffing furiously on a pipe.

The meeting was called, Sink began, "to see where we stand on the A7D." What we were going to do, he said, was to "level" with LTV and tell them the "whole truth" about the A7D. "After all," he said, "they're in this thing with us, and they have the right to know how matters stand."

"In other words," I asked, "we're going to tell them the truth?"

"That's right," he replied. "We're going to level with them and let them handle the ball from there."

"There's one thing I don't quite understand," I interjected. "Isn't it going to be pretty hard for us to admit to them that we've lied?"

"Now, wait a minute," he said angrily. "Let's don't go off half-cocked on this thing. It's not a matter of lying. We've just interpreted the information the way we felt it should be."

"I don't know what you call it," I replied, "but to me it's lying, and it's going to be damned hard to confess to them that we've been lying all along."

He became very agitated at this and repeated his "We're not lying," adding, "I don't like this sort of talk."

I dropped the matter at this point, and he began discussing the various discrepancies in the report.

We broke for lunch, and afterward, I came back to the plant to find Sink sitting alone at his desk, waiting to resume the meeting. He called me over and said he wanted to apologize for his outburst that morning. "This thing has kind of gotten me down," he confessed, "and I think you've got the wrong picture. I don't think you really understand everything about this."

Perhaps so, I conceded, but it seemed to me that if we had already told LTV one thing and then had to tell them another, changing our story completely, we would have to admit we were lying.

"No," he explained patiently, "we're not really lying. All we were doing was interpreting the figures the way we knew they should be. We were just exercising engineering license."

During this afternoon session, we marked some forty-three discrepant points in the report: forty-three points that LTV would surely spot on occasions where we had exercised "engineering license."

After Sink listed those points on the blackboard, we discussed each one individually. As each point came up, Sink would explain that it was probably "too minor to bother about," or that perhaps it "wouldn't be wise to open that can of worms," or that maybe this was a point that "LTV just wouldn't understand." When the meeting was over, it had been decided that only three points were "worth mentioning."

Similar conferences were held during August and September, and the summer was punctuated with frequent treks between Dallas and Troy, and demands by the Air Force to see the raw test data. Tempers were short and matters seemed to grow worse.

Finally, early in October 1968, Lawson submitted his resignation, to take effect on October 25. On October 18, I submitted my own resignation, to take effect on November 1. In my resignation, addressed to Russell Line, I cited the A7D report and stated: "As you are aware, this report contained numerous deliberate and willful misrepresentations which, according to legal counsel, constitute fraud and expose both myself and others to criminal charges of conspiracy to defraud ... The events of the past seven months have created an atmosphere of deceit and distrust in which it is impossible to work ..."

On October 25, I received a sharp summons to the office of Bud Sunderman. As chief engineer at the Troy plant, Sunderman was responsible for the entire engineering division. Tall and graying, im-

peccably dressed at all times, he was capable of producing a dazzling smile or a hearty chuckle or immobilizing his face into marble hardness, as the occasion required.

I faced the marble hardness when I reached his office. He motioned me to a chair. "I have your resignation here," he snapped, "and I must say you have made some rather shocking, I might even say irresponsible, charges. This is very serious."

Before I could reply, he was demanding an explanation. "I want to know exactly what fraud is in connection with the A7D and how you can dare accuse this company of such a thing!"

I started to tell some of the things that had happened during the testing, but he shut me off saying, "There's nothing wrong with anything we've done here. You aren't aware of all the things that have been going on behind the scenes. If you had known the true situation, you would never have made these charges." He said that in view of my apparent "disloyalty" he had decided to accept my resignation "right now," and said it would be better for all concerned if I left the plant immediately. As I got up to leave he asked me if I intended to "carry this thing further."

I answered simply, "Yes," to which he replied, "Suit yourself." Within twenty minutes, I had cleaned out my desk and left. Forty-eight hours later, the B.F. Goodrich Company recalled the qualification report and the four-disk brake, announcing that it would replace the brake with a new, improved, five-disk brake at no cost to LTV.

Ten months later, on August 13, 1969, I was the chief government witness at a hearing conducted before Senator William Proxmire's Economy in Government Subcommittee of the Congress's Joint Economic Committee. I related the A7D story to the committee, and my testimony was supported by Searle Lawson, who followed me to the witness stand. Air Force officers also testified, as well as a four-man team from the General Accounting Office, which had conducted an investigation of the A7D brake at the request of Senator Proxmire. Both Air Force and GAO investigators declared that the brake was dangerous and had not been tested properly.

Testifying for Goodrich was R.G. Jeter, vice-president and general counsel of the company, from the Akron headquarters. Representing the Troy plant was Robert Sink. These two denied any wrongdoing on the part of the Goodrich Company, despite expert testimony to the contrary by Air Force and GAO officials. Sink was quick to deny any connection with the writing of the report or of directing any falsifications, claiming to be on the West coast at the time. John Warren was the man who supervised its writing, said Sink.

As for me, I was dismissed as a high-school graduate with no technical training, while Sink testified that Lawson was a young, inexperienced engineer. "We tried to give him guidance," Sink testified, "but he preferred to have his own convictions."

About changing the data and figures in the report, Sink said: "When you take data from several different sources, you have to rationalize among those data what is the true story. This is a part of your engineering know-how." He admitted that

changes had been made in the data, "but only to make them more consistent with the over-all picture of the data that is available."

Jeter pooh-poohed the suggestion that anything improper occurred, saying: "We have thirty-odd engineers at this plant . . . and I say to you that is incredible that these men would stand idly by and see reports changed or falsified . . . I mean you just do not have to do that working for anybody . . . Just nobody does that."

The four-hour hearing adjourned with no real conclusion reached by the committee. But, the following day the Department of Defense made sweeping changes in its inspection, testing and reporting procedures. A spokesman for the DOD said the changes were a result of the Goodrich episode.

The A7D is now in service, sporting a Goodrich-made five-disk brake, a brake that works very well, I'm told. Business at the Goodrich plant is good. Lawson is now an engineer for LTV and has been assigned to the A7D project. And I am now a newspaper reporter.

At this writing, those remaining at Goodrich are still secure in the same positions, all except Russell Line and Robert Sink. Line has been rewarded with a promotion to production superintendent, a large step upward on the corporate ladder. As for Sink, he moved up into Line's old job.

Issues in Observing Groups

HAL B. GREGERSEN

Over the years considerable research has been conducted on the characteristics of groups, the dimensions of their growth, the functions that constitute their leadership, their decision-making processes, and other factors which provide insights into their effectiveness. A summary of this research follows which will enable an individual to understand the "how" and "why" of group behavior.

Basically, most groups are working toward some goal. Even informal bull sessions have informal goals. Our concern is to look at the dynamics that are present as a group moves along the "path" toward its goal. *Every* meeting and *every* group has its dynamics—its unique *pattern of forces.* These forces describe the interaction in the group—the interpersonal relationships, the communications problems, the way the members make decisions. Although these forces may exist in varying degrees, an examination of any group shows that they are always present. Understanding these dynamics—these characteristic aspects of group life—will help us work more effectively in group settings.

The following is a description of basic group dynamic concepts. In addition, a set of questions is presented to assist you in diagnosing your group's behavior.

1. *Background.* Every group has a history, consisting of both its previous experiences and the personal notions and attitudes which the members bring to the group. These bear directly upon the present activities of the group. Also, the previous responses and feelings of the group which have been developed affect its present interaction.

What is the history of the group?

How does this history affect the relationships of the members?

How does this history affect the work of the group?

2. *Participation.* Participation can be described in terms of who is speaking to whom, and how much speaking is being done and by whom. Participation patterns tell something about the status and the power in the group, and often indicate how effectively the group is using the resources of its members.

Who are the high and low participators? Why? Who talks to whom? Who keeps the ball rolling?

Do you see and shift in participation, e.g., highs become quiet; lows suddenly become talkative?

How are the silent people treated? How is their silence interpreted? Consent? Disagreement? Disinterest? Fear? Etc.

3. *Influence.* Influence and participation are not the same. Some people may speak very little, yet they capture the attention of the whole group. Others may talk a lot but are generally not listened to by other members.

Which members are high in influence?

Written by Hal B. Gregersen, University of California, Irvine.

That is, when they talk others seem to listen.

Which members are low in influence?

Others neither listen to nor follow them. Is there any shifting in influence? Who shifts?

Do you see any rivalry in the group?

4. *Communication.* This is primarily what people say, how they say it, and what effect it has. However, much significant communication is *non*verbal—in posture, facial expression, gesture, etc. In verbal communication, the clarity of expression and coherence of the presentation have an important influence on group effectiveness.

Do some members move in and out of the group, e.g., lean forward or backward in their chairs or move their chairs in and out? Under what conditions do they come in or move out? Which members frequently look away from the group?

Which members present their ideas clearly?

5. *Atmosphere.* At any given time a group's atmosphere is somewhere between "defensive" and "accepting." In a *defensive* atmosphere members are unable to communicate freely, to disagree with other members, or to expose ideas and feelings which run counter to the direction in which the group is going. But if the atmosphere is one of *listening, understanding, trusting*—in short, *accepting*—then the group will develop greater creativity, with more effective member relations.

Who seems to prefer a friendly, congenial atmosphere? Is there any attempt to suppress conflict or unpleasant feelings?

Who seems to prefer an atmosphere of conflict and disagreement? Do any members provoke or annoy others?

What signs of feelings do you observe in group members? Anger? Irritation? Frustration? Warmth? Excitement? Boredom? etc.

6. *Subgroupings.* Subgroups (sometimes called "cliques") often develop in groups and can greatly influence the group's effectiveness. Sometimes such subgroups form on the basis of friendships, sometimes because of a common need or interest at a particular stage of the group life, or sometimes because of antipathy toward other members or opposition to the direction of the group.

Is there any subgrouping? Sometimes two or three members may consistently agree and support each other or consistently disagree and oppose one another.

Do some people seem to be "outside" the group? Do some members seem to be "in"? How are those "outside" treated?

What are the issues around which subgroups appear to form?

7. *Norms.* Standards or ground rules may develop in a group that control the behavior of its members. Norms usually express what behaviors *should* or *should not* take place in the group. These norms may be clear to all members (explicit), known or sensed by only a few (implicit), or operating completely below the level of awareness of any group members.

Are certain areas avoided in the group (e.g., sex, religion, talk about present feelings in group)?

Are group members overly nice or polite to each other? Are only positive feelings expressed? Do members agree with each other too readily? What happens when members disagree?

Do you see norms operating about participation or the kinds of questions that are allowed?

8. *Procedures.* All groups operate with a certain set of procedures—that is, defined ways of getting work done (e.g., how an agenda is prepared and used, how votes are taken [by ballot or by hand]). If a group is to be effective, it must vary its procedures so that they are appropriate to the task at hand.

Is there any attempt to get all members

participating in a decision (consensus)?

Is there any evidence of a majority pushing a decision through over other members' objections? Do they call for a vote (majority support)?

Does anyone make any contributions which do not receive any kind of response or recognition (plop)? What effect does this have on the member?

9. *Goals.* Goals can be immediate and short-range, or long-range; they can emerge from the group or be imposed on it; they can be realistic in relation to the resources of the group, or completely unrealistic. Effective groups must continually check the appropriateness of their goals.

How does the group choose its goals?

Are the goals realistic and attainable, considering the resources of the group?

Does the group relate its immediate task to long-range group objectives?

10. *Dysfunctional behaviors.* These activities typically hinder the development of a group, its maintenance, and its ability to accomplish goals. In general, blocking functions are dysfunctional for group progression on any scale.

Aggressor —Deflating others' status; attacking the group or its values; joking in a barbed or semi-concealed way.

Blocker —Disagreeing and opposing beyond reason; resisting stubbornly the group's wish for personally oriented reasons; using hidden agenda to thwart the movement of a group.

Dominator —Asserting authority of superiority to manipulate group or certain of its members; interrupting contributions of others; controlling by means of flattery or other forms of patronizing behavior.

Showoff —Making a scene over one's lack of involvement; abandoning the group while remaining physically with it; seeking recognition in ways not relevant to group task.

Avoidance Behavior —Pursuing special interests not related to task; staying off subject to avoid commitment; preventing group from facing up to controversy.

11. *Leadership.* Leader behavior in a group can range from almost complete control of the decision making by the leader to almost complete control by the group, with the leader contributing his/her resources just like any other group member. A number of leadership functions must be performed by both the leader and other members of the group.

A. *Task functions.* These leadership functions are to facilitate and coordinate group efforts in the selection and definition of a common problem and in the solution of that problem.

Initiator —Proposing tasks or actions; defining group problems; suggesting a procedure.

Informer —Offering facts; giving expression of feelings; giving an opinion.

Clarifier —Interrupting ideas or suggestions; defining terms; clarifying issues before group.

Summarizer —Pulling together related ideas; restating suggestions; offering a decision or conclusion for group to consider.

Reality tester —Making a critical analysis of an idea; testing an idea against some data trying to see if the idea would work.

B. *Maintenance functions.* Functions in this category describe leadership activity necessary to alter or maintain the way in which members of the group work together, developing loyalty to one another and to the group as a whole.

Harmonizer —Attempting to reconcile disagreements; reducing tension; getting people to explore differences.

Gate keeper —helping to keep communication channels open; facilitating the participation of others; suggesting procedures that permit sharing remarks.

Consensus tester —Asking to see if a group is nearing a decision; sending up a trial balloon to test a possible conclusion.

Encourager —Being friendly, warm, and responsive to others; indicating by facial expression or remark the acceptance of others' contributions.

Compromiser —When his/her own idea or status is involved in a conflict, offering a compromise which yields status; admitting error; modifying an interest of group cohesion or growth.

GUIDELINES FOR GROUP OBSERVATION

Although these various aspects of group dynamics that have been discussed can be easily memorized, and awareness of how and an understanding of why they occur within groups is more difficult to attain. Often when a group has a task to perform, the group becomes so involved in the *task* of organizing for the activity that it is not able to remember accurately the *process* by which the task was accomplished. It can be useful for a neutral person who is not involved in the activity to observe and give feedback about the behavior of indi-

viduals during an actual group meeting. This observation process can sensitize group members, as well as the observer, to be more aware of the subtleties of group behavior in their day-to-day involvement.

When you are serving as a group observer your task is to provide feedback to group members about their behavior in the experience you are observing. You are to take no active part, but you should position yourself at a point where you can hear what is being said, see nonverbal behavior of as many participants as possible, and observe people on the periphery of the group.

As the group meeting proceeds, take notes of specifically what happens, who is involved, and so forth, so that you can refer to the notes when you verbally elaborate on them to the group members after they have completed the exercise. Avoid evaluations such as *good* and *bad;* simply describe the behavior of the people involved. If necessary, refer back to the specific descriptions of group dynamics and member roles in order to give specific feedback to group members.

By familiarizing yourself with the dynamics of a work or social group, your ability to perform effectively in groups will increase.

We've Got to Stop Meeting Like This

SHARON LOPEZ

Trying to beat the meeting blues? Here's how to run lively, *productive* sessions that your whole staff will enjoy.

Each week, Ruth Allen, the news director of KRLD–TV, in Dallas, Tex., presides over or attends at least 20 meetings. She holds daily editorial meetings, has frequent sessions to critique her news program and huddles almost every day with reporters and photographers. She has installed a new management team and meets with them regularly. In addition, as president of the local black professional communications society, she chairs a general meeting every month. "I spend most of my life in meetings," she observes.

She's not alone. According to a study by the New York-based management consultant firm Booz, Allen & Hamilton, most managers with an average salary of $40,000 or more spend half their time in meetings.

Meetings are often frustrating, redundant, rambling, unproductive and colossal time wasters. But it's a fact of business life that most critical decisions are made and many problems solved in the context of a meeting.

It is also true that when conducted well, meetings can be stimulating, challenging and worthwhile. Says Glenn Porter, deputy commissioner of the New York State Commerce Department: "Meetings serve to boost morale, build cohesiveness and share information. People can demonstrate their knowledge and learn what's going on in other departments. Certain ideas come out of the process, and these benefits can be lost without meetings. Effective meetings are a critical part of any business organization."

But what makes a meeting effective? What's the best way to avoid sessions rife with long, drawn out presentations, petty disagreements, people who love to hear themselves speak and those who simply prefer to spend their time in meetings, rather than work?

Organizing and presiding over a productive meeting requires skill and creativity. It takes someone who is willing to take charge and to trust his or her instincts to make the session work. Once the purpose of a meeting has been determined, the leader must be able to steer the discussion in the right direction, field questions, anticipate problems and, in general, control the tone and outcome. He or she must therefore wear many hats: conductor, moderator, coach and participant.

From department meetings to big boardroom conferences, there are many different types of meetings, and each should be handled differently to achieve the best results.

Porter, who heads a team of financial and business advocacy experts, categorizes meetings in terms of power relationships and designates them either vertical or horizontal.

In a vertical meeting, there is usually one person in charge. He or she has the final word. Meetings where decisions must be made fall into this category.

A horizontal meeting might involve a board of directors or an executive committee. Brainstorming and planning sessions, where the emphasis may not be on making a decision but rather finding out how the group feels about an issue, fall into this category.

The power relationship is more equal and there is more room for free-flowing conversation. Here, the desired result is to come up with a plan or to solve a problem.

It is important to understand which forum is most effective to accomplish your goals. Porter does an informal checklist before he calls a meeting.

"I stop and think, what is the objective? Can this be accomplished without a meeting? Can it be resolved by a memo or conference call?"

In deciding what you want to accomplish, it helps to write a one-line statement, for example, "The purpose is to explain to the staff a new overtime policy and how it will affect them." Or, "We want to get a clear understanding of how budget cuts will affect this department." Then make a list of all the items that need to be covered surrounding that theme.

Next, figure out who needs to attend. Many meetings are unproductive because the wrong people are there. In a preliminary discussion on the feasibility of a merger or acquisition, it would be important to first meet with the key financial and technical experts whose opinions can make or break the decision before involving everyone else. Otherwise, you'll have people who will not make a contribution or who will interrupt constantly to clarify points along the way.

Stephanie Winston, author of *The Organized Executive*, advises: "Make up an action agenda, which includes your objec-

tive. Do you want a recommendation to come out of this meeting? Do you want to decide on a course of action? Do you want information, or do you want suggestions for revisions on a report? Then come up with a list of specific questions or discussion topics. Devising this list will help to focus the interaction between meeting participants more tightly."

Richard Douglas, vice president for public affairs, Sun Diamond Growers of California, a Stockton, Calif.-based food manufacturer, holds monthly operational review meetings for the managers of the company's five subsidiaries. These meetings follow a standardized agenda. First, they review marketing strategies, then they look at government problems, industry problems and finally at the financial picture. With this formula, people know exactly what to expect.

Most managers agree that where possible, agendas should be distributed two to three days prior to the meeting. For example, before Douglas meets with the staff of the company magazine that he oversees, he sends copies of the agenda with a cover letter. The letter states the date, time, place and topic of discussion. The cover letter also states, "If you have any additions to this, please let me know. Please come fully prepared to make this a successful meeting." He has found this to be an effective way to circumvent lack of preparedness, which to him is the greatest cause of unproductive meetings.

Porter sends a similar letter with his agendas and has his secretary call to double-check all of the information with those who have received it. By reinforcing the meeting time, this helps cut down on lateness, a factor that also causes problems.

Winston advises: "Start on time. Don't wait for people unless it's the boss." Allen is particularly strict about enforcing meeting times. "In my mind, if one minute is wasted, I multiply that by twenty-eight, the number of people on my staff.

It's a gross mismanagement of time."

"With the agenda," she adds, "be flexible, but not too flexible. If things arise that aren't on the agenda, write them down. You will probably not be prepared to deal with them on the spot anyway. You can schedule another meeting to address them." She continues, "Prioritize your problems so that if the meeting has to be cut off, you've got the most important things out of the way."

It's important to take notes during the meeting. Porter makes sure that in addition to having the session recorded on tape, someone is in the room taking notes. That person can highlight or italicize the different tasks and assignments that are made and can easily review them before the meeting breaks up.

"The follow-up system is crucial," says Winston. "Sometimes assignments are made and they drop down the hole. When the manager asks what happened, no one knows. To prevent this, someone should note assignments and distribute them in a written memo."

A good participant is also important to the success of a meeting. "Be sure to speak up, but not in a disruptive or hostile way and make your opinions known," says Winston. "Managers are looking at their staffs to see if they come up with ideas. If you find that it's hard to keep your mind on things because the room is too hot or the presentation is too boring, take notes, even if it's not necessary. This helps to focus your attention, and forces you to think about what's being said. Also, handle yourself decorously, without putting others down.

"And," she adds, "if you're stuck in the meeting because of politics or status, but you're not really involved, don't read during the meeting. Bring something with you to write so it at least looks like you're taking notes and you're not completely wasting your time."

Avoid some of these snags that can ruin the most well-planned meeting:

Idlers. Some people enjoy meetings because they keep them away from their work. Winston says that the best time to hold a meeting is before lunch or near quitting time, because this provides built-in time limits.

People will often condense what they have to say to get out on time. If you find the meeting running longer than planned, cut the comments of meeting participants short.

Repeaters. When you find someone taking up a lot of time going over issues that have already been resolved, don't be afraid to jump in and say, "We appreciate hearing from you, but we have to move on to the next item."

Dominators. Some people try to make power plays and take over with their personal agenda. That's the time to say, "That's interesting, George. We're glad we heard from you. Mary, what's your point of view?"

Criticizers. It's up to the leader to keep drawing people back to the agenda at hand. Allen will say flatly to anyone who criticizes other people or departments, "That's not what we're here to talk about. We're here to discuss the news department, not production."

Interrupters. When people are all speaking at once and nothing is being said, simply say, "We can't all speak at once." Then designate the order that people should continue speaking. But Porter says all interruptions aren't necessarily destructive. Use your instincts to assess when it's okay to let the discussion flow. Porter, for instance, says he sometimes welcomes a phone call during a meeting. "It's a form of creative manipulation. If I don't like the tone of the meeting, I'll accept a call and then subtly change the direction of the conversation afterward. Or, if it's important to me to observe how people interact with one another," he says, "I'll tell them to continue the discussion and watch them while seemingly giving all of my attention to the phone call."

Who's to do it? Before the end of a meeting, be clear on who is supposed to do what. Says Douglas: "I always review what's been accomplished and who has what assignments and what the time frame is in which to complete them."

Managing meetings requires practice. By remembering to be well organized, to follow up and to let your instincts be your guide, you'll find the sessions that once seemed to be a waste of time can become lively, productive and worthwhile.

. . . The law of triviality. Briefly stated, it means that the time spent on any item of the agenda will be in inverse proportion to the sum involved.

C. Northcote Parkinson, *Parkinson's Law*

Too often it is assumed that the organization of a company corresponds to . . . an organization chart. Actually, it never does.

Fritz J. Roethlisberger and Wiliam J. Dickson

At the very highest level there is very little knowledge. They do not understand the opinion of the masses . . . Their bureaucratic manner is immense. They beat their gongs to blaze the way. They cause people to become afraid just by looking at them.

Mao Tse-Tung

I fear uniformity. You cannot manufacture great men any more than you can manufacture gold.

John Ruskin

A camel is a horse designed by a committee.

Author unknown

The symptoms of groupthink arise when members of the decision-making groups become motivated to avoid being too harsh in their judgments of their leaders' or their colleagues' ideas. They adopt a softline of criticism, even in their own thinking. At their meetings, all the members are amiable and seek complete concurrence on every important issue, with no bickering or conflict to spoil the cozy 'we-feeling' atmosphere.

Irving L. Janis, *Victims of Groupthink*

"That's the American way. If little kids don't aspire to make money like I did, what the hell good is this country?"

Lee Iacocca, (*Newsweek:* May 11, 1987)

EXERCISES

NASA Exercise

The challenge in decision making is to obtain the best information within limits of time and other resources. This is often very difficult because information does not exist in pure form. It is always filtered through people who may or may not get along with each other and who might not even care about a good decision. This exercise is a means to help you look at the process of gathering information, working out group procedures, analyzing different contributions, and handling conflict and motivation. The exercise is intended to help you examine the strengths and weaknesses of individual decision making.

The NASA exercise is used quite frequently; alternative situations based on the same behavioral principles include Winter Survival and Desert Survival. The Winter Survival scenario follows the NASA exercise and can be used in the same way.

INSTRUCTIONS

You are a member of a space crew originally scheduled to rendezvous with a mother ship on the lighted surface of the moon. Due to mechanical difficulties, however, your ship was forced to land at a spot some 200 miles from the rendezvous point. During landing, much of the equipment aboard was damaged, and because survival depends on reaching the mother ship, the most critical items available must be chosen for the 200–mile trip. On the next page are listed the fifteen items left intact and undamaged after the landing. Your task is to rank them in terms of their importance to your crew in reaching the rendezvous point. In the first column (step 1) place the number *1* by the most important item, the number *2* by the second most important, and so on, through number *15*, the least important. You have

fifteen minutes to complete this phase of the exercise.

After the individual rankings are completed, participants should be formed into groups having from four to seven members. Each group should then rank the fifteen items as a team. This group ranking should be a general consensus after a discussion of the issues, not just the average of each individual ranking. While it is unlikely that everyone will agree exactly on the group ranking, an effort should be made to reach at least a decision that everyone can live with. It is important to treat differences of opinion as a means of gathering more information and clarifying issues and as an incentive to force the group to seek better alternatives. The group ranking should be listed in the second column (step 2). The third phase of the exercise consists of the instructor's providing the expert's rankings, which

DIFFERING VIEWPOINTS ON THE IMPACT OF GROUPS

should be entered in the third column (step 3). Each participant should compute the difference between the individual ranking and the expert's ranking (step 4), and between the group ranking and the expert's ranking (step 5). Then add the two "difference" columns—the smaller the score, the closer the ranking is to the view of the experts.

NASA tally sheet

Items	Step 1 Your individual ranking	Step 2 The team's ranking	Step 3 Survival expert's ranking	Step 4 Difference between Steps 1 & 3	Step 5 Difference between Steps 2 & 3
Box of matches					
Food concentrate					
50 feet of nylon rope					
Parachute silk					
Portable heating unit					
Two .45 calibre pistols					
One case dehydrated Pet milk					
Two 100–lb. tanks of oxygen					
Stellar map (of the moon's constellation)					
Life raft					
Magnetic compass					
5 gallons of water					
Signal flares					
First aid kit containing injection needles					
Solar-powered FM receiver-transmitter					
TOTAL					
(The lower the score the better)				Your score	Team score

Winter Survival Exercise

THE SITUATION

You have just crash-landed somewhere in the woods of northern Minnesota or southern Manitoba. It is 11:32 A.M. in mid-January. The small plane in which you were traveling was destroyed except for the frame. The pilot and copilot have been killed, but no one else is seriously injured.

The crash came suddenly before the pilot had time to radio for help or inform anyone of your position. Since your pilot was trying to avoid a storm, you know the plane was considerably off course. The pilot announced shortly before the crash that you were eighty miles northwest of a small town that is the nearest known habitation.

You are in a wilderness area made up of thick woods broken by many lakes and rivers. The last weather report indicated that the temperature would reach minus twenty-five degrees in the daytime and minus forty at night. The men and women in your party are wearing business attire (including pants and jacket), street shoes, and overcoats.

While escaping from the plane your group salvaged the fifteen items listed below. Your task is to rank these items according to their importance to your survival.

You may assume that the number of persons in the group is the same as the number in your group and that you have agreed to stick together.

WINTER SURVIVAL DECISION FORM

Rank the following items to their importance to your survival, starting with "1" for the most important and proceeding to "15" for the least important:

DIFFERING VIEWPOINTS ON THE IMPACT OF GROUPS

Items	Step 1 Your individual ranking	Step 2 The team's ranking	Step 3 Survival expert's ranking	Step 4 Difference between Steps 1 & 3	Step 5 Difference between Steps 2 & 3
Compress kit with 28 ft., 2 in.-gauze					
Ball of steel wool					
Cigarette lighter without fluid					
Loaded .45 calibre pistol					
Newspaper (1 per person)					
Compass					
Two ski poles					
Knife					
Sectional air map made of plastic					
30 feet of rope					
Family-size chocolate bar (1 per person)					
Flashlight with batteries					
Quart of 85–proof whiskey					
Extra shirt and pants for each person					
Can of shortening					
TOTAL					
(The lower the score the better)				Your score	Team score

Intergroup Exercise

One of the interesting dimensions of organizational behavior is the relationship among individual goals, formally stated goals, and actual organizational activities. The way we assess our own and others' motives, the assumptions regarding criteria and strategy, and the dynamics of intragroup *and* intergroup *relationships all have an important impact on what really happens.*

This exercise will provide an opportunity to examine these and other aspects of group behavior and, perhaps more importantly, your own attitudes and values with respect to significant organizational issues.

Exercise objective. To win as many points as possible.

Exercise rules:

1. Each team will select a captain who transmits the team's decisions. The captain gives the referee the team's decision after each move. Also, each team will select two negotiators.
2. Each team has ten tanks and starts the game fully armed (i.e., all ten tanks are armed). When you disarm a tank you have a "dove." Normally each team has ten 3 × 5 cards with a tank on one side and a dove on the other. (A suitable substitute for tanks and doves would be a 3 × 5 card with an X on one side [armed] and the other side blank [unarmed].)
3. A game consists of at least two "sets." A set ends whenever a team "attacks," or after five moves, whichever comes first.
4. A "move" consists of a two-minute period when each team decides on its strategy. During each move a team may change two, one, or zero cards from an armed to an unarmed position. Or it may change two, one, or

zero cards from an unarmed to an armed position. At the end of the two-minute period the captain must announce the team's decision to the referee. The referee will *not* give either team information about the other team's move.

5. Either team can request negotiations [through the referee] with the other team after any move. The request to negotiate may be accepted or rejected by the other team. However, the team *must* negotiate after the first and third moves. Negotiations, on neutral ground, will last two minutes in the presence of the referee.
6. At the end of moves one through four, either team may announce an "attack" to the referee. At this time the set ends. The attacking team is charged five points for attacking. (If both teams announce an attack, they are both charged five points). Then the team with the greater number of tanks (determined by the referee, who has the score sheet) wins ten points for each tank it has over and above the tanks held by the other team.

7. If there is no attack prior to the fifth move, at the end of the fifth move each team receives five points for each dove.

Giant Food Company

To understand the subtleties of group decision making, it is necessary to have a keen awareness of the process by which individual objectives are translated into behavior in a dynamic group setting. This role play is an opportunity to try to achieve a decision satisfactory to you by acting as if you really were the character whose role you have been assigned. Try to accept the role in terms of contemporary implications. Let your feelings develop as if you actually were that individual. Should issues develop that are not covered by the role, adapt or innovate accordingly.

To conceptualize your role, it is usually best to read it carefully two or three times; then close the book and think about it for a few minutes. Do not read the other roles; try to develop an approach in terms of the information given and your own interpretation of how a person in that position would likely behave. After you have the role in mind, do not reread it during the process of the role play.

GENERAL SITUATION

You are a sales representative for Giant Food Company, a wholesale supplier of packaged food products. Most of your customers are large grocery chains, but you deal with the stores on an individual basis, depending upon their inventory needs. You also supply smaller independent grocery stores and some restaurants. You have a territory assigned to you in the Los Angeles area, and it is your responsibility to generate as much business as possible. You are compensated on a commission basis, and you must pay your own expenses.

You are responsible to check the stock in your customers' stores and to take orders to replace sold items. You also make recommendations to the store manager about marketing and display of your products, and you must compete with other distributors and products for shelf and display space. Your relationship with the store manager affects how your products will be displayed and stocked, and display and stocking greatly affect the sales volume.

Your sales manager has an office in the main warehouse. He is responsible for the allocation of company property that you may use in your work. A new car has been ordered and will soon be available to one of the sales representatives in your division.

The sales representatives pride themselves on the appearance and running condition of their cars and on their econo-

Adapted from game originally designated by N. Berkowitz and H. Hornstein.

my, as they must pay all of their automobile expenses. The sales representatives often entertain their customers as part of their sales program; they feel that the car plays a vital part in the impression they make and therefore that it affects subsequent sales.

Some facts about the sales manager and the sales representatives and their cars are the following:

Phil   14 years with the company, male, white, sales manager

Tom   19 years with the company, male, white, 2–year–old Toyota sedan

José   9 years with the company, male, Chicano, 5–year–old Chevrolet full-size sedan

Henry 5 years with the company, male, white, 4–year–old Ford mid-size sedan

Susan 3 years with the company, female, white, 4–year–old Datsun station wagon

Paul   6 months with the company, male, white, 6–year–old Plymouth mid-size sedan

INDIVIDUAL ROLES

Phil. You are the sales manager of the five sales representatives. Every year or two you get a new car for one of them and are faced with the problem of whom to give it to and how the other vehicles should be reallocated. Often there are hard feelings about your decision, because each person has reasons for feeling that he or she is entitled to the new car. In the past, no matter what you have decided, most of them consider it wrong. You are now faced with the problem of who is to receive the new car, a Ford subcompact station wagon, next week. This year you have decided to allow the group to solve the problem, and you will make them live with their decision. They can decide what is the most fair way to redistribute the cars that are now available. You don't want to take a position because you want

to do what they think is most fair.

Tom. You have a two-year-old Toyota, which runs well and has been an economical little car. You have been with the company in this position for nineteen years, however, and the Toyota is just not large enough to handle the promotion and display material you must take to your many customers. Sometimes you are forced to use your family station wagon. You have the greatest dollar volume of sales of all the sales representatives, and often you can't service your customers adequately or economically because you must make several trips to an area when you begin a new promotional campaign. You think the extra room in the Ford station wagon will be adequate, and you like the economy of the subcompact. You also feel that your seniority (longer service than the sales manager) and the volume of business entitles you to the new car.

José. You have a five-year-old Chevrolet sedan, which in its day was a very nice car. You enjoy the roomy interior, because you have developed a good volume of business over the last nine years. The car is something of a gas hog and is getting very expensive to run the distances you must go to reach your area, which is mostly in the suburbs. You also feel that you need a newer car to take your customers to lunch. The Chevrolet is getting somewhat shabby. You feel that one of the reasons why you still have this old car, when newer representatives have better cars, may be that you are a Chicano.

Henry. You have been with the company for five years and have a four-year-old Ford sedan. It is in fairly good shape, except for the right door, which is sprung and doesn't close tightly. That door has been an irritation since Susan backed into it two years ago in the parking lot. You feel that you deserve either the new car or her car, because she damaged yours. You don't think she should be trusted with the new car; she would probably just wreck it anyway. And she doesn't have enough business to justify it. You feel that you should receive the new car because it will help you build up your business.

Susan. You are the only woman in this position in a virtually all-male company. You feel that you are seen as an intruder and a radical, although you make every attempt to avoid that image. You expect to be treated as an equal. You have shown that your salesmanship is equal to or better than the men's. You have a four-year-old Datsun wagon. The body is OK, but the engine and the transmission, which were treated badly by the last person to use the car, are constantly giving you trouble. The Datsun has often been in the shop when you needed it, and the engine needs to be rebuilt or replaced. You need the new car so that you can be more reliable in the eyes of your customers. You think the men in the department would like to see you fail and have given you the old Datsun as a handicap. You have a good driving record, except for the time when Henry opened the door of his car just as you were backing up to the building to load display materials. He still blames you for his door, although it was really his fault.

Paul. You have been with the company only six months. You have taken over the area and the car of a former sales representative who retired and who for the past few years had been coasting and doing little to build up the business. In the past six months you have shown the company what can be done to turn around such a stagnant area. You have doubled your business and have begun to generate a group of prospective customers, whom you must win away from the competitors. You have the oldest car and feel that it is a definite hindrance to your work. It is also uneconomical, and it needs repair. You feel that you have shown what you can do and should be rewarded with the new car, as a shot in the arm to help you build up momentum.

To What Degree Does Concern With Individual Needs Make the Organization More Effective or, Conversely, Render it Incapable of Taking Essential Action?

"All right, everything must stop. The merger decision can wait. Edgar has a problem. Tell us about your hang-up, Edgar."

CASES

Ranch Supplies Company

John Watson, executive vice-president and general manager of Ranch Supplies Company (RSC), sat at his desk mulling over the events of the past few months, which had just climaxed in a serious clash between two of his key employees—George Cox and Dale Johnson. When John hired Dale, he had expected that a marketing team combining George's longtime field sales experience with Dale's recent UCLA business school training would result in great benefits to RSC. However, almost since the day Dale came to work, his relationship with George had deteriorated. And now George had just stormed into John's office and stated that he didn't want Dale to work with him on any more projects. John wondered what, if anything, he could do to help resolve the conflict between Dale and George.

BACKGROUND

Ranch Supplies was an international company that annually grossed close to 4 million dollars' worth of cattle tags, bull semen, and other herd management supplies. RSC was a subsidiary of Jones Enterprises, which was owned by Bill Jones. Bill had convinced John less than a year before to leave a prominent Chicago consulting firm to come to work for him at the head office of both companies, in Grand Junction, Colorado. John was promoted quickly from assistant to the president of Jones Enterprises to general manager of RSC (see Exhibit 1).

When John came into the RSC organization, he turned to George Cox to teach him the ropes of the cattle industry and RSC's part in it. George did not have a college education but had worked his way up through RSC's organization from one of the original salesmen to his present position as director of marketing. He was one of the old-timers in the organization, having been with RSC since before it was acquired by Jones Enterprises. He was responsible for setting up the original marketing distribution system for the Big Green Tag (considered the "Cadillac" of the cattle ear tag industry) and for organizing the company's A.I. (artificial insemination) program. George was considered by many at RSC to be one of the most valuable people in the organization because of his close involvement with the Big Green Tag and bull semen, the two major items distributed by the company.

In spite of George's long-time service with the company, Bill Jones had voiced the opinion that George was not vital to the organization. He recognized that George had great ability as a salesman and that he had successfully persuaded many of the owners of famous bulls to sign contracts granting RSC exclusive distributorship of their bulls' semen, but he did not think of George as a good administrator because he was hard-headed in

EXHIBIT 1   Ranch Supplies Company Organization Chart

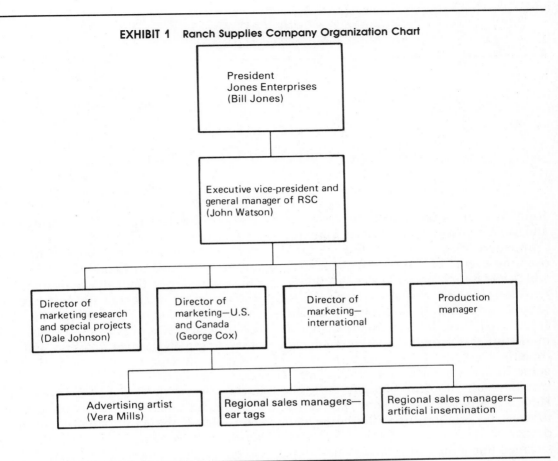

many ways and didn't like to delegate authority.

John voiced similar impressions about George's lack of administrative ability. He commented that George not only lacked administrative skill in keeping up on all the detail work that went along with the deals and commitments he made, but also liked to "feel as if he had total control over the company's marketing and distribution system." According to John, it seemed that George didn't like to have his operations subject to the approval of either John or Bill and that "he wants to be in my position as executive vice-president."

Unlike George, Dale Johnson had con-siderable formal business training. He and John had been classmates in the MBA program at UCLA. Dale was much more theoretical in his approach to solving problems than was George.

Dale originally came to work with the understanding that he would devote half of his time to Jones Enterprises and half to RSC; but because John had hired him and there was a greater need for him to help solve some of RSC's problems, he spent most of his time at RSC and had his office in the RSC building. John said that Dale was extremely creative in thinking of new ideas and ways to approach a problem but that he constantly hopped from one project to another, so that his work was disorganized. He often dreamed up projects on his own and started working on them. John also noted that Dale lacked the patience and skill needed to promote his ideas effectively within the organization. He added, however, that Dale was considered an important asset to the company because he had developed a point-of-purchase display that had proved successful in promoting RSC's new line of ear tag, the upright tag. RSC was planning to distribute another new tag in the near future, the stay-fast tag, which they hoped would be competitive in price with the "Fords and Chevrolets" of the industry and, at the same time, would not affect the sales of RSC's other ear tags. Dale was thought to be the person best qualified to develop a quality advertising and promotion campaign for the stay-fast tag.

THE CONFLICT

It was during the development of the promotion for the stay-fast tag that the clash between Dale and George first became evident. In deciding who would work on the project, John saw great potential in putting George and Dale together so that George's experience and Dale's training could be utilized. Dale and George were considered to be the best marketing men employed by RSC, and it was expected that they would cooperate with each other and coordinate their marketing efforts. However, even in the early stages of the project it was apparent that the relationship between the two was not cordial. It seemed that neither man was willing to compromise his own ideas. Soon the conflict became apparent to everybody in the office, for not only had George and Dale failed to present a unified proposal on the new marketing strategy, but George visibly shunned Dale each time they passed each other in the hallway.

John felt that there was little organizational pressure to make Dale and George work together: both reported to John di-

rectly, and there was no superior-subordinate relationship between the two (see Exhibit 1). The fact that Dale was considered staff and George was a line manager seemed to add to their unwillingness to cooperate.

John made the following observations about the two men:

Dale likes to be a one-man show. He does not desire to be a leader in a large organization, but he likes to be in charge of his projects. He doesn't like too many people under him. Dale is extremely creative, but many of his ideas are impractical. He has not yet learned to screen himself. For example, he has sometimes come to me for advice; and then, after I have advised him to do something a certain way, he has ignored my advice and done it his way.

George, on the other hand, is resentful of Dale because I hired him, and he doesn't want someone who is working for me to be a success. He also has difficulty in accepting people's weaknesses as well as their strengths, and, because Dale's impulsive nature annoyed him, he refused to work with him.

The growing tension between Dale and George came to a head when Dale was assigned a new box for the Big Green Tag.

Dale developed a box that seemed to bring approval from a good number of people in the company. After a prototype was approved, several hundred thousand boxes were ordered from an outside firm. During the development of the new box, Verla Mills, the company artist with whom Dale had been working on the new design, complained several times to George (her boss) that Dale was finicky and that he changed his mind too much.

After the newly designed box had been approved and ordered, Dale announced his decision that not only should the box graphics be changed, but all of RSC's products should be promoted under the acronym "RSC Tags," and new colors should be used in the graphics scheme. Dale took it upon himself to hire an outside advertising agency to come up with a new logo. When George found out about Dale's new project he nearly exploded. He stormed into John's office and told him that he flatly refused to work with Dale on any more projects. George re-fused to talk to Dale about the matter, but news of the problem soon got around to the rest of the office staff. John wondered what he could do to help resolve the conflict and get Dale and George to work together.

The Great Majestic Company

Robert Hoffman, the manager of the Great Majestic Lodge, was sitting at his desk and debating what he would say and what action he would take at a meeting with his bellmen, which was scheduled to begin in two hours. He had just weathered a stormy encounter with Mr. Tomblin, the general manager of the Great Majestic Lodge and several other recreational and lodging facilities in the area.

Mr. Tomblin was visibly upset by an action taken by the bellmen at Great Majestic Lodge three weeks ago. At the end of the explosive meeting, Mr. Tomblin roared, "Bob, I don't care if you fire the whole damn bunch! I want you to do something about this right now!"

BACKGROUND

Great Majestic Lodge was located in a popular park in the western United States. It was rather remote, yet offered all the modern conveniences featured at any fine metropolitan hotel. Because of its size and accommodations, the lodge was a favorite spot for large, organized tours. Most of the tours stayed one night and none stayed over two days. They were good moneymakers for the lodge because they always kept their schedules, paid their bills promptly, and were usually gone very early on checkout day.

Most of the employees hired by the Great Majestic Company were college students. This was an ideal situation, because the opening and closing dates of the lodge corresponded to most universities' summer vacations. The employees lived and ate at the company facilities and were paid $105 a month.

THE LODGE BELLMEN

The bellmen at the Great Majestic Lodge were directly responsible to the lodge manager, Mr. Hoffman. They were college students who, before being chosen for the bellman position, had worked for the company at least three summers. A total of seven were chosen on the basis of their past work performance, loyalty, efficiency, and ability to work with the public. Mr. Tomblin, the general manager, chose the bellmen himself.

The position of bellman was considered by the employees to be prestigious and important. In the eyes of the public, the bellmen represented the Great Majestic Lodge in every aspect. They were the first ones to greet the guests upon arrival, the people the guests called when anything was needed or went wrong, and the last ones to see the guests off upon their departure. Clad in their special cowboy apparel complete with personalized name tags and company insignia, the bellmen functioned as an effective public relations force for the Great Majestic Lodge, as well as providing prompt and professional service for each guest.

The bellmen all lived together in the back area of the most secluded employees' dorm at the Great Majestic Lodge. This facility was shared with most of the other lodge employees who had been with the company for two years or more. The older student-employees were especially close-knit, and all were looking forward to the time they would have the opportunity to be chosen as bellmen. The first-year employees usually occupied a dorm to themselves, adjacent to the seniority dorm. For the most part, a warm comradeship was experienced among all the staff at the lodge.

Traditionally, the bellmen had a comfortable relationship with Mr. Tomblin. This latest incident was of great concern for Mr. Hoffman. He realized that Mr. Tomblin was dead serious about firing them. It was midsummer, and it would be difficult to find qualified replacements. The bellmen this year had been especially productive.

The bellmen were paid a dollar per hour plus tips, which they pooled and divided equally at the end of each week. Daily tips averaged $20 per man. Hoffman was particularly concerned about the situation because it involved employees for whom he was directly responsible.

ORGANIZED TOURS

The bellmen had the responsibility of placing the tour luggage in the guests' rooms as soon as the bus arrived. The front desk provided them with a list of guests' names and the assigned cottage numbers. Speed was particularly impor-

tant, because the guests wanted to freshen up and demanded that their bags be delivered promptly.

On the morning of departure, the guests left their packed bags in their rooms while they went to breakfast. The bellmen picked up the bags, counted them, and then loaded them on the bus.

As payment for the service rendered by the bellmen, the tour directors paid fifty cents per bag. This was the standard gratuity paid by all tours. It was considered a tip, but it was included in the tour expenses by each company. On large tours, the tip could range as high as $75, although the average was $40.

THE JONES TRANSPORTATION AGENCY

The Jones Transportation Agency had a reputation throughout the area of being fair and equitable with their gratuities. However, one of their tour directors, Mr. Sirkin, did not live up to the company's reputation. On a visit to the Great Majestic Lodge, Mr. Sirkin had not given a tip. The bellmen knew their service to Mr. Sirkin had been very good. They were upset about the situation but assumed Sirkin had forgotten the tip in the rush before his tour departed. The tour was large and the tip would have amounted to $65.

Mr. Sirkin's tour also stayed at several other nearby resorts. Several of the Majestic Lodge bellmen knew the bellmen at the other lodges and, in discussing the situation, discovered that Mr. Sirkin had neglected the tip at each of the other lodges. It was apparent that Mr. Sirkin had made a profit of more than $180 on his four-day tour through the region.

THE LETTER

Upon hearing of Sirkin's actions, the Majestic Lodge bellmen decided that some action had to be taken. They immediately ruled out telling Mr. Hoffman. On previous occasions when there had been a problem, Mr. Hoffman had done very little to alleviate the situation.

Roger Sikes, a first-year bellman and a business undergraduate, suggested that a letter be written directly to the president of Jones Transportation Agency. He felt that the agency would appreciate knowing one of their tour directors had misused company funds. After some discussion, the other bellmen present agreed. Sikes prepared a detailed letter, which told the Jones president the details of the Sirkin incident. The bellmen didn't expect to recover the money from the tour, but they felt that this was the appropriate action to take.

Five of the bellmen signed the letter as soon as it was completed. Two more opposed but, after more discussion and considerable peer-group pressure, agreed to sign the letter. It was mailed with the expectation of a speedy reply and justice for the offending Mr. Sirkin.

REACTION TO THE LETTER

Three weeks after the bellmen's letter had been mailed to the Jones Transportation Agency, Mr. Tomblin was thumbing through his morning mail. He noticed a letter from his good friend Grant Cole, the president of the Jones Transportation Agency. Mr. Tomblin opened this letter first. Mr. Cole had written that there was a problem at the Great Majestic Lodge and he thought Mr. Tomblin should be made aware of it. He enclosed the letter from the bellmen and suggested that, if the bellmen had any problems with any Jones directors in the future, it might be wise for them to speak to Mr. Tomblin before any action was taken. Mr. Cole in-

formed Mr. Tomblin that Jones was investigating the Sirkin incident.

Mr. Tomblin was enraged. The bellmen had totally ignored their supervisor and had written a letter without first consulting any of the managers of the entire Great Majestic Company. This was not only a breach of company policy, but a personal humiliation for Mr. Tomblin.

Mr. Tomblin, yelling with outrage, leaped to his feet and charged through the lobby to Hoffman's office. He spotted bellman George Fletcher and ordered him to get out of his sight. The bewildered Fletcher quickly obeyed.

Robert Hoffman's meeting with Mr. Tomblin was an unpleasant experience. He had never seen Mr. Tomblin so upset at actions of employees. Mr. Tomblin was a proud man, and, because his pride had been hurt, he wanted revenge. He showed Hoffman the bellmen's letter and the reply from Grant Cole. Mr. Tomblin made it clear that he expected some quick action. Hoffman knew that the action had to meet Mr. Tomblin's approval. Hoffman's position as manager was suddenly placed in a precarious position.

There had been several employees in the lobby when Mr. Tomblin roared through. Hoffman knew the gossip would spread quickly throughout the lodge. The bellmen were well liked by the other employees and he knew they would be concerned about the bellmen's fate.

Hoffman called the still shaken George Fletcher into his office and told him to summon the off-duty bellmen for a meeting. After Fletcher left, Robert Hoffman attempted to think of alternatives that would satisfy Mr. Tomblin and also provide the expected quality service to the guests.

Northwest Industries

Northwest Industries was a growing company that manufactured recreational vehicles. One of the factories was located in Salem, Oregon. The recreational vehicle market was strong in the western United States and there was good demand for Northwest's products. The market reached its peak in mid-June and tapered off during the winter months. The factory tried to maintain a fairly constant production flow by building up inventories during the low winter months. During the summer months, a number of college students were hired to help boost production and bring inventory back to the desired level.

ORGANIZATION

The Salem plant had a three-leveled management structure (see Exhibit 1). Craig Hansen, age 52, was the general plant foreman. He had started working on the lines and had worked up to his position after seventeen years. Mr. Hansen knew "everything about trailers and could perform any separate job involved in the construction of a trailer within forty-five minutes." He was in charge of schedules for each run of trailers that was sent through. He also decided which line the trailer would go on and how long it would take to construct them. Mr. Hansen was serious about the business and conferred with Northwest's home office several times each week.

Joe Mackay, age 35, was the assistant plant foreman. His job was to help the foremen solve any problems they couldn't handle and to see that all plant safety rules and regulations were complied with. He also was responsible for raw materials inventory and ordering. The men viewed Joe as a walking bomb and therefore tried to stay out of his way. When he was called to help correct an error that had been made, Joe demanded to know who had made it and an explanation of how the workman could be so dumb.

Eight foremen comprised the third management layer. During the winter four of them worked in other areas of the plant and weren't involved in construction. Each foreman was assisted by a lead man, who helped manage the sixteen-man production crew. Foremen were salaried at $1500 per month, while lead men received 20 cents extra per hour, or $6.70 per hour.

Ted Nelson, age 28, was one of the regular foremen. He didn't have much, good or bad, to say about the college kids. In fact, he didn't say much about anything. On Ted's line, when a mistake was made, he would correct it himself and not say anything to the one who had made the mistake. If it happened again, Ted would point out the mistake to the worker and then correct it himself while the worker went back to the job. Ted also managed the time cards and handed out the paychecks.

Quality control in the plant was maintained by three inspectors who reported directly to Mr. Hansen. The inspector's position was considered prestigious, perhaps even more prestigious than foreman, even though both received the same sala-

EXHIBIT 1   Northwest Industries, Salem plant—Organization chart

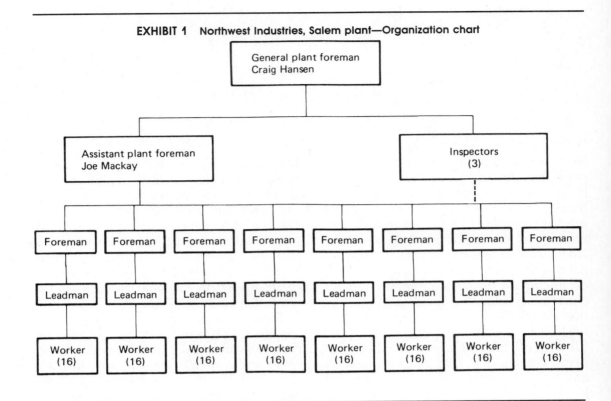

ry. Inspectors had to be especially knowl-edgeable and trustworthy and able to find production mistakes quickly.

Upon completion of each trailer, the foreman would call one of the inspectors, who would examine the trailer and test all components. Any defects were noted on a "squawk sheet." These "squawks" then had to be fixed before the inspector would sign the release form. An average trailer generally had four or five minor squawks, which a good "squawker" could repair within twenty or twenty-five minutes. The idea was to have a good squawker, so that people would not be pulled off the line and lose time to fix production errors.

Workers with some experience were hired at $4.50 per hour, and unskilled help started at $3.75 per hour. Provided the unskilled workers produced well, a raise would be given after two months on the job to $4.50 per hour. After four or five years, the workers usually earned $6.50 per hour.

The inspectors, the year-round work-ers, and the foremen were a very close-knit group. They enjoyed many activities together, such as parties, bowling, raft races, and, occasionally, light refresh-ments. Lunch and break times were looked forward to. All participated in a regular contribution to support the highly enjoyed numbers game, which accompa-nied each pay period, as well as to fund such things as birthday and sympathy cards.

Most of the employees at Northwest had completed high school and then start-ed work with the company. These fellows worked hard and took pride in what they were making. Most planned to stay with Northwest all their lives. About seventy-five employees worked year-round, with sixty-five seasonal workers helping out in the summer months.

Northwest's usual procedure was to run four of the eight production lines during the winter. During the summer, enough new people were hired to staff all eight lines. Most of the stations on a line required two people to complete each job, and ample space existed between stations to permit a trailer to sit between work areas. This spacing procedure facilitated line moves and allowed for the time differences in performing each job.

THE NEW PLAN

This year, Mr. Hansen had decided to eliminate some of the problems experienced in the past. Six of the foremen had been complaining about the inefficiency of those college kids, who were reported to be slow, stubborn know-it-alls. They admitted that the kids were hard to train and got bored easily but for the most part did a good job.

Mr. Hansen decided to run four lines as normal, leaving most of the older, regular employees on those lines. The younger people who were already working for the company were distributed to two of the other lines, and, as the college kids were hired, they were paired up with the younger but experienced workers for training. Mr. Hansen's strategy was that, as the college kids learned, they would be able to expand to the other two lines, and eventually all eight lines would be in full production.

The plan was readily adopted by the foremen. Four were assigned to the four lines with the regulars, and the other four were assigned in pairs to the two new lines, with one designated as the foreman and the other as assistant foreman.

The new plan seemed to be working well. Halfway through July, the plant was running at full production. The lines with the newer workers enjoyed working to-gether, and a substantial rivalry had been created between them and the older workers. Mr. Hansen had seen to it that the younger lines were given routine, long production runs to work on. These runs generally consisted of thirty or forty units that were exactly the same and thus the training period was minimized and errors were reduced. The other, more experienced lines were given the shorter runs to work on.

At first the rivalry was in fun, but after a few weeks the older workers became resentful of the remarks that were being made and felt that those kids should have to work on some of the more difficult runs. The younger lines easily met production schedules, and thus some spare time was left for goofing around. It wasn't uncommon for someone from the younger lines to go to another line, in guise of looking for some material, and then give the older workers a hard time. Some of the older workers resented this treatment and soon began to retaliate with sabotage. They would sneak over during breaks and hide tools, dent metal, install something crooked, or in other small ways do something that would slow production in the lines with the younger workers.

To Mr. Hansen everything seemed to be going quite well, and he was proud of himself and his plan. Toward the end of July, however, he began hearing reports of the rivalry and sabotage. As most of the longer production runs had been completed, Mr. Hansen decided that "those kids needed to quit playing around and get to work." He gave them some of the new runs, which were basically the same as before, except for a few changes in the interior walls and the wood roof.

Ted Nelson, the foreman of line C, one of the younger ones, heard about the new run coming on his line and decided to go ahead of the first trailer to help each station with the forthcoming changes. He carefully explained each change to the workers as the lead trailer came into their station and then went on to the next. The kids seemed to be picking up the changes okay, so that Ted didn't worry too much about the new run.

As the first trailer was pushed out, ready for inspection, Ted called the inspector. A half hour later, the inspector emerged with two pages of squawks—forty-nine of them. Not seeing Ted anywhere, the inspector called in Mr. Hansen and Joe to point out the uncommonly high number of squawks. It took about five minutes for things to completely explode. Ted walked on the scene just in time to hear Mr. Hansen yell to Joe, "Get that line into gear in one week and get those squawks fixed or fire the whole bunch!"

How Do You Identify a Potential Leader?

"Leadership experience? ... Well, I organized a strike once!"

4

Some Comments on the Challenge of Leadership

In ancient as well as modern times, few questions have so preoccupied people's minds as that of the nature of effective leadership. Individuals in every kind of organized activity have tried to grasp the secret; that is, how does one mobilize human resources in the accomplishment of a task? Although simple or universal explanations have so far proven to be inadequate, some considerations can be useful in approaching the concept of leadership.

First, most people ascribe real power to leaders. As organization members, professional consultants, or casual observers try to explain what is wrong in an organization, a likely diagnosis is "bad leadership." Conversely, when a company performs well, when an athletic team wins, or when a national economy is strong, the common explanation is "good leadership." Even with our limited understanding, leadership is still regarded as the panacea or the scapegoat in a high percentage of explanations of organizational performance.

Second, most people have strong value assumptions about how leaders *ought* to think, behave, and treat their subordinates. These assumptions can be drawn from philosophical, political, economic, military, or religious principles. And, although the evidence supporting the effectiveness of a leadership concept may be limited, that concept is still believed and preached as a matter of fundamental truth. Consequently, rational analysis is difficult.

A third problem is the description or classification of leadership styles. In past research we attempted to label leaders *authoritarian or democratic,* on the assumption that authoritarian leaders were interested in the *task* and that democratic leaders were interested in *people.* This over-simplification suggested that you could either be tough and get the job done or be soft and make the people happy. Subsequent evidence indicated that a leader could show both traits strongly, or both weakly, or some other combination. But the evidence also revealed that task-emphasis and people-emphasis were not necessarily opposite ends of the continuum.

Putting the leadership issue in historical perspective also helps clarify it. Early discussions of leadership focused almost exclusively on personality traits of individual leaders. It was felt that, by observing great military or religious leaders, identifying their character traits, and imitating them, the imitators in turn could become great leaders. But experience has shown us that people cannot easily adopt the characteristics of great leaders. Furthermore, we found that we could not define a precise set of leadership characteristics anyway. Great leaders seemed to have many different traits.

Successive studies concentrated on styles. It was argued that, even if we could not all be like great leaders of the past, we might be able to learn general principles of leadership. The vast number of "human relations" training programs reflected this emphasis. But this approach has enjoyed limited success.

Recent studies have shown that some authoritarian leaders were successful and some were not and that some democratic or participative leaders experienced great success and some seemed to flounder. The implication is that there is no optimal style that everyone could use. Clearly, circumstances have a significant impact on leadership. This realization led us to a contingency approach, which argues that leadership effectiveness is a function of many different factors—some of which are beyond the leader's control: (a) the characteristics of the leader, (b) the characteristics of the subordinates, (c) the nature of the task, (d) the organization structure and climate, and (e) the external environment of the organization.

A continuing indicator of the felt need for more effective leadership is the large number of leadership training programs. From the time of the "human relations" movement in the 1940s we have observed an almost unlimited number of training techniques and courses. The earlier supervisory training programs evolved into management development, which had a broader focus, and finally into organization development, which looks at the whole organization as a system. Organization development (OD) recognizes the inappropriateness of looking only at the leader in the analysis of organizational performance. The leader is very important but is not the only variable in the equation.

The articles in this section explore factors that affect the quality of leadership. While no article offers a list of simple steps on how to become a good leader, all suggest factors that need to be considered in the development of a leadership strategy.

Workingman and Management

ERIC HOFFER

There are many of us who have been workingmen all our lives and, whether we know it or not, will remain workingmen till we die. Whether there be a God in heaven or not; whether we be free or regimented; whether our standard of living be high or low—I and my like will go on doing more or less what we are doing now.

This sober realization need not be unduly depressing to people who have acquired the habit of work and who, like the American workingman, have the ingredients of a fairly enjoyable life within their reach. Still, the awareness of being an eternal workingman colors one's attitudes; and it might be of some interest to indicate briefly what the relations between management and labor look like when seen from his point of view.

To the eternal workingman, management is substantially the same whether it is made up of profit seekers, idealists, technicians, or bureaucrats. The allegiance of the manager is to the task and the results. However noble his motives, he cannot help viewing the workers as a means to an end. He will always try to get the utmost out of them; and it matters not whether he does it for the sake of profit, for a holy cause, or for the sheer principle of efficiency.

One need not view management as an enemy or feel self-righteous about doing an honest day's work to realize that things are likely to get tough when management can take the worker for granted; when it can plan and operate without having to

worry about what the worker will say or do.

The important point is that this taking of the worker for granted occurs not only when management has unlimited power to coerce, but also when the division between management and labor ceases to be self-evident. Any doctrine which preaches the oneness of management and labor— whether it stresses their unit in a party, class, race, nation, or even religion—can be used to turn the worker into a compliant instrument in the hands of management. Both Communism and Fascism postulate the oneness of management and labor, and both are devices for the extraction of maximum performance from an underpaid labor force. The preachment of racial unity facilitated the exploitation of labor in our South, in French Canada, and in South Africa. Pressure for nationalist and religious unity served, and still serves, a similar purpose elsewhere.

Seen from this point of view, the nationalization of the means of production is more a threat than a promise. For we shall be bossed and managed by someone, no matter who owns the means of production—and we can have no defenses against those who can tell us in all truth that we, the workers, own everything in sight and they, our taskmasters, are driving us for our own good. The battle between Socialism and Capitalism is to a large extent a battle between bosses, and it is legitimate to size up the dedicated Socialist as a potential boss.

One need not call to mind the example of Communist Russia to realize that the idealist has the making of a most formidable taskmaster. The ruthlessness born of self-seeking is ineffectual compared with the ruthlessness sustained by dedication to a holy cause. "God wishes," said Calvin, "that one should put aside all humanity when it is a question of striving for his glory." So it is better to be bossed by men of little faith, who set their hearts on toys, than by men animated by lofty ideals who are ready to sacrifice themselves and others for a cause. The most formidable employer is he who, like Stalin, casts himself in the role of a representative and champion of the workers.

Our sole protection lies in keeping the division between management and labor obvious and matter of fact. We want management to manage the best it can, and the workers to protect their interests the best they can. No social order will seem to us free if it makes it difficult for the worker to maintain a considerable degree of independence from management.

The things which bolster this independence are not utopian. Effective labor unions, free movement over a relatively large area, a savings account, a tradition of individual self-respect—these are some of them. They are within the worker's reach in this country and most of the free world, but are either absent or greatly weakened in totalitarian states.

In the present Communist regimes, unions are tools of management, worker mobility is discouraged by every means, savings are periodically wiped out by changes in the currency, and individual self-respect is extirpated by the fearful technique of Terror. Thus it seems that the worker's independence is as good an index as any for measuring the freedom of a society.

The next question is whether an independent labor force is compatible with efficient production. For if the attitude of the workers tends to interfere with the full unfolding of the productive process, then the workingman's independence becomes meaningless.

It has been my observation for years on the docks of San Francisco that, while a wholly independent labor force does not contribute to management's peace of mind, it can yet goad management to perfect its organization and to keep ever on the lookout for more efficient ways of doing things. Management on the San Francisco waterfront is busy twenty-four hours a day figuring out ways of loading and discharging ships with as few men as possible.

Mechanization became very marked on the waterfront after the organization of the present militant labor union in 1934. The fork lift and the pallet board are almost in universal use. There are special machines for handling sugar, newsprint, and cotton bales. There are new methods for handling coffee, rice, and wool. New arrangements and refinements appear almost every day. Here nobody has to be told that management is continually on the job. Certainly there are other factors behind this incessant alertness, and some of them play perhaps a more crucial role in the process of mechanization. But it is quite obvious that a fiercely independent labor force is not incompatible with efficient production.

Contrary to the doctrine propounded by some in the heyday of the Industrial Revolution, mechanization has not taught docility to "the refractory hand of labor." At least here on the docks, we know that we shall manage to get our full share no matter what happens. And it is a dull workingman who does not see in the machine the only key to the true millenium. For only mechanization can mitigate—if not cure—"the disease of work," as de Tocqueville calls it, which has tortured humanity since the first day of its existence.

To me the advent of automation is the culmination of the vying with God which began at the rise of the modern Occident. The skirmish with God has now moved all the way back to the gates of Eden. Jehovah and his angels, with their flaming and revolving swords, are now holed up inside their Eden fortress, while the blasphemous multitude with their host of machines are clamoring at the gate. And right there, in the sight of Jehovah and his angels, we are annulling the ukase that with the sweat of his brow man shall eat bread.

It is true, of course, that the cleavage between management and labor is a source of strain and strife. But it is questionable whether tranquility is the boon it is made out to be. The late William Randolph Hearst shrewdly observed that "whatever begins to be tranquil is gobbled up by something that is not tranquil." The constant effort to improve and advance is neither automatic nor the result of a leisurely choice between alternatives. In human affairs, the best stimulus for running ahead is to have something we must run from. The chances are that the millennial society, where the wolf and the lamb shall dwell together, will be a stagnant society.

The Manager's Job: Folklore and Fact

HENRY MINTZBERG

If you ask a manager what he does, he will most likely tell you that he plans, organizes, coordinates, and controls. Then watch what he does. Don't be surprised if you can't relate what you see to these four words.

When he is called and told that one of his factories has just burned down, and he advises the caller to see whether temporary arrangements can be made to supply customers through a foreign subsidiary, is he planning, organizing, coordinating, or controlling? How about when he presents a gold watch to a retiring employee? Or when he attends a conference to meet people in the trade? Or on returning from that conference, when he tells one of his employees about an interesting product idea he picked up there?

The fact is that these four words, which have dominated management vocabulary since the French industrialist Henri Fayol first introduced them in 1916, tell us little about what managers actually do. At best, they indicate some vague objectives managers have when they work.

The field of management, so devoted to progress and change, has for more than half a century not seriously addressed the basic question: What do managers do? Without a proper answer, how can we teach management? How can we design planning or information systems for managers? How can we improve the practice of management at all?

Our ignorance of the nature of managerial work shows up in various ways in the modern organization—In the boast by the successful manager that he never spent a single day in a management training program; in the turnover of corporate planners who never quite understood what it was the manager wanted; in the computer consoles gathering dust in the back room because the managers never used the fancy on-line MIS some analyst thought they needed. Perhaps most important, our ignorance shows up in the inability of our large public organizations to come to grips with some of their most serious policy problems.

Somehow, in the rush to automate production, to use management science in the functional areas of marketing and finance, and to apply the skills of the behavioral scientists to the problem of worker motivation, the manager—that person in charge of the organization or one of its subunits—has been forgotten.

My intention in this article is simple: to break the reader away from Fayol's words and introduce him to a more supportable,

and what I believe to be a more useful, description of managerial work. This description derives from my review and synthesis of the available research on how various managers have spent their time.

In some studies, managers were observed intensively ("shadowed" is the term some of them used); in a number of others, they kept detailed diaries of their activities; in a few studies, their records were analyzed. All kinds of managers were studied—foremen, factory supervisors, staff managers, field sales managers, hospital administrators, presidents of companies and nations, and even street gang leaders. These "managers" worked in the United States, Canada, Sweden, and Great Britain. In the insert is a brief review of the major studies that I found most useful in developing this description, including my own study of five American chief executive officers.

Research on managerial work

Considering its central importance to every aspect of management, there has been surprisingly little research on the manager's work, and virtually no systematic building of knowledge from one group of studies to another. In seeking to describe managerial work, I conducted my own research and also scanned the literature widely to integrate the findings of studies from many diverse sources with my own. These studies focused on two very different aspects of managerial work. Some were concerned with the characteristics of the work—how long managers work, where, at what pace and with what interruptions,

with whom they work, and through what media they communicate. Other studies were more concerned with the essential content of the work—what activities the managers actually carry out, and why. Thus, after a meeting, one researcher might note that the manager spent 45 minutes with three government officials in their Washington office, while another might record that he presented his company's stand on some proposed legislation in order to change a regulation.

A few of the studies of managerial work are widely known, but most have remained buried as single journal articles or isolated books.

Among the more important ones I cite (with full references in the bibliography) are the following:

- Sune Carlson developed the diary method to study the work characteristics of nine Swedish managing directors. Each kept a detailed log of his activities. Carlson's results are reported in his book *Executive Behavior.* A number of British researchers, notably Rosemary Stewart, have subsequently used Carlson's method. In *Managers and Their Jobs,* she describes the study of 160 top and middle managers of British companies during four weeks, with particular attention to the differences in their work.

- Leonard Sayles's book *Managerial Behavior* is another important reference. Using a method he refers to as "anthropological," Sayles studies the work content of middle- and lower-level managers in a large U.S. corporation. Sayles moved freely in the company, collecting whatever information struck him as important.
- Perhaps the best-known source is *Presidential Power*, in which Richard Neustadt analyzes the power and managerial behavior of Presidents Roosevelt, Truman, and Eisenhower. Neustadt used secondary sources—documents and interviews with other parties—to generate his data.
- Robert H. Guest, in *Personnel*, reports on a study of the foreman's working day. Fifty-six U.S. foremen were observed and each of their activities recorded during one eight-hour shift.
- Richard C. Hodgson, Daniel J. Levinson, and Abraham Zaleznik studied a team of three top executives of a U.S. hospital. From that study they wrote *The Executive Role Constellation*. These researchers addressed in particular the way in which work and socioemotional roles were divided among the three managers.
- William F. Whyte, from his study of a street gang during the Depression, wrote *Street Corner Society*. His findings about the gang's leadership, which George C. Homans analyzed in *The Human Group*, suggest some interesting similarities of job content between street gang leaders and corporate managers.
- My own study involved five American CEO's of middle- to large-size organizations—a consulting firm, a technology company, a hospital, a consumer goods company, and a school system. Using a method called "structural observation," during one intensive week of observation for each executive I recorded various aspects of every piece of mail and every verbal contact. My method was designed to capture data on both work characteristics and job content. In all, I analyzed 890 pieces of incoming and outgoing mail and 368 verbal contacts.

A synthesis of these findings paints an interesting picture, one as different from Fayol's classical view as a cubist abstract is from a Renaissance painting. In a sense, this picture will be obvious to anyone who has ever spent a day in a manager's office, either in front of the desk or behind it. Yet, at the same time, this picture may turn out to be revolutionary, in that it throws into doubt so much of the folklore that we have accepted about the manager's work.

I first discuss some of this folklore and contrast it with some of the discoveries of systematic research—the hard facts about how managers spend their time. Then I synthesize these research findings in a description of ten roles that seem to describe the essential content of all managers' jobs. In a concluding section, I discuss a number of implications of this synthesis for those trying to achieve more effective management, both in classrooms and in the business world.

SOME FOLKLORE AND FACTS ABOUT MANAGERIAL WORK

There are four myths about the manager's job that do not bear up under careful scrutiny of the facts.

I. Folklore: The manager is a reflective, systematic planner. The evidence on this issue is overwhelming, but not a shred of it supports this statement.

Fact: Study after study has shown that managers work at an unrelenting pace, that their activities are characterized by brevity, variety, and discontinuity, and that they are strongly oriented to action and dislike reflective activities. Consider this evidence:

Half the activities engaged in by the five chief executives of my study lasted less than nine minutes, and only 10% exceeded one hour (Mintzberg 1973). A study of 56 U.S. foremen found that they averaged 583 activities per eight-hour shift, an average of 1 every 48 seconds (Guest 1956). The work pace for both chief executives and foremen was unrelenting. The chief executives met a steady stream of callers and mail from the moment they arrived in the morning until they left in the evening. Coffee breaks and lunches were inevitably work related, and ever-present subordinates seemed to usurp any free moment.

A diary study of 160 British middle and top managers found that they worked for a half hour or more without interruption only about once every two days. (Stewart 1967, Carlson 1951).

Of the verbal contacts of the chief executives in my study, 93% were arranged on an ad hoc basis. Only 1% of the executives' time was spent in open-ended observational tours. Only 1 out of 368 verbal contacts was unrelated to a specific issue and could be called general planning. Another researcher finds that "in *not one single case* did a manager report the obtaining of important external information from a general conversation or other undirected personal communication" (Aguiler 1967).

No study has found important patterns in the way managers schedule their time. They seem to jump from issue to issue, continually responding to the needs of the moment.

Is this the planner that the classical view describes? Hardly. How, then, can we explain this behavior? The manager is simply responding to the pressures of his job. I found that my chief executives terminated many of their own activities, often leaving meetings before the end, and interrupted their desk work to call in subordinates. One president not only placed his desk so that he could look down a long hallway but also left his door open when he was alone—an invitation for subordinates to come in and interrupt him.

Clearly, these managers wanted to encourage the flow of current information. But more significantly, they seemed to be conditioned by their own work loads. They appreciated the opportunity cost of their own time, and they were continually aware of their ever-present obligations—mail to be answered, callers to attend to, and so on. It seems that no matter what he is doing, the manager is plagued by the possibilities of what he might do and what he must do.

When the manager must plan, he seems to do so implicitly in the context of daily actions, not in some abstract process reserved for two weeks in the organization's mountain retreat. The plans of the chief executives I studied seemed to exist only in their heads—as flexible, but often specific, intentions. The traditional literature notwithstanding, the job of managing does not breed reflective planners; the manager is a real-time responder to stimuli, an individual who is conditioned by his job to prefer live to delayed action.

II. Folklore: The effective manager has no regular duties to perform. Managers are constantly being told to spend more time planning and delegating, and less time seeing customers and engaging in negotiations. These are not, after all, the true tasks of the manager. To use the popular analogy, the good manager, like the good conductor, carefully orchestrates everything in advance, then sits back to enjoy the fruits of his labor, responding occasionally to an unforseeable exception.

But here again the pleasant abstraction just does not seem to hold up. We had better take a closer look at those activities managers feel compelled to engage in before we arbitrarily define them away.

Fact: In addition to handling exceptions, managerial work involves performing a number of regular duties, including ritual and ceremony, negotiations, and processing of soft information that links the organization with its environment. Consider some evidence from the research studies:

A study of the work of the presidents of small companies found that they engaged in routine activities because their companies could not afford staff specialists and were so thin on operating personnel that a single absence often required the president to substitute (see Choran).

One study of field sales managers and another of chief executives suggest that it is a natural part of both jobs to see important customers, assuming the managers wish to keep those customers (Davis 1957; Copeman 1963).

Someone, only half in jest, once described the manager as that person who sees visitors so that everyone else can get his work done. In my study, I found that certain ceremonial duties—meeting visiting dignitaries, giving out gold watches, presiding at Christmas dinners—were an intrinsic part of the chief executive's job.

Studies of managers' information flow suggest that managers play a key role in securing "soft" external in-

formation (much of it available only to them because of their status) and in passing it along to their subordinates.

III: Folklore: The senior manager needs aggregated information, which a formal management information system best provides. Not too long ago, the words *total information system* were everywhere in the management literature. In keeping with the classical view of the manager as that individual perched on the apex of a regulated, hierarchical system, the literature's manager was to receive all his important information from a giant, comprehensive MIS.

But lately, as it has become increasingly evident that these giant MIS systems are not working—that managers are simply not using them—the enthusiasm has waned. A look at how managers actually process information makes the reason quite clear. Managers have five media at their command—documents, telephone calls, scheduled and unscheduled meetings, and observational tours.

Fact: Managers strongly favor the verbal media—namely, telephone calls and meetings. The evidence comes from every single study of managerial work. Consider the following:

In two British studies, managers spent an average of 66 and 80% of their time in verbal (oral) communication (Stewart 1967; Burns 1954). In my study of five American chief executives, the figure was 78%.

These five chief executives treated mail processing as a burden to be dispensed with. One came in Saturday morning to process 142 pieces of mail in just over three hours, to "get rid of all the stuff." This same manager looked at the first piece of "hard" mail he had received all week, a standard cost report, and put it aside with the comment, "I never look at this."

These same five chief executives responded immediately to 2 of the 40 routine reports they received during the five weeks of my study and to four items in the 104 periodicals. They skimmed most of these periodicals in seconds, almost ritualistically. In all, these chief executives of good-sized organizations initiated on their own—that is, not in response to something else—a grand total of 25 pieces of mail during the 25 days I observed them.

An analysis of the mail the executives received reveals an interesting picture—only 13% was of specific and immediate use. So now we have another piece in the puzzle: not much of the mail provides live, current information—the action of a competitor, the mood of a government legislator, or the rating of last night's television show. Yet this is the information that drove the managers, interrupting their meetings and rescheduling their workdays.

Consider another interesting finding. Managers seem to cherish "soft" information, especially gossip, hearsay, and speculation. Why? The reason is its timeliness; today's gossip may be tomorrow's fact. The manager who is not accessible for the telephone call informing him that his biggest customer was seen golfing with the main competitor may read about a dramatic drop in sales in the next quarterly report. But then it's too late.

To assess the value of historical, aggregated, "hard" MIS information, consider two of the manager's prime uses for his information—to identify problems and opportunities (Wrapp 1967) and to build his own mental models of the things around him (e.g., how his organization's budget system works, how his customers buy his product, how changes in the economy affect his organization, and so on).

Every bit of evidence suggests that the manager identifies decision situations and builds models not with the aggregated abstractions an MIS provides, but with specific tidbits of data.

Consider the words of Richard Neustadt, who studied the information-collecting habits of Presidents Roosevelt, Truman, and Eisenhower:

> It is not information of a general sort that helps a President see personal stakes; not summaries, not surveys, not the *bland amalgams*. Rather ... it is the odds and ends of *tangible detail* that pieced together in his mind illuminate the underside of issues put before him. To help himself he must reach out as widely as he can for every scrap of fact, opinion, gossip, bearing on his interests and relationships as President. He must become his own director of his own central intelligence (Neustadt 1960, 153–154).

The manager's emphasis on the verbal media raises two important points:

First, verbal information is stored in the brains of people. Only when people write this information down can it be stored in the files of the organization—whether in metal cabinets or on magnetic tape—and managers apparently do not write down much of what they hear. Thus the strategic data bank of the organization is not in the memory of its computers but in the minds of its managers.

Second, the manager's extensive use of verbal media helps to explain why he is reluctant to delegate tasks. When we note that most of the manager's important information comes in verbal form and is stored in his head, we can well appreciate his reluctance. It is not as if he can hand a dossier over to someone; he must take the time to "dump memory"—to tell that someone all he knows about the subject. But this could take so long that the manager may find it easier to do the task himself. Thus the manager is damned by his own information system to a "dilemma of delegation"—to do too much himself or to delegate to his subordinates with inadequate briefing.

IV. Folklore: Management is, or at least is quickly becoming, a science and a profession.

By almost any definitions of *science* and *profession*, this statement is false. Brief observation of any manager will quickly lay to rest the notion that managers practice a science. A science involves the enaction of systematic, analytically determined procedures or programs. If we do not even know what procedures managers use, how can we prescribe them by scientific analysis? And how can we call management a profession if we cannot specify what managers are to learn? For after all, a profession involves "knowledge of some department of learning or science" (*Random House Dictionary*). (Andrews 1969).

Fact: The managers' programs—to schedule time, process information, make decisions, and so on—remain locked deep inside their brains.

Thus, to describe these programs, we rely on words like *judgment* and *intuition*, seldom stopping to realize that they are merely labels for our ignorance.

I was struck during my study by the fact that the executives I was observing— all very competent by any standard—are fundamentally indistinguishable from their counterparts of a hundred years ago (or a thousand years ago, for that matter). The information they need differs, but they seek it in the same way—by word of mouth. Their decisions concern modern technology, but the procedures they use to make them are the same as the procedures of the nineteenth-century manager. Even the computer, so important for the specialized work of the organization, has apparently had no influence on the work procedures of general managers. In fact, the manager is in a kind of loop, with increasingly heavy work pressures but no

aid forthcoming from management science.

Considering the facts about managerial work, we can see that the manager's job is enormously complicated and difficult. The manager is over-burdened with obligations; yet he cannot easily delegate his tasks. As a result, he is driven to overwork and is forced to do many tasks superficially. Brevity, fragmentation, and verbal communications characterize his work. Yet these are the very characteristics of managerial work that have impeded scientific attempts to improve it. As a result, the management scientist has concentrated his efforts on the specialized functions of the organization, where he could more easily analyze the procedures and quantify the relevant information (Gragson 1973).

But the pressures of the manager's job are becoming worse. Where before he needed only to respond to owners and directors, now he finds that subordinates with democratic norms continually reduce his freedom to issue unexplained orders, and a growing number of outside influences (consumer groups, government agencies, and so on) expect his attention. And the manager has had nowhere to turn for help. The first step in providing the manager with some help is to find out what his job really is.

BACK TO A BASIC DESCRIPTION OF MANAGERIAL WORK

Now let us try to put some of the pieces of this puzzle together. Earlier, I defined the manager as that person in charge of an organization or one of its subunits. Besides chief executive officers, this definition would include vice presidents, bishops, foremen, hockey coaches, and prime ministers. Can all of these people have anything in common? Indeed they can. For an important starting point, all are vested with formal authority over an organizational unit. From formal authority comes status, which leads to various interpersonal relations, and from these comes access to information. Information, in turn, enables the manager to make decisions and strategies for his unit.

The manager's job can be described in terms of various "roles," or organized sets of behaviors identified with a position. My description, shown in Exhibit 1, comprises ten roles. As we shall see, formal authority gives rise to three interpersonal roles, which in turn give rise to three additional interpersonal roles; these two sets of roles enable the manager to play the four decisional roles.

Interpersonal Roles:

Three of the manager's roles arise directly from his formal authority and involve basic interpersonal relationships.

1. First is the *figurehead* role. By virtue of his position as head of an organizational unit, every manager must perform some duties of a ceremonial nature. The president greets the touring dignitaries, the foreman attends the wedding of a lathe operator, and the sales manager takes an important customer to lunch.

The chief executives of my study spent

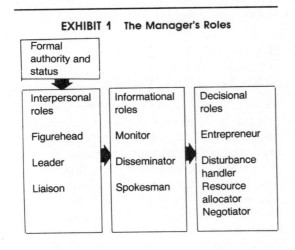

EXHIBIT 1   The Manager's Roles

12% of their contact time on ceremonial duties; 17% of their incoming mail dealt with acknowledgments and requests related to their status. For example, a letter to a company president requested free merchandise for a crippled schoolchild; diplomas were put on the desk of the school superintendent for his signature.

Duties that involve interpersonal roles may sometimes be routine, involving little serious communication and no important decision making. Nevertheless, they are important to the smooth functioning of an organization and cannot be ignored by the manager.

2. Because he is in charge of an organizational unit, the manager is responsible for the work of the people of that unit. His actions in this regard constitute the *leader* role. Some of these actions involve leadership directly—for example, in most organizations the manager is normally responsible for hiring and training his own staff.

In addition, there is the indirect exercise of the leader role. Every manager must motivate and encourage his employees, somehow reconciling their individual needs with the goals of the organization. In virtually every contact the manager has with his employees, subordinates seeking leadership clues probe his actions: "Does he approve?" "How would he like the report to turn out?" "Is he more interested in market share than high profits?"

The influence of the manager is most clearly seen in the leader role. Formal authority vests him with great potential power; leadership determines in large part how much of it he will realize.

3. The literature of management has always recognized the leader role, particularly those aspects of it related to motivation. In comparison, until recently it has hardly mentioned the *liaison* role, in which the manager makes contacts outside his vertical chain of command.

This is remarkable in light of the finding of virtually every study of managerial work that managers spend as much time with peers and other people outside their units as they do with their own subordinates—and, surprisingly, very little time with their own superiors.

In Rosemary Stewart's diary study, the 160 British middle and top managers spent 47% of their time with peers, 41% of their time with people outside their unit, and only 12% of their time with their superiors. For Robert H. Guest's study of U.S. foremen, the figures were 44%, 46%, and 10%. The chief executives of my study averaged 44% of their contact time with people outside their organizations, 48% with subordinates, and 7% with directors and trustees.

The contacts the five CEOs made were with an incredibly wide range of people: subordinates; clients, business associates, and suppliers; and peers—managers of similar organizations, government and trade organization officials, fellow directors on outside boards, and independents with no relevant organizational affiliations. The chief executives' time with and mail from these groups is shown in Exhibit 2. Guest's study of foremen shows, likewise, that their contacts were numerous and wide ranging, seldom involving fewer than 25 individuals, and often more than 50.

As we shall see shortly, the manager cultivates such contacts largely to find information. In effect, the liaison role is devoted to building up the manager's own external information system—informal, private, verbal, but nevertheless, effective.

Informational Roles:

By virtue of his interpersonal contacts, both with his subordinates and with his network of contacts, the manager emerges as the nerve center of his organizational unit. He may not know everything, but he typically knows more than

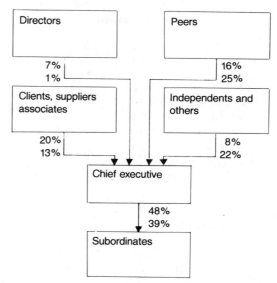

EXHIBIT 2 The Chief Executives' Contacts

Note: The top figure indicates the proportion of total contact time spent with each group and the bottom figure, the proportion of mail from each group.

any member of his staff.

Studies have shown this relationship to hold for all managers, from street gang leaders to U.S. presidents. In *The Human Group*, George C. Homans explains how, because they were at the center of the information flow in their own gangs and were also in close touch with the other gang leaders, street gang leaders were better informed than any of their followers (Homans 1950). And Richard Neustadt describes the following account from his study of Franklin D. Roosevelt:

> The essence of Roosevelt's technique for information gathering was competition. "He would call you," one of his aides once told me, "and he'd ask you to get the story on some complicated business, and you'd come back after a couple of days of hard labor and present the juicy morsel you'd uncov-

ered under a stone somewhere, and *then* you'd find out he knew all about it, along with something else you *didn't* know. Where he got this information from he wouldn't mention, usually, but after he had done this to you once or twice you got damn careful about *your* information (Neustadt 1960, 1957).

We can see where Roosevelt "got this information" when we consider the relationship between the interpersonal and informational roles. As leader, the manager has formal and easy access to every member of his staff. Hence, as noted earlier, he tends to know more about his own unit than anyone else does. In addition, his liaison contacts expose the manager to external information to which his subordinates often lack access. Many of these contacts are with other managers of equal status, who are themselves nerve centers in their own organization. In this way, the manager develops a powerful data base of information.

The processing of information is a key part of the manager's job. In my study, the chief executives spent 40% of their contact time on activities devoted exclusively to the transmission of information; 70% of their incoming mail was purely informational (as opposed to requests for action). The manager does not leave meetings or hang up the telephone in order to get back to work. In large part, communication *is* his work. Three roles describe these informational aspects of managerial work.

1. As *monitor,* the manager perpetually scans his environment for information, interrogates his liaison contacts and his subordinates, and receives unsolicited information, much of it as a result of the network of personal contacts he has developed. Remember that a good part of the information the manager collects in his monitor role arrives in verbal form, often as gossip, hearsay, and speculation. By virtue of his contacts, the manager has a natural advantage in collecting this soft information for his organization.

2. He must share and distribute much of this information. Information he gleans from outside personal contacts may be needed within his organization. In his *disseminator* role, the manager passes some of his privileged information directly to his subordinates, who would otherwise have no access to it. When his subordinates lack easy contact with one another, the manager will sometimes pass information from one to another.

3. In his *spokesman* role, the manager sends some of his information to people outside his unit—a president makes a speech to lobby for an organization cause, or a foreman suggests a product modification to a supplier. In addition, as part of his role as spokesman, every manager must inform and satisfy the influential people who control his organizational unit. For the foreman, this may simply involve keeping the plant manager informed about the flow of work through the shop.

The president of a large corporation, however, may spend a great amount of his time dealing with a host of influences. Directors and shareholders must be advised about financial performance; consumer groups must be assured that the organization is fulfilling its social responsibilities; and government officials must be satisfied that the organization is abiding by the law.

Decisional Roles:

Information is not, of course, an end in itself; it is the basic input to decision making. One thing is clear in the study of managerial work: the manager plays the major role in his unit's decision-making system. As its formal authority, only he can commit the unit to important new courses of action; and as its nerve center, only he has full and current information to make the set of decisions that determines the unit's strategy. Four roles describe the manager as decision-maker.

1. As *entrepreneur*, the manager seeks to improve his unit to adapt it to changing conditions in the environment. In his monitor role, the president is constantly on the lookout for new ideas. When a good one appears, he initiates a development project that he may supervise himself or delegate to an employee (perhaps with the stipulation that he must approve the final proposal).

There are two interesting features about these development projects at the chief executive level.

First, these projects do not involve single decisions or even unified clusters of decisions. Rather, they emerge as a series of small decisions and actions sequenced over time. Apparently, the chief executive prolongs each project so that he can fit it bit by bit into his busy, disjointed schedule and so that he can gradually come to comprehend the issue, if it is a complex one.

Second, the chief executives I studied supervised as many as 50 of these projects at the same time. Some projects entailed new products or processes; others involved public relations campaigns, improvement of the cash position, reorganization of a weak department, resolution of a morale problem in a foreign division, integration of computer operations, various acquisitions at different stages of development, and so on.

The chief executive appears to maintain a kind of inventory of the development projects that he himself supervises—projects that are at various stages of development, some active and some in limbo. Like a juggler, he keeps a number of projects in the air; periodically, one comes down, is given a new burst of energy, and is sent back into orbit. At various intervals, he puts new projects on-stream and discards old ones.

2. While the entrepreneur role describes the manager as the voluntary initiator of change, the *disturbance handler* role depicts the manager involuntarily responding to pressures. Here change is beyond the manager's control. He must act because the pressures of the situation are too severe to be ignored: strike looms, a major customer has gone bankrupt, or a supplier reneges on his contract.

It has been fashionable, I noted earlier, to compare the manager to an orchestra conductor, just as Peter F. Drucker wrote in *The Practice of Management:*

> The manager has the task of creating a true whole that is larger than the sum of its parts; a productive entity that turns out more than the sum of the resources put into it. One analogy is the conductor of a symphony orchestra through whose effort, vision, and leadership individual instrumental parts that are so much noise by themselves become the living whole of music. But the conductor has the composer's score; he is only interpreter. The manager is both composer and conductor (Drucker 1954).

Now consider the words of Leonard R. Sayles, who has carried out systematic research on the manager's job:

> (The manager) is like a symphony orchestra conductor, endeavouring to maintain a melodious performance in which the contributions of the various instruments are coordinated and sequenced, patterned and paced, while the orchestra members are having various personal difficulties, stage hands are moving music stands, alternating excessive heat and cold are creating audience and instrument problems, and the sponsor of the concert is insisting on irrational changes in the program (Sayles 1964).

In effect, every manager must spend a good part of his time responding to high-pressure disturbances. No organization can be so well run, so standardized, that it has considered every contingency in the uncertain environment in advance. Disturbances arise not only because poor managers ignore situations until they reach crisis proportions, but also because good managers cannot possibly anticipate all the consequences of the actions they take.

3. The third decisional role is that of *resource allocator*. To the manager falls the responsibility of deciding who will get what in his organizational unit. Perhaps the most important resource the manager allocates is his own time. Access to the manager constitutes exposure to the unit's nerve center and decision-maker. The manager is also charged with designing his unit's structure, that pattern of formal relationships that determines how work is to be divided and coordinated.

Also, in his role as resource allocator, the manager authorizes the important decisions of his unit before they are implemented. By retaining this power, the manager can ensure that decisions are interrelated; all must pass through a single brain. To fragment this power is to encourage discontinuous decision making and a disjointed strategy.

There are a number of interesting features about the manager's authorizing others' decisions. First, despite the widespread use of capital budgeting procedures—a means of authorizing various capital expenditures at one time—executives in my study made a great many authorization decisions on an ad hoc basis. Apparently, many projects cannot wait or simply do not have the quantifiable costs and benefits that capital budgeting requires.

Second, I found that the chief executives faced incredibly complex choices. They had to consider the impact of each decision on other decisions and on the organization's strategy. They had to ensure that the decision would be acceptable to those who influence the organization, as well as ensure that resources would not be overextended. They had to understand the various costs and benefits as well as the feasibility of the proposal. They also had to consider questions of timing. All this was necessary for the simple approval of someone else's proposal. At the same time, however, delay could lose time, while quick approval could be ill considered and quick rejection might discourage the subordinate who had spent months developing a pet project.

One common solution to approving projects is to pick the man instead of the proposal. That is, the manager authorizes those projects presented to him by people whose judgment he trusts. But he cannot always use this simple dodge.

4. The final decisional role is that of *negotiator*. Studies of managerial work at all levels indicate that managers spend considerable time in negotiations: the president of the football team is called in to work out a contract with the holdout superstar; the corporation president leads his company's contingent to negotiate a new strike issue; the foreman argues a grievance problem to its conclusion with the shop steward. As Leonard Sayles puts it, negotiations are a "way of life" for the sophisticated manager.

These negotiations are duties of the manager's job; perhaps routine, they are not to be shirked. They are an integral part of his job, for only he has the authority to commit organizational resources in "real time," and only he has the nerve center information that important negotiations require.

The Integrated Job

It should be clear by now that the ten roles I have been describing are not easily separable. In the terminology of the psychologist, they form a gestalt, an integrated whole. No role can be pulled out of the framework and the job be left intact. For example, a manager without liaison contacts lacks external information. As a result, he can neither disseminate the information his employees need nor make decisions that adequately reflect external conditions. (In fact, this is a problem for the new person in a managerial position, since he cannot make effective decisions until he has built up his network of contacts.)

Here lies a clue to the problem of team management. (Hodgson, Levinson, and Zaleznik 1965). Two or three people cannot share a single managerial position unless they can act as one entity. This means that they cannot divide up the ten roles unless they can very carefully reintegrate them. The real difficulty lies with the informational roles. Unless there can be full sharing of managerial information—and, as I pointed out earlier, it is primarily verbal—team management breaks down. A single managerial job cannot be arbitrarily split, for example, into internal and external roles, for information from both sources must be brought to bear on the same decisions.

To say that the ten roles form a gestalt is not to say that all managers give equal attention to each role. In fact, I found in my review of the various research studies that . . .

- sales managers seem to spend relatively more of their time in the interpersonal roles, presumably a reflection of the extrovert nature of the marketing activity;
- production managers give relatively more attention to the decisional roles, presumably a reflection of their concern with efficient work flow;
- staff managers spend the most time in the informational roles, since they are experts who manage departments that advise other parts of the organization.

Nevertheless, in all cases the interpersonal, informational, and decisional roles remain inseparable.

TOWARD MORE EFFECTIVE MANAGEMENT

What are the messages for management in this description? I believe, first and foremost, that this description of managerial work should prove more important to managers than any prescription they might derive from it. That is to say, *the manager's effectiveness is significantly influenced by his insight into his own work.* His performance depends on how well he understands and responds to the pressures and dilemmas of the job. Thus managers who can be introspective about their work are likely to be effective at their jobs. The insert offers 14 groups of self-study questions for managers. Some may sound rhetorical; none is meant to be. Even though the questions cannot be answered simply, the manager should address them.

Let us take a look at three specific areas of concern. For the most part, the managerial logjams—the dilemma of delegation, the data base centralized in one brain, the problems of working with the management scientist—revolve around the verbal nature of the manager's information. There are great dangers in centralizing the organization's data bank in the minds of its managers. When they leave, they take their memory with them. And when subordinates are out of convenient verbal reach of the manager, they are at an informational disadvantage.

I. The manager is challenged to find systematic ways to share his privileged information. A regular debriefing session with key subordinates, a weekly memory dump on the dictating machine, the maintaining of a diary of important information for limited circulation, or other similar methods may ease the logjam of work considerably. Time spent disseminating this information will be more than regained when decisions must be made. Of course, some will raise the

Self-Study Questions for Managers

1. Where do I get my information, and how? Can I make greater use of my contacts to get information? Can other people do some of my scanning for me? In what areas is my knowledge weakest, and how can I get others to provide me with the information I need? Do I have powerful enough mental models of those things I must understand within the organization and in its environment?

2. What information do I disseminate in my organization? How important is it that my subordinates get my information? Do I keep too much information to myself because dissemination of it is time-consuming or inconvenient? How can I get more information to others so they can make better decisions?

3. Do I balance information collecting with action taking? Do I tend to act before information is in? Or do I wait so long for all the information that opportunities pass me by and I become a bottleneck in my organization?

4. What pace of change am I asking my organization to tolerate? Is this change balanced so that our operations are neither excessively static nor overly disrupted? Have we sufficiently an-

alyzed the impact of this change on the future of our organization?

5. Am I sufficiently well informed to pass judgment on the proposals that my subordinates make? Is it possible to leave final authorization for more of the proposals with subordinates? Do we have problems of coordination because subordinates in fact now make too many of these decisions independently?

6. What is my vision of direction for this organization? Are these plans primarily in my own mind in loose form? Should I make them explicit in order to guide the decisions of others in the organization better? Or do I need flexibility to change them at will?

7. How do my subordinates react to my managerial style? Am I sufficiently sensitive to the powerful influence my actions have on them? Do I fully understand their reactions to my actions? Do I find an appropriate balance between encouragement and pressure? Do I stifle their initiative?

8. What kind of external relationships do I maintain, and how? Do I spend too much of my time maintaining these relationships? Are there certain types of people whom I should get to know better?

9. Is there any system to my time scheduling, or am I just reacting to the pressures of the moment? Do I find the appropriate mix of activities, or do I tend to concentrate on one particular function or one type of problem just because I find it interesting? Am I more efficient with particular kinds of work at special times of the day or week? Does my schedule reflect this? Can someone else (in addition to my secretary) take responsibility for much of my scheduling and do it more systematically?

10. Do I overwork? What effect does my work load have on my efficiency? Should I force myself to take breaks or to reduce the pace of my activity?

11. Am I too superficial in what I do? Can I really shift moods as quickly and frequently as my work patterns require? Should I attempt to decrease the amount of fragmentation and interruption in my work?

12. Do I orient myself too much toward current, tangible activities? Am I a slave to the action and excitement of my work, so that I am no longer able to concentrate on issues? Do key problems receive the attention they deserve? Should I spend more time reading

and probing deeply into certain issues? Could I be more reflective? Should I be?

13. Do I use the different media appropriately? Do I know how to make the most of written communication? Do I rely excessively on face-to-face communication, thereby putting all but a few of my subordinates at an informational disadvantage? Do I schedule enough of my meetings on a regular basis? Do I spend enough time touring my organization to observe activity at first hand? Am I too detached from the heart of my organization's activities, seeing things only in an abstract way?

14. How do I blend my personal rights and duties? Do my obligations consume all my time? How can I free myself sufficiently from obligations to ensure that I am taking this organization where I want it to go? How can I turn my obligations to my advantage?

---

question of confidentiality. But managers would do well to weigh the risks of exposing privileged information against having subordinates who can make effective decisions.

If there is a single theme that runs through this article, it is that the pressures of his job drive the manager to be superficial in his actions—to overload himself with work, encourage interruption, seek the tangible and avoid the abstract, make decisions in small increments, and do everything abruptly.

II. Here again, the manager is challenged to deal consciously with the pressures of superficiality by giving serious attention to the issues that require it, by stepping back from his tangible bits of information in order to see a broad picture, and by making use of analytical inputs. Although effective managers have to be adept at responding quickly to numerous and varying problems, the danger in managerial work is that they will respond to every issue equally (and that means abruptly) and that they will never work the tangible bits and pieces of informational input into a comprehensive picture of their world.

As I noted earlier, the manager uses these bits of information to build models of his world. But the manager can also avail himself of the models of the specialists. Economists describe the functioning of markets, operations researchers simulate financial flow processes, and behavioral scientists explain the needs and goals of people. The best of these models can be searched out and learned.

In dealing with complex issues, the senior manager has much to gain from a close relationship with the management scientists of his own organization. They have something important that he lacks—time to probe complex issues. An effective working relationship hinges on the resolution of what a colleague and I have called "the planning dilemma." (Hekimian and Mintzberg 1968). Managers have the information and the authority; analysts have the time and the technology. A successful working relationship between the two will be effected when the manager learns to share his information and the analyst learns to adapt to the manager's needs. For the analyst, adaptation means worrying less about the elegance of the method and more about its speed and flexibility.

It seems to me that analysts can help the top manager especially to schedule his time, feed in analytical information, monitor projects under his supervision, develop models to aid in making choices, design contingency plans for disturbances that can be anticipated, and conduct "quick-and-dirty" analysis for those that cannot. But there can be no cooperation if the analysts are out of the mainstream of the manager's information flow.

III. The manager is challenged to gain control of his own time by turning obligations to his advantage and by turning those things he wishes to do into obligations. The chief executives of my study initiated only 32% of their own contacts (and another 5% by mutual agreement). And yet to a considerable extent they seemed to control their time. There were two key factors that enabled them to do so.

First, the manager has to spend so much time discharging obligations that if he were to view them as just that, he would leave no mark on his organization. The unsuccessful manager blames failure on the obligations; the effective manager turns his obligations to his own advantage. A speech is a chance to lobby for a cause; a meeting is a chance to reorganize a weak department; a visit to an important customer is a chance to extract trade information.

Second, the manager frees some of his time to do those things that he—perhaps no one else—thinks important by turning them into obligations. Free time is made, not found, in the manager's job; it is forced into the schedule. Hoping to leave some time open for contemplation or general planning is tantamount to hoping that the pressures of the job will go away. The manager who wants to innovate initiates a project and obligates others to report back to him; the manager who needs certain environmental information establishes channels that will automatically keep him informed; the manager who has to tour facilities commits himself publicly.

The Educator's Job

Finally, a word about the training of managers. Our management schools have done an admirable job of training the or-

ganization's specialists—management scientists, marketing researchers, accountants, and organizational development specialists. But for the most part they have not trained managers (Livingston 1971).

Management schools will begin the serious training of managers when skill training takes a serious place next to cognitive learning. Cognitive learning is detached and informational, like reading a book or listening to a lecture. No doubt much important cognitive material must be assimilated by the manager-to-be. But cognitive learning no more makes a manager than it does a swimmer. The latter will drown the first time he jumps into the water if his coach never takes him out of the lecture hall, gets him wet, and gives him feedback on his performance.

In other words, we are taught a skill through practice plus feedback, whether in a real or a simulated situation. Our management schools need to identify the skills managers use, select students who show potential in these skills, put the students into situations where these skills can be practiced, and then give them systematic feedback on their performance.

My description of managerial work suggests a number of important managerial skills—developing peer relationships, carrying out negotiations, motivating subordinates, resolving conflicts, establishing information networks and subsequently disseminating information, making decisions in conditions of extreme ambiguity, and allocating resources. Above all, the manager needs to be introspective about his work so that he may continue to learn on the job.

Many of the manager's skills can, in fact, be practiced, using techniques that range from role playing to videotaping real meetings. And our management schools can enhance the entrepreneurial skills by designing programs that encourage sensible risk taking and innovation.

No job is more vital to our society than that of the manager. It is the manager who determines whether our social institutions serve us well or whether they squander our talents and resources. It is time to strip away the folklore about managerial work, and time to study it realistically so that we can begin the difficult task of making significant improvements in its performance.

Thinking and Learning About Leadership
THOMAS E. CRONIN

A. INTRODUCTION

Leadership is one of the most widely talked about subjects and at the same time one of the most elusive and puzzling. Americans often yearn for great, transcending leadership for their communities, companies, the military, unions, universities, sports teams, and for the nation. However, we have an almost love-hate ambivalence about power wielders. And we especially dislike anyone who tries to boss us around. Yes, we admire the Washingtons and Churchills, but Hitler and Al Capone were leaders too—and that points up a fundamental problem. Leadership can be exercised in the service of noble, liberating, enriching ends, but it can also serve to manipulate, mislead and repress.

"One of the most universal cravings of our time," writes James MacGregor Burns, "is a hunger for compelling and creative leadership." But exactly what is creative leadership? A *Wall Street Journal* cartoon had two men talking about leadership. Finally, one turned to the other in exasperation and said: "Yes, we need leadership, but we also need someone to tell us what to do." That is to say, leadership for most people most of the time is a rather hazy, distant and even confusing abstraction. Hence, thinking about or defining leadership is a kind of intellectual leadership challenge in itself.

What follows are some thoughts about leadership and education for leadership. These thoughts and ideas are highly personal and hardly scientific. As I shall suggest below, almost anything that can be said about leadership can be contradicted with counter examples. Moreover, the whole subject is riddled with paradoxes. My ideas here are the product of my studies of political leadership and my own participation in politics from the town meeting level to the White House staff. Some of my ideas come from helping to advise universities and foundations and the Houston-based American Leadership Forum on how best to go about encouraging leadership development. Finally, my thoughts have also been influenced in a variety of ways by numerous conversations with five especially insightful writers on leadership—Warren Bennis, James MacGregor Burns, David Campbell, Harlan Cleveland and John W. Gardner.

B. TEACHING LEADERSHIP

Can we teach people to become leaders? Can we teach leadership? People are divided on these questions. It was once widely held that "leaders are born and not made," but that view is less widely held today. We also used to hear about "natural leaders" but nowadays most leaders have learned their leadership ability rather than inherited it. Still there is much mystery to the whole matter. In any event, many people think colleges and universities should steer clear of the whole subject. What follows is a set of reasons why our institutions of higher learning generally are "bashful about teaching leadership." These reasons may overstate the case, but they are the objections that serious people often raise.

First, many people still believe that leaders are born and not made. Or that leadership is somehow almost accidental or at least that most leaders emerge from circumstances and normally do not create them. In any event, it is usually added, most people, most of the time, are not now and never will be leaders.

Second, American cultural values hold that leadership is an elitist and thus anti-American phenomenon. Plato and Machiavelli and other grand theorists might urge upon their contemporaries the need for selecting out and training a select few for top leadership roles. But this runs against the American grain. We like to think that anyone can become a top leader here. Hence, no special training should be given to some special select few.

Third, is the complaint that leadership training would more than likely be preoccupied with skills, techniques and the *means* of getting things done. But leadership for what? Leadership in service of what ends? A focus on *means* divorced from *ends* makes people—especially intellectuals—ill at ease. They hardly want to be in the business of training future Joe McCarthys or Hitlers or Idi Amins.

Fourth, leadership study strikes many as an explicitly vocational topic. It's a practical and applied matter—better learned in summer jobs, in internships or on the playing fields. You learn it on the job. You learn it from gaining experience, from making mistakes and learn from these. And you should learn it from mentors.

Fifth, leadership often involves an element of manipulation or deviousness, if not outright ruthlessness. Some consider it as virtually the same as learning about jungle-fighting or acquiring "the killer instinct." It's just not "clean" enough a subject matter for many people to embrace. Plus, "leaders" like Stalin and Hitler gave "leadership" a bad name. If they were leaders, then spare us of their clones or imitators.

Sixth, leadership in the most robust sense of the term is such an ecumenical and intellectually so all-encompassing a subject that it frightens not only the timid but even the most well educated of persons. To teach leadership is an act of arrogance. That is, it is to suggest one understands far more than even a well educated person can understand—history, ethics, philosophy, classics, politics, biography, psychology, management, sociology, law, etc . . . and to be steeped deeply as well in the "real world."

Seventh, colleges and universities are increasingly organized in highly specialized divisions and departments all geared to train specialists. While the mission of the college may be to educate "the educated person" and society's future leaders, in fact the incentive system is geared to training specialists. Society today rewards the expert or the super specialist—the data processors, the pilots, the financial whiz, the heart surgeon, the special team punt returners, and so on. Leaders, however, have to learn to become generalists and usually have to do so well after they have left our colleges, graduate schools and professional schools.

Eighth, leadership strikes many people (and with some justification) as an elusive, hazy and almost mysterious commodity. Now you see it, now you don't. So much of leadership is intangible, you can't possibly define all the parts. A person may be an outstanding leader here, but fail there. Trait theory has been thoroughly debunked. In fact, leadership is highly situational and contextual. A special chemistry develops between leaders and followers and it is usually context specific. Followers often do more to determine the leadership they will get than can any teacher. Hence, why not teach people to be substantively bright and well-read and let things just take their natural course.

Ninth, virtually anything that can be said about leadership can be denied or disproven. Leadership studies, to the extent they exist, are unscientific. Countless paradoxes and contradictions litter every manuscript on leadership. Thus, we yearn for leadership, but yearn equally to be free and left alone. We admire risk-taking, entrepreneurial leadership but we roundly criticize excessive risk-taking as bull-headedness or plain stupid. We want leaders who are highly self-confident and who are perhaps incurably optimistic—yet we also dislike hubris and often yearn for at least a little self-doubt (e.g., Creon in *Antigone*). Leaders have to be almost single-minded in their drive and commitment but too much of that makes a person rigid, driven and unacceptable. We want leaders to be good listeners and represent their constituents, yet in the words of Walter Lippmann, effective leadership often consists of giving the people not what they want but what they will learn to want. How in the world, then, can you be rigorous and precise in teaching leadership?

Tenth, leadership at its best comes close to creativity. And how do you teach creativity? We are increasingly made aware of the fact that much of creative thinking calls upon unconscious thinking, dreaming and even fantasy. Some fascinating work is being done on intuition and the nonrational—but it is hardly a topic with which traditional disciplines in traditional colleges are comfortable.

Leaders themselves often complain that the incentives for leadership are not as great as the disincentives. Many people shy away from leadership responsibilities saying it "just isn't worth it." A survey of some 1700 business, government and professional leaders revealed a number of striking reasons for this question. See Table 1.

C. RELATIONSHIPS

A few other initial observations need to be made about leadership. Chief among these is that the study of leadership needs inevitably to be linked or merged with the study of followership. We cannot really study leaders in isolation from followers, constituents or group members. The leader is very much a product of the group, and very much shaped by its aspirations, values and human resources. The more we learn about leadership, the more the leader-follower linkage is understood and reaffirmed. A leader has to resonate with followers. Part of being an effective leader is having excellent ideas, or a clear sense of direction, a sense of mission. But such ideas or vision are useless unless the would-be leader can communicate them and get them accepted by followers. A two-way engagement or two-way interaction is constantly going on. When it ceases, leaders become lost, out of touch, imperial or worse.

The question of leaders linked with followers raises the question of the transferability of leadership. Can an effective leader in one situation transfer this capacity, this skill, this style—to another setting? The record is mixed indeed. Certain persons have been effective in diverse set-

TABLE 1 What Leaders Say Are the Obstacles to Leadership in America

	Very Important	Somewhat Important	Not Important
The system does not favor the most capable individuals	54%	35%	11%
Our educational system does not provide people with leadership skills	48	37	15
American voters look for the wrong qualities in leaders	46	44	10
Leaders are not fully appreciated	23	49	28
Leaders are not given enough financial compensation	21	48	31
The pressures of leadership positions are too great	18	51	31
Leadership roles demand too much time	17	45	38
Potential leaders are deterred by fears of lack of privacy	16	43	41
The responsibilities of leadership roles appear too great	14	44	42
The times make effective leadership impossible	10	39	51

Source: The Connecticut Mutual Life Report on American Values in the '80s (Hartford, Conn.1981), p. 188.

tings. George Washington and Dwight Eisenhower come to mind. Jack Kemp and Bill Bradley, two well-known and respected members of Congress, were previously successful professional athletes. Scores of business leaders have been effective in the public sector and vice versa. Scores of military leaders have become effective in business or politics. Some in both. However, there are countless examples of those who have not met with success when they have tried to transfer their leadership abilities from one setting to a distinctively different setting. Sometimes this failure arises because the new group's goals or needs are so different from the previous organization. Sometimes it is because the leadership needs are different. Thus, the leadership needs of a military officer leading a platoon up a hill in battle may well be very different from the leadership requirements of someone asked to change sexist attitudes and practices in a large corporation or racist and ethnic hatred in an inner city. The leadership required of a candidate for office is often markedly different from that required of

a campaign manager. Leadership required in founding a company may be exceedingly different from that required in the company's second generation.

Another confusing aspect about leadership is that leadership and management are often talked about as if they were the same. While it is true that an effective manager is often an effective leader and leadership requires, among other things, many of the skills of an effective manager, there are differences. Leaders are the people who infuse vision into an organization or a society. At their best, they are preoccupied with values and the longer range needs and aspirations of their followers. Managers are concerned with doing things *the right way*. Leaders are more concerned with identifying and then getting themselves and their organizations focused on *doing the right thing*. John Quincy Adams, Herbert Hoover and Jimmy Carter were often good, sometimes excellent managers. Before coming to the White House, they were all recognized for being effective achievers. As businessmen, diplomats, governors or cabinet members, they excelled. As presidential leaders, they were found wanting. None was invited back for a second term. While none was considered an outright failure, each seemed to fail in providing the vision needed for the times. They were unable to lift the public's spirit and get the nation moving in new, more desirable directions.

As this brief digression suggests, being a leader is not the same thing as being holder of a high office. An effective leader is someone concerned with far more than the mechanics of office. While a good manager is concerned, and justifiably so, with efficiency, with keeping things going, with the routines and standard operating procedures, and with reaffirming ongoing systems, the creative leader acts as an inventor, risk taker and generalist entrepreneur—ever asking or searching for what is right, where are we headed and keenly sensing new directions, new possibilities and welcoming change. We need all the talented managers we can get, but we also need creative leaders. Ironically, too, an effective leader is not very effective for long unless he or she can recruit managers to help them make things work over the long run.

D. CHARACTERISTICS

One of the most important things to be said about leadership is that it is commonly very dispersed throughout a society. Our leadership needs vary enormously. Many of the great breakthroughs occur because of people well in advance of their time who are willing to agitate for change and suggest fresh new approaches that are, as yet, unacceptable to majority opinion. Many of the leadership needs of a nation are met by persons who do not hold high office and who often don't look or even act as leaders. Which brings us to the question of defining leadership. Agreement on a definition is difficult to achieve. But for the purposes at hand, leaders are people who perceive what is needed and what is right and know how to mobilize people and resources to accomplish mutual goals.

Leaders are individuals who can help create options and opportunities—who can help clarify problems and choices, who can build morale and coalitions, who can inspire others and provide a vision of the possibilities and promise of a better organization, or a better community. Leaders have those indispensable qualities of contagious self-confidence, unwarranted optimism and incurable idealism that allows them to attract and mobilize others to undertake demanding tasks these people never dreamed they could undertake. In short, leaders empower and help liberate others. They enhance the possibilities for freedom—both for people and organizations. They engage with followers in such a way so that many of the followers became leaders in their own right.

As implied above, many of the significant breakthroughs in both the public and private sectors of this nation have been made by people who saw all the complexities ahead of them, but so believed in themselves and their purposes that they refused to be overwhelmed and paralyzed by doubts. They were willing to invent new rules and gamble on the future.

Good leaders, almost always, have been get-it-all-together, broken-field runners. They have been generalists. Tomorrow's leaders will very likely have begun life as trained specialists. Our society particularly rewards the specialist. John W. Gardner puts it well:

> All too often, on the long road up, young leaders become "servants of what is rather than shapers of what might be." In the long process of learning how the system works, they are rewarded for playing within the intricate structure of existing rules. By the time they reach the top, they are very likely to be trained prisoners of the structure. This is not all bad; every vital system re-affirms itself. But no system can stay vital for long

unless some of its leaders remain sufficiently independent to help it to change and grow.

Only as creative generalists can these would-be leaders cope with the multiple highly organized groups—subsystems within the larger system—each fighting for special treatment, each armed with their own narrow definition of the public interest, often to the point of paralyzing *any* significant action.

Overcoming fears, especially fears of stepping beyond the boundaries of one's tribe, is a special need for the leader. A leader's task, as a renewer of organizational goals and aspirations, is to illuminate goals, to help reperceive one's own and one's organization's resources and strengths, to speak to people on what's only dimly in their minds. The effective creative leader is one who can give voice and form so that people say, "Ah, yes—that's what I too have been feeling."

Note too, however, that leaders are always aware of and at least partly shaped by the higher wants and aspirations and common purposes of their followers and constituents. Leaders consult and listen just as they educate and attempt to renew the goals of an organization. They know how "to squint with their ears." Civic leaders often emerge as we are able to agree upon goals. One analyst has suggested that it is no good for us to just go looking for leaders. We must first rediscover our own goals and values. If we are to have the leaders we need, we will first have to agree upon priorities. In one sense, if we wish to have leaders to follow, we will often have to show them the way.

In looking for leadership and in organizational affiliations—people are looking for *significance, competence, affirmation, and fairness.* To join an organization, an individual has to give up some aspect of his or her uniqueness, some part of their soul. Thus, there is a price in affiliating and in following. The leader serves as a strength and an attraction in the organization—but psychologically there is also a *repulsion* to the leader—in part because of the dependence on the leader. John Steinbeck said of American presidents that the people believe that, "they were ours and we exercise the right to destroy them." Effective leaders must know how to absorb these hostilities, however latent they may be.

The leader also must be ever sensitive to the distinction between *power* and *authority.* Power is the strength or raw force to exercise control or coerce someone to do something, while authority is power that is *accepted* as legitimate by subordinates. The whole question of leadership raises countless issues about participation and the acceptance of power in superior-subordinate relationships. How much participation or involvement is needed, is desirable? What is the impact of participation on effectiveness? How best for the leader to earn moral and social acceptance for his or her authority? America generally prizes participation in all kinds of organizations, especially civic and political life. Yet, we must realize too that a part of us yearns for charismatic leadership. Ironically, savior figures and charismatic leaders often, indeed almost always, create distance and not participation.

One of the most difficult tasks for those who would measure and evaluate leadership is the task of trying to look at the elements that make up leadership. One way to look at these elements is to suggest that a leader has various *skills,* also has or exercises a distinctive *style* and, still more elusive, has various *qualities* that may be pronounced. By skill, I mean the capacity to do something well. Something that is learnable and can be improved, such as speaking or negotiating or planning. Most leaders need to have *technical skills* (such as writing well); *human relations skills,* the capacity to supervise, inspire, build coalitions and so on, and also what might be called *conceptual skills*—the capacity to play with ideas, shrewdly seek advice and forge grand strategy. Skills can be examined. Skills can be taught. And skills plainly make up an important part of leadership capability. Skills alone, however, cannot guarantee leadership success.

A person's leadership style may also be critical to effectiveness. Style refers to how a person relates to people, to tasks and to challenges. A person's style is usually a very personal and distinctive feature of their personality and character. A style may be democratic or autocratic, centralized or decentralized, empathetic or detached, extroverted or introverted, assertive or passive, engaged or remote. This hardly exhausts the diverse possibilities—but is meant to be suggestive. Different styles may work equally well in different situations. However, there is often a proper fit between the needs of an organization and the needed leadership style. A fair amount of research has been done in this area—but, much more remains to be learned.

A person's *behavioral style* refers to one's way of relating to other people—to peers, subordinates, rivals, bosses, advisers, the press. A person's *psychological style* refers to one's way of handling stress, tensions, challenges to the ego, internal conflicts. Considerable work needs to be done in these areas—particularly if we are to learn how best to prepare people for shaping their leadership styles to diverse leadership situations and needs. But it is a challenge worth accepting.

James MacGregor Burns, in his book on *Leadership,* offers us yet one additional distinction worth thinking about. Ultimately, Burns says, there are two overriding kinds of social and political leadership: *transactional* and *transformational leadership.* The transactional leader engages in an exchange, usually for self-interest and with short-term interests in mind. It is, in essence, a bargain situation: "I'll vote for your bill if you vote for mine." Or "You do me a favor and I will shortly return it." Most pragmatic office-holders practice transactional leadership most of the time. It is commonly a practical necessity. It is the general way people do business and get their jobs done—and stay in office. The transforming or transcending leader is the person who, as briefly noted earlier, so engages with followers as to bring them to a heightened political and social consciousness and activity, and in the process converts many of those followers into leaders in their own right. The transforming leader, with a focus on the higher aspirations and longer range, is also a teacher, mentor and educator—pointing out the possibilities and the hopes and the often only dimly understood dreams of a people—and getting them to undertake the preparation and the job needed to attain these goals.

Of course, not everyone can be a leader. And rarely can any one leader provide an organization's entire range of leadership needs. Upon closer inspection, most firms and most societies have all kinds of leaders and these diverse leaders, in turn, are usually highly dependent for their success on the leadership performed by other leaders. Some leaders are excellent at creating or inventing new structures. Others are great task leaders—helping to energize groups at problem solving. Others are excellent social (or affective) leaders, helping to build morale and renew the spirit of an organization or a people. These leaders are often indispensible in providing what might be called the human glue that holds groups together.

Further, the most lasting and pervasive leadership of all is often intangible and noninstitutional. It is the leadership fostered by ideas embodied in social, political or artistic movements, in books, in documents, in speeches, and in the memory of great lives greatly lived. Intellectual or idea leadership at its best is provided by those—often not in high political or corporate office—who can clarify values and the implications of such values for policy. The point here is that leadership is not only dispersed and diverse, but interdependent. Leaders need leaders as much as followers need leaders. This may sound confusing but it is part of the truth about the leadership puzzle.

E. LEADERSHIP QUALITIES

In the second half of this essay, I will raise in a more general way, some of the qualities I believe are central to leadership. Everyone has their own lists of leadership qualities. I will not be able to discuss all of mine, but permit me to offer my list and then describe a few of the more important ones in a bit more detail.

Leadership Qualities— A Tentative List

- Self-knowledge/self-confidence
- Vision, ability to infuse important, transcending values into an enterprise
- Intelligence, wisdom, judgment
- Learning/renewal
- Worldmindedness/a sense of history and breadth
- Coalition building/social architecture
- Morale-building/motivation
- Stamina, energy, tenacity, courage, enthusiasm
- Character, integrity/intellectual honesty
- Risk-taking/entrepreneurship
- An ability to communicate, persuade/ listen
- Understanding the nature of power and authority
- An ability to concentrate on achieving goals and results
- A sense of humor, perspective, flexibility

Leadership consists of a spiral upwards, a spiral of self-improvement, self-knowledge and seizing and creating opportunities so that a person can make things happen that would not otherwise have occurred. Just as there can be a spiral upwards, there can be a spiral downwards—characterized by failure, depression, self-defeat, self-doubt, and paralyzing fatalism.

If asked to point to key qualities of successful leadership, I would suggest these:

Leaders Are People Who Know Who They Are and Know Where They Are Going

"What a man thinks about himself," Thoreau wrote, "that is what determines, or rather indicates his fate." One of the most paralyzing of mental illnesses is wrong perception of self. This leads to poor choosing and poor choosing leads to a fouled-up life. In one sense, the trouble with many people is not what they don't know, it is what they do know, but it is misinformed or misinformation.

Leaders must be self-reliant individuals with great tenacity and stamina. The world is moved by people who are enthusiastic. Optimism and high motivations count for a lot. They can lift organizations. Most people are forever waiting around for somebody to light a fire under them. They are people who have not learned the valuable lesson that ultimately you are the one who is responsible for you. You don't blame others. You don't blame circumstances. You simply take charge and help move the enterprise forward.

I am sure many of you have been puzzled, as I have been, about why so many talented friends of ours have leveled off earlier than needs to be the case. What is it that prevents people from becoming the best they could be? Often it is a lack of education, a physical handicap or a disease such as alcoholism. Very often, however, it is because people have not been able to gain control over their lives. Various things nibble away at their capacity for self-realization or what Abraham Maslow called self-actualization. Family problems, inadequate financial planning, and poor health or mental health problems are key factors that damage self-esteem. Plainly, it is difficult to handle life, not to mention leadership responsibilities, if a person feels they do not control their own lives. This emotional feeling of helplessness inevitably leads people to believe they aren't capable, they can't do the job. It also inhibits risk-taking and just about all the qualities associated with creativity and leadership.

Picture a scale from, at one end, an attitude of "I don't control anything and I feel like the bird in a badminton game"—to the other end of the scale where there is an attitude of "I'm in charge." Either extreme may be pathological, but plainly the higher up, relatively, toward the "I'm in charge" end of the scale, the more one is able to handle the challenges of transforming or creative leadership.

Thus, the single biggest factor is motivating or liberating would-be leaders in their attitude toward themselves and toward their responsibilities to others.

Leaders also have to understand the situations they find themselves in. As observed in Alice in Wonderland, before we decide where we are going, we first have to decide where we are right now. After this comes commitment to something larger and longer term than just our own egos. People can achieve meaning in their lives only when they can give as well as take from their society. Failure to set priorities and develop significant personal purposes undermines nearly any capacity for leadership. "When a man does not know what harbor he is making for, no wind is the right wind."

Setting Priorities and Mobilizing Energies

Too many people become overwhelmed with trivia, with constant close encounters of a third rate. Leaders have always to focus on the major problems of the day, and on the higher aspirations and needs of their followers. Leadership divorced from important transcending purpose becomes manipulation, deception and, in the extreme, is not leadership at all, but repression and tyranny.

The effective modern leader has to be able to live in an age of uncertainty. Priorities have to be set and decisions have to be made even though all the information is not in—this will surely be even more true in the future than it has been in the past. The information revolution has tremendously enlarged both the opportunities and the frustrations for leaders. Knowing what you don't know becomes as important as knowing what you do know. A willingness to experiment and explore possible strategies even in the face of uncertainty may become a more pronounced characteristic of the creative leader.

The creative priority setter learns both to encourage and to question his or her intuitive tendencies. Oliver Wendell Holmes, Jr., said that "to have doubted one's own first principles is the mark of a civilized man" and so it continues to be. The ability to look at things differently, and reach out for more and better advice is crucial. The ability to admit error and learn from mistakes is also vitally important.

Leaders need to have considerable self-confidence, but they also must have a dose of self-doubt. Leaders must learn how to communicate the need for advice and help, how to become a creative listener, how to empathize, and understand. In Sophocles' compelling play, *Antigone*, the tragic hero, King Creon, hears his son's advice but imprudently rejects it or perhaps does not even hear it. But it, Haemon's, is advice any leader should take into account:

Let not your first thought be your only thought. Think if there cannot be some other way. Surely, to think your own the only wisdom, and yours the only word, the only will, betrays a shallow spirit, an empty heart. It is no weakness for the wisest man to learn when he is wrong, know when to yield. . . .

So, father, pause and put aside your anger. I think, for what my young opinion's worth, that good as it is to have infallible wisdom, since this is rarely found, the next best thing is to be willing to listen to wise advice.

Leaders need to be able to discover their own strengths and the strengths of those with whom they work. They have to learn how to share and to delegate. They have to be able to make people believe they are important, that they are or can be winners. People yearn to think that what they are doing is something useful, something important. The transforming or creative leader knows how to nourish conviction and morale within an organization.

Good leaders know how to serve as morale-builders and renewers of purpose, able to get people to rededicate themselves to long-cherished but sometimes dimly understood values. Motivation is sometimes as much as 40 to 50 percent of the leadership enterprise. You can do very little alone with just faith and determination, yet you can do next to nothing without them. Organizations of all kinds need constantly to rediscover or renew their faith, direction, and sense of purpose.

Leaders Have to Provide the Risk-Taking, Entrepreneurial Imagination for Their Organizations and Communities

Leaders are able to see things in a different and fresh context. Warren Bennis suggests that creative leadership requires the capacity to recontextualize a situation. Willis Harmon suggests a leader is one who reperceives situations and challenges and comes up with new approaches, insights and solutions.

A third grade class begins and the teacher says: "Class, take out your pencils and paper and draw a picture of anything you can think of." Students begin to draw—balls, trees, automobiles, and so forth. Teacher asks Sally, in the second row: "What are you drawing?" Sally says, "I'm drawing a picture of God." Teacher says: "But no one has ever seen God, we don't know what he looks like." An undaunted Sally responds: "Well, they sure will when I get through!"

This little story illustrates the sometimes irrational self-confidence and "failure is impossible" factor that motivates the galvanizing leader. The founding revolutionaries in America, Susan B. Anthony, Martin Luther King, Jr., Saul Alinsky and countless others had the vision of a better and newer society and they, in effect, said, "They'll know a better or more just society when we get through."

Mark Twain once said, "a man is viewed as a crackpot until his idea succeeds." We need a hospitable environment for the dissenter and the creative individual. We need to avoid killing the spark of individuality that allows creativity to flourish. We kill it with rules, red tape, procedures, standard operating restrictions and countless admonitions "not to rock the boat."

Creativity is the ability to recombine things. To see a radio here and a clock there and put them together. Hence, the clockradio. Openmindedness is crucial. Too many organizations are organized with structures to solve problems that no longer exist. Vested interest grows up in every human institution. People all too often become prisoners of their procedures.

Psychologist David Campbell points out that history records a long list of innovations that come from outside the "expert" organization. (See also John Jewkes, *The Sources of Invention.*) The automobile was not invented by the transportation experts of that era, the railroaders. The airplane was not invented by automobile experts. Polaroid film was not invented by Kodak. Handheld pocket calculators were not invented by IBM, digital watches were not invented by watchmakers. Apple computers and herbal tea are yet two more examples. The list is endless and the moral is vivid.

Leaders get organizations interested in what they are going to become, not what they have been. Creative leadership requires also not being afraid to fail. An essential aspect of creative leadership is curiosity. The best way to have inventive ideas is to have lots of ideas, and to have an organization that welcomes fresh ideas—whatever their merit. As any scientist knows, the art of research requires countless experimentation and failure before you get the results you want, or sometimes the unexpected result that constitutes the true breakthrough.

Leaders recognize the utility of dreaming, fantasy and unconscious thinking. One advocate of creative thinking writes,

> Production of dramatically new ideas by a process of purely conscious calculation rarely seems to occur. Unconscious thinking, thinking which you are unaware of, is a major contribution to the production of new ideas....

Leaders Need to Have a Sense of Humor and a Sense of Proportion

Leaders take their work seriously, but do not take themselves too seriously. Humor relieves strain and enables people to relax and see things in a slightly different or fresh light. Effective leaders usually can tell a joke, take a joke, and tell a good story. They also usually know the art of telling parables. Lincoln, FDR and JFK come quickly to mind, while Hoover, Nixon and Carter were humorless men. Adlai Stevenson put it this way. "If I couldn't laugh, I couldn't live—especially in politics."

In this same light, leaders need to be able to share the credit. Leadership some-

times consists of emphasizing the dignity of others and of keeping one's own sense of importance from becoming inflated. Dwight Eisenhower had a slogan he tried to live by which went as follows: "There's no telling how much one can accomplish so long as one doesn't need to get all the credit for it."

Thus, leaders need to have a sense of proportion and a sense of detachment. They must avoid being workaholics and recognize that they will have to be followers in most of the enterprises of life and leaders only a small fraction of the time. Emerson put it well when he tried to answer the question, "What is Success?"

> To laugh often and love much, to win the respect of intelligent persons and the affection of children; to appreciate beauty; to find the best in others; to give one's self; to leave the world a lot better whether by a healthy child, a garden patch, or a redeemed social condition; to have played and laughed with enthusiasm and sung with exaltation, to know even one life has breathed easier because you have lived—this is to have succeeded.

Humor, proportion and also *compassion*. A person able to understand emotions and passion and at least on occasion to express one's self with passion and conviction. Enthusiasm, hope, vitality and energy are crucial to radiating confidence.

Leaders Have to Be Skilled Mediators and Negotiators, but They Also Have to Be Able to Stir Things Up and Encourage Healthy and Desired Conflict

An old Peanut's cartoon has a dejected Charlie Brown coming off a softball field as the game concludes. In exasperation he whines, "How can we lose when we are so sincere?" Sincerity or purity of heart are not enough to succeed in challenging leadership jobs.

The strength of leaders often lie in their tenacity, in knowing how to deal with competing factions, knowing when to compromise, when to amplify conflict, and when to move an organization or a community away from paralyzing divisiveness and toward a vision of the common good.

Most citizens avoid conflict and find conflicts of any kind painful. The truly effective leader welcomes several kinds of conflict and views conflict as an opportunity for change or revitalization.

Stirring things up is often a prerequisite for social and economic breakthrough. Women's rights, black rights, consumer protection, tax reform movements and even our election campaigns are occasions for division and conflict. They are a reality the leader has to learn to accept, understand and turn to his advantage. Harry Truman said,

> A President who's any damn good at all makes enemies, makes a lot of enemies. I even made a few myself when I was in the White House, and I wouldn't be without them.

George Bernard Shaw and others have put it only slightly differently. Reasonable people, they observe, adjust themselves to reality and cope with what they find. Unreasonable people dream dreams of a different or a better world and try to adapt the world to themselves. This discontent or unreasonableness is often the first step in the progress of a person as well as for a community or nation.

But be aware that "stirrer uppers" and conflict-amplifiers are often threatening in any organization or society. In the kingdom of the blind, the one-eyed man is king. This may well be, as the proverb has it. But in the kingdom of the one-eyed person, the two-eyed person is looked upon with considerable suspicion and may even be considered downright dangerous.

Thus, it takes courage and guts as well as imagination and stamina to be the two-eyed person in a one-eyed world. Harlan Cleveland points out that just about every

leader has had the experience of being in an office surrounded by experts. The sum of the meeting will be, "Let's do nothing cautiously." The leader is the one who has to say, "Let's take the first step." He or she is the functional equivalent of the first bird off the telephone wire, or what Texans call the "bell cow." The experts always have an excuse. They are like the losing tennis player whose motto is: "It's not whether you win or lose, it's how you place the blame."

An Effective Leader Must Have Integrity

This has been suggested earlier in several implicit ways, but it is perhaps the most central of leadership qualities. A leader must be able to see people in all of their relationships, in the wholeness of their lives and not just as a means to getting a job done, as a means for enhanced productivity.

Some may call it character, others would call it authenticity, compassion or empathy. Whatever we call it, character and integrity are much easier kept than recovered. People can see through a phony. People can readily tell whether a person has respect for others. Respect and responsibility generally migrate to those who are fair, compassionate and care about values, beliefs and feelings of others. A person who cannot rise above their prejudices usually fails. A person who permits a shell to be built up around their heart will not long be able to exercise creative leadership. Michael Maccoby captures this concern.

> The exercise of the heart is that of experiencing, thinking critically, willing, and acting, so as to overcome egocentrism and to share passion with other people ... and to respond to their needs with the help one can give.... It requires discipline, learning to concentrate, to think critically, and to communicate. The goal, a developed heart, implies integrity, a spiritual center, a sense

of "I" not motivated by greed or fear, but by love of life, adventure and fellow feelings.

A leader's integrity requires also that he or she not be captured by peer pressures, protocol, mindless traditions or conventional rules. The truly effective leader is able to see above and beyond normal constraints and discern proper and desirable ends. The leader also possesses a sense of history and a concern for posterity. This ability, an exceptional capacity to disregard external pressures, is the ability that separates leaders from followers.

The Leader Has to Have Brains and Breadth

In the future, even more so than in the past, only the really bright individuals will be leaders.

Harlan Cleveland highlights this quality well when he writes:

> It used to be that a leader was a two-fisted businessman who chopped up the jobs that needed to be done, then left everyone alone and roared at them if they didn't work right....
>
> Loud commands worked if one person knew all things, but because of the way we (now) make decisions, through committees, a person charging around with a loud voice is just in the way.

Today's leaders must widen their perspectives and lengthen the focal point of their thinking. Leaders today have to learn how to thread or weave together disparate parts and move beyond analytical to integrative thinking. This will require well-read, well-traveled persons who can rise above their specialities and their professions. It will require as well persons who are not afraid of politics, but who rather view the art of politics as the art of bringing about the difficult and the desirable.

F.   AMERICAN LEADERSHIP

The creative political leader must work in a tension-filled world between unity and dissent, majority rule and minority rights and countless other contradictions. Tocqueville said of us, "These Americans yearn for leadership, but they also want to be left alone and free." The political leader is always trying to reconcile this and other paradoxes—but the important point is to be able to live with the paradoxes and dilemmas. And beyond this, the political leader must also be able to create, and preserve, a sense of community and shared heritage, the civic bond that ties us—disparate and fiesty, rugged individualists together.

Effective leaders of today and tomorrow also know how to vary their styles of leadership depending on the maturity of their subordinates. They involve their peers and their subordinates in their responsibility networks. They must be good educators and good communicators. They also have to have that spark of emotion or passion that can excite others to join them in the enterprise.

Most effective leaders will also be effective communicators: good writers, good speakers and good conversationalists. A few noted scientists may get by with mumbling, but they are the exception. For so much of leadership consists nowadays in persuading and informing that someone who cannot communicate well, cannot succeed. To paraphrase George Orwell, "If people cannot communicate well, they cannot think well, and if they cannot think well, others will do their thinking for them."

America is especially good at training experts, specialists and managers. We have plenty of these specialist leaders, but they are almost always one-segment leaders. We are in special need of educating multi-segment leaders. Persons who have a global perspective and understand that the once tidy lines between domestic and international, and public and private are irretrievably blurred. Indispensible to a leader is a sense of breadth, the intellectual capacity to handle complex mental tasks, to see relationships between apparently unrelated objects, to see patterns in incomplete information, to draw accurate conclusions from inchoate data.

Vision is the ability to see all sides of an issue and to eliminate biases. Vision and breadth of knowledge put one in a strategic position—preventing the leader from falling into the traps that short-sightedness, mindless parochialism often set for people.

None of these qualities can guarantee creative leadership, but they can, when encouraged, provide a greater likelihood of it. We need all the leadership we can get—in and out of government. The vitality of nongovernmental America lies in our ability to educate and nourish more citizen-leaders. Those of us who expect to reap the blessings of freedom and liberty must undergo the fatigues of supporting it and provide the leadership to sustain it.

G. LEARNING ABOUT LEADERSHIP

Permit me to return again to the question of whether leadership can be learned, and possibly taught. My own belief is that students cannot usually be taught to be leaders. But students, and anyone else for that matter, can profitably be exposed to leadership, discussions of leadership skills and styles, and leadership strategies and theories. Individuals can learn in their own minds the strengths as well as limitations of leadership. People can learn about the paradoxes and contradictions and ironies of leadership, which however puzzling, are central to appreciating the diversity and the dilemmas of problem-solving and getting organizations and nations to function.

Learning about leadership means recognizing bad leadership as well as good. Learning about leadership means understanding the critical linkage of ends and means. Learning about leadership also in-

volves the study of the special chemistry that develops between leaders and followers, not only the chemistry that existed between Americans and Lincoln, but also between Mao and the Chinese peasants, Lenin and the Bolsheviks, between Martin Luther King, Jr., and civil rights activists, between Jean Monnet and those who dreamed of a European Economic Community.

Students can learn to discern and define situations and contexts within which leadership has flourished. Students can learn about the fallibility of the trait theory. Students can learn about the contextual problems of leadership, of why and when leadership is sometimes transferable, and sometimes not. Students can learn about the crucial role that advisors and supporters play in the leadership equation. Students can also learn about countless problem-solving strategies and theories, and participate in role playing exercises that sharpen their own skills in such undertakings.

Students of leadership can learn widely from reading biographies about both the best and the worst leaders. Plutarch's *Lives* would be a good place to start. Much can be learned from mentors and from intern-participant observing. Much can also be learned about leadership by getting away from one's own culture and examining how leaders in other circumstances go about the task of motivating and mobilizing others. Countless learning opportunities exist that can sharpen a student's skills as a speaker, debater, negotiator, problem clarifier and planner. Such skills should not be minimized. Nor should anyone underestimate the importance of history, economics, logic, and a series of related substantive fields that help provide the breadth and the perspective indispensable to societal leadership.

Above all, students of leadership can make an appointment with themselves and begin to appreciate their own strengths and deficiencies. Personal mastery is important. So too the ability to use one's intuition, and to enrich one's creative impulses. John Gardner suggests, "It's what you learn after you know it all that really counts." Would-be leaders learn to manage their time more wisely. Would-be leaders learn that self-pity and resentment are like toxic substances. Would-be leaders learn the old truth that most people are not for you or against you but rather pre-occupied with themselves. Would-be leaders learn to break out of their comfortable imprisonments; they learn to cast aside dull routines and habits that enslave most of us. Would-be leaders learn how to become truly sharing and caring people—in their families, their professions and in their communities. And would-be leaders constantly learn too that they have more to give than they have ever given, no matter how much they have given.

Let me conclude by paraphrasing from John Adams:

> We must study politics (and leadership) and war (and peace) that our sons (and daughters) have the liberty to study mathematics and philosophy, geography, natural history and naval architecture, navigation, commerce, and agriculture, in order to give their children a right to study painting, poetry, music, architecture, statuary, tapestry, and porcelain.

Power Failure in Management Circuits

ROSABETH MOSS KANTER

The position, not the person, often determines whether a manager has power

When one thinks of "power," one often assumes that a person is the source of it and that some mystical charismatic element is at work. Of course, with some people this is undoubtedly so; they derive power from how other people perceive them. In organizations, however—says this author—power is not so much a question of people but of positions. Drawing a distinction between productive and oppressive power, the author maintains that

the former is a function of having open channels to supplies, support, and information; the latter is a function of these channels being closed. She then describes three positions that are classically powerless: first-line supervisors, staff professionals, and, surprisingly, chief executive officers. These positions can be powerless because of difficulties in maintaining open lines of information and support. Seeing powerlessness in these positions as dangerous for organizations, she urges managers to restructure and redesign their organizations in order to eliminate pockets of powerlessness.

Power is America's last dirty word. It is

easier to talk about money—and much easier to talk about sex—than it is to talk about power. People who have it deny it; people who want it do not want to appear to hunger for it; and people who engage in its machinations do so secretly.

Yet, because it turns out to be a critical element in effective managerial behavior, power should come out from undercover. Having searched for years for those styles or skills that would identify capable organization leaders, many analysts, like myself, are rejecting individual traits or situational appropriateness as key and finding the sources of a leader's real power.

Access to resources and information and the ability to act quickly make it possible to accomplish more and to pass on more resources and information to subordinates. For this reason, people tend to prefer bosses with "clout." When employees perceive their manager as influential upward and outward, their status is enhanced by association and they generally have high morale and feel less critical or resistant to their boss (Pelz 1952, 209). More powerful leaders are also more likely to delegate (they are too busy to do it all themselves), to reward talent, and to build a team that places subordinates in significant positions.

Powerlessness, in contrast, tends to breed bossiness rather than true leadership. In large organizations, at least, it is powerlessness that often creates ineffective, desultory management and petty, dictatorial, rules-minded managerial styles. Accountability without power—responsibility for results without the resources to get them—creates frustration and failure. People who see themselves as weak and powerless and find their subordinates resisting or discounting them tend to use more punishing forms of influence. If organizational power can "ennoble," then, recent research shows, organizational powerlessness can (with apologies to Lord Acton) "corrupt" (Kanter 1977,

164–205), (Kipnis 1976).

So perhaps power, in the organization at least, does not deserve such a bad reputation. Rather than connoting only dominance, control, and oppression, *power* can mean efficacy and capacity—something managers and executives need to move the organization toward its goals. Power in organizations is analogous in simple terms to physical power: it is the ability to mobilize resources (human and material) to get things done. The true sign of power, then, is accomplishment—not fear, terror, or tyranny. Where the power is "on," the system can be productive; where the power is "off," the system bogs down.

But saying that people need power to be effective in organizations does not tell us where it comes from or why some people, in some jobs, systematically seem to have more of it than others. In this article I want to show that to discover the sources of productive power, we have to look not at the *person*—as conventional classifications of effective managers and employees do—but at the *position* the person occupies in the organization.

WHERE DOES POWER COME FROM?

"The effectiveness that power brings evolves from two kinds of capacities: first, access to the resources, information, and support necessary to carry out a task; and, second, ability to get cooperation in doing what is necessary. (*Exhibit I* identifies some symbols of an individual manager's power.)"

Both capacities derive not so much from a leader's style and skill as from his or her location in the formal and informal systems of the organization—in both job definition and connection to other important people in the company. Even the ability to get cooperation from subordinates is strongly defined by the manager's clout outward. People are more responsive to bosses who look as if they can get

EXHIBIT I Some common symbols of
a manager's organizational power
(influence upward and outward)

To what extent a manager can—

Intercede favorably on behalf of someone in trouble with the organization

Get a desirable placement for a talented subordinate

Get approval for expenditures beyond the budget

Get above-average salary increases for subordinates

Get items on the agenda at policy meetings

Get fast access to top decision makers

Get regular, frequent access to top decision-makers

Get early information about decisions and policy shifts

more for them from the organization.

We can regard the uniquely organizational sources of power as consisting of three "lines":

1. *Lines of supply.* Influence outward, over the environment, means that managers have the capacity to bring in the things that their own organizational domain needs—materials, money, resources to distribute as rewards, and perhaps even prestige.

2. *Lines of information.* To be effective, managers need to be "in the know" in both the formal and the informal sense.

3. *Lines of support.* In a formal framework, a manager's job parameters need to allow for nonordinary action, for a show of discretion or exercise of judgment. Thus managers need to know that they can assume innovative, risk-taking activities without having to go through the stifling multi-layered approval process. And, informally, managers need the backing of other important figures in the organization whose tacit approval becomes another resource they bring to their own work

unit as well as a sign of the manager's being "in."

Note that productive power has to do with *connections* with other parts of a system. Such systemic aspects of power derive from two sources—job activities and political alliances:

1. Power is most easily accumulated when one has a job that is designed and located to allow *discretion* (nonroutinized action permitting flexible, adaptive, and creative contributions), *recognition* (visibility and notice), and *relevance* (being central to pressing organizational problems).

2. Power also comes when one has relatively close contact with *sponsors* (higher-level people who confer approval, prestige, or backing), *peer networks* (circles of acquaintanceship that provide reputation and information, the grapevine often being faster than formal communication channels), and *subordinates* (who can be developed to relieve managers of some of their burdens and to represent the manager's point of view).

When managers are in powerful situations, it is easier for them to accomplish more. Because the tools are there, they are likely to be highly motivated and, in turn, to be able to motivate subordinates. Their activities are more likely to be on target and to net them successes. They can flexibly interpret or shape policy to meet the needs of particular areas, emergent situations, or sudden environmental shifts. They gain the respect and cooperation that attributed power brings. Subordinates' talents are resources rather than threats. And, because powerful managers have so many lines of connection and thus are oriented outward, they tend to let go of control downward, developing more independently functioning lieutenants.

The powerless live in a different world. Lacking the supplies, information, or support to make things happen easily, they may turn instead to the ultimate weapon of those who lack productive power—oppressive power: holding others back and punishing with whatever threats they can muster.

POSITIONS OF POWERLESSNESS

Understanding what it takes to have power and recognizing the classic behavior of the powerless can immediately help managers make sense out of a number of familiar organizational problems that are usually attributed to inadequate people:

• The ineffectiveness of first-line supervisors.
• The petty interest protection and conservatism of staff professionals.

• The crises of leadership at the top.

Instead of blaming the individuals involved in organizational problems, let us look at the positions people occupy. Of course, power or powerlessness in a position may not be all of the problem. Sometimes incapable people *are* at fault and need to be retrained or replaced. (See the ruled insert for a discussion of another special case, women.) But where patterns emerge, where the troubles associated with some units persist, organizational power failures could be the reason. Then, as Volvo President Pehr Gyllenhammar concludes, we should treat the powerless not as "villains" causing headaches for everyone else but as "victims" (Gyllenhammar 1977, 133).

EXHIBIT II Ways organizational factors contribute to power or powerlessness

Factors	Generates power when factor is	Generates powerlessness when factor is
Rules inherent in the job	few	many
Predecessors in the job	few	many
Established routines	few	many
Task variety	high	low
Rewards for reliability/predictability	few	many
Rewards for unusual performance/innovation	many	few
Flexibility around use of people	high	low
Approvals needed for nonroutine decisions	few	many
Physical location	central	distant
Publicity about job activities	high	low
Relation of tasks to current problem areas	central	peripheral
Focus of tasks	outside work unit	inside work unit
Interpersonal contact in the job	high	low
Contact with senior officials	high	low
Participation in programs, conferences, meetings	high	low
Participation in problem-solving task forces	high	low
Advancement prospects of subordinates	high	low

First–Line Supervisors

Because an employee's most important work relationship is with his or her supervisor, when many of them talk about "the company," they mean their immediate boss. Thus a supervisor's behavior is an important determinant of the average employee's relationship to work and is in itself a critical link in the production chain.

Yet I know of no U.S. corporate management entirely satisfied with the performance of its supervisors. Most see them as supervising too closely and not training their people. In one manufacturing company where direct laborers were asked on a survey how they learned their job, on a list of seven possibilities "from my supervisor" ranked next to last. (Only company training programs ranked worse.) Also, it is said that supervisors do not translate company policies into practice—for instance, that they do not carry out the right of every employee to frequent performance reviews or to career counseling.

In court cases charging race or sex discrimination, first-line supervisors are frequently cited as the "discriminating official" (Fulmer 1976, 40). And, in studies of innovative work redesign and quality of work life projects, they often appear as the implied villains; they are the ones who are said to undermine the program or interfere with its effectiveness. In short, they are often seen as "not sufficiently managerial."

The problem affects white-collar as well as blue-collar supervisors. In one large government agency, supervisors in field offices were seen as the source of problems concerning morale and the flow of information to and from headquarters. "Their attitudes are negative," said a senior official. "They turn people against the agency; they put down senior management. They build themselves up by always complaining about headquarters, but prevent their staff from getting any information directly. We can't afford to have such attitudes communicated to field staff."

Is the problem that supervisors need more management training programs or that incompetent people are invariably attracted to the job? Neither explanation suffices. A large part of the problem lies in the position itself—one that almost universally creates powerlessness.

First-line supervisors are "people in the middle," and that has been seen as the source of many of their problems (Kanter and Stein 1979). But by recognizing that first-line supervisors are caught between higher management and workers, we only begin to skim the surface of the problem. There is practically no other organizational category as subject to powerlessness.

First, these supervisors may be at a virtual dead end in their careers. Even in companies where the job used to be a stepping stone to higher-level management jobs, it is now common practice to bring in MBAs from the outside for those positions. Thus moving from the ranks of direct labor into supervision may mean, essentially, getting "stuck" rather than moving upward. Because employees do not perceive supervisors as eventually joining the leadership circles of the organization, they may see them as lacking the high-level contacts needed to have clout. Indeed, sometimes turnover among supervisors is so high that workers feel they can outwait—and outwit—any boss.

Second, although they lack clout, with little in the way of support from above, supervisors are forced to administer programs or explain policies that they have no hand in shaping. In one company, as part of a new personnel program supervisors were required to conduct counseling interviews with employees. But supervisors were not trained to do this and were given no incentives to get involved. Counseling was just another obligation. Then managers suddenly encouraged the workers to bypass their supervisors or to put pressure on them. The personnel staff brought them together and told them to demand such interviews as a basic right. If supervisors had not felt powerless before, they did after that squeeze from below, engineered from above.

The people they supervise can also make life hard for them in numerous ways. This often happens when a supervisor has himself or herself risen up from the ranks. Peers that have not made it are resentful or derisive of their former colleague, whom they now see as trying to lord it over them. Often it is easy for workers to break rules and let a lot of things slip.

Yet first-line supervisors are frequently judged according to rules and regulations while being limited by other regulations in what disciplinary actions they can take. They often lack the resources to influence or reward people; after all, workers are guaranteed their pay and benefits by someone other than their supervisors. Supervisors cannot easily control events; rather, they must react to them.

In one factory, for instance, supervisors complained that performance of their job was out of their control: they could fill production quotas only if they had the supplies, but they had no way to influence the people controlling supplies.

The lack of support for many first-line managers, particularly in large organizations, was made dramatically clear in another company. When asked if contact with executives higher in the organization who had the potential for offering support, information, and alliances diminished their own feelings of career vulnerability and the number of headaches they experienced on the job, supervisors in five out of seven work units responded positively. For them *contact* was indeed related to a greater feeling of acceptance at work and membership in the organization.

But in the two other work units where there was greater contact, people per-

ceived more, not less, career vulnerability. Further investigation showed that supervisors in these business units got attention only when they were in trouble. Otherwise, no one bothered to talk to them. To these particular supervisors, hearing from a higher-level manager was a sign not of recognition or potential support but of danger.

It is not surprising, then, that supervisors frequently manifest symptoms of powerlessness: overly close supervision, rules-mindedness, and a tendency to do the job themselves rather than to train their people (since job skills may be one of the few remaining things they feel good about). Perhaps this is why they sometimes stand as roadblocks between their subordinates and the higher reaches of the company.

Staff Professionals

Also working under conditions that can lead to organizational powerlessness are the staff specialists. As advisers behind the scenes, staff people must sell their programs and bargain for resources, but unless they get themselves entrenched in organizational power networks, they have little in the way of favors to exchange. They are seen as useful adjuncts to the primary tasks of the organization but inessential in a day-to-day operating sense. This disenfranchisement occurs particularly when staff jobs consist of easily routinized administrative functions which are out of the mainstream of the currently relevant areas and involve little innovative decision making.

Furthermore, in some organizations, unless they have had previous line experience, staff people tend to be limited in the number of jobs into which they can move. Specialists' ladders are often very short, and professionals are just as likely to get "stuck" in such jobs as people are in less prestigious clerical or factory positions.

Women Managers Experience Special Power Failures

The traditional problems of women in management are illustrative of how formal and informal practices can combine to engender powerlessness. Historically, women in management have found their opportunities in more routine, low-profile jobs. In staff positions, where they serve in support capacities to line managers but have no line responsibilities of their own, or in supervisory jobs managing "stuck" subordinates, they are not in a position either to take the kinds of risks that build credibility or to develop their own team by pushing bright subordinates.

Such jobs, which have few favors to trade, tend to keep women out of the mainstream of the organization. This lack of clout, coupled with the greater difficulty anyone who is "different" has in getting into the information and support networks, has meant that merely by organizational situation women in management have been more likely than men to be rendered structurally powerless. This is one reason those women who have achieved power have often had family connections that put them in the mainstream of the organization's social circles.

A disproportionate number of women managers are found among first-line supervisors or staff professionals; and they, like men in those circumstances, are likely to be organizationally power-

less. But the behavior of other managers can contribute to the powerlessness of women in management in a number of less obvious ways.

One way other managers can make a woman powerless is by patronizingly overprotecting her: putting her in "a safe job," not giving her enough to do to prove herself, and not suggesting her for high-risk, visible assignments. This protectiveness is sometimes born of "good" intentions to give her every chance to succeed (why stack the deck against her?). Out of managerial concerns, out of awareness that a woman may be up against situations that men simply do not have to face, some very well-meaning managers protect their female managers ("It's a jungle, so why send her into it?").

Overprotectiveness can also mask a manager's fear of association with a woman should she fail. One senior bank official at a level below vice president told me about his concerns with respect to a high-performing, financially experienced woman reporting to him. Despite *his* overwhelmingly positive work experiences with her, he was still afraid to recommend her for other assignments because he felt it was a personal risk. "What if other managers are not as accepting of women as I am?" he asked. "I know I'd be sticking my neck out; they would take her more because of my endorsement than her qualifications.

And what if she doesn't make it? My judgment will be on the line."

Overprotection is relatively benign compared with rendering a person powerless by providing obvious signs of lack of managerial support. For example, allowing someone supposedly in authority to be bypassed easily means that no one else has to take him or her seriously. If a woman's immediate supervisor or other managers listen willingly to criticism of her and show they are concerned every time a negative comment comes up and that they assume she must be at fault, then they are helping to undercut her. If managers let other people know that they have concerns about this person or that they are testing her to see how she does, then they are inviting other people to look for signs of inadequacy or failure.

Furthermore, people assume they can afford to bypass women because they "must be uninformed" or "don't know the ropes." Even though women may be respected for their competence or expertise, they are not necessarily seen as being informed beyond the technical requirements of the job. There may be a grain of historical truth in this. Many women come to senior management positions as "outsiders" rather than up through the usual channels.

Also, because until very recently men have not felt comfortable seeing women as businesspeople (business clubs have traditionally excluded women), they have tended to seek each other out for informal socializing. Anyone, male or female, seen as organizationally naive and lacking sources of "inside dope" will find his or her own lines of information limited.

Finally, even when women are able to achieve some power on their own, they have not necessarily been able to translate such personal credibility into an organizational power base. To create a network of supporters out of individual clout requires that a person pass on and share power, that subordinates and peers be empowered by virtue of their connection with that person. Traditionally, neither men nor women have seen women as capable of sponsoring others, even though they may be capable of achieving and succeeding on their own. Women have been viewed as the *recipients* of sponsorship rather than as the sponsors themselves.

(As more women prove themselves in organizations and think more self-consciously about bringing along young people, this situation may change. However, I still hear many more questions from women managers about how they can benefit from mentors, sponsors, or peer networks than about how they themselves can start to pass on favors and make use of their own resources to benefit others.)

Viewing managers in terms of power and powerlessness helps explain two familiar stereotypes about women and leadership in organizations: that no one wants a woman boss (although studies show that anyone who has ever had a woman boss is likely to have had a positive experience), and that the reason no one wants a woman boss is that women are "too controlling, rules-minded, and petty."

The first stereotype simply makes clear that power is important to leadership. Underneath the preference for men is the assumption that, given the current distribution of people in organizational leadership positions, men are more likely than women to be in positions to achieve power and, therefore, to share their power with others. Similarly, the "bossy woman boss" stereotype is a perfect picture of powerlessness. All of those traits are just as characteristic of men who are powerless, but women are slightly more likely, because of circumstances I have mentioned, to find themselves powerless than are men. Women with power in the organization are just as effective—and preferred—as men.

Recent interviews conducted with about 600 bank managers show that, when a woman exhibits the petty traits of powerlessness, people assume that she does so "because she is a woman." A striking difference is that, when a man engages in the same behavior, people assume the behavior is a matter of his own individual style and characteristics and do not conclude that it reflects on the suitability of men for management.

Staff people, unlike those who are being groomed for important line positions, may be hired because of a special expertise or particular background. But management rarely pays any attention to developing them into more general organizational resources. Lacking growth prospects themselves and working alone or in very small teams, they are not in a position to develop others or pass on power to them. They miss out on an important way that power can be accumulated.

Sometimes staff specialists, such as house counsel or organization development people, find their work being farmed out to consultants. Management considers them fine for the routine work, but the minute the activities involve risk or something problematic, they bring in outside experts. This treatment says something not only about their expertise but also about the status of their function. Since the company can always hire talent on a temporary basis, it is unclear that the management really needs to have or considers important its own staff for these functions.

And, because staff professionals are often seen as adjuncts to primary tasks, their effectiveness and therefore their contribution to the organization are often hard to measure. Thus visibility and recognition, as well as risk taking and relevance, may be denied to people in staff jobs.

Staff people tend to act out their powerlessness by becoming turf-minded. They create islands within the organization. They set themselves up as the only ones who can control professional standards and judge their own work. They create sometimes false distinctions between themselves as experts (no one else could possibly do what they do) and lay people, and this continues to keep them out of the mainstream.

One form such distinctions take is a combination of disdain when line managers attempt to act in areas the professionals think are their preserve and of subtle refusal to support the managers' efforts. Or staff groups battle with each other for control of new "problem areas," with the result that no one really handles the issue at all. To cope with their essential powerlessness, staff groups may try to elevate their own status and draw boundaries between themselves and others.

When staff jobs are treated as final resting places for people who have reached their level of competence in the organization—a good shelf on which to dump managers who are too old to go anywhere but too young to retire—then staff groups can also become pockets of conservatism, resistant to change. Their own exclusion from the risk-taking action may make them resist *anyone's* innovative proposals. In the past, personnel departments, for example, have sometimes been the last in their organization to know about innovations in human resource development or to be interested in applying them.

Top Executives

Despite the great resources and responsibilities concentrated at the top of an organization, leaders can be powerless for reasons that are not very different from those that affect staff and supervisors: lack of supplies, information, and support.

We have faith in leaders because of their ability to make things happen in the larger world, to create possibilities for everyone else, and to attract resources to the organization. These are their supplies. But influence outward—the source of much credibility downward—can diminish as environments change, setting terms and conditions out of the control of the leaders. Regardless of top management's grand plans for the organization, the environment presses. At the very least, things going on outside the organization can deflect a leader's attention and drain energy. And, more detrimental, decisions made elsewhere can have severe consequences for the organization and affect top management's sense of power and thus its operating style inside.

In the go-go years of the mid–1960s, for example, nearly every corporation officer or university president could look—and therefore feel—successful. Visible success gave leaders a great deal of credibility inside the organization, which in turn gave them the power to put new things in motion.

In the past few years, the environment has been strikingly different and the capacity of many organization leaders to do anything about it has been severely limited. New "players" have flexed their power muscles: the Arab oil bloc, government regulators, and congressional investigating committees. And managing economic decline is quite different from managing growth. It is no accident that when top leaders personally feel out of control, the control function in corporations grows.

As powerlessness in lower levels of organizations can manifest itself in overly routinized jobs where performance measures are oriented to rules and absence of change, so it can at upper levels as well. Routine work often drives out nonroutine work. Accomplishment becomes a question of nailing down details. Short-term results provide immediate gratifications and satisfy stockholders or other constituencies with limited interests.

It takes a powerful leader to be willing to risk short-term deprivations in order to bring about desired long-term outcomes. Much as first-line supervisors are tempted to focus on daily adherence to rules, leaders are tempted to focus on short-term fluctuations and lose sight of long-term objectives. The dynamics of such a situation are self-reinforcing. The more the long-term goals go unattended, the more a leader feels powerless and the greater the scramble to prove that he or she is in control of daily events at least. The more he is involved in the organization as a short-term Mr. Fix-it, the more out of control of long-term objectives he is, and the more ultimately powerless he is likely to be.

Credibility for top executives often comes from doing the extraordinary: exercising discretion, creating, inventing, planning, and acting in nonroutine ways. But since routine problems look easier and more manageable, require less change and consent on the part of anyone else, and lend themselves to instant solutions that can make any leader look good temporarily, leaders may avoid the risky by taking over what their subordinates should be doing. Ultimately, a leader may succeed in getting all the trivial problems dumped on his or her desk. This can establish expectations even for leaders attempting more challenging tasks. When Warren Bennis was president of the University of Cincinnati, a professor called him when the heat was down in a classroom. In writing about this incident, Bennis commented, "I suppose he expected me to grab a wrench and fix it" (Bennis 1976).

People at the top need to insulate themselves from the routine operations of the organization in order to develop and exercise power. But this very insulation can lead to another source of powerlessness—lack of information. In one multinational corporation, top executives who are sealed off in a large, distant office, flattered and virtually babied by aides, are frustrated by their distance from the real action (Kanter and Stein 1979).

At the top, the concern for secrecy and privacy is mixed with real loneliness. In one bank, organization members were so accustomed to never seeing the top leaders that when a new senior vice president went to the branch offices to look around, they had suspicion, even fear, about his intentions.

Thus leaders who are cut out of an organization's information networks understand neither what is really going on at lower levels nor that their own isolation may be having negative effects. All too often top executives design "beneficial" new employee programs or declare a new humanitarian policy (e.g., "Participatory management is now our style") only to find the policy ignored or mistrusted because it is perceived as coming from uncaring bosses.

The information gap has more serious consequences when executives are so insulated from the rest of the organization or from other decision makers that, as Nixon so dramatically did, they fail to see their own impending downfall. Such insulation is partly a matter of organizational position and, in some cases, of executive style.

For example, leaders may create closed inner circles consisting of "doppelgängers," people just like themselves, who are their principal sources of organizational information and tell them only what they want to know. The reasons for the distortions are varied: key aides want to relieve the leader of burdens, they think just like the leader, they want to protect their own positions of power, or the familiar "kill the messenger" syndrome makes people close to top executives reluctant to be the bearers of bad news.

Finally, just as supervisors and lower-level managers need their supporters in order to be and feel powerful, so do top executives. But for them sponsorship may not be so much a matter of individual endorsement as an issue of support by larger sources of legitimacy in the society. For top executives the problem is not to fit in among peers; rather, the question is whether the public at large and other organization members perceive a common interest which they see the executives as promoting.

If, however, public sources of support are withdrawn and leaders are open to public attack or if inside constituencies fragment and employees see their interests better aligned with pressure groups than with organizational leadership, then powerlessness begins to set in.

When common purpose is lost, the system's own politics may reduce the capacity of those at the top to act. Just as managing decline seems to create a much more passive and reactive stance than managing growth, so does mediating among conflicting interests. When what is happening outside and inside their organizations is out of their control, many people at the top turn into decline managers and dispute mediators. Neither is a particularly empowering role.

Thus when top executives lose their own lines of supply, lines of information, and lines of support, they too suffer from a kind of powerlessness. The temptation for them then is to pull in every shred of power they can and to decrease the power available to other people to act. Innovation loses out in favor of control. Limits rather than targets are set. Financial goals are met by reducing "overhead" (people) rather than by giving people the tools and discretion to increase their own productive capacity. Dictatorial statements come down from the top, spreading the mentality of powerlessness farther until the whole organization becomes sluggish and people concentrate on protecting what they have rather than on producing what they can.

When everyone is playing "king of the mountain," guarding his or her turf jealously, then king of the mountain becomes the only game in town.

TO EXPAND POWER, SHARE IT

In no case am I saying that people in the three hierarchical levels described are always powerless, but they are susceptible to common conditions that can contribute to powerlessness. *Exhibit III* summarizes the most common symptoms of powerlessness for each level and some typical sources of that behavior.

I am also distinguishing the tremendous concentration of economic and political power in large corporations themselves from the powerlessness that can beset individuals even in the highest positions in such organizations. What grows with organizational position in hierarchical levels is not necessarily the power to accomplish—productive power—but the power to punish, to prevent, to sell off, to reduce, to fire, all without appropriate concern for consequences. It is that kind of power—oppressive power—that we often say corrupts.

The absence of ways to prevent individual and social harm causes the polity to feel it must surround people in power with constraints, regulations, and laws that limit the arbitrary use of their authority. But if oppressive power corrupts, then so does the absence of productive power. In large organizations, powerlessness can be a bigger problem than power.

David C. McClelland makes a similar

EXHIBIT III Common symptoms and sources of powerlessness for three key organizational positions

Position	Symptoms	Sources
First-line supervisors	Close, rules-minded supervision	Routine, rules-minded jobs with little control over lines of supply
	Tendency to do things oneself, blocking of subordinates' development and information	Limited lines of information
	Resistant, underproducing subordinates	Limited advancement or involvement prospects for oneself/subordinates
Staff professionals	Turf protection, information control	Routine tasks seen as peripheral to "real tasks" of line organization
	Retreat into professionalism	Blocked careers
	Conservative resistance to change	Easy replacement by outside experts
Top executives	Focus on internal cutting, short-term results, "punishing"	Uncontrollable lines of supply because of environmental changes
	Dictatorial top-down communications	Limited or blocked lines of information about lower levels of organization
	Retreat to comfort of like-minded lieutenants	Diminished lines of support because of challenges to legitimacy (e.g., from the public or special interest groups)

distinction between oppressive and productive power:

"The negative ... face of power is characterized by the dominance-submission mode: if I win, you lose.... It leads to simple and direct means of feeling powerful (such as being aggressive). It does not often lead to effective social leadership for the reason that such a person tends to treat other people as pawns. People who feel they are pawns tend to be passive and useless to the leader who gets his satisfaction from dominating them. Slaves are the most inefficient form of labor ever devised by man. If a leader wants to have far-reaching influence, he must make his followers feel powerful and able to accomplish things on their own.... Even the most dictatorial leader does not succeed if he has not instilled in at least some of his followers a sense of power and the strength to pursue the goals he has set" (McClelland 1975, 263).

Organizational power can grow, in part, by being shared. We do not yet know enough about new organizational forms to say whether productive power is infinitely expandable or where we reach the point of diminishing returns. But we do know that sharing power is different from giving or throwing it away. Delegation does not mean abdication.

Some basic lessons could be translated from the field of economics to the realm of organizations and management. Capital investment in plants and equipment is not the only key to productivity. The productive capacity of nations, like organizations, grows if the skill base is upgraded. People with the tools, information, and support to make more informed decisions and act more quickly can often accomplish more. By empowering others, a leader does not decrease his power; instead he may increase it—especially if the whole organization performs better.

This analysis leads to some counterintuitive conclusions. In a certain tautological sense, the principal problem of the powerless is that they lack power. Powerless people are usually the last ones to whom anyone wants to entrust more power, for fear of its dissipation or abuse. But those people are precisely the ones who might benefit most from an injection of power and whose behavior is likely to change as new options open up to them.

Also, if the powerless bosses could be encouraged to share some of the power they do have, their power would grow. Yet, of course, only those leaders who feel secure about their own power outward— their lines of supply, information, and support—can see empowering subordinates as a gain rather than a loss. The two sides of power (getting it and giving it) are closely connected.

There are important lessons here for both subordinates and those who want to change organizations, whether executives or change agents. Instead of resisting or criticizing a powerless boss, which only increases the boss's feeling of powerlessness and need to control, subordinates instead might concentrate on helping the boss become more powerful. Managers might make pockets of ineffectiveness in the organization more productive not by training or replacing individuals but by structural solutions such as opening supply and support lines.

Similarly, organizational change agents who want a new program or policy to succeed should make sure that the change itself does not render any other level of the organization powerless. In making changes, it is wise to make sure that the key people in the level or two directly above and in neighboring functions are sufficiently involved, informed, and taken into account, so that the program can be used to build their own sense of power also. If such involvement is impossible, then it is better to move these people out of the territory altogether than to leave behind a group from whom some power has been removed and who might resist and undercut the program.

In part, of course, spreading power means educating people to this new definition of it. But words alone will not make the difference; managers will need the real experience of a new way of managing.

Here is how the associate director of a large corporate professional department phrased the lessons that he learned in the transition to a team-oriented, participatory, power-sharing management process:

"Get in the habit of involving your own managers in decision making and approvals. But don't abdicate! Tell them what you want and where you're coming from. Don't go for a one-boss grass roots 'democracy.' Make the management hierarchy work for you in participation. . . .

"Hang in there, baby, and don't give up. Try not to 'revert' just because everything seems to go sour on a particular day. Open up—talk to people and tell them how you feel. They'll want to get you back on track and will do things to make that happen—because they don't really want to go back to the way it was. . . . Subordinates will push you to 'act more like a boss,' but their interest is usually more in seeing someone else brought to heel than getting bossed themselves."

Naturally, people need to have power before they can learn to share it. Exhorting managers to change their leadership styles is rarely useful by itself. In one large plant of a major electronics company, first-line production supervisors were the source of numerous complaints from managers who saw them as major road blocks to overall plant productivity and as insufficiently skilled supervisors. So the plant personnel staff undertook two pilot programs to increase the supervisors' effectiveness. The first program was based on a traditional competency and training model aimed at teaching the specific skills of successful supervisors. The second program, in contrast, was designed to empower the supervisors by directly affecting their flexibility, access to resources, connections with higher-level officials, and control over working conditions.

After an initial gathering of data from supervisors and their subordinates, the personnel staff held meetings where all the supervisors were given tools for developing action plans for sharing the data with their people and collaborating on solutions to perceived problems. But then, in a departure from common practice in this organization, task forces of supervisors were formed to develop new systems for handling job and career issues common to them and their people. These task forces were given budgets, consultants, representation on a plantwide project steering committee alongside managers at much higher levels, and wide latitude in defining the nature and scope of the changes they wished to make. In short, lines of supply, information, and support were opened to them.

As the task forces progressed in their activities, it became clear to the plant management that the hoped-for changes in supervisory effectiveness were taking place much more rapidly through these structural changes in power than through conventional management training; so the conventional training was dropped. Not only did the pilot groups design useful new procedures for the plant, astonishing senior management in several cases with their knowledge and capabilities, but also, significantly, they learned to manage their own people better.

Several groups decided to involve shop-floor workers in their task forces; they could now see from their own experience the benefits of involving subordinates in solving job-related problems. Other supervisors began to experiment with ways to implement "participatory management" by giving subordinates more control and influence without relinquishing their own authority.

Soon the "problem supervisors" in the "most troubled plant in the company" were getting the highest possible perform-ance ratings and were considered models for direct production management. The sharing of organizational power from the top made possible the productive use of power below.

One might wonder why more organizations do not adopt such empowering strategies. There are standard answers: that giving up control is threatening to people who have fought for every shred of it; that people do not want to share power with those they look down on; that managers fear losing their own place and special privileges in the system; that "predictability" often rates higher than "flexibility" as an organizational value; and so forth.

But I would also put skepticism about employee abilities high on the list. Many modern bureaucratic systems are designed to minimize dependence on individual intelligence by making routine as many decisions as possible. So it often comes as a genuine surprise to top executives that people doing the more routine jobs could, indeed, make sophisticated decisions or use resources entrusted to them in intelligent ways.

In the same electronics company just mentioned, at the end of a quarter the pilot supervisory task forces were asked to report results and plans to senior management in order to have their new budget requests approved. The task forces made sure they were well prepared, and the high-level executives were duly impressed. In fact, they were *so* impressed that they kept interrupting the presentations with compliments, remarking that the supervisors could easily be doing sophisticated personnel work.

At first the supervisors were flattered. Such praise from upper management could only be taken well. But when the first glow wore off, several of them became very angry. They saw the excessive praise as patronizing and insulting. "Didn't they think we could think? Didn't they imagine we were capable of doing this kind of work?" one asked. "They must have seen us as just a bunch of animals. No wonder they gave us such limited jobs."

As far as these supervisors were con-cerned, their abilities had always been there, in latent form perhaps, but still there. They as individuals had not changed—just their organizational power.

Participative Management: Quality vs. Quantity

RAYMOND E. MILES and J.B. RITCHIE

Just as other vintage theoretical vehicles have demonstrated amazing durability on the academic stage, the theory of partici-pative management has shown a remark-able facility for holding the spotlight of debate in the management literature. For this and other theories, however, it should be noted that it is often clever direction and staging, rather than substance, which sustains audience interest.

Having signaled this caveat, we must admit to some feeling of trepidation as we suggest another inquiry into this now middle-aged set of concepts. We do so, however, because we believe some of the recent findings from our continuing re-search on the process and effects of par-ticipation justify further examination of this theory. We should add that our re-search and its implications are unlikely to do much to resolve the polemics between those who view participation as the solu-tion to all organizational ailments and those who consider it a humanistic pallia-tive which threatens the moral fiber of managerial prerogatives. Nevertheless, we feel our findings may prove valuable

to the much larger group for whom the concept of participation is neither pan-acea nor plague, but simply confusing.

In our view, a prime source of confu-sion surrounding the concept of participa-tion is its purpose. We noted this confu-sion a few years ago (Miles 1965), drawing from our research the conclu-sion that most managers appeared to hold at least two different "theories" of partici-pation. One of these, which we labeled the **Human Relations** model, viewed partici-pation primarily as a means of obtaining cooperation—a technique which the man-ager could use to improve morale and re-duce subordinate resistance to his policies and decisions. The second, which we la-beled the Human Resources model, recog-nized the untapped potential of most or-ganizational members and advocated participation as a means of achieving di-rect improvement in individual and orga-nizational performance. Predictably, managers viewed the Human Relations model as appropriate for their subordi-nates while wanting their superior to fol-low the Human Resources logic.

Our recent research draws attention to a closely related, and probably equally important, source of confusion involving the *process* of participation. Our earlier descriptions of the purpose of participation under the Human Relations and Human Resources models implied that it is not only the degree of participation which is important, but also the nature of the superior-subordinate interaction. Upon reflection, the notion that both the quality and quantity of participation must be considered seems patently obvious. Rather surprisingly, however, the quality variable in the participative process has been infrequently specified in management theory, and even more rarely researched.

The lack of specific focus in theory or research on the quality aspect of the participative process has led, in our view, to the promulgation of a simple "quantity theory of participation," a theory which implies only that some participation is better than none and that more is better than a little. Clearly, a concept which, whether intended or not, appears to lump all participative acts together in a common category ignores individual and situational differences and is therefore open to a variety of justified criticism. It is just such a simplified view that allows its more vitriolic critics to draw caricatures extending the participative process to include a chairman of the board consulting with a janitor concerning issues of capital budgeting—the sort of criticism which brings humor to journal pages but contributes little to our understanding of participation.

Recognizing these key sources of confusion, our current studies have been aimed at increasing our understanding of the process of participation under the Human Relations and Human Resources models. Specifically, we have attempted, within a large sample of management teams, to identify and measure the amount of superior-subordinate consultation and a dimension of the quality of this interaction—the superior's attitude which reflects the degree to which he has confidence in his subordinates' capabilities.

(Our research approach and findings are described in a later section.) As indicated, in our theoretical framework both the quantity and quality of participation are important determinants of subordinate satisfaction and performance. For these analyses, we have focused on the impact of these variables, both separately and jointly, on the subordinate's satisfaction with his immediate superior. Our findings, we believe, clarify the role which quality plays in the participative process and add substance to the Human Relations—Human Resources differentiation.

In the following sections we explore further the concepts of quantity and quality of participation, integrate these into existing theories of participative management, and examine the implications of our research for these theories and for management practice.

THE QUALITY CONCEPT AND MANAGEMENT THEORY

A simple, and we believe familiar, example should assist us in firmly integrating the quantity-quality variables into the major theories of participative management and perhaps demonstrate, in part at least, why we are concerned with this dimension. Most of us have had the following experience:

> An invitation is received to attend an important meeting (we know it is important because it is carefully specified as such in the call). A crucial policy decision is to be made and our views and those of our colleagues are, according to the invitation, vital to the decision.
>
> Having done our homework, we arrive at the meeting and begin serious and perhaps heated discussion. Before too long, however, a light begins to dawn, and illuminated in that dawning light is the fact that the crucial decision we had been called together to decide . . .

With a cynical, knowing smile, the typical organization member completes the sentence by saying "had already been made." It is helpful, however, to push aside the well-remembered frustration of such situations and examine the logic of the executive who called the meeting and the nature of the participative process flowing from his logic.

We can easily imagine (perhaps because we have frequently employed the same logic) the executive in our example saying to himself, "I've got this matter pretty well firmed, but it may require a bit of selling—I'd better call the troops in and at least let them express their views." He may even be willing to allow some minor revisions in the policy to overcome resistance and generate among his subordinates a feeling of being a part of the decision.

PURPOSES OF PARTICIPATION

Clearly defined in our example and discussion is the tight bond between the purpose of participation and the quality of ensuing involvement. And, underlying the purpose of participation is the executive's set of assumptions about people—particularly his attitudes concerning the capabilities of his subordinates.

Three theoretical frameworks describe this linkage between the manager's basic attitudes toward people and the amount and kind of consultation in which he is likely to engage with his subordinates. It is worth a few lines to compare these theory systems and to apply them to our example. Listed chronologically, these frameworks are:

- The Theory X—Theory Y dichotomy described by the late Douglas McGregor (1960, 1967).
- The System I, II, III, IV continuum defined by Rensis Likert (1961, 1967).
- Our own Traditional, Human Relations, Human Resources classification

(Miles 1966; Miles, Porter, and Craft 1966).

TERMINOLOGY

We have been criticized for referring to an essentially autocratic (nonparticipatory) style of management as traditional. Such a style is no longer traditional in the sense that it is prescribed, taught, or openly advocated by a majority of modern managers. Our research suggests that most managers consider such a style to be socially undesirable and few will admit adherence to it in concept or practice.

Nevertheless, we would argue that many if not most of our institutions and organizations are still so structured and operated that this style is alive and well today in our society. Many schools, hospitals, labor unions, political parties, and a substantial number of business enterprises frequently behave, particularly at the lower levels, in a manner which can only be described as autocratic. Thus, even though their policy statements have been revised and some participative trappings have been hung about, the main thrust of their activity is not greatly changed from what it was twenty, thirty, perhaps even fifty years ago—they behave in a traditional manner toward the structure and direction of work. Further, the assumptions of the Traditional model are, in our view, still widely held and espoused in our society—the rhetoric has improved, but the intent is the same. These assumptions seem to us still to be a part of our "traditional" approach to life. If our views are accurate, Traditional model is therefore still an appropriate tag.

McGregor's Theory X, Likert's System I, and our Traditional model describe autocratic leadership behavior coupled with tight, unilateral control, and little or no subordinate participation in the decision process. Theory X and the Traditional model explicitly delineate the superior's assumptions that most people, including subordinates, are basically indolent, self-centered, gullible, and resistant to change and thus have little to contribute to the decision-making or control process. Focusing more on descriptive characteristics and less on an explicit set of assumptions, Likert's System I manager is pictured only as having no confidence or trust in his subordinates. At the other extreme, Theory Y, System IV, and our Human Resources model define a style of behavior which involves subordinates deeply in the decision process and emphasizes high levels of self-direction and self-control. Again, both Theory Y and the Human Resources model make the logic underlying such behavior explicit—that most organization members are capable of contributing more than demanded by their present jobs and thus represent untapped potential for the organization, potential which the capable manager develops and invests in improved performance. A System IV superior is described simply as one having complete confidence and trust in subordinates in all matters. In between these extremes fall Likert's Systems II and III and our Human Relations model. Systems II and III describe increasing amounts of subordinate participation and self-control, as their superior's attitudes toward them move from "condescending" to "substantial, but not complete" confidence and trust. Our Human Relations model views the superior as recognizing his subordinates' desire for involvement but doubting their ability to make meaningful contributions.

THEORY AND MANAGEMENT PRACTICE

Comparing these frameworks with our example, it is clear that the executive calling the meeting was not operating at the Theory X, System I, Traditional end of the participative continuum. Had he followed the assumptions of these models, he would simply have announced his deci-

sion, and if a meeting were called, used it openly to explain his views. Similarly, it seems doubtful that our executive was following the Theory Y, System IV, or Human Resource models. Had he been, he would have called the meeting in the belief that his subordinates might make important contributions to the decision process and that their participation would possibly result in constructing a better overall policy. He would have had confidence and trust in their ability and willingness to generate and examine alternatives and take action in the best interest of the organization.

Instead, the meeting in the example and those from our own experience seem to be defined almost to the letter by our Human Relations logic and the behavior described in Likert's Systems II and III. The casual observer, and perhaps even the more naive participant, unaware of the reasoning of the executive calling the meeting, might well record a high level of involvement during the session—participation high both in quantity and quality. Most of the participants, however, would be much less charitable, particularly about the meaningfulness of the exercise. They would sense, although the guidance was subtle, that at least the depth of their participation was carefully controlled, just as they would be equally alert to the logic underlying the meeting strategy.

ALTERNATIVE THEORIES

Having described varying degrees of quantity and quality of participation flowing from alternative theories of management, and having attempted to link to common experience through our meeting example, it is not difficult to conjecture about the relationships between these variables and subordinate satisfaction. We would expect subordinate satisfaction to move up and down with both the quantity and the quality of participation, and there is already some evidence, with regard to the amount of participation, at least, that it does. Thus, we would expect, particularly within the managerial hierarchy, that their satisfaction would be lowest when both quantity and quality of participation were lowest—as the Traditional model is approached—the highest when both quantity and quality are high—when participation moves toward the type described in the Human Resources model.

Predicting satisfaction under the Human Relations model is less easy. If the superior's behavior is blatantly manipulative, we might expect satisfaction to be quite low despite high participation. But, if the superior's logic were less obvious, even to himself, we might expect his subordinates to be somewhat pleased to be involved in the decision process, even if their involvement is frequently peripheral.

We cannot precisely test the impact of these models on subordinate satisfaction, but our recent research does provide some evidence with regard to these conjectures, and it is therefore appropriate that we briefly describe the method of our investigation and look at some of our findings.

RESEARCH APPROACH

The findings reported here were drawn from a broader research project conducted among management teams (a superior and his immediate subordinates) from five levels in six geographically separated operating divisions of a west coast firm (Blankenship and Miles 1968; Roberts, Blankenship, and Miles 1968). The 381 managers involved in the study ranged from the chief executive of each of the six divisions down through department supervisors.

From extensive questionnaire responses we were able to develop measures of the three variables important to these analyses: *quantity of participation, quality of participation,* and *satisfaction with im-*

mediate superiors. Our measure of quantity of participation was drawn from managers' responses to questions concerning how frequently they felt they were consulted by their superior on a number of typical department issues and decisions (Ritchie and Miles 1970). This information allowed us to classify managers as high or low in terms of the amount of participation they felt they were allowed. For a measure of quality of this participation, we turned to the responses given by each manager's superior. The superior's attitudes toward his subordinates—his evaluation of their capabilities with regard to such traits as judgment, creativity, responsibility, perspective, and the like—were analyzed and categorized as high or low compared to the attitudes of other managers at the same level. Finally, our satisfaction measure was taken from a question on which managers indicated, on a scale from very satisfied to very dissatisfied, their reactions to their own immediate superiors.

FINDINGS

The first thing apparent in our findings, as shown in each of the accompanying figures, is that virtually all the subjects in our study appear reasonably well satisfied with their immediate superiors. This is not surprising, particularly since all subjects, both superiors and subordinates, are in managerial positions. Managers generally respond positively (compared to other organization members) on satisfaction scales. Moreover, supporting the organization's reputation for being forward looking and well managed, most participants reported generally high levels of consultation, and superiors' scores on confidence in their subordinates were typically higher than the average scores in our broader research.

Nevertheless, differences do exist, differences which, given the restricted range of scores, are in most instances highly significant in statistical terms. Moreover, they demonstrate that both the quantity and the quality of participation are related to managers' feelings of satisfaction with their immediate superiors.

As shown in Figure 1, the quantity of participation achieved is apparently related to managers' feelings of satisfaction with their superiors. (The taller the figure—and the smaller the numerical score—the more satisfied is that group of managers.) Managers classified as low (relative to the scores of their peers) in terms of the extent to which they are consulted by their superiors are less well satisfied than those classified as high on this dimension. The difference in the average satisfaction score for the low consultation group (2.13) falls between the satisfied and the so-so (somewhat satisfied—somewhat dissatisfied) categories. For the high consultation group, the score (1.79) falls between the satisfied and the highly satisfied categories.

A slightly stronger pattern of results is apparent when managers are grouped in terms of the amount of confidence which their superiors have in them (Figure 2). Managers whose superiors have relatively high trust and confidence scores are significantly more satisfied (1.72) than their colleagues (2.16) whose superiors have relatively lower scores on this dimension.

Finally, our results take on their most interesting form when managers are cross-classified on both the quantity and the quality dimensions of participation. As shown in Figure 3, the progression in satisfaction is consistent with our theoretical formulation. Especially obvious is the comparison between managers classified as low both in amount of consultation received and the extent to which their superior has confidence in them (2.26) and managers who are rated high on both variables (1.55). Of interest, and relevant to our later discussion, managers whose superiors have high confidence in them but who are low in amount of participa-

tion appear slightly more satisfied (1.95) than their counterparts who are high in amount of participation but whose superiors are low in terms of confidence in their subordinates (2.05).

LINKING FINDINGS TO THEORY

The bulk of our findings, particularly as illustrated in Figure 3, thus appear to support our conjectures. Managers who least value their subordinates' capabilities and who least often seek their contributions on department issues have the least well satisfied subordinates in our study. It would probably be incorrect to place the Traditional (Theory X, System I) label on any of the managers in our sample, yet those who, relative to their peers, lean closest to these views do so with predictable results in terms of subordinate satisfaction.

Similarly, managers who, relative to their peers, are both high in their respect for their subordinates' capabilities and who consult them regularly on departmental issues also achieve the expected results. Precise labeling is again probably inappropriate, yet managers whose attitudes and behavior are closest to the Human Resources (Theory Y, System IV) model do in fact have the most satisfied subordinates.

Further, those managers who consult their subordinates frequently but who have little confidence in their ability to make a positive contribution to department decision making, and thus who fall nearest to our Human Relations model, have subordinates who are more satisfied than those under the more Traditional managers but are significantly less satisfied than the subordinates of Human Resources managers.

The majority of our findings support the major formulations of participative management theory, but they also suggest the need for elaboration and clarification.

FIGURE 1 Amount of Superior Consultation and Subordinate Satisfaction

Low consultation | High consultation

1 Very satisfied 4 Dissatisfied
2 Satisfied 3 Somewhat satisfied / Somewhat dissatisfied 5 Very dissatisfied

FIGURE 2 Superior's Confidence in Subordinates and Subordinate Satisfaction

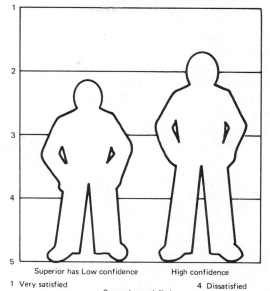

Superior has Low confidence | High confidence

1 Very satisfied 4 Dissatisfied
2 Satisfied 3 Somewhat satisfied / Somewhat dissatisfied 5 Very dissatisfied

FIGURE 3 Effects of Amount of Consultation and Superior's Confidence in Subordinates on Subordinate Satisfaction

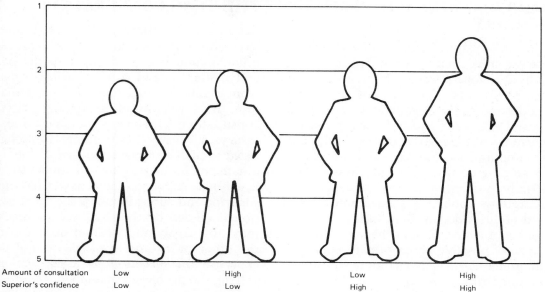

Amount of consultation   Low   High   Low   High
Superior's confidence   Low   Low   High   High

1 Very satisfied   2 Satisfied   3 Somewhat satisfied/Somewhat dissatisfied   4 Dissatisfied   5 Very dissatisfied

This need is brought to attention by the total pattern of our findings, and particularly by the results for one of our categories of managers—those high in superiors' confidence but relatively low in participation. Recall that, while the differences were not large, this group had the second highest average satisfaction score in our sample—the score falling between that of the Human Relations (high participation, low superior confidence) group and that of the Human Resources (high on each) group. Moreover, for the two groups characterized by high participation, there is substantially higher satisfaction for those whose superior reflects high confidence in his subordinates. Clearly, any theory which focused on the amount of participation would not predict these results. Rather, for these managers at least, the quality of their relationship with their superiors as indicated by their superiors' attitude of trust and confidence in them appears to modify the effects of the amount of participation.

IMPLICATIONS FOR THE THEORY

The quality dimension of the theory of participative management has not been fully developed, but its outlines are suggested in our own Human Resources model and in McGregor's Theory Y framework. McGregor stressed heavily the importance of managers' basic attitudes and assumptions about their subordinates. In expanding on this point (McGregor 1967, 79), he suggested that a manager's assumptions about his subordinates' traits and abilities do not bind him to a single course of action. Rather, he argued that a range of possible behaviors are appropriate under Theory Y or Human Resources assumptions—a manager with high trust and confidence in his subordinates could and should take into account a variety of situational and personality factors in de-

ciding, among other things, when and how to consult with them. Extending this reasoning, one can even imagine a Theory Y or Human Resources manager actually consulting with his subordinates less often than some of his colleagues. Nevertheless, the nature and quality of participation employed by such a manager, when it occurs, would presumably be deeper and more meaningful, which would be reflected in high levels of subordinate satisfaction and performance.

This view of the super-subordinate interaction process, emphasizing as it does the quality of the interaction rather than only the amount, can be employed to answer three of the more pervasive criticisms of participative management. These criticisms—each of which is probably most accurately aimed at the simple quantity theory of participation—focus on the inappropriateness of extensive consultation when the superior is constrained by time, technology, and his own or his subordinate's temperament.

THE TIME CONSTRAINT

"In a crisis, you simply do not have time to run around consulting people." This familiar explication is difficult to debate, and in fact, would receive no challenge from a sophisticated theory of participation. In a real building-burning crisis, consultation is inappropriate, and unnecessary. A crisis of this nature is recognized as such by any well-informed subordinate and his self-controlled cooperation is willingly supplied. The behavior of both superior and subordinate in such a situation is guided by the situation and each may turn freely and without question to the other or to any available source of expertise for direction or assistance in solving the problem at hand.

Many crises, however, do not fit the building-burning category, and may be much more real to one person, or to one level of management, than to those below him. Our experience suggests that managers may not be nearly as bound by their constraints as they frequently claim to be, or if they are constrained, these limits are either known in advance or are open to modification if circumstances demand. Rather, in many instances it appears that managers employ the "time won't permit" argument primarily to justify autocratic, and at least partially risk-free behavior. If he succeeds, the credit is his; if he fails, he can defend his actions by pointing out that he had no time to explore alternatives.

Such self-defined, or at least self-sustaining, crises are most frequently employed by the manager with a Human Relations concept of participation—one who views participation primarily as a means of obtaining subordinate cooperation and who focuses mainly on the amount of formal involvement required. The crisis itself can be employed in place of participation as the lever to obtain cooperation and there is clearly no time for the sort of routine, frequently peripheral consultation, in which he most often indulges.

Conversely, the manager with high trust and confidence in his subordinates' capabilities, the Human Resources manager, is less likely to employ the time constraints as a managerial tactic. In real crises he moves as rapidly as the situation demands. He is, however, more likely, because of his normal practices of sharing information with his subordinates, to have a group which is prepared to join him in a rapid review of alternatives. He is unconcerned with involvement for the sake of involvement and thus his consultation activities are penetrating and to the point. His subordinates share his trust and feel free to challenge his views, just as he feels free to question their advice and suggestions openly.

THE TECHNOLOGY BARRIER

"Look, I've got fifteen subordinates scattered all over the building. What do you expect me to do—shut down the plant and call a meeting every time something happens?" This argument is obviously closely linked to the time constraint argument— technology is a major factor in determining the flow and timing of decisions. Similarly, it too flows from a Human Relations—quantity oriented view of participation.

A good manager obviously does not regularly "stop the presses" and call a conference. He has confidence in his subordinates' abilities to handle problems as they appear and to call him in when the problem demands his attention. This confidence is, however, reinforced by joint planning, both one-to-one and across his group of subordinates, before the operation gets under way. Having agreed in advance on objectives, schedules, priorities, and procedures, involvement on a day-to-day basis may be minimal. The manager in this instance does not seek participation to obtain cooperation with his views. Both the manager and his subordinates view the regularly scheduled work planning and review sessions as important because they result in well-considered solutions to real problems.

THE TEMPERAMENT BARRIER

"I'm simply not the sort who can run around to his subordinates asking them how things are going—it's just not my style." The manager who made this statement did so somewhat apologetically, but there was little for him to be apologetic about. He had a high-performing group of subordinates, in whom he placed high trust and confidence, who were in turn highly satisfied with their boss. Further, while he did not seek their views on a variety of routine departmental matters, and his subordinates did not drop in to his office to chat, he freely shared all departmental information with them and on a regular basis worked with his subordinates in coordinating department plans and schedules. In addition, he practiced a somewhat formal but effective form of management by objectives with each of his subordinates.

This manager and, unfortunately, many of the more outspoken critics of participative management, tend to feel that consultation must be carried out in a gregarious, back-slapping manner. Joint planning is a decision-making technique, and not a personality attribute. Extreme shyness or reserve may be an inhibiting factor, but is not an absolute barrier. Trust and confidence in subordinates can be demonstrated as effectively, if not more effectively, by action, as by words.

Similarly, as suggested earlier, the manager who holds a Human Resources view of participation acknowledges personality and capability differences among his subordinates. He feels a responsibility to the organization and to his subordinates to assist each to develop continuously his potential for making important contributions to department performance. He recognizes that individuals move toward the free interchange of ideas, suggestions, and criticisms at different paces. However, by demonstrating his own confidence in his subordinates' capabilities and in their potential, he tends to encourage more rapid growth than other managers.

CONCLUDING COMMENTS

Our continuing research on the purpose and process of participative management has, in our view, contributed additional support for the Human Resources theory of participation. It has emphasized that when the impact on subordinates is considered, the superior's attitude toward the traits and abilities of his subordinates is equally as important as the amount of consultation in which he engages.

This not-so-startling finding allows expansions and interpretations of modern theories of participation to counter criticisms which may be properly leveled at a simple quantity theory of participation. However, although our findings have obvious implications for both theory and management behavior, they too are open to possible misinterpretation. It is possible to read into our findings, as some surely will, that subordinate consultation may be neglected, that all that matters is that the superior respect his subordinates.

Such a philosophy—tried, found wanting, and not supported by our findings—is embodied in the frequent statement that "all you need to do to be a good manager is hire a good subordinate and turn him loose to do the job as he sees fit." Such a philosophy, in our view, abdicates the superior's responsibility to guide, develop, and support his subordinates. The most satisfied managers in our sample were those who received high levels of consultation from superiors who valued their capabilities. It is our view that effective participation involves neither "selling" the superior's ideas nor blanket approval of all subordinate suggestions. Rather, it is most clearly embodied in the notion of joint planning where the skills of both superior and subordinate are used to their fullest.

Our findings emphasize the importance of attitudes of trust and confidence in subordinates, but they do not indicate their source. It is possible, but unlikely, that those superiors in our sample who reported the highest levels of trust and confidence in their subordinates did so because their subordinates were in fact of higher caliber than those of their colleagues. Within our large sample of managers, several indicators—education, age, experience, for example—suggest that managers' capabilities are roughly evenly distributed across levels and divisions within the organization.

Another possible reason for differences in superiors' attitudes on this dimension is that they are caused by interaction with subordinates, rather than being a determinant of the nature of this interaction. That is, the manager, who attempts consultation which is highly successful increases his confidence in his subordinates and thus develops broader involvement. This seems to be a highly plausible explanation which has implications for management development. In fact, there is growing evidence that managers who experiment with participative techniques over lengthy periods do develop both a commitment to such practices and additional trust in their subordinates.

Getting the Best From Foreign Employees

LENNIE COPELAND and LEWIS GRIGGS

Each culture has its expectations for the roles of boss and employee. What one culture encourages as participatory management, another sees as managerial incompetence. What one values as employee initiative and leadership, others consider selfish and destructive of group harmony.

There's nothing inherently natural or carved in stone about the way bosses or workers are supposed to act. Every country has a heritage that has created expectations for people in certain positions. The methods of modern business, *your* business, must not clash with those traditional expectations. You must understand the way things *are* before you can hope to be effective in existing organizational systems or before you can change the status quo.

LEADERS GET AND USE POWER DIFFERENTLY

In many countries, authority in business and government is inherited. Key positions are filled from certain families; hence authority is vested in the person rather than in the position. Elsewhere, a manager may command respect by virtue of position, age, or influence. In either case, the foreign manager does not have to prove a right to leadership. American managers, on the other hand, often feel respect must be *earned* through achievement or fair handling of subordinates. Thus, American managers overseas try to *prove* something that their local employees have already *assumed*. A Mexican manager working for an American firm described one vice-president who, he says, "tried to win our respect by showing how hard he worked for the company. Yet he had only a superficial interest in the rest of us. He had it backwards. Of course, we respected him—he was the vice-president. But that was about all."

Rule 1: Authority Figures Must Look and Act the Part

The respect of workers depends on appearance of strength and competence, but what comes across as strong and competent is not the same everywhere. In Mexico, *machismo* is important. In Germany, polish, decisiveness, and breadth of knowledge give a manager stature. This is not to say that you should adopt without restraint any of the more blatant symbols of power in a country; it is foolish to appear arrogant or superior to local workers. The point is, you should behave appropriately for your role, or your employees may be confused.

Americans are peculiar in their concentration of interest and effort into a few activities. With few exceptions, industrial leaders in the United States are known only for their corporate identity. Latin American management emphasizes the total person. Leaders are respected as multidimensional social beings who are family leader, business leader, intellectual, and patron of the arts. French and Italian industry leaders are social leaders. In Germany, power can be financial, political, entrepreneurial, managerial, or intellectual; of the five, intellectual power seems to rank highest. Many of the heads of German firms have doctoral degrees and are always addressed as "Herr Doktor."

It Helps to Know the Signals of Rank. In most countries, power is more visible than it is in America, where great pains seem to be taken by the most powerful to appear ordinary. Abroad, people are often shocked when they see American executives pushing a shopping cart or mowing a lawn, or when they see American children working at summer jobs. Local personnel get confusing signals from our behavior.

To communicate rank or to estimate the power of a foreigner, you have to know the local accoutrements of success or position. Style of dress, possessions, office setting, even titles do not all mean the same in different countries. Appearance and clothing are extremely important to the Latin Americans. Arab and American businessmen seem to value large offices, expensive automobiles, and magnificent homes. British offices of important people may be quite cramped and much more conservatively appointed. Ostentatious displays of power are considered bad form by the Germans.

Authority is also supported by proper decorum and distance. Managers exude rank by how they behave and interact with employees. Codes of conduct are unwritten but nevertheless firm. In Belgium, a newly appointed executive in a major American accounting firm went early to his office one morning to "meet the guys." Leaving his jacket in his office, he sauntered about, stopping to chat with employees of all levels. His good intentions backfired: He upset the routine by arriving earlier than is customary among senior executives (10 A.M.), and violated protocol by talking with employees who were not his "direct-reports." His casual dress and familiar attitude toward the employees caused great amazement and offense—and it became extremely difficult for him to gain respect in the company.

Rule 2: In Relationship–Oriented Societies, Show Personal Concern for Employees

Generally, outside Europe, Canada and the United States, it is good business to take a strong personal interest in the problems of both customers and employees. You must work at truly understanding their concerns. You must be accessible, available, and personal. People in other countries have extremely different commitments and expectations about how they should be treated by an employer.

In the Soviet Union and Eastern Europe, the factory or state farm is the paternalistic provider of many services, such as day care, schools, and medical clinics. Many younger workers live in dorms and use the *kollektiv* (group) vacation facilities and Pioneer camps for the children. The Japanese also provide seemingly unlimited services to their corporate members: housing, recreation, schools, day care, even marriage-broker assistance. Some firms provide hot meals to be taken home. The Arab expects his boss to help with personal problems—sickness in the family, debt, or other misfortune. In Africa, a manager might make loans to personnel, to be repaid on payday. Foreigners working for Western companies miss that kind of concern.

Budget Hours of Talk—and Listening—Into Your Week. In Asia, the Arab world, and Latin America, a manager needs a warm personalized approach, demonstrated by appearing at birthday parties and soccer games, walking through the work areas often, recognizing people by name, talking to workers and—even more important—*listening* to them. In Latin America and China, it is important to drop in periodically for social visits with workers, inquiring about their health and morale without mentioning work problems. Without singling out any individual, the group should be complimented liberally to give everyone "face."

Paradoxically, even where openness is not a local trait, Americans should not try to keep secrets from employees. If you tell one person something, tell them all—they will all hear it anyway and it's better that they get it straight from you without distortion. Explaining your actions will help avoid or allay rumors that can be severely detrimental to your goals.

"Personalized Style" Does Not Mean

"Personal" in the Way Americans Usually Mean it. There is an art to making warm, supportive personal contact that is not too familiar and that does not bring the executive down to a subordinate's level, causing loss of respect or face or violating privacy. There are signs of respect in tone of voice and manner that denote grades of inferiority and superiority in hierarchical societies. Most Americans are not raised with a strong sense of class distinction. Nevertheless, you should be able to recognize its manifestations.

DECISION MAKING AND DELEGATION

American managers all over the world, from Germany to Turkey to India, have been astonished to find multilevel approval needed for the authorization of routine items, and poor communication between

Risky Incentive Plan

An American executive in Japan announced that he would send his company's most successful salesman and his family on a holiday abroad. To the American's surprise, the salesmen were uninterested. He had offered the prize to *one* of them only. Everyone else would be a loser. Not only that: Japanese like to travel, but not with their wives.

The American changed the reward to a trip for all if they met the sales target. They did. But then the section chief told him: "Four of the salesmen are first-year people who don't participate in things like this. I would like to return their tickets and distribute the cash evenly among all the office girls and people in other departments who participated in the success."

SOURCE: Condensed from *Doing Business in Japan*, JETRO, 1982

echelons of management. In so many places, companies are still run very much from above, and everything must trickle up to the top executive's office. Even where efforts have been made to delegate decision-making power within an organization, local business people continue to insist on seeing the head person, and employees continue to seek the approval of their superiors.

French, Italian, and German executives generally believe that a tight reign of authority is needed to obtain adequate job performance, and managers feel there is more prestige in directing than in persuading. Employees do not try to influence their supervisors. In India and South America, too, those with authority believe employees want a strong boss who gives orders, and workers do not question the actions of their managers.

Where an American group of employees might normally have a give-and-take discussion and present the boss with a recommendation (perhaps reached by vote and majority rule), the German group will expect the boss to give instructions. An American manager who tries to get German workers to make a group decision may be told, "No, let the foreman decide." If the American manager insists it has to be their decision, each member of the group will state a preference and then again expect the boss to decide. Insistence on the part of the manager will be met by more opposition.

England's colonial and civil service heritage left an emphasis on decentralized decision making, but management analysts say that despite considerable lip service to the contrary, decision making in Great Britain generally remains the prerogative of highly placed management. Democratic and decentralized management ideals frequently clash with a leader's class consciousness or basic lack of faith in the decision-making abilities of subordinates.

Rule 3: Involve People in Ways They Understand

You can't expect an uninitiated East Indian or Latin American or Italian to understand participatory management. The only way to get them to participate in any meaningful way is by teaching and guiding, slowly and gradually. It will take time to change deeply ingrained customs, and in the process you will have to deal with confusion and tension. You also risk losing control. If a supervisor's efforts are taken for ignorance or weakness, foreign workers may disregard the supervisor and pursue their own inclinations.

Arab and African Executives Have Strong Traditions of Consultation in Decision Making. Tribal leaders have practiced council meetings or "palaver" for milennia. The consultation tradition is supported by the Koran and sayings of Mohammed. Senior members of the ruling families or the community are still consulted on matters of importance; in other matters the family is often asked for input. The consultation method is used almost to the exclusion of joint decision-making or delegation of decision-making responsibility. Arab executives say the practice continues because it works: It is a good human-relations technique, diffusing potential opposition, and it actually produces good input. Arabs prefer consultation on a person-to-person basis; they hate committees and group meetings. Arabs make decisions in an informal and unstructured manner.

Some of our professional business approaches seem to them rigid and impersonal. Their heritage is not one of enclosed offices but of open spaces, tents, and generous hospitality. As a result, you may find your meetings interrupted by the constant commotion of people coming and going, telephone calls, and servants offering beverages. If you insist on a more formal style, you may be at a disadvantage.

Because Far Eastern Cultures and Religions Tend to Emphasize Harmony and the Perfectability of Humans, Group Decision Making Predominates. Despite Japanese emphasis on rank and status, business emphasizes group participation, group harmony, and group decision making. The Japanese manager is a facilitator whose role is not to take charge but to improve the initiatives of others and nurture an environment in which employees work together for the good of the company. The Japanese executive plays a key role in decision making, but not a lonely role. Responsibility for the corporation's success rests with all employees.

The bottom-up style of Japanese decision making can be unnerving for Westerners accustomed to the issuance of orders from above. Americans in Japanese-run companies complain, "Our Japanese executives seem to be waiting to rubber-stamp our initiatives, while the American executives are waiting for the Japanese top management to establish objectives." Without objectives from above, the Americans don't know what to initiate.

Managing Japanese employees is by no means a passive function. When a Japanese employee brings in a proposal, you must suggest and encourage, and perhaps send that person back for more answers until the proposal is improved enough to warrant being referred higher in the organization where the same questioning process will be continued.

While employees are involved in the decision-making process, the Japanese system does not require that all participants approve of all actions. Their seals on a document containing a decision indicate satisfaction that their point of view has been fairly heard, not necessarily their full approval of a decision. The Japanese consensus-making process may take a long time, but once a decision has been reached, it will be implemented quickly, because details have been worked out and support won in advance of the decision.

In Taiwan, Hong Kong, Singapore, and South Korea, Confucianism very much affects management practices. Harmony and benevolent paternalism are the guiding principles, and business units are run like families. Managers are paternalistic figures to employee "children," and just as a parent is responsible for the child's behavior, so the manager is responsible for the employee's performance. When employees do not do well, their "parents" lose face. There is a strong sense of family pulling together: No employee alone can be responsible for the company. Consensus is important.

In China, too, workers must be involved. The paramount task of a supervisor is to create a cooperative work atmosphere and sense of common purpose. The Chinese ritual of "taking the mass line" is

---

Set Clock on Local Time

When Dick Burns was the assistant general manager for Sears' overseas buying office in Hong Kong, his superiors complained to him that the employees were coming in too late each morning. They did come late, but they also worked until seven or eight each night. When management at home became irritated with the apparent lack of work discipline, Burns was told to get the people in earlier. He passed the order along: "I get in here at nine, and from now on I want everybody here at nine." The employees did exactly as they were told—all arrived promptly at nine, and left at four forty-five. A lot of work did not get done. Eventually Burns told the employees to go back to their old ways—and they got back to their normal, highly productive rate.

one the visitor to China must learn in order to manage people effectively. The process involves calling meetings of senior and middle-level staff to explain the importance of work goals and methods before a job begins. Employees make suggestions, and having been consulted, are inclined to feel that the job warrants their effort. These managers then convey the "mass line" message down to the workers. The Chinese resist being pushed, and the Westerner who cannot finesse the local management practices may encounter foot-dragging among personnel.

WORK ETHIC AND MOTIVATION

Americans perceive many foreigners as poor workers. "No work ethic," we say, meaning "lazy." Yet a universal concern of Japanese, Swiss, and others who take over American firms or invest in the United States is that perpetual problem of getting the American labor force to produce. The problem boils down not to laziness but to conflict between culturally different patterns of job behavior, management styles, and the role that work plays in the employee's life. To get performance out of people, you have to understand the local meaning of "work ethic."

Rule 4: Know Why People Work and How the Job Fits Into Their Life

If you want a road built from Oesso to Brazzaville, start at Oesso. Your crew will work harder to get to the big city, a place they want to go, than they will if going through a jungle to nowhere. You must recognize the reality of what drives the people you are managing. In Japan, employees are wedded to their company. Their attention and energies are concentrated on the company—their personal life is their company life, and its future is their future. Compared to Americans,

who are job- rather than company-oriented, the Japanese are generally much better informed about their company's business, and easily step outside their own tasks to help colleagues. American business is more segmented and cellular; parochial attitudes prevail. Americans "mind their own business" and feel little loyalty to a company. When we are displeased with salaries, company policies, or personalities, we resign.

The Latin American, on the other hand, tends to work not for a company or for a job, but for an individual. People strive for personal power. Relationships and loyalties are much more personalized, and managers can get performance only by effectively using personal influence and working through individual members of a group. Among Turks and Arabs, too, the individual is supreme, although inextricably integrated with family and society. Employees tend to be evaluated on their loyalty to superiors more than on actual job performance.

Familiarity Breeds Confusion

An American manager at the beginning of his term in France rented a large and beautiful apartment and invited everyone in his office to this place for a big party. The French were horrified—first, most French employees are not invited into the privacy of their boss's home; and second, he had invited employees of all levels in the organization and their spouses, people who normally did not mix socially and who would not know what to say to one another. But they had to go because of his high position in the company. Once at the apartment, of course, they were not blind to the evidence of the American's affluence and personal memorabilia. The party was a disaster, with long-term repercussions.

Australians say they "go to work to get vacation." They have the shortest working hours in the world, and they need their frequent "smoke-ohs" (smoking breaks) during the day. To the French, the *qualité de la vie* is what matters. Until recently, the French government had a minister in charge of quality of life. The French cling to their free time and vacations: They resist working overtime and have the longest vacations in the world, by law a minimum of five weeks a year. German firms, too, are moving in this direction. However, both French and Germans usually exert themselves during work hours, and have a reputation of being productive and concerned with quality.

Rule 5: There's no Race if Nobody Wants to Run

In America, competition is the name of the game: Everyone wants to be a winner. Elsewhere, competition in the workplace means everyone loses, either because people go off in their own directions or because they stop dead in their tracks.

In Greece they say: "Two Greeks will do badly what one will do well." Greek teams work well only when a strong leader is available to set goals and settle conflicts. In South America, a team is likely to get stuck in power plays among equally strong-willed individuals. Generally speaking, in countries where people are inexperienced in cooperative working relationships, leadership and responsibilities should be delineated clearly. If class, race, and other social divisions are strong, it is important to be sensitive to intergroup hostilities and social practices.

Where cooperation is an art form, as in Japan, Taiwan, and other Asian countries, creating competition can bring work to a halt. The goal is to maintain group harmony, but you can effectively stir competition against those outside the group. Needless to say, Japanese concern for harmony does not keep Japanese companies from competing all-out with U.S. firms.

Rule 6: Use the Right Carrot for the Culture

Carefully consider incentives and rewards—what's appropriate and effective at home may produce surprising results abroad. A financial bonus for a star performer could easily humiliate a Japanese, Chinese, or Yugoslav employee.

Individual goals are highly personal in any country; people are not the same, nor is an individual necessarily consistent over time. Aspirations may change at different stages of a career. Nevertheless, there are patterns that prevail in different countries, and it is useful to know them.

In America, money is a driving force. A satisfactory wage is essential, or an American will be extremely discontented. Elsewhere, managers are more likely to emphasize respect, family or job security, good personal life, social acceptance, advancement, or power.

In some countries, rewards for workers are limited. In Russia, there are few motivational options, and bonuses are the norm, based on a percentage of salary. Asked what would motivate Soviets, the official at the USSR consulate in San Francisco says, "discipline." An American who lived in Moscow says that money is not a motivator because there is practically nothing to buy. Yet there is a tremendous craving for Western goods, and people can be rewarded with *things* instead of cash. If you make Western goods available to a Soviet citizen, however, never accept payment and always make clear that it is a gift, because it is illegal for you to sell to Soviets.

Carrots Are Not Green—Don't Forget Nonfinancial Rewards. Many observers say the reward that seems to work best in many places is appreciation. In Taiwan, the most highly sought reward is affection and social recognition from the top. Cash bonuses are given out across the board, but departments compete for top management's public praise at the annual celebration.

Japanese companies do offer cash rewards to individuals, but payments are nominal. Matsushita Electric gave a factory worker $13 for suggesting a device to stop solder from dripping down the endplates of television sets and causing short circuits. Another worker received $100 for 60 suggestions accepted in a year. At Mitsubishi Electric, ten members of a quality circle jointly received a cash reward of $200 for suggesting the best cost-reduction idea of the year. Most companies prefer to rely on nonfinancial rewards. At some plants, rectangular cards are hung from the ceiling directly above some of the workers, showing the production count or marking the group for its excellent performance.

There are many alternatives to money: job security, vacations, parties, gifts, sports or health facilities, services, prestigious titles, and public or private praise, to mention a few. The rule is to match the reward with the values of the culture. The wrong reward can be as insulting as extra time off given to the American manager who still hasn't taken last year's vacation.

SUPERVISING PEOPLE

Rule 7: Avoid Blame, Avoid Shame

Nobody likes to be criticized, especially in front of others. But Americans sometimes fail to take the sting out of "helpful" comments. In the United States, one is supposed to accept criticism as valuable feedback; an employee might even thank a manager for being frank. It is a big mistake to behave this way anywhere else in the world, however—with the possible exception of Australia.

To Arabs, Africans, Asians, and Latin Americans, preservation of dignity is an all-important value. Those who lose self-respect, or the respect of others, dishonor both themselves and their families. Public criticism is intolerable. If you use harsh words, or even contradict a person, foreigners will unite in antagonism against you. The result of a confrontation with employees or servants will be such a shock that they may leave the job. In a unionized work situation, there might be some kind of employee action. When irreconcilable positions are reached, a third-party mediator is often crucial.

Experienced travelers say that, reward systems aside, the only way to enforce a standard of performance is by courteous exhortation, lots of explanation and conversation, humor, and an appeal to the foreigner's sense of cooperation. Jim Kelso, after 22 years with Occidental Petroleum in Indonesia and Libya, says: "Keep telling them, 'Good try ... That's great ... What would happen if you tried it this way?' Never make it personal or emotional." If you fail and cause loss of face, enmity will be undying.

Rule 8: Supervising is a Job That is Never Done

A magnificent new hotel in China, equipped with the most modern accoutrements and grandly decorated, soon looks shabby: tiles become loose, potted plants die, and the paint peels. In Mexico, a stunning necklace, obviously made with much skill and time, is precariously held together by the flimsiest of tin clasps. In Cairo, an ambitious development project is announced, but then fails to materialize.

International travelers find a pattern of incompleteness that is most frustrating. The American manager wants to assume that once something is planned and under way, the hard part is over. Not so. In many places, just as much attention must be given to the final stages and to continuing maintenance. The expectation around the world is that managers must follow up on a job once it is assigned.

Supervisors also encounter a lack of support, both in newly opened and well-established offices and plants. Skills they consider fundamental are unavailable, and on-the-job training becomes necessary just to keep an operation going. Americans are especially irked that secretaries do not take responsibility, as we define it. They may speak English, but they are not educated in clerical skills, and can't whip out memos or set up a filing system. They are not trained that way. In Japan, they only serve tea and handle personal things. Many of the demands made by an American boss can be very disturbing to them. One Bechtel manager says it made his Japanese secretary physically ill when he tried to make her take responsibility.

HIRING AND FIRING

Western work discipline, such as regular office hours, quality standards, honesty, and avoidance of conflict of interest are not part of the value system everywhere. Pilfering, neglect of machinery and equipment, absenteeism, and bribery are problems worldwide. Employees and managers may feel no compunction about using company assets and company time for their own personal benefit, even to the extent of starting small businesses using company supplies.

Rule 9: Think Creatively About Where to Find Employees

Sources of personnel vary widely from country to country, and you will have to find people in unaccustomed places. In Thailand, men tend toward the civil service and the legal profession, so business-women are a valuable resource in all segments of business. In developing countries such as Ethiopia, managerial candidates may be found among an educated elite, or among former military officers, who are more likely to have some

technical training and refined work values. British managers come from the population at large, but French managers are drawn from the elite educational institutions. Only 6 percent of Italian personnel managers come from blue-collar families, compared with 38 percent in the United States. In developing countries, it may be necessary to bring in "third-country nationals" or search for nationals within U.S. graduate schools.

Regardless of the work assigned to them, individuals with certain family or educational status often expect the same respect at work that they receive in their local communities. Thus, young university graduates in Latin America, the Middle East, and parts of the Far East may refuse "degrading" dirty work or manual training. Often, when a young man gets a degree, he expects immediately to have a plush office, staff, and an exorbitant salary, even though he has had no managerial experience or business training. The hiring process should take these sentiments into consideration. In some jobs it may be best to hire totally inexperienced workers who have not learned work habits that clash with your needs. Often trainability is more important than prior training or experience.

Rule 10: There is More to a Job Applicant Than Work Qualifications

What Western society condemns as nepotism, another values as family loyalty. When a foreign company is acquired, numerous relatives, family members, and friends may be found employed in key positions.

When one American multinational corporation set up a model operation in Pakistan, the American managers had to deal with job-seeking relatives of customs officials and government officials. The first year was difficult—often approval to import needed materials depended on the hiring of someone's nephew. The company worked hard to be firm without being arrogant, and adopted a policy of hiring relatives who had the skills but not those who didn't.

Once management established a reputation for being fair, a singular level of trust was attained. The plant became Pakistani-run in only five years—an outstanding success. The lesson is that you need not adopt the local hiring norms, but if you don't, you must be sensitive in your handling of the situation. The company was able to make clear that in return for providing top-notch training, opportunity, and good pay, management expected an unusual degree of responsibility.

Cultural Collision

Not long ago, the supervisor on an American oil rig in Indonesia was almost killed, simply because he shamed an employee. Exasperated by the poor performance of an Indonesian employee, the manager exploded and barked at his timekeeper, "Tell that man to pack his bags and take the next boat to shore." Even with his limited English, the worker could tell he was being criticized and guessed he was being fired. Within moments, a mob of outraged Indonesians had grabbed the fire axes that lined the rig's scaffolding and went after the American, chasing him around the deck. He escaped and barricaded himself in his quarters. The angry crew was chopping down the door and virtually upon him when help arrived.

This incident is a dramatic example of cultural collision. The American manager had violated certain principles of behavior that are profoundly important to Indonesians. First, he lost his temper in a culture where peace, harmony, and emotional restraint are all-important. Second, he disregarded the Indonesian's distinct concept of fairness. Superiors in Indonesia are expected to deal with their subordinates as fathers deal with children, sternly but sympathetically. Third, he shamed the man in front of others. One simply *never* berates an Indonesian in public.

The American boss tends to look at employees in many separate, but not equally important, categories. "Bill is the best salesman in the business," we hear, "and he also plays a great game of tennis." To the American, it is the work performance that is of primary importance. The employer considering hiring an individual in America will weigh evidence of the applicant's potential strengths and weaknesses in performing the job.

In Islamic countries, the employee's personality and social behavior in the workplace are more notable than his specific knowledge or skills. A Moslem manager might easily say, "Hussein is a nice man. I am most pleased to have such a fine person with my company who is also such a good engineer." A manager considering two job applicants will be less concerned about previous experience or education if the individual seems well-intentioned and able to learn. He is more likely to ask: Is the employee a good person? Do I like him? Does he need the job financially? Will he be loyal? And, finally, Would it please God to provide him this job?

The Job Interview May Be Unlike Anything You Have Seen at Home. An American executive recruiting a Lebanese office manager was surprised when the young man brought his uncle to the interview and the uncle did all the talking. In Lebanon, it would be immodest for a job applicant to speak highly of himself, hence the need for a spokesman who can expound on the applicant's merits. In India and Pakistan, an interviewee presents school records, diplomas, and awards, all of which are closely scrutinized by the interviewer.

In China workers will very modestly present their talents. For the American, an interview is a lesson in humility beyond most Westerner's experience. Even the most highly skilled job applicants will minimize their skills, and the employer will have to know their history or see evidence of their work to get the true picture.

Rule 11: Don't Assume Any Foreign Appearance Will Do

An American advertiser recently thought he was being culturally sensitive by hiring a Chinese–American woman to produce his commercial in Japan. Fortunately, she told him how wrong he was. There is still tremendous animosity between the Chinese and Japanese. Moreover, a second-generation Chinese- or Japanese–American is far from the real thing. Along the same lines, a South American complains, "It's a real insult when they send down a Latin exile to manage us."

Another common management mistake is to send a U.S. manager to the company's operations in one single country and then bring the manager back to the home office as the expert for the entire area. A year in Egypt does not make anyone an Arab expert, nor does a year in Venezuela make anyone a South American expert. Any such "expert" should have at least a second-country assignment to provide exposure to differences as well as to fundamental similarities. As one expert suggests, the aim is to *beware* of generalizing from one country to another, but also *be aware* of what they do have in common.

Rule 12: Easy to employ, difficult to discharge

International managers struggle with the problem of finding good personnel, but a tougher problem is getting rid of employees who don't work out. From Switzerland to Mexico to Indonesia, the unsentimental American "hire and fire" habit seems unnaturally brutal to foreign employees. Foreign personnel are usually more firmly attached to their company, and they are used to being protected during their working lives. Firing is never abrupt or taken lightly.

Foreign workers are protected by strong labor laws and union rules, and the employer who is unaware of them will risk costly lawsuits and penalties.

Ignorance of the law is no excuse. A Mexican labor law, for example, gives workers complete protection. After a 30-day trial period, they are regarded as virtually permanent employees. British law protects a manager against "loss of office." Belgian labor laws are among the toughest in the world, and Belgian social benefits are the most liberal in Europe.

In Indonesia, you can't fire people without a long process of government red tape. An employer must give three written warnings over a year, specifying the bad work, with written copies distributed to certain officials. A manager must meet with the employee to suggest changes in performance, and do it diplomatically. One old hand advises, "Offer him a transfer somewhere else in the company, and over three years you can move him from job to job until he can be eased down to the kitchen and out the back door."

In the USSR, workers are guaranteed jobs—the government boasts there is no unemployment—and only serious infractions justify dismissal. Visitors to Russia must hire Soviets through the UPDK (Agency to Provide Assistance to the Diplomatic Corps), the agency that supplies all personnel. You can fire an employee, but the UPDK is not likely to make a replacement for a long time.

Even where laws do not tie employee to employer, firing is not without consequences. In the Taiwanese and other paternalistic cultures, dismissal is considered the failure of the superior, who has failed to get adequate performance from his "child." It is better to shift unsatisfactory workers to "uncles" in other departments.

Personnel Problems Are Not Easier in a Joint Venture. You can't always rely on your foreign partners to play fair when it comes to choosing local staff, and you must beware of becoming a dumping ground for all the people your partner doesn't want. It is common company practice to divert people who are no longer needed in one company into ventures considered less important. But if you ac-cept these rejects, it is virtually impossible to get rid of them, and you have little choice but to try to get the best you can out of them.

A great deal, of course, depends on the motivations of your foreign partner in entering a business relationship. The more the foreigners have invested in the joint venture and the more concerned they are for its success, the less likely they are to give you poor personnel. Executives with experience in foreign joint ventures and partnerships say that quality of staffing must be clearly defined during negotiations; it is too late after a deal is made.

Formal Mentoring Programs Are No Panacea

REBA L. KEELE, KATHY BUCKNER, and SHERI J. BUSHNELL

Because of American corporations' preoccupation with developing managers through mentor relationships, some human resources departments have established formal programs in which each newcomer is assigned to an experienced person as a "protégé." These programs, however, are based on a misunderstanding of what makes developmental relationships valuable in career development; success with formal mentoring programs is primarily fortuitous, and is dependent upon the organization's culture. In fact, assigned mentor-protégé programs may inhibit employee development rather than enhance it.

The point missed by many advocates of mentoring is that while mentors do indeed provide emotional, appraisal, instrumental, and informational support, so do a wide variety of other relationships. The table compares the mentor-protégé relationship to a social network of many different kinds of developmental relationships. For human resource managers to assume that mentoring is essential in developing managers is a mistake that may have negative consequences. Relationships with many people, of varying intensities and types, will accomplish the same result as a single-mentor relationship, without its potential limitations for the organization and the individual.

Formal mentoring programs, in which older managers are assigned to younger ones, generally have been successful only in organizations where they have not been needed. Misconceptions about why successful programs worked, and about the nature of mentor relationships may inspire other companies to attempt to establish them. Recently we were approached by representatives of a manufacturing company concerned about the relatively flat hierarchy in their organization, with its implications of career plateauing at a fairly young age. The human resources department had decided that a mentoring program would fill its need. The problem with this proposal was that they did not understand what mentoring is; the value of other developmental relationships; and what it would take for their company to make such a program work.

WHAT IS MENTORING?

Mentoring relationships are relatively exclusive, intensive, mentor-controlled, and voluntary. They require a high personal investment. Such relationships cannot be assigned. If an assigned relationship does succeed, success is the result of the luck of the draw, or a different relationship has been labeled a mentor-protégé relationship.

For example, a frequently mentioned successful "mentor" program exists at the Internal Revenue Service. The IRS calls its experienced executives "coaches." What the IRS *has* created is a development program for managers who have been identified by a rigorous selection process as candidates for the district director position. These candidates participate in a six-month program designed to create opportunities for a strong social network and to expose them to the tasks required of district directors. (One candidate spent time in 15 different cities over the six-month training period.)

These candidates have no formal work requirements and no boss. Each is assigned to a high-ranking official, who is available to them mainly through telephone and computer networks because of travel limitations. This coach helps the candidates synthesize and integrate their experience. Although not a true mentoring system, this program is likely to be successful. Because of the cross-functional opportunities, the candidate has to interact with many different people on work-related tasks. However, it may have the problems of any fast-track management development program, including the potential relative neglect of employees not on this track.

What about other formal programs? Security Pacific National Bank selected as mentors only those executives who al-

---

Mentor Relationships vs. Social Networks

Mentor-Protégé Relationship	*Social Network Relationships*
Relatively exclusive.	May include hundreds of people.
Long-term, but time limited (2–10 years).	Varying durations, depending on many factors.
High investment, strong ties.	Strong and weak ties.
Almost always with superior.	Includes ties with higher-ups, peers, employees, and outsiders.
More focus on mentor's agenda.	More focus on own agenda.
Mentor has more relative power in relationship.	More power lies with individual.
Limited availability, especially to women and minorities.	Available to more people.
Dependent on mentor's resources.	Broader resource base.
Source of emotional, appraisal, instrumental, and informational support (one relationship).	Source of emotional, appraisal, instrumental, and informational support (many relationships).

ready had a track record of developing other people. The protégés were people for whom a particular opening was being targeted. They were given formal training in career goals and management techniques, and the "mentors" served as a resource for solving problems in the protégés' jobs.

At the Jewel Companies, certain managers were assigned as mentors because of their recognized talent and ability to teach. All managers were evaluated on their efforts to develop lower-level employees. In this organization, support for a mentoring system has been demonstrated by a pattern of protégés succeeding their mentors as chief executive officer. Thus, there is a strong corporate culture that reinforces management development.

COMMON FACTORS

We propose that successful formal mentoring programs have the following characteristics:

1. They are a small part of management development programs for selected fast-track employees. The more closely the program resembles a true mentoring program, the fewer protégés can be involved, because of the time demands of such relationships.
2. They emphasize *coaching*, rather than mentoring. The relationship is limited by its task-oriented focus, and by a specific time period or job goal.
3. The organization's culture supports developing managers, and there are formal or informal rewards for doing so.

POTENTIAL NEGATIVE EFFECTS

If formal mentoring programs *can* contribute to developing managers, why do we express such concern about their es-

tablishment? We believe they have potentially negative consequences that would not be present in a program emphasizing a broader range of relationships.

The protégés' high expectations about the mentor and his or her role in their career progress are unlikely to be met. The word "mentor" has a trainload of connotations, and any program labeled "mentoring" almost certainly will accomplish less—and require more—for most participants than they had expected. This may lead to disappointment and possibly resentment.

The time involved in developing a "mentor" relationship and the importance placed on it by a formal program may lead protégés to pay too little attention to developing connections with other people essential to their success in the organization. The most effective general managers in one study numbered their first-name relationships in the hundreds. Building that kind of extended network requires energy and time.

There never could be enough mentors for everyone who might want one. Therefore, few potential protégés are offered the opportunity to be mentored, and assigned mentors may not have adequate skills in developing others, or their own careers may be stymied.

The more highly selective the mentoring program, the more likely it is that it will suffer from problems common to most fast-track programs. These include discouraging those not selected and tempting employees to seek visibility rather than invest in long-term, less visible efforts.

If mentors are not direct supervisors of protégés, there is risk of creating or exacerbating problems between the protégés and their immediate supervisors and peers. However, it is not advisable to assign direct supervisors as mentors, because inequities between those supervised result.

The most important consequence of formal mentoring programs is also the most subtle. Mentors take the blame for protégés' mistakes, acting as protectors until employees are established enough to withstand direct criticism. Mentors are *responsible* for showing the ropes of the organization to protégés, who in turn give mentors at least partial credit for their successes. To the extent that this happens, protégés are less likely to pay attention to the need for their own active involvement in learning essential skills and knowing essential people.

ENCOURAGING DEVELOPMENTAL RELATIONSHIPS

Since all these potential consequences could be serious for the organization or individual, what do we recommend as an approach to encouraging effective relationships in management development?

An organization's primary goal should be to create conditions conducive to *network formation*, rather than to assign mentors. While many of the same conditions also would encourage mentoring, there should be subtle but critical differences in focus. The protégé who expects to have an assigned mentor may defer personal responsibility for his or her career development. The mentor is to be a protector, coach, and guide, thus assuming some measure of responsibility for the protégé's success or failure.

However, the central person in a network understands that making contact with many people can extend one's resources. Others may sponsor, protect, guide, and coach—just as the mentor does—but the responsibility for choosing network members and building connections belongs to the individual.

What are the characteristics of organizations which foster network formation?

1. They have opportunities for cross-departmental interaction.
2. Their reward systems reinforce the development of peers and lower-level employees.
3. They emphasize the use of diverse and complementary people in teams whenever appropriate.
4. Their teams include persons not identified as on the "fast track."
5. They educate all employees on how to build relationships and get things done in that organization.

CONCLUSION

While mentoring relationships can be extremely helpful, they are not readily available for most employees, and formal programs may create unintended problems. We recommend that organizations instead consider the extent to which their structure and culture encourage employees at all levels to build networks of relationships that contribute to their job effectiveness.

It's Time to Punt Those Macho Old Metaphors

J.B. RITCHIE

"What this outfit needs is fewer tight ends and more wide receivers." With that terse football metaphor, the chief executive of a large corporation tried to summarize his company's problems and suggest a solution. It was clear he assumed that his insight would be understood and accepted by other company executives.

What he failed to realize was that his metaphor was deeply flawed, as are those used by so many managers. It communicated a narrow, shallow view of the firm's woes, betrayed his own inability to articulate a careful analysis, alienated employees who found the metaphor inappropriate and confused those unfamiliar with football.

In consulting with dozens of corporations each year, I witness the extensive use and powerful impact of spoken and written metaphors. To explain or clarify complex situations, executives commonly draw on simpler and less ambiguous images in life.

Although this can be an effective way to make a point, the misuse of metaphors often leads to serious problems. The way we talk and write frames the way we look at the world and shapes the way we think.

The sports metaphor, along with two other common and outmoded images—military and cowboy metaphors—can become obsessive and may distort and limit thoughtful analysis. Thus, organizations

Reprinted by permission of the Los Angeles Times and the author.

frequently lose the capacity to think and act appropriately because they are trapped unconsciously in an irrelevant, or even destructive, paradigm.

Years ago, when I started working with the telecommunications industry, I became aware of the use of metaphors as a management device. Some of the metaphors were helpful, but many were rooted in the irrelevant past—the traditional Ma Bell monopoly. In meetings and memos, telephone company employees frequently referred to their firm as a "protective family."

This means, of course, that since you do not fire your kids, neither do you terminate workers. This value created severe conflicts when a streamlined telephone company no longer needed so many employees.

Employees also spoke of "universal service"—the idea that they had to provide all telephone-related services. They also talked as though they were the only ones who could possibly provide telephone services properly. And they spoke with contempt for anyone who would dare challenge them, question their authority and, ultimately, compete with them.

In rejecting new ideas, especially from younger managers, people in the telecommunications industry and other businesses sometimes would say that an individual had not yet earned his or her spurs and thus didn't have the right to suggest policy.

These employees and their managers

were operating under what I call the cowboy management metaphor. They had the notion that they were riding a sort of infinite prairie or range over which they had exclusive control. Like the cowboy, they had to do everything within that sphere. The cowboy cooks meals, makes his bed at night, herds and brands cattle, shoots the bears. When confronted by an enemy, he relies on his cunning, his fists or his six-shooter.

The notion that "a Smith & Wesson beats four aces"—a phrase I've heard many times—is a cowboy prescription for a company's problem. It justifies extreme, often slightly illegal, behavior when more rational means aren't working. But it is just when the stakes are high and the road rough that metaphors gather strength and become dangerous. At that point, they not only reflect the organization's or leader's philosophy and style, but they tend to reinforce narrow thinking that can exacerbate a problem.

That is not to say that metaphors are never useful. They can be a powerful, even elegant, means of sharing a larger vision and its subtleties. The combination of richness and brevity is compelling. Examples include terms that reflect love, support and acceptance, used by companies such as Hewlett-Packard that want to foster a spirit of cooperation.

The issue, then, is not whether metaphors ought to be used at all, but which are appropriate under which circumstances. Is the metaphor a refinement of good analysis or a substitution for it? Do the "football games" played in the board room really improve the company, or do they place a "scoreboard" in a setting where there shouldn't be one?

Keeping score may work in sports, but what of the destructive behavior it inspires or justifies where people need support and understanding instead of a win-at-all-costs value system? And what of these metaphors' overwhelming male perspective in an increasingly mixed-gender workplace?

In the most effective organizations today, I see declining use of male-oriented, simplistic metaphors and increasing use of music metaphors. The symphony conductor, who oversees men and women expert at playing only one or two instruments, works splendidly as a metaphor for leadership in the contemporary workplace where high specialization is the norm.

The conductor must know his or her musicians well and carefully coordinate their efforts. The musicians all play off the same score, but each contributes his or her own skill and personal artistic sense.

More broadly, the ideas of harmony, consonance, balance, beauty, beat, key and complexity are widely applicable. These concepts work so well in so many situations, in fact, that I frequently prescribe music metaphors for managers who want to tap into the power of figurative language without the harmful side effects they risk with the older metaphors.

It appears, then, that the *macho* metaphors of the past are receding from view but still are all too frequent. For those who fight it, old habits die hard. But effectiveness in today's work world must begin with a broader, more realistic picture of the people who make up organizations—and most are no longer just living out boyhood games and dreams.

"There are no bad regiments only bad colonels."

Napoleon

"All decisions should be made as low as possible in the organization. The charge of the Light Brigade was ordered by an officer who wasn't looking at the territory."

Robert Townsend, Up the Organization

It's said that a good manager may get his team between five and ten more wins a year than a middling skipper would, and a bad manager may cost his team even more games than that. The game is basically very simple. If you get good players, you win. I've never seen a manager win a pennant. Players win pennants.

Sports Illustrated (April 13, 1981)

"Leadership is figuring out which way your people are going and running fast enough to get in front of them."

Gandhi

Managers are hired to be fired.

Sports Illustrated (April 13, 1981)

BILLY MARTIN, Manager

	HIRED	FIRED
Minnesota Twins	1969	1969
Detroit Tigers	1971	1973
Texas Rangers	1973	1975
New York Yankees	1975	1978
New York Yankees (Rehired)	1979	1979
Oakland A's	1980	1982
New York Yankees (Rehired)	1982	1983
New York Yankees (Rehired)	1985	1985
New York Yankees (Rehired)	1987	1988

EXERCISES

Supervisory Style Exercise

While many factors can determine the effectiveness of supervisory behavior, this exercise highlights the relationship between a supervisor's assumptions about people and his or her leadership strategy.

Part of the class should develop a supervisory approach based on the first set of assumptions (Supervisor X) and another part on the second set (Supervisor Y). Then compare the strategies based on different assumptions.

SUPERVISOR X

You are a supervisor in a manufacturing plant and are responsible for the production of a small group of workers. According to personnel manning requirements, your group is fully staffed. As far as you know, there is no problem with machine operation, and the quality of raw materials seems to be consistently high.

While your group has had a good history of satisfactory performance, in recent weeks the quality and quantity of production have both declined substantially.

On the basis of the following assumptions, which you believe to be true regarding people generally, what would you do to correct the current situation and to prevent it from recurring in the future?

1. People are basically lazy, have an inherent dislike of work, and will go to great lengths to avoid work assignments.
2. People generally must be closely controlled, directed, and threatened with punishment in order to obtain satisfactory performance.
3. People generally want to avoid responsibility and prefer the security of a less demanding job.
4. People need a clear-cut organization hierarchy with each job spelled out in great detail.

SUPERVISOR Y

You are a supervisor in a manufacturing plant and are responsible for the production of a small group of workers. According to personnel manning requirements, your group is fully staffed. As far as you know, there is no problem with machine operation, and the quality of raw materials seems to be consistently high.

While your group has had a good history of satisfactory performance, in recent weeks the quality and quantity of production have both declined substantially.

On the basis of the following assumptions, which you believe to be true regarding people generally, what would you do to correct the current situation and to prevent it from recurring in the future?

1. People basically enjoy productive work and receive a great deal of satis-

faction from making a worthwhile contribution to the organization.
2. People will exercise a great deal of self-direction and self-control in solving organizational problems and performing their job.

3. People generally will accept and seek responsibility in order to satisfy achievement and ego needs.
4. People have a great deal of untapped potential and can make a substantial contribution in defining their job.

Leadership Exercise

T–P Leadership Questionnaire: An assessment of style *

In your attempt to achieve results through different leadership approaches, you might focus on one technique or goal. For example, you may see some leaders dealing with general directions, leaving details to subordinates. Other leaders focus on specific details with the expectation that subordinates will carry out orders. Depending on the situation, both approaches can be effective. The important issue is the ability to identify relevant dimensions of the situation and behave accordingly.

In this exercise you can identify your relative emphasis on two dimensions of leadership—"task orientation" and "people orientation." These are not opposite approaches, and an individual can be high or low on either or both.

* The T–P Leadership Questionnaire was adapted from Sergiovanni, Metzcus, and Bruden's revision of the Leadership Behavior Description Questionnaire, *American Educational Research Journal* 6 (1969): 62–79.

Goal

To evaluate oneself in terms of task orientation and people orientation.

Group size

Unlimited.

Time Required

Approximately forty-five minutes.

Materials

1. T–P Leadership Questionnaire.
2. T–P Leadership–Style Profile Sheet.

Process

1. Fill out the T–P Leadership Questionnaire.
2. Before the questionnaires are scored, it may be appropriate to discuss the concept of shared leadership as a function of the combined concern for task and people.
3. In order to locate oneself on the Leadership–Style Profile Sheet, each group participant will score his own questionnaire on the dimensions of task orientation (T) and people orientation (P).
4. The T–P Leadership Questionnaire is scored as follows:
   a. Circle the item number for items 8, 12, 17, 18, 19, 30, 34, and 35.
   b. Write the number 1 in front of a *circled item number* if you responded S (seldom) or N (never) to that item.
   c. Also write a number 1 in front of *item numbers not circled* if you responded A (always) or F (frequently):
   d. Circle the number 1's which you have written in front of the following items: 3, 5, 8, 10, 15, 18, 19, 22, 24, 26, 28, 30, 32, 34, and 35.
   e. *Count the circled number 1's.* This is your score for concern for people. Record the score in the blank following the letter P at the end of the questionnaire.
   f. *Count uncircled number 1's.* This is your score for concern for task. Record this number in the blank following the letter T.
5. Follow directions on the Leadership–Style Profile Sheet. A discussion of implications members attach to their location on the profile would be appropriate.

Variations

1. Participants can predict how they will appear on the profile prior to scoring the questionnaire.
2. Paired participants already acquainted can predict each other's scores. If they are not acquainted, they can discuss their reactions to the questionnaire items to form some basis for this prediction.
3. The leadership styles represented on the profile sheet can be illustrated through role-playing. A relevant situation can be set up, and the "leaders" can be coached to demonstrate the styles being studied.
4. Subgroups can be formed of participants similarly situated on the shared leadership scale. These groups can be assigned identical tasks to perform. The data generated can be processed in terms of morale and productivity.

T–P leadership questionnaire

Directions: The following items describe aspects of leadership behavior. Respond to each item according to the way you would most likely act if you were the leader of a work group. Circle whether you would most likely behave in the described way: always (A), frequently (F), occasionally (O), seldom (S), or never (N).

A F O S N   1.   I would most likely act as the spokesman of the group.

A F O S N   2.   I would encourage overtime work.

A F O S N   3.   I would allow members complete freedom in their work.

A F O S N   4.   I would encourage the use of uniform procedures.

A F O S N   5.   I would permit members to use their own judgment in solving problems.

A F O S N   6.   I would stress being ahead of competing groups.

A F O S N   7.   I would speak as a representative of the group.

A F O S N   8.   I would needle members for greater effort.

A F O S N   9.   I would try out my ideas in the group.

A F O S N   10.   I would let members do their work the way they think best.

A F O S N   11.   I would be working hard for a promotion.

A F O S N   12.   I would tolerate postponement and uncertainty.

A F O S N   13.   I would speak for the group if there were visitors present.

A F O S N   14.   I would keep the work moving at a rapid pace.

A F O S N   15.   I would turn the members loose on a job and let them go to it.

A F O S N   16.   I would settle conflicts when they occur in the group.

A F O S N   17.   I would get swamped by details.

A F O S N   18.   I would represent the group at outside meetings.

A F O S N   19.   I would be reluctant to allow the members any freedom of action.

A F O S N   20.   I would decide what should be done and how it should be done.

A F O S N   21.   I would push for increased production.

A F O S N   22.   I would let some members have authority which I could keep.

A F O S N   23.   Things would usually turn out as I had predicted.

A F O S N   24.   I would allow the group a high degree of initiative.

A F O S N   25.   I would assign group members to particular tasks.

A F O S N   26.   I would be willing to make changes.

A F O S N   27.   I would ask the members to work harder.

A F O S N   28.   I would trust the group members to exercise good judgment.

A F O S N   29.   I would schedule the work to be done.

A F O S N   30.   I would refuse to explain my actions.

A F O S N   31.   I would persuade others that my ideas are to their advantage.

A F O S N   32.   I would permit the group to set its own pace.

A F O S N   33.   I would urge the group to beat its previous record.

A F O S N   34.   I would act without consulting the group.

A F O S N   35.   I would ask that group members follow standard rules and regulations.

T_____   P_____

T–P leadership-style profile sheet

Name_____ Group_____

Directions: To determine your style of leadership, mark your score on the *concern for task* dimension (T) on the left-hand arrow below. Next, move to the right-hand arrow and mark your score on the *concern for people* dimension (P). Draw a straight line that intersects the P and T scores. The point at which the line crosses the *shared leadership* arrow indicates your score on that dimension.

SHARED LEADERSHIP RESULTS FROM BALANCING CONCERN FOR TASK AND CONCERN FOR PEOPLE.

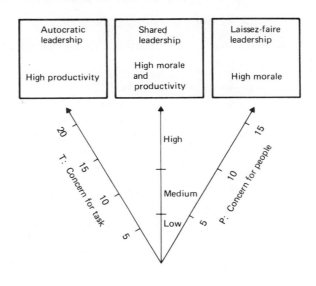

Who's in Charge Around Here?

Those in leadership roles never have perfect information regarding people or performance. Making good decisions with limited information is a real challenge. This role play is an opportunity for you to explore the process of deciding on an acceptable strategy in an awkward situation.

Try to think and act as if you really were the character whose role you have been assigned. Think of the role in terms of contemporary implications, and let your feelings develop as if you actually were involved. Should issues develop that are not covered by the role, adapt or innovate accordingly.

To conceptualize your role, it is usually best to read it carefully two or three times; then close the book and think about it for a few minutes. Do not read the other roles; try to develop an approach in terms of the information given and your own interpretation of how a person in that position would likely behave. After you have the role in mind, do not reread it during the process of the role play.

GENERAL INFORMATION

This incident takes place in a government agency in a large metropolitan area. Mr. Hall is the division manager, Cynthia is currently working as his staff assistant for special projects, and Jason is the supervisor in the department where Cynthia was previously a case worker.

Jason has been in his position for three months. He replaced Louise, who moved to another agency. One month ago Jason fired Cynthia. She immediately filed a complaint and, after a hearing by Mr. Hall, was reinstated. However, her case worker position had been filled in the meantime, and she was appointed as staff assistant to Mr. Hall, Jason's immediate superior.

ROLE FOR JASON

You are the department supervisor re-

sponsible for ten case workers and several supporting staff members. When you replaced Louise three months ago, you realized that things were very sloppy in the department. Many people were putting in six-hour days, and complaints were coming from clients and other agency units that depended on your department. After you talked to each case worker and held several department meetings, most of the staff members really went to work—all except Cynthia and one other, a man who voluntarily resigned. Cynthia acted as if she owned the place. She did a poor job with her clients, and no one in the department could stand her. Finally, after working with her for two months, you couldn't see any hope for changing her and feared that, if you didn't let her go, the morale of the unit would go down. So, you called her in and, following what you thought were the proper steps, terminated her.

Then, a few days later, she filed a complaint with Mr. Hall, your boss. Without even calling you in to discuss the issue, he considered the situation and rehired her. This made you a little suspicious. You remembered hearing that Cynthia "Had something" on Mr. Hall. Anyway, you were grateful that you had filled her slot prior to her rehiring, so that she couldn't be reassigned to your department. But instead, of all things, she was assigned to work as Mr. Hall's staff assistant.

With her appointment, morale really did go down. Everyone was saying that the way to get promoted was to do a bad job. Things were beginning to settle down until last week, when Cynthia came to your office to give you instructions on a project she was responsible for. This was too much; you blew up and told her where to go. Then Mr. Hall called to tell you that you would have to work with Cynthia. You requested to talk to him about the whole situation. You must somehow warn Hall about Cynthia—you think she will ruin his operation just as she almost ruined yours. He agreed to talk, and you are now on your way to his office.

ROLE FOR MR. HALL

One thing after another! Why can't your department supervisors do their job and quit griping over every little thing! Jason, one of your new supervisors, who is sort of on trial, has just requested a conference to complain about your staff assistant, Cynthia. So, you guess you will have to talk to him.

Before he comes in, you try to reconstruct in your mind the events preceding the incident. Jason took over a pretty good department from Louise, who left to take a better job. At first you thought he would be OK. He did eliminate some recurring problems, but then you started getting a few complaints. One guy quit and wrote a nasty letter to you, claiming that Jason would ruin the department. You assumed this was sour grapes. Then

Cynthia, whom you have known for some time, said that things were really bad and that anyone who showed any initiative was suppressed. In fact, Jason seemed irritated by anyone who moved out on his or her own. Anyway, he did a dumb thing when he fired Cynthia. He didn't even follow the civil service procedure. In addition, all of Cynthia's performance reports said she was exceptional. You couldn't fire someone who didn't have even one bad mark in her personnel file.

Cynthia filed a complaint and came in to talk to you. You had always thought she had a lot of potential, and because a formal hearing would reinstate her anyway, you decided to hire her as your staff assistant.

That turned out to be a great move. She has taken responsibility for many projects, followed up on them, and relieved you of several troublesome details. Everything is going well except for Jason. His department has shown steady improvement in several areas, but in situations where he must occasionally work with Cynthia, he seems totally unwilling to cooperate. This can't go on, and so you have agreed to talk to him about the problem and resolve it once and for all. Because Cynthia is involved in the whole thing, you have invited her to join the meeting. Both of them are on their way to your office.

ROLE FOR CYNTHIA

For the last three weeks you have been working as a staff assistant for special projects. Your boss, Mr. Hall, is a great guy to work for, and he supports you whenever you have a problem with any of the department supervisors. This job is a great improvement over your previous assignment as a case worker under Jason.

You are not exactly sure what happened when you were working under Jason, but somehow you think he was out to get you. Things were great when Louise was department supervisor. Everyone got along well. Then Jason came in and really turned things upside down. He kept the staff so long in meetings that no one ever had time to do his or her job. Jason seemed to give you ten things to do at once, and then he blew up when you didn't get them all done. He harassed another case worker so much that the poor guy had to quit, or have a nervous breakdown. Morale and efficiency dropped, and finally you had a little discussion with Mr. Hall, whom you knew socially, to tell him what was going on. Mr. Hall said he would look into it. You think Jason found out, because the next day he told you you were through.

You waited a couple of days and then filed a complaint with Mr. Hall. He called you in, listened carefully to your account, and then told you he would be glad to have you come to work for him. Besides, Jason had not followed proper procedures for termination.

Things went well until you had to contact Jason in connection with a project. When you went to talk to him, he acted as though he had gone crazy. He told you to get out of his office and never come back. You reported this to Mr. Hall, who called Jason to straighten things out. This didn't seem to solve the problem, and Jason requested a conference with Mr. Hall. Because you are a central figure in the whole thing, Mr. Hall invited you to join in. You are on your way to Mr. Hall's office.

The Perfect Manager is Just Around the Corner

"When I grow up? Well, my goal is to become the chief executive officer of a large multinational conglomerate, assume control at a time when its price-earnings ratio and earnings per share are very low, turn it around, and make it a model of economic efficiency and the talk of wall street. But first and most important, I must be a human being responsible to the needs of society."

CASES

How Iacocca Won the Big One

In the summer of 1961, a varying group of six to 12 men began to meet one night a week in the Fairlane Inn, a motel on Michigan Avenue in Dearborn, Mich. Their leader was Lee A. Iacocca, vice-president of Ford Motor Co. and general manager of its Ford Div. since November, 1960. Out of those meetings, free from the pressures of the office a mile or so away, came the Mustang. And out of the success of the Mustang came first a group vice-presidency, an executive vice-presidency, and finally, last week, the presidency of Ford Motor Co. for Lee Iacocca, just past his 46th birthday.

The Mustang was the great divide in Iacocca's career, a career that has brought him to the top so rapidly that the stops along the way have been blurred. Before the Mustang, he was brash, opinionated, aggressive—and unknown. When he was made vice-president, recalls Donald N. Frey, now president of General Cable Corp. and, for several incandescent years a principal Iacocca lieutenant, "half the people in the company didn't know who he was, and the other half couldn't pronounce his name." After the Mustang sold 419,000 in a 12–month period, Iacocca was brash, opinionated, aggressive—and successful. "The worst that was said of him," says Frey, "was that he would be

president or be fired. The best was that he would be president."

WINNING STYLE

The motel meetings and the subsequent Mustang history were typical of Iacocca's management mode and illustrate how he rose so fast, developed his loyal team, and was able to supplant in Henry Ford II's esteem such an experienced auto man as Semon E. Knudsen, whom Chairman Ford fired as president in September, 1969, only 19 months after recruiting him from General Motors. The presidency has been vacant since then. They also hint at how he now will handle the challenges of imports and markets of the future.

The Fairlane meetings were held to study population trends, Ford's product line, the auto market, and assorted other factors. Iacocca believes in ideas, in rubbing people together to create ideas—about their own jobs or someone else's. He grabs for facts and seems to absorb them by osmosis. The "Fairlane Group" eventually decided Ford needed a new car for the young people coming into the market.

Selling a new car to the company's top men "took tremendous courage," a participant recalls. "It was so soon after the Edsel that you can imagine the cold stares." Iacocca marshaled his material, and put on a brilliant performance that convinced his hostile audience.

Iacocca had earlier demonstrated his ability to present his ideas, when, as car marketing manager of the Ford Division, he was charged with introducing the Falcon in 1959. Chase Morsey, Jr., now executive vice-president of RCA Corporation and formerly a Ford marketing executive, remembers the Falcon presentation well. "His instincts are good and he has great taste in the way things are done," he says. The Falcon performance caught the eye of Henry Ford, but Iacocca already had his sponsors in the company: Robert S. McNamara, briefly Ford president in 1960, and Charles Beecham, the man Iacocca calls his mentor.

FAST LEARNER

Beecham, who retired a few years ago as vice-president of marketing, has a blunt and simple explanation of how and why Lee Iacocca rose so fast: "Lee learned how the wheels meshed together to make money for Ford Motor Co." Iacocca began learning under Beecham's tutelage in 1946 in the Chester (Pa.) district sales office. "The basic fundamentals in this business are how to make more money," says Beecham, "and he learned that by working with dealers." One time, Beecham sent Iacocca out to a dealer who was having sales and business problems and told him not to come back until he straightened the dealer out. It took three months.

Iacocca was still in the Chester office when he pushed a program called "56 for 56" (a 1956 Ford on a $56–a–month installment plan); most people now say Iacocca conceived the program; Beecham agrees, but with some hesitation. The program attracted the attention of McNamara, then Ford Div. general manager. When Beecham, by that time sales manager of the division, needed more staff, McNamara approved Iacocca's appointment as truck manager. "Suddenly," recalls Thomas Tierney, now head of his own

Dallas-based public relations firm, but then in truck promotion, "everybody in the division began to think and talk trucks. He believes in what he is doing, and has the ability to put together a team that believes in him."

Iacocca is the first man with actual dealer selling experience at the helm of Ford Motor Co. He knows what will sell cars, though his way of selling sometimes abrades associates. After he became car marketing manager in 1957, he went hell-for-leather for racing—when the company was trying to demonstrate a concern for safety. "He knew Ford was right on the safety thing, but he knew racing would sell cars." Indeed, one Iacoccaism well known around Ford is: "You race 'em on Sunday and sell 'em on Monday."

BOOKKEEPING

By all accounts, Iacocca has a tremendous capacity to learn, as well as a tremendous drive to work. He is widely regarded as a marketing man, but insiders respect his knowledge of finance and management. One man remembers that Iacocca began keeping books on people early in his career at the Ford Div. "He would take the books over to Mr. Ford and discuss people with him."

The key book was one in which Iacocca kept a record of a manager's own objectives for each quarter, along with the manager's own grading of how he had done. Says one close associate in awe: "I looked at mine one time and it was all marked up. He actually keeps track of you."

In that way, Iacocca has built up his own team, with a nucleus of men who were with him in the Chester office: Matthew S. McLaughlin, now president of Ford Marketing Corp.; John Naughton, vice-president and general manager, Ford Div.; Bennett Bidwell, vice-president and general manager of Lincoln–Mercury Div.; Frank Zimmerman, marketing manager of Ford Div.; and J. William Benton, sales manager of Lincoln–Mercury.

He drives his men hard, and in return, he pays them well—"one year my bonus exceeded my salary," recalls an aide—and exacts fierce loyalty. He is going to need all of that. The auto industry has entered the most difficult period in its history. Detroit has not yet found the answer to competition from abroad—unless it is in Ford's Pinto and GM's Vega. The pressures for greater safety and a cleaner environment will substantially change the design and performance of cars and emphasize the cost squeeze, and yet-undetermined living patterns may demand new types of cars. The auto market abroad is growing faster than in this country.

To these problems, Iacocca brings weaknesses as well as strengths. He knows little about the foreign segments of the business, which now will come under his direction, along with the company's other operations. His bluntness is building up opponents in Washington. Along with GM President Edward N. Cole, Iacocca has been getting firmer and firmer in his public statements that the industry cannot meet the stringent 1975 antipollution requirements. He and Henry Ford have derided the air bag as a safety device, defying government opinion.

But when it comes to product and profit, Iacocca's record is sparkling—with the Mustang, Maverick, and Pinto. Few outsiders ever recognized that the Mustang's drive train—the most expensive part of the car—was largely paid for by its prior use in the Falcon, and that this helped Ford's first car named for a horse to make money like crazy.

So Iacocca watchers are confident he will come up with products to meet all problems. Says one: "He's damned smart. He knows the company and knows products. I really think the company may do some dramatic things under him."

Upheaval in the House of Ford

Power struggles are nothing new at Ford Motor Co., but the one that climaxed last week was a stunner. After weeks of futile maneuvering to save his job, Lee Iacocca, 53, the hard-driving, cigar-chomping president of the world's fourth largest manufacturing company, found himself quite bluntly sacked by his equally tough-minded boss, Chairman Henry Ford II. It was the culmination of months of behind-the-scenes quarreling between two of the auto

industry's most respected—and often feared—executives. The end came for Iacocca following a day of stormy meetings of the ten-member organization committee of the company's outside directors at Ford's headquarters in Dearborn, Mich. Afterward, Iacocca denied widely published reports that he had asked his boss, "I have been with the company 32 years. What have I done wrong?" And that Ford had replied, "I just don't like you." In fact, Ford was recently heard to say, "I haven't liked you for two years."

The icily frank appraisal, like a line out of *Wheels*, sums up a relationship between two strong-willed men that was never warm and has been deteriorating for several years. "The body chemistry wasn't right," said Henry W. Gadsden, one of the several outside directors who hoped that the president could stay on. Both Ford and Iacocca can be at times charming, abrasive, cordial and arch. A clash of their personalities was all but inevitable from the moment that Ford, the celebrated heir who liked to remind subordinates that "my name is on the building," elevated Iacocca, the ambitious hired manager, to president in 1970. Early rumored to have the inside track on the job of chief executive upon Ford's retirement at the age of 65 in 1982, Iacocca made the mistake of encouraging subordinates to regard him as the dauphin. That did not sit well with Chairman Ford, who thought that Iacocca had too many rough edges, and whose company has always been headed by a member of the first family of American industry.

Ford has grown increasingly preoccupied with providing for an orderly transition before the eventual takeover of his job by another Ford—most likely his only son, Edsel, 29, an executive of Ford of Australia Ltd. The first open signs of Henry Ford's determination to nudge Iacocca aside came 15 months ago. In a maneuver that infuriated Iacocca, who throughout his presidency had alone reported directly to the chairman, Ford set up a three-man "office of the chief executive" composed of himself, Iacocca and Vice Chairman Philip Caldwell, 57.

The change diluted Iacocca's control over day-to-day operations, and sent him on a supersecret scouting mission for a possible job as assistant and heir apparent to J. Stanford Smith, chief executive of International Paper Co. The talks came to nothing. Iacocca's role at Ford was reduced still further only a month ago when Ford expanded the office of the chief executive to include his brother William Clay Ford, 53, owner of the Detroit Lions football team. At the time the internal structure of the office was modified so that Iacocca could no longer report to the chairman at all but instead had to deal through Caldwell.

In the past several weeks, Iacocca launched a fevered campaign to gather support from among the company's outside directors. Though some backed him, it was a pointless effort, since the chairman has the power to pick whomever he wishes as president.

Iacocca has been one of the most skillful managers in the auto industry's modern history. His quick decisions and his flair for styling not only brought him a spectacular rise at Ford in the early 1960s but was a key reason that the company overcame its stodgy image of earlier years. He made the Falcon a hot seller by adding bucket seats and a bigger engine as an option, captured a large piece of the youth market by making Ford cars conspicuous on the racing circuit. He is proudest of his revitalization of the company's dealer network, but industry historians may remember him most for the Mustang. He helped design the sporty car for Everyman with his own hands, and put it into production in 1964. By personally orchestrating a snappy marketing campaign, Iacocca logged 419,000 Mustang sales in the first year, still a record for new models.

The company that he leaves is in fine shape (last year sales jumped from $29 billion to $38 billion, and earnings rose from $983 million to $1.7 billion), but it will miss Iacocca's talents. Warned Ed Mulane, president of the Ford Dealer Alliance, which represents 1,200 car and truck outlets; "Iacocca is the only guy with charisma. He was able to slot in the right product at the right time."

In the past year the company has also been distracted by a series of lawsuits and reported scandals. Executives are worried by persistent rumors within the company that one top official may have misused hundreds of thousands of dollars in business-related travel expenses. In a totally unrelated matter, Henry Ford himself last month became the subject of a bizarre stockholder lawsuit by New York Attorney Roy Cohn, which accused Ford and other company officers of taking $750,000 in illegal kickbacks from a catering concern, Canteen Corp., a charge that Ford denies vigorously. The Justice Department is also investigating allegations that Ford executives paid $900,000 to an Indonesian government official in return for an aerospace communications contract.

On top of that, Iacocca's firing could lead to further departures by managers. Almost always when a top executive is removed, his close supporters and recruits become vulnerable. Chairman Ford is said to be looking closely at a number of General Motors executives to replace some Iacocca loyalists. The automakers may be in for a period of industry wide executive raiding.

Iacocca is not the first mighty executive to be cast off by Henry Ford II. When Ford was only 27, he led other family members in a celebrated coup that forced his aged and autocratic grandfather, the original Henry Ford, to relinquish power. Then, in a series of historic confrontations in 1945, he forced the resignation of Director Harry Bennett, who to keep his own *de facto* control over the company had surrounded himself with a gang of hired thugs. In 1969 Ford unceremoniously canned President Semon ("Bunky") Knudsen, in large part at the urging of Iacocca, who was Knudsen's rival for power. When asked why he was letting Knudsen go, Ford simply answered: "It just didn't work out."

Nine years later, Lee Iacocca sat on the gold-colored couch in his office and remarked that the boss had used ironically similar words to justify his own ouster. "Mr. Ford said it's just one of those things, we're going to do it and that's it."

MR. UPWARD AUTOMOBILITY

Lee Iacocca thought he had a better idea. An eager young sales manager in the 1950s, he figured he would pep up a dull convention of 1,100 Ford salesmen by proving in a live demonstration that if he dropped an egg from a 10-ft.–high ladder onto Ford's new crash-padded dashboard, the egg would not break. He was wrong. Until last week, that was one of the very few times that Iacocca came close to having egg on his face. After 32 years with Ford, the plain-spoken son of an Italian immigrant was a Horatio Alger—hero on wheels, a paradigm of upward automobility. Yet unlike others who have risen through the sober, polyester-clad ranks of America's most important industry, Iacocca is perpetually outspoken, fashionably dressed in European worsteds and as obviously at ease in a barroom throbbing with used-Ford salesmen as in a hearing room full of Senators. If humans can be said to have automotive analogues, Iacocca suggests nothing so much as a Ford Mustang, that stylish-yet-democratic car whose creation is perhaps Iacocca's greatest triumph.

Lido Anthony Iacocca was born in Allentown, Pa., into what can be described as a Ford family. His father drove a Model T, launched one of the nation's earliest rent-a-car agencies, made and lost several pre-Depression fortunes by renting Fords and trading in local real estate. Young Lido decided he wanted to enter the auto business, preferably with Ford. He got an engineering degree at nearby Lehigh University, signed on with Ford as a trainee, earned a master's in engineering at Princeton and then surprised Ford recruiters by rejecting a quiet career in automatic transmissions for the tough world of sales.

In ten years as a salesman, Iacocca sold so many cars that Ford Vice–President Robert McNamara brought him to Detroit as marketing director for Ford trucks. In 1960, at the precocious age of 36, Iacocca attained what was at one time his life's goal, a Ford vice presidency (in charge of the Ford Division). It was not a complete triumph; his plan had been to be there by age 35. "He had a schedule for himself as to what amount of money he would like to be making," his wife Mary once said, "Like maybe in five years he might like to be making $5,000 and in ten years $10,000. It was on a little scrap of paper."

Though a millionaire several times over by now, he lives with his wife and younger daughter (their other daughter is at college in the East) in a comparatively modest 13–room Colonial home in suburban Bloomfield Hills, and is active in Detroit area civic and charitable groups. He likes jazz and Big Band music, but has no hobbies. His close friends tend to come from outside the auto industry, and he has made a point of avoiding the social circles of "Mister Ford," as Iacocca and other Ford executives respectfully call their ruler. Iacocca once explained, "I don't want to be fired for something I said to Mister Ford at the 21 Club."

By that standard, Iacocca will be officially free to buy the boss a drink after Oct. 15, the day he goes off the payroll and, not coincidentally, his 54th birthday. By allowing Iacocca to stay on until then, Ford will be swelling Iacocca's annual pension to more than $100,000, though the de-hired executive is hardly the retiring type. He has given "no thought to what I'm going to do at all, literally none," he says. "Education, business, government, fishing—I don't know." He would not mind being an independent Ford dealer. "Maybe there is such a thing as a new life. I've got to do a lot of thinking about it."

Editor's note:

In November 1978, just a few months after he was fired as President at Ford, Iacocca became President of Chrysler Corporation. In the next three years Chrysler lost $3.5 billion—the largest loss of any American company in history. In 1979, it took an act of Congress to grant federal guarantees on $1.5 billion of Chrysler loans. This congressional "bail-out" was, and still is, a very controversial issue. In 1982 Iacocca announced a profit for the troubled company, and in 1983 repaid the federal loan. *Time* magazine said (March 12, 1983), "Chrysler's recovery is largely Iacocca's doing, a triumph of brains, bluster and bravado." Some at Chrysler "worship the guy" and others refer to him as the "Ayatollah" Iacocca.

Fables for Management: The Ill–Informed Walrus *

"How's it going down there?" barked the big walrus from his perch on the highest rock near the shore. He waited for the good word.

Down below, the smaller walruses conferred hastily among themselves. Things weren't going well at all, but none of them wanted to break the news to the Old Man. He was the biggest and wisest walrus in the herd, and he knew his business—but he had such a terrible temper that every walrus in the herd was terrified of his ferocious bark.

"What will we tell him?" whispered Basil, the second-ranking walrus. He well remembered how the Old Man had raved and ranted at him the last time the herd caught less than its quota of herring, and he had no desire to go through that experience again. Nevertheless, the walruses noticed for several weeks that the water level in the nearby Arctic bay had been falling constantly, and it had become necessary to travel much farther to catch the dwindling supply of herring. Someone should tell the Old Man; he would probably know what to do. But

who? and how?

Finally Basil spoke up: "Things are going pretty well, Chief," he said. The thought of the receding water line made his heart grow heavy, but he went on: "As a matter of fact, the beach seems to be getting larger."

The Old Man grunted. "Fine, fine," he said. "That will give us a bit more elbow room." He closed his eyes and continued basking in the sun.

The next day brought more trouble. A new herd of walruses moved in down the beach, and with the supply of herring dwindling, this invasion could be dangerous. No one wanted to tell the Old Man, though only he could take the steps necessary to meet this new competition.

Reluctantly, Basil approached the big walrus who was still sunning himself on the large rock. After some small talk, he said, "Oh, by the way, Chief, a new herd of walruses seems to have moved into our territory." The Old Man's eyes snapped open, and he filled his great lungs in preparation for a mighty bellow. But Basil added quickly, "Of course, we don't anticipate any trouble. They don't look like herring-eaters to me. More likely interested in minnows. And as you know, we don't bother with minnows ourselves."

The Old Man let out the air with a long sigh. "Good, good," he said. "No point in our getting excited over nothing then, is there?"

Things didn't get any better in the weeks that followed. One day, peering down from the large rock, the Old Man noticed that part of the herd seemed to be missing. Summoning Basil, he grunted peevishly, "What's going on, Basil? Where is everyone?" Poor Basil didn't have the courage to tell the Old Man that many of the younger walruses were leaving every day to join the new herd. Clearing his throat nervously he said, "Well, Chief, we've been tightening up things a bit. You know, getting rid of some of the deadwood. After all, a herd is only as good as the walruses in it."

"Run a tight ship, I always say," the Old Man grunted. "Glad to hear that all is going so well."

Before long, everyone but Basil had left to join the new herd, and Basil realized that the time had come to tell the Old Man the facts. Terrified but determined, he flopped up to the large rock. "Chief," he said, "I have bad news. The rest of the herd has left you." The Old Walrus was so astonished that he couldn't even work up a good bellow. "Left me?" he cried. "All of them? But why? How could this happen?"

Basil didn't have the heart to tell him, so he merely shrugged helplessly.

"I can't understand it," the Old Walrus said. "And just when everything was going so well."

MORAL: What you like to hear isn't always what you need to know.

L.J. Summers Company

Jon Reese couldn't think of a time in the history of L.J. Summers Company when there had been as much anti-company sentiment among the workers as had emerged in the past few weeks. He knew that Mr. Summers would place the blame on him for the problems with the production workers because Jon was supposed to be helping Mr. Summer's son, Blaine, to become oriented to his new position. Blaine had only recently taken over as production manager of the company (see Exhibit 1). Blaine was unpopular with most of the workers, but the events of the past weeks had caused him to be resented even more. This resentment had increased to the point that several of the male workers had quit and all the women in the assembly department had refused to work.

The programs that had caused the resentment among the workers were instituted by Blaine to reduce waste and lower production costs, but they had produced completely opposite results. Jon knew that on Monday morning he would have to explain to Mr. Summers why the workers had reacted as they did and that he would have to present a plan to resolve the employee problems, reduce waste, and decrease production costs.

COMPANY HISTORY

L.J. Summers Company manufactured large sliding doors made of many narrow aluminum panels held together by thick rubber strips, which allowed the door to

EXHIBIT 1   L. J. Summers Company Organization Chart

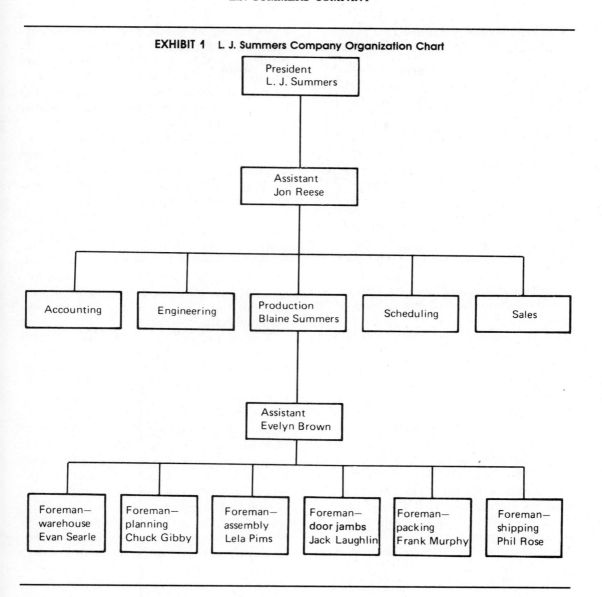

collapse as it was opened. Some of the doors were as high as eighteen feet and were used in buildings to section off large areas. The company had grown rapidly in its early years due mainly to the expansion of the building program of the firm's major customer, which accounted for nearly 90 percent of Summers' business.

When L.J. Summers began the business, his was the only firm that manufac- tured the large sliding doors. Recently, however, several other firms had begun to market similar doors. One firm in particular had been bidding to obtain business from Summers' major customer. Fearing that the competitor might be able to un- derbid his company, Mr. Summers began urging his assistant, Jon, to increase effi- ciency and cut production costs.

CONDITIONS BEFORE THE COST REDUCTION PROGRAMS

A family-type atmosphere had existed at Summers before the cost reduction programs were instituted. There was little direct supervision of the workers from the front office, and no pressure was put on them to meet production standards. Several of the employees worked overtime regularly without supervision. The foremen and workers often played cards together during lunchtime, and company parties after work were common and popular. Mr. Summers was generally on friendly terms with all the employees, although he was known to get angry if something displeased him. He also participated freely in the daily operations of the company.

As Mr. Summers' assistant, Jon was responsible for seeing to it that the company achieved the goals established by Mr. Summers. Jon was considered hardworking and persuasive by most of the employees and had a reputation of not giving in easily to employee complaints.

Blaine Summers had only recently become the production manager of Summers. He was in his early twenties, married, and had a good build. Several of the workers commented that Blaine liked to show off his strength in front of others. He was known to be very meticulous about keeping the shop orderly and neat, even to the point of making sure that packing crates were stacked "his way." It was often commented among the other employees how Blaine seemed to be trying to impress his father. Many workers voiced the opinion that the only reason Blaine was production manager was that his father owned the company. They also resented his using company employees and materials to build a swing set for his children and to repair his camper.

Blaine, commenting to Jon one day that the major problem with production was the workers, added that people of such caliber as the Summers' employees did not understand how important cost reduction was and that they would rather sit around and talk all day than work. Blaine rarely spoke to the workers but left most of the reprimanding and firing up to his assistant, Evelyn Brown.

Summers employed about seventy people to perform the warehousing, assembly, and door-jamb building, as well as the packing and shipping operations done on the doors. Each operation was supervised by a foreman, and crews ranged from three men in warehousing to twenty-five women in the assembly department. The foremen were usually employees with the most seniority and were responsible for quality and on-time production output. Most of the foremen had good relationships with the workers.

The majority of the work done at Summers consisted of repetitive assembly tasks requiring very little skill or training; for example, in the pinning department the workers operated a punch press, which made holes in the panels. The job consisted of punching the hole and then inserting a metal pin into it. Workers commented that it was very tiring and boring to stand at the press during the whole shift without frequent breaks.

Wages at Summers were considered to be low for the area. The workers griped about the low pay but said that they tried to compensate by taking frequent breaks, working overtime, and "taking small items home at night." Most of the workers who worked overtime were in the door-jamb department, the operation requiring the most skill. Several of these workers either worked very little or slept during overtime hours they reportedly worked.

The majority of the male employees were in their mid-twenties; about half of them were unmarried. There was a great turnover among the unmarried male workers. The female employees were either young and single or older married women. The twenty-five women who worked in production were all in the assembly department under Lela Pims.

THE COST REDUCTION PROGRAMS

Shortly after Mr. Summers began stressing the need to reduce waste and increase production, Blaine called the foremen together and told them that they would be responsible for stricter discipline among the employees. Unless each foreman could reduce waste and improve production in his department, he would either be replaced or receive no pay increases.

The efforts of the foremen to make the workers eliminate wasteful activities and increase output brought immediate resistance and resentment. The employees' reactions were typified by the following comment: "What has gotten into Chuck lately? He's been chewing us out for the same old things we've always done. All he thinks about now is increasing production." Several of the foremen commented that they didn't like the front office making them the "bad guys" in the eyes of the workers. The workers didn't change their work habits as a result of the pressure put on them by the foremen, but a growing spirit of antagonism between the workers and the foremen was apparent.

After several weeks of no apparent improvement in production, Jon called a meeting with the workers to announce that the plant would go on a four-day, ten-hour-a-day work week in order to reduce operating costs. He stressed that the workers would enjoy having a three-day weekend. This was greeted with enthusiasm by some of the younger employees, but several of the older women complained that the schedule would be too tiring for them and that they would rather work five days a week. The proposal was voted on and passed by a two-to-one margin. Next Jon stated that there would be no more un-supervised overtime and that all overtime had to be approved in advance by Blaine. Overtime would be allowed only if some specific job had to be finished. Those who had been working overtime protested vigorously, saying that this would only result in lagging behind schedule, but Jon remained firm on this new rule.

Shortly after the meeting, several workers in the door-jamb department made plans to stage a work slowdown so that the department would fall behind schedule and they would have to work overtime to catch up. One of the workers, who had previously been the hardest working in the department, said, "We will tell them that we are working as fast as possible and that we just can't do as much as we used to in a five-day week. The only thing they could do would be to fire us, and they would never do that." Similar tactics were devised by workers in other departments. Some workers said that if they couldn't have overtime they would find a better paying job elsewhere.

Blaine, observing what was going on, told Jon, "They think I can't tell that they are staging a slowdown. Well, I simply won't approve any overtime, and after Jack's department gets way behind I'll let him have it for fouling up scheduling."

After a few weeks of continued slowdown, Blaine drew up a set of specific rules, which were posted on the company bulletin board early one Monday morning (see Exhibit 2). This brought immediate criticism from the workers. During the next week they continued to deliberately violate the posted rules. On Friday two of the male employees quit because they were penalized for arriving late to work and for "lounging around" during working hours. As they left they said they would be waiting for their foreman after work to get even with him for turning them in.

That same day the entire assembly department (all women) staged a work stoppage to protest an action taken against

---

EXHIBIT 2 Production Shop Regulations

1. Anyone reporting late to work will lose one half hour's pay for each five minutes of lateness. The same applies to punching in after lunch.
2. No one is to leave the machine or post without the permission of the supervisor.
3. Anyone observed not working will be noted and if sufficient occurrences are counted the employee will be dismissed.

Myrtle King, an employee of the company since the beginning. The action resulted from a run-in she had with Lela Pims, foreman of the assembly department. Myrtle was about 60 years old and had been turned in by Lela for resting too much. She became furious, saying she couldn't work ten hours a day. Several of her friends had organized the work stoppage after Myrtle had been sent home without pay credit for the day. The stoppage was also inspired by some talk among the workers of forming a union. The women seemed to favor this idea more than the men.

When Blaine found out about the incident he tried joking with the women and in jest threatened to fire them if they did not begin working again. When he saw he was getting nowhere he returned to the front office. One of the workers commented, "He thinks he can send us home and push us around and then all he has to do is tell us to go back to work and we will. Well, this place can't operate without us."

Jon soon appeared and called Lela into his office and began talking with her. Later he persuaded the women to go back to work and told them that there would be a meeting with all the female employees on Monday morning.

Jon wondered what steps he should take to solve the problems at L.J. Summers Company. The efforts of management to increase efficiency and reduce production costs had definitely caused resentment among the workers. Even more disappointing was the fact that the company accountant had just announced that waste and costs had increased since the new programs had been instituted, and the company scheduler reported that Summers was farther behind on shipments than ever before.

Different People Have Different Reasons for Joining Organizations

"Isn't there any other reason you would like a job with this organization other than 'Want to work within the system to destroy it'?"

5

Survival and Growth in Organizations of the Future

In a time of declining productivity, increasing foreign competition, frequent plant closings, and record numbers of bankruptcies, organizations can no longer just assume that they will continue to grow or even that they will survive. Developments in our society are forcing organizations to change at an ever-increasing rate. Pressures for change come from many different directions.

Consumer groups have demanded safer, pollution-free, and more reliable products at lower prices. Their activities include class action suits against automobile manufacturers, product boycotts, and requests for drug recalls, increased airline safety, and more specific labelling information.

Another source of change is employees. Almost daily we find a new group pressing its demands: public school teachers strike, farm workers demonstrate for a more liveable wage, air traffic controllers participate in a work slowdown. Employees, individually and in groups, have long been active in encouraging organizations to change.

The number of state and federal government agencies pressing for change has increased dramatically in recent years: the Equal Employment Opportunity Commission enforces affirmative action in the hiring and promoting of minorities and women; the Environmental Protection Agency is trying to reduce water and air pollution; the Occupational Safety and Health Act was passed to require employers to make workplaces safer for employees; the National Labor Relations Board can require a company to bargain collectively with a certified bargaining agent.

Special-interest groups, such as the Sierra Club, the Veterans of Foreign Wars, the American Medical Association, the NAACP, and Common Cause, have adopted a variety of strategies to change organi-

SURVIVAL AND GROWTH IN ORGANIZATIONS OF THE FUTURE

zations. (The list of interested groups also includes foreign govern-ments, suppliers, stockholders, political parties, and the like.) They have used demonstrations, published reports on abuses, boycotted oth-er organizations, lobbied state and federal legislatures, and engaged in mass media campaigns.

Organizations that respond well to environmental pressures survive and grow. Other organizations, less responsive to changes in their envi-ronment, become less competitive. For example, major changes in fed-eral regulation of the airline industry during the late 1970s and the increased foreign competition in the automobile industry during the 1980s brought new challenges and problems to companies in the United States. Why were some firms able to respond quickly to these changes and continue as viable operations while other firms were slow to re-spond? There is no simple answer. But, as we have suggested, there are many pressures for change, and an organization needs a strategy for responding to those pressures.

A simple cone can help us think about the process of coping with environment.

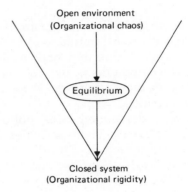

Open environment
(Organizational chaos)

Equilibrium

Closed system
(Organizational rigidity)

The top of the cone represents the openness of the environment and the almost unlimited resources (e.g., products, technologies, ideas, or-ganization structures, assumptions) that the organization can use to cope with its environment. As an organization adopts a strategy with its accompanying limitations, it is forced to move down the cone into a more structured situation affording fewer alternatives. Ideally, an orga-nization reaches a point of equilibrium if it acquires sufficient struc-ture to operate effectively but retains adequate flexibility to cope with environmental pressures for change. As the organization loses its abili-ty to cope, it encounters serious difficulty and may eventually die. In fact, because of external variables, self-imposed restrictions, and rigidi-ty, the natural tendency of an organization is to die. Only through great skill on the part of its members can an organization achieve equilibri-um with its environment and avoid death.

But how can managers and employees help their organizations find equilibrium and be appropriately responsive to the environment? The materials in this section were selected to present concepts and ideas for thinking about these issues.

READINGS

Choosing Strategies for Change

JOHN P. KOTTER and LEONARD A. SCHLESINGER

"From the frying pan into the fire," "let sleeping dogs lie," and "you can't teach an old dog new tricks" are very well-known sayings born of the fear of change. When people are threatened with change in organizations, similar maxims about certain people and departments are trotted out to prevent an altercation in the status quo. Fear of change is understandable, but because the environment changes rapidly, and it has been doing so increasingly, organizations cannot afford not to change. One major task of a manager, then, is to implement change, and that entails overcoming resistance to it. In this article, the authors describe four basic reasons people resist change. They also describe various methods for dealing with the resistance and provide a guide to what kinds of approaches will work when the different types of resistance occur.

"It must be considered that there is nothing more difficult to carry out, nor more doubtful of success, nor more dangerous to handle, than to initiate a new order of things" (Machiavelli).

In 1973, The Conference Board asked 13 eminent authorities to speculate what significant management issues and problems would develop over the next 20 years. One of the strongest themes that runs through their subsequent reports is a concern for the ability of organizations to respond to environmental change. As one person wrote: "It follows that an acceleration in the rate of change will result in an increasing need for reorganization. Reorganization is usually feared, because it means disturbance of the status quo, a threat to people's vested interests in their jobs, and an upset to established ways of doing things. For these reasons, needed reorganization is often deferred, with a resulting loss in effectiveness and an increase in costs." (Bower and Walton 1973).

Subsequent events have confirmed the importance of this concern about organizational change. Today, more and more managers must deal with new government regulations, new products, growth, increased competition, technological developments, and a changing work force. In response, most companies or divisions of major corporations find that they must undertake moderate organizational changes at least once a year and major changes every four or five (Allen 1978).

Few organizational change efforts tend to be complete failures, but few tend to be entirely successful either. Most efforts encounter problems; they often take longer than expected and desired, they sometimes kill morale, and they often cost a great deal in terms of managerial time or emotional upheaval. More than a few organizations have not even tried to initiate needed changes because the managers involved were afraid that they were simply incapable of successfully implementing them.

In this article, we first describe various causes for resistance to change and then outline a systematic way to select a strategy and set specific approaches for implementing an organizational change effort. The methods described are based on our analyses of dozens of successful and unsuccessful organizational changes.

DIAGNOSING RESISTANCE

Organizational change efforts often run into some form of human resistance. Although experienced managers are generally all too aware of this fact, surprisingly few take time before an organizational change to assess systematically who might resist the change initiative and for what reasons. Instead, using past experiences as guidelines, managers all too often apply a simple set of beliefs—such as "engineers will probably resist the change because they are independent and suspicious of top management." This limited approach can create serious problems. Because of the many different ways in which individuals and groups can react to change, correct assessments are often not intuitively obvious and require careful thought.

Of course, all people who are affected by change experience some emotional turmoil. Even changes that appear to be "positive" or "rational" involve loss and

uncertainty (1973). Nevertheless, for a number of different reasons, individuals or groups can react very differently to change—from passively resisting it, to aggressively trying to undermine it, to sincerely embracing it.

To predict what form resistance might take, managers need to be aware of the four most common reasons people resist change. These include: a desire not to lose something of value, a misunderstanding of the change and its implications, a belief that the change does not make sense for the organization, and a low tolerance for change.

PAROCHIAL SELF–INTEREST

One major reason people resist organizational change is that they think they will lose something of value as a result. In these cases, because people focus on their own best interests and not on those of the total organization, resistance often results in "policies" or "political behavior." (Zaleznik and Kets de Vries 1975; Miles 1978). Consider these two examples:

• After a number of years of rapid growth, the president of an organization decided that its size demanded the creation of a new staff function—New Product Planning and Development—to be headed by a vice-president. Operationally, this change eliminated most of the decision-making power that the vice-presidents of marketing, engineering, and production had over new products. Inasmuch as new products were very important in this organization, the change also reduced the vice-presidents' status which, together with power, was very important to them.

During the two months after the president announced his idea for a new product vice-president, the existing vice-presidents each came up with six or seven reasons the new arrangement might not work. Their objections grew louder and louder until the president shelved the idea.

• A manufacturing company had traditionally employed a large group of personnel people as counselors and "father confessors" to its production employees. This group of counselors tended to exhibit high morale because of the professional satisfaction they received from the "helping relationships" they had with employees. When a new performance appraisal system was installed, every six months the counselors were required to provide each employee's supervisor with a written evaluation of the employee's "emotional maturity," "promotional potential," and so forth.

As some of the personnel people immediately recognized, the change would alter their relationships from a peer and helper to more of a boss and evaluator with most of the employees. Predictably, the personnel counselors resisted the change. While publicly arguing that the new system was not as good for the company as the old one, they privately put as much pressure as possible on the personnel vice president until he significantly altered the new system.

> Political behavior emerges before and during organizational change efforts when what is in the best interests of one individual or group is not in the best interests of the total organization or of other individuals and groups.

While political behavior sometimes takes the form of two or more armed camps publicly fighting things out, it usually is much more subtle. In many cases, it occurs completely under the surface of public dialogue. Although scheming and ruthless individuals sometimes initiate power struggles, more often than not those who do are people who view their potential loss from change as an unfair violation of their implicit, or psychological, contract with the organization

(Schein 1965).

MISUNDERSTANDING AND LACK OF TRUST

People also resist change when they do not understand its implications and perceive that it might cost them much more than they will gain. Such situations often occur when trust is lacking between the person initiating the change and the employees. (Argyris 1970). Here is an example:

• When the president of a small midwestern company announced to his managers that the company would implement a flexible working schedule for all employees, it never occurred to him that he might run into resistance. He had been introduced to the concept at a management seminar and decided to use it to make working conditions at his company more attractive, particularly to clerical and plant personnel.

Shortly after the announcement, numerous rumors begin to circulate among plant employees—none of whom really knew what flexible working hours meant and many of whom were distrustful of the manufacturing vice-president. One rumor, for instance, suggested that flexible hours meant that most people would have to work whenever their supervisors asked them to—including evenings and weekends. The employee association, a local union, held a quick meeting and then presented the management with a nonnegotiable demand that the flexible hours concept be dropped. The president, caught completely by surprise, complied.

> Few organizations can be characterized as having a high level of trust between employees and managers; consequently, it is easy for misunderstandings to develop when change is introduced. Unless managers surface misunderstandings and clarify them rapidly, they can lead to resistance. And that resistance can easily catch change initi-

ators by surprise, especially if they assume that people only resist change when it is not in their best interest.

DIFFERENT ASSESSMENTS

Another common reason people resist organizational change is that they assess the situation differently from their managers or those initiating the change and see more costs than benefits resulting from the change, not only for themselves but for their company as well. For example:

• The president of one moderate-size bank was shocked by his staff's analysis of the bank's real estate investment trust (REIT) loans. This complicated analysis suggested that the bank could easily lose up to $10 million, and that the possible losses were increasing each month by 20 percent. Within a week, the president drew up a plan to reorganize the part of the bank that managed REITs. Because of his concern for the bank's stock price, however, he chose not to release the staff report to anyone except the new REIT section manager.

The reorganization immediately ran into massive resistance from the people involved. The group sentiment, as articulated by one person, was: "Has he gone mad? Why in God's name is he tearing apart this section of the bank? His actions have already cost us three very good people (who quit), and have crippled a new program we were implementing (which the president was unaware of) to reduce our loan losses."

Managers who initiate change often assume both that they have all the relevant information required to conduct an adequate organization analysis and that those who will be affected by the change have the same facts, when neither assumption is correct. In either case, the difference in information that groups work with often leads to difference in analyses, which in turn can lead to resistance. Moreover, if the analysis made by

those not initiating the change is more accurate than that derived by the initiators, resistance is obviously "good" for the organization. But this likelihood is not obvious to some managers who assume that resistance is always bad and therefore always fight it. (Lawrence 1954).

LOW TOLERANCE FOR CHANGE

People also resist change because they fear they will not be able to develop the new skills and behavior that will be required of them. All human beings are limited in their ability to change, with some people much more limited than others. (Watson 1969). Organizational change can inadvertently require people to change too much, too quickly.

Peter F. Drucker has argued that the major obstacle to organizational growth is managers' inability to change their attitudes and behavior as rapidly as their organizations require. (Drucker 1954). Even when managers intellectually understand the need for changes in the way they operate, they sometimes are emotionally unable to make the transition.

It is because of people's limited tolerance for change that individuals will sometimes resist a change even when they realize it is a good one. For example, a person who receives a significantly more important job as a result of an organizational change will probably be very happy. But it is just as possible for such a person to also feel uneasy and to resist giving up certain aspects of the current situation. A new and very different job will require new and different behavior, new and different relationships, as well as the loss of some satisfactory current activities and relationships. If the changes are significant and the individual's tolerance for change is low, he might begin actively to resist the change for reasons even he does not consciously understand.

People also sometimes resist organizational change to save face; to go along with the change would be, they think, an admission that some of their previous decisions or beliefs were wrong. Or they might resist because of peer group pressure or because of a supervisor's attitude. Indeed, there are probably an endless number of reasons why people resist change. (Zaltman and Duncan 1977).

Assessing which of the many possibilities might apply to those who will be affected by a change is important because it can help a manager select an appropriate way to overcome resistance. Without an accurate diagnosis of possibilities of resistance, a manager can easily get bogged down during the change process with very costly problems.

DEALING WITH RESISTANCE

Many managers underestimate not only the variety of ways people can react to organizational change, but also the ways they can positively influence specific individuals and groups during a change. And, again because of past experiences, managers sometimes do not have an accurate understanding of the advantages and disadvantages of the methods with which they *are* familiar.

EDUCATION AND COMMUNICATION

One of the most common ways to overcome resistance to change is to educate people about it before-hand. Communication of ideas helps people see the need for and the logic of a change. The education process can involve one-on-one discussions, presentations to groups, or memos and reports. For example:

• As a part of an effort to make changes in a division's structure and in measurement and reward systems, a division manager put together a one-hour audio-visual presentation that explained the

changes and the reasons for them. Over a four-month period, he made this presentation no less than a dozen times to groups of 20 or 30 corporate and division managers.

An education and communication program can be ideal when resistance is based on inadequate or inaccurate information and analysis, especially if the initiators need the resistors' help in implementing the change. But some managers overlook the fact that a program of this sort requires a good relationship between initiators and resistors or that the latter may not believe what they hear. It also requires time and effort, particularly if a lot of people are involved.

PARTICIPATION AND INVOLVEMENT

If the initiators involve the potential resistors in some aspect of the design and implementation of the change, they can often forestall resistance. With a participative change effort, the initiators listen to the people the change involves and use their advice. To illustrate:

• The head of a small financial services company once created a task force to help design and implement changes in his company's reward system. The task force was composed of eight second- and third-level managers from different parts of the company. The president's specific charter to them was that they recommend changes in the company's benefit package. They were given six months and asked to file a brief progress report with the president once a month. After they had made their recommendations, which the president largely accepted, they were asked to help the company's personnel director implement them.

We have found that many managers have quite strong feelings about participation—sometimes positive and sometimes negative. That is, some managers feel that there should always be participation during change efforts, while others feel this is virtually always a mistake. Both attitudes can create problems for a manager, because neither is very realistic.

When change initiators believe they do not have all the information they need to design and implement a change, or when they need the whole-hearted commitment of others to do so, involving others makes very good sense. Considerable research has demonstrated that, in general, participation leads to commitment, not merely compliance (Marrow, Bowers, and Seashore 1967). In some instances, commitment is needed for the change to be a success. Nevertheless, the participation process does have its drawbacks. Not only can it lead to a poor solution if the process is not carefully managed, but also it can be enormously time consuming. When the change must be made immediately, it can take simply too long to involve others.

FACILITATION AND SUPPORT

Another way that managers can deal with potential resistance to change is by being supportive. This process might include providing training in new skills, or giving employees time off after a demanding period, or simply listening and providing emotional support. For example:

• Management in one rapidly growing electronics company devised a way to help people adjust to frequent organizational changes. First, management staffed its human resource department with four counselors who spent most of their time talking to people who were feeling "burnt out" or who were having difficulty adjusting to new jobs. Second, on a selective basis, management offered people four-week minisabbaticals that involved some reflective or educational activity away from work. And, finally, it spent a great deal of money on in-house education and training programs.

Facilitation and support are most helpful when fear and anxiety lie at the heart of resistance. Seasoned, tough managers often overlook or ignore this kind of resistance, as well as the efficacy of facilitative ways of dealing with it. The basic drawback of this approach is that it can be time consuming and expensive and still fail (Zaltman and Duncan 1977). If time, money, and patience just are not available, then using supportive methods is not very practical.

NEGOTIATION AND AGREEMENT

Another way to deal with resistance is to offer incentives to active or potential resistors. For instance, management could give a union a higher wage rate in return for a work rule change; it could increase an individual's pension benefits in return for an early retirement. Here is an example of negotiated agreements:

• In a large manufacturing company, the divisions were very interdependent. One division manager wanted to make some major changes in his organization. Yet, because of the interdependence, he recognized that he would be forcing some inconvenience and change on other divisions as well. To prevent top managers in other divisions from undermining his efforts, the division manager negotiated a written agreement with each. The agreement specified the outcomes the other division managers would receive and when, as well as the kinds of cooperation that he would receive from them in return during the change process. Later, whenever the division managers complained about his changes or the change process itself, he could point to the negotiated agreements.

Negotiation is particularly appropriate when it is clear that someone is going to lose out as a result of a change and yet his or her power to resist is significant. Negotiated agreements can be a relatively easy way to avoid major resistance, though, like some other processes, they may become expensive. And once a manager makes it clear that he will negotiate to avoid major resistance, he opens himself up to the possibility of blackmail (Nierenberg 1968).

MANIPULATION AND CO-OPTATION

In some situations, managers also resort to covert attempts to influence others. Manipulation, in this context, normally involves the very selective use of information and the conscious structuring of events.

One common form of manipulation is co-optation. Co-opting an individual usually involves giving him or her a desirable role in the design or implementation of the change. Co-opting a group involves giving one of its leaders, or someone it respects, a key role in the design or implementation of a change. This is not a form of participation, however, because the initiators do not want the advice of the co-opted, merely his or her endorsement. For example:

• One division manager in a large multi-business corporation invited the corporate human relations vice president, a close friend of the president, to help him and his key staff diagnose some problems the division was having. Because of his busy schedule, the corporate vice-president was not able to do much of the actual information gathering or analysis himself, thus limiting his own influence on the diagnoses. But his presence at key meetings helped commit him to the diagnoses as well as the solutions the group designed. The commitment was subsequently very important because the president, at least initially, did not like some of the proposed changes. Nevertheless, after discussion with his human relations vice-president, he did not try to block them.

Under certain circumstances co-optation can be a relatively inexpensive and easy way to gain an individual's or a group's support (cheaper, for example, than negotiation and quicker than participation). Nevertheless, it has its drawbacks. If people feel they are being tricked into not resisting, are not being treated equally, or are being lied to, they may respond very negatively. More than one manager has found that, by his effort to give some subordinate a sense of participation through co-optation, he created more resistance than if he had done nothing. In addition, co-optation can create a different kind of problem if those co-opted use their ability to influence the design and implementation of changes in ways that are not in the best interests of the organization.

Other forms of manipulation have drawbacks also, sometimes to an even greater degree. Most people are likely to greet what they perceive as covert treatment and/or lies with a negative response. Furthermore, if a manager develops a reputation as a manipulator, it can undermine his ability to use needed approaches such as education/communication and participation/involvement. At the extreme, it can even ruin his career.

Nevertheless, people do manipulate others successfully—particularly when all other tactics are not feasible or have failed. (Kotter 1977, 125). Having no other alternative, and not enough time to educate, involve, or support people, and without the power or other resources to negotiate, coerce, or co-opt them, managers have resorted to manipulating information channels in order to scare people into thinking there is a crisis coming which they can avoid only by changing.

EXPLICIT AND IMPLICIT COERCION

Finally, managers often deal with resistance coercively. Here they essentially force people to accept a change by explicitly or implicitly threatening them (with the loss of jobs, promotion possibilities, and so forth) or by actually firing or transferring them. As with manipulation, using coercion is a risky process because inevitably people strongly resent forced change. But in situations where speed is essential and where the changes will not be popular, regardless of how they are introduced, coercion may be the manager's only option.

Successful organizational change efforts are always characterized by the skillful application of a number of these approaches, often in very different combinations. However, successful efforts share two characteristics: managers employ the approaches with a sensitivity to their strengths and limitations (see *Exhibit 1*) and appraise the situation realistically.

The most common mistake managers make is to use only one approach or a limited set of them *regardless of the situation.* A surprisingly large number of managers have this problem. This would include the hard-boiled boss who often bogged down owing to unanticipated problems. Efforts that involve a large number of people, but are implemented quickly, usually become either stalled or less participative.

SITUATIONAL FACTORS

Exactly where a change effort should be strategically positioned on the continuum

EXHIBIT I Methods for Dealing With Resistance to Change

Approach	Commonly used in situations	Advantages	Drawbacks
Education + communication	Where there is a lack of information or inaccurate information and analysis.	Once persuaded, people will often help with the implementation of the change.	Can be very time-consuming if lots of people are involved.
Participation + involvement	Where the initiators do not have all the information they need to design the change, and where others have considerable power to resist.	People who participate will be committed to implementing change, and any relevant information they have will be integrated into the change plan.	Can be very time-consuming if participators design an inappropriate change.
Facilitation + support	Where people are resisting because of adjustment problems.	No other approach works as well with adjustment problems.	Can be time-consuming, expensive, and still fail.
Negotiation + agreement	Where someone or some group will clearly lose out in a change, and where that group has considerable power to resist.	Sometimes it is a relatively easy way to avoid major resistance.	Can be too expensive in many cases if it alerts others to negotiate for compliance.
Manipulation + co-optation	Where other tactics will not work, or are too expensive.	It can be a relatively quick and inexpensive solution to resistance problems.	Can lead to future problems if people feel manipulated.
Explicit + implicit coercion	Where speed is essential, and the change initiators possess considerable power.	It is speedy, and can overcome any kind of resistance.	Can be risky if it leaves people mad at the initiators.

in *Exhibit 2* depends on four factors:

1. The amount and kind of resistance that is anticipated. All other factors being equal, the greater the anticipated resistance, the more difficult it will be simply to overwhelm it, and the more a manager will need to move toward the right on the continuum to find ways to reduce some of it. (Lorsch 1976).
2. The position of the initiator vis-a-vis the resistors, especially with regard to power. The less power the initiator has with respect to others, the more the initiating manager *must* move to the left on the continuum. (Lorsch 1976). Conversely, the stronger the initiator's position, the more he or she can move to the right.
3. The person who has the relevant data for designing the change and the energy for implementing it. The more the initiators anticipate that they will need information and commitment from others to help design and implement the change, the more they must move to the right (Lorsch 1976). Gaining useful information and commitment requires time and the involvement of others.
4. The stakes involved. The greater the short-run potential for risks to organizational performance and survival if the present situation is not changed, the more one must move to the left.

Organizational change efforts that ignore these factors inevitably run into problems. A common mistake some managers make, for example, is to move too quickly and involve too few people despite the fact that they do not have all the information they really need to design the change correctly.

Insofar as these factors still leave a manager with some choice of where to operate on the continuum, it is probably best to select a point as far to the right as

---

EXHIBIT 2   Strategic Continuum

Fast	Slower
Clearly planned.	Not clearly planned at the beginning.
Little involvement of others.	Lots of involvement of others.
Attempt to overcome any resistance.	Attempt to minimize any resistance.

Key situational variables

The amount and type of resistance that is anticipated.

The position of the initiators vis-a-vis the resistors (in terms of power, trust, and so forth).

The locus of relevant data for designing the change, and of needed energy for implementing it.

The stakes involved (e.g., the presence or lack of presence of a crisis, the consequences of resistance and lack of change).

---

possible for both economic and social reasons. Forcing change on people can have just too many negative side effects over both the short and the long term. Change efforts using the strategies on the right of the continuum can often help develop an organization and its people in useful ways. (Been 1979).

In some cases, however, knowing the four factors may not give a manager a comfortable and obvious choice. Consider a situation where a manager has a weak position vis-a-vis the people whom he thinks need a change and yet is faced with serious consequences if the change is not implemented immediately. Such a manager is clearly in a bind. If he somehow is not able to increase his power in the situation, he will be forced to choose some compromise strategy and to live through difficult times.

IMPLICATIONS FOR MANAGERS

A manager can improve his chance of success in an organizational change effort by:

1. Conducting an organizational analysis that identifies the current situation, problems, and the forces that are possible causes of those problems. The analysis should specify the actual importance of the problems, the speed with which the problems must be addressed if additional problems are to be avoided, and the kinds of changes that are generally needed.
2. Conducting an analysis of factors relevant to producing the needed changes. This analysis should focus on questions of who might resist the change, why, and how much; who has information that is needed to design the change, and whose cooperation is essential in implementing it; and what is the position of the initiator vis-a-vis other relevant parties in terms of power, trust, normal modes of interaction, and so forth.
3. Selecting a change strategy, based on the previous analysis, that specifies the speed of change, the amount of preplanning, and the degree of involvement of others; that selects specific tactics for use with various individuals and groups; and that is internally consistent.
4. Monitoring the implementation process. No matter how good a job one does of initially selecting a change strategy and tactics, something unexpected will eventually occur during implementation. Only by carefully monitoring the process can one identify the unexpected in a timely fashion and react to it intelligently.

Interpersonal skills, of course, are the key to using this analysis. But even the most outstanding interpersonal skills will not make up for a poor choice of strategy and tactics. And in a business world that continues to become more and more dynamic, the consequences of poor implementation choices will become increasingly severe.

Hard Hats in the Boardroom: New Trends in Workers' Participation

WARNER P. WOODWORTH

This incident in the late 1970s was a jarring revelation to these truck company officials that a chasm was growing between the executive suite and the workers on the factory floor. To them, it suggested a different world of work, conflicting values

within the organization's culture, and a poignant lesson about the growing sophistication of today's new generation of workers.

Fueled by declining productivity rates and a national economic crisis, American managers and trade unions are seeking to invent new organizational approaches to industrial effectiveness. Numerous firms have launched quality circle programs as executives become enamored with the ideas and techniques of Japanese practices. Instead of looking eastward to the Orient for answers, we may see that the trends most significant to American industry are to be found in Europe. It is from there that we derive our roots—the Judeo–Christian ethic, our major theories of political democracy, economic development, and indeed, most of the underpinnings of our contemporary culture.

I propose to review the thrust of recent events in the European workplace and perhaps extrapolate from them shifts America might expect in the coming decade. As we reflect on changes in European political and economic spheres, are there any signs that similar seeds have been planted in American soil? What parallels are emerging in the United States? Finally, we will explore several frameworks for a restructuring of organizational power that are beginning to emerge in the 1980s and discuss their implications.

After 150 years, Europe is again giving birth to a new industrial age. The first was a technological revolution, an era of mechanization and mass production, of assembly-line organizational logic and the triumph of the machine. The second industrial revolution going on now is a transformation of power, a shifting of ec-

---

I asked the young, long-haired worker on the truck assembly line what it was like to have a job in this company. "They're running this plant like F.W. Taylor back in 1910!" Later, I returned to the front office for a meeting with the company's top management. Upon hearing of the assembly-worker's comment, the response of the executives was unanimous: "Who is F.W. Taylor?"

—Organizational consultant

---

onomic and political control in society from the few to the masses, from the owners to the producers of labor, from the haves to the have-nots. The results are yielding significant outcomes as the social structure is altered, as political expectations change, as a new psychology of entitlement emerges, and the nature of work itself is redefined.

Today in many advanced countries of Europe, a job no longer means simply arriving on time, operating a machine, and producing one's quota of quality products. Work has been infused with the notion of individual rights, the quality of working life, and the democratizing of corporate bureaucracy from the shop floor to the boardroom. Whether the national rhetoric is capitalistic or socialistic, the underlying thrust is a push for participation and power. For millions of workers across Europe, new institutional forms have been created in order to guarantee the redistribution of power. The range of these mechanisms makes up a phenomenon known as Industrial Democracy.

Instead of merely reporting to work and receiving orders for the day, the new worker's role is one of decision maker and policy setter. The experiments of the 1950s and 1960s have become institutionalized in the 1970s. Indeed, the past decade in Europe can be characterized as the most sweeping economic reform of the century. While the arguments from the political left and right vary on *how* to distribute the fruits of labor throughout society, the debate about whether to share the benefits of production more widely is all but over.

Immediately after World War II, France began the drive toward industrial democracy by establishing mandatory works councils in 1945. Germany went further in 1947, allocating to workers one-third of the board of directors' seats in the coal and steel industries. However, an explosion giving rise to full-fledged industrial democracy has culminated in over thirty changes in corporate-union relations among some ten countries in the past decade alone. Below is a sampling of these developments which empower workers and labor with new organizational and economic clout in different nations:

The Netherlands establishes works councils (1971)

Sweden passes one-third codetermination law (1972)

Austria legislates labor constitution (1973)

Britain creates Bullock Commission (1974)

Denmark establishes codetermination system (1974)

Sweden considers Meidner profit-sharing plan (1975)

Norway creates work environment act (1976)

Germany passes 50–50 codetermination law (1978)

The sum total of these legislative and social innovations means profound indus-

trial change. A more focused description of major types of change will suggest the flavor of these alternatives in the reform of industrial relations.

COLLECTIVE BARGAINING

The fundamental basis for union-management relations in Europe is still the labor contract, although it is built on a foundation of cooperation, in contrast to the adversary system of the United States. Trade union membership is high, often exceeding 90 percent of the work force, and includes not only blue-collar employees, but white-collar and managerial personnel in many countries. In contrast to the dominant bread-and-butter concerns of bargaining in America, the agenda of European labor unions in recent years has been broadened to include safety and health, joint decision making, and social rights of workers. Sweden, for example, established a Democracy at Work law in 1977 which essentially tore the lid off issues once considered managerial prerogatives. On the other hand, Italian unions have achieved industrial democracy gains

---

Industrial democracy: The new revolution

For us, the question is whether the workers are to control their own destinies, or be subjected to ever more intensive and minute control themselves, as the power of the oligarchs becomes ever more arbitrary and ever more irresponsible.

—Coates & Topham (p. 240) Great Britain

We demand steps be taken to fight against the extreme divisions of labor, loss of skills, and the subservience of man to machines.

—Policy Paper on Industrial Democracy, French Trade Union, CGT

A Smorgasbord of Workplace Democratization

What we are insisting from Lucas is a move away from weapons production for the arms trade—toward socially useful production: goods accessible to all, products which conserve resources and improve the environment.

—Member of Lucas Aerospace Combine Shop Stewards Committee (British labor strategy to combat mass layoffs through creation of alternative technology).

through collective bargaining rather than political means. In many cases the unions have used arbitration along with legislation to widen the focus from wages and working conditions to employment policies, capital investments, production schedule, and new plant construction.

WORKPLACE DEMOCRACY

The participation of workers at the shop-floor level of the firm has become a major focal point for industrial democracy. Early experiments in British coal mines and Swedish automobile assembly plants have led to widespread attempts to alter the relationship between the individual and the machine. Specific tactics and terms may vary: Norwegian work restructuring, job enrichment, British sociotechnical systems, Swedish autonomous work teams, and labor-management cooperation. The important goal is to restore meaning and growth to the work experience. Most European nations have as a high priority the improving of the quality of working life, illustrated in Germany's expenditure of over $100 million in the past five years to carry out research under the Humanization of the Work Act. The underlying principle seems to be that if workers participate in the design and execution of shopfloor activities, there will ensue a more productive process and higher-quality results, as well as a closer correspondence between bureaucratic organizational life and genuine societal democracy.

WORKS COUNCILS

National legislation exists which mandates the formation of a works council at the enterprise in numerous European countries—France, the Netherlands, Sweden, Belgium, and so on. Usually the councils are established as union-management consultative bodies to monitor factory working conditions and strengthen operations. These councils may range from groups of "all talk/no action" to very powerful committees which basically run the business. Usually between 10 and 20 in number, membership is either decided by one's formal position in the company or union hierarchy or by the election of representatives. In Belgium, the works councils are mainly an advisory body to top management, while in Italy and the Netherlands they are union-dominated and heavily control company decisions. In the latter case the councils have access to corporate information about future plans and financial data. Executives must involve the council in such decisions as plant relocations, mergers, product development, and layoffs. The councils have veto power over safety issues, changes in pensions and profit-sharing, and disciplinary policies. Operating a works council consumes a good deal of the time and energy of management and labor, but many argue the effort pays off as the council becomes a vehicle through which decisions get reached and plans are implemented.

CODETERMINATION

In attempting to mitigate against a rebirth of nazism after World War II, the West German government attempted to democratize the economy by giving workers board of directors representation in key industries. Since then, the percentage of workers' board seats has grown from 33 percent to parity (50 percent) in Germany, and similar legislation is now on the books in the Scandinavian countries, France, the Netherlands, and Austria. The Bullock Commission Report of Great Britain advocated a similar structure for U.K. industries, but the political support for such a move has not yet been achieved. Recently, the European Economic Community organization has recommended a two-tier board system for all European companies in which the top level would have equal representation for workers and owners, with a second-level board consisting wholly of upper management, accountable as a group to the top board. Some nations mandate codetermination only in certain industries, and only in large companies. On the other hand, Sweden requires labor representation on the board of all firms employing (25) or more people. In most cases of codetermination, the trade union power seems to be mostly information; i.e., access to profit-and-loss statements and employee relations data rather than workers' using their power to redirect or block corporate activities.

INCOME REDISTRIBUTION

Perhaps the potentially most profound and far-reaching European changes have to do with worker participation in the corporate financial picture. The essence of sharing in the profits of a firm, however, is not simply a question of depositing an extra bonus in one's bank, but broadranging societal control. The ultimate goal is for the masses to obtain decision-making power through widespread stock ownership—a fundamental form of democratizing the economy. Such ideas are largely in the proposal stage at present, as labor leaders and economists advocate trade union control of the means of production throughout Europe. The first of this legislation to succeed will probably occur in Sweden, where the Meidner Plan is likely to be implemented since the Social Democrats' return to power in late 1982. This plan would turn 20 percent of the country's corporate profits over to a central fund administered by the union. Such a move would give labor virtual control of Sweden's economy within several years by creating a political economy of a Third Way, an alternative to the traditional dichotomy of having to choose between capitalism or socialism. Another illustration of a macro approach to economic democracy can be seen developing out of Yugoslavia's system in Eastern Europe.

There, workers' self-management has emerged as a radical and unique means by which all factories are socially owned, workers are elected to manage the firm, and major corporate decisions are decided democratically by voting.

While the shifts toward worker participation have perhaps been more dramatic in Europe, the American case suggests the seeds of change. From human relations training and organizational development techniques which emphasized trust and working together but left the central issue of organizational power untouched, the push today in countless firms is on the Quality of Working Life (QWL). The underlying thrust seems to be that *it is not enough to do things differently; what is needed is to do different things.*

Hundreds of firms, like Procter & Gamble and Westinghouse, have designed and built new plants based on a logic of "small is beautiful." These new wave factories tend to be single-storied facilities with plenty of sunlight, access to the out-of-doors, and brightly colored work spaces. Rather than ten thousand workers packed into crowded pigeonholes, the new firms

---

Parallels in America

There are no bad people, only bad management.

—Group Executive Vice-President, General Electric Corporation

I think most of us are looking for a calling, not a job. Most of us, like the assembly-line worker, have jobs that are too small for our spirit. Jobs are not big enough for people.

—*Working*, by Studs Terkel (p. xxiv)

usually have 500 employees at the maximum, a size that is more consistent with human-scale organizations. Such enterprises do not suffer from hierarchical overkill, but are simpler to understand and generate feelings of belonging to the company family. Smallness enhances the possibility that when difficulties emerge, the organization is not so large and complex that problems are unchangeable. A number of other aspects of today's new plants reveal the cumulative effect of change: no time clocks; no uniforms; teams of workers doing their own scheduling, hiring, and firing; quality control; light maintenance; often without even immediate supervisors.

Meanwhile, dramatic alterations are also appearing in the old manufacturing industries of the Northeast. To combat community deterioration caused by strikes, low productivity, and runaway plants, dozens of cities have created area labor-management committees. Among the most widely heralded successes are those of Muskegon, Michigan and Jamestown, New York, where union officials, industrial owners and managers, and elected representatives of the public have created regional councils engaged in cooperative problem-solving. In many cases such efforts have led to reduced work stoppages, improved health and safety records, the retention of once-threatened jobs, and revitalization of the regional economy. These new forums for anticipatory joint planning, rather than post facto reactions to a crisis, have resulted in job guarantees, improved percentages of corporate bids on new work, redesign of plant layouts, and community-wide commitment to a different quality of life.

The present "era of labor concessions" has not been so much a period of union givebacks, but a tradeoff. In numerous cases workers have agreed to not demand wage increases and even to reductions in benefits or other settlements which minimize costs to the firm. However, labor has sought and gained power in exchange for such agreements, illustrated by the following recent sampling of new contracts: Ford and General Motors agreed with the United Auto Workers not to close down assembly plants and to reduce outside competitive buying of parts; American Telephone and Telegraph agreed to consult electrical workers' "technological change committees" before any innovations were implemented; the United Rubber Workers won the right to inspect Uniroyal's books in exchange for concessions; workers at Pan American, Chrysler, and a number of smaller firms gained seats on the board of directors so they could monitor corporate performance and have access to critical financial data.

Perhaps a fundamental sign of the new industrial revolution in America is the shift toward workers' self-management and employee ownership. Sharing in the fruits of one's labors has been an evolutionary idea for some years, illustrated by the proliferation of profit-sharing schemes, Scanlon plans, and the more recent program of Improshare. However, more recently, employee stock ownership has mushroomed. In some cases, the workers simply obtain stock through special company arrangements, illustrated by Hallmark Cards or Sears, Roebuck, and Company (which is 20 percent employee-owned). In other instances, employees gained major blocks of stock through some sort of financing package, such as the Chrysler autoworkers obtaining 15 percent of the company's stock, 12 million shares, as part of the bailout plan, a figure which will rise to 25 percent by 1984. In hundreds of cases during the last five years, small business entrepreneurs have turned their firms over to their employees upon retirement, workers and communities have fought imminent plant closings through the tactic of a worker buyout, and thousands of jobs have been salvaged.

All told, today there are over 5,000

worker-owned firms across the country. In Poland when the heroic trade union, Solidarity, demanded as one of its core economic reforms a program of workers' self-management and ownership, the regime criticized the union proposal as bourgeois capitalism. In contrast, in the United States when one speaks of worker ownership, the idea is often rejected as socialism. Curiously, recent legislation reveals the notion of employee ownership to have widespread bipartisan support in Congress and even in the White House. So today worker ownership is growing, from 17 plywood corporations in the Northwest to an insurance company in Washington where workers elect their own managers. From a New Jersey automotive parts plant GM agreed to sell to its UAW workers to the $500 million-a-year Rath Packing Company in Iowa where workers control 11 of 17 seats on the board of directors. From the Chicago and Northwestern Railroad to the *Milwaukee Journal*. From large-scale agricultural co-ops to new wave collectives in light industry, crafts, and other economic alternatives. The idea was embraced by the newest and largest employee-owned firm in the country, a steel mill in Weirton, West Virginia which is being bought by 10,000 steelworkers and has become the eighth largest steel company in America. It has also caught hold in Philadelphia, where over 20 A & P food stores were closed late last year. Now an ingenious plan has been launched to reopen the stores under a new name with a heavy dose of worker participation and the funneling of profits into a fund to buy up the stores by the employees.

While the transporting of the new industrial revolution across the Atlantic is far from complete, the winds seem to be blowing in this direction. Although we should not overstate the similarities between Europe and America, the "Europeanization" of U.S. industry tends to look like the future. A key difference is that much of the shift in power to American workers is coming about through voluntary agreements between unions and companies, not because of political alliances and state-mandated legislation typified by much of Europe. In other words, while the thrust of the change is similar, the means differ and seem to be based on a distinctly American approach in which the federal government stays out. Another factor which distinguishes change between the two continents is that in the United States there is generally not a coherent policy among employers' associations or international labor organizations regarding workers' participation. Rather, the process is occuring in piecemeal fashion. There have been several exceptions, such as the creation of plant-level labor-management committees throughout the steel industry and the General Motors–UAW formal commitment to participative structurers which ensure a higher quality of working life. But the norm seems to be that the union local and/or plant management propose changes which lead to bottom-up empowerment.

In attempting to analyze QWL as an approach to organizational change, it may be useful to look at the whole picture

---

Quality of Working Life Frameworks

For 30 years Earl Murray has been tagging meat in the shipping department of the Rath Packing Company. Currently, he spends one day a month in a new role as a worker on the firm's board of directors. Out in the plant, he's a typical member of the 2,000–member union. In the boardroom he's a champion of the view from below in the analysis of company operations.

from different angles. One view that might be taken arises from consideration of the *level* of worker participation (shown in Table 1).

To explain this chart, let us begin with the lowest level of participation, *Terms and working conditions*. In America, the labor contract has been the historical vehicle for worker participation, as collective bargaining set the pay, benefits, duties, and otherwise defined the relationship between management and labor. Essentially, it boiled down to an assumption that "management's job is to manage and workers do the work."

A step-up in participation has developed over the past few years in cases where the union has been invited to become a partner with management in the administration of the firm. Under the rubric of *participative management*, Ford Motor Company has created employee involvement committees in over a hundred plants across the country in which workers and supervisors jointly assess problems and brainstorm possible solutions. Quality of working life specialists at General Motors have labored for a number of years to bring UAW and management representatives together for team-building programs in which trust and a new level of open dialogue are established for joint management of the factory.

During the decade of the 1970s, Dana Corporation increased productivity 126 percent by involving most of its 24,000 workers in participative management programs. Cummins Engine, General Foods, and others began to restructure decision making so that work teams became self-managing. Prominent European parallels consist of the Swedish new plant designs, sociotechnical redesign of work experiments in Britain, and so on.

Other efforts have raised the degree of organizational participation even higher, to a third level—the inclusion of workers in a firm's *governance*. Examples from Europe consist of work councils at the plant level in France, the Netherlands, and Belgium, and codetermination of the corporation in the cases of West Germany, Austria, and Scandinavia. The most widely heralded example of codetermination in the U.S. was the election of United Auto Workers President Douglas Fraser to the board of Chrysler Corporation in 1980. More recently, a union representative was elected to the board of Pan American World Airways to improve organizational effectiveness in the face of mounting losses. In other firms, such as Donnelly Mirrors, all employees are represented in an elected committee which sets all policy for personnel issues in the corporation.

Perhaps the most powerful level of participation is that of *legally owning a business*. European instances include Yugoslavian self-management, worker buyouts in Sweden, Britain's Scott Baker Commonwealth, and the 80 industrial cooperatives in Mondragon, Spain, which employ 20,000 workers in an intricate network which includes a worker bank, R & D center, engineering school, and housing complex. Worker ownership in America may arise from a profit-sharing program which gives employees a stake in the business, as illustrated by firms like Eastman Kodak which are partially owned by employees. Or the ownership may include over 50 percent of the stock held by the workers as is the case with South Bend Lathe, Bates Fabric, Rath Packing Company, and Hyatt–Clark Industries. In the latter case, for instance, workers are empowered to elect three di-

TABLE 1	Levels of Organizational Participation
Ownership—Stock control	
Governance—co-determination of policy	
Management—administration	
Terms and working conditions—Labor Agreements	

rectors of the company. They have set up an extensive system of worker participation and will directly own 100 percent of the stock ten years after taking over what was once a General Motors roller bearing facility.

To look at QWL from another angle, three basic *forms* of participation may exist (see Table 2).

One form is the involvement of the *individual*—an employee approaches management with ideas and criticisms. These may be verbal or written, solicited or unsolicited, and are often obtained through such programs as an open-door policy or suggestion box. A second form is that of *group* activity—quality circles, Scanlon committees, semi-autonomous or autonomous work teams, and so on. The third form is *organizational*, which, in contrast to the two direct approaches, is representational. Illustrations of this include the Management Councils created in Westinghouse Corporation in which representatives from supervisory ranks in various departments are elected to open up channels of communication, make recommendations regarding management needs, and so on.

TABLE 2 Forms of Participation

Individual—Direct
Group—Direct
Organizational—Representative

The Future

We encourage and support the shared responsibility of all people at Oldsmobile toward a common goal: producing a quality product at a competitive price, in an atmosphere of cooperation and shared recognition, in which everyone has the opportunity to participate in the decision-making process.

—Mission statement, Management-Union Steering Committee, Oldsmobile Division and United Auto Workers Local 652

Another angle from which a different perspective of organizational change appears is to look at a scale of participative power. Table 3 attempts to suggest a hierarchy of decision making and is illustrated with examples from cases discussed above. While the range of worker input varies considerably, one might argue that the higher on the ladder worker participation in decisions goes, the more potential exists for genuine workers' control and organizational democracy.

A central thesis of this report is that the impetus for organizational change in the United States has its roots in European culture, not Japan. Shifting worker expectations, "new breed" values about one's job, and the current economic crisis enlarge the context for an increasingly democratic organizational life. The range of recent behavioral science theories, managerial practices, and labor proposals are designed to give workers more of a voice, heightened autonomy, and an enlarged share of responsibility in company operations.

There seem to be two basic premises for changes toward worker participation, whether at the factory floor or in the boardroom. One is pragmatic rationale which argues that such participation will ensure corporate profits, improve productivity, and better utilize the firm's human resources. The other view stems from an ideological premise that until the rights of the individual penetrate the company gates, the fundamental ideals of a participatory democracy in society will not be achieved.

While the thrust of industrial democracy seems to portend a future of dramatic alterations in the social and economic infrastructure of modern society, this movement in America is not without its problems and failures. One of the best-known cases of a worker takeover, the Vermont Asbestos Group, was a large financial success, but the worker-owners eventually lost a controlling interest in the stock and the firm has recently reverted to a more traditional system. Similarly, the worker participation experiments that the Harvard Project on Technology, Work, and Character launched in 1972 with Harmon International Industries and the UAW in Bolivar, Tennessee have either been dismantled or extensively altered from an earlier, progressive form to more of a status quo organization.

Doubts and resistance to genuine democratization of industry are articulated in many management and trade union circles. Executive attitudes often reflect the view a CEO recently expressed to me that the current crisis over productivity and hard economic times is forcing business to seek employee input and listen to shopfloor-level ideas. His expectation, though, is couched in the hope that when the economy bounces back, channels from below will be blocked and the fortress-type practices of the past will again become the *modus operandi*.

Organized labor also has its concerns about joint union-management problem-solving. Said an official of the International Association of Machinists and Aereospace Workers, "We have a feeling that if we get into bed with management, there's going to be two people screwing the workers instead of one." And certain aspects of industrial democracy are referred to as "rainbow chasing" by Thomas Donahue, executive assistant to the president of the AFL–CIO, who argues: "We do not seek to be a partner in management—to be most likely the junior partner in success and the senior partner in failure."

Regardless of the controversies surrounding these new mechanisms for change and worker participation, the likelihood is that the radical alterations of the recent past will become norm within a decade or two. Cosmetic changes of the organization's facade will die quickly. But the substantive shifts of power beginning to occur suggest a future groundswell that will lead us into the twenty-first century. These changes are exploding from the guts and the heart of middle America. Top management and union officials who do not begin to articulate a coherent vision of a truly democratized society may be overthrown by the hard hats now clamoring at the gates.

TABLE 3 Range of Participation in Decisions

Word Station Decisions	Day-to-day Team Management	Technology and Planning	Business Procucts	Profits Distribution and Investment
Collective bargaining decisions regarding job bidding, place of work, etc.	Labor-management committees, quality, circles: GM, Ford	Sociotechnical design, layout new plant start-ups: Volvo, Saab, Procter & Gamble, General Foods	Worker involvement in the creation of new product lines, socially beneficial products: Scott Baker, Rath Packing	Control of financial budget and corporate investments: Mondragon, U. S. Plywood co-ops

A Billion Levi's Later

ED CRAY *

How the Levi Strauss Company Has Combined Business
Success With Its Own Brand of Social Responsibility.

They are ubiquitous, virtually universal, 60 threads to the inch, the seams sewn in orange. Their fading indigo stretches from San Francisco to the Far East and beyond. They are even bootlegged to the walls of the Kremlin. Their brand name has become the generic term for all blue denim pants, and, despite competition, Levi Strauss & Co.'s 100–year–old western work pants still lead an industry caught up in the great leisure-time boom.

Guaranteed to shrink and fade, workaday Levi's are an unlikely foundation on which to build the world's largest clothing manufacturer, a $1.5–billion-a-year corporation marketing 1,500 different garments in 70 countries. But then Levi Strauss is an unlikely company. Publicly traded just since 1971, the 125–year–old multinational is still controlled by heirs of the founder Levi Strauss, a Bavarian Jew who migrated to the United States in 1848. The family tradition runs deep, in-

Reprinted from *Politics Today*. Reprinted by permission of author.

* Ed Cray is The Director of Metro Training at the Los Angeles Times whose book, Levi's, was published by Houghton Mifflin. Cray, who also teaches journalism at the University of Southern California, is at work on a biography of Geroge C. Marshall.

fusing the corporation with a sense of social responsibility much praised in the business press and rarely imitated in the business world.

"It's in the genes," punned the shirt-sleeved chairman of the board, Walter Haas, Jr. It *is* the jeans, and their offspring, that have made it possible for Haas and his brother Peter, president and chief executive officer, to pursue their youthful ambition to make Levi Strauss the best corporation in America.

What Wall Street once regarded as a funny little San Francisco pants manufacturer may not be the best corporation in America; it depends on one's measure. But it has been an unparalleled financial success.

Just 30 years ago, the company had modest sales of $11 million. Some $3 million of that total came from wholesaling other firms' products. But a succession of shrewd business moves and some serendipitous sociological trends transformed the mundane pants first into a youthful symbol of protest, and then into the vestment of leisure in America. As the post-World War II baby boom children grew, faded blue denim became a national uniform associated with the relaxed lifestyle of the West. California, as in other things, set the pace. Levi's dominated the market there before they took over the rest of the nation.

The denim phenomenon carried with it the three major jeans manufacturers: Levi Strauss; Blue Bell with its lower-priced Wrangler brand; and VF with its high-quality H.D. Lee label. With its strong western image and a youth-oriented advertising campaign, Levi Strauss consistently outsells its combined rivals by wide margins (by $214 million this year alone).

The Haas brothers themselves rose through the ranks, gradually assuming control from their father, Walter Haas, Sr., and from their uncle, Daniel Koshland. And as they did they methodically expanded the company's product line. First slacks, then boys' pants; a women's wear line and sportswear followed. Meanwhile, the jeans business prospered beyond the most optimistic of corporate forecasts.

In 1964 Levi Strauss introduced Sta-Prest, the first successful permanent press, and that caught on with even the most haughty department stores. By 1968, the company (then privately held) had annual sales of more than $200 million. Ten years later, that figure has grown more than 700 percent. Profits have more than stayed apace, rising from $12.1 million in 1968 to $129.8 million this year. (If one looks at profits as a percentage of capital investment, the company's performance is particularly impressive: according to *Fortune,* in 1977 Levi Strauss was among the ten most profitable firms in the country.)

The great leisure-time boom—and the "California" lifestyle contagion—spread overseas, carried by Levi's jeans. Levi Strauss International has become a $500 million-a-year enterprise with 27 factories dotted about the globe. (Last year the firm signed an agreement with the Hungarian government that will introduce red-tabbed Levi's to Iron Curtain countries on a formal basis. That might reduce the black market price in Russia: $100–a–pair, used.)

In conventional terms, Levi Strauss is a rousing success. It is the largest of 22,000 American clothing manufacturers; beyond the men's jeans market, it is the second largest manufacturer of branded boy's wear (just behind Sear's house brand), the largest of sport-coat manufacturers, and, in just five years, one of the four largest shirtmakers in the country. But the Haas brothers, and the executives they have brought up through the ranks with them, do not measure success solely by the bottom line. The firm's first stock prospectus, issued when Levi Strauss went public, devoted one of three paragraphs in the legal description of the company to this:

> The Company's social responsibilities have for many years been a matter of strong conviction on the part of its management. Well before legal requirements were imposed, the Company was an "equal opportunity employer." In 1969, the Company received one of *Business Week* magazine's first two "Business Citizenship" awards in the field of human resources.

The corporation's underwriters think this paragraph was the first such announcement in a stock prospectus. The Haases have worked to institutionalize within the company their personal sense of social concern. The brothers have also tried to inspire similar feelings in other companies, where "social responsibility" is most often confined to self-serving institutional advertising, tax-deductible charity, and legally mandated equal employment opportunity.

The Haases see social responsibility as more. "It's really integrity in dealing with the public, with customers, with employees, with the communities in which we live. And this is where business has such a bad image," said Walter Haas. "There hasn't been integrity there."

For Levi Strauss, integrity begins with high quality, backed by a liberal merchandise-return policy. That was the case in 1873, when the company introduced the Two House brand denim pants, and it still applies, a billion pairs of pants later. The quality of the garments produced at Levi Strauss factories is closely monitored. Eighty-four people, with a budget of $1.3 million annually, police the company's purchases and the end product. Levi Strauss customarily rejects as substandard about 5 percent of the more than 250 million yards of fabric it buys annually. (The total yardage used would wrap a bandage around the equator almost five times; the rejected fabric would stretch from San Francisco to Melbourne.)

The standards are rigidly applied. The 13.5–ounce denim used in the famed jeans is produced largely by one American mill, and has been for more than 35 years. What is found to be flawed is rejected by Levi Strauss. Denim has been in short supply, and what Strauss rejects gets snapped up by less persnickety competitors in the United States and abroad.

Standards are not relaxed for expediency's sake. The company postponed for a year production of double-knit leisure suits, and thus missed the great boom of 1972, because Product Integrity repeatedly rejected the sampled piece goods as substandard. While Levi's merchandisers fretted and other companies scored, Product Integrity stood firm. Similarly, designers and merchandisers in women's wear, acutely aware of timing in that fashion-oriented market, repeatedly seek relief, and repeatedly find their fabrics rejected and returned to the mills.

Such striving for quality is not unique to Levi Strauss, to be sure; other corporations undertake similar efforts, but how many of them are willing to exchange a million garments (with a wholesale value of $7 million) to back up the pledge each year? Despite the costs, the return policy has been in effect for as long as anyone can remember. Walter Haas, Sr., who is now 88 years old, recalls that it hasn't changed since he joined the company in 1919. "If you don't give quality," he says, "you're responsible. It's as simple as that. Maybe that is one of the reasons we have been successful—because we have curious ideas."

The idea that Levi's should be durable, whether it's curious or not, has generated customer loyalty beyond dollar measure. The company regularly gets unsolicited letters from customers bragging that *their* pants lasted five or ten years, or seven unwashed months in a Cuban prison, or through high school, marriage and pregnancy. Doctors and grateful parents write in claiming that little Johnny's Levi's saved him from severe injury when he fell off: (a) his bike, (b) the cliff, or (c) the roof.

Consumer affection for Levi's is unrivaled by any product since Henry Ford's Model T. Presumably, the affection could be measured in dollars if one but knew how.

But profit is not the only motive here. In an era of inch-thick contracts and phalanxes of attorneys, Levi Strauss still feels free to do business with suppliers in its own quirky fashion. For 30 years the company has contracted for the manufacture of pants with a relatively small firm in Sedalia, Missouri. The J.A. Lamy Co. gave up its own branded lines long ago and now makes only Levi's. It is totally vulnerable to takeover, yet for 30 years the contract between Lamy and Levi Strauss has been no firmer than a handshake.

Levi Strauss & Co. has unique values, and a new employee has some learning to do. The president of Levi's Womenswear Division, Jim McDermott, explains that "If you make a mistake in buying a fabric, you don't go back to the mill and say, 'I'm Levi's, and if you don't bury it I'll cut you off.' You eat your mistake. We made a commitment and we live with it."

Commitment means a lot to McDermott, who came to Levi Strauss because of a broken promise. He had been a salesman for General Foods' Jello Division when the company "screwed around with the bonus arrangement they had and I got pissed off." McDermott quit, went to an employment agency, and was dispatched to Levi Strauss as a clerk. Thirteen years later, McDermott is president of a $26–million-a-year division and a corporate vice-president.

The commitment also turns inward. Managers of many corporations refer to their workers as "family." The decision lasts as long as labor relations are amicable.

Levi Strauss managers, especially the older ones with the most seniority, also look upon their coworkers warmly. And they reminisce about when the company was small, when the production manager knew every woman on the line and knew her husband's name and how her children were doing in school, when the Haases loaned money to hard-put workers, or paid extraordinary medical bills.

In 30 years of explosive growth, from 2,000 to 32,000 employees around the world, much of the paternalism has dissipated. "The Haases are trying to hold onto it," says Ed Pera, manager of the company's Canadian operations. "We're losing that feeling for people. The Haases are extremely upset about it."

Because the Haases themselves can no longer personally give employees that sense of family, they have tried to institutionalize it. When Levi Strauss first topped the billion-dollar sales mark in 1975, the board of directors voted to give the 2,700 home-office employees company stock. And a $50 check went to each of the firm's 23,000 far-flung workers. The company paid the income taxes on the bonuses. Altogether, the gesture cost Levi Strauss $2.1 million.

On its own motion—no union contract or retirement plan mandated it—the company increased pensions of its 800 retirees in 1975 and 1976 by as much as 80 percent in order to cover increases in the cost of living. The additional outlay of $250,000 each year is modest, though over the next 15 years it will likely total some $1.75 million.

Past retirees automatically get boosts to keep them abreast of present retirees, again at the instance of the company. The only rationale is that "it's the right thing to do," as vice-president and director Paul Glasgow put it.

The examples go on and on. After purchasing a clothing maker called Oberman in an effort to expand Levi's production quickly, Strauss gave the 3,000 Oberman employees who came with the factory full credit for the years they had worked in Oberman plants.

To a corporation selling 40 percent of men's denim pants in the United States and making $129 million in profits, these sums are not great burdens. Still, how many of the other 241 U.S. companies with more than a billion dollars in annual sales are so keen to share their wealth?

The generosity, according to Ernest Griffes, the manager of employee benefits, stems from a "basic tradition of sincere concern for the welfare and security of employees." Because of their scope, such efforts are necessarily impersonal, the corporate equivalent of a family tradition. So it isn't particularly surprising that Walter Haas should be proudest of a more modest program of his, one that could be funded from petty cash. It was his idea to hire older people to pay monthly visits to retirees in San Francisco and Knoxville, Tennessee. The visitors bring gifts, sometimes food, and make certain that the retirees are cared for. "I really don't understand why more companies don't do it. It doesn't cost much, and we want people to know that we care about them, even after they've stopped working for us."

It is hard to see how unpublicized visits to old people have any bearing on Wall Street's yardstick of corporate excellence—return on investment. Certainly, there are no more hours at the salvage table to be wrung from Mary Rossi, who, at 101 years of age, remembers Levi Strauss himself.

In 1978 Levi Strauss began awarding shares of stock to all employees with five years of service, one share for each year. The initial distribution to 8,800 workers dealt off 60,000 shares with a market value of $1.7 million.

Employee stock ownership is not a new concept at Levi Strauss. The firm seems to have been one of the first to permit employees to be shareholders. Between 1912 and 1971, the year the company went public, about a thousand workers bought shares, frequently at bargain prices. When "LeviStr" went on the Big Board, 29 current and former employees became instant millionaires, and scores of others, including a stock clerk whose shares were worth more than $340,000, found themselves comfortably fixed for life.

As a matter of practice, union-negotiated benefit increases are automatically extended to the 25 percent of the workers not enrolled in unions. And that turns out to be good for business. Levi Strauss has lost just five week's work to strikes since it was first unionized in 1935. Negotiations with the three unions in Strauss plants— Teamsters in one distribution center, the United Garment Workers, and the Amalgamated Clothing and Textile Union elsewhere—are low-key. "As long as you're fair," said Max Cowan, national production manager of the $700–million-a-year Jeans Division, "it doesn't make much difference whether you have a labor union or you don't."

Levi Strauss has been a corporate overachiever in equal employment opportunity. Already integrated in its California facilities, the firm began hiring blacks in segregated Blackstone, Virginia, in 1957. Community opposition was strong, and at one point the company feared it was going to lose the plant's output. But Levi Strauss insisted on integrating and since it was the town's biggest employer, it prevailed. Levi Strauss has been totally integrated since.

With many companies, entry-level jobs for unskilled blacks and browns are one thing, promotions another. Levi Strauss is doing relatively well, but management is acutely aware that its proportions of minorities don't reflect the population. Minorities now constitute 14 percent of all company managers, 20 percent of the professionals, and one-third of the technicians. Percentages are inching up year by year largely because of promotions from within. Sewing machine operators rise to jobs as line managers; clerks become merchandisers. It is, in fact, an extension of the company policy of old: "Hire an office boy when the president retires." Two of the five current division presidents began as shipping clerks in the stock room.

Though women make up 80 percent of Levi Strauss's employees, until the women's movement became strong, the company was no more sensitive to sexual discrimination than other corporations were. Only a few women survived competition and prejudice to rise to middle management positions. Once discrimination was understood for what it was, Levi Strauss moved to put things right. According to its 1977 annual report, women now make up 22 percent of the officials and managers, 40 percent of the professionals, and 8 percent of its (at one time all-male) domestic sales force of 600 persons.

The Haases and others at Levi Strauss are very much aware that social responsibility is good business and that it contributes to profits. Walter Haas explains, "We can compete with IBM or Procter and Gamble and all the others for the top graduate school students because they want to identify with a company that has this philosophy. And that assures our success 20 years from now."

If Levi Strauss does right by its customers, suppliers and employees, with whom it has a direct mercantile relationship, the corporation also perceives a responsibility to the larger community. Its company-sponsored community relations teams in the towns and cities in which the corporation has facilities are the broadest based, most innovative, and probably the most altruistic of the Levi Strauss programs.

Volunteers at each of the domestic facilities seek out worthy local projects, then support them. The Levi Strauss foundation sometimes helps with cash contributions, but it has other interests.

The Clovis, New Mexico boyswear manufacturing plant was selected as having the outstanding community relations team in 1976. Its members had, among other things, visited nursing homes, given a Christmas party at a mental retardation center, collected toys and clothes for a children's home, and so on. In an era of six-figure corporate donations to causes, such efforts appear modest, and they are. But in Clovis, which has a population of 28,495, they are noticed, and they have counterparts in teams at 50 other company plants and distribution centers.

Indeed such employee teams are mandated company policy. Not all plant managers are enthusiastic, but the efforts of their CRT are taken into account when bonuses are awarded.

Approximately one-third of the firm's sales, and something less than one-third of its profits, come from overseas operations. Corporate policy stresses strongly identifying Levi Strauss with the host country. Only 10 percent of its international managers are American citizens. Each of the overseas groups has been transformed into a self-sustaining manufacturing and sales entity; European goods are made and distributed in Europe. Far Eastern goods are marketed in the Orient. Prices are necessarily higher, and sales are thus limited, but Levi Strauss thereby becomes a local manufacturer, without the aura of a rich American corporation exploiting the local economy.

Except for some sweaters made in the Far East, Levi Strauss does not take advantage of cheaper foreign labor to manufacture goods overseas for sale in the United States. That, of course, places Levi Strauss at a substantial disadvantage domestically. Smaller, more fashion-oriented manufacturers such as Faded Glory, Brittania, Jag and Chemin-de-fer rely on cheap foreign labor, workers paid as little as 40 cents an hour (compared to the American minimum wage of $3.60), to produce their one-season, high-markup garments. Geared for the long haul, and for repeat business, Levi Strauss forgoes the quick profits.

Overseas operations are governed by a thick book of corporate policy statements, the most important of which are two from its "Code of International Business Principles":

> The Company is committed to operating well above the minimum legal standard such that its conduct and intentions are above question ... The Company subscribes to the belief that its operations should provide benefits to ... the host country as well as its stockholders and investors. The Company affirms that all its investments will be in harmony with the social, economic and environmental priorities of the host countries and that it intends to conduct its business in such a way as to earn acceptance and respect.

Every multinational company doing business today makes policy statements of platitudes. At Levi Strauss, they are taken seriously. The company does no business in South Africa and Rhodesia. And it has closed its operations in Indonesia, in part because of the common local practice of paying bribes for the most routine of services.

For all the good intentions, overseas managers do transgress. In 1976 and 1977, Levi Strauss announced that four of its people had passed $145,000 in bribes, in the form of so-called license fees expected to be paid by foreigners. Levi Strauss reported the payments to the Securities and Exchange Commission and dismissed the officers involved for violating corporate policy.

In June the company agreed to pay $3.5 million to Californians who had bought Levi's jeans between 1972 and 1975. The agreement settled a suit filed by the state's attorney general charging that Levi Strauss salesmen had threatened to close accounts with retailers who discounted Levi's jeans. The company, in this matter, did not admit guilt but settled nevertheless.

Good corporate citizenship of the sort practiced by Levi Strauss does not just happen. Nor can it be legislated, not exactly. Governments may permit tax credits for charitable contributions and corporations will make charitable contributions. But no tax credit could account for Levi Strauss's charitable impulses. Congress may mandate reforms in pension plans, and cunning tax lawyers will find loopholes. Making certain that retired workers are well cared for stems from a sense of duty foreign to bottom-line economics and legal obligation.

Walter Haas, Jr., much honored for his efforts to promote social responsibility among his peers, now has stopped giving speeches about it. "They don't do any good," he says.

Of course what business and industry are not inclined to do government will require. Business people can complain that there is too much government regulation already—of air and water pollution, of occupational safety and equal employment opportunity, of product safety and efficacy, of warranties, pension plans and energy conservation. But the government intruded only after the private sector flagrantly failed to live up to minimal standards of social responsibility.

For the most part corporations now care mainly about a single measure of business performance: profit and loss. Which is why Levi Strauss is such a fascinating anomaly.

Breaking Through

Women on the Move

In one of the most significant trends of the 1980s, women are steadily toppling barriers and assuming leadership in fields that traditionally have been closed to them.

The process is slow, arduous, often un-

noticed. While the numbers are still small, the attitude changes they signal are enormous.

A decade ago, the nation's space program allowed no women as astronauts. Now it has eight.

Ten years ago, even the largest U.S. banks could count on one finger their number of female vice-presidents. Now some giant banks have more than 100 women as vice-presidents and one or two as senior vice-presidents.

In 1972, women in companies with 100 or more employees held only 1 of 8 management jobs. Now they occupy 1 of 5. Ten years ago, 13 women served in the House of Representatives. Next January, 21 will serve, a record. Just over 300 women sat in state legislatures in 1972. The current figure exceeds 900.

And until last year, the Supreme Court was a monastic sanctum. Now it has Associate Justice Sandra O'Connor.

Statistics can deceive. A different set of figures, equally valid, shows that women—who are 51.3 percent of the U.S. population—still comprise only 5 percent of executives in the 50 top corporations, 10 percent of the astronauts, 12 percent of state legislators, 2 percent of U.S. senators.

Clearly, though the walls are crumbling around preserves that are still male dominated. Once the trailblazers breach the barriers, others follow close behind.

The momentum can be seen in the legal field. In 1960, only 3.3 percent of lawyers and judges were women. Since then, the figure has jumped four times. And, as Justice O'Connor has noted, women make up a third to a half of today's law-school classes.

Some women leaders in nontraditional fields are well known: Rosalyn Yalow, the second woman in history—after France's Marie Curie—to win the Nobel Prize in medicine; Sherry Lansing, the ex-model and script reader who became president of 20th Century–Fox movie studios; Sarah Caldwell, the conductor who founded the Opera Company of Boston and was the first woman to wield a baton at the Metropolitan Opera in New York.

Yet most of today's female pioneers are not household names. Thelma Estrin? A professor of engineering at the University of California at Los Angeles who helped pioneer the application of computer technology to brain research. Eugenie Clark? Biologist, University of Maryland professor of zoology, world renowned as an expert on sharks. Barbara Newell? Former president of Wellesley, now chancellor of Florida's university system. Nelle Nugent and Liz McCann? Toast-of-New-York producers whose hits include "Dracula," "The Elephant Man" and "The Life and Adventures of Nicholas Nickleby."

They and the six women whose stories follow demonstrate that it is now possible for women to reach high levels in almost any career. Numerically, women are still getting off the ground in positions of leadership. But, as the space program shows, they are finding that literally even the sky is no limit.

"JUST ANOTHER ASTRONAUT"

HOUSTON

When Sally Ride slips into her fireproof blue coveralls and blasts into orbit next April aboard the Challenger shuttle, she will become an instant heroine as the first U.S. woman in space.

A 31–year–old astrophysicist with a doctorate from Stanford, Ride takes pains to downplay her gender: "I am just another astronaut. There's nothing I'm going to be doing in space that I will be doing because I am a woman."

Still, women in space are a rare breed. Only two, both from the Soviet Union, have orbited the earth so far. Women in the physical sciences are not all that common, either. Of 3,124 people who earned U.S. doctorates in that field last year, only 380 were females.

Ride, who will help operate the spacecraft's intricate robot arm during a six-day mission, says she entered her field at a good time "in that the women's movement, coming when it did, helped me a lot. Women now are coming at an even better time."

Her own timing was perfect. She began job hunting in 1977—the year the National Aeronautics and Space Administration announced it was accepting astronaut applications for the first time since the late 1960s and that women would be considered. Until then, Ride says, "it hadn't occurred to me that it was even an option."

Mailing a postcard, she applied—as did 1,000 other women and 7,000 men. Nine months later, in January of 1978, Ride was one of six women chosen among the space agency's 35 new astronaut recruits. Two more women were selected in 1980, and females now number eight of the total corps of 78.

When Ride joined the space program, she found many male engineers "in white shirts, ties and short haircuts who had been working on the space program 20 years and didn't know what to expect" of their new female colleagues.

The way to overcome their suspicions, she found, was to prove right off the bat that she knew what she was doing. Now she spends 12 to 16 hours a week in shuttle-flight simulations and 15 hours a month in a T–38 jet trainer. Recently she married astronaut Steven Hawley.

Ride says she has not thought much beyond the April mission, noting: "Going up in the shuttle is enough of a major milestone." But one thing is certain: She wants to stay with NASA and hopes to fly in space again.

SARAH PETERSON

"WOMEN HAVE TO BE TWICE AS GOOD"

ORLANDO, Fla. Pauline Hartington grew up in Rhode Island and prepared herself for a traditionally feminine job—schoolteacher. But when she looked for work 29 years ago, beginning teachers were earning $2,400 a year. So she joined the Naval Reserve, which offered $4,200.

That started a military career that even-

tually saw her vault to the rank of rear admiral—the second woman to achieve such status—and to her present job as commander of the Naval Training Center here. At 51, she oversees a staff of 2,500 military personnel, 3,000 civilians and a student population of 10,000.

Even though her family has been supportive, she says: "I guess my mother could not understand a daughter who never married. I told her I married the Navy."

Along the way, Hartington became the first woman naval officer to attend the National War College for advanced military studies. She also was the first woman appointed secretary of the Joint Chiefs of Staff. On loan from the Navy, she helped set up the civilian personnel office for President Johnson's war on poverty program. As a young officer, she handled policy decisions involving the Navy's undergraduate education and foreign language programs.

Looking back, Hartington recalls that 29 years ago the highest Navy rank women could achieve was commander, "and you had only a 1 percent chance of that." Since last year, women have been allowed to compete for any rank, and their duties have become more varied. "I envy the young women who have the opportunity to go to sea," she says. "I wish I'd been born later. God, I would have loved to have gone to sea."

Hartington wears her uniform almost everywhere, but she remains a species many men cannot identify. In an airport once, an elderly man noticed her gold braid, shook his head and marveled: "You must fly the really big ones." Waitresses still often call her "Hon," and she grits her teeth when male civilians greet her at social gatherings by kissing her on the cheek and cooing: "That's the first time I've ever kissed an admiral!"

The admiral worries about some of the Navy's new women recruits. "They're content to be mediocre," she laments. In her own trek to the top, she says, "everywhere you went, you had to keep re-inventing the wheel, re-proving that you were indeed capable. If somebody else went home at 4, you had to stay until 6." On her desk is a plaque that reads: "Women have to be twice as good."

Hartington, who says she has had "a grand time" in the Navy, recalls the sacrifices—"the theater tickets I've torn up, the dinners I've called off or arrived at 2 hours late." But she insists: "It's paid off. I'm 'Good Old Dependable'—and that's not a bad reputation to have."

LINDA K. LANIER

BELIEVE IN YOURSELF

WASHINGTON, D.C. Anne Wexler is a consummate "pol." She's a lobbyist on occasion for big business and, at other times, a strategist for the Democratic party.

She heads a political consulting firm, Wexler and Associates, which she started last year. Before that, she was the top female adviser to Jimmy Carter with the title of assistant to the President for public liaison.

Now, as a lobbyist, she represents such firms as Bendix Corporation and Aetna Life & Casualty Company. As a politician, she is an adviser to former Vice President Walter Mondale, the Democratic Congressional Campaign Committee and the House Democratic Caucus. In the recent campaign, the Democratic leadership accepted one bit of advice from a select group of six consultants that includes Wexler: Raise the issue of whether GOP-inspired federal budget cuts are fair to minorities, the poor and the elderly.

Wexler, 52, is equally at home dealing with Republicans. "She works both sides of the aisle," notes one admiring Washington insider.

Wexler says she got into politics "because I love it." She started as a volunteer in Connecticut in Eugene McCarthy's 1968 presidential campaign. In 1970, she was one of two women in the country managing campaigns for U.S. Senate candidates. "We both lost," she recalls. Later she married her candidate, Joseph Duffey. He recently became Chancellor of the University of Massachusetts.

Professionally, Wexler's forte is rallying apparently disparate local-interest groups into a coalition behind a cause. Her guiding principle: "All politics is local, which means a national policy cannot succeed unless it has local support. You can't ignore the people. You have to reach out." A key congressional staffer calls her "the best grass-roots lobbyist in town."

Wexler insists that being a woman has never hindered her in politics. "I was not aware of any problem," she says. "Or if there was one, I just ignored it. My advice to other women wanting to enter politics is: Believe in yourself. Trust your own judgement. If you're a pro, you'll be taken seriously."

SUSANNA McBEE

I DIDN'T THINK IT WAS POSSIBLE

SUN PRAIRIE, Wis. In 1980, Marjorie S. Matthews of the United Methodist Church became the first woman to be elected bishop of a major U.S. denomination. Yet she does not consider herself a pioneer in the women's movement.

"I never felt I was doing anything unusual," says the 66–year–old bishop, who is serving a four-year term as leader of Wisconsin's 131,000 United Methodists.

But the question of her sex was critical when she decided, while working as a secretary in 1959, that she would become a missionary. "I never dreamed of being a preacher or pastor because I didn't think it was possible for a woman," she recalls.

At the time, Matthews did not have the educational background for missionary work, and her minister in Alma, Mich., suggested that she take Methodist correspondence courses to become a "local pastor," one who serves congregations too small to have a full-time preacher.

She did, and spent many Sundays in the 1960s driving rural roads between two tiny Michigan churches. Later she attended seminary, becoming a full pastor in the United Methodist Church in 1970. Ultimately she earned master's and doctor's degrees from Florida State University. Divorced, she has a son and three grandchildren.

As pastor and preacher, Bishop Matthews recalls, she found that objections to female clergy did not originate in her congregations as might have been expected but instead came from pastors of other denominations: "I remember calling on an elderly couple in Michigan who said another clergyman told them they were doomed because they had a woman pastor. That's pretty upsetting to elderly people, but I convinced them it wasn't so. I said what the church was doing was proper, or it would fade away."

Even male colleagues in her own church did not accept her instantly. Recalling her early days as a district superintendent, she says: "The first time I met with my peers, the other superintendents—all male—carried on business just as if I were not there and as though I didn't have anything to say. It took some tuning on their part to recognize that I was speaking with some ability about the district I was in."

Even now the bishop occasionally gets letters quoting the Bible for support in questioning the propriety of a woman's holding high religious office. "If you read the Bible literally," she notes in reply to such criticism, "then you're going to say no one could be a disciple unless you were 30 years old and of the Jewish faith."

Such letters indicate that changes in attitudes come slowly. "Women in seminaries today who think all the problems have been solved aren't seeing the situation correctly," Bishop Matthews says. "They would face culture shock if they were appointed to a highly conservative area."

STEVE HUNTLEY

DEALING AT THE TOP

NEW YORK
Dalila Rodriguez is 36, married, mother of two children ages 6 and 11—and a vice-president of Manufacturers Hanover Trust Company, one of the nation's largest banks.

Rodriguez says she always thought of herself as a career woman: "I never set any limitations."

Working for "Manny-Hanny" is like working for a small city: The bank has 20,900 employees, 800 of them vice presidents and 110 senior vice-presidents. Rodriguez is one of about 80 women to reach the vice-presidential level, including two senior VPs.

She grew up in Puerto Rico, daughter of a San Juan businessman. After four years of studying to become a pharmacist at the University of Puerto Rico, she left school without getting a degree.

Rodriguez and her husband came to New York, and in 1971 she was hired as a credit investigator at Manufacturers Hanover. She quickly moved into a year-long management-training program "because I had shown some initiative and a certain amount of aggressiveness."

Promotions have come steadily—from branch lending officer to branch assistant secretary to an assistant vice-president in international lending and finally, last February, to vice-president. Rodriguez manages a 650–million–dollar Latin American lending portfolio. On occasion she travels there and deals with banks, governments and private businesses in a region unaccustomed to treating females as equals. To her, the male environment she works in is a challenge.

"One should always try to excel," she says. "I make it a point to be organized. I had to prove that I could handle anything a single person or a man with a family could. I've never said I can't travel because of my children. I make arrangements to have my family well taken care of while I'm gone."

Whatever reservations her male colleagues may have had about women in banking, Rodriguez says attitudes are changing—especially in younger men. "They treat women on an equal basis, and they are more receptive to having a woman as a boss," she reports.

How does a woman make it in banking? Says Rodriguez: "Success is a matter of ability and performance—and personality. For a job like mine, you need to be self-confident and aggressive. You are dealing with people at the top. It's a matter of how you protect assets. Are you going to give the bank away, or improve its profits?"

PAT LYNCH

THERE'S A REAL DIFFERENCE

CHICAGO

Hanna Holborn Gray, president of the University of Chicago, was not sure she could pursue an academic career when she got married in graduate school 28 years ago.

At that time, she recalls, "it was kind of assumed that if you got married, you dropped out of the academic job market. I thought I would have to be flexible."

She was. After her marriage to Charles M. Gray, she did not drop out. Instead, she taught at Harvard for five years. When her husband was appointed to the history faculty of the University of Chicago in 1960, she moved, too, becoming a fellow at a private research institution.

The next year, Gray joined the UC faculty herself, also teaching history.

Gradually she shifted from teaching to administration. "For a long time, I didn't think it was the kind of work I was ready for."

But soon she became dean of the College of Arts and Sciences at Northwestern University, then provost of Yale University, later acting president there and finally, in 1978, president of UC. The fact that her husband, still a Chicago history professor, now works for her "is no problem at all," she says. "We think of ourselves as independent professionals and colleagues. It's kind of built into us."

On difficulties women face in higher education, Gray says: "It isn't terribly easy for women to be encouraged in academic institutions." But she adds: "I haven't experienced any sense that the men of the university regarded me as somewhat different or strange—someone requiring them to change their locker-room language."

Gray, 52, recalls her early days as a dean at Northwestern: "The naval commander in charge of the ROTC unit came to meet me in his dress whites and addressed me as 'Sir.' It was almost a caricature. He didn't salute, but I thought he might."

However, she contends that the academic realm is different from other professions once women overcome initial hurdles: "After you've been accepted as a colleague, the move as a woman to becoming president doesn't reawaken the early opposition—unlike the situation that often occurs when a woman becomes a chief executive in a corporation."

Gray contends that the job she holds "is a symptom of a larger change that's coming about." She adds: "It would be great to have it come along faster. Yet, you can see there's a real difference from the way things were before."

MARY GALLIGAN

The Touchy Issue of Sexual Harassment

ANNE McGRATH *

At first glance, the woman's complaint seemed to be a clear-cut case of retaliation. Her boss had found her performance woefully lacking at annual review time—too many absences, chronic tardiness, failure to carry out her day-to-day duties. Following that bad review, the secretary had come to Chris Landauer, then a personnel director for one of Gannett's newspapers, and counterattacked, charging her boss with sexual harassment. She claimed that he had made inappropriate advances both inside and outside the office, continually touching her even after she'd asked him to stop, and she blamed him for her reluctance to come to work.

As she does with every allegation of sexual harassment, Landauer, who is now director of personnel at Gannett headquarters, treated this one seriously. After hearing the secretary out, Landauer sent her home for the day. Next, she called the supervisor into her office to hear his side of the story. Landauer confronted him with the woman's account of his behavior and he said that yes, he had asked his secretary out and had even phoned her at home—he thought that by contacting her there he was doing a good job of keeping his personal life out of the office. Landauer also found other people to corroborate the victim's story.

* *Anne McGrath is associate editor for personal finance at* U.S. News & World Report.

After confirming both sides of the story, Landauer concluded the secretary was on the level and discussed possible solutions with her. The woman was subsequently transferred to another department, where, in turn, she was promoted within six months. The supervisor, who had had an excellent record before this, seemed to be merely a young and inexperienced manager whose style in dealing with women was flirtatious. He was suspended for two weeks without pay, lost his annual salary increase, and Landauer and another manager counseled him on his behavior. Gannett also sent the supervisor to a seminar that dealt with the issues of harassment and women in the workplace.

Such episodes on the job front have become increasingly common in recent years—with increasingly serious results for the companies involved. As last summer's Supreme Court decision in the case of *Meritor Savings Bank v. Vinson* shows, improper handling of sexual harassment allegations can leave a company open to costly litigation. With its decision in favor of Mechelle Vinson, the Supreme Court put American businesses on notice: No longer can companies afford to look benignly on acts of sexual harassment—or look the other way. The Court ruled that former employee Vinson—who claimed that she had been repeatedly forced to yield to her supervisor's sexual advances—had the right to sue the bank, even without proof that she'd been economically harmed.

"The Court said it is sufficient that the climate at work be a hostile one—that a worker be treated differently because of sex," explains Sarah Burns, legal director for the National Organization for Women. And while the court rejected the notion that companies are automatically liable for acts of harassment, it ruled that a firm may well find itself liable for a supervisor's actions even if management is unaware of the offending behavior. Penalties can also be severe. "Damages have run from $2,000 to $1.4 million," notes Burns. "I've seen cases reported as high as $2 million."

In the past, harassment was not a major concern in the workplace. Companies often looked the other way, unwilling to recognize the seriousness of what was taking place. "This attitude, plus the fear that they are somehow responsible for this unwanted attention or that their jobs are at stake, often makes the victims afraid to speak up," says Susan Schroeer, a human resources consultant.

The corollary, as any astute manager knows, is that when employees feel powerless, everyone suffers. Morale founders. Absenteeism and turnovers mount, and productivity declines. Sexual harassment is one problem area in which top managers must take the offensive by warning employees of the negative repercussions of harassment and, most important, having a viable plan of action to follow should it occur.

In assessing your own company's policies, take a look at the atmosphere around your office. Is crude language or off-color humor permissible in your domain? "As a manager, you have to say, 'It's okay to have fun, but not at someone else's expense,'" says Schroeer.

Next, make certain your employees know where to turn if they feel they have been the target of harassment. Is there a neutral committee or ombudsman for a victim to contact, particularly when her immediate supervisor is the problem? Or is your company set up like Gannett and Du Pont, where an open-door policy allows employees to speak to a manager other than their own or turn to the personnel department? Research and learn the proper course of action and convey the rules to your staff as well.

If, despite all your best efforts, an employee comes to you with a sexual harassment complaint, first, be sure to take the allegation seriously. Respect the fact that sexual advances are a subjective matter—that what qualifies as innocent flirtation to one person may be an offensive and threatening come-on to another—and do not express any feelings of disbelief. "Managers have to be very careful," warns Schroeer. "You are the company's representative, and if you imply that a person is merely overreacting and dismiss the complaint, your attitude may be taken to represent the entire company's attitude if a lawsuit is later filed."

On the other hand, don't respond with instant belief and anger, either. "Be objective," warns Landauer. To protect your own future credibility with subordinates, as well as the company's legal position, it is crucial to assure both sides a fair hearing.

Try to get the complete picture from the victim. The employee will probably be upset and fearful and have a tendency to focus on her feelings; it's up to you to probe for concrete details. What is it, exactly, that makes her feel harassed? Word for word, what comments were made? Where, and in what context? Was there any physical contact? How was she touched? When, precisely, did each offense occur? Were there any witnesses?

Immediately file a formal complaint with the appropriate body in your company, usually the personnel department. "It shouldn't wait for fifteen minutes," says Landauer. "If harassment is going on, the situation could become more explosive."

It might also be wise to give the employee a leave of absence or a temporary assignment to another department until the situation calms down.

When the complainant is removed from the scene, either you or the neutral investigating body should meet with the accused person and discuss the charge. "I explain the concern and ask the person to tell me what might have led to the complaint," says Landauer. "I ask for a description of the parties' relationship, as well as whether he or she recalls the incidents the other person has described. Did the person making the charges ever complain directly to the accused?"

Once you have determined that harassment has occurred, some form of corrective action should take place. Sometimes, as in the case mentioned above, the sexual innuendoes were made innocently enough. Other times, the perpetrator of the harassment knew precisely what he or she was doing and why. Be certain that the punishment fits the crime. Has the guilty party used his or her position to tie a subordinate's success to the granting of sexual favors? "If it's a power play, I'd think about dismissal or a probationary period," says Chicago-based management consultant Marilyn Moats Kennedy. On the other hand, the accused may be an old-school sort who is genuinely bewildered to discover that his affectionate pats and winks have angered women co-workers. "In that situation, I'd do some team-building," says Kennedy. "I'd tell the man it was up to him to change the women's attitudes."

To be sure your firm's defenses are strong and up-to-date, here's what you as a manager can do. If your company has not already awakened to the need, insist upon an explicit, written policy prohibiting sexual harassment. Employees have to know that management will not tolerate abusive behavior—that if they're victimized, charges will be taken seriously.

A blanket antidiscrimination state-ment in the company's employee handbook will no longer do the trick. It is important that management spell out the specifics. AT & T's corporate policy states that "AT & T prohibits sexual harassment of its employees in any form. Such conduct may result in disciplinary action up to and including dismissal. Specifically, no supervisor shall threaten or insinuate either explicitly or implicitly that an employee's submission to or rejection of sexual advances will in any way influence any personnel decisions regarding the person's employment, wages, advances, assigned duties, shifts or any other conditions of employment or career development." That statement is backed up by a nine-page document that clarifies what sort of behavior will be disciplined—including subtle harassment such as flirtation, off-color jokes and suggestive pictures.

Be certain that your company includes in its policy a set of clear-cut procedures that employees should follow when victimized. "We underscore the importance of the open-door policy," says Madelyn Jennings, senior vice president of personnel at Gannett. "Our employees are aware that they have recourse beyond their own managers."

As a manager, you should take the time to train both your workers and their supervisors in how to recognize and handle offensive behavior. You should emphasize that this is a serious matter and stress that they should know how to respond. If need be, turn to an outside source—the new educational videos and consultants who specialize in handling sexual harassment—and have them coach all personnel on exactly what behavior won't be tolerated and how to respond should it occur.

For even the most competent manager, dealing sensitively with employees' inter-relationships—not to mention their fear, anger and humiliation—is a tough job. As is the case with most destructive workplace conflicts, the best way to handle sexual harassment is to create an environment in which such behavior would be out of the question from the beginning.

Black Managers: The Dream Deferred

EDWARD W. JONES, JR.

In force for a generation, equal opportunity laws have brought blacks in large numbers into corporate managerial ranks. Starting from almost total exclusion, blacks now hold positions of responsibility, with prestige and income that our parents often thought impossible. Between 1977 and 1982 alone, according to the Bureau of Labor Statistics, the proportion of minority managers rose from 3.6% to 5.2%. EEO data from 1982 show that of all "officials and managers," 4.3% were blacks (including 1.6% black females) and 20.4%, white females. The companies that led this progress deserve commendation for their efforts in recruiting, hiring, and promoting not only blacks but also other minority members and women too.

Yet in the midst of this good news there is something ominous. In conversations with black managers, I hear expressions of disappointment, dismay, frustration, and anger because they have not gained acceptance on a par with their white peers. They find their careers stymied and they are increasingly disillusioned about their chances for ultimate success. They feel at best tolerated; they often feel ignored.

A sampling of headlines from the last few years underscores these perceptions: "Black Professionals Refashion Their Careers" (*New York Times*, November 29, 1985), "Many Blacks Jump Off The Corporate Ladder: Feeling Their Rise Limited" (*Wall Street Journal*, August 2, 1984), "Progress Report on the Black Executive: The Top Spots Are Still Elusive" (*Business Week*, February 20, 1984), "They Shall Overcome: Black managers soon learn that getting through the corporate door is only the first of their problems" (*Newsweek*, May 23, 1983), "Job–Bias Alert: Roadblocks Out Of The Closet" (*Wall Street Journal*, May 17, 1982).

Little information exists about minority participation in the top rungs of America's largest companies. But two surveys of *Fortune* "1000" companies by the recruiting firm Korn Ferry International show that as of 1979 and 1985 these businesses have not made even a dent in moving minorities and women into the senior ranks. The 1979 survey of 1,708 senior executives cited three as being black, two Asian, two Hispanic, and eight female. The 1985 survey of 1,362 senior executives found four blacks, six Asians, three Hispanics, and 29 women. I think it's fair to say that this is almost no progress at all.

A CEO of a multibillion-dollar, multinational company framed the issue: "I'm concerned. The curve of progress has started to flatten more than it should relative to the effort we've made. I need to know how to be successful in moving up competent but diverse people who are not clones of those above them."

But not enough like him seem to be concerned. A 1983 survey of 785 business opinion leaders ranked affirmative action for minorities and women as twenty-third out of 25 human resource priorities, almost last (Sirota and Alper Associates 1983). Today, unlike the 1960s, equal opportunity is not an issue on the front burner of national or corporate concerns. For many reasons, the prevailing theme of fairness has been replaced by calls for protection of individual liberties and self-help. No one wants to listen to a bunch of complaining minorities. From many perspectives, the problem is seen as solved. It is yesteryear's issue.

My research for this article has convinced me that many of the top executives of our largest companies are committed to fairness and to promoting qualified minorities into positions of responsibility. As one white senior executive put it, "No thinking person would pick a white manager for promotion over a more qualified black manager." In most instances he's probably right. The problem is the influence of unconscious, unthinking criteria on the choice.

This article is based on three years of research, including hundreds of interviews of men, women, whites, blacks, and other minorities; of senior, middle, and junior managers; and of professionals in management, education, consulting, psychology, sociology, psychiatry, and medicine. They included more than 30 black executives, each earning at least $100,000, and more than 200 black managers, most MBAs.

My purpose here is to report on this research, to inform concerned executives of the issues as perceived by black manag-

ers. I am not trying to prove anything, only to report and to offer direct testimony on where black managers stand, the progress they have made, the problems that exist, the way blacks feel, and what seems difficult and unresolved.

'COLORBLIND' COMPANIES

There is a problem that the statistics don't reflect. Listen to four higher level black executives who have achieved some credibility and status in the business world:

"There was strong emphasis in the seventies for getting the right numbers of black managers. But now we're stagnating, as if the motivation was to get numbers, not create opportunity. I get the sense that companies have the numbers they think they need and now don't think anything more needs doing. Some companies are substituting numbers that represent the progress of white women and camouflaging and ignoring the lack of progress for black managers altogether. Many companies hired aggressive, self-motivated, high-achieving blacks who are now feeling deep frustration. Some have left, others stay but are fed up. Some can take more pain, others just throw up their hands and say to hell with it."

"When you work your way up, try to conform, and even job hop to other companies only to confront the same racial barriers—well, it's debilitating. I just don't want to go through that again."

"I went into corporate America to shoot for the top, just like my white classmates at business school. But the corporate expectation seemed to be that as a black I should accept something that satisfied some other need. Corporations are saying, 'We want you to be just a number in a seat representing a particular program. Stay in your place.' The psychological contract made by corporations is unfulfilled for black high achievers. We're dealing with a breach of contract."

"We can have all the credentials in the world, but that doesn't qualify us in the minds of many white people. They can train the hell out of us and we can do well, but they may still think of us as unqualified. Old biases, attitudes, and beliefs stack the cards against us."

These are typical statements black managers make in private. When you hear them over and over, you have to believe there's something very real about them. The myth is that companies are color-blind. "We don't tolerate discrimination of any kind, and we've instituted procedures to make that a fact," is a typical comment by a white executive. More accurately, discrimination is ever present but a taboo topic—for blacks as well as whites. If you want to move up, you don't talk about it.

When top executives talk about hiring at the lower end, it's not taboo. Often it's actually obligatory for the sake of affirmative action. But when a black middle manager thinks he (or she) has been held back by a white boss because of race, he faces a tough choice. If he remains silent, he is stigmatized by the boss's action and may find his career pigeonholed. But if he speaks up, he is liable to be marked "too sensitive, a troublemaker, not a team player" and lose in the long run even if he proves unfairness.

So highly charged is this topic in corporations that I had to guarantee all interviewees anonymity. Candor might put companies at risk of being embarrassed and careers of being ruined. One executive, noting that blacks are few in his industry, declined to fill out a questionnaire *anonymously* for fear he would be identified. One white consultant said he lost a great deal of business after performing a survey for a large company in which he reported that black managers were accurate when they complained of unfair treatment. "They never called me back after that," he told me, "and other companies I had dealt with for years didn't call either. The word spread that I couldn't be trusted, and I was blackballed."

On a Treadmill

Corporations and educational institutions have given thousands of black managers the background to move up to more responsible positions. The corporate door is open, but access to the upper floors is blocked. Ironically, companies that led in hiring the best prepared blacks have the worst problem because their protégés' expectations of success are proportionate to their preparation.

To expand on the impressions obtained in interviews, I conducted two surveys of black MBAs. The first was a 23–page questionnaire mailed to 305 alumni of the top five graduate business schools. I received 107 back, without follow-up, for a response rate of 35%. More than 98% of the respondents believe that corporations have not achieved equal opportunity for black managers; 90% view the climate of support as worse than for their white peers; and 84% think that considerations of race have a negative impact on ratings, pay, assignments, recognition, appraisals, and promotion. Some 98% agreed with a statement that subtle prejudice pervades their own companies, and more than half said the prejudice is overt. Less than 10% said their employers promote open discussion of racial issues.

In the survey I listed 15 words and phrases that persons I had interviewed used to describe the climate for blacks in their organizations. To elicit more information (though admittedly in an unscientific fashion: ten of the descriptions were negative and five positive), I asked respondents to select those that "best describe the organizational climate for black managers." The answers, in percentage of total respondents, were:

Indifferent	59%	Encouraging	24%
Patronizing	41%	Psychologically un-healthy	21%
Reluctant to accept blacks	40%		
		Unfulfilling	20%

SURVIVAL AND GROWTH IN ORGANIZATIONS OF THE FUTURE

Whites are resent-ful	20%	Reactionary	10%
Supportive	15%	Negative	7%
		Untenable	7%
Positive	11%	Unwholesome	7%
Open in its communication	10%	Trusting of blacks	4%

A number of respondents volunteered 18 other descriptions, of which 12 were negative. I included all 33 terms in an expanded question (contained in a shorter questionnaire) that I distributed at a meeting of some 200 black graduates of a variety of schools. I received 75 returns.

Getting the most mentions were these descriptions: supportive in words only (50%), lacks positive direction (41%), has a policy of tokenism (33%), reluctant to accept blacks (33%), and indifferent (33%). The favorable descriptions that received the most mentions were encouraging (17%) and positive (15%).

It doesn't matter whether, by some impossible objective standard, these people are right or wrong; what counts is how they feel. My findings contrast sharply, by the way, with opinions offered from 1979 through 1984 by some 5,000 white managers and other professionals in the data base of Opinion Research Corporation. Only 28% of them indicated they lack confidence in their employers' appraisal systems. In my first sample, 90% of the black MBAs declared that blacks are treated worse in appraisals than whites at the same levels.

Here are three illustrations of why black managers are frustrated and angry. First, however, a caveat. To condense into a few paragraphs events that transpired over a number of months may oversimplify them, but they do help clarify the attitude of black managers who feel rejected. The white executive who reads these accounts may think, "I'm sure there were other reasons for this. There must have been something about the person that made him unsuitable for more responsi-

bility." But the people I interviewed and surveyed repeated the same kind of story time after time.

• For more than ten years, John has held the number two post in his department in a large Midwestern chemical company. Some years ago, when his superior, a white, became ill, John filled in for him. After John's boss, who was a vice president, died of a heart attack two years ago, his skip-level boss, a senior vice president, named John acting department head while the company searched for a replacement. During the next 14 months, John repeatedly said he'd like the job and was qualified, but the senior VP said they wanted to start fresh. "We want to reorient the department," he would say, or "We didn't like the way the department was run; Wally was too involved in side issues." But each candidate who came along was less qualified than John.

Finally the company lured a white executive with all the right credentials away from a prime competitor at a salary much higher than John's boss had received. It was the first time the company had brought in an outsider at such a high level. John, who is still number two in the department, is convinced that top management simply did not want a black vice president. "I've searched and searched in my mind for the reason they didn't appoint me," he said when I interviewed him. "All the excuses don't apply to me. They were always critical of my boss, but not of me. I had good ideas for the department and was excited about the prospect of running it, but they never were interested. The reason always comes down to race. They wouldn't have treated a white manager this way."

• Then there is Ron, a bright young administrator for a financial services company in California. In his second assignment, Ron accomplished in one year what his boss had said would take him three and was rewarded with a hefty raise and a transfer to a more difficult slot. There his group again decimated the plan, achieving sales levels in 18 months that the company had predicted would take three years. Again Ron was given praise, a raise, and a transfer—but no promotion.

Meanwhile, whites who had joined the company as trainees with Ron were promoted once and some of them twice. Ron was disillusioned. "My career is getting behind to the point I don't think I can catch up now," he told me. His color must have been a big factor in the way he had been treated, he claimed, because he had played according to all the rules, had outperformed his white peers, and had still come up short.

• Bill's division was part of a company newly acquired by a large multinational enterprise located on the West Coast. Hired through a headhunter by the new parent, he was the first black manager in his division. Between the time Bill was appointed and the day he walked into his office, an executive who had opposed Bill's selection had been promoted and as a vice president was two steps above Bill as his boss's boss. Despite Bill's repeated requests, his immediate superior gave him no written objectives. But all of Bill's colleagues told him they liked his direction.

The only indication that race was even noticed was a comment from a sales manager whose performance Bill's division relied on: "I don't normally associate with blacks." Bill learned later that other managers were telling his boss that he was hard to work with and unclear in his plans. His boss did not confront Bill with these criticisms, just hinted at possible problems. Only later did Bill put them together into the indictment they really were.

After six months, out of the blue, he was put on probation. According to Bill's superior, the vice president said he "did not feel Bill could do the job" and suggested to him that Bill accept severance pay and look for other work. Bill decided to stick it out for pride's sake; he knew he could do the job. His work and educational records had proven him to be a winner.

During the following six months, his division performed ahead of plan. Bill was getting compliments from customers and colleagues. His boss assured him that he had proved his worth, and the probation would be lifted. It was. A few months later, Bill's boss finally agreed to set written objectives and scheduled a meeting with him. But when Bill walked into his superior's office, he was surprised to see the VP there too. The purpose of the meeting was not to set objectives but to place Bill back on probation, or give him severance pay, because he did not "seem to be the right man." Bill left the company and started his own business.

It's noteworthy that Bill, Ron, and John all worked for "equal opportunity employers." Are these cases unusual? Listen to the testimony of a black I interviewed, a vice president of a large insurance company: "White executives at my level say they don't see race as a factor. This is contrary to my perceptions. When I say race, I refer to what is happening to all blacks. White executives choose to see these situations as issues of personal shortcomings. They say, 'We have to look at the possibility of upward mobility of blacks on an individual basis.' But when I look at it on an individual basis, I see all blacks being treated the same way. Therefore, I come to the conclusion that black managers are being treated as a group."

'Colorism'

Racism is too highly charged a word for my theme. When some people think of *racist* they picture overt bigotry and hatred, the burning cross, the shout "nigger"—things our country has rejected by law. For black managers, what gives them a disadvantage is deep-seated attitudes that may not even be consciously held, much less manifest themselves in provable illegal behavior.

For this discussion I'll use the word *colorism* to mean an attitude, a predisposition to act in a certain manner because of a person's skin color. This means that people tend to act favorably toward those with skin color like theirs and unfavorably toward those with different skin color. Study after study shows that colorism exists among white Americans; whereas they generally have an automatically positive internal picture of other whites, they don't have one of blacks. It takes an effort to react positively toward blacks (Crosby, Bromely and Saxe 1980, 546).

A 1982 survey of Ivy League graduates, class of '57, helps explain colorism. For them "dumb" came to mind when they thought of blacks. Just 36% of the Princeton class, 47% at Yale, and 55% at Harvard agreed with the statement, "Blacks are as intelligent as whites" (*Wall Street Journal* May 21, 1982). These are graduates of three leading universities who are now approaching their 50s, the age of promotion into senior corporate positions. Though current data are unavailable, in the mid–1950s two-fifths of the American business elite were graduates of these three schools (Keller 1953, 202).

All people possess stereotypes, which act like shorthand to avoid mental overload. We are products of all we have experienced directly or indirectly from infancy. Stereotypes will never be eliminated; the best we can do is bring people to a level of awareness to control their impact. Most of the time stereotypes are mere shadow images rooted in one's history and deep in the subconscious. But they are very powerful. For example, in controlled experiments the mere insertion of the word black into a sentence has resulted in people changing their responses to a statement (Sedlacek and Brooks 1970, 971).

One reason for the power of stereotypes is their circularity. People seek to confirm their expectations and resist contradictory evidence, so we cling to beliefs and stereotypes become self-fulfilling (Snyder 1982, 60). If, for example, a white administrator makes a mistake, his boss is likely to tell him, "That's OK. Everybody's entitled to one goof." If, however, a black counterpart commits the same error, the boss thinks, "I knew he couldn't do it. The guy is incompetent." The stereotype reinforces itself.

While blatant bigotry is a problem in organizations, neutrality may be an even greater obstacle to blacks. While an estimated 15% of white Americans are extremely antiblack, 60% are more or less neutral and conform to socially approved behavior (Pettigrew 1981, 116). According to Joseph Feagin, a sociologist at the University of Texas at Austin, "Those managers and executives who are the biggest problem are not the overt racial bigots. They are people who see discrimination but remain neutral and do nothing about it. These are the people who let racially motivated behavior go unnoticed, unmentioned, or unpunished. These are the people who won't help."

Advancement in organizations obviously requires support from the top; and as they step through the maze of obstacles, aspirants try earnestly to pick up signals from those in power so they can tell which way the winds blow. Black managers feel obliged to use a color lens in interpreting those signals. A white male passed over for a choice assignment may wonder about his competence or even whether his style turned somebody off: "Was it my politics? My clothes? My laugh?" Blacks will ponder those things too, but the final question they must ask themselves is, "Was it my color?"

Of course, a decision about a promotion is a subjective thing. For blacks, colorism adds an extra layer of subjectivity. An outplacement consultant (white) who has worked for a number of the largest U.S. corporations referred to "a double standard that boils down to this: the same qualities that are rewarded in white managers become the reason the black manager is disliked and penalized." A black personnel executive explained the double standard this way: "If you're aggressive then you're arrogant, but if you're not aggressive then you're not assertive. You try to be right in the middle, and that's impossible."

Studies show that senior executives are generally taller than average. Height is thus an advantage in moving up the corporate ladder—but not necessarily if you're black. "I was interviewing with a white vice president over cocktails for an opening in his organization," recalled one black executive. "I've always had a good track record and, as you can see, I'm not very large. After a few drinks he told me that he liked me, but if I were a big black guy with large muscles, he wouldn't even consider me for the job."

The corporate posture is that there is no race problem. Perhaps in the attitude of the person at the very top that's true, but not lower down. A black VP of a large East Coast bank said, "Our president talks about adhering to equal opportunity, and every year he sends out this letter saying he's firmly committed to equal opportunity. And I believe he's serious. But as the message gets to middle managers, it's lost." Another black manager put it this way, "The general may give the orders, but it's the sergeant who decides who gets liberty and who gets KP."

At the "sergeant's" level, competition is conditioned by colorism. "It's not a conspiracy, it's an understanding," said a black personnel director at a New England-based food distribution company. "Whites don't get together and say, 'Let's do it to this black guy.' That doesn't happen. Say Joe Blow, a black manager, is

vying against ten white guys for a promotion to the assistant VP level. The ten white execs will behave in such a way as to hold Joe Blow back. They'll act independently of each other, possibly without any collusion. But given the opportunity to push Joe Blow ahead or hold Joe Blow back, they'll each hold him back."

Those who seek to step into upper management are playing a new and more complicated game. The stakes are higher and the rules are often less well defined, if they exist at all. So it is here in the middle management passage where the issue of prejudice is most acute.

To get ahead, a person depends on informal networks of cooperative relationships. Friendships, help from colleagues, customers, and superiors, and developmental assignments are the keys to success. Outsiders, or people treated as outsiders (no matter how talented or well trained), rarely do as well. Black managers feel they are treated as outsiders, and because of the distance that race produces they don't receive the benefit of these networks and relationships. Few win bosses as mentors. Moreover, they rarely get the vote of confidence from superiors that helps them to move up step-by-step and allows them to learn the business. These assignments would give them the expertise, exposure, and knowledge necessary for promotion to top posts.

What senior executives would support the promotion to their peer group of somebody they envision as stupid, lazy, dishonest, or preoccupied with sex (the prevailing racial throwbacks among whites about blacks)? This attitude permeates an entire organization because the corporate climate and culture reflect the unspoken beliefs of senior executives, and middle managers, desiring to be senior executives, conform to these norms. This statement by a black middle manager, a woman, illustrates the impact that a closed circle can have on blacks' aspirations:

"A black manager who worked for me deserved a merit raise. I came to the appraisal meeting with all the necessary documentation. There were three or four 40- to 50-year-old white men arguing for *their* people without any documentation. I was the only one supporting my manager, and I was the only one that saw him as eligible. I was overruled just by the sheer vote of it. It turned out to be a matter of 'Joe, you did a favor for me last week, so I'll support you in getting your person in this week. You owe me one, old buddy.'"

"You can try to legitimize the process by saying, 'We all got together and we went through a democratic process, so it was done fairly.' This process was democratic if by that you mean you have one vote in a group of buddies where everyone votes. But a lot of who gets what pay increase and who is put up for promotion is the underlying political buddy system. It's a matter of who believes in who, and each person's prejudices and beliefs come into play to decide the outcome."

A white consultant told me, "White managers aren't comfortable sponsoring black managers for promotion or high-visibility assignments. They fear ostracism from other whites." As a consequence, black executives are shunted into slots out of the mainstream. Here is the testimony of three of them, one from the pharmaceuticals industry, one from an insurance company, and a manufacturer:

"Too often black managers are channeled into The Relations, as I call them—the community relations, the industrial relations, the public relations, the personnel relations. These may be important functions, but they are not the gut functions that make the business grow or bring in revenues. And they're not the jobs that prepare an executive to be a CEO."

"The higher you go, the greater the acceptance of blacks for limited purposes, such as for all those programs that reach out to communities for various projects, the velvet ghetto jobs. And you become an expert on blacks. At my company, if an issue has anything to do with blacks, they come and ask me. On black purchasing they ask me. Hell, I don't have anything to do with purchasing, but because I'm black they think I ought to know something about it."

"White managers don't want to include black managers in the mainstream activities in corporations. Even blacks who have line responsibilities, to the extent that they can be pushed aside, are being pushed aside. They ask you to take a position of visible prominence not slated to the bottom line and give you financial rewards rather than leadership. It's all for outside appearance. But money doesn't relieve a poverty of satisfaction and spirit."

PRESSURE TO CONFORM

"Business needs black executives with the courage and insight to help us understand issues involving equal opportunity," John deButts, former CEO of AT & T, once said. "They must tell us what we need to know, not just what they think we want to hear." But black managers are often afraid to risk their careers by speaking their minds.

In most organizations, conformity is an unwritten rule. If you don't conform, you can't be trusted—especially for higher positions. Black managers try to conform to the corporate values regarding race, and female managers, the values regarding women. If race is "not an issue," acceptance means you are expected to pretend race is not an issue. "A lot of black managers," one black executive told me, "are afraid that if they stand up and take an active role in some black concern, even though they believe it's the right issue, people will say, 'Oh, he's black and just standing up for blacks as any black would.'"

Moreover, some white managers become defensive if prejudice is mentioned. After all, it's un-American to be prejudiced, and who wants to be un-American? So white and black managers, fearful of confronting the issue, take part in a charade. "There is often less than total candor between blacks and whites at any level, and the higher up you go the more that is true," says psychiatrist Price Cobbs. "There is mutual patronizing and misreading, making blacks and whites unable to exchange ideas and express their feelings."

At each step up the organizational pyramid, of course, there are fewer positions. But the slots for minority members are even more limited. This creates an additional game—king (or queen) of the little hill—in which minority members and women compete against each other for the tiny number of near-top jobs available to them. And the first one who gets to the top of this smaller hill is sorely tempted to fend off, rather than help, other minority players.

Attempts by black managers to convince white superiors they are trustworthy, safe, and therefore acceptable manifest themselves in different ways. One black executive explained, "It might take the form of a manager not wanting a black secretary—not so much because he thinks the individual is unqualified, but because he's concerned about how his superiors and peers might perceive them. 'Hey,' they might say, 'that's a black operation over there, so it can't be too effective.'"

Here are some true stories that illustrate running a gauntlet:

• Al, who aspired to the lower rungs of senior management, had to fill a vacancy in his organization. The most qualified candidate was another black manager, George. Al's company was an "equal opportunity employer," but he worried that if he promoted George he would be perceived as favoring blacks and therefore would be unacceptable as an executive. So he promoted a less qualified white candidate. George initiated a suit for discrimination, the company settled, and Al resigned.

• Bob was an ambitious person who changed employers when passed over for promotion. After a year at his new job, he saw that white managers he thought to be inferior performers were being promoted above him. Actually, many of the company's black managers were becoming vocal about a perceived pattern of favoritism toward white managers, who were faring better on appraisals, assignments, promotions, and pay. So that his superiors would see him in a positive light, Bob didn't associate openly with other black managers—but he privately encouraged their efforts to speak up. They should be the "bad guys" while he played the "good guy" in the hope that at least one black might be the first to crack the color barrier at a high level.

In meetings with black managers, senior executives would say that they recognized that blacks were not moving up fast enough, but it takes time and the blacks should not be too pushy. Bob told the white executives, "I don't see why you're even meeting with those guys. They're a bunch of complainers." Two months later, Bob was the first black to be promoted to the executive level.

• Charlie, a junior executive, did not wear race on his sleeve but was straightforward and honest on the subject. One day several lower level black managers sought his advice on correcting what they saw as a pattern of discrimination stunting their careers. Charlie concluded that senior management ought to know about their concerns, and he agreed to arrange a meeting with top officers. Two days before the meeting, the president took Charlie aside in the executive dining room and said, "Charlie, I'm disappointed that you met with those people. I thought we could trust you."

• Ellen, a politically astute black manager, noted that promotions for black managers in her organization diminished coincident with an increase in promotions for white females. Ellen skewed promotions in favor of white females and was a regular participant in meetings about women's issues. She would not promote black males because they were "undependable." Ellen was surprised when a white male declined a promotion because the black male who trained him "was more deserving."

The twist that colorism puts on the maneuvering of ambitious managers is not a new phenomenon. Jews and Italians (among Irish, and other ethnic newcomers in America) have tried to pass as less Jewish or less Italian than their Jewish or Italian colleagues. Obviously it is more difficult for blacks to overcome white executives' feelings about color, but they, like whites, will use what tactics they can to get ahead. But for blacks it's more than merely changing roles like changing hats. Adopting a white value system often means unconsciously devaluing other blacks—and ultimately themselves.

Race & Sex

Another phenomenon that black managers are talking about is "substituting the lesser evil." In their evident push to demonstrate progress toward equal opportunity, some companies are promoting white women in lieu of black men and women. Many of the black managers I interviewed mentioned this phenomenon. Of all the complex interracial issues, certainly the most controversial is the combination of race and sex. The white male-black female, black male-white female relationships are very sensitive matters. Here the most primitive feelings interact, and the stereotypes come boiling to the surface.

At higher levels of organizations, white women have problems in achieving acceptance that in some ways are like those of blacks. Even so, race poses the bigger barrier. According to Price Cobbs, the psychiatrist, "There will be far more white women in the old boys' club before there are large numbers of blacks—men or women."

Since white women comprise 40% of the U.S. population, compared with blacks' 12%, they naturally should move into positions of power in greater numbers than blacks. What seems to be happening, however, is the movement upward of white women at the expense of blacks—men and women. Black managers are concluding that senior executives who are uncomfortable promoting blacks into positions of trust and confidence—those positions that lead to the top jobs—feel less reluctant to promote white females to these posts. "It's as if there is a mind-set that says, 'We have a couple of women near the executive suite—we've done our job,' and they dismiss competent blacks," one black executive said. "It's corporate apartheid," said another.

If the comfort level is a big factor in an invitation to enter the executive suite, it is understandable that white women will get there before blacks. After all, the mothers, wives, and daughters of top officers are white women, and they deal with white women all their lives—but only rarely with black men and women. And they are likely to view white women as being more from their own social class than black men and women.

Stereotypes no doubt play a role here too. One study indicates that the higher the white male rises in the corporate hierarchy, the less likely he is to hold negative stereotypes about women but the more likely he is to hold negative stereotypes about blacks (Fernandez 1981, 80).

Black women, of course, seemingly have to overcome issues of both race and sex. But these combined drawbacks may cause less resistance than that experienced by black men. A study of biracial groups concluded that black women are not perceived in the same sexual role as white women or in the same racial role as black men. Within a social context, black females are more readily accepted in roles of influence than black males. The author of the study reasoned that white society has historically allowed more assertive behavior from black women than black men because black women are considered to be less dangerous (Adams 1983, 69).

If personal comfort levels are a main criterion for advancement, black women are less threatening and therefore more acceptable to white male executives and so will advance faster and farther than black men. Recently *Fortune* magazine found that "the figures for black men tell a disturbing story. From 1976 to 1984, black men lost ground relative to both white women and black women" (Fisher 1985, 29).

Balancing Act

Most black managers feel that to satisfy the values and expectations of the white corporate hierarchy they must run a gauntlet of contradictory pressures. Running the gauntlet means smarting from the pain of prejudice even as white colleagues deny that your reality of race has any impact. It means maintaining excellent performance even when recognition ·is withheld.

It means being smart but not too smart. Being strong but not too strong. Being confident but not egotistical to the point of alienation. Being the butt of prejudice and not being unpleasant or abrasive. Being intelligent but not arrogant. Being honest but not paranoid. Being confident yet modest. It means seeking the trust and respect of fellow blacks and acceptance by whites. Speaking out on issues affecting blacks but not being perceived as a self-appointed missionary or a unifaceted manager expert only on black subjects. Being courageous but not too courageous in areas threatening to whites.

It means being a person who is black but not losing one's individuality by submersion into a class of "all blacks," as perceived by whites. Defining one's self while not contradicting the myriad definitions imposed by white colleagues. Being accepted as a leader for whites and not being seen as an Uncle Tom by blacks. Being a person who is black but also a person who is an authentic human being.

Some black managers are becoming psychological contortionists, struggling to play by the rules of this game. Feelings of self-worth and self-esteem are vital ingredients of mental health. High-achieving black managers are particularly vulnerable to depression if they strive for what white peers attain only to find that the objects of their desire are withheld. The knowledge that these goals should be attainable because of educational preparation and intellectual capability makes the conflict sharper and black managers that much more vulnerable to depression (Thomas and Sitlen 1972, 49). According to Price Cobbs, the level of outrage and indignation among black managers exceeds that of black Americans who are unemployed. Another psychiatrist I talked to adds: "Those black managers in the potentially greatest psychological trouble are the ones who try to deny their ethnicity by trying to be least black—in effect, trying to be white psychologically."

According to Abraham Zaleznik, a social psychologist at the Harvard Business School, if companies promote only those blacks "who are going along with the values of others, they are eliminating those blacks who have more courage, leadership potential, and a better sense of self worked out. This would be tragic because it would attack the very basis of building self-esteem based on an individual's unique capabilities."

WHERE TO FROM HERE?

The picture of frustration and pain that I have drawn is the reality for many, but certainly not all, black managers. I have stressed what is the predominant condition. Most black managers are convinced that their best is never seen as good enough, even when their best is better than the best of white colleagues. The barrier facing black managers is no less real than a closed door. But in the minds of many of their superiors, if people can't make it on their own, it must be their own fault.

I am not talking about the disadvantaged but about high achievers, those blacks who are most integrated into the fabric of our country's white-oriented culture. Yet because of colorism many of these best qualified managers are seen as unqualified "affirmative action hires." (Even so, affirmative action should not be a distasteful term—though it is in Washington these days. Its objective is to ensure that all qualified persons compete on a level playing field.)

What will be the outcome if many of America's best educated and best prepared blacks are not allowed to succeed, and if our country's leaders, including those in corporations, no longer care about this issue? Everyone may agree that "a mind is a terrible thing to waste," but are we not contradicting ourselves if we make waste matter of some of our best black managerial minds or relegate them to the scrap heap of human potential? How hypocritical will we appear in America if "equal opportunity" becomes primarily a white female slogan and the law is used to construct a system akin to corporate apartheid in which the positions of power and authority are nearly all held by whites? What will today's black managers say to their children if one day they ask, "Why don't I have the opportunity you had, and what did you try to do about it?"

Just as one cannot be a little bit pregnant, corporations cannot have a little bit of equal opportunity. There is unlimited opportunity, based on uniform rules, or equal opportunity does not exist. If, at a certain higher level, opportunity appears to peak because no blacks have ever been

at such a level, blacks and whites may perceive that blacks could never—and therefore should never—be promoted there. They don't satisfy the "prototype" for an executive at that level, and therefore, among those who are competing for advancement, they are less appealing as candidates than their white competitors.

So their effectiveness as managers, even in their present roles, becomes an issue. Such a perception combines with ego adjustments of whites working for blacks (whites who may never have been subordinate to a black person before) to make effective leadership by a black much more difficult. Who wants to work for someone not seen as a winner? Or someone with a questionable future?

Will black managers ever be allowed to move up the organization and succeed in the old-fashioned way, by earning it? They must be allowed to fail as well as succeed. In other words, they must be treated the same as white managers.

The first step is to accept how deeply rooted our feelings are about race and color, then remove the taboo from candor on racial realities. We must open up communication and not deny or pretend. Corporations cannot manage attitudes, but they can manage behavior with accountability, rewards, and punishment, as in all other important areas of concern. What gets measured in business gets done, what is not measured is ignored.

The commitment must come from the top down—that of course is obvious. But more than sincerity is needed from the board of directors down through the management structure: commitment, example, and follow-through. Unless the CEO influences the corporate culture to counter the buddy system by compelling all managers to focus on competence and performance rather than comfort and fit, the in-place majority will merely perpetuate itself and the culture will continue to default to traditional racial etiquette and attitudes.

Equal opportunity will not be achieved by promoting one or two high-profile, "most acceptable" blacks into the executive suite, putting a black on a board of directors, or bringing in one or two "name" blacks from outside and bypassing middle management. A fair chance means that black managers can move ahead and still be genuine, that they don't have a psychological gauntlet imposed on them. Fairness means that successful black managers can be role models. A fair chance means that there can be black division heads of marketing, production, and strategic planning, as well as urban affairs and community relations. It also means that black executives can become part of the headquarters elite and report directly to the CEO, not only as vice presidents but as senior and executive vice presidents. It means black executives can be CEOs.

Where do we go from here? The answer lies in our vision for America: whether we want a land of opportunity for all Americans based on individual dignity and respect, or a land of advantage and disadvantage based on skin color. Whether we want a nation where competence and character will be the criteria for leadership, or whether color will ordain that Americans stay in a place determined in the minds and by the values of others. Senior corporate executives can help decide the outcome. Where do they choose to go from here?

Business Ethics: A Manager's Primer

GENE LACZNIAK

The application of different ethical maxims to a given situation may produce divergent ethical judgments. The 14 propositions given here should enable management to deal with the subject of business ethics with confidence.

Too many business managers have been shortchanged in their business education. They have been cheated because during their college years their business professors failed to integrate ethical issues into management education. While some practicing managers have taken courses in "business ethics" or "social responsibility," they typically have not learned to appreciate fully the crucial role that ethics plays in business decision making. To a large degree this has happened because many business educators shy away from integrating ethics into mainstream business classes such as marketing, finance, and production.

Why do educators find it so difficult to teach business ethics or, for that matter, to address ethical issues when dealing with other topics of business strategy? Largely for the following three reasons.

Reprinted by permission from BUSINESS Magazine. "Business Ethics: A Manager's Primer," by Gene Laczniak, January–March, 1983.

First, many business educators pride themselves on their analytical approach; in contrast, addressing ethics is associated with a softer type of analysis, and occasionally with a preachy mentality. This might be deemed the *soapbox factor*. A second closely related cause is that the foundation for meaningful remedies in the area of business ethics is perceived as subjective and unscientific. In other words, many business professors feel that ethics is too elusive a subject for extended lecture treatment. This constitutes the *soft factor*. Third, some business educators believe that dealing with business ethics in the classroom will have little or no lasting effect upon the morality of their students; this might be labeled the *superfluous factor*. Consequently, a great many business educators have not given business ethics its proper due in the classroom because of their perceptions that the subject is soapboxish, soft, and superfluous.

This article compiles and analyzes some propositions that are useful for understanding business ethics. These propositions are grouped into three categories: (1) propositions that serve as useful foundations; (2) descriptive propositions; and (3) proscriptive propositions.

PROPOSITIONS THAT SERVE AS USEFUL FOUNDATIONS

Proposition 1: Ethical Conflicts and Choices Are Inherent in Business Decision Making. This proposition is a logical springboard for appreciating the importance of business ethics because it legitimates the inseparability of business decisions and moral consequences. Substantial support for this postulation is available. One classic study of business ethics reported that at some point in their careers 75% of the responding managers felt a conflict between profit considerations and being ethical (Baumhart 1961, 6). Later studies noted that the majority of

managers questioned also felt this pressure to be unethical (Brenner and Molander 1977, 52–71). Similarly, another widely publicized study indicated that 65% of the managers surveyed sometimes felt pressure to compromise their personal ethical standards (Carroll 1975).

More importantly, this proposition can provide the business manager with the motivation to discover and analyze the numerous ethical implications of current business practices. For example:

- Is it ethical for pharmaceutical companies to market infant formula in developing countries as an alternative to breast feeding when it is common knowledge that sanitary containers and unpolluted water are frequently not available and that babies will be deprived of the immunological benefits inherent in breast milk?
- Is it proper for a public relations firm to attempt to bolster the worldwide image of a country accused of numerous human rights violations?
- Is it moral for a firm to ship a product designated unsafe in one market, such as the United States, to another market where the regulations do not apply?

Every business manager can add examples to the ones just noted. The point is that this proposition emphasizes that the ethical implications of business practices are legion.

Proposition 2: Proper Ethical Behavior Exists on a Plane Above the Law. The Law Merely Specifies the Lowest Common Denominator of Acceptable Behavior. This proposition undercuts the argument that legality is the only criterion for judging acceptable behavior. If this proposition does *not* hold, the study of ethics is extraneous. While some members of the legal profession may challenge this postulate, the entire field of moral philosophy rests on its inherent truth. This proposition provides a rationale for examining the compelling argument that ethical propriety and legality do not necessarily coincide. For example, it is not *illegal* to exhort children to ask their parents to buy a product promoted *via* a commercial on a children's television show. Whether such a practice is *unethical,* because it exploits the gullibility of children, can be vigorously debated.

In addition, this proposition provides an opportunity to explore some fundamental differences between legal and ethical perspectives. For instance, the law is a *reactive* institution that applies to situations only after they have occurred. Ethics is usually more *proactive,* attempting to provide guidance prior to a situation's occurrence. Similarly, within the law, a transgression must be proven beyond a reasonable doubt, whereas from an ethical perspective, an action is morally wrong independent of conclusive proof that it in fact took place. For example, suppose the quality control manager of an electrical supply house knowingly sends out Christmas tree lights that could potentially short out because of a design defect and thereby cause a fire. The lights, however, do not malfunction. Legally, the manager is not culpable because no harm occurred; ethically, a violation of trust has clearly occurred. Thus this proposition embodies the concept that the realm of ethics provides guidance for managerial actions and supplements the requirements provided by law.

Proposition 3: There is no Single Satisfactory Standard of Ethical Action Agreeable to Everyone That a Manager Can Use to Make Specific Operational Decisions. Few business executives would question this generalization. This proposition establishes that advocating a particular moral doctrine is not the point of examining the issue of ethics. Rather, while there are many ethical perspectives of great worth, the issue of morality *in general* is

at question. In other words, the power and impact implicit in managerial decisions demands an examination of the responsibility for those actions. Thus, ethical considerations are properly examined in reference to the managerial process.

Proposition 4: Managers Should Be Familiar With a Wide Variety of Ethical Standards. Several ethical maxims are used as the theoretical foundation for a variety of industry statements on ethics. Typical of the more simplistic maxims are:

> *The utilitarian principle* —Act in a way that results in the greatest good for the greatest number.
> *The professional ethic* —Take only actions that would be viewed as proper by a disinterested panel of professional colleagues.
> *The golden rule* —Act in the way you would expect others to act toward you.
> *Kant's categorical imperative* —Act in such a way that the action taken under the circumstances could be a universal law or rule of behavior.
> *The TV test* —A manager should always ask, "Would I feel comfortable explaining to a national TV audience why I took this action?"

Obviously, these maxims are difficult to apply to specific situations and can sometimes lead to conflicting resolutions, particularly if analyzed in the context of *case situation.* For example, consider the case of a sales representative who, against stated company policy, routinely pads his expense account vouchers 10% to 15%. However, he does this with the knowledge that his fellow sales representatives and his supervisor do the same thing and tacitly approve of this action. In this circumstance, does the golden rule justify the behavior? Wouldn't the professional ethic imply that the practice should cease? This is a rudimentary illustration, but it underscores the fact that various modes of moral reasoning exist and that the application of different ethical maxims to a given situation may produce divergent ethical judgments.

Proposition 5: The Discussion of Business Cases or of Situations Having Ethical Implications Can Make Managers More Ethically Sensitive. Perhaps this is the most debatable of the five propositions ventured thus far because a certain substantial segment of business educators and managers would question its truth. The position of this group is that academic course work cannot instill integrity in a future manager. They believe that students come into the classroom with a relatively intransigent morality. Therefore, classroom efforts directed at personal values are an exercise in futility (Miller and Miller 1976, 39–43).

Notice, however, that the proposition as stated promises only the *potential* for increased sensitivity to ethical concerns, not wholesale changes in morality. One expert provides some limited support for this proposition when he reports that a sample of MBA graduates who took a course in business ethics seemed to develop ethical sensitivity over a period of time (Purcell 1977). Furthermore, other researchers have contended that the academic community has the responsibility to provide courses in business ethics regardless of their effect (Konrad 1978, 54–57). In the view of these experts, such offerings will not transform personalities overnight but will stimulate thinking about ethical issues. In short, sufficient justification exists for encouraging discussion among managers about business ethics, and for the expectation that the effort will have some moral payoff in the business world.

In summary, the five foundation propositions provide a rationale for business ethics as (1) an area of significant managerial concern, (2) distinct from the realm of law, (3) an area, like many areas of management, that has few pat answers but (4) worth exploring because of its rel-

evance to effective and responsible management decision making.

DESCRIPTIVE PROPOSITIONS

With these five foundation propositions, the business manager is now ready to address the specific process of ethical behavior as it occurs in the organization. Unfortunately, little can be definitively stated about how ethical or unethical behavior evolves in a business firm. In part, this is why business ethics are considered subjective or soft—a dimension that was referred to earlier. Nevertheless, a few useful, general propositions can be established for ethics in the organization.

Proposition 6: There are Diverse and Sometimes Conflicting Determinants of Ethical Action. These Stem Primarily From the Individual, From the Organization, From Professional Norms, and From the Values of Society. This proposition underscores the multiple influences that characterize the business environment and shape ethical actions; it also highlights the complexity of pressures that can be part of resolving an ethical question. Consider, for example, the following sample situation:

> *Smith University holds as part of its endowment portfolio a large block of stock in the multinational Jones Company. The stock was donated to Smith University by the founder of the Jones Company. The Jones Company is heavily involved in apartheid-ruled South Africa. Members of the university community, especially students and faculty, are pressuring the university to immediately sell all its Jones Company stock. Some members of the community where Smith University is located have even threatened to picket Smith classes. Mr. Courtney, vice president of Finance at Smith and a former diplomat, knows Jones Company to be a model corporate citizen in South Africa, treating black and white employees alike. However, the management of Jones Company supports the existing South African gov-*

ernment. Furthermore, Courtney believes the Jones Company stock is extremely depressed at this time and that its sale would not be in the best interest of the endowment fund, the major source of student scholarships. Should Courtney and Smith University sell the stock immediately?

Notice the multiple pressures that may be present in a situation such as this: *Societal* pressures dictate selling the securities. Moreover, Courtney's *personal* beliefs, stemming from his religion and philosophy, make him shudder at the inflexibility of the South African government. On the other hand, *organizational* pressures dictate restraint, since Courtney and other officers of the university feel the Jones securities will soon appreciate in value. Similarly, from a *professional* viewpoint, Courtney knows that the sale of the Jones stock would be a symbolic act at best and at worst a slap in the face to a company that has been a Good Samaritan in South Africa and a close friend to the university. How does Courtney resolve these conflicting pressures? No precise answer exists. Somehow he takes the various viewpoints into consideration and recommends an action with which he is comfortable. It is even possible that his recommendation, whatever it is, will be overruled at a higher level of the organization.

The foregoing examination of Proposition 6 suggests another proposition. In the last analysis, Courtney must make a decision that will have ethical consequences. Ultimately, the factors and subfactors to which ethics are attributable—influences such as religion, professional norms, societal expectations, and organizational pressures—somehow combine to shape an *individual* decision that is associated with Courtney and according to which Courtney could be morally judged. This leads to the next proposition.

Proposition 7: Individual Values Are the Final Standard, Although Not Necessarily the Determining Reason for Ethical Be-

havior. The upshot of Proposition 7 is that multifaceted influences affecting the likelihood of ethical action by the decision maker will ultimately be reflected in an individual decision. The action taken will be perceived by others as embodying the ethical values of the decision maker. Introduction of this proposition helps business-people realize the individual responsibility inherent in managerial decision making. In other words, no matter what factors lead a manager to make a particular decision, there is a measure of individual responsibility that cannot be denied because in the last analysis the decision was made by a given manager. For example, the product manager who knowingly sends a shipment of unsafe products to retail stores cannot avoid individual culpability by claiming that economic pressures in the organization necessitated the action.

One major organizational implication of Proposition 7 is that management should strive to maintain a laudatory *organizational* ethic because this dimension is somewhat controllable by the organization. This lessens the likelihood that organizational considerations will pressure the individual manager to compromise his or her personal beliefs and behave unethically. Conversely, a high organizational ethic could induce a manager with low integrity to behave more properly. For example, the American Telephone and Telegraph Corporation (AT & T) provides all employees with a copy of a booklet that states that if employees report to outside sources the improper behavior of AT & T management or employees, no disciplinary or retaliatory action will ever be taken.

Proposition 8: Consensus Regarding What Constitutes Proper Ethical Behavior in a Decision–Making Situation Diminishes as the Level of Analysis Proceeds From Abstract to Specific. Put another way, it is easy to get a group of managers to agree *in general* that a practice is improper;

however, casting that practice in a specific set of circumstances usually reduces consensus. For example, almost all businesspeople will agree that stealing by employees is wrong. But consider the following specific question: Is it alright for a manager to unwittingly take a few pens and pads of paper home for personal use? What about a stapler? A calculator? A typewriter? What if the pens will be used by orphans to play games at a charity picnic? Where does one draw the line?

Even a simplistic example like this can cause debate. The difficulty is compounded as the circumstances become more involved. In any event, Proposition 8 emphasizes the uncertain environment in which managers necessarily function as they attempt to make the ethically proper decision. Consider the following ethical precepts—with which all businesspeople would agree—along with the complication introduced by some hypothetical situation-specific examples.

- *Business has the obligation to honestly report financial progress and potential to holders of company debt and equity. Situation:* The annual report of the Columbia Railroad Co. reports that the firm has financially outperformed all its competitors. This was largely due to the sale of some highly appreciated Manhattan real estate. The income from this transaction is noted with only a footnote in the financial statement. Columbia avoided having the income classified as a special treatment "extraordinary item" because of some complex legal maneuvers and because it has other real estate assets that might provide similar profits in the future. Should the income from the real estate be highlighted more clearly in the annual report?
- *Business has the obligation to treat potential, current, and past employees fairly. Situation:* Employee Harry Har-

ris is apprehended stealing tools and equipment valued at $500 from the company. Company policy calls for dismissal in such instances. However, Harris is 63 years old—two years from pension—and has had a clean slate until this incident. Is it ethical for the company to fire him at this point in his career?

- *Business has the obligation to provide consumers with facts relevant to the informed purchase of a product or service. Situation:* The Doe Co. manufactures Clean & Gleem, an all-purpose cleaning concentrate that consumers mix with four parts water. Clean & Gleem has been sold this way for 25 years. A recent issue of *Consumer Reports* indicates that Clean & Gleem will clean just as effectively if mixed with eight parts water. Thus, consumers need only use half as much concentrate. Should the Doe Co. inform customers of this fact? Would it be unethical not to do so?

In summary, Proposition 8 and these examples of some specific "tough choice" cases provide some insight into the difficulty of steering an ethically proper course.

Proposition 9: The Moral Tone of an Organization is Set by Top Management. Stated another way, the organization is but a lengthened shadow of the morality of persons in charge. For instance, one study found that managers ranked the behavior of superiors as the strongest single factor in deterring unethical behavior (Baumhart 1961, 6). Similar results are reported in more recent studies (Newstrom and Ruch 1975, 29–67).

The organizational implications of this proposition are clear. If employees take their cues concerning ethical behavior from top management, then the first line of responsibility for setting high ethical standards falls to these corporate executives. The following example partially embodies the proposition:

> An employee embezzled $20,000 over several years. When confronted with the incriminating evidence, the employee was not contrite and expressed the belief that he was just as entitled to the company's money as any member of top management. He pointed out that upper management dipped into petty cash for lunch money, used company stamps to mail Christmas cards, and had company personnel help with yard work at their personal residences.

Numerous other real-world examples of this proposition abound. The J.C. Penney Co. is a classic illustration of a company with a reputation for high ethical standards along with a record unblemished by any major scandal. Much of the credit must go to the founder, who was so convinced that ethics and profit were compatible that the company's outlets were originally called the "Golden Rule" stores. In contrast, many of the so-called "dirty tricks" and the political whip cracking of the Nixon administration can be explained by the win-at-all-costs philosophy of the men at the top.

Proposition 10: The Lower the Organizational Level of a Manager, the Greater the Perceived Pressure to Act Unethically. At first glance, this proposition might seem contradictory to Proposition 9. After all, if the moral tone of an organization resides in top management, why the concern with the subsidiary levels of management? The answer lies in the fact that while a *general ethical climate* is established by an organization's superiors, many of the operational decisions that have ethical implications will actually be made at levels other than top management. Thus because the frequency of decision making is greater, the lower-level manager may simply have more opportunities to behave ethically or unethically. Furthermore, it may be that the areas of responsibility of middle man-

agement are treated as profit centers for purposes of evaluation. Consequently, anything that takes away from profit—including ethical behavior—is perceived by lower-level management as an impediment to organizational advancement and recognition.

Surveys of managers seem to confirm that ethical conflict is felt most strongly by lower-level managers (Carroll 1975, 53–71). Thus, top management's exhortations and policy regarding ethics will be a factor in ethical behavior at these levels of management, but only *one* factor. If organizational advancement and salary adjustments are made primarily by the rule of bottom-line unit performance, pressure will exist on middle managers to compromise ethical standards if profit can be served. In this sense, the "ethical buck" stops at the bottom rather than the top of the organization.

Top management should recognize that ethical pressure points will exist at all levels of the organization. Therefore, a sanctimonious statement of a manager's standards does not discharge a firm's duty to foster high ethical standards. Efforts should be made to communicate to all levels of management that ethical behavior will be monitored and will be rewarded accordingly. This proposition reminds business managers that they will be involved in potential ethical conflicts when they enter the organization. The proposition also implies that mechanisms, such as codes or policy statements, that could be used by top management to communicate an ethical commitment "down the line" should be examined for their usefulness to middle management.

Within the context of Proposition 10, it is interesting to note that some analysts have speculated that managers behave more ethically as they grow older—a kind of "mellowing" factor. Since managers in top management are usually older than those at the lower level, this might partially explain why the younger, middle managers feel greater pressures to compromise their personal ethics. Similarly, one can reason that top-level managers have attained career success already; thus they have the luxury of subscribing to high ethical norms, while lower-level managers must still prove themselves, which perhaps requires a more aggressive (and likely less ethical) posture. This "mellowing" hypothesis is controversial and does not yet merit the status of a proposition.

Proposition 11: Individual Managers Perceive Themselves as More Ethical Than Their Colleagues. This postulate is the product of many studies of ethics in management. Typically, it evolves because of the following situation: An individual manager is interviewed by a researcher or reporter about a specific questionable practice, such as the use of invisible ink to track questionnaires after respondents have been promised confidentiality. The manager responds that X% of his colleagues would participate in such a practice but, of course, he or she would not. Thus, more than anything else, this proposition emphasizes the human tendency of managers to discuss ethics in a manner that will protect themselves from incrimination or to rationalize their own uprightness.

One implication of this proposition is that the actual ethical norms of businesspeople are probably more accurately reported in what they say their typical colleague would do in a situation than in what they report they themselves would do. The introduction of this proposition serves to remind the business manager of the difficulty of maintaining one's objectivity when one is involved in analyzing ethical questions that hold personal ramifications. Propositions 6 through 11 are limited in number but in fact establish some fundamental insights into the realm of business ethics. Namely:

• Multiple factors influence ethical deci-

sion making. Some are controllable, some are not. Ultimately, the final decision regarding an ethical question is strongly motivated by the manager's individual values.

• Consensus regarding ethical propriety is difficult to achieve when evaluating many specific situations; moreover, managers have a tendency to overstate their own ethical sensitivity.

• Ethical pressures are felt most acutely by lower- and middle-level managers who look to top management for behavioral cues but are themselves confronted with many difficult decisions.

PROSCRIPTIVE PROPOSITIONS CONCERNING ETHICS

Propositions regarding business ethics, while easy to postulate, are difficult to propose with the confidence that they will have a significant impact on the organization. One is reminded of the quip by Mark Twain, "To be good is noble. To tell people to be good is even nobler and much less trouble." Nevertheless, organizations with a reputation for impeccable ethical conduct have cultivated and enhanced their outstanding moral demeanor with organizational adjustments that have had an impact on ethical performance. The following propositions focus on such organizational strategies.

Proposition 12: Effective Codes of Ethics Should Contain Meaningful and Clearly Stated Provisions Along With Enforced Sanctions for Noncompliance. A code of ethics or some other formal statement of ethical concern is the minimum commitment to organizational social responsibility all firms should be expected to make. Unfortunately, the vast majority of executives have little confidence in the effectiveness of codes in improving morality because of their vagueness and the difficulty of enforcing them (Brenner and Molander 1977, 52–71). All too often such codes have become meaningless public relations gimmicks. Still, codes are not without value. They represent a public commitment regarding the prohibition of practices and can diffuse potential ethical problems. For example, consider the purchasing agent who wonders whether it is proper to accept a bottle of 12–year–old Scotch whiskey at Christmastime from a sales representative. He may reason that there is no explicit quid pro quo expected and that since the gift is given at holiday time, the practice is acceptable. Nevertheless, the manager makes this assessment half-heartedly, because he knows the sales representative's firm has several contracts pending and the practice looks suspicious. A specific code statement that prohibits the giving or receiving of gifts with a value of more than $5 would have eliminated the ethical question concerning the gift.

Successful codes tend to be those that are specific *and* enforced. To anticipate every ethical contingency that can arise in a business situation and to hope to include it in a code is both naive and unrealistic. However, certain specific ethical problems tend to arise in particular industries, and these problems require the special scrutiny of management. For instance:

- Producers of heavily sugared products must face the question of how ethical it is to advertise to children, given both the persuasibility of this group and their susceptibility to tooth decay.
- Companies selling whole life insurance must question the ethics of promoting a financial institution that can lock an individual into a low return on investment in perpetuity.

Almost every business environment suggests some relatively unique ethical questions.

The question of code enforcement is a matter of behavioral psychology. Unless members of the organization see a code of ethics monitored and subsequently enforced with visible sanctions, they will ascribe little organizational importance to the code. The implication of Proposition 12 is that a code of ethics that is not enforced is a code of ethics without teeth, and it will be treated as such by personnel at all levels in an organization.

Proposition 13: Employees must have a nonpunitive, fail-safe mechanism for reporting ethical abuses in the organization. This postulate raises the issue of "whistle blowing" and its role in the firm. On one hand, no corporation likes to have its dirty linen aired in public without an opportunity to examine internally its own transgressions. On the other hand, a real commitment to ethical propriety demands that clear abuses of organizational morality will be condemned and dealt with accordingly, no matter how they come to light. In recent years, too many corporate Serpicos have gone public with substantial abuses, only to be hounded by their own organizations. Organizations dedicated to high ethical standards should provide mechanisms that will assure channels of communication and subsequent protection for whistle blowers. Operationally, this sort of program requires the explicit support of high-level administrators. If top management might be involved in the transgressions, employees should be made aware of an audit committee of the board (chaired by a member independent of management, such as an outside director) to whom information can be given.

Admittedly, such a program can be difficult for management to accept. The possibility of undue negative publicity caused by an overzealous or alarmist employee is a risk. Some issues are difficult to resolve. For example, a financial auditor discovers a foreign payoff that was made several years ago by the now retired chief executive officer. Should this skeleton be allowed to leave the corporate closet? Yet, such dilemmas are the price of developing a climate of ethical responsibility in the organization.

Proposition 14: Every Organization Should Appoint a Top-level Manager or Director to Be Responsible for Acting as an Ethical Advocate in the Organization. In an organization committed to high moral standards, ethical responsibility falls into everyone's domain. But as with many things, unless someone is appointed to direct the effort the responsibility dissolves among the many. One researcher has insightfully proposed the concept of the ethics advocate—a top manager or director whose responsibility would be to elucidate the ethical implications of management's decisions (Purcell 1975, 4–11). For example, if a corporation is planning to shut down a plant in a particular community, the ethical advocate would seek to clarify what, if any, moral responsibility the company had to the community where the plant was located. Similarly, the representative would outline what ethical responsibilities the company has to the employees who might be discharged because of the plant shutdown. In short, the ethical advocate would serve as the verbal conscience of the corporation. Both Cummins Engine Co. and the Monsanto Corp. have introduced such positions into their organizations.

Notice that these three propositions—Propositions 12, 13, and 14—provide the business manager with a battery of questions that can be used to initially evaluate the ethical posture of an organization:

• Does the organization have a code of ethics? Is it specific? Is it enforced?
• Has the organization attempted to identify ethical concerns unique to its industry and operations?
• What is the organization's policy toward whistle blowers? What mechanisms are available to report ethical

abuses? Internal channels? External channels?
• Has top management communicated its concern for a commitment to high ethical standards? How has this been practically demonstrated?
• Is there someone in the organization who serves as an ethical advocate or ombudsman? What are this person's specific responsibilities?

CONCLUSION

Certainly, it can be said that there is not a great deal of definitive knowledge regarding the process that leads managers to behave ethically. It is also conceded that the precise philosophical perspective managers ought to use to make ethical decisions is open to debate. Whether it be moral intuition, a particular theory of distributive justice, utilitarianism, or some other framework, reasonable people can disagree on whether a particular decision is ethically proper or not. A few will also continue to maintain that such discussions and frameworks will never have a pragmatic influence on managerial behavior. In this sense the study of business ethics remains somewhat soft, relatively subjective, arguably superfluous, and prone to a soapbox mentality.

Nevertheless, the strength of such arguments is overstated. While business ethics may be an area that is relatively soft, certain solid propositions that are supported in multiple research studies and in the practices of progressive companies can be transmitted to current and future business managers. Rather than embodying a soapbox mentality, the purpose of these propositions is to sensitize the manager to some of the realities of ethics in the organization. The fact that ethical questions are unavoidable, that subordinates look to top management for behavioral cues, and so on, are bits of managerial acumen that should be well-ingrained in the future business executive. These propositions also describe some pragmatic mechanisms that have been utilized by organizations to develop a progressive ethical climate. Numerous executives testify to the worth of these propositions as an aide to moral responsibility. Thus one may realistically view business ethics as an area consisting of a limited number of solid, successfully adapted propositions that can sensitize managers to their ethical responsibility as organizational decision makers. On these propositions business practitioners can begin to build, supplement, and amplify the necessary discussion of ethics that must take place in the boardroom and beyond.

Whistleblowing

MYRON PERETZ GLAZER and PENINA MIGDAL GLAZER

The costs are high, the results uncertain. So why do some people risk all to reveal fraud and waste in their organizations?

When Morton Thiokol engineers Allan McDonald and Roger Boisjoly testified before the Presidential commission investigating the Challenger disaster about problems with the rocket's O-ring seals, their honesty was applauded by the commission and the public. Company management had a different reaction. As a reward for testifying, the two men were transferred to menial jobs. Although later reinstated, both for a time joined that small army of unsung heroes, American whistleblowers.

If you've worked for long in any area of business or government, you too have probably come across some blatant examples of waste, fraud or corruption. Maybe they were bad enough that you tried to do something about them. Most of us don't. But what about the few who do, the ethical resisters who blow the whistle on mis-

management and dishonesty? What makes them act when the rest of us look the other way?

In recent years, we have interviewed and corresponded at length with 55 whistleblowers and many of their spouses. Kathy Laubach, the wife of one resister, expresses clearly what seemed to be their major motivation, a strong belief in individual responsibility: "A corrupt system can happen only if the individuals who make up that system are corrupt. You are either going to be part of the corruption or part of the forces working against it. There isn't a third choice. Someone, someday, has to take a stand; if you don't, maybe no one will. And that is wrong."

Vincent Laubach joined the Department of the Interior (DOI) in 1981 and was assigned to investigate the failure of strip-mining companies to pay required fines and reclamation fees for the use of public lands. A conservative Republican with a long and successful career as a prosecuting attorney, Laubach believed that he had a mandate from the newly elected Reagan administration to collect the millions of dollars that the coal operators had withheld. He soon learned that his commitment was not shared by his superiors.

When Laubach complained to the Inspector General's office that he wasn't being allowed to do his job, an official there reported the allegations to Laubach's superiors at DOI. They immediately ordered Laubach to cease contacts with anyone outside his office; a few months later, when he traveled to the Mayo Clinic for a job-related back injury, they said he was AWOL and fired him. Despite serious physical problems, Laubach contested the firing during a lengthy grievance procedure. At the same time, he and Kathy pursued his case in the press and with members of Congress.

In 1984, a House subcommittee concluded that the Interior Department had "flouted the law" and "failed miserably" in enforcing the strip-mining legislation. As a result of a 1982 court decision in a suit filed by various environmental groups, the Environmental Defense Fund now monitors collection efforts by DOI's Office of Surface Mining. This action confirmed Laubach's initial charges, but for months there was no official recognition that he had been unfairly fired. Finally, in 1985 an agreement restored Laubach's right to his job and paid him $24,000 to cover his legal fees. The agreement was negotiated by the Government Accountability Project (GAP is a Washington-based organization that defends whistleblowers) and the Solicitor General's office of the DOI.

While Laubach has been vindicated, he is far from satisfied. For one thing, the department has still failed to collect the $150 million to $200 million in assessed fines and fees. For another, the Laubachs believe that Vince's case was settled favor-

ably only after intense pressure from friends in Congress, national media attention and the service of excellent attorneys. Few whistleblowers are so fortunate. The federal administrative review process still resolves very few cases in their favor.

The strong belief in individual responsibility that drives ethical resisters is often supported by feelings of professional ethics, religious values or allegiance to the community. Irwin Levin, for example, became a supervisor in the Brooklyn Office of Special Services for Children in 1979 and found that cases of serious child abuse and even death were not being properly investigated. He was unable to persuade his superiors to take remedial action, and similar complaints to his union were ignored; officials didn't want to criticize their own members.

Levin then took his allegations to the president of the City Council, who referred the matter back to his agency without demanding a public investigation. "Once I discovered that the commissioners would not act," Levin told us, "I knew that if I didn't do something, nobody would."

Levin sent case records to community leaders, but they ignored his pleas, apparently fearing that any investigation would reflect unfavorably on the entire community. In retaliation for making the documents available to outsiders, the Office of Special Services charged Levin with releasing confidential information. He was demoted, fined and transferred to a job in which he had virtually no work to do for years.

Levin was vindicated only after a long-delayed Inspector General's investigation supported his charges and Mayor Edward Koch personally ordered his reinstatement. Despite this restitution and the wide publicity his charges received, Levin still wonders whether he should have passed on his information anonymously. The personal costs of public disclosure have been high, and he doubts whether children are more fully protected now than when he first blew the whistle.

In the mid 1970s, Grace Pierce, a doctor employed by a pharmaceutical company, protested what she considered to be needlessly large amounts of saccharine being used in an antidiarrhea drug for infants. "I do the research," she explained. "I'm responsible. I feel responsibility as a physician first. My responsibility to the corporation is second."

Another doctor, Mary McAnaw, echoed these ideas in protesting a 1980 drug study that she felt would injure patients at the Veterans Administration Hospital in Leavenworth, Kansas: "I know it may sound hackneyed today but I believe it: The only thing necessary for evil to prevail is for good men to do nothing. That sentence kept recurring to me. I felt if I didn't do anything, who will?"

In another confrontation, Demetrios Basdekas, an engineer working for the Nuclear Regulatory Commission, balked at licensing a plant that he considered unsafe. He did not believe that the company had the required backup controls in the event of an accident:

"I cannot envision anything more important than the health and safety of the public in this generation and the effects on future generations as well.... I decided not to go along. I accepted it as a reasonable price for me to pay. I was an engineer who had a good paycheck coming in, but at the same time I felt an essential responsibility that came along with it."

For some resisters, religious beliefs are a crucial element in their decision. Bert Berube had worked for the General Services Administration (GSA) for many years as an engineer. When he was made director of the Office of Systems Acquisition in the Washington office in 1978, he began to challenge decisions that he felt resulted in waste of public funds and in construction and maintenance of unsafe facilities. His complaints created resentment rather than action, and he was de-moted and transferred in 1978 to a position with no responsibility.

He was made regional administrator of GSA's National Capital Region after Ronald Reagan was elected President. In his campaign, Reagan had praised government employees who exposed fraud and waste. When the abuses continued, however, Berube resumed his complaints and in 1983 he was fired. Although Berube knew that speaking out might hurt his family, he believed that he alone had to make the decision:

"Your conscience is something you deal with yourself. It is not a committee action. It is whether you believe it is right or wrong, a question of religious faith. I am the one who is going to be held accountable by God for what I do in my life. My wife is not nor are my children."

Other whistleblowers mentioned strong feelings about their obligation to the community. Starting in 1982, several workers at the construction site of the Comanche Peak nuclear plant in Glen Rose, Texas, testified before the Nuclear Regulatory Commission about their fears that violations of safety regulations endangered the land. Stan Miles, an ironworker, expressed his feelings this way:

"I was born in this state and it means a lot more to me than just a place to live. I've never gone out of the state to work. I like the people here. It's changed a lot since I was a boy. For instance, where I was born in west Texas, real west Texas, you didn't have car trouble without the next person stopping, and if he had to drive 80 miles out of his way, he did, and you didn't have to pay him anything.

"That's gone—all gone and for the sake of a dollar bill. They took something that was priceless and ruined it for something made of paper. Because if you poison the water with nuclear wastes, you poison the land. How can the dollar bill replace that?"

Virtually all of the ethical resisters we studied had long histories of successful employment. They were not alienated or politically active members of movements advocating major changes in society. On the contrary, they began as firm believers in their organizations, convinced that if they took a grievance to superiors, there would be an appropriate response. This naiveté led them into a series of damaging traps. They found that their earlier service and dedication provided them with little protection against charges of undermining organizational morale and effectiveness.

Punishment took many forms—transfer, demotion, firing, blackballing, personal harassment and intimidation. The first step was usually to undermine the effectiveness and reputation of whistleblowers by isolating them or assigning them to lesser duties or none at all. Under these conditions, they could no longer see sensitive documents or take part in conversations with colleagues that might influence policy or reveal new damaging information.

When Basdekas testified before a Congressional committee in 1976 about the dangers of improperly constructed nuclear plants, he was reassigned to far less desirable work and quarters. Unpleasant as his treatment was, Basdekas believes it would have been far worse if some people in Congress had not been watching.

"I was put in an office with no windows and no heat controls, a building that used to be the FBI storage building. That would be OK if there was no other space available. But right across the hall from me there was a nice office with windows, heat controls, desk, chairs, table, the whole works. And it was empty.

"I was refused a promotion for 11 years—from 1973 to 1984. Finally, despite explicit warning from my management not to go ahead, I requested an impartial outside evaluation and finally received a long overdue promotion. That was part of the cost, but it was not the major part by a long shot."

The punishment of Basdekas involved isolation, transfer and the end of career advancement. In the case of Billie Garde, a single mother of two children, retaliation was directed more at her personal life. In 1980 she left her position as schoolteacher and joined the Census Bureau in Muskogee, Oklahoma. She found herself working for a man who wanted her to falsify civil-service test scores to help him get unqualified applicants onto the payroll. He was also involved in sexual exploitation:

"He wanted me to hire a harem of young women from among my former students to sleep with visiting political officials. He could not have been more explicit about what he wanted to do. And I could not have been more unbelieving. I thought he was nuts."

When Garde refused to falsify scores or recruit students as he wanted, her boss set out to get her. "When he discovered that my ex-husband was interested in getting custody of my kids, he called me in and said that Larry wanted custody and he was going to help him get it, if I didn't conform. I just flipped out. I went home and was absolutely terrified."

Garde spent weeks trying to persuade the Census Bureau to conduct an inquiry. Finally, another woman also complained, and Garde's boss was informed of the allegations and an impending investigation. The next day he fired her.

Outraged but in some ways relieved, Garde left for Washington, D.C., to look for work while her children stayed with their father, as they did each summer. She declined an interview with a reporter from an Oklahoma newspaper until it became clear to her that the Census Bureau had no intention of proceeding with the investigation. Garde then told the reporter all she knew. The story ran the day her daughters were to leave Oklahoma to join her in Washington; they never arrived.

"My former superior went to a lawyer in Muskogee with Larry. Then the lawyer and Larry went to the courthouse. The judge was getting off the elevator and the lawyer said to the judge, 'This is Larry Garde. He's married to the woman involved in the Census scandal. He doesn't want to send the kids back.' And the judge signed the order and changed custody from me to him. No notice, no hearing, no nothing ... just boom!

"Later that day I phoned Larry and he said, 'You're never going to see the kids again.' Larry was convinced I was going to jail. All of the lies the man had told about me then came out of Larry's mouth. I thought, 'He got me.' "

Laubach, Levin, Garde and the others all had three major goals. They wanted the courts, a Congressional committee or some other outside authority to investigate and uphold their charges. Second, they sought to clear their own names and salvage their reputations. Finally, they wanted reinstatement, eligibility for promotion, serious work assignments and recognition as competent workers.

The 55 resisters we dealt with had mixed results in achieving these goals. Recreating careers required flexibility about the kind of work, its geographical location and, often, a willingness to accept less money. For most ethical resisters, time was a crucial factor. There were many devastating months or even years of dislocation, unemployment and temporary jobs.

Most of the resisters have restored at least a semblance of their former financial and emotional lives. A few have built satisfying and rewarding careers as a direct result of their protests; many others have had to accept lower income and less prestige. Miles, the fervent Texan, has worked at various jobs in the past two years, some of them outside Texas. Berube, twice demoted or fired for rocking the GSA boat, has started a woodworking business with his son. Pierce, whose suit against the pharmaceutical company for "damage to her professional reputation,

dissipation of her career, loss of salary, as well as seniority and retirement benefits," was rejected by the courts, is now in private medical practice in New Jersey.

McAnaw's concern about the abuse of human subjects in a study at the VA Hospital in Leavenworth, Kansas, was substantiated by the Food and Drug Administration. Nonetheless, her earlier transfer to a hospital in Kansas City was upheld by a judicial ruling. The 80–mile daily round trip takes a heavy toll on her family, but she is pleased that her new superiors treat her as a respected member of the surgery staff.

Garde, who recovered the custody of her daughters with the help of GAP, has graduated from law school. She is now director of GAP's Environmental Whistleblower Protection Clinic in Washington, D.C. In this position, she works with and defends resisters but urges others to provide information anonymously. The costs of public disclosure, she feels, are often simply too great.

A few resisters—such as the late Karen Silkwood, former policeman Frank Serpico and, most recently, Marie Ragghianti, former head of the Board of Pardons and Paroles for the State of Tennessee—have become nationally known through movies about them. They have successfully brought public attention to major social problems.

Others, such as Ernest Fitzgerald of the Pentagon and Hugh Kaufman and William Sanjour of the Environmental Protection Agency, remain within the government, ready to testify about government inefficiency and irresponsibility. A third group of resisters seeks to provide financial and other support for their fellow ethical resisters by working with GAP and other public-interest groups.

Bill Bush of Huntsville, Alabama, is in some ways a member of all three groups. After successfully challenging age discrimination in National Aeronautics and Space Administration personnel policies,

Bush was reinstated but given a job that involved fewer tasks and produced an increasing sense of alienation. Instead of quitting, he has become deeply involved with what he calls "his family of whistleblowers."

Bush, now the hub of an elaborate national network, maintains a computer file on hundreds of workers who have challenged authority. Dissenters call him constantly for information, advice and emotional support. Bush uses every opportunity to inform Congress, the press, watchdog agencies and scholars about people in trouble. Despite what he suffered during years of isolation within the agency, he feels he has dramatically improved the ethical quality of his own life:

"In spite of the avalanche of hatred I brought upon myself, I learned for the first time the pleasures of assisting others in trouble. My associates began to confide in me about their concerns, personal and public. Helping others and participating in nonviolent activism are personally more rewarding than selfishness and passivism."

Voices of Experience

The ethical resisters we worked with know the costs and rewards of whistleblowing through hard-won personal experience. We wondered what advice they had for young people who were thinking of following their example. Among the 21 resisters and spouses who responded to our question in letters, phone calls and personal conversation, only three flatly advised others not to come forward. One of them summed up the reasons this way:

"My advice to potential whistleblowers can be summarized in two words: 'Forget it!'

"But if you can't forget it, then leak the information, making sure that your name isn't associated with it.

"Finally, if you can't do the above, then at least find out what it takes to be a successful whistleblower and the possible consequences. Be prepared to be ostracized, have your career come to a screeching halt and perhaps even be driven into bankruptcy."

The other whistleblowers had a variety of suggestions, most of them included in a list of 10 suggestions offered by Shirley Stoll, a nurse clinician who exposed patient abuse in a Veterans Administration hospital. The words in italics are comments from some of the others that expand or modify Stoll's points.

1. Have the facts and be able to prove them.
2. Act with deliberate thought and care—do not act rashly or in haste.
3. Go through channels unless you are reporting on a supervisor. Then report to his or her boss.

   Don't make the mistake of thinking that someone in authority, if only he or she knew what was going on, would straighten the whole thing out. That can be fatal.

4. Expect the worst: the loss of your job at least.

5. Be prepared to go all the way no matter how far you have to push it.

   Don't tilt at windmills; don't waste your strength and courage fighting a battle you know you will lose. There are more than enough fights around that offer a chance of winning.

6. Know that you will be criticized and humiliated.
7. Do not threaten action unless you mean to follow through. Promise your antagonists action and give it to them, such as by going to the media. They will only act to remedy the prob-

lem when they know you will follow through on your promise.

8. Consult your loved ones—try to get their concurrence and agreement about what you are doing. You will need their support.

The trials you undergo will either cement together or tear apart your marriage.

9. Do not expect that your life will ever be the same. It will not. You will maintain your self-respect by doing the right thing. You will also suffer losses such as income and possibly health or relationships.

10. Finally, remember that there is nothing on Earth as strong as belief in yourself and your God.

Remember the words of Hugh Kaufman, a resister who still works for the Environmental Protection Agency: "If you have God, the law, the press and the facts on your side, you have a 50–50 chance of winning."

Today's Success—Tomorrow's Challenge: An Attitude Toward the Future

J.B. RITCHIE and HAL B. GREGERSEN

Mark Twain is said to have remarked that he was concerned with the future because that was where he was going to spend the rest of his life. We suspect that it is the inevitability of that logic that both frightens and encourages managers or other individuals as they contemplate the transition from present to future states. They find themselves trying to decide along the lines of maintaining and protecting the present world (and protecting themselves in the process) versus pursuing a new world and preparing to take advantage of stimulating and exciting opportunities. An individual's reaction to the challenge can be placed somewhere between two extremes. At one end of the continuum is an almost catatonic state induced by the fear

Reprinted by permission from *The Michigan Business Review*, May 1973, © 1973 by *The Michigan Business Review*. Revised by author, 1984.

and frustration of a changing and uncertain future. At the other end is a sort of euphoric attitude generated by the feeling that any change will be an interesting experience and very likely an improvement. As people place themselves along that continuum, a variety of issues must be considered.

What are some of the important points to consider as we attempt to understand our attitude toward changes in the future? One of the first points that should be mentioned is that in the process of formulating our attitude toward change, we are also determining a part of that future. Within certain constraints one can only think what one is prepared to think and do what one is prepared to do. Short of a catastrophe, our response to impending events—the cognitive and behavior patterns we are prepared to employ—will be substantially determined by the attitudes and skills we are now forming (or have already formed). Except for a forced confrontation, people will not be receptive to a better way of doing something if their minds are only prepared to mentally repeat yesterday's procedure. One cannot respond to a threatening situation in an analytical problem-solving fashion without preparation to receive, process, and evaluate information under stress. The attitude that facilitates this behavior must exist prior to the decision situation; otherwise, the individual will simply be a victim of events. A classic illustration of this point is a major corporation's response to the prospects of a copying machine during the mid–1950s. After considering the potential future uses of such a device, the following conclusion was stated: "Nothing will ever replace carbon paper." Someone was not very well prepared to think about the future!

A second dimension of our attitude toward the future is whether we can distinguish between "problems of failure" and "problems of success." The problem of failure comes when an action does not produce the desired result. In contrast, if the action does produce a positive outcome, the problem of success comes when we cannot cope with the results of psychological, organizational or technical reality created by the new situation. The question has some interesting implications because we are not accustomed to thinking about problems resulting from success.

FAILURE VERSUS SUCCESSES

As you think about it, so often when we hear about the challenge of our times we are presented with an inventory of the many failures of our social, economic, and political institutions. We hear criticisms of virtually every program and organization. These accusations are stated by a variety of individuals: politicians who do not like an incumbent administra-

tion, students who do not like the university curriculum, business executives who are chafing under the restrictive regulations of a government bureaucracy, the young who reject the rules and values of the old, environmentalists who want clean air and water, minorities who desire their share of economic returns. Clearly, it is not difficult to generate a lengthy list of serious problems which await solution; however, is it reasonable to portray present problems as always being a result of past failures?

We would argue that a negative array of failures is only one way to view the problems created by a series of events. Rather than focusing on the failures of the system as the cause of a problem—or source of a challenge—we contend that it is most often the successes or achievements of our complex organizational society which pose the more significant challenge. In many areas where criticism is directed, we find that we have attained exactly what we set out to achieve—whether we now agree or disagree with the set of criteria for that achievement, by some measure we have been successful. However, success in one area does not necessarily replicate itself in other areas. A singular success must be understood, controlled, and integrated into a larger or newly established organizational framework. For example, recent implementation of the quality circles concept into hundreds of American organizations was mainly a replication of singular success in the Japanese business world. With little regard for the different aspects of American industry, many innovative U.S. organizations are now recognizing the futility of blindly expanding a singular success into broader organizational contacts. On the other hand, the failure of a program is more straightforward—you drop it, or try to make it work next time. But with success you must create new ways to incorporate the results of the success into the overall system. The new, offtimes unanticipated demands which have been generated as a result of affluence or education, growth or technology, are usually much more challenging than correcting the past mistakes of a static system.

SOME EXAMPLES

It seems to us unfortunate, for example, to talk about the failure of our education systems (although there are some dramatic failures) when a more interesting challenge is to cope with the success of it. We set out to educate and train more of our population, and now we are upset when that educated, trained population demands exactly what we taught them to look for in life: opportunities to achieve their goals in the workplace, equality under the law, credibility in business and government, answers supported by good evidence rather than authoritarian fiat, etc. The dilemma comes when the rest of our societal institutions are not equipped to respond to the needs and demands of educated and affluent individuals.

Another example comes from the field of data processing, computers, and management information systems. Some years ago we observed great enthusiasm to make dramatic movement into this area. Many organizations made enormous expenditures installing new systems. Over a period of time, many of these investments were not recovered; consequently, people were asking why. We heard many managers say that the system was a failure. But, was it really the system? The system often did exactly what it was supposed to do—generate a great deal of information to be used in management decision-making. The problem was that many people did not know what information they needed or wanted. The information overload was not a failure of the system; it was the success of the system. The failure was that managers did not know how to use it—they became victims rather than masters of technology.

FUTURE SHOCK

A third consideration in thinking about the future can be drawn from Alvin Toffler's books, *Future Shock* and *The Third Wave*. Nearly two decades ago, Bennis and Slater expressed many predictions about the composition of future organizations in *The Temporary Society*. Briefly, Bennis and Slater predicted that the most constant thing within our future organizations would be continual change. Drawing upon Bennis and Slater's perspective, Toffler stretches their predictions beyond the organizations of the late '70s into the society of tomorrow. In *Future Shock*, Toffler argued that we are now a part of an "environment so ephemeral, unfamiliar, and complex as to threaten millions with adaptive breakdown." This breakdown is "future shock." Future shock is what happens to individuals when the substance and pace of change overpower the individual, "when he is required to operate above his adaptive range." The problem comes not from a particular change which we cannot handle; rather, it is the fact that so many things are changing that we need a new set of assumptions to deal with the "temporary society." Toffler says we are living in a world of transience, novelty, and diversity. Our norms have become a temporary house, car, neighborhood, friendship, job, etc. Things move so fast that all of our possessions, relationships, and values become part of a "throw-away" society. Demands change so fast that there is no time for long-term stability in our activities. "Good" products, procedures, and criteria are often outdated or obsolete before they are even generally known. The solution Toffler suggests to help us come to terms with the future is his "theory of adaptation—an understanding of trends, how people respond to change, and most importantly, how *you* respond. With that understanding, he claims, the individual can attain serenity within an environment of confusion.

In addition to individuals confronting a state of "future shock," organizations which are merely collectives of individuals will also need to contend with the various pressures toward substantive organizational change. For example, in *The Third Wave*, Toffler raises an intriguing question about what goals organizations of the future will pursue. Instead of a corporation maximizing its profit as its sole goal, Toffler suggests that the effective corporation of the future will have multiple bottom lines. Such a corporation will probably pursue a variety of goals in areas such as "social, environmental, informational, political, and ethical" issues "in addition to the traditional financial bottom line."

From yet another perspective, the novelist Chaim Potok approaches the concept of "future shock" in terms of a core identity. For him, individuals need to have firm roots in a culture that provides a clear identity. After they comprehend their own values and those of their immediate environment (e.g., family, friends, religious or occupational community), then they can more confidently venture out into the broader environment of other cultures and ideas without being overcome by "future shock." Instead, by knowing one's own culture, people encounter a newly found world of ideas, peoples, or technology with a core-to-core confrontation which will not only be destructive but can be the basis of great creativity and innovation. In short, one must first know what ideas and values influence actions; and only then can one consistently enter the broader "marketplace of ideas." The challenge, then, is to develop ways to learn about your environment and yourself.

NEEDS AND MOTIVATION

Our last issue deals specifically with the elusive problem of understanding behavior. It has already been suggested that the future may be influenced by what an individual thinks, values, and anticipates. When we ask why one thinks and behaves in certain ways, we are talking about motivation. In order to understand or change how we feel about the future, it may be helpful to explore a concept of motivation. For purposes of illustration, we shall build on the theory of Abraham Maslow. In *Toward a Psychology of Being*, Maslow's thesis is that we operate on a hierarchy of needs and that a satisfied need is not a motivator. These needs are rank ordered as follows (see figure 1):

1. Basic needs—physiological demands, rest, food
2. Security needs—order, control, predictability
3. Social needs—affection, belongingness, love
4. Ego needs—prestige, self-respect, identity
5. Self-actualization needs—ultimate self-fulfillment

The argument is that a lower need must be reasonably satisfied before the next higher level need can command a major part of the individual's attention. All of the needs are likely operating at all times to some extent—it is a question of relative emphasis or dominance of a certain need depending on the degree of overall need satisfaction. The logic that "man lives by bread alone" has some basis when man has no bread. But, what happens when there is plenty of bread? Does the intensity of effort in acquiring food remain the same? At this point the concern over having a secure home, community, nation, and future may lead to substantial effort. As a certain degree of security is attained, the individual is more concerned with having a status home, car, country club membership, or whatever else provides social recognition. At this point he becomes more concerned with pleasing other individuals because the lower-order needs are basically taken care of.

As you move up the hierarchy (to the

FIGURE 1 Need hierarchy in individual motivation

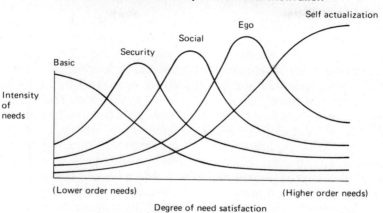

right on Figure 1), it becomes more and more difficult to satisfy the complex interaction of needs. This nexus of needs also seems to require more sophisticated manipulation in order to fulfill them. Such is the case in moving from social to ego types of needs. The ego needs play to the "identity crisis" of our current generation.

Many of our current human resource training and development programs are formulated around the pop psychology emphasis of past years which encouraged people to "look out for number one," to "win through intimidation," and to "pull your own strings." Such programs are a reflection of the quest to answer such questions as: "Who am I?" "Where do I fit in?" and "What do I think of myself?", and "How can I get more out of the organization than I put into it?"

A major problem in this pursuit of self-interests is the disregard for others' dignity and well-being. A prime example of these egotistic pursuits is when managers return from certain training programs anxious to try out new skills in confrontation and assertiveness when others have not attended the program. Many of these "politically sensitized" managers are con-vinced that they will never become the victim of organizational politics. But, does that individual care about someone else becoming the victim? In our experience, rarely. As this quest for "self" turns into a competitive game at the cost of other individuals or organizations, one slowly becomes trapped in the culture of narcissism—unless one moves to a more noble definition of self-actualization.

SIGNIFICANCE OF SELF–ACTUALIZATION

The last need on the hierarchy—self-actualization—is most difficult to describe. The youth talk about "doing their own thing" as a way to express a desire for self-fulfillment. We search for examples of individuals who act only for the intrinsic satisfaction which comes from the process rather than just the external rewards. The ultimate "religious ethic" of serving one's fellow men may be this type of phenomenon. While we may debate the purity of an individual's motives when altruism or selflessness is imputed to someone's behavior, the idea of intrinsic satisfaction is very strong. And, there does seem to be some evidence of a higher or-der quest where values are most impor-tant. These have found success on another level, when higher values lead to more successful organizations. (See Peters and Waterman's *In Search of Excellence*.)

From this very abbreviated framework we can observe some possible explana-tions for current and future problems. For example, it is estimated that forty years ago about 40 percent of the popula-tion were confronted with low-income poverty conditions. That means that most of the people in the United States were close to the bottom of the need hierarchy. Their goals were quite direct—higher in-come and greater security. Since the be-ginning of World War II, however, that percentage has declined remarkably. By 1950 it was down to about 30 percent, 1960 about 20 percent, 1970 about 10 per-cent. Following that trend line, poverty should now be eradicated. Instead, it is up to about 15 percent. What we saw was a large block of society moving up the need hierarchy until the early eighties. In the seventies, education and economic growth had placed the majority of the population in that area of need satisfac-tion where social and ego needs domi-nate. This does not mean that we forgot lower-order needs—we just added to them. There were at least three important consequences which resulted from this "progress."

STRIVING FOR HIGHER ORDER NEEDS

One consequence was that these people were demanding satisfaction of more complex needs. They still required that lower-order needs continued to be satis-fied, but greater energy was going into so-cial- and ego-type goals. Money was for prestige and pleasure rather than only food and security. This made many more conflicting demands on our institutions than had been made before the seventies.

Part of the problem was that most of our institutions were created during a time when lower-order needs had been domi-nant, and therefore many jobs reflected those inappropriate assumptions. Many managers assumed that employees were like they were in the forties and fifties. They should be thankful for a job and be loyal to the boss. These older assumptions may hold for those at the lower end of the hierarchy; however, they appear inade-quate as you move toward the middle and upper end. In fact, with a skilled, mobile, affluent work force you heard a well-known management consultant saying that "organization loyalty is a weakness, not a virtue."

A second consequence of the general movement to higher-order needs came from a special sector of the educated, af-fluent population—women. How could one expect an educated or trained woman with a house full of labor-saving devices, a car, no small children, and a world full of things to be done, to sit home and be content? It seemed that women's libera-tion pressures inevitably came from women in whom higher-order needs were waiting to be realized.

A third consequence resulting from a majority of people striving after higher-order needs was seen in the minority who were still at the lower end of the needs hierarchy. When the poor had a lot of company during the great Depression, things were not so bad. But by the seven-ties the distance was more obvious, and they clearly saw "coercive comparisons" between the rich and the poor. The con-clusions of the statistical comparisons were brutal, frustrating, and insulting. About 8 percent of the total population was at the bottom, while over 30 percent of the black population was in the same cellar position. Since advertising and other norms of society were geared to people with higher-order needs, the reali-zation of the poor's position was more poignant. Also, people at the bottom of the hierarchy seemed to feel as a matter of right that they should have been at the point where the majority of people had established the "standard of living." This meant that the greater the education and affluence of a society, the greater the tension and strain from those still at the bottom.

What we observe, then, is that we had been very successful in providing higher income with a relative degree of security for many people. But, by default, we expected the same organizations and policies which provided for satisfaction of those lower-order needs to also take care of the higher-order ones. And, we have good evidence that it did not automatically work—our corporations, schools, and governments were continually challenged because they were trying to serve needs which were no longer predominant. We continually yearned for the "good old days"; in fact, the goals of those people who had lived in the "good old days" were very clearly to obtain education and affluence—the very conditions which created incompatability with the organizations of the "good old days." The situation is analogous to giving someone a great deal of money and then being upset when he or she buys expensive things. Over a period of time, we realized that by developing people who had acquired higher-order needs through schooling or other forms of socialization, we created a very incongruous world by expecting them to continue behaving on the assumptions of lower-order needs.

THE SHIFT IN NEEDS

Resulting from the past organizational emphasis on fulfilling lower needs, we wanted in the early eighties to modify our organizations in order to satisfy higher needs. With a major push toward a society which would fulfill our social, ego and self-actualization needs, many organizations began to shift their direction. As re-

ported and advocated in books such as Ouchi's *Theory Z* or Peters and Waterman's *In Search of Excellence*, many managers are set on the infusion of deeply held values into the organization's members on an explicit and/or implicit basis. Peters and Waterman argue that the most successful organizations of today are those which inculcate their organizations with an over-arching value system which would satisfy the higher-order needs. In hopes of attaining a fulfillment of social, ego, and self-actualization needs, the apparent organizational success of these changes is that employees will probably act upon deeply held organizational values rather than just to satisfy external constraints.

Clearly, the success of the "best companies" presented by Peters and Waterman is the permeation of commonly shared values—an answer to the question of "Who am I?" or "Who are we?" However, with the development of loyal and obedient employees, what might be a failure of this "success"?

If an organization demands loyalty to an overarching set of organizational values, what might happen to the individual who refuses to wholly accept the organization's values? Individuals now seek a feeling of who they are from other organizations in addition to their work organization. In fact, the actual success of a value-laden organization may well cause the subsequent failure of forcing a single set of values upon a wide variety of individuals. Indeed, Toffler suggests that the corporation of the future will not be homogenous. Rather, the future organization will be a breeding ground for heterogeneity. Following the logic of organizational variety, Toffler asserts that organizations will not be single-purpose organizations. On the contrary, such future organizations will be multi-purpose.

Another part of this shift in needs can be placed in historical perspective. Most of the people in current leadership positions in formal institutions experienced two dramatic events which influenced their assumptions about needs, goals, and behavior. These events were the Depression and World War II. Here we saw the two lower-order needs under attack. The success of our victory over these threats carried with it a strong commitment to carefully protect oneself against any future threat in those areas. Thus, we observed a great emphasis on financial security and military protection. These concerns are not felt in the same way by the current generation. For the most part they have not experienced real threats to the basic and security needs—although many more are beginning to experience these threats. For the most part, however, they start out at a social need level and take the lower ones for granted. The lesson seems clear: We must learn how to live with the consequences of our achievement or lack thereof.

We have discussed some considerations relating to an attitude toward the future. We have tried to raise some questions, which if carefully answered might help in developing a constructive approach to the future. We have tried to suggest some concepts, which if incorporated into those answers might provide insight regarding the fast-moving and complex environment we must live in. And lastly, we have tried to suggest that the conditions we find ourselves in are not cause to give up in despair—the new demands and conflicts we observe are not because of failure; rather, they reflect progress. The challenge of the future is to understand our world and develop the competence to deal with it—it is not an easy task. We must study. We must think. We must be open-minded. And many of us must change! But this is not a new demand—it has been done before, and it can be done again!

"The name of the game in the 1980's is quality. We must get back out of the wild growth of the curriculum and get back into some core of knowledge—history, philosophy, theology, language, literature, mathematics, science, art, and music. Otherwise we are just graduating trained seals."

The Reverend Theodore Hesburgh, President Notre Dame University (Retired)

It is remarkable how willing American business people are to make the current quarter look better at the expense of the future, to sacrifice the future to make this year's bottom line a little more attractive or less embarrassing. The American approach stands in sharp contrast to Japan's sophisticated business leadership, which often does just the opposite, sacrificing now in order to have a healthy future.

John Naisbitt, *Megatrends*

"We have no problems with sex discriminating in our company. Women are treated the same as men. Recently we hired a female chemical engineer. She is a great little girl and is working out very well."

Male middle manager

When the only tool you have is a hammer, you tend to treat everything as if it were a nail.

Abraham Maslow

"Take care of the means, and the end will take care of itself."

Gandhi

"The effective executive focuses on contribution. He looks up from his work and outward toward goals. He asks: What can I contribute that will significantly affect the performance and the results of the institution I serve?"

Peter Drucker, *The Effective Executive*

"Do not wait for the last judgment. It takes place everyday."

Albert Camus

EXERCISES

Organizational Profile Exercise

Many comments have been made with respect to accurate identification of the strengths and weaknesses of organizations. It is important that you develop more than just an intuitive feel for what is going on. There are a variety of different ways to obtain such a profile. (Discussion with different management or organizational consultants would clearly illustrate this point.) However, many of the methods involve some sort of questionnaire. The following exercise is an abbreviated version of one of the best known instruments in the field. It was developed by Rensis Likert and is more fully explained in his books, *New Patterns of Management* and *The Human Organization.*

In this exercise you should think of an organization you are familiar with (perhaps one in which you are currently involved or one you have been part of in the past). Describe that organization by indicating the most accurate statement with respect to each organizational variable. You have a range of twenty points along the scale to describe the relative

Adapted from Rensis Likert, *The Human Organization*, pp. 197–211. Copyright © 1967 by McGraw–Hill, Inc. Reproduced by permission.

degree of each item.

After describing this organization, you should now think of an *ideal* organization—not a mythological one, but one you think would be most effective. What characteristics do you think you would see in this type of organization? Describe this organization with another color or marking. Then connect the set of points for your actual organization in a vertical profile. Do the same for your ideal organization.

If you are like most people, the ideal organization will be a profile to the right of your actual organization. This raises the question of changing organizations to make them more effective and, in turn, more rewarding. You might discuss this topic in groups or in class.

You will notice the systems referred to in the headings on the profile sheet. These classifications identify the differences in overall description of the general organization climate. In Likert's model overall responses which fall in the range of each of the four systems are defined as follows: System 1—Exploitive authoritative; System 2—Benevolent authoritative; System 3—Consultative; System 4—Participative Group.

SURVIVAL AND GROWTH IN ORGANIZATIONS OF THE FUTURE

Profile of Organization Characteristics

	Organizational variables	System 1	System 2	System 3	System 4
Leadership	1. How much confidence is shown in subordinates?	None	Condescending	Substantial	Complete
	2. How free do they feel to talk to superiors about job?	Not at all	Not very	Rather free	Fully free
	3. Are subordinates' ideas sought and used, if worthy?	Seldom	Sometimes	Usually	Always
Motivation	4. Is predominant use made of (1) fear, (2) threats, (3) punishment, (4) rewards, (5) involvement?	1, 2, 3 occasionally 4	4, some 3	4, some 3 and 5	5, 4 based on group
	5. Where is responsibility felt for achieving organization's goals?	Mostly at top	Top and middle	Fairly general	At all levels
	6. How much cooperative teamwork exists?	None	Little	Some	Great deal
Communication	7. What is the direction of information flow?	Downward	Mostly downward	Down and up	Down, up and sideways
	8. How is downward communication accepted?	With suspicion	Possibly with suspicion	With caution	With a receptive mind
	9. How accurate is upward communication?	Often wrong	Censored for the boss	Limited accuracy	Accurate
	10. How well do superiors know problems faced by subordinates?	Know little	Some knowledge	Quite well	Very well
Decisions	11. At what level are decisions made?	Mostly at top	Policy at top, some delegation	Broad policy at top, more delegation	Throughout but well integrated
	12. Are subordinates involved in decisions related to their work?	Not at all	Occasionally consulted	Generally consulted	Fully involved
	13. What does decision-making process contribute to motivation?	Nothing, often weakens it	Relatively little	Some contribution	Substantial contribution
Goals	14. How are organizational goals established?	Orders issued	Orders, some comments invited	After discussion, by orders	By group action (except in crisis)
	15. How much covert resistance to goals is present?	Strong resistance	Moderate resistance	Some resistance at times	Little or none
Control	16. How concentrated are review and control functions?	Highly at top	Relatively highly at top	Moderate delegation to lower levels	Quite widely shared
	17. Is there an informal organization resisting the formal one?	Yes	Usually	Sometimes	No—same goals as formal
	18. What are cost, productivity, and other control data used for?	Policing, punishment	Reward and punishment	Reward, some self-guidance	Self-guidance problem-solving

What—Me Change?

Organizations often encounter obstacles in their attempts to change or to adapt to a changing environment. Sometimes this obstacle is a person or persons in key positions within the organization. This role play is an opportunity to understand the frustrations and the dynamics of confronting roadblocks and dealing with them. Let your feelings develop as they would if you actually were the individuals described in your role. Should issues develop that are not covered by the role, adapt or innovate accordingly.

To conceptualize your role, it is usually best to read it carefully two or three times. Do not read the other roles. Then close the book and think about it for a few minutes. Try to develop an approach in terms of the limited information given and your own interpretation of how a person in that position would probably behave. After you have the role in mind, do not reread it during the process of the role play.

ROLE FOR MIKE

You have been with a small manufacturing firm for eighteen years. For the past seven years you have been plant manager. You have developed your management and control systems over the years, and you feel that you have been doing a pretty good job. The plant had been doing pretty well until the last two years. Recently a competitor has taken away some of your old accounts. These past customers have told you that they are getting a better price, better service, and better quality from the competitor. You think that the supervisors who work for you probably are to blame for the slow orders and lowered quality as well as the salespeople who deal directly with the accounts. In the past few weeks you have become aware of some problems among the supervisors. Not only have they seemed very dissatisfied and surly to you, but they have not been following established procedures that you have developed. The company president has called you in and told you that several of the supervisors have reported that they have met with resistance from you every time they have tried to improve and change things. You resent the implication that you are against improvement. It is just that tried-and-true methods have been developed and have worked until now. Some of their new schemes are too radical even to consider. The supervisors have apparently been doing things behind your back for some time now and finally they have made this attempt to undermine your position with the president. You resent this deeply, because if you hadn't brought them along and trained them, they would still be working on the production line. The president has told you to work out the problem with them. He is tired of hearing about it, and, if you can't solve it internally, he will have to take some action. You think it is about time that these young upstarts be put in their place and understand who is boss. You think George is the ringleader and have called him in to lay down the law. You want to talk to George and George alone, and when you have straightened him out you will bring all the supervisors together.

ROLE FOR GEORGE

You have been with a small manufacturing firm for six years. You worked into your present position, supervisor of the assembly department, from the production line. You have been supervisor for two years. In those two years you have tried to implement changes that you had recognized as necessary even when you worked on the line. Mike, the plant manager and your immediate supervisor, has been a roadblock to every change you have tried to make. You are becoming very frustrated, and the feeling is shared by the other supervisors as well as the salespeople who have to face customers when the orders are not on time or are of poor quality. You have gotten them together and have talked about the problem but have come to no solutions. You and Jim, a salesman, have gone to the president to explain what is happening and what you have tried to do about it. He was sympathetic but told you that he expected you to handle it at your level and go directly to Mike about it. If you can't come to any reasonable solutions, then he may have to take more drastic action, but not until Mike has had a chance to deal with the problem himself.

You are now prepared to confront Mike directly with your feelings about the way things are going. You expect him to react negatively and defensively, because he always has before when you make suggestions. He reacts as if any suggestion for improvement is a personal attack on his competence. Things have finally gone on

long enough, and if changes aren't made you will quit. You have just received a call from Mike to come to his office immediately. You can tell he is mad. Jim is here with you right now, and you invite him to go along even though Mike implied that you come alone.

ROLE FOR JIM

You are a sales representative for a small manufacturing firm. Over the years you have built up a sizable clientele who use your company's products. You have recently lost some major accounts, and it is hurting your income, because you work on a commission. You are no longer sure how much quality or reliability you can promise your customers, because your promises have repeatedly been broken by the plant in the past year or two. You have expanded your sales, while the plant is still running as it did several years ago. They have made no effort to gear up for increased business. The plant manager's response to having lost the business is, "We have all we can do anyway, we don't need their work." This hurts you, and furthermore you have no incentives to acquire new customers because you don't expect to be able to keep them. You have tried to talk to Mike about the problem, but he doesn't even recognize it as a problem. He thinks things are going along fine, and if he does see problems, he always blames them on someone else. You have talked to the supervisors of the different departments, and they have tried but haven't been allowed to innovate. Finally you and George went to see the company president about it. You are talking to George when he gets a call from Mike to come and see him immediately. The tone of his voice tells you he is mad. Probably he got wind of the visit with the president. He tells George to come to his office alone, but the two of you decide that you will go together. You intend to stay at the meeting with Mike and tell him what's on your mind.

Most People (and Organizations) Would Sooner Die Than Change—and Most Do

"I recognize your fresh, innovative, and creative perspective. However, here we prefer stale, traditional, tried-and-true thinking."

CASES

Universal Bank

INTRODUCTION

Brian Baker had just come from a meeting with one of Universal Bank's executive vice-presidents, Bob Jasper, and his head was spinning. Jasper has asked Brian to go to Mexico City and put out some fires in the bank's local branch. During the oil boom years, Universal Bank's Mexico operation had been one of the most profitable units in the organization. No one anticipated the severity of the economic collapse which sent banks reeling. Universal was no different—they had over a hundred million dollars in outstanding loans in Mexico. Although they had been able to renegotiate most loans, top management was on edge because several big loans were due in the next six to twelve months. Bob Jasper decided that Brian Baker was the bank's best shot at guiding Universal through a rough year ahead. His technical competence in loan operations, his language ability, and his international experience and savvy made him the obvious choice.

BACKGROUND

Brian had an MBA from the University of Michigan. He came to work for Universal Bank in New York after graduating, and quickly demonstrated both his technical

This case was prepared by Alan Hawkins under the direction of J.B. Ritchie, Brigham Young University, May 1983.

and leadership skills. The first few years were exciting and challenging. In addition, his fast-track status had given him both prestige and financial comforts more quickly than he had hoped for. Brian, his wife Kathryn, and their two children lived in an old, but very attractive, house in a nice suburb. Kathryn finished her law degree at Michigan at the same time that Brian graduated, and they moved to New York. For two years, Kathryn worked on the legal staff of a large, multinational chemical company. When her first child was born, she decided to take time off to be with her child and redecorate the house—something she had wanted to do for some time. But the second child was born soon after the first, and the strain of two small children eventually caused a mild depression for Kathryn. Brian encouraged her to go back to work. She was able to go back to work part-time for her previous employer, and with the variety and outside stimulation she was soon feeling much better.

However, shortly after Kathryn started back to work, Brian began to feel restless. He had thrived on the challenge and adventure that he received from his work for the first few years. Now he had settled into a more comfortable routine at work. Also, with two children, he felt the burden of family responsibilities. Life wasn't as exciting as it once was.

It wasn't long, though, before that all

changed. Universal was opening a branch in Buenos Aires, and Brian was selected to go down and get it off the ground. His technical skill, leadership, energy, and language ability made him an excellent candidate. "This is just the break you need, Brian," his boss, Sam Stewart, told him when he offered him the position. "A stint abroad is all you need to make you top management material. Management is really high on the branch down there and you'll be in the limelight. Do a good job and you'll probably come back as my boss!"

Brian had no doubts about accepting the position, but Kathryn was much less enthusiastic. Her company wanted her to come to work full-time now, and for the first time she was feeling confident about her abilities as a lawyer. In addition, the kids were just starting school and she was concerned how they would react to such a major change. Where would they live? What about school for the kids? How long would they be down there? She was unable to get a satisfactory answer to any of these questions and the uncertainty was overwhelming.

But eventually Brian was able to convince her to go, with the promise that they would be gone no longer than a couple of years and that when they got back she could return to her career. When Brian accepted the job, they had less than a month to sell the house and make all of the necessary arrangements before they had to leave.

ARGENTINA

For the first year in Buenos Aires, Brian hardly saw his family. He worked 16–hour days and traveled frequently. It was exactly what Brian wanted: challenge, autonomy, responsibility, and excitement. Professionally, he felt good about his own development, and the new branch was progressing well. His only major complaint was that headquarters didn't seem to take much notice of what he was doing. In contrast to what Sam Stewart told Brian when he offered him the job, there was no limelight. If a report was late or inaccurate, he would get a phone call from someone in accounting; otherwise, Brian felt as if no one back home was really paying much attention—especially to him. Brian's major source of information and help was the South American regional supervisor—but he only came by every two or three months.

Brian's fluency in Spanish helped him to adjust quickly to the Argentine culture. He developed a taste for the local food and enjoyed participating in holiday festivities. This helped his Argentine subordinates to accept him and to work well with him.

Unfortunately, it took longer for Kathryn to adjust to Argentina. With Brian rarely home and the kids attending a British school, she was lonely, and her depression began to creep back. She fought it by immersing herself in studying the language and by visiting museums and other cultural and historical sites.

After about a year in Buenos Aires, Brian became aware of a legal position at the U.S. Embassy there. The job included working with immigration cases, visas, and some sticky international licensing problems. Kathryn applied for the position and was hired. Although apprehensive of her ability to speak the language, she was happy to be using her legal skills again, and quickly made some good friends.

At that point, things were going pretty well for the Bakers. Even though Brian still wasn't around much, Kathryn and the kids took advantage of school breaks and holidays to travel to scenic spots along Argentina's vast coastline. Five years passed, and the Bakers were still not anxious to return to the states. But a series of events combined to quickly force their return.

First, Kathryn had become involved

with a local human rights movement that was ruffling some feathers in the Argentine government. Some local government officials who were acquainted with Brian began to put some pressure on him to rein her in, but to no avail. Then suddenly, Brian's father died of a heart attack, and Brian returned to New York for the funeral. While he was there he talked with top management about the progress he was making in Buenos Aires.

"You've done an outstanding job down there, Brian," said one executive vice-president, "and we're appreciative of what you've done. You've single-handedly put Universal Bank on the map in South America. None of our other branches have been able to do so well in so short a time. But it's time for you to move on, Brian. You're too talented to be stuck in right field for your whole career. Train one of your local subordinates down there to replace you, and come back as soon as you can."

Brian couldn't help but feel like the rug had just been pulled out from under him. The ostensible reason that management wanted him back was to further his career. But he wondered if the real reason had more to do with Kathryn's human rights activities and the bank's wanting to prevent any conflict with the Argentine government.

A spirit of gloom hung over the Bakers as they prepared to leave Buenos Aires. Eventually, they resigned themselves to returning, and even decided it was for the best. Brian's mother was calling almost weekly wondering when they would be home. She would need to depend on Brian more now that her husband had died. Moreover, the kids were almost teenagers, and both Brian and Kathryn believed that it was important for the kids to have more stability through these years. If they waited any longer to return to the U.S., it would just make it more difficult for the kids to make the transition. With a feeling of sadness, yet also a feeling of pride for what they had accomplished during the last five and a half years, Brian and Kathryn shipped the last boxes, packed their bags, and returned home to New York.

THE REPATRIATION

Coming home wasn't easy. There were no "Welcome Back" banners for Brian when he came back to work. In fact, the first day back he wondered if he was even in the right place. He had never seen half the employees before, and some major restructuring of the organization left him confused about the direction of the domestic operation. But there were bigger problems. All of his peers that he used to work with in New York were well up the hierarchy. There was no clear position open for Brian when he returned, and no one seemed all that interested in taking him on board.

"They're out of touch with domestic operations," was an opinion frequently expressed about repatriated managers at Universal Bank. "They walk around dazed for six months, and when they finally come out of shock, they think they should run the show. Overseas they had it all to themselves, but back here they forget we're a team."

Brian was assigned to work on a few projects while waiting for some position to open up for him. He felt that the projects hardly used the skills and abilities he had developed over the past five years in Buenos Aires. His lack of commitment to the projects only aggravated the situation, confirming to other people in the company that he was no longer a team player.

Meanwhile, the Baker children were having a difficult time making the readjustment to American life. In terms of their educational level, they were well ahead of their peers. Socially, though, they were seen as odd, even stuffy, and had difficulty making friends. They had missed a crucial socialization period, and they were now being "socialized" the hard way. The $125 a week the Bakers were paying a child psychologist didn't seem to help much. Brian felt responsible for the problems his kids were having, and had a hard time dealing with the resultant guilt. We should never have gone to Buenos Aires in the first place, he thought to himself.

Kathryn was the only member of the family who seemed to be adjusting well. She went to work full-time on the legal staff of the same company that she had worked for before they left. The company had recently opened up a new manufacturing facility in Argentina, and her language ability, her familiarity with the local legal system and cultural norms, and her contacts made her extremely valuable to the company. She had several opportunities to travel back to Argentina on business. Brian tried not to be jealous of her success, but with his career seemingly stalled and her career just beginning to skyrocket, there was tension between them. Brian was hoping that returning to the U.S. would give him more time to spend with the family. He did spend more time with the kids, but Kathryn's work didn't allow her as much time at home as Brian would have liked. It was evident to Brian that five and a half years in Buenos Aires working 70–hour weeks had left their marriage relationship strained. But he was uncertain how to change things.

After six months of Brian's working on insignificant projects, no position had opened up for him. He was angry, frustrated, and wanted to quit but didn't feel they could afford it. Despite Kathryn's in-come, they were still struggling financially. When they returned to the U.S., real estate prices had soared and their new mortgage required both incomes. They had become accustomed to the perks and the good life they were able to enjoy while in Buenos Aires due to Brian's large salary and bonuses. Financially, they felt worse off than before they left for Argentina six years earlier. Because of their current money situation, Brian hung on, hoping that he would soon be able to find a more challenging position.

That's when Bob Jasper called Brian into his office and asked him to put out the fires in Universal's Mexico City branch. "I know you've been a little dissatisfied since you got back from Buenos Aires, Brian. I admit that we've really screwed up with a lot of our repatriated managers. But things are going to change. I want you to go down to Mexico and get them through this rough period ahead. I give you my word that I'll bring you back in one year as a senior vice-president. You're the best manager we've got, Brian. We're counting on you. I'll need your decision on Monday. Take a few days off to think about it."

Brian was excited by the offer, but uncertain what to do. How would the family react? When Brian mentioned the offer to Kathryn, she was visibly shaken and upset. They tried to talk about it, but the discussion didn't get anywhere.

"We'll talk about it Saturday when I get back," Kathryn said. The next morning she left on a business trip. Brian asked his mother to come and stay with the kids for a couple of days. Then he jumped in the car and headed for the Catskills to do some hard thinking.

DMG Corporation

Dennis Brown and Sharon Wayment had been hired as consultants at DMG Corporation to conduct a survey of the attitudes of the professional employees. Over the past months they had been gathering data through employee interviews on various issues of concern. From the data, they determined that top management needed to consider employee concerns in four areas: (1) career development for professionals, (2) the role of professional women, (3) computer training, and (4) communications.

In each of these areas Sharon and Dennis were conducting more specific interviews and also checking with a number of other organizations to see what they had been doing to successfully address these concerns. For each of these four areas, Sharon and Dennis were preparing a summary of employee concerns and recommendations for Richard Chrisman, the Vice–President of Employee Relations, to review and submit to top management. Currently, they were working on the issues which were of concern to the professional women at DMG.

In 1977, there had been only two pro-

This case was prepared by Joan Dixon, Kate Kirkham and Paul H. Thompson under the direction of Kirkham and Thompson.

fessional women employed by DMG—one in accounting and one in personnel—in addition to the secretaries and clerks. Over the next five years, the number of women in professional positions had increased to 27 women working in engineering, marketing, accounting, and administration (see Table 1). Considering the small number of women compared with the number of men in the organization, management felt that significant progress had been made toward increasing the number of women in professional positions. Interviews with managers indicated they felt very good about the women they had hired because they had qualifications equal to or better than those of the men who had been hired in the same time period, and they were doing very good work.

However, as Sharon and Dennis reviewed the information they had gathered, they observed that there were differing views of what women were experiencing in the organization. For example, the response to a survey taken in the engineering department about whether women were treated the same as men underscored this difference in perception. Of the 45 engineers interviewed, 39 reported that there was no problem—

TABLE 1 Professional Employees of DMG Corporation

	Engineering	Marketing	Accounting	Administration	Total
Men	337	36	57	48	478
Women	13	4	3	7	27
Total	350	40	60	55	505

women and men were treated the same. However, of the six respondents who indicated that women were not being treated equally, five were women.

In preparation for the meeting with Mr. Chrisman, Sharon and Dennis compiled a set of interviews which represent-ed the most frequently expressed attitudes concerning professional women (Appendix A). They also prepared a summary of programs which had been implemented in other companies to address the needs of women (Appendix B).

Appendix A:
Individual Interviews

1. Product Specialist in Marketing

Marilyn: I found no discrimination against women here. Oh, a few people make uncalled-for comments, but that's not the company's fault. Most people here try to accept women.

Consultant: Are there any who don't?

Marilyn: It's usually secretaries who are a problem. It makes me mad when women won't accept women. They say, "Are you a *secretary?*" Women have as much problem accepting women professionals as men do. For example, men flirt with our secretary, but I can't flirt with her. So we have to develop a whole new role relationship just for us. I'm the only woman she types for, so it's hard for us to learn to work together. With customers, it's different. I've had some customer contact in the eight months I've been here, but I've had no problems because I'm a woman. But people from other countries sometimes comment on my being the only woman in the meeting.

Consultant: What about the men you work with? Are they ever a problem?

Marilyn: I work with a lot of men my age. That's no problem. You just have to establish the rules. For example, if we travel, we just set the rules. I don't see problems with stereotyping either. My boss is a bit unusual in hiring a woman. He thinks women can do the job. He is nice and courteous.

Consultant: How has your boss been helpful to you?

Marilyn: He has asked me if I've had any problems being accepted, and that has helped. I don't make a big issue of sexist comments. He also is responsible for helping me get a mentor. My mentor isn't up-and-coming in the company, but he's helped me to understand the market, the job, etc. He's older and is not going much higher. I initiated the contact after my boss told me to go talk to him. Now we talk almost every day. He's been very helpful to make me more effective. He's the best resource I could have.

Consultant: Why do you think he helps you?

Marilyn: He wants to help the company be more effective. He also has three daughters and is aware of women's need for mentors. He says, "I want you to help me learn how to work with women." So I tell him if he makes a sexist comment.

Consultant: Do you think a women's support group would be helpful here?

Marilyn: I suppose a support group would be helpful if it were positive. They could suggest things to do. Women don't have the hard times they used to; they can take more initiative now. I go out to eat with women and with guys in our department. For a while I was the one who organized the group to eat lunch.

2. Financial Analyst

Cindy: Some of us (all women) have discussed the issue among ourselves and feel a support group or women's association could make a very positive contribution to the company. So three weeks ago a couple of us approached some of our managers to get some feedback on the idea. Those we talked to directly were quite positive about the matter, but now we're hearing rumors that some people think we're planning to picket the plant. Somehow it got blown all out of proportion. We've never even thought of picketing the plant.

Consultant: What did you hope to accomplish with a support group?

Cindy: Mostly an opportunity to get together and develop constructive ideas about how to cope with problems. There is a danger that it could just become a complaining session. We need to focus on something positive and have company sponsorship to support and direct us to work constructively.

We want to make other women and men aware of the problem. We'd like to see them do something for male managers on this issue. They have the responsibility to prevent discrimination against women.

Consultant: What kind of discrimination do you see?

Cindy: All kinds. Sexism is rampant in my department. My boss is very sexist. He lets it be known by frequently joking about women. He makes comments on women drivers, women should stay at home, etc. His favorite line is "Some dumb broad did it." I confront him by joking back, but it's not very effective. His boss is aware of this, but he doesn't confront him on it. There are not enough women in the organization to stand up and create an awareness. Top management doesn't have to deal with it. There aren't many women in management.

Consultant: Is the problem just with your boss, or do other men in your department act the same way?

Cindy: It's all of them. The men play racquetball together. I play racquetball, but I'm never invited to play with them. The boss and the men go to lunch together; I'm never invited. The men go out together after work; I'm not invited. The boss has had all of the men reporting to him over to his house, but I've never been invited to his house. My peers make negative comments about other women. Maybe they are threatened by women. They'll come in and a woman will be using the computer terminal. They'll say, "She's always at the terminal. I'm tired of waiting for her." She's not at the terminal any more than they are.

You know, it's funny. The men seem to feel at ease with the female secretaries. They go to lunch with them all the time. But they ignore the female professionals. They seem to be trying to isolate the women professionals. All of the men in our department are married and their wives stay home with the kids. So these men don't have any way to understand women professionals.

Consultant: If the general manager wanted to improve the situation for women, what could he do?

Cindy: He could do more for the development of women's careers. There is no company commitment to this. For example, I feel like I've been stuck in a corner of the accounting department. I'm not even trained to be an accountant. I'm a financial analyst. And I know a woman MBA who was hired at the same time as two male MBAs. She was hired at a lower salary and one job grade lower. She was just as well qualified. It really upsets me that this company doesn't recognize and reward qualified women.

Consultant: Anything else besides job assignment and career development?

Cindy: Well, yes. It would be nice to have a combined task force of men and women to discover and deal with problems, to make sure that women are supported by their superiors and peers. Recently, I was left in charge for two days when the boss was gone. One of the men went to our boss's boss and said, "I don't have to report to a 28–year–old woman, do I? I don't have to do what she tells me, do I?" The boss said no. That really made me mad. What am I supposed to do? Where do I go for support when my own superiors won't back me up?

3. **Engineering Department: Group interview With Male Supervisors**

Consultant: Let's talk about the situation for women. What kind of experience are they having here?

Joe: It's better than it used to be.

Mack: They have hired a lot of women in recent years. The company has really made an effort to get women into the organization.

Fred: We just hired a chemical engi-

neer. She's our best little girl.

Steve: The women are getting recognized. They're pulling their own weight.

Joe: Women are accepted just like the men. They are treated just like any other engineer. The real problem is out in the plant.

Consultant: What do you mean?

Joe: They have a different attitude down there. They think women are sick all the time.

Fred: The real problem is that the women aren't able to lift things, so men back off and don't work as hard. They only respond to the tough approach.

Mack: That's true. I sometimes hesitate to send one of the girls out to the plant because she may not be forceful enough to deal with them.

Fred: Yeah, I've seen the guys out there give some of our girls a real hard time.

Consultant: You mean sexual harassment?

Fred: Well, it's mostly teasing. They'll whistle or say something about how nice they look. Sometimes they are real slow about doing what the girls ask them to do.

Consultant: What about here? Are the women treated equally in the Engineering department?

Mack: No problem, the company has given us lectures on discrimination and awareness. We have very specific instructions on sexual harassment.

Joe: The company has done a lot for women. One girl is in upper management already. I don't think they have done as much for minorities. The women are moving very fast. The company is not promoting minorities as fast.

Consultant: Do you mean women are being given special treatment?

Fred: Women take more sick leave

than men. The company has been lenient on that.

Mack: Yes, and some of the men are resentful of women who have more time off on sick leave.

Joe: But there are also plenty of guys who take lots of sick leave; they just aren't as noticeable as the women. Before, when I said women were being promoted faster than the minorities, I didn't mean they were getting special treatment. I meant that the minorities were being neglected more. I haven't seen anything special in treatment or recruitment of women.

Fred: I've noticed it's easier for women to switch departments than it is for men.

Consultant: Why would that be?

Fred: I don't know. I guess they're trying to fill quotas.

Consultant: Have you noticed any times when women are specifically discriminated against on a particular job?

Steve: We had a case like that just last month.

Consultant: What happened?

Steve: I got a report from the plant that produces one of the electrical components we design. They'd hit some real snags. I wanted to take all four members of my design team down there so we could work on the problem on site. It was a two- or three-day trip. I took the request to my boss, who okayed the trip, but then he said, "Of course, Susan won't be going." I couldn't change his mind. He just didn't think it was proper for a woman to make that trip with us.

Consultant: What about informal gatherings? Do you involve the women in activities such as going to lunch or playing tennis or golf after work?

Mack: Sometimes we do, but they don't like to do the same kinds of things we do. They'd be bored.

Joe: Anyway, they always get together and do "girl things" like have parties when someone has a baby.

4. Female Engineers: Group Interview

Consultant: What has hindered you in your effort to become effective engineers?

Pam: Mainly the fact that I have a math degree rather than an engineering degree. But there has also been some kidding about my being a woman.

Consultant: How do you respond?

Pam: I say, "Women have as many brains as you do." Some men don't take it very well when I say that.

Karen: Kidding isn't the only difficult part about being a woman here. There is a lot of stereotyping. At school there was a more liberal atmosphere. But coming to work here was like stepping back ten years. Here men compare you to their wives, not to other engineers. They treat you more like a woman than another engineer. It's a subtle influence, but it's there.

Pam: Some men ask me, "What are you doing here? Why aren't you home having a family?" Other men are jealous; they say, "You ought to be rich because you have two salaries in your family." You can hear jealousy in their comments.

Karen: Some of the managers get upset when women take sick leave. One woman told her supervisor that she was pregnant, and he said, "I don't like that; you'll miss too much work." I think his reaction was discriminatory.

Consultant: Does she still work here?

Karen: No; when the baby came, she requested a one-year leave of absence, but the company wouldn't do it, so she had to just quit. I've seen her recently. She does a little consulting on the side to keep a toe in the door. She'd like to continue full-time when her son gets older.

Pam: Another problem is that managers treat exempt and non-exempt people quite differently. If exempt women take extra sick leave, they don't get in trouble, but if non-exempt women take extra sick leave, they get into trouble.

Consultant: What do you do when someone makes a sexist comment?

Karen: Sometimes I get mad, then I confront him. I try to make him look stupid. The people who are five years older than me are more conservative than those who are 50 years old. The 30–year–olds are more of a problem. Maybe it's because I'm more tolerant of the older engineers.

Consultant: I note that the men call women "girls" here.

Pam: I don't mind being called a girl, but some women don't like it. Our secretary keeps correcting them when they call her a girl. But to me, the way they treat me is more important than what they call me. My supervisor does something I don't like. He walks by the copy machine and comes to my desk and asks me to make two copies for him. It would be faster for him to do it for himself.

Consultant: Do you tell him you don't like that?

Pam: No, I don't like it, but I don't tell him.

Consultant: Does he do the same to others in the department?

Pam: Yes, he gives copying work to the other two women and the one man who is new. The old-timers say that it used to get to them, to do copying for him. Maybe he just does it with new employees. But since three of us are women, it doesn't look right to me.

Consultant: Who do you talk with about your work?

Pam: I talk with my husband and the other women in the department. I don't go to my supervisor very often.

Karen: My husband has also helped me a lot. He tells me when I'm being too sensitive. He helps me keep a good perspective on what's happening. I often get told by men in the department that I'm too sensitive. I don't know if I'm too sensitive. Sometimes it bothers me to hear negative comments about women.

Consultant: What do you think about having a women's support group?

Pam: A lot of managers would get upset if there was such a group. They'd be afraid that it would become a union; so women don't want a support group. A lot of managers discriminate against women in promotions. We have only one woman supervisor out in the plant, and the men call her names behind her back. Many men don't want to work for a woman. We don't have a women's support group in the company, but we know what's happening with other women because we talk to each other.

Consultant: What improvements would you like to see?

Pam: Equal promotion for men and women. Equal job assignments. I have problems—for example, I go to the plant to check a motor and men will say, "What is a pretty girl like you doing down here getting dirty?" I get less harassment here because my husband works in the department.

Karen: Don't treat women differently. Treat men and women the same. Back up the women, be supportive, don't laugh at sexist comments. Women don't need special assistance, but they need confidence building. Many women lack self-confidence. Women are treated as second-class citizens in their up-bringing.

Appendix B:
Programs Implemented by Other Companies
To Deal With Professional Women's Issues

1. Awareness Seminars (one- or two-day sessions):
   • Men and women working together
   • Professional development for women
   • Career opportunities within the corporation
   • Managing a diverse workforce
2. Support Groups for Women:
   • A peer group who could meet to discuss common challenges and problems
3. Monthly Noontime Programs for Women
   • Educational programs

   • Networking
   • Scientific and engineering development
   • Guest speakers
   • Career discussions
4. Company Newsletter:
   • Include articles about women and issues of concern to professional women
5. Task Force:
   • Enlist both men and women to study management practices, policies, behaviors, etc. which discriminate against women, and recommend action to be taken.

Hovey and Beard Company

PART 1

The Hovey and Beard Company manufactured wooden toys of various kinds: wooden animals, pull toys, and the like.

Abridged and adapted from "Group Dynamics and Intergroup Relations" by George Strauss and Alex Bavelas in *Money and Motivation* by William Foote Whyte. Copyright ©1955 by Harper & Row Publishers, Inc. By permission of the publishers.

One part of the manufacturing process involved spraying paint on the partially assembled toys. The operation was staffed entirely by women.

The toys were cut, sanded, and partially assembled in the wood room. Then they were dipped into shellac, following which they were painted. The toys were predominantly two-colored; a few were made in more than two colors. Each color required an additional trip through the paint room.

For a number of years, production of these toys had been entirely handwork. However, to meet tremendously increased demand, the painting operation had recently been re-engineered so that the eight women who did the painting sat in a line by an endless chain of hooks. These hooks were in continuous motion, past the line of women and into a long horizontal oven. Each woman sat at her own painting booth, so designed as to carry away fumes and to backstop excess paint. The women would take a toy from the tray beside her, position it in a jig inside the painting cubicle, spray on the color according to a pattern, then release the toy and hang it on the hook passing by. The rate at which the hooks moved had been calculated by the engineers so that each woman, when fully trained, would be able to hang a painted toy on each hook before it passed beyond her reach.

The women working in the paint room were on a group bonus plan. Since the operation was new to them, they were receiving a learning bonus which decreased by regular amounts each month. The learning bonus was scheduled to vanish in six months, by which time it was expected that they would be on their own—that is, able to meet the standard and to earn a group bonus when they exceeded it.

PART 2

By the second month of the training period, trouble had developed. The women learned more slowly than had been anticipated, and it began to look as though their production would stabilize far below what was planned for. Many of the hooks were going by empty. The women complained that the hooks were going by too fast, and that the time-study man had set the rates wrong. A few women quit and had to be replaced with new women, which further aggravated the learning problem. The team spirit that the management had expected to develop automatically through the group bonus was not in evidence except as an expression of what the engineers called "resistance." One woman whom the group regarded as its leader (and the management regarded as the ringleader) was outspoken in making the various complaints of the group to the foreman: "The job was a messy one, the hooks moved too fast, the incentive pay was not being correctly calculated, and it was too hot working so close to the drying oven."

PART 3

A consultant who was brought into this picture worked entirely with and through the foreman. After many conversations with him, the foreman felt that the first step should be to get the women together for a general discussion of the working conditions. He took this step with some hesitation, but he took it on his own volition.

The first meeting, held immediately after the shift was over at 4:00 in the afternoon, was attended by all eight women. They voiced the same complaints again: The hooks went by too fast, the job was too dirty, the room was hot and poorly ventilated. For some reason, it was this last item that they complained of most. The foreman promised to discuss the problem of ventilation and temperature with the engineers, and he scheduled a second meeting to report back to the women. In the next few days the foreman had several talks with the engineers. They and the superintendent felt that this was really a trumped-up complaint, and that the expense of any effective corrective measure would be prohibitively high.

The foreman came to the second meeting with some apprehension. The women, however, did not seem to be much put out, perhaps because they had a proposal of their own to make. They felt that if several large fans were set up so as to circulate the air around their feet, they would be much more comfortable. After some discussion, the foreman agreed that the idea might be tried out. The foreman and the consultant discussed the question of the fans with the superintendent, and three large propeller-type fans were purchased.

PART 4

The fans were brought in. The women were jubilant. For several days the fans were moved about in various positions until they were placed to the satisfaction of the group. The women seemed completely satisfied with the results, and relations between them and the foreman improved visibly.

The foreman, after this encouraging episode, decided that further meetings might also be profitable. He asked the women if they would like to meet and discuss other aspects of the work situation. The women were eager to do this. The meeting was held, and the discussion quickly centered on the speed of the hooks. The women maintained that the time-study man had set the hooks at an unreasonably fast speed and that they would never be able to reach the goal of filling enough of them to make a bonus.

The turning point of the discussion came when the group's leader frankly explained that the point wasn't that they couldn't work fast enough to keep up with the hooks, but they couldn't work at that pace all day long. The foreman explored the point. The women were unanimous in their opinion that they could keep up with the belt for short periods if they wanted to. But they didn't want to because if they showed they could do this for short periods, they would be expected to do it all day long. The meeting ended with an unprecedented request: "Let us adjust the speed of the belt faster or slower, depending on how we feel." The foreman agreed to discuss this with the superintendent and the engineers.

The reaction of the engineers to the suggestion was negative. However, after several meetings, it was granted that there was some latitude within which variations in the speed of the hooks would not affect the finished product. After considerable argument with the engineers, it was agreed to try out the women's ideas.

With misgivings, the foreman had a control with a dial marked "low, medium, fast" installed at the booth of the group leader; she could now adjust the speed of the belt anywhere between the lower and upper limits that the engineers had set.

PART 5

The women were delighted, and spent many lunch hours deciding how the speed of the belt should be varied from hour to hour throughout the day. Within a week the pattern had settled down to one in which the first half hour of the shift was run on what the women called medium speed (a dial setting slightly above the point marked "medium"). The next two and one-half hours were run at high speed; the half hour before lunch and the half hour after lunch were run at low speed. The rest of the afternoon was run at high speed with the exception of the last 45 minutes of the shift, which was run at medium.

In view of the women's reports of satisfaction and ease in their work, it is interesting to note that the constant speed at which the engineers had originally set the belt was slightly below medium on the dial of the control that had been given the women. The average speed at which the women were running the belt was on the high side of the dial. Few, if any, empty hooks entered the oven, and inspection showed no increase of rejects from the paint room.

Production increased, and within three weeks (some two months before the scheduled ending of the learning bonus) the women were operating at 30 to 50 percent above the level that had been expected under the original arrangement. They were collecting their base pay, a considerable piece-rate bonus, and the learning bonus which, it will be remembered, had been set to decrease with time and not as a function of current productivity. The women were earning more now than many skilled workers in other parts of the plant.

PART 6

Management was besieged by demands that this inequity be taken care of. With growing irritation between superintendent and foreman, engineers and foreman, superintendent and engineers, the situation came to a head when the superintendent revoked the learning bonus and returned the painting operation to its original status. The hooks moved again at their constant, time-studied designated speed; production dropped again; and within a month, all but two of the eight girls had quit. The foreman himself stayed on for several months but, feeling aggrieved, then left for another job.

Metropolitan Police Department

On June 17, 1968, Verl Iverson, commander of the ninth division of the Metropolitan Police Department, was trying to figure out some way of motivating the people in his division to wear the new equipment provided by the city as accessories to the basic uniform. For two years, the city and department officials had been trying to institute a change in the accessories to the uniform worn by the city police and had met with much unanticipated resistance from both the old-timers and the rookies on the force. Verl had just had an encounter with Phil Snead, a deputy chief of the department, over the long-drawn-out process of changing over to the new equipment. Chief Snead left Verl with an ultimatum: that officers who had not changed over to the new equipment in two weeks should be given an official reprimand including days off without pay.

THE NEW UNIFORM

In the mid-sixties, the chief of police of the Metropolitan Police Department as well as a number of city officials received numerous letters from the public suggesting that the police uniforms worn by the force were outdated and that they gave the policemen a "gestapo" look. Being concerned about public image, the chief of police formed a committee and assigned it the task of recommending changes in the uniform to remove the gestapo look while maintaining the efficiency of the uniform as a piece of equipment. After months of research and evaluation, the committee selected several items of new equipment to be field tested. The results of the field tests, in general, were seen as favorable, and a go-ahead was given to start to issue the new equipment to academy graduates.

The parts of the uniform that were

changed included the hat, the pants belt, and the Sam Browne belt (the belt used to carry handcuffs, holster, and other accessories). The hat was changed to a rounded-top style instead of the old eight-pointed style. The new pants belt had a Velcro fastener instead of the conventional buckle and was lined with Velcro strips on the inside. The new Sam Browne was very different from the traditional style. Like the pants belt, it was lined with Velcro on the inside; to fasten it to the pants belt, the pants belt was reversed and its exposed Velcro lining was pressed against the Velcro on the reverse side of the Sam Browne. (The old Sam Browne belt was attached to the old pants belt with leather straps.)

The city had gone to considerable expense to make the uniform convey what was thought to be the image of an efficient police officer. It was felt that the removal of the silver buckles from the pants and accessories belts, the rounding of the crown of the hat, and other minor modifications achieved the goal of obtaining a uniform without the gestapo look.

RESPONSE TO THE CHANGE

Verl knew that the city officials and high-echelon law enforcement officers who were pushing the change in uniform were very committed to the change, and there appeared to be no way to convince them to return to the old-style accessories. All of this had been decided two years ago after heated discussions between the committee and representatives of the law enforcement officers. Verl also knew that many of the officers on the force were opposed to wearing some of the new pieces of equipment.

The opposition to the new gear had been so strong that twice the city had had to postpone the date set for it to be worn by all personnel. Until this point, the city had supplied all new academy graduates with the new equipment and had allowed those who were on the force prior to the introduction of the new pieces to wear what was initially issued them or, in the case of the older officers, what they had purchased themselves.

The opposition to the new equipment was mainly directed at the new pants belt and the new Sam Browne belt. The officers complained that the Velcro cut through the belt loops of their pants, that the Sam Browne belt was uncomfortable, and that it didn't hold up well. Verl knew that many of the old-timers were a little on the heavy side and that the old wide leather belt slipped down comfortably underneath the "overhang" but the new Velcro-lined belt was not as adjustable.

The older officers had voiced the opinion that the new Sam Browne was unsafe. The Sam Browne was a very important accessory to a police officer. Almost every piece of equipment was attached to the belt, including keys, handcuffs, whistle, and revolver. Each officer had a slightly different way of wearing the Sam Browne. Each could find any piece of equipment in a split second. In emergencies and dangerous situations, it was vital that the officer have easy and quick access to his equipment. The old-timers complained that once they had become accustomed to their particular way of carrying equipment on the belt, a change to a new system could cause confusion and delay in an emergency and might cost an officer's life.

The newer officers had also voiced a strong bias against the new belts. After graduating from the academy and beginning service on the force, almost without exception each officer bought the old-style Sam Browne and pants belt and discarded the new ones issued by the city. The younger officers said that the new belt was not worn by anyone but rookies on the force and that wearing the belts identified a "green" officer both to other officers on the force and to people on the street, who might treat a new cop with less respect than they would an experienced policeman.

During the course of the last two years, the department had tried everything to get the officers to wear the belts, from threats of days off to an animated cartoon showing the benefits of the new equipment. Verl agreed with the points brought up by the officers. He also thought that the equipment change was a waste of time and money. He knew that within a year or two he would retire and that he had reached the highest level he would attain on the force. Nevertheless, he felt a great deal of pressure to get the officers to change. Verl felt that he was in a difficult spot, and he wondered how he could develop a strategy that would satisfy the city council, the chief of police, and the policemen in his department.

John Higgins

In 1962, Leonard Prescott, vice-president and general manager of Weaver-Yamazaki Pharmaceutical of Japan, believed that his executive assistant, John Higgins, had been losing his effectiveness in representing the U.S. parent company because of his extraordinary identification with the Japanese culture.

Weaver Pharmaceutical, with extensive international operations, was one of the largest U.S. drug firms. Its competitive position depended heavily on research and development. Sales activity in Japan had begun in the early 1930s through distributorship by Yamazaki Pharmaceutical, a major producer of drugs and chemicals in Japan. World War II disrupted sales, but Weaver resumed export sales to Japan in 1948 and captured a substantial market share. To prepare itself for increasingly keen competition from Japanese producers in the foreseeable future, Weaver decided to undertake local production of

some of its product lines. In 1953 the company began its preliminary negotiations with Yamazaki, which culminated in the establishment of a jointly owned and operated manufacturing subsidiary in 1954.

Through the combined effort of both parents, the subsidiary soon began to manufacture sufficiently broad lines of products to fill the general demands of the Japanese market. Importation from the United States was limited to highly specialized items. The company did a substantial amount of research and development (R & D) on its own, coordinated through a joint committee of both parents to avoid unnecessary duplication of efforts. The subsidiary had turned out many new products, some of which were marketed successfully in the United States and elsewhere. Weaver management considered the Japanese operation to be one of the most successful of its international ventures. It felt that the company's future prospects were quite promising, especially since there was steady improvement in Japan's standard of living.

The subsidiary was headed by Shozo

Suzuki, who as executive vice-president of Yamazaki and president of several other subsidiaries limited his participation in Weaver–Yamazaki to determination of basic policies. Day-to-day operations were managed by Prescott, who was assisted by Higgins and several Japanese directors. Though several other Americans were assigned to the venture, they were concerned with R & D and held no overall management responsibilities.

The Weaver Company had a policy of moving American personnel from one foreign post to another with occasional tours in the international division of the home office. Each assignment generally lasted for three to five years. Since there was only a limited number of expatriates, the personnel policy was flexible enough to allow an employee to stay in a country for an indefinite period of time if he or she desired. A few Americans had stayed in one foreign post for over ten years.

In 1960, Prescott replaced the former general manager, who had been in Japan since 1954. Prescott was an old hand at international work, having spent most of his twenty-five-year career with the company in its international work. He had served in India, the Philippines, and Mexico and had spent several years in the home office's international division. He was delighted with the challenge to expand the Japanese operations. After two years there, Prescott was pleased with the progress the company had made and felt a sense of accomplishment in developing a smoothly functioning organization.

He became concerned, however, with the notable changes in Higgins's attitude and thinking. Prescott felt that Higgins had absorbed and internalized the Japanese culture to such a point that he had lost the U.S. point of view. Higgins had "gone native," so to speak, and this change resulted in a substantial loss of his administrative effectiveness.

Higgins was born in a small Midwestern town; after high school in 1950, he entered his state university. Midway through college, he was drafted. Since he had shown an interest in languages by taking German and Spanish in college, he was given an opportunity to attend the Army Language School for intensive training in Japanese. After fifteen months he was assigned as an interpreter and translator in Tokyo. While in Japan, he took further courses in Japanese language, literature, and history. He made many Japanese friends, fell in love with Japan, and vowed to return there for a period to live. In 1957, Higgins returned to college. Since he wanted to use the language as a means rather than an end in itself, he finished his college work in management rather than in Japanese. He graduated with honors in 1958 and joined Weaver. After a year in the company training program he was assigned to Japan.

Higgins was pleased to return to Japan, not only because of his love for Japan, but also for the opportunity to improve the "ugly American" image abroad. Because of his language ability and interest in Japan, he was able to intermingle with broad segments of the Japanese population. He noted that Americans had a tendency to impose their value systems, ideals, and thinking patterns upon the Japanese, believing that anything American was universally right and applicable. He felt indignant about American attitudes on numerous occasions and was determined to do something about it.

Under both Prescott and his predecessor, Higgins's responsibilities included troubleshooting with major Japanese customers, attending trade meetings, negotiating with government officials, conducting marketing research projects, and helping with day-to-day administration. Both bosses sought his advice on many difficult and complex administrative problems and found him capable.

Prescott mentally listed a few examples to describe what he meant by Higgins's "complete emotional involvement" with the culture of Japan. In 1961, Higgins married a Japanese woman who had studied in the United States and graduated from a prestigious Japanese university. At that time, Higgins asked for and received permission to extend his stay in Japan for an indefinite period. This seemed to Prescott to mark a turning point in Higgins's behavior.

Higgins moved to a strictly Japanese neighborhood, relaxed in a kimono at home, used the public bath, and was invited to weddings, neighborhood parties, and even Buddhist funerals. Although Weaver had a policy of granting two months' home leave every two years with paid transportation for the employee and his or her family, Higgins declined his trips, preferring to visit remote parts of Japan with his wife.

At work, Higgins had also taken on many characteristics of a typical Japanese executive. He spent a great deal of time listening to the personal problems of his subordinates, maintained close social ties with many of the men in the organization, and had even arranged marriages for some of the young employees. Consequently, many employees sought Higgins's attention to register their complaints and demands with management. These included requests for more liberal fringe benefits in the form of recreational activities and acquisition of rest houses at resort areas. Many employees also complained to Higgins about the personnel policy that Prescott had installed. This involved a move away from promotion based on seniority to one based on superior's evaluation of subordinates. The employees asked Higgins to intercede on their behalf. He did so and insisted that their demands were justified.

Although Prescott felt it helpful to learn the feelings of middle managers from Higgins, he did not like having to deal with Higgins as an adversary rather than an ally. Prescott became hesitant to ask Higgins's opinion because he invariably raised objections to changes that were contrary to the Japanese norm. Prescott believed that there were dynamic changes taking place in traditional Japanese customs and culture. He was confident that many of the points Higgins objected to were not tied to existing cultural patterns as rigidly as Higgins seemed to think. The opinion was bolstered by the fact that many Japanese subordinates were more willing to try out new ideas than Higgins was. Prescott further thought that there was no point in a progressive American company's merely copying the local customs. He felt that the company's real contribution to Japanese society was in bringing in new ideas and innovations.

Recent incidents had raised some doubts in Prescott's mind as to the soundness of Higgins's judgment, which Prescott had never before questioned. For example, there was a case involving the dismissal of a manager who in Prescott's opinion lacked initiative, leadership, and general competency. After two years of continued prodding by his superiors, including Prescott himself, the manager still showed little interest in self-improvement. Both Higgins and the personnel manager objected vigorously to the dismissal because the company had never done this before. They also argued that the man involved was loyal and honest and that the company was partially at fault for having kept him on for the last ten years without spotting the incompetency. A few weeks after the dismissal, Prescott learned accidentally that Higgins had interceded on behalf of the fired employee and had gotten Yamazaki Pharmaceutical to take him on. When confronted, Higgins simply said that he had done what was expected of a superior in any Japanese company.

Prescott believed these incidents to be symptomatic of a serious problem. Higgins had been an effective and efficient manager. His knowledge of the language and the people had proved invaluable. On numerous occasions, his American friends envied Prescott for having a man of Higgins's qualifications as an assistant. Prescott also knew that Higgins had received several outstanding offers to go with other companies in Japan. Prescott felt that Higgins would be far more effective if he could take a more emotionally detached attitude toward Japan. In Prescott's view, the best international executive was one who retained a belief in the fundamentals of the U.S. point of view while also understanding foreign attitudes. This understanding, of course, should be thorough or even instinctive, but it also should be objective, characterized neither by disdain nor by strong emotional attachment.

QUESTIONS

1. How would you contrast the attitudes of Higgins and Prescott toward the implementation of U.S. personnel policies in the Japanese operations?
2. What are the major reasons for these differences in attitude?
3. If you were the Weaver corporate management person responsible for the Japanese operations and the conflict between Higgins and Prescott had come to your attention, what would you do? Be sure to identify some alternatives and then make a recommendation.

ANNOTATED BIBLIOGRAPHY

SECTION 1

"The Cultural Awareness Hierarchy: A Model For Promoting Understanding" (Muniz, P. and Chasnoff, R.)

Batdorf, L.L. "Culturally Sensitive Training." *Training and Development Journal*, August 1980, 28–41.

Benedict, R. *Patterns of Culture*. Boston: Houghton-Mifflin, 1959.

SECTION 2

"On the Folly of Rewarding A, While Hoping for B" (Kerr, S.)

Barnard, C.I. *The Functions of the Executive*. Cambridge, Mass.: Harvard University Press, 1964.

Blau, P.F. and Scott, W.R. *Formal Organizations*. San Francisco: Chandler, 1962.

Fiedler, F.E. "Predicting the Effects of Leadership Training and Experience from the Contingency Model." *Journal of Applied Psychology* 56 (1972): 114–119.

Garland, L.H. "Studies of the Accuracy of Diagnostic Procedures." *American Journal Roentgenological, Radium Therapy Nuclear Medicine* 82 (1959): 25–38. In one study of 14,867 films for signs of tuberculosis, 1,216 positive readings turned out to be clinically negative; only 24 negative readings proved clinically active, a ratio of 50 to 1.

Kerr, S. "Some Modifications in MBO as an OD Strategy." *Academy of Management Proceedings* (1973): 39–42. (a)

Kerr, S. "What Price Objectivity?" *American Sociologist* 8 (1973): 92–93. (b)

Litwin, G.H. and Stringer, R.A., Jr. *Motivation and Organizational Climate*. Boston: Harvard University Press, 1968.

Perrow, C. "The Analysis of Goals in Complex Organizations." In A. Etzioni (Ed.), *Readings on Modern Organizations*. Englewood Cliffs, N.J.: Prentice-Hall, 1969.

Scheff, T.J. "Decision Rules, Types of Error, and Their Consequences in Medical Diagnosis." In F. Massarik and P. Ratoosh (Eds.), *Mathematical Explorations in Behavioral Science*. Homewood, Ill.: Irwin, 1965.

Simon, H.A. *Administrative Behavior*. New York: Free Press, 1957. In Simon's terms, a decision is "subjectively rational" if it maximizes an individual's valued outcomes so far as his knowledge permits. A decision is "personally rational" if it is oriented toward the individual's goals.

Swanson, G.E. "Review Symposium: Beyond Freedom and Dignity." *American Journal of Sociology* 78 (1972): 702–705.

Webster, E. *Decision Making in the Employment Interview*. Montreal: Industrial Relations Center, McGill University, 1964.

"A New Strategy for Job Enrichment" (Hackman, J.R. et al.)

Ford, N.R. *Motivation Through the Work Itself*. New York: American Management Association, 1969.

Hackman, J.R. and Lawler, E.E. "Employee Reactions to Job Characteristics." *Journal of Applied Psychology Monograph* (1971): 259–286.

Hackman, J.R. and Oldham, G.R. *Motivation Through the Design of Work: Test of a Theory*. Technical Report No. 6. Department of Administrative Sciences, Yale University, 1974.

Hackman, J.R. and Oldham, G.R. "Development of the Job Diagnostic Survey." *Journal of Applied Psychology* (1975): 159–170.

Herzberg, F. *Work and the Nature of Man*. Cleveland: World, 1966.

Herzberg, F. "One More Time: How Do You Motivate Employees?" *Harvard Business Review* (1968): 53–62.

Herzberg, F., Mausner, B., and Snyderman, B. *The Motivation to Work.* New York: John Wiley & Sons, 1959.

Paul, W.J., Jr., Robertson, K.B. and Herzberg, F. "Job Enrichment Pays Off." *Harvard Business Review* (1969): 61–78.

Turner, A.N. and Lawrence, P.R. *Industrial Jobs and the Worker.* Cambridge, Mass.: Harvard Graduate School of Business Administration, 1965.

Walters, R.W. and Associates. *Job Enrichment for Results.* Cambridge, Mass.: Addison-Wesley, 1975.

"Managerial   Problem-Solving   Styles" (Hellriegel, D. and Slocum, J.)

"An Interview: The Management Style of John deButts." *Harvard Business Review*, January-February 1974, 34–42.

Boyatzis, R.E. "The Need For Close Relationships and the Manager's Job." *Organizational Psychology: A Book of Readings*, (Eds.) D.A. Kolb, I.M. Rubin and J.C. McIntyre. Englewood Cliffs, N.J.: Prentice-Hall, 1974, pp. 183–7.

Hall, Calvin S. and Gardner Lindzey. *Theories of Personality.* New York: John Wiley, 1970.

Jung, Carl G. *Collected Works*, (Eds.) Herbert Read, Michael Fordham and Gerhard Adler. Princeton, N.J.: Princeton University Press, 1953.

Kilman, Ralph H. and V. Taylor. "A Contingency Approach to Laboratory Learning: Psychological Types Versus Experimental Norms." *Human Relations*, December 1974, pp. 891–909.

McKenney, James L. and P.G. Keen. "How Managers' Minds Work." *Harvard Business Review*, May-June 1974, pp. 79–90.

Myers, I.B. and K.C. Briggs. *Myers-Briggs Type Indicator.* Princeton, N.J.: Educational Testing Service, 1962.

Ross, Irwin. "The View From Stewart Mott's Penthouse." *Fortune*, March 1974, pp. 134–5.

Terkel, Studs. *Working.* New York: Pantheon Books, 1974.

Vanderwicken, Peter. "Irving Shapiro Takes Charge at duPont." *Fortune*, January 1974, pp. 70–81.

Wehr, Gerhard. *Portrait of Jung: An Illustrated Biography*, New York: Herder and Herder, 1971.

Wiggins, Nancy. "Individual Differences in Human Judgments: A Multivariate Approach" in *Human Judgment and Social Interactions*, (Eds.) Leon Rappaport and David A. Summer. New York: Holt, Rhinehart and Winston, 1973.

SECTION 3

"Assets and Liabilities in Group Problem Solving: The Need For an Integrative Function" (Maier, N.R.F.)

Crozier, W.J. "Notes on Some Problems of Adaptation." *Biological Bulletin* 39 (1920): 116–129.

Duneker, K. "On Problem Solving." *Psychological Monographs* 58 (1945): 5, Whole No. 270.

Hamilton, W.F. "Coordination in the Starfish. III. The Righting Reaction as a Phase of Locomotion (Righting and Locomotion)." *Journal of Comparative Psychology* 2 (1922): 81–94.

Hoffman, L.R. "Conditions for Creative Problem Solving." *Journal of Psychology* 52 (1961): 429–444.

Hoffman, L.R. "Group Problem Solving." In L. Berkowitz (Ed.), *Advances in Experimental Social Psychology.* Vol. 2 New York: Academic Press, 1965. Pp. 99–132.

Hoffman, L.R., Harburg, E., and Maier, N.R.F. "Differences and Disagreement as Factors in Creative Group Problem Solving." *Journal of Abnormal and Social Psychology* 64 (1962): 206–214.

Hoffman, L.R., and Maier, N.R.F. "The Use of Group Decision to Resolve a Problem of Fairness." *Personnel Psychology* 12 (1959): 545–559.

Hoffman, L.R., and Maier, N.R.F. "Quality and Acceptance of Problem Solutions by Members of Homogenous and Heterogeneous Groups." *Journal of Abnormal and Social Psychology* 69 (1964): 264–271.

Hoffman, L.R., and Maier, N.R.F. "Valence in the Adoption of Solutions by Problem-Solving Groups. II. Quality and Acceptance as Goals of Leaders and Members." Unpublished manuscript, 1967 (mimeo).

Kelley, H.H., and Thibaut, J.W. "Experimental Studies of Group Problem Solving and Process." In G. Lindzey (Ed.), *Handbook of Social Psychology*. Cambridge, Mass.: Addison-Wesley, 1954. Pp. 735–785.

Maier, N.R.F. "Reasoning in Humans. I. On Direction." *Journal of Comparative Psychology* 10 (1930): 115–143.

Maier, N.R.F. "The Quality of Group Decisions As Influenced By the Discussion Leader." *Human Relations* 3 (1950): 155–174.

Maier, N.R.F. *Principles of Human Relations*. New York: Wiley, 1952.

Maier, N.R.F. "An Experimental Test of the Effect of Training on Discussion Leadership." *Human Relations* 6 (1953): 161–173.

Maier, N.R.F. *The Appraisal Interview*. New York: Wiley, 1958.

Maier, N.R.F. "Screening Solutions to Upgrade Quality: A New Approach to Problem Solving Under Conditions of Uncertainty." *Journal of Psychology* 49 (1960): 217–231.

Maier, N.R.F. *Problem-Solving Discussions and Conferences: Leadership Methods and Skills*. New York: McGraw-Hill, 1963.

Maier, N.R.F., and Hayes, J.J. *Creative Management*. New York: Wiley, 1962.

Maier, N.R.F., and Hoffman, L.R. "Using Trained 'Developmental' Discussion Leaders to Improve Further the Quality of Group Decisions." *Journal of Applied Psychology* 44 (1960): 247–251. (a)

Maier, N.R.F., and Hoffman, L.R. "Quality of First and Second Solutions in Group Problem Solving." *Journal of Applied Psychology* 44 (1960): 278–283. (b)

Maier, N.R.F. and Hoffman, L.R. "Organization and Creative Problem Solving." *Journal of Applied Psychology* 45 (1961): 277–280.

Maier, N.R.F. and Hoffman, L.R. "Group Decision in England and the United States." *Personnel Psychology* 15 (1962): 75–87.

Maier, N.R.F. and Hoffman, L.R. "Financial Incentives and Group Decision in Motivating Change." *Journal of Social Psychology* 64 (1964): 369–378. (a)

Maier, N.R.F. and Hoffman, L.R. "Types of Problems Confronting Managers." *Personnel Psychology* 17 (1964): 261–269. (b)

Maier, N.R.F. and Hoffman, L.R. "Acceptance and Quality of Solutions as Related to Leaders' Attitudes Toward Disagreement in Group Problem Solving." *Journal of Applied Behavioral Science* 1 (1965): 373–386.

Maier, N.R.F. and Maier, R.A. "An Experimental Test of the Effects of 'Developmental' vs. 'Free' Discussions on the Quality of Group Decisions." *Journal of Applied Psychology* 41 (1957): 320–323.

Maier, N.R.F. and Solem, A.R. "The Contribution of a Discussion Leader to the Quality of Group Thinking: The Effective Use of Minority Opinions." *Human Relations* 5 (1952): 277–288.

Maier, N.R.F. and Solem, A.R. "Improving Solutions by Turning Choice Situations Into Problems." *Personnel Psychology* 15 (1962): 151–157.

Maier, N.R.F. and Zerfoss, I.F. "MRP: A Technique for Training Large Groups of Supervisors and Its Potential Use in Social Research." *Human Relations* 5 (1952): 177–186.

Moore, A.R. "The Nervous Mechanism of Coordination in the Crinoid Antedon Rosaceus." *Journal of Genetic Psychology* 6 (1924): 281–288.

Moore, A.R. and Doudoroff, M. "Injury, Recovery and Function In an Aganglionic Central Nervous System." *Journal of Comparative Psychology* 28 (1939): 313–328.

Osborn, A.F. *Applied Imagination.* New York: Scribner's, 1953.

Schneirla, T.C. and Maier, N.R.F. "Concerning the Status of the Starfish." *Journal of Comparative Psychology* 30 (1940): 103–110.

Solem, A.R. "Almost Anything I Can Do, We Can Do Better." *Personnel Administration* 28 (1965): 6–16.

Thibaut, J.W. and Kelley, H.H. "*The Social Psychology of Groups.*" New York: Wiley, 1961.

Wallach, M.A. and Kogan, N. "The Roles of Information, Discussion and Consensus in Group Risk Taking." *Journal of Experimental and Social Psychology* 1 (1965): 1–19.

Wallach, M.A., Kogan, N. and Bern, D.J. "Group Influence on Individual Risk Taking." *Journal of Abnormal and Social Psychology* 65 (1962): 75–86.

Wertheimer, M. *Productive Thinking.* New York: Harper, 1959.

"The Abilene Paradox: The Management of Agreement" (Harvey, J.B.)

Argyris, C. *Intervention Theory and Method: A Behavioral Science View.* Addison-Wesley, 1970. Gives an excellent description of the process of "owning up" and being "open," both of which are major skills required if one is to assist his organization in avoiding or leaving Abilene.

Camus, A. *The Myth of Sisyphus and Other Essays.* Vintage Books, Random House, 1955. Provides an existential viewpoint for coping with absurdity, of which the Abilene Paradox is a clear example.

Harvey, J.B. and Albertson, R. "Neurotic Organizations: Symptoms, Causes and Treatment." Parts I and II. *Personnel Journal* (September and October 1971). A detailed example of a third-party intervention into an organization caught in a variety of agreement-management dilemmas.

Janis, I.L. *Victims of Groupthink.* Houghton-Mifflin Co., 1972. Offers an alternative viewpoint for understanding and dealing with many of the dilemmas described in the "Abilene Paradox." Specifically, many of the events that Janis describes as examples of conformity pressures (that is, group tyranny) I would conceptualize as mismanaged agreement.

Slater, P. *The Pursuit of Loneliness.* Beacon Press, 1970. Contributes an in-depth description of the impact of the role of alienation, separation, and loneliness (a major contribution to the Abilene Paradox) in our culture.

Walton, R. *Interpersonal Peacemaking: Confrontation and Third Party Consultation.* Addison-Wesley, 1969. Describes a variety of approaches for dealing with conflict when it is real, rather than phony.

"Intergroup Problems in Organizations" (Schein, E.H.)

Blake, R.R. and Mouton, J.S. "Reactions to Intergroup Competition under Win-Lose Conditions." *Management Science* 7 (1961): 420–435.

Blake, R.R. and Mouton, J.S. "Headquarters—Field Team Training for Organizational Improvements." *Journal of the American Society of Training Directors* 16 (1962).

Janis, I.L. and King, B.T. "The Influence of Role Playing on Opinion Change." *Journal of Abnormal and Social Psychology* 69 (1954): 211–218.

Sherif, M., et al. *Intergroup Conflict and Cooperation: The Robbers Cave Experiment.* Norman, Oklahoma: University Book Exchange, 1961.

SECTION 4

"The Manager's Job: Folklore and Fact" (Mintzberg, H.)

Aguilar, F.J. *Scanning the Business Environment.* New York: Macmillan, 1967. P. 102.

Andrews, K.R. "Toward Professionalism in Business Management." (March-April 1969): 49. A more thorough, though rather different, discussion of this issue.

Burns, T. "The Directions of Activity and Communication in a Departmental Executive Group." *Human Relations* 7, no. I (1954): 73.

Carlson, S. *Executive Behaviour.* Stockholm: Strömbergs, 1951. The first of the diary studies.

Choran, I. Unpublished study. Reported in Mintzberg, *The Nature of Managerial Work.*

Copeman, G.H. *The Role of the Managing Director.* London: Business Publications, 1963.

Davis, R.T. *Performance and Development of Field Sales Managers.* Boston: Division of Research, Harvard Business School, 1957.

Drucker, P.F. *The Practice of Management.* New York: Harper & Row, 1954. Pp. 341–342.

Grayson, C.J., Jr. in "Management Science and Business Practice." (July-August, 1973): 41. Grayson explains why, as chairman of the Price Commission, he did not use those very techniques that he himself promoted in his earlier career as a management scientist.

Guest, R.H. "Of Time and the Foreman." *Personnel* (May 1956): 478.

Hekimian, J.S. and Mintzberg, H. "The Planning Dilemma." *The Management Review* (May 1968): 4.

Hodgson, R.C., Levinson, D.J. and Zaleznik, A. *The Executive Role Constellation.* Boston: Division of Research, Harvard Business School, 1965. Discussion of the sharing of roles.

Homans, G.C. *The Human Group.* New York: Harcourt, Brace & World, 1950. Based on the study by William F. Whyte entitled *Street Corner Society,* rev. ed. (Chicago: University of Chicago Press, 1955).

Livingston, J.S. "Myth of the Well-Educated Manager." (January-February 1971): 79.

Mintzberg, H. *The Nature of Managerial Work.* New York: Harper & Row, 1973. Contains all the data from my study.

Neustadt, R.E. *Presidential Power.* New York: John Wiley, 1960. Pp. 153–154 (italics added) and p. 157.

Sayles, L.R. *Managerial Behavior.* New York: McGraw-Hill, 1964. P. 162.

Stewart, R. *Managers and Their Jobs.* London: Macmillan, 1967.

Wrapp, W.E. "Good Managers Don't Make Policy Decisions." (September-October 1967): 91. Wrapp refers to this as spotting opportunities and relationships in the stream of operating problems and decisions: in his article Wrapp raises a number of excellent points related to this analysis.

"Power Failure in Management Circuits" (Kanter, R.M.)

Bennis, Warren. *The Unconscious Conspiracy: Why Leaders Can't Lead.* New York: AMACOM, 1976.

Fulmer, William E. "Supervisory Selection: The Acid Test of Affirmative Action," *Personnel,* November-December, 1976, p. 40.

Kanter, R.M. *Men and Women of the Corporation.* New York: Basic Books, 1977.

Kanter, R.M. and Barry Stein, eds. *Life in Organizations.* New York: Basic Books, 1979.

Kipnis, David. *The Powerholders.* Chicago: University of Chicago Press, 1976.

McClelland, David C. *Power: The Inner Experience.* New York: Irvington Publishers, 1975.

Pelz, Donald C. "Influence: A Key to Effective Leadership in the First-Line Supervisor," *Personnel,* November 1952.

"Participative Management: Quality vs. Quantity" (Miles, R.E. and Ritchie, J.B.)

Blankenship, L.V. and Miles, R.E. "Organization Structure and Management Decision Behavior." *Administrative Science Quarterly* (June 1968): 106.

Likert, R. *New Patterns of Management.* New York: McGraw-Hill, 1961.

Likert, R. *The Human Organization.* New York: McGraw-Hill, 1967.

McGregor, D. *The Human Side of Enterprise.* New York: McGraw-Hill, 1960.

McGregor, D. *The Professional Manager.* New York: McGraw-Hill, 1967.

Miles, R.E. "Human Relations or Human Resources?" *HBR* (July-August 1965): 149.

Miles, R.E. "The Affluent Organization." *HBR* (May-June 1966): 106.

Miles, R.E., Porter, L.W. and Craft, J.A. "Leadership Attitudes Among Public Health Officials." *American Journal of Public Health* (December 1966): 1990.

Ritchie, J.B. and Miles, R.E. "An Analysis of Quantity and Quality of Participation as Mediating Variables in the Participative Decision-Making Process." *Personnel Psychology* (Autumn 1970): 347. A more detailed analysis of these data.

Roberts, R.L., Blankenship, V. and Miles, R.E. "Organizational Leadership, Satisfaction, and Productivity: A Comparative Analysis." *Academy of Management Journal* (December 1968): 401.

SECTION 5

"Choosing Strategies for Change" (Kotter, J.B. and Schlesinger, L.A.)

Allen, S.A. "Organizational Choice and General Influence Networks for Diversified Companies." *Academy of Management Journal* (September 1978): 341. Recent evidence on the frequency of changes.

Argyrus, C. *Intervention Theory and Method.* Reading, Mass.: Addison-Wesley, 1970. P. 70.

Beer, M. *Organization Change and Development: A Systems View.* Pacific Palisades, Calif.: Goodyear, 1979.

Bower, M. and Walton, C.L., Jr. "Gearing a Business to the Future." In *Challenge to Leadership.* New York: The Conference Board, 1973. P. 126.

Drucker, P.F. *The Practice of Management.* New York: Harper & Row, 1954.

Greiner, L.E. "Patterns of Organization Change." *HBR* (May-June 1967): 119.

Greiner, L.E. and Barnes, L.B. "Organization Change and Development." In Dalton and Lawrence (Eds.), *Organizational Change and Development.* Homewood, Ill.: Irwin, 1970. P. 3.

Kotter, J.P. "Power, Dependence, and Effective Management." *HBR* (July-August 1977): 125, 135.

Lawrence, P.R. "How to Deal with Resistance to Change." *HBR* (May-June 1954): 49. Reprinted as *HBR* Classic (January-February 1969): 4.

Lorsch, J.W. "Managing Change." In Lawrence, Barnes, and Lorsch (Eds.), *Organizational Behavior and Administration.* Homewood, Ill.: Irwin, 1976. P. 676.

Luke, Robert A., Jr. "A Structural Approach to Organizational Change." *Journal of Applied Behavioral Science* (September-October 1973): 611.

Machiavelli, N. *The Prince*

Marrow, A.J., Bowers, D.F. and Seashore, S.E. *Management by Participation.* New York: Harper & Row, 1967.

Miles, R.H. *Macro Organizational Behavior.* Pacific Palisades, Calif.: Goodyear, 1978. Chapter 4. A discussion of power and politics in corporations.

Nierenberg, G.I. *The Art of Negotiating.* Birmingham, Ala.: Cornerstone, 1968. An excellent discussion of negotiation.

Schein, E.H. *Organizational Psychology.* Englewood Cliffs, N.J.: Prentice-Hall, 1965. P. 44.

Tagiuri, R. "Notes on the Management of Change: Implication of Postulating a Need for Competence." In Kotter, Sathe, and Schlesinger (Eds.), *Organization.* Homewood, Ill,: Irwin, 1979. A good discussion of an approach that attempts to minimize resistance.

Watson, G. "Resistance to Change." In Bennis, Benne and Chin (Eds.), *The Planning of Change.* New York: Holt, Rhinehart, and Winston, 1969. P. 489. A discussion of resistance that is personality based.

Zaleznik, A., deVries, K. and Manfred, F.R. *Power and the Corporate Mind.* Boston: Houghton-Mifflin, 1975. Chapter 6. A discussion of power and politics in corporations.

Zaltman, G. and Duncan, R. *Strategies for Planned Change.* New York: John Wiley, 1977. Chapters 3 and 4.

"Hard Hats in the Boardroom" (Woodworth, W.P.)

Coates, K. and Topham, T. "Participation of Control?" In K. Coates (Ed.), *Can the Workers Run Industry?* London: Sphere Books, 1968. Pp. 227–240.

Donahue, T. International Conference on Industrial and Labor Relations. Montreal, May 26, 1976.

Dujmovic, I. "Modern Management and Workers' Self-Management in Yugoslavia." Paper presented at the Second International Conference on the Economics of Workers' Self-Management, Istanbul, July 16–19, 1980 (mimeo).

Eide, R. and Ohman, B. *Economic Democracy Through Wage Earner Funds.* Stockholm: Arbetslivscentrum, 1980.

IDE (International Research Group). "The Role of Formal Norms in the Introduction of Industrial Democracy." *Economic Analysis and Workers' Management.* Vol. 15, No. 3, 1981. Pp. 353–364.

Jenkins, D. "Beyond Job Enrichment: Workplace Democratization in Europe." *Working Papers for a New Society.* Vol. 2, No. 1, 1975. Pp. 51–57.

Johnson, A.G. and Whyte, W.F. "The Mondragon System of Worker Production Cooperatives." *Industrial and Labor Relations Review.* Vol. 31, No. 1, 1977. Pp. 18–30.

Kissler, L. and Sattel, U. "Codetermination in the Course of Time." Paper presented at the Tenth World Congress, International Sociological Association, Mexico City, August 16–21, 1982.

"The New Industrial Relations." *Business Week.* May 11, 1981, pp. 84–98.

Stokes, B. *Worker Participation—Productivity and the Quality of Working Life.* Washington, D.C.: Worldwatch Institute, 1978.

Terkel, S. *Working.* New York: Pantheon, 1974.

Woodworth, W.P. "Towards A Labor-Owned Economy in the United States." *Labour and Society.* Vol. G, No. 1, 1981. 41–56.

Zwerdling, D. *Democracy at Work.* Washington, D.C.: Association for Workplace Democracy, 1978.

"Black Managers: The Dream Deferred" (Jones, E.W.)

Adams, Kathryn. "Aspects of Social Context As Determinants of Black Women's Resistance to Challenges." *Journal of Social Issues*, vol. 39, no. 3, 1983.

Crosby, Faye, Steven Bromley and Leonard Saxe. "Recent Unobtrusive Studies of Black and White Discrimination & Prejudice: A Literature Review." *Psychological Bulletin.* vol. 87, no. 3, 1980.

Fernandez, John. *Racism and Sexism in Corporate Life.* Lexington, Mass.: Lexington Books, D.C. Heath, 1981.

Fisher, Anne B. "Good News, Bad News and an Invisible Ceiling." *Fortune*, Sept. 16, 1985.

Keller, Suzanne. *Beyond the Ruling Class: Strategic Elites in Modern Society.* New York: Random, 1953.

Pettigrew, Tom. "The Mental Health Impact," in *Impacts of Racism On White Americans*, (Eds.) Benjamin P. Bowser and Raymond G. Hunt. Beverly Hills: Sage, 1981.

Sedlacek, William E. and Glenwood C. Brooks, Jr. "Measuring Racial Attitudes in a Situational Context." *Psychological Reports.* vol. 27, 1970.

Sirota & Alper Associates. A survey conducted in 1983.

Snyder, Mark. "Self-Fulfilling Stereotypes." *Psychology Today,* July 1982.

Wall Street Journal, May 21, 1982.

Thomas, Alexander and Samuel Sitlen. *Racism and Psychiatry.* Secaucus, N.J.: Citadel, 1972.

INDEX